International Economics

THE IRWIN SERIES IN ECONOMICS

Consulting Editor
LLOYD G. REYNOLDS
Yale University

International Economics

CHARLES P. KINDLEBERGER, Ph.D.
Ford Professor of Economics
Massachusetts Institute of Technology

FIFTH EDITION • 1973

RICHARD D. IRWIN, Inc. Homewood, Illinois 60430
IRWIN-DORSEY LIMITED Georgetown, Ontario

Fifth Edition

First Printing, March 1973

ISBN 0-256-01435-3
Library of Congress Catalog Card No. 72–92424

Printed in the United States of America

Preface

This quinquennial revision was intended to be a minor one after the far-reaching reorganization of the 4th edition, but it got out of hand. Professor Peter Lindert's suggestions were so stimulating, that I was moved to go much further than I had intended, if perhaps not all the way he indicated. The first half of the book remains much as before, but Parts III, IV, and V have been thoroughly restructured. A chapter on money in the adjustment process has been added, and one on national policies with respect to direct investment. To make room for these, and to continue the slimming campaign begun in 1968 after the 1963 edition hit 686 pages, a considerable amount of historical material has been eliminated, and the substances of several chapters redistributed. The chapter on international monetary arrangements has been completely rewritten to keep pace with not only the facts,[1] but also the writer's evolving notions.

To assist the student in reviewing, a number of concepts, words of art, and bits of significant jargon, not already covered in the boldface side headings, have been put in boldface type.

I am unable to thank here by name all the teachers and students who wrote in with corrections, suggestions, corrections. Their interest is deeply appreciated, and I have tried to reply to the point and thank them by letter. The professor who pointed out that Billy Rose's world championship was in shorthand, not typing, distressed me. After reflection, however, I decided to ignore historical fact in favor of apt illustration. Professors Lloyd G. Reynolds and Carlos Diaz-Alejandro of Yale University, however, deserve mention with Professor Lindert of the University of Wisconsin, for their valuable suggestions for improvements. Mary East typed, cut, and pasted. I am grateful to them all.

February 1973   C. P. KINDLEBERGER

---

[1]Not all the facts. No account could be taken of the devaluation of the dollar on February 12, 1973, after a heavy speculative attack.

CONTENTS

International Economics and Economics in General. Differences in Kind. Factor Mobility. Different Moneys. Balance-of-Payments Adjustment. Different National Policies. Separate Markets. Politically Different Units. International Economic Problems. Scheme of the Book.

PART I
THE THEORY OF INTERNATIONAL TRADE

Law of Comparative Advantage. Production Possibilities Curves. Constant Costs. Increasing Opportunity Costs. Factor Proportions. Trade and Factor Efficiency. Equalization of Factor Prices. Increasing Returns.

The Law of Reciprocal Demand. Offer Curves. Supply and the Offer Curve. Indifference Curves. The Terms of Trade. The Gains from Trade. Different Tastes. Identical Factors—Identical Tastes. More Commodities, More Countries. General Equilibrium.

The Simple Assumptions of Heckscher-Ohlin Comparative Advantage. Changes in Tastes. Changes in Factor Endowments. Technological Change —Making Old Goods More Cheaply. Factor Growth and Technological Change. Changes in Technology—New Goods. Shifting Comparative Advantage. Meeting or Setting the International Standard. Marketing. Need for a New Theory in Manufactured Goods?

Trade and Growth. Export-Led Growth in 19th-Century Developing Economies. Export-Led Growth in Industrial Leaders. Export-Led Growth in Developed Countries Today. The Penalties of the Head Start. The Terms of Trade. Engel's Law, Biased Factor and Technological Change, and

Monopoly. The Impact of Internal Conditions. Neoimperialism, Neo-colonialism and Exploitation. Import Substitution.

Transport Costs and Price Equality. Transport Costs in Partial Equilibrium. The Impact of Transport Costs. The Rationale of Transport Costs. Supply-Oriented Commodities. Market Orientation. Footloose Industries. Location Economics.

PART II
COMMERCIAL POLICY

Eight Effects. The Protective Effect. The Consumption Effect. The Revenue Effect. The Redistribution Effect. Infant-Industry Argument. Tariff Factories. Effective Rate of Protection. The Terms-of-Trade Effect. The Competitive Effect. The Income and Balance-of-Payments Effects. The Reciprocal Trade Agreements Program. Nontariff Barriers. Export Quotas Abroad. Barriers to Trade in Agriculture. Noneconomic Arguments.

Elements of Public Finance. Government Activity and Comparative Advantage. Differences in Rates of Tax. Different Tax Systems. State Trading. Economic Warfare. Trade among Socialist Countries. East-West Trade.

Competitive Trade? Monopoly and Monopsony. Cartels. Cartel Policy. Market Separation. Price Discrimination. Discriminating Monopsony. Dumping and Reverse Dumping. Trade Restrictions against Dumping. The Dilemma of Policy.

Commodity Price Stabilization. Financial Devices. Developed-Country Protection in Primary Products. Import Substitution. Preferences for Manufactures from Developing Countries. Export Incentives and Subsidies. Asymmetric Rules.

Custom Unions and Free Trade Areas. The Theory of Customs Unions. The Real World. The Dynamic Effects of Customs Union. Beyond Customs Union. Some Lesser Problems of Customs Unions and Free Trade Areas. EEC's Special Regime for Agriculture. Regional Integration among Developing Countries.

Merits of the Price System. Demerits of the Price System. Alternatives to the Price System. Efficiency and Welfare. The Case for Multilateral Trade.

The Conditions Needed for Free Trade. The Theory of the Second Best. The Burden of Proof. Social versus Economic Goals.

PART III
FACTOR MOVEMENTS

Labor Migration. The International Labor Market. The Patterns of Labor Movement. The European Labor Market. Does Emigration Benefit the Sending Country? Does Immigration Benefit the Receiving Country? Cosmopolitan Migration Policy. Technical Assistance. Freedom of Movement and Social Integration.

Forms of Long-Term Capital. New Bond Issues. Foreign and Domestic Investment. Institutional Pattern of Lending. Government Control. Capital Movements and Welfare. The Feasibility of Controlling Capital Movements. Borrowing to Finance Imports. Tied Loans. The Project Basis for Loans. Capacity to Absorb Capital. Cumulative Lending. The Need to Borrow Interest. Debt Service Ratio.

Direct Investment as Capital Movement. Monopolistic Competition. Bilateral Monopoly: Direct Investment in Resource Industries in Developing Countries. Direct Investment and Welfare. The International Corporation. Direct Investment and the Balance of Payments. In the Home Country. The Impact on the Balance of Payments of the Host Country.

Instinctive Reactions. Foreign Enterprise and Exports. Foreign Control. Market Failure. Restricting Nonessentials. Mitigating the Effects of Foreign Investment. Joint Ventures. Selectivity. Limiting Take-Overs. Excluding Foreigners from the Local Capital Market. Taking the Package Apart. Cartels. Disinvestment and Disappearing Investment. The Burke-Hartke Bill. Government Guarantees and Insurance. A Forum for Resolving Conflicts over Direct Investment.

PART IV
THE ADJUSTMENT PROCESS

Functions of the Foreign Exchange Market. International Clearing. Credit Function. The Euro-Dollar Market. Hedging. Arbitrage. The Foreign Exchange Rate. Types of Intervention. The Foreign Exchange Market and the Balance of Payments.

Purposes. Definition. Economic Transactions. Balance-of-Payments Accounting. Balances within the Total. The Merchandise-Trade Balance. The Current-Account Balance. Basic Balance. The Balance on Regular Transactions. The Balance Settled by Official Transactions. Autonomous versus Compensatory Items. Banker versus Trader. The Figures. The Balance of Indebtedness.

PART V
BALANCE-OF-PAYMENTS ADJUSTMENT AND INTERNATIONAL MONETARY ARRANGEMENTS

Fund. Seasonal Adjustment through Short-Term Capital Movements. Speculation. Mobile Short-Term Capital and Monetary Policy. Destabilizing Speculation. Speculation and the Equilibrium Rate. Moral Suasion. Discount Policy. Domestic Offsets. The IMF and Speculation. The Basle Agreement. The General Arrangements to Borrow and Enlarging the Fund's Quotas. Confidence. The Gold-Exchange Standard. Flexible Exchange Rates and the Movement of Short-Term Capital.

LIST OF FIGURES

xiv

LIST OF TABLES

Chapter 1

THE STUDY OF INTERNATIONAL ECONOMICS

International Economics and Economics in General

Study of international economics can be justified—if there be a need to do so—on two bases, one applicable to the professional economist and the other to the general citizen. To the former, international economics is sometimes thought to be different in kind from other branches of economics, but it is more usually regarded as different only in degree. In any case it is held to merit attention because it richly illustrates the complexity of the general-equilibrium system as it interrelates the pure theory of allocation and exchange (microeconomics) with monetary and income adjustment (macroeconomics). For the citizen, some capacity to handle the concepts of international economics would appear to be a necessity as the world approaches the 21st century, to enable him to form opinions on the wide-ranging argument as to whether international economic relationships are benign or exploitative, and to make choices, as a voter, between more international interdependence and what appears to be a rising tide of nationalism or neomercantilism, with attention turned inward to domestic problems. If resources are scarce—an assumption which underlies all economics and which, if not self-evident for material goods in an age of affluence, is at least true for the citizen's time and attention—it may be necessary to choose between expanding trade, an effective international monetary system, and assistance to developing nations on the one hand; and domestic problems of urban decay, limited opportunities for minorities of all kinds, and pollution on the other.

Differences in Kind

In classical economics, the principles which determined relative values or prices differed between interregional and international trade because factors of production—labor and capital, if not land—were mobile within a country but immobile between countries. Some economists point up the

1

difference that interregional trade takes place between economic units using the same money, whereas in international trade one national money must be exchanged into another by means of a foreign exchange market before a transaction can be completed. Or the adjustment mechanism works one way within a country and differently between countries, because regions share among themselves through a national budget, whereas national systems of taxation and expenditure remain distinct. The several points of emphasis can be combined into the general statement that interregional differs from international economics in the same way that national differs from international politics: a nation represents a consensus, with a policy-making apparatus in government which effects choices for the totality. The world economy lacks government with binding power of decision.

It is important, however, to underline one aspect of interregional and international trade which distinguishes them both from the rest of economics. In these subjects space becomes important. General-equilibrium theory normally appears to operate as if a specific national economy were located at a single point in space and national economics were separate points close beside one another. Goods and services then move in costless fashion. In interregional and international trade this is shown not to be so. For many purposes the assumption of costless transfer is borrowed from general-equilibrium theory. But for others, it is explicitly laid aside. In Chapter 6 we discuss the effects of space on prices, the movements of goods, and the location of industry.

Factor Mobility

In differentiating international from domestic trade, classical economists stressed the behavior of the factors of production. Labor and capital were mobile within a country, they believed, but not internationally. Even land was mobile within a country, if we mean occupationally rather than physically. The same land, for example, could be used alternatively for growing wheat or raising dairy cattle, which gave it a restricted mobility.

The importance of this intranational mobility of the factors of production was that returns to factors tended to equality within, but not between countries. The wages of Frenchmen of a given training and skill were expected to be more or less equal; but this level of wages bore no necessary relation to those of comparable Germans or Italians, Englishmen or Australians. If a weaver received higher wages in Lyons than in Paris, Parisian weavers would migrate to Lyons in sufficient numbers to bring down wages there and raise them in Paris, until equality had been restored. But no such forces are at work between Lyons and Milan, Dresden, Manchester, or New Bedford. The wages of weavers in these cities are independently determined and can fluctuate without affecting one another. The same equality of return within a country, but inequality internationally, was believed to be true of land and capital

Today it is thought that this distinction of the classical economists has been made too rigidly. There is some mobility of factors internationally: Immigration has been important for the United States and is currently of great significance to the economic life of Australia, Argentina, and Israel, to name but a few examples. Emigration has been a factor in the economic life of many European countries, but perhaps outstandingly of Ireland (now Eire) and Italy. Perhaps the most interesting aspect of migration in the postwar period, however, has been the mass movement, affecting as many as four million workers, from the Mediterranean countries of Portugal, Spain, southern Italy, Yugoslavia, Greece, and Turkey northward across the mountains, especially to France, Germany, and Switzerland. The movement slowed up at the end of the 1960s as economic growth in Europe settled down to a slower pace and some countries, such as Switzerland, found themselves overwhelmed by the large proportion of foreigners, but it did not reverse itself. There is even a sense in which it is now possible to think of a European market for labor.

There is also some considerable degree of immobility within countries. The example used of Paris and Lyons is particularly unapt because the French do not typically move about. Migration within the United States takes place on a broad scale under the influence of major forces such as war. The invasion of Ohio, Michigan, and Illinois by Southerners in and immediately following World War I was paralleled by a similar movement to California and Texas in World War II. But movement on this scale is not normal.

It may be accurate to say that there is a difference of degree in factor mobility interregionally and internationally and that in the usual case people will migrate within their own country more readily than they will emigrate abroad. Identity of language, customs, and tradition cannot be assumed between parts of the same country, but they are more likely than between countries.

Capital is also more mobile within than between countries. It is not, however, completely mobile within countries; and regional differences in interest rates do exist. At the same time, it is not completely immoble between countries. We shall see in Part III what happens when capital moves from country to country.

To the extent that there are differences in factor mobility and equality of factor returns internationally as compared with interregionally, international trade will follow different laws. If there is a shift in demand from New England pure woolens to southern synthetic woolen compounds, capital and labor will move from New England to the South. If, however, there is a shift in demand from French to Italian silk, no such movement of capital and labor to Italy takes place. Some other adjustment mechanism is needed.

Different Moneys

To many economists, and especially to the man in the street, the principal difference between domestic and international trade is that the latter involves the use of different moneys. A dollar is accepted in California and in Maine. But the Swiss franc, which is the coin of the realm in Basel, must be converted into French francs or German deutsche marks before it can be used to buy goods in Strasbourg in France or Freiburg in Germany, each but a few miles away.

With a little more sophistication, however, it is evident that the important fact is not the different moneys so much as the possibiliy of change in their relative value. When Switzerland, Belgium, and France belonged to the Latin Monetary Union and all three francs were convertible into each other on a one-for-one basis, an individual would be almost indifferent whether he held one franc or another, unless he were on the verge of making a purchase. For actual buying, it was necessary to have the unit acceptable to the seller; but if exchange rates were fixed, currencies convertible, and both were expected to remain so, one currency was as good as another.

This aspect of international trade is evidently linked to the mobility of capital. One of the reasons capital moves freely in the United States is that a dollar is a dollar from Florida to Minnesota (although not necessarily in purchasing power from 1932 to 1973). There are other reasons for the internal mobility of capital, such as the existence of a single law covering creditor and debtor which makes debts more readily collectible, but the elimination of all currency risks and uncertainty is an outstanding one. If the exchange rate may move, the mobility of capital is likely to be affected. In some cases, capital movements will be increased: the prospect of appreciation of the German mark or the Japanese yen causes speculators in other countries to convert their dollars, pounds, francs, etc., into DM or yen. But the risk of a change in the value of foreign currencies on balance tends to make people keep their capital at home. On the other hand, after a long period of stable exchange rates, capital becomes more venturesome in moving over the world, and international mobility approaches that which obtains within countries.

If all currencies of the world were on the gold standard at fixed and unchanging rates, then, as we shall see in greater detail later, exchange rates would be fixed. Different countries have different Phillips curves (representing the tradeoff between price stability and employment), or different degrees of monetary discipline, or different experiences affecting their supply of exports or demand for imports which require them to follow different foreign-exchange policies. It is this difference in policies rather than the existence of different national moneys which distinguishes foreign from domestic trade.

Balance-of-Payments Adjustment

One of the most puzzling aspects of the difference between interregional and international economics is that regions virtually never have payments problems whereas countries, especially of late, seem to be continously out of balance-of-payments equilibrium. This is related to the monetary question just discussed. It is partly owing to greater mobility of capital within than between countries, which means that internal disequilibria are automatically financed. But it is also a consequence of the fact that regions share with one another through the national budget; such sharing exists only to a limited degree internationally.

Suppose West Virginia suffers a depression because of the substitution for coal of natural gas from Texas. Under the U.S. system of progressive taxation and social security benefits, the state will pay less income tax to the federal government and receive more in payments for unemployment benefits and old-age pensions and perhaps will enjoy an increase in federal public works. The loss of exports of coal will be compensated not only by emigration and capital inflows, but by a reduction in tax outpayments and an increase in government inpayments. The built-in stabilizer is automatic and operates without regard to policy. There may be no action on the part of West Virginia, but there will be interaction between its citizens and those of the national government.

Different National Policies

Not only is there no or very little automatic sharing through a budget in international trade; different needs lead countries to pursue divergent national policies, and not only with respect to foreign-exchange rates. National policies differ in a wide matter of domestic matters affecting international economic relations—wages, prices, competition, investment, business regulation, etc.—and often involve interference directly in international economic intercourse in tariffs, exchange controls, nontariff barriers, and the like.

The liberal economist of a somewhat earlier day had the answer to this. If all national policies in the field of international economic relations were identical, then differences of incidence would be comparable to those that follow in a region. Governmental policy should be one of noninterference in the working of certain tried and true measures or rules of thumb, handed down by tradition. These measures were the gold standard, the small and balanced budget, and free trade. The policy of laissez-faire or noninterference applied only to trade. Positive measures were called for in the monetary and fiscal areas. If these rules were obeyed, the state would not interfere, and trade would be conducted only among firms and consumers whose nationality did not matter. There would be no reason to think of the French market for wheat, since there would be no need to distinguish between French consumers and those of any other national group.

Separate Markets

Apart from purposeful state interference, however, national markets are frequently separate. On occasion, the reason for this separation will be interference by the state for national reasons. The British drive cars on the left. The French drive on the right. These traffic regulations are decreed by governments for national traffic safety. Since it is safer to sit close to the side of the car which passes the stream of traffic coming in the opposite direction, the British use right-hand-drive cars, the French left-hand. To export automobiles to foreign markets requires a variety of design changes which slow down the assembly line, raise costs, and separate markets to some extent.

But markets are also separated by language, custom, usage, habit, taste, and a host of other causes of difference. Standards differ. Some goods are designed in inches, feet, pounds, and short tons; some in metric measurements. Even within the nonmetric system, the Americans reckon oil in barrels per day, the British in short tons per year. Export and import trade must get outside of the culture of the domestic market to become acquainted with different goods, described in different words, using differing measurements, bought and sold on different terms, for different currency units. Australia, New Zealand, and the United Kingdom shifted to the decimal system in money to simplify economic calculation in the age of the computer; but the British are preparing to convert to the metric system in weights and measures as they join the Common Market, to enable their producers and consumers to gain more from integration into the wider European market—in the long run after the costs of adjustment have been overcome.

Politically Different Units

These cultural distinctions between markets, important in the absence of different national measures, have led political scientists to take a look at the nature of countries. This brings us to perhaps the most significant distinction of all. A country organizes itself into a political unit, which it does so successfully, because its citizens and subjects have a sense of cohesion or belonging together. There may be more or less power applied from the top to repress deviations from the national pattern of behavior.

But there must be some centripetal force, or the country falls to pieces. The point was emphasized by Ortega y Gasset in *Invertebrate Spain* in explaining how the centrifugal forces of regional antagonism, class warfare, and individual distrust shook the weak central government in the 1930s and led to the Spanish Civil War.

This cohesion of the national group helps to explain national differences in tastes and custom, which are dividers of national markets. It also explains the fact of national economic policies. Government has a responsibility to the national group which transcends its responsibility, in the liberal formulas, to the nationals of other countries or to a world code. In the 19th century this was true to a lesser extent than it is today, with the increase of national sentiment and the breakdown of the old international community. It has frequently been said that members of the *haute bourgeoisie*—upper middle class—of widely different countries were closer spiritually to each other a hundred years ago than they were to the working class of their own community. Under these circumstances, an international code was possible. The task of producing and enforcing a code of international economic behavior is much more difficult today. The difference between interregional and international trade is that trade between regions is trade among members of the same group, whereas trade between countries runs between different cohesive units. Friedrich List a hundred years ago expressed it: "Domestic trade is among us; international trade is between us and them."

The development of rules and institutions for international economic relations was making considerable progress in the postwar period (outside of the bloc of Socialist countries) when several changes took place. To some extent national cohesion broke down, particularly in the developed world where young people increasingly disagreed with the values of the older generation. While this problem lies outside the frame of reference of this book, the loss of legitimacy and consensus in national social, political, and economic life has turned attention away from the international economy to rebuilding the domestic polity. In the international sphere, moreover, the nature of the central problem changed, and the issues multiplied.

International Economic Problems

For a time in recent history, the citizen's task of understanding the world was helped by the fact that one economic problem at a time seemed to dominate the international stage. While the countries of the world might not find a solution to this problem until some time after its importance diminished, they could at least agree what the problem was. In the 1920s, the issue was how to transfer the reparations Germany was required to pay to the Allies under the Treaty of Versailles and how to transfer the sums due under Allied war debts to the United States. In the 1930s it was world depression, the need to restore employment at home in ways which would not "beggar thy neighbor."

After World War II, the international economic problem changed again. In the late 1940s the principal item on the agenda was reconstruction in Europe and the Far East. Then came, in the 1950s, the expansion of trade after the constrictions of World War II and the Great Depression, followed by the restoration of convertibility of other currencies after the dollar shortage of the immediate postwar period. In this period, a beginning was made in the economic development of countries which were termed successively "backward," "less developed" and then **"developing."** By the late 1960s and 1970s the list of international issues was lengthening: assistance to economic development; integration of the countries of Europe and perhaps elsewhere; the Euro-dollar market, operating independently of any national jurisdiction; the "deficit" in the balance of payments of the United States that replaced former surpluses; nontariff barriers to trade, when successive mutual reductions had brought tariffs to historically low levels; preferences for developing countries in manufactures; and agreement on international monetary arrangements. Most recently, a more fundamental question has arisen as to whether international solutions are possible at all, and if possible, desirable.

It is widely noted, insistently by such an observer as the Swedish economist Gunnar Myrdal, that the large expansion of trade since 1950 has widened the gap in levels of living between the developed and the developing countries (outside of those of the latter that produce oil), rather than narrowing it, as international trade theory holds it can (should? does?).

A substantial body of thought maintains that the alleged internationalism of leading segments of opinion, in the United States especially but also in Western Europe, is a disingenuous disguise for **neoimperialism** and **neocolonialism.**

Neomercantilism—the attempt of a country to enrich itself even at the expense of the rest of the world—is less regarded as unethical conduct. In fact, free trade is considered in some quarters to be the neomercantilism of the rich.

American leadership in removing obstacles to trade and capital movements (but not migration of labor) is judged in places to be less an attempt to provide the public good of a well-functioning international economic system and more an exploitative means of American imperialism. Europe (led by France), the developing countries through the United Nations Conference on Trade and Development (UNCTAD), and even Canada have experienced increasing nationalism and intensified feelings antipathetical to the United States.

"First things first," "Mind your own business," "Heaven helps those who help themselves," "Charity begins at home,"—all have become slogans virtually as moral as "Do unto others as you would they would do unto you," and "Love thy neighbor as thyself." The private national good is said to be consonant with the public international good, at least in the long run.

For some purposes—in Europe, Africa, Asia, and Latin America—bigger is better. Economic integration is needed to build scale and efficiency. A European currency must be built as a counterweight to the dollar. The Organization of Petroleum Exporting Countries (OPEC) and the Andes Pact among the countries of western South America represent attempts to overcome the weakness in bargaining power of the single country, opposed to the economic might of the United States or of the Organization for Economic Cooperation and Development (OECD) of the developed countries of Western Europe, the United States, Canada, and Japan. In other cases (e.g., Cuba and Chile), there is believed to be no need to tie up either with the world economy or with regional or functional neighbors; escape from foreign "exploitation" gives a country an enormous boost in output and income.

In some formulations, all international economics is at basis international politics. The object of international intercourse is not wealth but power. At the opposite, Marxist extreme, of course, this notion is stood on its head: The purpose of national power is wealth.

In one radically different point of view, dependence of any kind, of child on parents, student on teacher, wife on husband and of one country on trade with another—even mutual dependence or interdependence—is regarded as exploitation. In a world of affluence there is no need for international trade or even interregional trade between city and countryside. The city grows its own food through hydroponics; the country produces its own manufactures and materials—to the extent it chooses to indulge in them—through the magic of modern chemistry and computerized machine tools. With no scarcity there is no need for economics. With participatory democracy, there is no need for order. On this showing, economics and political science have no place in the world.

The student as citizen must be aware of these issues in international economics and ultimately formulate some response to them for himself. In the pages that follow, we will try to refrain from delivering conclusions while we present the analytical tools necessary to deal with the ideas. The book is addressed more to the embryonic economist than to the citizen, although it is hoped that the citizen will gain from mastery of the professional analysis. It is recognized, of course, that those with faith in a strong national, ideological, or analytical point of view will not accept such a disclaimer.

Scheme of the Book

The book deals first with microeconomic aspects of international economics—the pure theory of trade and the theory of commercial policy, and then with macroeconomic policy—the adjustment mechanism, the movement of capital, the balance of payments, and the international monetary system. There is some slight expositional inconvenience in that one must discuss, say, the balance-of-payments aspects of tariffs before the adjustment process has been dealt with. But this inconvenience is far less important than the gain in logical form. Part I deals with the pure theory of trade and the effects on it of changes in technology, economic development, and transport costs. Part II covers commercial policy. Part III deals with factor movements, including one chapter on the migration of labor, a chapter on portfolio capital, and two chapters—one of analysis and one on policy—dealing with direct investment. Parts I to III are the portion of the book dealing with microeconomic analysis. In Part IV we develop the tools of macroeconomic analysis, with chapters on the foreign exchange market, the balance of payments, and the roles of price, income, and money in the adjustment mechanism. Finally in Part V we come to adjustment policies, including international monetary arrangements suitable for a world of nation-states.

Summary

International economics differs from domestic or interregional trade in degree. Factor mobility is greater between regions than between countries; and equalization of factor prices is therefore greater. National markets also differ more widely than regional markets on grounds of tastes, customs, habits. But international trade can also be distinguished in kind from domestic trade. It runs between different political units, each with a sovereign government responsible for the well-being of the unit. This accounts for differences in national economic policies—in monetary, exchange, trade, wage, and similar areas.

Interregional and international trade are both concerned with problems of overcoming space.

International economics is worth separate attention from those undertaking to study economics because it combines the microanalytical problems of allocation and exchange with the macroeconomic problems of money, incomes, exchange rates, and payments adjustment. The questions currently posed for the student as citizen cannot be answered professionally without the use of political and other value judgments. But the analysis is useful in providing the tools for addressing serious issues of today's world which the citizen cannot escape.

BIBLIOGRAPHICAL NOTE

Additional reading is provided in separate chapters on an annotated basis, to distinguish between treatments of the same material on different levels, both less and more difficult, to point the student in the direction of deeper treatments of portions of it, and to provide references for particular points made in the text (since there are no reference-type footnotes). These are grouped separately under "Texts," "Treatises, Etc.," and "Points." Since economists are concerned especially with price, particular attention is paid to paperback editions which the student may want to add to his library.

The textbooks most frequently referred to (by last name of author and chapter number) are, in order of increasing analytical difficulty, for the pure theory of trade:

H. R. Heller, *International Trade, Theory and Empirical Evidence* (rev. ed., Englewood Cliffs, N.J.: Prentice-Hall, Inc., 1973), with brief discussion of data following each presentation of a concept.

R. Findlay, *Trade and Specialization* (Harmondsworth, England: Penguin Books, 1970) (paperback).

B. Södersten, *International Economics* (New York: Harper and Row, 1970).

M. C. Kemp, *The Pure Theory of International Trade and Investment* (Englewood Cliffs, N.J.: Prentice-Hall, Inc., 1969), which is rigorous.

On the monetary aspects of the subject, see:

R. W. Stevens, *A Primer on the Dollar in the World Economy, United States Balance of Payments and International Monetary Reform* (New York: Random House, 1972) (paperback).

H. G. Grubel, *The International Monetary System: Efficiency and Practical Alternatives* (Harmondsworth, England: Penguin Books, 1969) (paperback).

L. B. Yeager, *International Monetary Relations* (New York: Harper & Row, Publishers, 1966).

R. A. Mundell, *International Economics* (New York: The Macmillan Company, 1968).

Under "Treatises" we shall refer to standard articles on the subject. A number of these have been collected into bound volumes of readings, including especially:

American Economic Association, *Readings in the Theory of International Trade* (Homewood, Ill.: Richard D. Irwin, Inc. [formerly Philadelphia: The Blakiston Co.], 1949).

American Economic Association, *Readings in International Economics* (Homewood, Ill.: Richard D. Irwin, Inc., 1967). These two volumes are collections of outstanding articles from the periodical literature.

J. N. Bhagwati, ed., *International Trade, Selected Readings* (Harmondsworth, England: Penguin Books, 1969) (paperback).

R. N. Cooper, ed., *International Finance, Selected Readings* (Harmondsworth, England: Penguin Books, 1969) (paperback).

L. H. Officer and T. D. Willett, eds., *The International Monetary System, Problems and Proposals* (Englewood Cliffs, N.J.: Prentice-Hall, Inc., 1969) (paperback).

The writer will perhaps be forgiven if he refers frequently to J. N. Bhagwati, R. W. Jones, R. A. Mundell, and J. Vanek, eds., *Trade, Balance of Payments and Growth* (Amsterdam: North-Holland Publishing Company, 1971), a collection of recent essays.

In addition to these essays, there will be occasional reference to the monographic literature, especially to:

J. E. Meade, *The Theory of International Economic Policy*, Vol. I, *The Balance of Payments* (New York: Oxford University Press, Inc., 1951).

J. E. Meade, *A Geometry of International Trade* (London: George Allen & Unwin, Ltd., 1952).

J. E. Meade, *The Theory of International Economic Policy*, Vol. II, *Trade and Welfare* (New York: Oxford University Press, Inc., 1955).

Other articles in the major professional journals will be referred to by abbreviations:

AER—American Economic Review

EIF—Essays on International Finance (Princeton)

EJ—Economic Journal (London)

Econ—Economica (London)

JIE—Journal of International Economics

JPE—Journal of Political Economy

MS—The Manchester School

OEP—Oxford Economic Papers

PSIF—Princeton Studies in International Finance

QJE—Quarterly Journal of Economics

RE & S—Review of Economics and Statistics

SP—Staff Papers (of the International Monetary Fund)

SPIE—Special Papers in International Economics (Princeton)

Since many courses require term papers on international economic problems, it may be useful to list the major international sources of statistical and other material. Domestic statistical yearbooks, annual economic reports (of the President or the Chancellor of the Exchequer), monthly and annual trade and financial statistics, etc., must of course be consulted for some problems.

The two major sources for current data are: International Monetary Fund (IMF), *International Financial Statistics* (monthly), which is organized by countries; and United Nations (UN), *Monthly Bulletin of Statistics* (monthly), where data for a wide number of countries are gathered by function.

For detailed international trade data, the UN's *Direction of World Trade* (monthly) and its *Yearbook of International Trade Statistics* may be consulted.

An important source of statistical and other economic information is the Organization for Economic Cooperation and Development (OECD) in Paris, which deals especially with the developed countries.

In addition to these statistics, the United Nations publishes a series of useful annual reports and in some instances quarterly bulletins of analysis from its headquarters in New York and its regional commissions for Europe, Latin America, Asia, and the Far East and Africa. Particularly outstanding are the annual *Economic Survey of Europe in 19——* and the *World Economic Report*.

The Bank for International Settlements has issued an *Annual Report* on international financial questions since 1931. It is the authoritative source on Eurocurrency markets.

Central-bank monthly bulletins and annual reports are a mine of information, and many, like the *Federal Reserve Bulletin*, serve up not only national but also comparative international statistics.

The contracting parties to the General Agreement on Tariffs and Trade

(GATT) have put out an annual report entitled *International Trade,* followed by the appropriate year, since 1952.

The two outstanding sources of information on world economic questions, of course, are *The New York Times* and *The Economist* (London weekly).

Especially useful sources of fact, opinion, and policy discussion for the 1970s are:

U.S., Commission on International Trade and Investment Policy (Williams Commission), *United States International Economic Policy in an Interdependent World, Report of the President,* plus Volumes I and II of *Papers Submitted to the Commission on International Trade and Investment Policy* (Washington, D.C.: Superintendent of Documents, July 1971) (paperback).

National Planning Association, *U.S. Foreign Economic Policy for the 1970s: A New Approach to New Realities, with Supporting Papers,* Planning Pamphlet No. 130 (Washington, D.C., November 1971), an establishment view.

J. N. Bhagwati, ed., *Economics and World Order: From the 1970's to the 1990's* (New York: The Macmillan Company, 1972), a "humanistic and radical" approach.

M. A. G. van Meerhaeghe, *International Economic Institutions,* 2d ed. (London: Longman, 1971), describing machinery for international economic regulation.

Finally student and teacher alike should bear in mind the flood of useful and stimulating material which flows, at least in the United States, from the legislative process. Much in the way of fact and opinion can be gleaned from a variety of sources when legislation is before Congress—hearings before committees of the Congress, reports commissioned by these same bodies, information (or propaganda) from the Executive Branch, from lobbies, including such representative bodies as the U.S. Chamber of Commerce and the AFL–CIO and such disinterested groups as the Committee on Economic Development and the League of Women Voters. Particularly useful are the compendiums and hearings before the Joint Economic Committee of the Congress of the United States on international aspects of the U.S. economy. This material is rich in nuggets of fact and opinion, but difficult to find one's way through.

SUGGESTED READING

Texts

See Heller, chap. 1.

Treatises, Etc.

The major work distinguishing interregional from international trade is B. Ohlin's *Interregional and International Trade* (Cambridge, Mass.: Harvard University Press, 1933; rev. ed., 1967). This pioneering study advances the proposition that international trade differs but little from interregional trade as it attempts a complete revision of the theory of international trade.

See also G. Haberler, *The Theory of International Trade* (London: Macmillan & Co., Ltd., 1937) chap. 1; and J. Viner, *Studies in the Theory of International Trade* (New York: Harper & Bros., Publishers, 1937), appendix A.

M. von N. Whitman, "International and International Payments Adjustment, A Synthetic View," *PSIF*, No. 17 (1967) explores the macroeconomic aspects of the differences in adjustment between and within national economics and provides a useful summary of the literature.

Points

For the connections between international economics and international politics, see, at a fairly elementary level, C. P. Kindleberger, *Power and Money* (New York: Basic Books, 1970). For the view that dependence, even interdependence, is exploitation see J. Galtung, "The Future of Human Society," *Futures, The Journal of Forecasting and Planning*, 2 (June 1970).

The economist view counter to this sociologist view is provided by R. N. Cooper, *The Economics of Interdependence: Economic Policy in the Atlantic Community* (New York: McGraw-Hill Book Company, 1968).

PART I

The Theory of International Trade

<table>
<tr><td>Chapter
2</td><td># THE PURE THEORY OF INTERNATIONAL TRADE: SUPPLY</td></tr>
</table>

THE PURE THEORY OF
INTERNATIONAL TRADE:
SUPPLY

**Chapter
2**

The pure theory of international trade is concerned with basic questions of production and exchange at the barter level, without the intervention of money and monetary problems, and without (though they could be brought into the analysis) international movements of capital or income transfers. The issue is what goods a country will export and import and at what relative prices, or terms of trade. The classical and neoclassical answers to this issue are given in the next two chapters. More complicated answers which derive from more varied assumptions are set forth in the three chapters which follow.

Interferences with trade and their removal on a universal or discriminatory basis are considered in Part II. The questions posed by national moneys, their exchange for one another, and balance-of-payments adjustments are left for much later in the book.

Law of Comparative Advantage

The classical economists asked what goods would be traded between two countries because they thought the answer for trade between countries was different from that for trade within a country. Within a country, a region produces the goods it can make cheaper than other regions. The value of a commodity within a country, moreover, is determined by its labor content. If the product of a certain industry can be sold for more than the value of the labor it contains, additional labor will transfer into that industry from other occupations to earn the abnormal profits available there. Supply will expand until the price is brought down to the value of the labor it contains. Similarly, if a commodity sells for less than the worth of its labor, labor will move away into other lines until the gap is closed. The tendency of wages toward equality within a country results in prices of goods equal to their labor such as to equalize the return to labor in all occupations and regions. If wages are higher in California than in Massachusetts, labor will migrate to California. This will lower

17

wages in California and raise them in Massachusetts, and the movement will continue until the return to labor is equated in the two regions. After labor has spread itself among several regions to equalize wages, these regions will produce and sell to each other what each region can make the cheapest. Its advantage in such commodities over other regions will be absolute. Therefore the theory of trade applicable to regions of a country is the theory of absolute advantage.

Classical economists thought that the labor theory of value valid in trade within a country cannot be applied between nations, since factors of production are immobile internationally. If wages are higher in the United States than in Britain, they stay higher, for migration cannot take place on a scale sufficient to eliminate discrepancies. Under these circumstances, the classical economists asked, what will the United States sell to Britain and Britain to America?

Let us assume two countries and two commodities. If each country can produce one good cheaper (i.e., with less labor) than it can be produced in the other, as in the case of domestic trade, each will have an advantage in the production of one commodity and a disadvantage in the production of the other. Each country will then be anxious to export the commodity in which it has an advantage and import the commodity in which it has a disadvantage. The position is suggested in the following table, where wheat can be produced more cheaply in the United States and cloth more cheaply in Britain. The United States has an absolute advantage in wheat and an absolute disadvantage in cloth. It will export wheat and import cloth, which, with the numerical values given, may be assumed to exchange one for the other at something like the rate of one yard of cloth for one bushel of wheat:

Production of One Man in One Week

Product	In United States	In United Kingdom
Wheat	6 bushels	2 bushels
Cloth	2 yards	6 yards

But suppose that the labor content of both wheat and cloth is less in the United States than in Britain. Suppose that instead of merely 2 yards of cloth per week a man in the United States can produce 10. The position is then as follows:

Production of One Man in One Week

Product	In United States	In United Kingdom
Wheat	6 bushels	2 bushels
Cloth	10 yards	6 yards

It is evident that labor is more efficient in the United States than in the United Kingdom, and wages in the United States will be higher on that account. By assumption however, migration will not take place to equalize wage rates.

Trade cannot now follow the decree of absolute advantage, and a new principle is needed to take its place. This was developed by David Ricardo more than 150 years ago, in the law of comparative advantage. Ricardo observed that in cases similar to ours, while the United States had an absolute advantage over Britain in both wheat and cloth, it had a greater advantage in wheat than in cloth. He concluded that a country would export the product in which it had the greater advantage, or a comparative advantage, and import the commodity in which its advantage was less, or in which it had a comparative disadvantage. In this example the United States would export wheat and import cloth, even though it could produce cloth more efficiently than Britain.

The reasoning underlying this conclusion may be demonstrated arithmetically. Without international trade, wheat and cloth would exchange for one another in each country at their respective labor contents, which would differ as between the two countries. In the United States, 6 bushels of wheat, or one week's labor, would buy 10 yards of cloth. In Britain, by the same token, 6 bushels of wheat—three weeks' labor in the less productive country—would buy 18 yards of cloth. If the United States through trade can get more than 10 yards of cloth for 6 bushels of wheat (or more than 1⅔rds yards of cloth per bushel of wheat), it will pay it to do so. It cannot hope to get more than 18 yards of cloth for 6 bushels of wheat (3 yards of cloth for a single bushel). This is the price which cloth producers in Britain can get without trade, and there is no reason for them to enter into foreign trade and be worse off.

Similarly, if Britain can get more than 2 bushels of wheat for 6 yards of cloth (more than one third of a bushel of wheat per yard of cloth), it will pay it to export cloth and buy wheat. But it cannot hope to get more than six tenths or three fifths of a bushel per yard—the American wheat farmers' price without trade.

For effective comparison, the prices should be quoted the same way. At any price for cloth cheaper than 10 yards (of cloth) for 6 bushels (of wheat), that is, for any more than 10 yards for 6 bushels, the United States will gain by shifting resources out of cloth into wheat and importing cloth. Similarly, at a price of cloth which would involve Britain giving up less than 18 yards for 6 bushels (equal to 6 yards for 2 bushels), it will pay Britain to move its labor out of wheat into cloth and import wheat in exchange for cloth rather than grow grain itself. Trade raises the price of wheat and lowers the price of cloth in the United States; it raises the price of cloth and lowers the price of wheat in Britain. Even when one country can produce both commodities more efficiently than another country, both can gain from specialization and exchange, provided that the efficiency advantage is greater in some commodity or commodities than in others.

On the basis of this type of demonstration, the classical economists concluded that international trade does not require offsetting absolute advantages but is possible where a comparative advantage exists. It goes without saying but must be said, as it is frequently forgotten, that a comparative advantage is always (and by definition) accompanied by a comparative disadvantage.

Production Possibilities Curves

The labor theory of value on which this analysis rested was subsequently rejected as invalid. The tendency for the return to labor to be equal throughout a country was seen by observation to be weak and faltering. Labor is not homogeneous. If there is an increase in the demand for barrels, the wages of coopers will rise above those of smiths, with whom they are not interchangeable. It became recognized that there is not one great class of labor with a single wage but a series of noncompeting groups among which the tendency to equalization of wages, at least in the short run, is weak or nonexistent.

A more fundamental objection, however, which would apply even if labor were homogeneous and commanded one price in a perfectly competitive market, is that goods are not produced by labor alone but by various combinations of all the factors of production: land, labor, and capital. To compare the labor content of two commodities—say, gasoline and textiles, or meat and shoes—gives an erroneous view of relative values. Gasoline production requires far more capital per unit of labor than textiles, and meat output more land than shoes. Variable proportions of factors in the production of different commodities make it impossible to use the labor theory of value, however qualified.

An escape from this impasse has been provided by Gottfried Haberler in the theory of **opportunity costs.** The cost of wheat in the long run is how much cloth a country has to give up to get additional units of wheat. It makes little difference whether the factors which leave the production of cloth are all suited to the output of wheat or not. The question is simply how much of one commodity must be given up to get more of the other.

The notion of opportunity cost is illustrated in international trade theory with production possibilities or transformation curves. Instead of saying that a week's labor will produce either 6 bushels of wheat or 10 yards of cloth, one says that all the factors of production can produce either 6 bushels of wheat or 10 yards of cloth per some appropriate unit of time, or some intermediate combination of them. In Figure 2.1, where the

FIGURE 2.1. Production Possibilities Curves, Constant Opportunity Costs

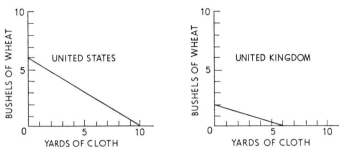

vertical axis represents wheat and the horizontal axis cloth, the U.S. curve means that the resources of the United States, in the absence of foreign trade, can be used entirely to produce wheat, in which case 6 bushels (per capita per week) can be produced, exclusively for cloth, in which case output will consist of 10 yards per man-week, or some appropriate intermediate combination, such as 3 bushels of wheat and 5 yards of cloth. The production possibilities curve does not tell what will in fact be produced. More information is needed for this purpose, on the side of demand. It merely sets out what the possibilities are.

Constant Costs

A straight-line production possibilities curve, such as those in Figure 2.1, indicates constant opportunity costs. At the limits in the United States, resources can produce either 6 bushels of wheat or 10 yards of cloth. Moreover for any resources shifted out of cloth into wheat or vice versa, 10 units of cloth must be given up to get 6 units of wheat, or the other way round. Six bushels of wheat for 10 yards of cloth is the domestic rate of transformation in production at all points along the production possibilities curve, whether all or only a small proportion of total resources is reallocated between industries.

A straight-line production possibilities curve represents more than constant opportunity costs. In the absence of trade, and provided that the economy produces something of both commodities, the slope of the straight line can be taken as a price. Wheat and cloth will exchange under autarky (no trade) in the United States at 6 bushels for 10 yards. At any higher price for cloth, e.g., 7 bushels for 10 yards, it will pay the economy to shift resources out of wheat, where they earn only 6 bushels per man-week, into cloth, where they can produce 10 yards and exchange them for 7 bushels. The supply of wheat will decline and that of cloth will increase until the price ratio of 6 to 10 is restored. Producers are in equilibrium only when the price of the two goods equals the domestic rate of transformation in production. Without trade and with constant opportunity costs and demand such that both commodities are produced, the price must equal the slope of the production possibilities curve.

Let us now take a look at what happens when trade opens up between the United States and Britain. Figure 2.2 shows the two production pos-

FIGURE 2.2.   International Trade under Constant Opportunity Costs, 1

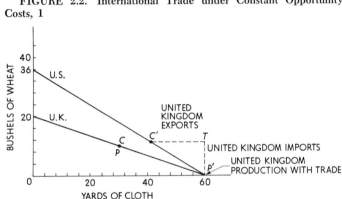

sibilities curves superimposed upon each other and blown up to the same scale. Instead of showing the production possibilities curves as 6 wheat / 10 cloth for the United States and 2 wheat / 6 cloth for Britain, the scales are enlarged and equated at the cloth end. Without trade, 60 yards of cloth will exchange for 36 bushels of wheat in the United States. In Britain, 60 yards of cloth will exchange for only 20 bushels of wheat.

Assume that demand conditions are such that before trade the United Kingdom has been producing and consuming 10 bushels of wheat and 30 yards of cloth (at point P or C on Figure 2.2) on its production possibilities and price line. With a price different from 60:20 made possible by trade, the United Kingdom would be able to reach a higher level of consumption. If it could trade at the U.S. price, for example, it could move from point C to C' where it could consume 12 of wheat and 40 of cloth— a clear gain of both cloth and wheat. It could do this, it may be observed, if it produced only cloth and exchanged 20 of its total output of 60 for 12 bushels of wheat of the United States. British production changes from P to P', consumption from C to C', made possible by exports and imports represented by the dashed lines converging at T. The horizontal dashed line $C'T$ represents exports of cloth, which, subtracted from total production, leave the amount consumed domestically. The vertical dashed line $P'T$ represents wheat imports. The ratio at which exports and imports exchange for each other—i.e., the slope of the hypotenuse of the right-angle triangle formed by them, $C'P'$, is the price line of the United States. In this case the United States has not benefited from foreign trade, exchanging wheat for cloth at 6:10 before and after trade. Production has changed. Twelve additional bushels of wheat are produced and 20 yards less of cloth.

The price after trade may be the same as the price before trade for one of the parties. It cannot be the same for both. Both countries must trade at the same price. Since their prices had differed before trade and are the same after trade, the price of at least one must have altered. The post-trade price can, however, differ from pretrade prices for both. It may, for example, settle at 60 yards of cloth for 28 bushels of wheat, as indicated in Figure 2.3. In this case, both parties will gain. The United Kingdom

FIGURE 2.3. International Trade under Constant Opportunity Costs, 2

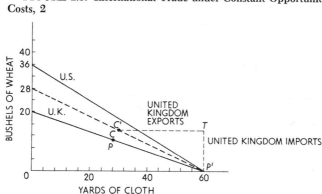

will not gain as much as in the previous example, but the United States will share the gains from foreign trade. To demonstrate the fact of the U.S. gain diagrammatically, it is necessary to shift the wheat and cloth axes, or to quote both prices with a common point on the wheat axis, in order to show the U.S. opportunity cost curve lying inside the British. It is clear enough without an additional diagram, however, that if the United States can obtain 60 yards of cloth by exchanging any less than 36 bushels of wheat—at best as little as 20 bushels, which is Britain's no-gain price, but short of this some such improved price as 28 bushels—the country has gained in trade.

Under conditions of constant opportunity costs one country must be fully specialized, and both may be. Before trade, both countries produce some of both goods. The prices at which they produce and consume differ. After trade, the price at which both produce, consume, and trade must be the same. If the price represents the pretrade or no-gain price for one country it need not be specialized. But if the prices for both improve, with constant opportunity costs, both must be specialized or producers will not be in equilibrium, with price differing from the domestic rate of transformation in production.

Increasing Opportunity Costs

Our production possibilities curves thus far have been those in which opportunity costs were constant and the ratio between commodity costs was equal to price. But the notion that all resources can equally well produce either of two commodities involves an assumption as extreme as the discarded labor theory of value. If all resources are not equally at home in the production of wheat or cloth, but some, such as land and outdoors men, are better at wheat, and others, such as spindles, looms, and city folk, are better at cloth, we may have a situation of increasing costs. Some resources may be equally adaptable to wheat or cloth production, but not all are.

The production possibilities curve, under increasing costs, is concave to the origin at *O*. In Figure 2.4*a*, for example, where a production possi-

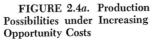

FIGURE 2.4*a*. Production Possibilities under Increasing Opportunity Costs

FIGURE 2.4*b*. Production with Increasing Opportunity Costs

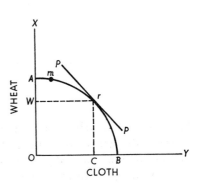

bilities curve *A–B* is shown, wheat and cloth are fairly substitutable for one another between points *r* and *t* on the curve. To the left of *r*, however, one can get only a small increase in wheat by giving up cloth, primarily because the resources taken out of the production of cloth are not suitable for the production of wheat. Possibly there will be no land with which to combine the labor previously in the textile industry. Similarly, to the right of *t*, a country can get only a little bit more of cloth by giving up a relatively large amount of wheat.

Under increasing costs, the production possibilities curve is not identical with a price curve, as in the case of constant costs. The price at which wheat will exchange for cloth cannot be determined by the production possibilities curve by itself, but can be found only with the assistance of data on demand. The complex of problems presented by demand will be taken up in the following chapter. At the moment, however, it may be noted that price is indicated by a straight line between the X and Y axes, the slope of which represents the ratio at which cloth will exchange for wheat, and that production, under a transformation curve representing increasing costs, will take place at the point on the curve tangent to the price in the market. In Figure 2.4b, production will take place at r, on the production possibilities curve, AB, whenever the price is the slope of the line p–p. At r, production will consist of O–W units of wheat and O–C units of cloth. If the economy produced cloth and wheat at point m on the production possibilities curve, the price p–p could not be sustained. At this price there would be too much wheat in relation to cloth or too little cloth in relation to wheat. The unsold quantity of wheat and the unsatisfied demand for cloth would require a change in price to maintain production at m.

If demand keeps the price at p–p, however, it will be possible to earn a higher return in cloth than in wheat, and resources will shift out of wheat into cloth, moving production from m toward r. This shift of resources will continue until, given the price p–p and the production possibilities curve A–B, an optimum allocation of resources is reached at point r. At this point, the marginal rate of transformation in production will be equal to the marginal rate of transformation through trade.

Foreign trade will take place under increasing costs in broadly the same way as under constant costs, except that complete specialization of a country in a single commodity is not so likely. Figure 2.5 shows such a case. Before trade the U.K. price of wheat in terms of cloth is p–p, with production at Z. Omitting several steps discussed in the next chapter by which the price ratio between wheat and cloth after trade is determined, the opening up of trade is assumed to raise the price of cloth in terms of

FIGURE 2.5. International Trade under Increasing Opportunity Costs

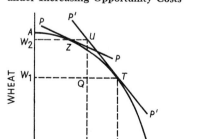

wheat to $p'-p'$. Here $p'-p'$ is a higher price for cloth than $p-p$ (and a lower one for wheat) because more wheat is obtained for a given amount of cloth.

It now pays the United Kingdom to shift resources from the production of wheat into cloth, moving the point of production from Z to T and exchanging cloth for wheat in foreign trade. The higher the price for cloth, the more resources should be taken out of wheat and put into cloth. Production will settle at that point where the new price is tangent to the production possibilities curve, i.e., where the price line is equal to the marginal rate of transformation in production.

Exactly how much cloth is exchanged for wheat is again indeterminate with the analytical tools we have developed. Consumption will take place somewhere along the price line, $p'-p'$, to the left of T—say at U. Let us assume that demand conditions yield the consumption point U. The United Kingdom will then produce $O-C_2$ of cloth and $O-W_1$ of wheat at point T; export C_1-C_2 of cloth and import W_1-W_2 of wheat; and consume $O-W_2$ of wheat and $O-C_1$ of cloth. The quantities C_1-C_2 and W_1-W_2 are equal to $Q-T$ and $Q-U$, which by simple geometry, are exchangeable for one another at the price ratio $p'-p'$. Through trade, Britain will have been enabled to consume more wheat and cloth than it could produce for itself with its own production possibilities.

The failure of specialization to become complete, of course, is due to decreasing returns. As factors less suited for the production of cloth are drawn into that industry, per-yard production costs rise. As factors less suited for production of wheat are drawn from the farms, per-bushel costs of wheat fall. The opposite occurs in the United States. The cost ratios between the two countries may well be equalized before either country specializes in a single product.

Deprived of the labor theory of value and expressed in terms of opportunity costs, the law of comparative advantage is still valid. In a two-good world if one country is more efficient in producing both goods than another country, it profits by concentrating on the product in which it has a greater or comparative advantage and buying the good in which it has a comparative disadvantage. The basic criterion is that with trade it gets a higher price for its specialty or pays a lower price for the commodity in which it is relatively not so productive.

The law of comparative advantage has general validity. Billy Rose, a well-known New York character of a generation ago, was a theatrical impresario and a world champion typist. Despite his championship it paid him to employ a secretary. While he had an absolute advantage over his secretary in typing, his advantage in this activity was narrow compared to that in his other occupation. It therefore paid him and his secretary to specialize.

More generally speaking, if the price of X in terms of Y is lower abroad than at home, it will pay a country to shift resources out of X and into Y, trading Y for X until the prices of X and Y (abstracting from transport costs) are equal at home and abroad. But in these terms the law of comparative costs comes closer to being a law of comparative prices. This would be the case if there were nothing economists could say further about it.

In answer to the question put by the classical economists, the law of comparative costs says that a country exports those products that are comparatively cheap in price at home and imports those that are comparatively expensive. But economics can say more than this.

Factor Proportions

If international trade is based on differences in comparative costs, the curious student will proceed to the next question: What makes for differences in comparative costs? Why do the transformation curves of various countries differ?

The answer given to this question by Swedish economist Bertil Ohlin is twofold: Different goods, he stated, require different factor inputs; and different countries have different factor endowments. If wheat is technologically best produced with lots of land relative to labor and capital, countries that have an abundance of land will be able to produce wheat cheaply. This is why Australia, Argentina, Canada, Minnesota, and the Ukraine export wheat. On the other hand, if cloth requires much labor relative to capital and land, countries that have an abundance of labor—Hong Kong, Japan, India—will have a comparative advantage in cloth manufacture and be able to export it.

In Appendix A we show how transformation curves are derived from production functions for commodities. It is noted there that there may be some ambiguity about the technological factor proportions involved in producing a given commodity. Where these factor proportions are technically unalterable, we can agree that one commodity is more labor intensive than another. Oil refining is more capital intensive than cabinetmaking, and hydroelectric power generation unambiguously requires land, in the form of specialized waterpower sites. But in the production of many commodities, there is a range within which one factor can be substituted for another. Eggs can be produced by chickens roaming the range, using land, or cooped up in batteries of nests, where capital substitutes for land and labor. It is impossible to say that one of these commodities is more capital intensive or labor intensive than another until we know more about the possibilities of factor substitution and the factor availabilities.

The factor endowments explanation of trade further rests on the assumption that each country has the same technological possibilities of producing a given good, i.e., that the production functions are the same in both countries. This assumption will be modified in Chapter 4, where we explore the existence of trade based on technological differences between countries.

Again there is considerable difficulty in defining what a factor is for the purpose of using this explanation. For one thing, to define factors broadly as land, labor, and capital is to overlook the point that these factors are not homogeneous for many purposes but divide into noncompeting groups. It is not enough to have land to raise sheep, but one must have grazing land; nor can minerals be produced by land in general, but only by certain ore-bearing types. Many natural resources are so-called specific factors, limited to one or a few countries. If one defines factors narrowly and makes separate factors out of noncompeting groups or specific factors, it turns out that much trade is based on absolute advantage, the existence of a factor in one country but not in its trading partner. One can keep the explanation of comparative advantage developed by Ohlin from the insights of his teacher, Eli Heckscher, and overlook noncompeting groups and specific factors, or one can define factors narrowly and give up their broad explanation of why prices differ before trade.

Related to noncompeting groups of labor is the question whether one can, in fact, separate capital from labor, particularly when some industries are intensive of skilled labor, which takes education, or capital, to produce. Investment in human capital, as education has been called, may produce a comparative advantage in research-type industries. We say more on this in Chapter 4.

Another difficulty is that it is hard to separate goods from factors, especially when one recognizes that much of world trade is in intermediate goods, those sought not for final consumption but for use in making other goods. It is not necessary to import copper, lacking copper mines, if one can import copper ore. Britain could produce cotton cloth without growing cotton by dint of importing the fiber. But this means that the Heckscher-Ohlin account of comparative advantage should be linked not with commodities so much as with activities. Mining copper ore must be done in countries with ore deposits, but refining copper can be done anywhere in the world that the abundant capital, skilled labor, and copper ore can be combined. The fact that Japan imports iron ore from Australia and coal from the United States suggests that trade in intermediate goods has reduced the importance of specific factors as an explanation of comparative advantage.

Despite the difficulty of deciding how broadly or narrowly to define factors and whether to relate factors to commodities or economic activities, most economists regard the Heckscher-Ohlin explanation of trade as broadly true. The United States is thought to be well endowed with capital and to export capital-intensive goods. Foreign countries are more favorably situated with respect to labor and sell labor-intensive products to the United States. A study by Wassily Leontief, however, greatly disturbed the serenity in which these conclusions were held by purporting to demonstrate statistically that the labor content of U.S. exports was higher than that of this country's imports, and the capital content of imports exceeded that of exports. These findings are still being debated. The debate has been highly useful in producing a thorough examination of the underlying basis of the Ohlin doctrine. For the purpose of what follows in this book, the Leontief claim is taken as not proven, and the Ohlin explanation of U.S. trade, modified for technology as in Chapter 4, is held to be presumptively true.

Trade and Factor Efficiency

What about trade between two countries with the same factor proportions and different factor efficiencies (and, what we have yet to discuss, the same tastes)? Suppose we have two countries, Sweden and Austria, with the same proportions of land, labor, and capital, but with these factors of production more efficient in Sweden than in Austria. Let us assume that labor is more efficient in Sweden than in Austria not because it is combined with more capital and land; it merely works harder in every industry. And Swedish land is richer, let us assume, than Austrian; and Swedish machinery more highly developed. Can trade take place then?

The answer is no. Austrian factors of production will receive less income than Swedish because of their reduced effectiveness in production; but this will not help trade, because all factors receive proportionately less. The production possibilities curves of the two countries will resemble those set forth in Figure 2.6, showing the Austrians capable of producing less

FIGURE 2.6. Different Real Costs; Identical Comparative Costs

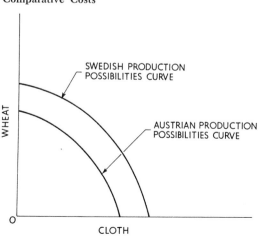

than the Swedes. But if tastes are the same in the two countries, the prices of wheat in terms of cloth and cloth in terms of wheat—to restrict ourselves to our two familiar commodities—will be the same. When the Austrian production possibilities curve is adjusted to a common point with the Swedish, as must be done following the technique of this chapter, it will be seen that the shape of the two curves is identical. This clinches the point that with identical tastes and identical comparative costs trade is impossible.

It follows from this that it is not the efficiency of factors as a whole which creates a basis for trade but the existence of factor differences, or of differences in factor efficiency which are not the same for all commodities and which are not offset by differences in tastes. If Austrian people were more efficient in cloth because they had a predilection for city life and were less efficient in agriculture, the basis for a difference in relative prices and for trade would exist.

The fact is, of course, that Austria and Sweden have roughly the same factor proportions and do trade to a considerable extent. This is because the real world does not conform to our two-country, two-commodity model. In a multicommodity world, two countries with roughly the same factor proportions will find a number of commodities which they can profitably exchange directly.

Equalization of Factor Prices

Trade takes place when relative prices differ between countries and continues until these relative differences—aside from transportation costs—have been eliminated. In the absence of transportation costs, in fact, trade would equalize relative commodity prices. In a more roundabout way, it may be noted further, trade tends to bring about the equalization of factor prices.

The export of products of the abundant factor increases the demand for its services and makes them relatively less abundant. The import of products embodying large amounts of scarce factors makes those factors less scarce in the domestic market. Exports will raise the price of the abundant and cheap factor; imports will reduce the return to the scarce and expensive factor. For example, the export of farm products from the United States raises the income of agricultural land and hence its value, while the import of precision instruments reduces the scarcity and hence the return to the type of skilled labor employed in this field.

Under certain limited conditions, this tendency toward factor-price equalization will be carried to the point where factor prices are fully equalized. The assumptions are highly restrictive. There must be as many or more commodities than factors; broadly similar tastes; identical production functions of a simple character, different as between the two commodities and each providing a limited degree of factor substitution; no transport costs or other barriers to trade to inhibit full commodity price equalization; perfect competition; and something of every commodity produced and consumed in every country after trade. Appendix B contains a formal proof of the proposition with two commodities and two factors.

How significant the tendency to factor-price equalization through trade in the real world is has been sharply debated. It is claimed, for example, that trade between developed and less developed countries widens the gap in living standards (and factor prices such as wages) rather than narrows it, and it is evident after centuries of trade that there are still poor as well as rich countries. The result may be due to other factors which overwhelm any tendency to equalization, or it may derive, as radical thinkers believe, from the nature of neoimperialist or neocolonial trade. Even though the theorem is not generally true, it is likely that it is more than an intellectual curiosity. If the assumptions for full factor-price equalization do not prevail everywhere in the world, the analysis is nonetheless relevant among broadly similar countries, as in the European common market, and it focuses attention on significant consequences of trade. Trade tends to raise the price of the abundant factor and weaken the price of the scarce factor, and where trade is based on differences in factor endowments, this repercussion of trade on factor prices is vastly important, politically as well as economically.

Increasing Returns

All this has been described in terms of constant and decreasing returns. Economic theorists, moreover, object to discussion of increasing returns because where economies are internal to the firm the assumption is not consistent with the assumption of perfect competition. With competition, increasing returns to the firm would quickly lead to its expansion, until one firm took over an industry, the country, or the world. Economies external to the firm are accepted as legitimate but thought not to be very extensive.

But increasing returns based on internal economies have always played a role in discussion of international trade theory and policy, usually in connection with the infant-industry argument for a tariff. This can be justified in one of two ways: as a reflection of a long-run cost curve which falls, i.e., moves down and to the right historically, even though at any point in time it is sloping upward; and more recently, as discovered by the theorists, through "learning by doing," in which unit cost is correlated not with current scale but with cumulative production over time, and the downward path of cost cannot be foretold. In both cases, and where the economies are external to the firm, diagrammatic representation of increasing returns must be undertaken with care, since the path toward lower costs is irreversible.

Increasing returns may be diagrammed in several ways. In Figure 2.7a the production possibilities curve *AQB* is convex to the origin and shows decreasing costs of automobiles in terms of agricultural machinery and of agricultural machinery in terms of automobiles, starting from the position *Q* where the price of automobiles in terms of agricultural machinery is given as *p–p*. If the increasing returns are due to internal economies, *Q* is an unstable equilibrium which cannot exist under competitive condi-

FIGURE 2.7*a*. Increasing Returns, Two Commodities

FIGURE 2.7*b*. Decreasing Opportunity Costs, One Commodity

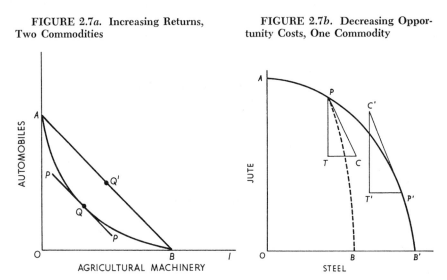

tions. Any slight disturbance, increasing the price of automobiles in terms of agricultural machinery, i.e., flattening the *p–p* line, will make producers shift out of agricultural machinery into automobiles. They will, however, be unable to find a new equilibrium position until they have shifted all their resources and arrive at *A*. If originally the price of agricultural machinery has risen, i.e., if the *p–p* line had become steeper, there would have been a pull toward *B* which would have to continue until *B* was reached.

In Figure 2.7*b*, the problem is not so much decreasing opportunity costs as the departure of private from social costs. One form this departure can take is that of economies external to the firm. The production possibilities curve *A–B′* represents the social transformation curve between jute and steel, but entrepreneurs, given market prices of factors of production which, let us say, exaggerate the real costs of making steel, operate as if the production possibilities curve were *A–P–B*. Under these circumstances they will produce at *P*, trade *P–T* of jute for *T–C* of steel, and consume at *C*, which is below the social transformation curve. If there were some way to equate private to social costs, the production point would move to *P′*, the country would export *T′–P′* of steel and import *C′–T′* of jute to end up much better off.

Under increasing costs there is no reason for relative prices in two countries with roughly the same sort of resources and comparable tastes to differ sufficiently to disclose comparative advantages which will lead to trade. And yet it is known that trade takes place among industrial countries, with roughly the same factor proportions, such as Britain, Germany, Japan, and the United States, and that between countries with different factor proportions some trade takes place in like, but not quite identical, goods. Twenty-five percent of Britain's imports consist of finished manufactured goods, and 33 percent of the imports of the United States. This trade is of the sort based on specialization which springs from increasing returns.

While increasing returns may be inadmissible in the short run as largely incompatible with static equilibrium, their long-run historical validity makes Figure 2.7a an important explanation of the rise of trade. Differences in comparative costs come about not only because of differences in factor endowments but also through specialization in different commodities. To a degree the choice of whether the United States or Britain specializes in one kind of an automobile or another, or this tractor or that, may be determined by historical accident. The fact is that, with each country specialized, a basis for trade exists, since each can produce one good cheaper than the other.

When increasing returns are due to internal economies of scale, Figure 2.7a represents the position only momentarily as the country in question is poised between specialization in automobiles or agricultural machinery. After a choice has been made, capital committed, and capacity built, the production possibilities curve will no longer be convex to the origin but will resemble the more normal curves in previous diagrams.

The other diagram, Figure 2.7b, illustrates a standard argument for tariffs. This fact will merely be noted here, since tariffs will not be addressed until Chapter 7. If a tariff on steel (or possibly an export tax on jute combined with a subsidy on steel) can move entrepreneurs from the transformation curve A–B to A–B', the welfare of the country in Figure 2.7b can be improved.

Summary

The basis for trade, so far as supply is concerned, is found in differences in comparative costs. One country may be more efficient than another, as measured by factor inputs per unit of output, in the production of every possible commodity; but so long as it is not equally more efficient in every commodity, a basis for trade exists. It will pay the country to produce more of those goods in which it is relatively more efficient and to export these in return for goods in which its absolute advantage is least.

Differences in comparative costs arise because of the fact that different countries have different factor endowments and because different commodities are best produced with a predominance of one or another factor. Trade arises out of differences in relative factor prices but assists in narrowing them.

Differences in factor endowments explain the large portion of total trade that is represented by economic interchange between the temperate zones and the tropics, between densely populated industrial communities and sparsely settled agricultural lands in the temperate zone, not to mention mining communities and countries with other specialized resources. But trade may also flourish between countries with similar factor endowments, particularly industrial areas, owing to differences in comparative costs produced by historically increasing returns.

Comparative costs thus furnish the basic ingredient of the answer to the classical question: What commodities will a country buy and sell in international trade? It is not the whole answer, since we have been concentrating on supply to the complete neglect of demand. But the subject of demand, as we shall see in the next chapter, can appropriately be covered in providing the answer to the second classical question: At what price will these goods be traded?

SUGGESTED READING

See Suggested Reading for Chapter 3, and Appendixes A and B.

Chapter 3	THE PURE THEORY OF INTERNATIONAL TRADE: DEMAND

The Law of Reciprocal Demand

There is a temptation to say that the law of comparative costs determines what commodities will be bought and sold in foreign trade, while the law of reciprocal demand sets the prices at which they will be traded. Some economic literature comes close to stating this, and many students learn the theory of foreign trade with some such generalization. But it is not quite true. In general-equilibrium theory, of course, demand and supply together determine the quantities of goods bought and sold and their prices. In a famous analogy Alfred Marshall compared demand and supply to the upper and lower blades of a pair of scissors, neither of which can do the cutting alone. For ease of exposition, however, we will follow the development of classical theory for a distance and approach something like an analytical separation of supply and demand.

Let us go back to our simple example of wheat and cloth produced in a man-week in the United States and Britain:

Production of One Man in One Week

Product	In United States	In United Kingdom
Wheat	6 bushels	2 bushels
Cloth	10 yards	6 yards

Before trade, wheat and cloth will exchange at 6:10 in the United States and 6:18 in the United Kingdom. These will be the limits beyond which the price after trade will not settle. Britain will be unwilling to pay more for 6 bushels of wheat than 18 yards of cloth; the United States will not want to accept less than 10 yards for the same amount of wheat. The United States is indifferent to foreign trade at 6:10; it makes no difference whether it exports wheat and imports cloth or produces both at home. But at this price, when it gets all the gain, Britain will be eager to trade. Conversely, Britain will be indifferent to trade, and the United States eager for it, at 6:18. Where, then, will the price settle?

There may be a tendency for the lazy theorist to split the difference and suggest 6 bushel of wheat for 14 yards of cloth. This was the method we used, arbitrarily, in the last chapter. But the technique cannot be defended. John Stuart Mill found the answer to the difficulty. More information is needed to settle on a price. In addition to production costs, there must be data on demand. What counts is the strength of the U.S. demand for wheat and cloth and the reciprocal strength of the British demand for the same products. The price at which foreign trade will take place is determined by what Mill called the "law of reciprocal demand."

The nature of the interacting demands can be illustrated by the device of stationing an auctioneer in mid-Atlantic. He has the task of finding a price to apply in both countries, where the exports of wheat that the United States is willing to ship against imports of cloth will match the exports of cloth that Britain is willing to sell for wheat. Too high a price for cloth in terms of wheat will call forth offers of cloth from Britain and demands for wheat, but inadequate offers of wheat or calls for cloth. Conversely, too high a price for wheat in terms of cloth will burden the auctioneer with unsought wheat from the United States and more bids than offers for cloth.

If the two countries are of unequal size, the reciprocal aspect of demand may not come into play at all. The price ratio of the larger country will prevail, and the smaller country can sell as much cloth or wheat to the other as it chooses at the established given price. This is the importance of being unimportant. In theory at least, the small country can reap large gains from trade. Guatemala, which cannot dream of manufacturing cash registers for years to come, can buy them at the U.S. price and sell coffee at the price determined by Brazil and the United States. The case of trading at the price ratio existing in the larger country before trade, which is one limit of profitable trade, may be more frequent than the classical economists have suspected. But where demand and supply in one country or the other are not so large as to overwhelm demand and supply in the other, the law of reciprocal demand comes into play to settle price.

Offer Curves

The theory behind Mill's law of reciprocal demand has been portrayed graphically with so-called offer curves. These start out with a somewhat different geometrical perspective than production possibilities curves. In Figure 3.1*a* we show a price ratio between X and Y, which is the same as the production possibilities curve with constant costs. As a production possibilities curve, we are concerned with the increase in the production of one good as the output of the other is decreased, i.e., in the absolute values

FIGURE 3.1a. Relative Prices of X and Y

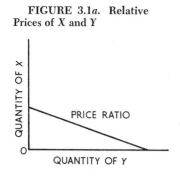

FIGURE 3.1b. Relative Prices of X and Y

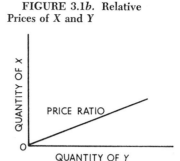

of the curve. As a price, however, we are interested merely in the quantity of X which has the same value as a quantity of Y, i.e., in the slope of the line. In this case the negative slope, that is, the downward slope from left to right, has no significance, and we can draw the line X with a positive slope from the origin (O). In Figure 3.1b the price ratio between X and Y can be extended any distance to show what quantity of X will be exchanged for what quantity of Y.

The offer curve of a country, i.e., the amount of wheat it is willing to offer for cloth, may start out like this price curve. In any event, the price line is a limit beyond which the offer curve cannot go. This has already been stated and is obvious enough; no country will export products for less in the way of imports than it can produce in import-competing goods at home. For a small amount of imports, moreover, a country may be indifferent whether it produces at home or buys at the same price in foreign trade, so that the offer curve, shown in Figure 3.2, may follow for a distance the price line in the absence of trade, shown in Figure 3.1b.

Beyond this distance, however, the offer curve moves away from the

FIGURE 3.2. Britain's Offer Curve of Cloth (demand for wheat)

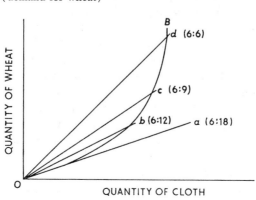

no-trade price line. Figure 3.2 portrays the British offer curve, *O–B,* which shows the amounts of cloth Britain will offer at various prices for given amounts of wheat. Line *a* is the ratio at which cloth and wheat exchange in the absence of trade (6 bushels against 18 yards). The offer curve can be regarded as a supply curve in international trade, representing various amounts of cloth Britain is willing to exchange against specific amounts of wheat. Or it can be regarded as a demand curve (of a special sort), indicating the amounts of wheat Britain is interested in acquiring for specified amounts of cloth. The offer curve is derived by ascertaining the amount of cloth Britain wants to exchange for wheat or of wheat it wants to acquire against cloth, at various prices for the two commodities, one in terms of the other. The prices are represented by rays from the origin. The offer curve connects up the amounts Britain wants to trade at various prices and includes the straight-line portion where Britain is indifferent whether it trades or not.

Beyond the portion of the curve where it is indifferent to trade, Britain is likely to offer less and less cloth for wheat as more and more wheat becomes available. In part, this will be because Britain wants wheat less; in part because cloth becomes more valuable as its supply is reduced through exports. At some point such as *d* Britain may be unwilling to give up any more cloth for additional wheat. At this point Britain's offer curve, interpreted as a demand for wheat against cloth, has unitary elasticity in that it is prepared to offer only the same amount of cloth for larger amounts of wheat. As a supply of cloth offered for wheat, the offer curve has zero elasticity, since the supply of cloth is invariant to increasing amounts of wheat offered in exchange. The point to be noted is that the elasticity of the offer curve can be interpreted in various ways: as an import elasticity, reflecting the change in imports corresponding to a change in price; as an export elasticity, representing the change in exports associated with a change in price; or as a total elasticity, which is the percentage change in imports relative to the percentage change in exports at a point on the curve. The most usual concept of elasticity of the offer curve, used for example in Appendix D, is the import elasticity.

The offer curve is not an ordinary demand or supply curve, of course. As a demand curve, for example, it expresses the demand for one commodity (imports) in terms of the supply of another (exports), whereas the normal demand curve expresses the demand for a given commodity in terms of money. The money measure used, however, is price per unit, not total money spent. If the second commodity be regarded as money, which is possible, the offer curve would be a demand curve in terms of quantities of commodities against total amount of money. It would be a total revenue curve, as opposed to a demand curve, which compares quantity with average revenue per unit.

The British offer curve of cloth for wheat has been given in Figure

FIGURE 3.3*a*. U.S. Offer Curve of Wheat (demand for cloth)

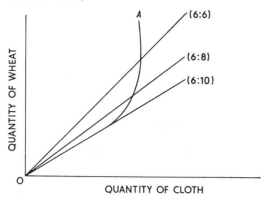

FIGURE 3.3*b*

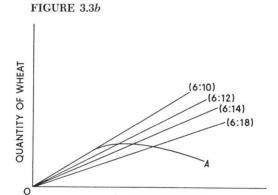

3.2. A similar curve for the United States is shown in Figure 3.3*a*, starting from the 6:10 domestic U.S. ratio rather than the British ratio of 6:18. But there is no one to offer wheat for cloth at prices for cloth above 6:10. The real issue is what the United States will trade at lower prices for cloth or at higher prices for wheat. The offer curve must bend down, as in Figure 3.3*b*.

If the offer curves for the United States and Britain now are taken on the same basis, they will cross. This point (*P* in Figure 3.4) will show where our auctioneer would get the same price for wheat and cloth in both countries (*O–P*) and equal amounts of wheat and cloth exported and imported by the United States and Britain. At any other point than *P* (say, *t*) the United States would be willing to pay broadly as much wheat as at *P* for a good deal less cloth. But for this amount of cloth, Britain is willing to accept a good deal less wheat, as indicated by the point *w*. Neither *t* nor *w* can serve as a point of equilibrium, because the **terms of**

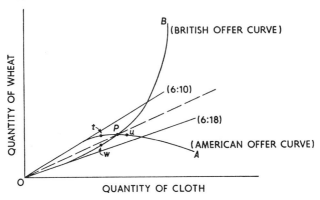

FIGURE 3.4. Law of Reciprocal Demand: Intersection of Two Offer Curves

trade implied by the ray from the origin to each point do not suffice to clear the market. At the relatively high price for wheat in terms of cloth represented by O (w, for example), the British would offer only a small amount of cloth, and the United States would want considerably more (see point u).

Supply and the Offer Curve

The identification of the offer curve with the law of reciprocal demand conveys an impression that prices in international trade are determined by demand alone and not by production costs. This would be the case if exchanges were undertaken with fixed initial endowments of goods rather than goods produced currently. The late Frank D. Graham of Princeton attacked the law of reciprocal demand as appropriate only to trade in antiques and old masters. But the criticism goes too far. The offer curve embodies production as well as demand, as implied by the remark that in the case of a constant opportunity cost, it starts out to follow the no-gain price line derived from the straight-line production possibilities curve. A more general demonstration is offered to the curious student in Appendix C.

But demand has an important role to play. To demonstrate this, we must master another geometric technique, that of the indifference curve.

Indifference Curves

The indifference curve may be compared with a contour line. A single curve represents a single level of satisfaction or utility, made up of varying combinations of two goods. Let us take our familiar products, wheat and cloth. The indifference curve a–a in Figure 3.5a shows an example in

FIGURE 3.5*a.* Single
Indifference Curve

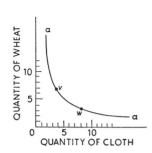

FIGURE 3.5*b.* Indiffer-
ence Map

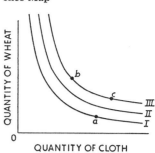

which a consumer is indifferent whether he has 7 bushels of wheat and
4 yards of cloth (*v*), or 3 bushels of wheat and 8 yards of cloth (*w*), or
any other combination which may be read off the same curve. It will be
observed that the single indifference curve is convex to the origin and flat-
tens out to become asymptotic to the axes at each end. After a certain
point, as in offer curves, a consumer is unwilling to give up any more
wheat simply to get more cloth, of which he already has plenty, or, at the
other end, to lose more scarce, valuable cloth for redundant wheat.

The single indifference curve represents the combination in which a
consumer with a given utility level would purchase two commodities as
the price between them is varied. The notion of price here takes us back
to the example we used in the previous chapter, which was demonstrated
again in Figure 3.1*a.* The indifference curve is made up of a series of points
designating quantities of wheat and cloth, respectively, which would be
bought with a given income at a series of prices ranging between infinity
and zero for wheat in terms of cloth. The same thing may be said in still
another way. At a given price, the consumer with a level of real income
indicated by a given indifference curve will consume the quantity of the
two commodities indicated by the point of tangency of the price line to
the indifference curve.

Like contour lines, indifference curves are arranged in maps in which
the parallel lines indicate progress in the indicated direction from a lower
degree of satisfaction (or altitude) to a higher. In Figure 3.5*b,* for example, point *b* on indifference curve *III* is taken to represent a higher level
of satisfaction or welfare than point *a* on indifference curve *I,* even though
it has more wheat and less cloth. The extra wheat is more than sufficient
to compensate for the loss of cloth. Point *c,* where there is more of both, is
clearly superior in satisfaction to point *a,* and the consumer is indifferent
between *c* and *b.*

The higher branches of economic theory raise a difficult question about
community indifference curves. It is agreed that the indifference map of

an individual is conceptually satisfactory and could be set down if anyone could be found who was sufficiently confident of the logic and stability of his tastes to submit to questioning. If an individual believes that he is better off than he was before with 5 more bushels of wheat and 2 less yards of cloth—substantially better off—there is no one to gainsay him. But there may be objection, it is suggested, to the notion that the community is better off with an average of 5 bushels more and 2 yards less. Some members of the community lose the cloth, while others gain the wheat. Who can say that the increase in satisfaction of the one is greater than the decrease in satisfaction of the other? Or if the changes are evenly distributed, there is still a problem if there are some who vastly prefer cloth over wheat and others with opposite tastes. In this case it is impossible to say that the gain of the wheat devotees outweighs the loss in satisfaction of the cloth addicts. Levels of satisfaction or welfare cannot be compared from one person to another.

These are real difficulties, as we shall see later in our discussion of commercial policy. If one group in the community is better off as a result of some action but others are in a worse position, it is impossible to say how the welfare of the community as a whole has been affected. The change in income distribution where people have different tastes produces a new indifference map whose contours intersect those of the original. But indifference curves are only useful when they do not intersect. Intersecting curves imply that utility level *I* is sometimes superior to and sometimes inferior to utility level *II*, an intolerable state of affairs. Despite these difficulties, however, we continue to use indifference curves—although with caution. One basis for so doing is the simplifying assumptions that the tastes of the community can be described by the tastes of an individual, that these are consistent from one period to another, and that there is no change in income distribution. These assumptions are clearly contrary to realism. Another justification used by welfare economists has been the "compensation principle": If it is clear that the beneficiaries of a change in price have enough additional income to compensate (or bribe) the losers for their loss, and some left over, the new position represents an improvement. If the wheat addicts can afford to underwrite the losses of the cloth addicts, and the cloth addicts are not anxious to bribe the wheat addicts to abstain from trade, trade unambiguously makes possible an improvement in utility, whether in fact compensation takes place or not.

However unrealistic, the community indifference curve is schematically a neat device. In the first place, it provides us with the answer to the price at which wheat and cloth will be traded in the two communities with decreasing returns and in the absence of trade. The price which will prevail in a single market is that which is tangent both to the production possibilities curve (*AB*) and to the highest possible indifference curve (in this case curve *II*). Production and consumption will both take place, in the absence of trade, at this point of tangency. This is shown by point Q in Figure 3.6. At any point on a higher indifference curve (say, t) the quantities of wheat and cloth involved are beyond the capacity of the economy to produce. At any point on a lower indifference curve, satisfaction can be increased by shifting production toward wheat away from cloth, or vice versa. Point r, for example, represents the quantities of wheat and cloth that consumers would take at a price for wheat and cloth in terms of each other tangent to indifference curve I at r.

FIGURE 3.6. Indifference Curves, Production Possibilities Curve without Trade

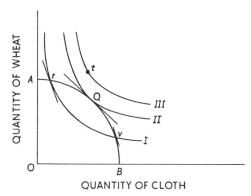

But, at this price, maximum production would require output at v. Let the student who has doubts refer back to Figure 2.4*b* and the discussion it brought on. The price of cloth is so high in terms of wheat that resources will be shifted from wheat to cloth. But this production cannot be sold at these prices. There is far too much cloth and far too little wheat to satisfy consumers, who at this price would consume more wheat and less cloth. In order to get rid of output, the price of wheat will have to be raised and that of cloth lowered. This means another shift of production from v. And so it would oscillate, first consumers and then producers dissatisfied with the combinations of wheat and cloth until a stable equilibrium is found at the point where the production possibilities curve is tangent to the highest possible indifference curve.

As long as decreasing returns exist, there will always be such a point. (And only one point.) While there is only one production possibilities curve, there are an infinite number of indifference curves which can be drawn representing infinitesimally small increases in real income. If these indifference curves do not intersect, as we assume they do not, any production possibilities curve must produce one point of tangency to a family of indifference curves.

The slope of this tangent is the price line. It is also the **marginal rate of**

substitution in consumption on the indifference curve and the **marginal rate of transformation** on the production possibilities curve. When the price ratio equals the marginal rate of substitution in consumption, consumers are in equilibrium. When the price ratio equals the marginal rate of transformation in production, producers are in equilibrium. When the marginal rate of substitution in consumption equals the marginal rate of transformation in production, without external trade, producers and consumers are both in equilibrium, and markets are cleared at existing prices.

The Terms of Trade

The indifference curve analysis can now be applied to the problem of trade between two open economies to indicate the quantities of goods bought and sold and the price at which they are traded (frequently referred to as the terms of trade), though the diagrams become somewhat complex. Let us assume that the United States and Britain have different production possibilities curves (increasing costs) but the same set of indifference curves. In the absence of foreign trade, production (and consumption) will take place at the points of tangency to the production possibilities curves which are also tangent to the highest possible indifference curves. In Figure 3.7, these points are *c* in the United States and *d* in

FIGURE 3.7. **Trade with Identical Tastes, Different Factor Endowments**

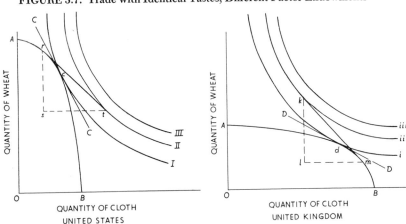

Britain. The tangents themselves, *C–C* and *D–D*, represent the prices at which wheat and cloth are traded in terms of each other in the United States and Britain before trade has been opened.

With the opening of trade, the amounts of wheat and cloth exported and imported in the two countries and the price at which they will be exchanged will be determined by parallel lines of equal length tangent to the respective production possibilities curves and tangent to a higher indifference curve. These lines, r–t in the United States and k–m in Britain, run in opposite directions from the production possibilities curves in order to reach higher indifference curves. The requirement that the lines must be parallel, or of the same slope, fulfills the condition that the prices in the two countries must be the same after trade is open, if transport costs be disregarded. The requirement that they be of equal length, as well as of the same slope, is in satisfaction of the necessary condition that exports of one country shall be imports of the other. It should be observed that Britain's exports of cloth (l–m) are equal to U.S. imports (s–t), while the U.S. exports of wheat (r–s) are equal to imports by Britain (k–l).

The effects of trade with different production possibilities curves and identical indifference curves are to make each country more specialized in production and less specialized in consumption. In both cases production slides farther along the production possibilities curve toward the output of the commodity for which the factors are most effective. Given the shape of the curves portrayed in Figure 3.7, however, consumption tends to move in the other direction—more toward equality, as the scarce commodity in each country becomes cheaper after importation.

While it is generally believed that countries are rather specialized in production and have broadly similar tastes in consumption, the shape of the indifference curves drawn in Figure 3.7 has no fundamental validity. Tastes (and hence indifference curves) may differ, as well as supply conditions. Indeed, as we shall see presently, trade is possible with identical supply conditions and different tastes. Whatever may be the indifference maps or supply conditions, however, trade is possible when the equilibrium prices in two countries without trade are different. Under these circumstances, there will be a new price at which it is possible for one or both to gain from exchange. In mathematical terms, trade is possible when the two countries find lines of equal length and slope which run from a tangency with the production possibilities curve of each country to a tangency with a higher indifference curve in one or both.

The Gains from Trade

The gains from trade in Figure 3.7 are measured separately for each country, and represent the added utility as the country moves from one indifference curve to a higher one, from *I* to *II* for the United States and *i* to *ii* for the United Kingdom. The diagram has a precision which is misleading, and special care must be exercised in attempting to compare one country's gains with those of another, except in the limiting case when for one country the posttrade price is virtually unchanged from the pretrade price. In this instance, the country in question gets no gain, and its trading partner gets all.

The difficulties with measuring and comparing gains from trade are several: indifference curve analysis has all the problems of aggregation discussed above. In addition, it is based on ordinal rather than cardinal utility: *III* is higher than *II*, and *II* higher than *I*, so that *III* is higher than *I*, but in no case can one say by how much without an explicit social welfare function, which converts ordinal into measurable cardinal utility. All the more is it impossible to compare the distance between *III* and *II* with that between *ii* and *i* without an international social welfare function, which says that a dollar of gain for one country is equal to one dollar (or two dollars or fifty cents) of gain for the other.

Again, if tastes change, a new indifference map is needed, and one cannot even say that a single country is better off (ordinally), compared with the position before the change in tastes.

Finally, in the real world, it is operationally difficult, approaching impossibility, to measure the change in prices before and after trade, or, from a given trading position, to estimate how much prices would be changed if trade were suddenly eliminated.

In these circumstances it is hard for the economist to make much sense out of the remarks of those, including representatives of other social sciences, who claim that the only acceptable trade is that in which the gains from trade are divided "equally," or who read into given trade situations a large measure of "exploitation." The crude analytical approximation of the gains from trade used by the economist—the change in the price of the export good between the no-trade and the posttrade positions, weighted by the volume of exports—is of little or no help.

Appendix C provides an exposition of a technique for putting offer curves, production possibilities curves, and consumption indifference maps on the same diagram. In fact, the production possibilities curve and the consumption indifference map are used to construct a trade indifference map from which the offer curve is derived. While the technique takes some time to master, for even the partially serious student it is worthwhile. It will not help him in deciding whether the gains from trade are divided "fairly" in the world, but he can benefit from acquaintance with the analytical difficulties.

Different Tastes

The possibility of trade between countries with the same factor endowment and different tastes has already been mentioned. Two countries can produce wheat or rice equally well but, as consumers, rank them differently. Figure 3.8 illustrates this case. In the absence of trade, wheat is more expensive than rice in the country that prefers wheat to rice, and rice more expensive than wheat in the other. The opening of trade equalizes prices in the two countries and enables each country to move its consumption to a higher indifference curve by exchanging wheat for rice or the opposite. In this instance—the converse of the more usual case, in which tastes are more or less the same and factors differ—trade permits each country to specialize less in production and more in consumption. The explanation is that, prior to trade, each country used resources for the fa-

FIGURE 3.8. Trade with Identical Factor Endow-ments, Different Tastes

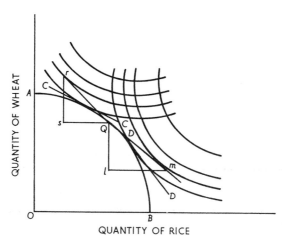

QUANTITY OF WHEAT

QUANTITY OF RICE

vored commodity that were more suited to the product it did not prefer. In the bread-eating country, for example, land suited to rice production was used, in the absence of trade, to grow wheat. With trade possible, this land can yield a higher return in terms of satisfaction by growing rice, which is now exchanged for wheat.

Identical Factors—Identical Tastes

The basis for trade between countries with identical factors under increasing returns was set forth in the last chapter. Here it is necessary only to add the indifference curves which portray the demand side of the position. This is done in Figure 3.9. Identical tastes were implicitly assumed in the discussion in Chapter 2, so that no further explanation is required. In the absence of trade, production is at point p in both countries. After trade begins and after producers in both countries have become aware of the possibility of economics of scale, production in one country will shift to the limit of the production possibilities curve, at either A or B, and that in the other country will be likely to shift to the other extreme. Under these circumstances, trade takes place to shift consumption in both countries to a higher indifference curve, i.e., to point p' on indifference curve II.

FIGURE 3.9. Trade with Identical Factor Endowments, Identical Tastes, Increasing Returns

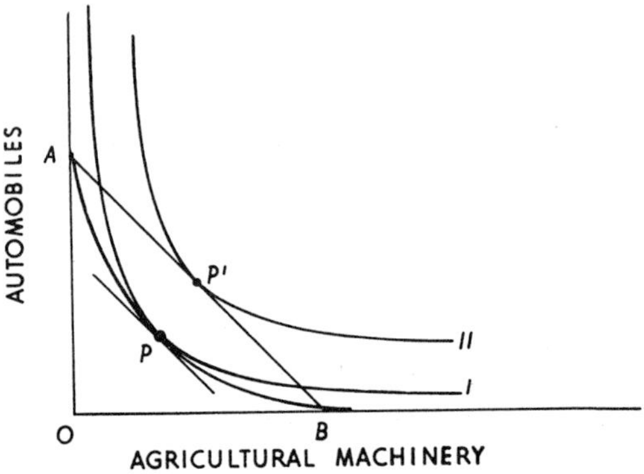

More Commodities, More Countries

The analysis of this chapter has been limited to two countries and to two goods. There are a number of economists who believe that the analysis is fundamentally altered if it is broadened to include more countries and more commodities. The majority, however, do not accept this view, believing that the two-country, two-commodity analysis is capable of extension, by means of a variety of techniques, to the more intricate and more realistic models.

Given, say, five commodities produced in each of two countries, these can be ranged in order of comparative advantage in each country. Initially one can say only that a country will export the commodity in which it has the largest advantage and import the commodity in which its disadvantage is greatest. The question of whether it will export or import the three commodities between these limits will then depend upon the balance of trade. If the demand for imports of the commodity offering a large disadvantage is very great, it may have to export all four of the other commodities, given the nature of the foreign demand for them, to balance its accounts.

More than two countries can be handled by aggregating all but one into a special country called "Rest of the World" and treating it as a single entity. But this may hide certain problems rather than illuminate them. These we save for Chapter 11, "Economic Integration."

General Equilibrium

In its most general form, the answer to the first two questions raised by the classical economists reduces to the statement that what goods will be produced and the prices at which they will be traded will be determined by supply and demand and that the supply and demand for goods will both determine and be determined by the supply and demand for factors of production.

The system of equilibrium is an interacting one. In each country, the prices of goods are equal to **marginal rates of transformation in production,** behind which stand factor endowments, factor prices, and production functions (which embody a technology for converting factor inputs into goods outputs), and to the **marginal rates of substitution in consumption,** behind which lie tastes, income levels, and income distribution. Moreover in the absence of transport costs, the prices of goods are the same in the several countries, with prices and rates of transformation in production, in consumption, and in international trade all the same and one country's exports paying for its imports. When a change occurs in factor endowments, tastes, technology, transport costs, and the like, the whole system changes and there are shifts of production possibilities, indifference, and demand and supply curves, which have been directly affected by the change, as well as shifts along other curves. Goods prices and factor prices will change. In the usual case, moreover, there will be complications from the existence of money, money incomes, savings, exchange rates and capital movements.

A fundamental aspect of economic analysis is that the profession is best at saying what will happen under conditions of **partial equilibrium,** when a change occurs only in a narrow part of the system and its repercussions over the whole system can be ignored. In partial equilibrium one assumes "other things equal," or *ceteris paribus.* In general equilibrium, on the other hand, it is necessary to trace interactions and feedbacks throughout the system. Instead of *ceteris paribus,* one must work with the assumption of *mutatis mutandis,* changing those things which ought to be changed, for those who fail to recall this Latin ablative absolute. As we shall see below, international economics is filled with situations in which the initial temptation to use partial analysis must be resisted because the feedbacks and interactions are significant.

This concludes our presentation of the pure theory of international trade in its classical and neoclassical form. The next task is to make the picture more realistic, by relaxing some of the assumptions underlying it. In the next chapter we get away from the assumptions of fixed factor endowments on the one hand and, on the other, those of fixed production functions, a given technology, or what Frank W. Taussig used to call "a given state of the arts." In Chapter 5 we explore the possibility that the classical theory of comparative advantage cannot apply to the less developed countries because their situation departs from the classic assumptions in a variety of particulars, especially their inability to shift smoothly and costlessly along the production possibilities curve and their lack of perfect competition in goods and factor markets. The final chapter in this part, Chapter 6, lends verisimilitude to an otherwise unconvincing tale by introducing transport costs.

Summary

Ricardo answered the question of what commodities are exported and imported by stating that this will be determined by the law of comparative cost; Mill answered the question of what prices will rule in international trade by stating that this would be determined by the law of reciprocal demand. It was necessary to find a price which would exchange all the goods that one country had to sell for all that the other wanted to offer. Intersecting offer curves show how this law operates.

But this analysis tended to submerge the effect of changes in supply. A diagrammatic analysis has been developed which combines production possibilities curves for supply with community indifference maps for demand. There are some difficulties posed by the community indifference maps, but they are used nonetheless. In the absence of trade, production and consumption will both take place at the tangent between the production possibilities curve and the highest indifference curve. With trade, it is possible to effect gains which carry each country beyond its production possibilities curve. Trade will take place at a price the same in each country, tangent to the production possibilities curve and a higher (for at least one country) indifference curve. This price line is then the hypotenuse of a right-angle triangle in which the other legs measure exports and imports.

The theory of international trade starts off with factor supplies, technology, tastes, and similar givens in a number of countries and integrates them into a general-equilibrium system in which goods and factor prices are related to one another. Goods move between countries, factors do not. In the two-commodity, two-country, two-factor case, producers and consumers are in equilibrium as the prices of the traded goods (the marginal rate of transformation of the goods in trade) equals the marginal rate of transformation in production and the marginal rate of substitution in consumption.

SUGGESTED READING

Texts

See Peter B. Kenen, *International Economics*, Foundations of Modern Economics Series, 3d ed. (Englewood Cliffs, N.J.: Prentice-Hall, Inc., 1971) (paperback) for a less rigorous treatment. See also Heller, chaps. 2–6; Findlay, chaps. 2–4; and Kemp, chaps. 2 and 3. Excerpts from classical writing are presented in W. R. Allen, *International Trade Theory: Hume to Ohlin* (New York: Random House, Inc., 1965) (paperback).

Treatises, Etc.

For the technical literature, see the articles cited in the Suggested Reading in Appendixes A and B. Beyond this, there is an infinitude of choice. See especially American Economics Association, *Readings in the Theory of International Trade,* the section on "Price Theory and International Trade," with articles by Leontief, Samuelson, Williams, Heckscher and Graham; American Economic Association, *Readings in International Economics,* part I on "The Theory of Comparative Advantage," with papers by R. Robinson, Metzler, Samuelson, Rybczynski, Johnson and Kenen, plus those in part III, "Trade Policy and Welfare," by Baldwin and Haberler; and Bhagwati, *International Trade,* with Lancaster and Jones on the Heckscher-Ohlin theorem and Samuelson on the gains from trade, a 1962 article which follows his 1939 paper in *Readings in the Theory of International Trade.*

On more than two factors and commodities, see the papers by Jones, and Vanek and Bertrand in Bhagwati et al., *Trade, Balance of Payments and Growth.* For modern classic articles in international trade theory (not really a contradiction) see *The Collected Scientific Papers of P. A. Samuelson,* Vols. I and II, edited by J. E. Stiglitz (Cambridge, Mass.: The M.I.T. Press, 1966), and Vol. III, edited by R. C. Merton (1972). See especially, in addition to the articles cited above, in Vol. III, "An Exact Hume-Ricardo-Marshall Model of International Trade" (from *JIE,* February 1971).

Surveys of international trade theory are popular and will introduce the student to a much wider selection of bibliographical material, if that is needed. See especially those by Haberler (*SPIE,* No. 1, July 1961), Corden (*SPIE,* No. 7, March 1965) and Bhagwati (*EJ,* March 1964), reprinted with an addendum in Bhagwati's *Trade, Tariffs and Growth, Essays in International Economics* (Cambridge, Mass.: The M.I.T. Press, 1969). The enlarged survey has a bibliography of 208 items.

B. Ohlin's statement of the general-equilibrium position is a useful one in prose. See *Interregional and International Trade* (Cambridge, Mass.: Harvard University Press, 1933: rev. ed. 1967), chaps. 5–7 and 13. This theory is presented mathematically by J. L. Mosak, *General Equilibrium Theory in International Trade* (Bloomington, Ind.: Principia Press, 1944). A linear programming solution to comparative advantage is given in R. Dorfman, P. A. Samuelson, and R. M. Solow, *Linear Programming and Economic Analysis* (New York: McGraw-Hill Book Co., Inc., 1958) chap. 5 and especially pp. 117–21.

Points

J. B. Condliffe, *The Commerce of Nations* (New York: W. W. Norton & Co., Inc., 1950), gives an excellent account of the development of laissez-faire in the 19th century which makes useful supplementary reading. See especially chapters 6–8 and 13.

The teacher who wants to illustrate the theory of comparative advantage in practice is referred to G. D. M. MacDougall's essay in American Economic Association, *Readings in International Economics;* B. Balassa, "An Empirical

Demonstration of Classical Comparative Costs," *RE & S*, August 1963; and R. M. Stern, "British and American Productivity and Comparative Costs in International Trade," *OEP*, October 1962. An attempt to apply the theory to reality is set out in chaps. 3–5 in C. P. Kindleberger, *Foreign Trade and the National Economy* (New Haven, Conn.: Yale University Press, 1962) (paperback).

COMPARATIVE STATICS OF TRADE: CHANGES IN TASTES, FACTOR ENDOWMENTS, TECHNOLOGY

The Simple Assumptions of Heckscher-Ohlin Comparative Advantage

In addition to the two-by-two-by-two assumptions of most analysis in the pure theory of trade—two countries, two commodities, two (homogeneous) factors—the theory generally abstracts from a number of other circumstances which make it somewhat unrealistic. It is assumed, for example, that tastes, factor endowments, and technology are fixed, that information is costless and ubiquitous. It is necessary to relax these assumptions, and this is best done one at a time, in comparative statics. We reserve for the next chapter a statement of the objection to free trade raised by developing countries, which is largely built on dynamic arguments.

So doubtful is the assumption that the same technology is available all over the world (and the labor with the identical technological capacity) that many economists believe that the Heckscher-Ohlin theory, however much it may apply to trade in primary products such as foodstuffs and raw material, is of little relevance to trade in manufactured goods, except possibly those of the simplest kind.

Changes in Tastes

We need not spend much time with tastes. It is sufficient to point out that the analysis based on opening up trade between two countries that had never traded before predicates a gain from trade on the existence of fixed tastes unchanged by the fact of newly opened trade. This of course is highly unrealistic. Trade has many origins—the exchange of gifts between primitive tribes; the plundering of the Middle East by Europeans during the Crusades or of Europe by Scandinavian pirates; and the opening of the western hemisphere by Spanish, Portuguese, and English explorers. In most historical origins of trade, the initial exchanges involved the creation of new wants, as well as their satisfaction. Tastes change with trade, even as trade satisfies existing wants more fully.

The point has significance beyond recalling the origin of cotton, muslin, sugar, and even tariffs as Arabic words, or the introduction of tobacco, rum, and the potato from North America to Europe. Ragnar Nurkse has pointed to the **demonstration effect** under which underdeveloped countries have learned about the existence of goods in developed nations which will lighten their burdens, satisfy their physical appetites, and titillate their innate sense of self-expression or exhibitionism. When modern methods of production are introduced into some particularly primitive societies, it is necessary to introduce modern methods of consumption. With the initiation of plantation cultivation of fruit, sugar, rubber, tea, and the like, there must come a change in the diet of native laborers, and the varied native subsistence fare must be replaced by staple imported foodstuffs. With the alteration in the pattern of living, there may be a worsening in the nutritional level of the diet and increased dietary deficiences.

When the price of exports rises with trade or that of imports falls, with all tastes and means of production unchanged, trade may be said to result in an unambiguous gain for a country as a whole, leaving aside the distribution of the gain within the country and the difficulties inherent in measuring the extent of the gain. But when the improvement in the terms of trade is accompanied by a shift in tastes in favor of imports, leading to an increase in demand for them, the case is not so clear. One can say that there is an improvement, as compared with the hypothetical case of increasing the demand for imports without satisfying it. A new want coming into existence along with trade to fill it, however, involves a departure from the classical assumptions and raises doubt as to the classical conclusion of gain. As mentioned briefly in the last chapter, with the change in tastes there is a change in the consumption indifference map as well as the trade indifference map, to use the jargon of Appendix C, and hence there is no basis for measuring gains or losses from trade.

There is some basis for thinking that the demonstration effect is stronger today than, say, before World War I. To take what may seem to be a trivial example but one of some importance for international trade, international exchanges increased greatly in the 19th century without bringing about any substantial homogeneity of taste in dress, diet, consumers' goods, or cultural pursuit. Such is less and less true. Trade in Europe in the 19th century continued side by side with different styles of national diet and cooking: The British was distinct from the Continental breakfast, and on the Continent itself Italian, French, German, and Scandinavian cooking all differed. Today the Indochinese complain that the native Asian breakfast is giving way to European eggs, bacon, and coffee; in Japan, rice is increasingly abandoned in favor of wheat; and Coca-Cola is a trademark known round the world. Demonstration effect is more significant for underdeveloped countries that frequently want to import—Swiss watches, British bicycles, and U.S. fountain pens at the most primitive level—before they have earned or arranged to borrow the necessary exchange. This possible source of disequilibrium will concern us in Part V. But even between developed countries these changes in taste which come with the introduction of new goods are significant, as the shift in American taste toward European products such as small cars demonstrates. And technology changes, of course, bring new tastes along with them. As often said, not only is necessity the mother of invention, but invention is the mother of necessity.

It is not enough to cultivate a taste for Cadillacs and caviar; one must be able to afford them. A Swedish economist lately turned politician, Staffan Burenstam Linder, built a theory of trade in manufactures on the basis of similar tastes, in turn linked to not widely dissimilar incomes. Assume, for example, two countries with identical consumption indifference maps but widely differing levels of income. In one sense their tastes are identical; in another they are dissimilar. The poor country spends 80 percent of its income on food; the rich perhaps 5 percent. The rich country spends let us say 20 percent of its income on transport (automobiles, airplane tickets, road construction, and the like), the latter only 3 percent. Rising income and differing income elasticities of demand—the percentage change in consumption of a given item relative to the percentage change in income—mean that even with fundamentally identical wants, the marginal rates of substitution of goods in consumption will differ between the rich and the poor.

Linder's theory is that countries at roughly the same level of income will trade a great deal with each other, exchanging one sort of differentiated product for another. Fiats are sold to Britain and British Fords to Italy. Peugeots exchange for Volkswagens. The gains from trade in these exports and imports are relatively limited, measured by how much the price of exports would decline or the price of the import competing would rise if the trade were cut off. In a welfare sense, therefore, faster growth of trade among the developed countries than between the developed and developing countries is not conclusive proof of more rapid gains from trade.

Linder's theory starts from the point that manufacturers produce first for the domestic market and then spill over into foreign markets. We return to this shortly in dealing with technological change as a basis for trade. But note here that the new goods are sold first to those countries with roughly the same level of income that are in a position to develop a taste for the new goods.

Changes in Factor Endowments

Tastes do not stand still, and neither do factor endowments. We can illustrate the impact of changes in factor endowments best, however, if we assume that tastes and technology are unaltered, while factor endowments grow. Capital and population are the factors that grow. Land presumably does not, and may even shrink through depletion (although this, as are so many general statements, is subject to qualification: land can expand in an economic sense through changes in technology which may make old ore deposits useful, for example, and through capital investment, as in reforestation and in new discovery, which seems to have run its course on this terrestrial globe but may not have so far as the universe is concerned). Suppose we start with the simple case of a two-country, two-commodity, two-factor model, based on capital and labor, where capital and labor grow in the same proportion, with technology and tastes fixed.

It is intuitively evident, and can be demonstrated with the geometry of Appendix A, that with an equal expansion of the two factors and no change in technology, the production possibilities curve will be expanded by pushing out evenly in all directions. In Figure 4.1, the production pos-

FIGURE 4.1. Effect of Neutral Expansion of Production Possibilities Curve on Trade

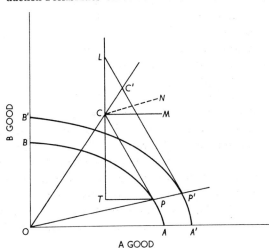

sibilities curve *A–B* will now become *A'–B'*. But what happens to trade and to the terms of trade? The answer, as the answer to every question in economics at this level of generality, is "It depends." But this answer is not enough to satisfy the teacher, and the student must go on to explain what it depends on. It depends first on the position with respect to demand, and second on the shape of the other offer curve.

In Figure 4.1, let the triangle *T–P–C* represent trade before factor growth, with exports, *T–P*, being exchanged for imports, *C–T*, at the terms of trade, *P–C. P* is the production point and *C* the consumption. The operational trick is to find out what happens to production and consumption with growth at the same terms of trade as before. If it turns out that the country wants to trade more at the old terms of trade, it is likely that it is going to have to accept a lower price for its exports and pay more for its imports. If, on the other hand, it wants to trade less, again at the original terms of trade, the outcome is likely to be the reverse: a higher price for exports and cheaper imports.

Since the growth of the production possibilities curve has been uniform, the production point *P'* on the new production possibilities curve *A'–B'* will lie on a straight-line ray from the origin *O–P*, which intersects *A'–B'* at *P'*. This is the result of the underlying linear homogeneous production functions, and unchanged terms of trade (as assumed), *P'–C'*. The question is now what happens to demand. If a right angle such as *L–C–M* is drawn with its origin at *C*, increased income from increased overall output will mean that the demand for both the A-good and the B-good expand, unless one of them is an inferior good. If we rule out inferior goods, the new consumption point has to lie within the triangle *L–C–M*. A neutral assumption is that the income elasticity of demand for the two goods is unity, i.e., that at the same price, goods A and B will be consumed in exactly the same proportions with the enlarged income as with the smaller. This possibility would put the new consumption point on a straight-line ray from the origin through *C*. With this assumption it is now clear what will happen: line segment *P'–C'* is parallel to and longer than *P–C*, which means that at the same terms of trade as before, the country would want to offer more of commodity A for more of commodity B. Its offer curve would have moved out to the right as in Figure 4.2. Un-

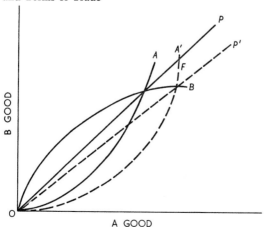

FIGURE 4.2. Effect of Neutral Expansion of Production and Homothetic Indifference Map on Trade and Terms of Trade

less the offer curve that *A* faces is a straight line, such as *O–P* in Figure 4.2, the terms of trade will shift against the expanding country, as shown by the dotted line in the same illustration.

But there is no need for demand to be homothetic, as the condition of consumption in fixed proportions with expanding income and constant price is called. If the path of consumption with increasing income but constant prices, the so-called **Engel's curve** (of which there is one curve for every possible price), through *C* is steeper than *C–C'*, demand favors the import good. With the demand for the B good income elastic, *A* will want to trade even more than the amounts of exports and imports implicit in the length and slope of *P'–C'*, and the market-clearing terms of trade, assuming *A* faces a *B* offer curve of less than infinite elasticity, will deteriorate still more. Indeed, the Engel's curve can favor the export good, for a bit, and *A* will still want to trade more of the A-good for more of the B-good because its expansion of production possibilities for the A-good exceeds its demand bias in favor of it. If a dotted line *C–N* is drawn exactly parallel to *P–P'* in Figure 4.1 and if the Engel's curve follows this line, *A* will want to trade the same amount before growth as after, and the terms of trade will remain unchanged. If the curve falls below it, demand favors the export good more than export production possibilities have grown, and the offer curve in Figure 4.2 will shift to the left of the original, *O–A*, *A*'s trade will fall, and its terms of trade will improve. But if the Engel's path cuts the *P'–L* curve anywhere above *C–N*, the terms of trade will decline, provided that the foreign offer curve is not infinitely elastic, or a straight line.

Of course there is no need for the production possibilities curve to expand neutrally, pushing out symmetrically along its whole length. If the A-good is capital intensive, and capital grows but not labor, the production possibilities curve will evidently grow in an **export-biased** fashion, as in Figure 4.3*a*. Or the factor which is intensively used in the import industry may be the one with the only or the greater expansion, as in Figure 4.3*b*. Note that growth can now be more than merely export or

FIGURE 4.3*a*. Export-Biased Growth

FIGURE 4.3*b*. Import-Biased Growth

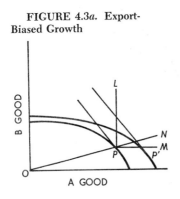

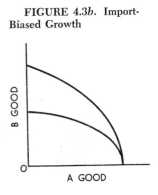

import biased. In Figure 4.3*a* a right angle set with its origin at *P* marks the boundaries within which growth can be defined to be import biased, neutral, or export biased. But on the production side, the tangency of the old price line to the new production possibilities curve can lie outside these limits, as at *P'*, where growth is **ultraexport biased.** This occurs when with new production possibilities and the old trading price, the country will produce not only more of the export but positively less of the import good. Growth now necessarily worsens the terms of trade (allowing for less than an infinitely elastic offer curve facing the country) so long as there are no inferior goods. And **ultraimport-biased** growth (not shown in Figure 4.3*b*) necessarily improves the terms of trade with the same qualifications.

Let us see if we can use this theoretical framework to say anything useful about the real world. First we should note that (as stated in the next chapter) the less developed countries claim the terms of trade tend against them because they have ultrabiased export growth, with an import-biased demand. This means that after growth, at the original terms of trade they would offer much more in the way of exports and, with higher incomes, would want much more in the way of imports, the production of which declines under ultrabiased growth. This shifts out the offer curve and worsens the terms of trade. There is more to their story, but the analysis is suggestive.

Second, it is of some interest to show the position of the United States with regard to natural resource products. Land, as already indicated, is a complex factor of production. In a given state of the arts, land can be increased by discovery or reduced by depletion, or, simultaneously, both. But the factor resource, land, as indeed every factor, can only be defined in terms of a technological process. An innovation will expand or contract the amount of land viewed as an economic agent. Land bearing low-grade taconite ores became an economic resource only after the taconite refining process was discovered.

It is hard to know whether, in the economic history of the United States since the Civil War, land has been an expanding, fixed, or contracting factor. For some purposes, such as oil production, land was enormously abundant and is now relatively scarce. In other minerals, depletion has exhausted the richest deposits. But discoveries and improvements in technology continue. Drilling for oil takes place in the continental shelf in the Gulf of Mexico, offshore in the Pacific, on the North Slope in Alaska, and is planned, or threatened, off Georges Bank in the Atlantic. Improvements in refinery techniques have just about reached the point where it will pay to extract oil from the abundant shales of the Rocky Mountain area. Land, the fixed factor, is seen to be subject to all sorts of changes.

If we assume land fixed, for purposes of illustration, and capital and labor growing together at a steady pace, the nature of comparative advantage may be seen to change. The United States used to be an exporter of a wide variety of metals and minerals. Now it is a net importer of all but two—coal and molybdenum. Copper, zinc, lead, iron, and especially oil, which we used to export, are now on a net import basis. Figure 4.4

FIGURE 4.4. Schematic Representation of the Change in U.S. Land-Intensive Commodities from Comparative Advantage to Comparative Disadvantage

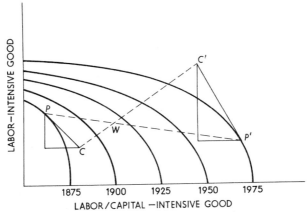

Source: J. Vanek, *The Natural Resource Content of United States Foreign Trade, 1870–1955* (Cambridge, Mass.: The M.I.T. Press, 1963).

shows a stereotyped representation of the nature of the change. The vertical axis measures land-intensive goods; the horizontal axis, on the other hand, represents the goods embodying primarily labor and capital. The inner production possibilities curve, marked 1875, shows a strong specialization in land-intensive production, which is in part exchanged for labor/capital-intensive goods. With the passage of time, the shape of the production possibilities curve changes. Land is fixed, and capital and labor grow. Production possibilities in the land-intensive product increase somewhat, as more capital and labor will produce more land-intensive products even with land unchanged. But the production possibilities curve grows mainly to the right. By 1920, as the figure is drawn, the production possibilities curve is fairly balanced on the scales shown. By 1950, it is skewed in favor of labor/capital-intensive products in place of its original skewness in the opposite direction.

The dotted line P–P' represents the locus of points of tangency to the successive production possibilities curves, where production has taken place. C–C' signifies the path of consumption. To the left of the intersection, i.e., prior to about 1920 as shown on the figure, land-intensive products were exported and labor/capital-intensive products imported. After 1920, or thereabouts, when the curves intersect, the trade position was reversed. The United States exported labor/capital-intensive products and imported the products of land.

This representation is, of course, purely schematic. It departs from reality in a hundred ways—two goods, constant technology, a fixed factor, incomplete specialization, and so forth. Problems of defining land-intensive products make it impossible to pin down when the change from an export to an import basis occurred in minerals. It was probably more nearly after World War II than after World War I. Nonetheless, the demonstration has validity in a very broad sense and helps illustrate how comparative advantages change with factor growth.

Technological Change—Making Old Goods More Cheaply

The analysis of technological change in existing goods follows broadly the same analysis as changes in factor proportions, but with a vast number of complications which we will eschew. Production functions can change so that the same factor combinations can produce more goods than before; or the technological change can be biased in such a way as to save more of one factor than the other. Saving a factor is equivalent to increasing its quantity. It is intuitively obvious that an unbiased and equal technological change in both commodities is exactly the same as a proportionate increase in both factors. Unless demand is biased in an offsetting way, and unless the offer curve facing the country is infinitely elastic, the country will have to give up at least some of its potential gain from greater technological efficiency in reduced terms of trade. Similarly, unbiased technological change in one commodity will lead to export- or import-biased expansion of the production possibilities curve, as in growth of a single factor.

Biased technological growth is more complex. If there is biased growth in the export good which augments the abundant factor, this will lead to export-biased growth, in fact to ultraexport-biased growth, since there are two tendencies working to expand exports. And biased technological growth in the import-competing good which augments the scarce factor will lead to ultraimport-biased growth. In between there are evidently a variety of intermediate cases, such as growth in the import sector which saves the abundant factor, or growth in the export sector which augments the scarce factor where one cannot say much without the specific data.

Factor Growth and Technological Change

While factor growth and technological change can be analytically distinguished, they may occur simultaneously or quasi simultaneously in the real world to maintain a comparative advantage in a given commodity.

During the interwar period, for example, the United States was losing its comparative advantage in agriculture. Agricultural products, which had represented 47 percent of U.S. exports in 1922–24, dwindled to 25 percent by 1937–39. Farm policies, including price supports, played a role in this deterioration, but one which we ignore. To a considerable extent the deterioration was the result of an increase in the price of labor which made a number of these commodities unable to compete in price on the world market.

Shortly before and during the course of World War II, however, a quasi revolution occurred in U.S. agriculture. Machinery and fertilizer, plus new techniques of dry farming in wheat and irrigation in cotton, raised yields and, especially, labor productivity. A number of farm products which had been exported on the basis of land-intensive comparative advantage could now be exported once more because they were capital intensive in a capital-intensive country. Others, such as rice, linseed, soybeans, and Turkish tobacco which had been imported changed over to an export basis.

The position was possibly even more striking in coal. Successive changes in technology developed successively larger stream shovels for open-pit mining until they reached the present 2,400-ton size capable of removing 80 tons of overburden in one bite. Investment costs in mining rose sharply, but labor costs declined still more so that despite high wage rates, the unit cost of coal fell (during a period of inflation). The depletion of land has been more than offset by the improvement in technology, with the result that coal has become an export product.

Changes in Technology—New Goods

Some years ago, Irving Kravis undertook an empirical investigation of the Heckscher-Ohlin theorem, looking especially to see if labor-intensive exports were produced by especially low-wage labor, and found to his evident surprise that in virtually every country the exporting industries were those that paid the highest wage rates. What a country produced and exported, he decided, was what it had "available," i.e., the goods its entrepreneurs and innovators developed. Availability meant an "elastic" supply. It did no good for a country to have the cheap labor to produce, say, transistors, if in fact it lacked inventors, or for an inventor to license the invention if the country lacked the innovators, entrepreneurs, skilled workmen, and so on, needed to produce the product. This theory challenged the assumption of the classical doctrine that technology was the same all over the world.

A good deal of work has been done in pursuing this and other leads into the technological basis for trade in new goods. Donald B. Keesing, for example, pushed forward to rescue the Heckscher-Ohlin analysis by exploring the connection between exports and high expenditure on research and development and between exports and advanced labor skills, such as those embodied in scientists and engineers. When the top commodity groups with the highest research effort—computers, electronics, nuclear energy, space equipment, and aircraft—are separated from 14 other major industries, it appears that the former export four times as much per dollar of sales as the latter. Or the measures can be put in terms of skilled labor as a percent of total employment. Whatever the measure, it has been found that U.S. exports have had a high technological component and that many of these exports diminish or disappear when the technological lead of the United States narrows or is lost.

Linder, as mentioned earlier, notes that inventions in new goods occur in rich goods where the markets are best for new experiences or cheaper ways of satisfying old needs. He asserts that exports start out as goods produced for the local market. This assumes that few if any products are developed originally for export. The student may amuse himself trying to develop counterexamples, such as Swiss wristwatches, produced in particular volume during World War I by a small country located on the borders of two warring countries, too busy to produce the necessary timepieces for their own use; or Christmas tree ornaments exported by a non-Christian country, such as Japan, on the basis of cheap labor.

Trade may thus be based on a **technological gap,** created either by a substantial endowment of the necessary knowledge of skills, or by the market for new goods, or both. But few countries long maintain a monopoly of the knowledge needed to make anything. Invention and innovation may give a country an absolute advantage for a time, but they are followed in relatively short order by imitation, which leads back to the conditions of similar production functions worldwide—the assumption underlying the Heckscher-Ohlin basis for trade.

Raymond Vernon has generalized this pattern of experience into what he calls the **product cycle** or cycle in the life of a new product. It is first "new," then maturing as it spreads to other industrialized countries, and finally standardized. Computers are at one end of the spectrum today, and textiles, leather goods, rubber products, and paper at the other. Some years ago a British economist suggested that automobiles would turn out to be the textiles of tomorrow. The spread of automobile production into the developing countries of Asia and Latin America—largely with heavy protection, but with exports emerging in copious quantities from Japan at long last—suggests that the good is trembling on the verge of "standardization."

The product cycle can be illustrated with the stylized diagram in Figure 4.5. In the early stage of development, with time measured along the horizontal axis, the innovation and production begin in, say, the United States, at period t_0 (the invention may have occurred anywhere; what

FIGURE 4.5. Export Cycle of a Commodity in Which Innovation Leads to Exports and Imitation Abroad Ultimately Leads to Imports

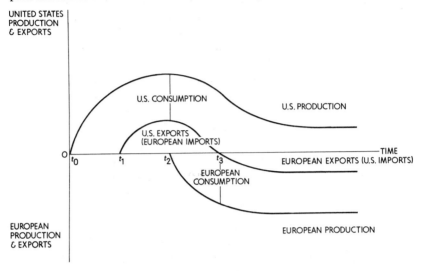

counts is the first commercial production). At t_1 exports begin from the United States which are imports and consumption in Europe, where quantities are measured negatively below the horizontal axis. At t_2 production begins in Europe. Vernon is interested in the question whether and when U.S. producers establish facilities for production abroad, but that subject will not engage us until Chapter 15. Whosoever's production it is, it substitutes for imports (exports of the United States), which decline, and may even turn into exports (U.S. imports at t_3 in Figure 4.5). This will occur if when the product has passed through the stage of "maturity" to "standardization," it turns out to have a high wage component that gives the comparative advantage, on a common technology, to Europe.

Shifting Comparative Advantage

A series of studies of the product cycle has been undertaken in particular industries which suggests that the pace of imitation is speeding up. In synthetic fibers, G. C. Hufbauer noted that comparative advantage is not based on raw materials. Countries that produce wood pulp (Canada and Sweden) and those with petroleum feed stock (in the Middle East and, for example, Venezuela) are notably not engaged in the production of fibers. In this industry, trade started with a technological breakthrough leading to a technological gap, became supported by economies of scale, ultimately spread through imitation, and became widely disseminated. In the end, comparative advantage shifted away from the innovators and settled to rest on wage costs, or factor proportions. A similar study in petrochemicals traced the product cycle in a closely related field.

A steady comparative advantage in research-intensive goods produces one structure of trade. The product cycle relates to a single good in which comparative advantage is lost and may turn into comparative disadvantage. The two can be combined into a dynamic process in which comparative advantage in new goods continues over a changing range of goods. The possibility that this explained U.S. trade was put forward as early as 1929 by John H. Williams. The notion languished as a general explanation although it survived in a number of studies of particular industries.

Erik Hoffmeyer observed the evolving character of U.S. trade in office machinery. At the earliest stage, U.S. innovators pioneered in typewriters, adding machines, and cash registers. With their increasing use in the domestic market, producers began to export them. With the passage of time, however, relatively simple machines were widely produced abroad on the one hand, and replaced by production in the United States of more complex machinery on the other. With time, therefore, the United States imported mechanical typewriters, adding machines, and so on, and exported electric typewriters, cash registers, and data processing machinery.

A thesis at the Massachusetts Institute of Technology on international trade in motion pictures observed that the United States pioneered in many film innovations and that after each one—the feature-length picture, talkies, color, wide-screen movies, and so on—there was a surge of exports. After a lag, based on the need to see whether the innovation would succeed and the time to imitate it, foreign producers followed suit. When the technology was widely known and adopted, the United States might or might not continue to export, or trade in differentiated products might move in both directions.

A recent study traces the diffusion of semiconductors within the United States and outward to Britain, France, Germany, and Japan—and could have done so to the lesser producers in Hong Kong and Taiwan—combining the product cycle in a single commodity and its major innovations. In this instance, lack of economies of scale assisted diffusion, but learning by doing and a rapidly advancing product made imitation dangerous.

Meeting or Setting the International Standard

For a country to break into international trade as an imitator, it must produce to an international standard of quality or suffer a penalty in lower prices. This is true in primary products and simple manufactures, as well as in complex manufactures. During the Civil War, in the 1860s, when Egypt and India sold cotton while the South was blockaded, it was said that Indian cotton was full of dirt. Almost 100 years later Turkish wheat broke into the world market with difficulty because it was said to be full of "rocks and mice." Japan long suffered a reputation as a producer of shoddy goods.

But where goods are manufactured and enjoy economies of scale, it can happen that a country with a small domestic market is forced to manufacture standardized products because its producers cannot produce enough for domestic needs to lower prices sufficiently to enter the world market. Jacques Drèze, a Belgian economist, explains that his country concentrates on production and exports not only by broad classes of goods such as semifinished iron and steel, flat glass, and photographic film, but also within categories of goods which vary in degree of standardization. The country produces white china, but not colored or decorated, and within automobile components, it produces batteries, tires, windows, upholstery fabrics, wiring harness and radiators, which are standardized among producers, rather than engines, bodies, and their parts, which vary more widely among producers, models, and countries.

This point may explain Belgian trade but cannot be a general case, since there are many small countries—Scandinavia, the Netherlands, Switzerland, for example—which export highly differentiated products, not all of which are immune from economies of scale. The scale is achieved through exporting rather than the home market alone, which seems to account for Danish silver, glass, and furniture; Dutch electrical equipment; Swedish machinery, ball-bearings, and telephones; Dutch electrical appliances; and Swiss watches and pharmaceuticals.

Marketing

It is not enough for the good to be produced cheaply and in acceptable quality. It must be sold, or to put it another way, it must be bought. Japan was slow in breaking into the international automobile and camera markets, despite cheap, good products, because it needed time to set up a system of dealers in the case of automobiles, and to get consumer acceptance of their products through advertizing and arrange distribution channels for the cameras.

In the 1920s, Czechoslovakia felt itself squeezed between Germany and the Soviet Union and made strong efforts to market its glassware, porcelain, jewelry, musical instruments, etc., in Britain and the United States. Once department store buyers included Prague on their normal itinerary, the problem was solved so long as costs and prices could be held down. In similar fashion, Italian success in knitted wear and shoes, based on high style and cheap labor, depended critically on enlisting the support of department store buyers, which eliminated the need for dealers who sold. So important is the marketing function that Italian firms making electrical appliances find it worthwhile to sell them under different trademarks in foreign markets—witness Hoover buying its vacuum cleaners in Italy and distributing them in Britain under its own label, or Zanussi merging with Phillips of the Netherlands to find outlets for its refrigerators and other household appliances.

Need for a New Theory in Manufactured Goods?

Do the existence of technological change and rising real income which demands improvements in goods alter the fundamental case for trade based on factor proportions? An attempt to resolve this issue in a conference of economists failed to reach a clear-cut decision. Changing incomes, tastes, technology, factor proportions, etc., complicate the analysis. Whether the change in degree is sufficient to constitute a change in kind is perhaps at basis a philosophical riddle depending upon definitions, rather than anything which can be handled on a yes-no level.

At this conference, Hufbauer assembled seven theories of the basic composition of trade in manufactures, ranging from the orthodox Heckscher-Ohlin doctrine based on factor proportions down to the Linder heterodoxy which emphasized trade in goods similar to those produced at home for the home market. Between them lay theories emphasizing "human skills," "scale economies," "stages of production," "technological gap," and "product cycle" which overlap and merge into each other and can be regarded as legitimate descendants of the Heckscher-Ohlin doctrine, rather than its antithesis. The attempt was made to test the relative theories against trade data. Some support was found for each. We are left then with the rather awkward position that there is an established explanation of trade, the Heckscher-Ohlin theory, but that manufactures conform to it only after its modification to make the underlying assumptions more realistic. The unreality of the assumptions of neoclassical theory, however, are not sufficient to justify its discard. Students still have to learn it, and as we shall see later, there is enough truth in the basic theory, and especially in the corollaries and implications for policy, that it serves as the basis for analysis of interferences with trade.

Summary

The classical theory of comparative advantage gives an answer to the question of what products will be exported and imported, at what prices, and who will gain from trade, in a world of fixed tastes, fixed resources, and fixed technology. This static world no longer exists, however, if it ever did. Tastes change, particularly as the demonstration effect impresses one country with the articles of consumption or means of production developed in another.

The impact of changes in factor endowments on trade is tested by seeing how trade at the original terms of trade would be affected by the changes. Neutral growth, with the most neutral possible demand assumption (homothetic indifference curves), will lead to an expansion of the desire to trade at the old terms of trade. This will displace the offer curve in such a way as to expand trade and worsen the terms of trade, provided the foreign offer curve is not infinitely elastic. Changes in factor endowments may be biased in favor of exports or against them, and they may meet biased demand conditions which accentuate or offset (in whole or part) such production bias. Ultrabias in production, however, determines the outcome, provided there are no inferior goods.

Technological change can take place in cost reductions for old goods or in the introduction of new ones. The former can be treated generally as if they were equivalent to changes in factor endowments. The introduction of new goods in one country ahead of others, however, gives rise to exports which are not related, in the short run at least, to factor endowments. The trade of the United States, for example, seems to have been strongly influenced by the introduction of new products, although these are associated with a special factor, scientists and engineers engaged in research and development.

SUGGESTED READING

Texts

See C. P. Kindleberger, *Foreign Trade and the National Economy* (New Haven, Conn.: Yale University Press, 1962) (paperback), chap. 4, "Technology."

Treatises, Etc.

The most important article on factor growth and trade is "Economic Development and International Trade" in H. G. Johnson's *Money, Trade and Growth* (Cambridge, Mass.: Harvard University Press, 1962) reprinted in American Economic Association, *Readings in International Economics*. In this theoretical line, see also R. Findlay and H. Grubert, "Factor Intensities, Technological Progress and the Terms of Trade," *OEP*, February 1959; and P. Bardhan, "International Differences in Production Functions, Trade and Factor Prices," *EJ*, March 1965. See also H. G. Johnson's essay, "The Theory of Trade and Growth, A Diagrammatic Analysis," in Bhagwati et al., *Trade, Balance of Payments and Growth*.

A major source dealing with technology and trade is R. Vernon, ed., *The Technology Factor in International Trade* (New York: National Bureau of Economic Research, 1970). The paper in this work by G. C. Hufbauer is referred to under the section above, "Need for a New Theory in Manufactured Goods?" and its bibliography of 81 items contains references to the work of Keesing, Kravis, Douglass, Vernon (on the product cycle), Drèze, et al.

Points

The full-length studies of innovation, trade, and imitation in particular industries are G. K. Douglass, "Product Variation and International Trade in Motion Pictures," Massachusetts Institute of Technology thesis, 1963; G. C. Hufbauer, *Synthetic Materials and the Theory of International Trade* (London: Gerald Duckworth & Co. Ltd., 1966); R. B. Stobaugh, Jr., "The Product Life Cycle, U.S. Exports and International Investment," D.B.A. thesis, Harvard Business School, June 1968; and J. E. Tilton, *International Diffusion of Technology: The Case of Semiconductors* (Washington, D.C.: The Brookings Institution, 1971).

On the possibility that automobiles will become a ubiquitous manufacture, see Sir D. MacDougall, "A Lecture on the Dollar Problem," *Econ*, August 1954, p. 196.

Chapter **TRADE AND GROWTH IN**

5 **DEVELOPING ECONOMIES**

Trade and Growth

The intimate connection between trade and growth, both growth based on factor accretion and that rooted in technological change, should have been made clear in the preceding chapter. But the fairly optimistic conclusion that trade responds to and changes with growth is not universally shared. On the contrary, the less developed countries today are more or less united in believing that the path to growth does not lead through trade. Ragnar Nurkse made a distinction between growth in the 19th century, which was on the whole led by exports, and that in the 20th, which, with the exception of the oil-producing and the developed countries, is not. Exports can be a leading sector in growth or a lagging one. It is the view of the less developed countries (which dominate the United Nations Conference on Trade and Development [UNCTAD], organized in 1964 and the most recent meeting of which was at Santiago, Chile, in April 1972), that blame for the limited help they get from trade can be laid at the door of the developed countries. Before we address this issue, however, and seek a reply to it, it may be useful to look at the 19th-century experience more generally and that of the developed countries today, where trade abets growth rather than discourages it.

Export-Led Growth in 19th-Century Developing Economics

The developing countries of the 19th century were for the most part empty lands. As they filled up, they needed to acquire many products from abroad, which implied a need to export and borrow capital. The exports consisted for the most part in what the Canadian economic historian Harold A. Innis has called "staples" and from which he developed a **staple theory** of trade and growth. Some products contributed much more to growth than others. Furs, for example, helped but little, since they required very high land/labor and land/capital ratios: only a couple of Indians

70

and a canoe per 100 square miles, perhaps; and little transport was needed to ship the beaver pelts to European markets, where they were used to make felt hats. Lumber and metals, on the other hand, increased the need for farming to feed the labor force. The spread of wheat went hand in hand with the extension of railroads into the interior and large-scale shipping to deliver the product to Europe, with room on the return voyage to bring settlers in bulk.

Douglass V. North has applied staple theory to the growth of the United States, suggesting that the major forces for expansion in the early 19th century were associated with various products, some more than others, and wheat more than cotton.

The process by which one product stimulates (or does not stimulate) the production of others and thereby encourages growth has been called **linkages** by Albert O. Hirschman. Forward linkages are found when new production makes a bulky material so cheap that industry is attracted to the area to take advantage of cheap inputs. Backward linkages occur when an industry needs inputs and creates such a strong demand for them that new industries spring into being to satisfy the need.

Staple theory went beyond forward and backward linkages to discuss the effect of a new industry on technological change—whether it stimulated and encouraged it or not—and on income distribution. In the Pacific Northwest, for example, the lumber industry, with cheap stands of timber, produced a local and remote market with high per capita incomes which attracted service and other industries to the location. Such a country as Denmark, which became rich through exporting meat and dairy products to Britain, found itself gradually becoming an industrial country without the need for tariff protection as local industries grew up to supply the demand of the farmers both for inputs for the farms and for consumption goods.

The linkages of staple industries had to meet a response. The guano industry of Peru in the 19th century needed labor, but since the local Indians would not serve, the exploiters of the deposits of natural fertilizer brought in Chinese coolies. (One hundred years later, the fish-meal industry met a much greater local response that led to the establishment of boat-building and machinery industries to serve the export industry.) Other factors had to be brought from abroad as well—capital, transport, and management. In some cases of economic growth today, as, for example, mining in Africa, the stimulus to the development of nearby farming was present, but since the African natives did not react to it, the opportunity gave rise to immigration of European settlers to provide the needed food. The difference between the 19th- and the 20th-century experience in export-led growth in primary products may then be less the conditions of international markets than the capacity of the economies to respond to economic signals. Or perhaps the economy could respond but once. A classic article by Hla Myint suggests that the plantation economies of the 19th century achieved a once-and-for-all improvement in technology which was not followed up by further technological change. Partly this was because the foreign planters made a great deal of money and saw no reason to alter the system, while native laborers lacked education or an opportunity to become entrepreneurs. Partly it was because the nature of many plantation crops such as rubber, coffee, cocoa, and coconuts, with a long period of waiting between the initial planting of the trees or bushes and the subsequent attainment of full-scale production, discouraged agricultural experimentation by the individual planter. Myint asserted that once-and-for-all technological change was followed by fossilization.

Export-Led Growth in Industrial Leaders

The 19th century was distinguished by export-led growth not only in the "regions of recent settlement"—largely British dominions and the former colonies represented by the United States. Then, as today, the industrial leader found markets abroad, both for old products newly produced at lower costs and for new products. In the first half of the 19th century, Britain, for example, developed export markets in cotton textiles, iron rails, locomotives, ships, and coal. It was good while it lasted, but it bred resentment in potential competitors. Alexander Hamilton and Henry Carey in the United States and Friedrich List in Germany developed a system of national economy, in opposition to the worldwide free-trade view of Adam Smith. Free trade was satisfactory for the industrial leader, they maintained, but harmful to countries that had not yet industrialized. Increasing returns to scale in manufacturing, or decreasing costs, made it necessary to provide infant-industry protection to the lagging countries with potentiality for industry, to prevent dominance by the country which was first in the field with the Industrial Revolution. The argument is one which continues today.

Export-Led Growth in Developed Countries Today

Export-led growth today perhaps works through similar linkages, but the analysis emphasizes rather different factors. In postwar Europe and Japan, for example, the process started with technological change. This reduced export prices and made it possible to sell more goods abroad in competition with other foreign producers. Most of these goods in which technological change took place were income elastic, i.e., demand for them grew rapidly as income increased (in contrast to the demand for the primary commodities produced in the developing countries, of which more below). But the process became a positive feedback one, so long as the developed countries had extra factors with which to expand: an increase in productivity through new investment or technological change, or both, led to lower prices and more exports, which led to more profits, more investment, lower prices, and more exports. The process continued as resources, largely labor, were drawn from occupations of low productivity, such as agriculture, elsewhere in the economy or from abroad. Capital was formed from profits. Only when the economies ran out of labor in the first half of the 1960s was the positive feedback process of export-led growth interrupted.

Initial technological change represented (much of it) imitation and closing of the wide technological gap which existed between the United States and other developed countries at the end of the war. Some of the change led to import substitution, which when carried far enough leads to exports, after the local producers take over first the entire market and then sell abroad. But much of the change in Europe and Japan went beyond imitation to innovation—*vide* Volkswagen and Sony. It was helped by the European Common Market and rapid growth in neighboring countries. While plans for growth emphasized investment in domestic industries and social capital, the lead in expansion was usually taken by exports. The Japanese and Italian cases are particularly striking as modernization in export industries led export prices to fall in a world of creeping inflation.

The Penalties of the Head Start

There may be ultimate disadvantages to the head start as well as initial benefits. The developing countries' contention that manufactured goods are superior to primary production as a basis for trade and a stimulus to growth rests on the alleged superiority of the former over the latter in two respects: the facts (beliefs?) that manufactures are subject to increasing returns to scale, and primary production to decreasing returns, and that manufactures create more productive linkages than do foodstuffs and raw materials. But production and export of manufactured goods can lead to fossilization of the economic structure of a country, or may not be proof against it. Britain's exports of textiles, rails, galvanized iron sheets, and railroad equipment did not lead at the end of the 19th century into electrical equipment, chemicals, and automobiles. When the early staple manufactures were no longer wanted by Europe and the United States, instead of developing new products, Britain sold the old to new markets—the colonies and dominions, with Empire preference. Until a few years ago when Flemish industry picked up through foreign investment, Belgian observers complained that their industrial structure, based on foreign trade in capital-intensive products of slow technological growth such as semifinished iron and steel, flat glass, china, soda ash, and fertilizers, was thoroughly fossilized.

The Terms of Trade

Developing countries today complain that they are unable to follow the example either of the industrial leaders of the 19th century, or that of Germany, France, Italy, and Japan today. The reason, they assert, is that the external conditions they face are different. In particular, their spokesman, Raul Prebisch, insists the terms of trade of less developed countries are secularly declining.

Before we analyze the Prebisch contention about the terms of trade, it is useful to say a few words about this concept, which is easily misinterpreted. The terms-of-trade concept, as already made clear in Chapter 3, is the relation between the prices of exports and the price of imports. In barter trade, this is given either as $\frac{Px}{Pm}$, i.e., the price of exports divided by the price of imports, or $\frac{Qm}{Qx}$, the quantity of imports divided by the quantity of exports. Since the relative price of exports in such a diagram as Figure 3.4 is the amount of imports one can get for one's exports, these amount to the same thing when $PxQx = PmQm$, i.e., when the value of exports is equal to the value of imports. (If the student divides $PxQx = PmQm$ by $PmQx$, he will find that $\frac{Px}{Pm} = \frac{Qm}{Qx}$). The $\frac{Px}{Pm}$ version is called the **net barter terms of trade**; the $\frac{Qm}{Qx}$, the **gross barter terms of trade.** It is not entirely clear how these uncommunicative terms crept into the jargon of economists, but they were adopted by Frank Taussig and Jacob Viner, and the rest of us are stuck with them.

A higher price for exports with the same price for imports, a lower price for imports with the same price for exports, a larger volume of imports for the same volume of exports (with balanced trade), or a smaller volume of exports for the same volume of imports (again when $PxQx = PmQm$) is a favorable development in the terms of trade. The less developed countries claim, however, that the price of their exports is going down relative to the price of imports over time—an unfavorable change.

When trade is not balanced and $\frac{Px}{Pm} \gtreqless \frac{Qm}{Qx}$, the net barter terms of trade differ from the gross barter terms. The latter become, on the whole, uninteresting since they may reflect less price movements than changes in the balance of payments, and even capital movements. Most reference, therefore, is to the net barter terms of trade, and when one reads "terms of trade" without qualification, one should think $\frac{Px}{Pm}$. This is a concept such as farm parity, which represents the relationship between the prices at which farmers sell and those at which they buy.

But like parity, the net barter terms of trade do not convey much meaning in their unqualified form. For one thing, prices can be held very high, but if sales volume falls off, raising the price of exports can overdo it. Opposite to the old joke "we lose a little on every sale, but, boy, do we have volume!" is the exact antithesis, "We make a big profit on every sale, but we don't sell much." Accordingly, the idea was developed of weighting the net barter terms of trade by the volume of exports. If export prices rise but volume falls off equally, this measure—called the **income terms of trade**—shows no change. The same concept is sometimes called the "**capacity to import.**" It is obvious that if, over the long run, $PxQx$ must equal $PmQm$, $\frac{PxQx}{Pm}$ determines Qm, or the volume that the country can import. The less developed countries in fact say that they cannot change Px, or Pm, or Qx, so their volume of imports, Qm, is determined for them. $\frac{PxQx}{Pm}$ is a superior concept to $\frac{Px}{Pm}$ for the purposes of the less developed countries. But the latter is the one usually employed.

When these concepts are applied to more than one commodity on a side, it should be obvious, we have to use index numbers. Instead of $\frac{Px}{Pm}$ for the net barter terms of trade, we use

$$\frac{Px_1}{Pm_1} \div \frac{Px_0}{Pm_0}$$

where 1 and 0 represent two periods in time. Here it is vitally important to make sure that the base year is a representative period. When the Agricultural Adjustment Act chose 1909–14 as the base on which to measure parity, it was because this was a particularly favorable period for farmers. Similarly, the British seem always to measure changes in their terms of trade from 1938, when they were the most favorable in the nearly 100 years between 1870 and the present. Conversely, the less developed countries today choose a base of 1950, when primary product prices soared sky-high under the influence of the outbreak of the war in Korea.

But the volume of exports and the choice of a base year are not all that's wrong with the net barter terms of trade as a measure of welfare. One must also take productivity into account. In the previous chapter it was noted that technological change of the most neutral sort worsens the terms of trade. But this does not mean that the country is worse off. It can be, as will be indicated later in this chapter. But typically what it means is that the country is sharing some of its improvement in productivity with its customers. With changing efficiency, the net barter terms of trade are distinctly misleading as a measure, as the farm population in the United States is unwilling to acknowledge in its insistence on parity. One ought to take into account the improvement in productivity as well.

Suppose export prices fall 10 percent relative to import prices, as measured from a suitable base year, but export costs have fallen 20 percent. The country is clearly better off. The concept used to express this is called the **single factoral terms of trade**—again a monstrous piece of jargon—which is given as $\frac{Px}{Pm} \cdot Zx$ where Zx stands for productivity in exports.

(This expression should be adjusted, of course, for changes from a suitable chosen base period.) The "single" in this designation differentiates it from the **double factoral terms of trade** or $\frac{Px}{Pm} \cdot \frac{Zx}{Zm}$, which takes account not only of productivity in the country's exports, but also the productivity of foreign factors in the country's imports. The single factoral terms of trade is a much more relevant concept than the double factoral. We are interested in what our factors can earn in goods, not what our factor services can command in the services of foreign factors.

Related to productivity abroad, moreover, is a question of the quality of the goods imported. This is of some considerable relevance to the Prebisch claim, because coffee, copper, cotton, and so on (to stay alliterative) are roughly the same goods today that they were 50 years ago, whereas the price index of imports is not likely to have taken full account of the improvement in quality of automobiles, radios, petroleum-refining equipment, and trucks.

Further on the issue of whether the criterion of net barter terms of trade is the appropriate one for the distribution of the gains from trade between developing and developed countries, a distinction may be made between the terms of trade on merchandise alone and those on goods and services in combination. Its importance is that some of the "price" in the export price level in the developing countries is attached to value added by foreign factors of production. If the price of exports rises, for example, and profits on foreign investment rise sufficiently to account for all of the increase in the price of exports, the local economy has not gained. Putting it this way is not likely to give much comfort to the less developed countries. But suppose the price of exports declines, and the return on investment declines as well. In this case the country is no worse off, while the net barter merchandise terms of trade would lead one to think it was. What is needed for deeper analysis, then, is the terms of trade on the current account of the balance of payments as a whole, not merely merchandise, or the terms of trade on domestic value added, sometimes called "returned value."

One further extension of this point pertains to transport costs, which will be discussed more fully in the next chapter. The merchandise terms of trade are generally given at border values, i.e., f.o.b. (free on board) for exports, and c.i.f. (cost, insurance, freight) for imports. If the country carries none of either its exports or its imports, this is a good measure for merchandise and the transport account in the balance of payments. But this condition is unlikely to be fulfilled. And it is especially unlikely that the reciprocal of the merchandise terms of trade of a trading partner measured f.o.b. for exports and c.i.f. for imports will accurately reflect the terms of trade of a country. In his original work, Prebisch could find few terms-of-trade series for Latin America going back to 1870 and assumed that the Latin-American series would be the reciprocal of the British series. But this is not so. If transport costs decline relative to the costs of merchandise, as has been the case since 1870, the merchandise terms of trade of two trading partners can both simultaneously improve. Export prices in both cases are unchanged, for example, while import prices decline because of cheaper transport.

For all these theoretical and statistical reasons one cannot accept the Prebisch case that the terms of trade of the less developed countries have persistently moved against any particular group of less developed countries such as Latin America. But there is nonetheless something to the case.

Engel's Law, Biased Factor and Technological Change, and Monopoly

The case can be made that the changes in demand, factor growth, and technology discussed in the previous chapter tend to operate, on balance, systematically against less developed and in favor of the more developed countries. Their effect is partly on the net barter terms of trade and partly on the volume of trade, or the gross barter terms. But let us take the items one by one.

Engel's law states that as income grows, the demand for food grows less than proportionately. This is a law of pervasive importance in economic growth, with profound side effects in such questions, for example, as the necessity for the political importance of farmers to decline with the passage of time. To the extent that income elasticities determine the volume of exports, and to the extent that the less developed countries grow foodstuffs in a world of growing income per capita, the demand for their exports will grow more slowly than the demand for manufactured exports.

The last sentence is a highly qualified one, however. The less developed countries export coffee, tea, rice, tropical fruit, sugar, fats and oils, and other foodstuffs, but they also export products of high income elasticity. Most of these are raw materials, such as rubber, nonferrous metals, iron ore, diamonds, lumber, and of course oil, but some, like meat and wine, are foodstuffs. Moreover, the volume of exports depends partly on income per capita, but also on population growth. And exports depend only partly on income elasticity abroad. To the extent that a developing country can produce them cheaply, and the potential importer abroad does not shut them off with protective policies, exports can grow through a competitive effect as well as through income changes. Canada, Australia, the United States, and Argentina took over the European market for grain in the 19th century from local farmers. Japanese textiles grew on the basis not of income elasticities, but cheapness.

As mentioned in the previous chapter, factor growth and technological change in the developed countries seem biased in some considerable degree against the less developed countries. Not only is demand biased, through Engel's law, but capital grows faster than population (and land), and technology makes it possible to substitute capital for land and labor, which the less developed countries have in relative abundance. Synthetics in rubber, silk, cotton, quinine, petroleum, fertilizer, and so on are part of this movement. More and more elaborate manufacture, so that a dollar's worth of raw material is worked up into higher and higher amounts of the finished product, is another. Thin coating in tin and printed circuits which save copper are only two examples which come to mind. A smaller and smaller portion of final demand is therefore provided by the raw material producer.

Finally, the less developed countries assert that the terms of trade are governed in part by differences in the competitive situation as between the developed and the less developed countries. An increase in productivity in the developed world is likely to lead to no decline in price, as administered pricing diverts the increase in productivity first into higher profits and then into higher incomes for productive factors. In the less developed countries, on the other hand, a high degree of competitiveness among countries leads to lower prices rather than higher factor incomes. The less developed countries give away more of their gains in productivity because of monopolistic competition abroad and more nearly perfect competition among them.

The Impact of Internal Conditions

The less developed countries tend to blame the environment in which they operate for the fact that they are unable, as they insist, to grow through trade as other countries have done. The terms of trade run against them, and the fault lies in conditions in the developed countries. Before this case can be accepted, however, it is necessary to explore whether there are circumstances within the less developed countries which contribute to the result. At least four possibilities have been examined in the literature: their inability to transform; their need for intermediate goods; disequilibrium in factor markets; and misallocation of resources through misguided protectionism.

The theory of comparative advantage assumes that a country can smoothly and costlessly adjust production along its production possibilities curve. It also implies that when a country invests additional resources in growth it does so in response to the price system. This implies that if the foreign offer curve is relatively inelastic it does not use its resources to expand export capacity but grows in import-biased fashion.

Figure 5.1 shows an offer curve, O–T–A, of a less developed country

FIGURE 5.1. Adverse Terms of Trade through Growth

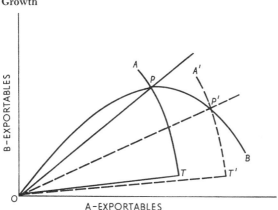

which is highly skewed in production. The offer curve is kinked because the country is fully specialized in the production of A-exportables and cannot expand its production at higher prices.[1] Intersecting B's offer curve at P, A gets substantial gains from trade, but it has to be careful about growth. If its production possibilities grow only in the A-good, growth is ultrabiased and extends the offer curve down and to the right, as for example to O–T'–A'. This sharply worsens the terms of trade, from O–P to O–P'. Under the conditions shown, where B's offer curve is inelastic, it is possible that growth in A will leave it worse off than before, what Jagdish N. Bhagwati, echoing Marx's expression about the immiserization

---

[1] The force of this statement cannot be seen by a student who has not worked through Appendix C, which links the production possibilities curve to the offer curve. For those who have, the O–T segment of the offer curve represents the constant cost portion of the production possibilities frontier.

of the poor, has called **"immiserizing growth."** This means that the loss in the terms of trade has outweighed the increase in production possibilities. While the outward shift of the production possibilities curve would normally have been expected to put a country on a higher consumption indifference curve, it ends up on a lower one, as in Figure 5.2. The answer, of

FIGURE 5.2. "Immiserizing Growth": Ending up on a Lower Consumption Indifference Curve after Growth

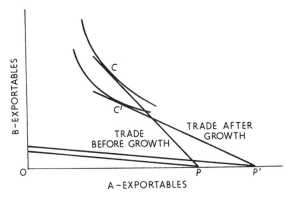

course, is not to forswear growth, but to avoid growth in a commodity facing inelastic demand. The law of comparative advantage must be interpreted marginally: in the two-good case, if the marginal revenue from growth in the export good is negative, comparative advantage urgently requires that growth be limited to the "import good."

Figure 5.1 shows one important point about the trade of the less developed countries, however, that was mentioned earlier but is worth repeating because it is often overlooked. *A* may not be able to gain much from growth, but it obtains substantial gains from trade at *O–T–A* in Figure 5.1. The contrast is with the position portrayed in Figure 5.3, where *A* and *B*, with highly similar production possibilities and tastes as reflected in their offer curves, do not lose much in terms of trade from growth but have limited gains from trade to begin with. The complaint of the less developed countries that the growth of world trade has been largely among the developed countries ignores the point that it is the gains from trade that count, not mere volume.

One reason *A* in Figure 5.1 may grow in the export-biased direction is because that is all it knows how to do. Resources may not be readily shiftable to the import-competing industry because of lack of complementary resources or other friction. Another reason, cited by Linder, is that imports from *B* may kill off the import-competing industry, as British textile exports to India killed off the handicrafts, and free trade between Ireland

FIGURE 5.3. Trade between Developed Countries with
Limited Gains

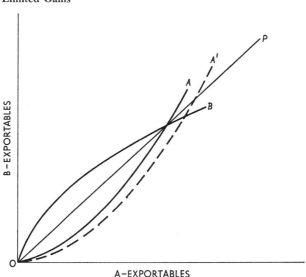

and England after 1801 led Irish industry to collapse and drove its population to seek work across the Irish Channel. When it is impossible to make
a living in the import-competing industry, growth takes place in the export industry until it goes too far and loses the gains from trade which were
originally substantial.

One alleged reason that the law of comparative advantage should not
be applied to the less developed countries is that factor prices in these
countries do not always reflect social marginal productivities. Suppose, for
example, that there is disguised unemployment in agriculture, that is,
labor employed which has a real marginal product below its money wage,
and possibly as low as zero, while at the same time wages are high in
manufacturing. Because wages are low in agriculture and high in manufacturing, it will appear that the country has a comparative advantage
in agriculture and a disadvantage in industry. But if the social marginal
product is still lower in agriculture than in industry, it will pay to shift
workers from agriculture to industry, which may require interference in
trade. The position may be illustrated by Figure 5.4, where the terms of
trade cut the production possibilities curve at P, and trade lands consumption within the production possibilities curve at C rather than on the
curve itself at some point such as T (where the country might export
either good, depending on demand conditions). Or the position can be
summed up by stating that the case violates the condition of full trading
equilibrium, $P = DRT_P = FRT_T = DRS_C$, where P is price, DRT_P is the

**FIGURE 5.4. Trade When Private Costs
Do Not Reflect Social Costs**

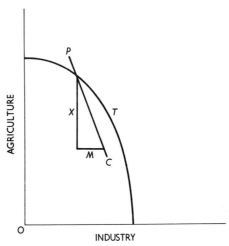

domestic rate of transformation in production, FRT_T is the foreign rate of transformation in trade, and DRS_C is the domestic rate of substitution in consumption. The case where factor prices do not reflect social marginal productivities, which has been put forward as an argument against trade or in favor of a tariff (by Mihail Manoilescu in the 1930s and Everett E. Hagen more recently) rests on the fact that with noncompetitive factor markets, the market price of goods differs from DRT_P.

The third argument that the less developed countries should not follow the path of free trade, in addition to their inability to transform and the failure of market prices to reflect social values, rests on the existence of intermediate goods that are needed in relatively fixed proportions in many productive processes and that the less developed countries cannot produce for themselves. If enough of these intermediate goods—fuel, iron and steel, cement, lumber, and so on—is not imported, domestic resources cannot be fully utilized, since the possibilities of substituting domestic resources for imports are limited, and since they are needed together for production. Thus far, the trading problem of the less developed countries is no different from that of the developed states, who equally depend on imported supplies of intermediate goods to keep their economies going.

But Linder, who emphasizes the importance of intermediate goods, maintains that the less developed countries cannot solve their intermediate goods problem in the same way that the developed countries can. This is partly because their capacity to transform is more limited, so that their requirements are proportionately larger. The fact gives them an import minimum of capital equipment (for growth) and of raw materials and fuel needed for maintaining existing capacity in operation. They may at the same time be constrained by an export maximum, based on the inelasticity of the foreign offer curve for primary products and their inability at an early stage of growth to produce and market finished manufactures. The problem arises where the import minimum exceeds the export maximum, leaving a foreign exchange gap. In this circumstance, the opponents of classical trade theory assert, it is necessary for the less developed countries systematically to cut down on imports of goods which they can make for themselves or do without (without affecting domestic factor use). This means, in effect, import substitution for consumers' goods.

Neoimperialism, Neocolonialism and Exploitation

The lack of progress of trade in the developing countries is so distressing to them and to many students of the subject that the accusation is made that the developing countries suffer from neoimperialism or neocolonialism. Imperialism and colonialism, in which a mother country imposes its will on its empire or colonies through the naked use of political power, backed by force, are generally recognized as no longer applying. Since World War II, in fact, a wave of liberation from colonial and imperial ties has created roughly 50 newly independent countries. The claim is made, however, that political does not bring economic independence. The developed countries, and, in some formulations, particularly the United States, impose their will on developing countries, particularly in trade and investment and to some extent through the use of foreign aid, administered either directly or through "international bodies" which the developed countries control. In one interesting interpretation, neoimperialism always existed side by side with overt imperialism, and the classic example of comparative advantage used by Ricardo, the exchange of bolts of British cloth against pipes of Portuguese wine, is not free trade at all but neocolonialism: Britain forced Portugal through the Treaty of Methuen in 1703, and earlier trade treaties, to specialize in unrewarding primary production and to abstain from stimulating and profitable manufactures— before the Industrial Revolution.

The facts of imperialism and colonialism with their use of force are broadly clear, though interpretations differ markedly as to whether the basic drives to imperialism in Europe after 1885 were economic gain (as in the Belgian Congo and the Boer War), economic gain for a limited group in the imperial power, or political prestige. Whatever its origins, moreover, empire preferences, restrictions on colonial shipping and production, and the gobbling up of, say, good sugar land in Cuba by American carpet-baggers in the turmoil following the Spanish-American war are not in doubt. The issues connected with investment and foreign aid in developing countries must be left for later in the book. But the question of how much the developed countries "exploit" the developing countries through trade today is a tough nut to crack for all but the convinced extremes.

It is first necessary to define exploitation, and this is not easy, despite the facility with which the word comes to the lips of those discussing children, students, women, blacks, Indians, chicanos, and other minority groups.

A distinguished economist once defined it as a higher price than the minimum which the "exploiting" country would accept and continue to trade. This means, presumably, the no-gain trade position indicated in Chapter 2 in the discussion of constant opportunity costs, or the virtually straight-line rays from the origin of the offer curves in Figure 5.1, as far as T in the O–A offer curve, and about halfway to P along the O–B curve. This implies that any country that gains from trade exploits its partner, and that when both gain, as is normal the way we draw the diagrams, they mutually exploit each other. This departs from the ordinary use of the word in which there must be an exploiter and an exploited. Moreover, if there is exploitation when there are gains from trade, trade means exploitation by definition. This takes us close to the notion expressed in Chapter 1 that dependence, even interdependence, is exploitation—and undesirable. It may be noted that the economist in question modified this interpretation.

In another version, perhaps offhand and not necessarily to be taken seriously as an expression of mature thought, a sociologist said in a lecture that one country exploits another when the gains from trade, including the spinoffs (called linkages above) are divided unequally. In Chapter 3, we suggested the difficulties that abound in trying to weigh one country's gains from trade against those of another, except in the limiting case when one country has no gain and the other gains all. If spinoffs in the form of stimuli to development are added to the gains from trade measured as the change in price before and after trade, weighted by the trade volume, the question of scientific definition and measurement becomes inordinately complex. The lecturer went on to say that there are more spinoffs in manufacturing than in primary production. If he believed that spinoffs are more important than the gains from trade as measured is comparative statics, it follows that primary producers are exploited by definition.

In the usual economic analysis, exploitation is reserved for intervention in the competitive market process and is measured by the difference between the marginal returns (of a good or factor) under competitive conditions on the one hand, and monopoly or monopsony (a monopoly buyer) on the other. With bilateral monopoly, a monopolist facing a monopolist, there is again mutual exploitation, although one may outweigh the other. In this sense, the developing countries are exploited if their terms of trade are turned against them by monopoly and monopsony—the possibility mentioned on p. 78. On the other hand, the developing countries may be said to be guilty of exploitation—neoimperialism or neocolonialism—if in their commodity agreements (such as that in oil) they raise the price above the competitive level.

With duress, monopoly, or monopsony, the case may be clear. What about the circumstances where bargaining power is unevenly divided because of wide differences in income, wealth, productive capacity, knowledge, etc? Is the United States a neoimperialist because it trades with developing countries without first providing them with the productive alternatives that it enjoys at home by virtue of its skilled labor force and accumulated capital? The fact that developing countries are highly specialized in the production and export of a few primary products and lack the capacity to transform their productive structures toward a wider range of manufactures limits their bargaining power.

For trade under unequal bargaining conditions to be regarded as exploitative or not depends on what one considers as the reasonable alternative. If the alternative to such trade is to push for improving the productive structure of the developing countries and to limit their dependence on trade, then trade at the asymmetrical stage is exploitative, and only waiting until development has been accomplished is nonexploitative. But if the alternatives lie between trade and no trade and no development, with the developed countries setting about producing the raw materials and agricultural products themselves, without importing, then no trade is exploitative and trade is nonexploitative. In short, when a rich man employs a poor man to work on his place for minimum wages, it is exploitative in one sense; but when he does not hire him and the alternative is unemployment, it is exploitative in another.

But perhaps the use of pejorative words is not helpful, and it is better to describe in detail exactly how one interprets the facts of particular situations.

Import Substitution

In the process of growth, domestic production replaces imports. This is a wholly normal process. Increased productivity in export industry leads to higher incomes which are spent on items first imported but produced locally as the market grows. As productivity in exports increases, the same output can be obtained for fewer resources; those freed may be attracted into import-competing enterprise through the price system. In Denmark, as noted, exports of dairy products, bacon and eggs provided the income spillover for local industry to grow great under free trade and ultimately itself develop export markets in manufactures. Import substitution is therefore a natural concomitant of growth. But there is import substitution as a natural process and import substitution as a policy; they are not necessarily the same thing, nor do they necessarily lead to the same result.

In his classic pioneering study of growth, *The Conditions of Economic Progress,* Colin Clark observed that with growth, resources transferred from primary production (agriculture, fishing, forestry, and sometimes mining) to secondary production (manufacturing) and tertiary output (services). This is the result of Engel's law. But it is one thing to observe what happens in growth and another to set out to grow by constructing a manufacturing sector. This is the fallacy of *post hoc ergo propter hoc* (after this, therefore because of this). The path to growth may lead through more efficient agriculture to a manufacturing sector which is built up as a spillover from the income increase generated by the primary sector. But to invest resources in a manufacturing sector as a planned policy may not lead to growth. By the same token, import substitution as observed historically is no warrant for applied policies of import substitution, which may end up producing the wrong thing at too high a cost.

Under the advice of Raul Prebisch, Hans W. Singer, Gunnar Myrdal and others, however, most of the less developed countries have set about to meet their foreign exchange gap by import substitution in consumers' goods. Where the country does face an offer curve of unit import elasticity or less, this is the economic course, since an enlarged volume of exports would lead to a lower return in value. But import substitution frequently takes off on its own and reaches the point where the country in question spends more resources to acquire goods domestically than it would need to produce goods for export and transform them into the needed goods through trade. Where exchange rates are overvalued, domestic factor prices fail to reflect social marginal returns, and trade is restricted so that goods prices fail to reflect the foreign rate of transformation through trade. It is frequently impossible any more to know whether a country would do better to expand or cut down on trade, and in what goods.

A further discussion of these issues must wait until Chapter 10, when we discuss the commercial policy appropriate to the developing countries.

Summary

Trade was an engine of growth for the open lands for the 19th century and for the leader in the Industrial Revolution, Great Britain. Export-led growth is also a modern phenomenon in postwar Europe and Japan. In the 19th century, trade in some staples contributed more to growth than others, through linkages which stimulated other industry or technological change. But linkages require a response, and when there was none locally, the stimulus turned abroad and led to enclaves cut off from the local economy.

Today's less developed countries, except for oil producers, expect little growth from trade. This is partly because of the world environment, in which the terms of trade are believed to turn systematically against the less developed countries, and partly the result of conditions in the countries themselves. On the first score, it is maintained that the developed countries grow with antitrade-biased demand and antitrade-biased factor growth and technological change. In addition, monopolistic competition among the developed countries and more competitive conditions of production in the less developed ones hurt the terms of trade of the latter. On the second score—conditions in the developing countries—their capacity to take advantage of the opportunities for growth presented by trade is restricted by inability to transform, i.e., to shift resources where they can earn the highest return; by the fact that factor and goods prices do not reflect social marginal productivities, by a heavy dependence on imports of intermediate and capital goods for growth, and by full utilization of their resources at a time when an export maximum exists.

As a consequence of these circumstances in the world and within the countries, many developing states actively seek to substitute domestic production for imports. In so doing, they run grave risk of misallocating resources to wasteful uses.

Whether or not trade between developed and developing countries is described as neoimperialism or exploitative depends on the definitions given to these terms and what are considered to be realistic alternatives to trade in today's circumstances. When definitions and alternatives are not widely agreed upon, pejorative terms lead to misunderstanding.

In the course of developing the foregoing points, the chapter also expounded various concepts of the terms of trade and distinguished between the volume of overall trade and the volume of trade embodying substantial gains.

SUGGESTED READING

Texts

G. M. Meier, *International Trade and Economic Development* (New York: Harper & Row, Publishers, 1963; rev. and extended, 1967) has an excellent treatment and a large bibliography.

Treatises

On the 19th century see R. Nurkse, *Problems of Capital Formation and Patterns of Trade and Development* (London: Oxford University Press, 1967) (paperback). This is two small books published together, the latter of which, the Wicksell Lecture given in 1959, is the relevant one. See also M. H. Watkins, "A Staple Theory of Economic Growth," *Canadian Journal of Economics and*

Political Science, May 1963; and H. Myint, "The Gains from International Trade and Backward Countries," *Review of Economic Studies,* 1954–55. Bhagwati's essay on "Immiserizing Growth" is reprinted in American Economic Association, *Readings in International Economics.* See also the essays by Corden and Johnson on trade and growth, and R. E. Caves, "Export-led Growth and the New Economic History" in Bhagwati et al., *Trade, Balance of Payments and Growth.*

On the terms of trade, see C. P. Kindleberger's monograph, *The Terms of Trade* (New York: The Technology Press and John Wiley & Sons, Inc., 1956).

The views of Prebisch, spokesman for the less developed countries, are set forth in many publications, the latest available of which is United Nations Conference on Trade and Development, *Towards a New Trade Policy for Development,* A Report by the Secretary-General of the Conference (New York: United Nations, 1964). See S. B. Linder, *Trade and Trade Policy for Development* (New York: Frederick A. Praeger, Inc., 1967).

H. Chenery's "Patterns of Industrial Growth," *AER,* March 1960, outlines how domestic production substitutes for imports over time.

Points

D. V. North's interpretation of early U.S. history in terms of export-led growth is to be found in *The Economic Growth of the United States, 1790–1860* (Englewood Cliffs, N.J.: Prentice-Hall, Inc., 1961). Hirschman's point about linkages is from *The Strategy of Economic Development* (New Haven, Conn.: Yale University Press, 1958). A study of modern export-led growth is R. M. Stern's *Foreign Trade and Economic Growth in Italy* (New York: Frederick A. Praeger, Inc., 1967). The difference in impact of trade on growth in Peru between the 1860s and the 1960s is illustrated in J. Levin, *The Export Economics* (Cambridge, Mass.: Harvard University Press, 1960), part I; and M. Roemer, *Fishing for Growth: Export-led Development in Peru, 1950–1967* (Cambridge, Mass.: Harvard University Press, 1970).

The historical treatment of trade between Britain and Portugal as exploitative is in S. Sideri, *Trade and Power, Informal Colonialism in Anglo-Portuguese Relations* (Rotterdam: Rotterdam University Press, 1970).

E. F. Penrose's definition of exploitation referred to on p. 84 is contained in "Profit-Sharing between Producing Countries and Oil Companies in the Middle East," *EJ,* June 1959. The definition of exploitation as unequal gains from trade, including spinoffs, was offered by J. Galtung in a lecture at the Graduate School of International Affairs in Geneva, Switzerland, in February 1972.

For a Marxist attitude that trade between developed and developing countries cannot aid the latter so long as they are capitalistic, see T. E. Weisskopf, "Capitalism, Underdevelopment, and the Future of Poor Countries," in Bhagwati, *Economics and World Order.*

The reference to the Hagen article is "An Economic Justification of Protectionism," *QJE,* November 1958.

Chapter 6

TRANSPORT COSTS AND LOCATION THEORY

Transport Costs and Price Equality

The introduction of transport costs into the analysis of international trade disturbs the conclusion that international trade equalizes the prices of traded goods in the trading countries. If, in the absence of transport costs, our old friends, wheat and cloth, would have exchanged on a one-to-one basis, the necessity to overcome costs of transport would make the import good more expensive in both countries and the export good less valuable. In the United States, for example, wheat might exchange for cloth at 8 bushels for 12 yards, while in Britain the ratio would be 8 yards for 12 bushels. The implications of this may be illustrated in diagrammatic form. In Figure 6.1, the British offer curve of cloth for wheat and the American offer curve of wheat against cloth cross at point P. But with transport costs, the price ratios in the two countries must differ, so that the line from O through P cannot be taken as the price in both countries. The effect of transport costs of both goods is represented by the angle formed by O–P', the price in the United States, and O–P'', the price in Britain.

But these prices cannot solve the problem. At O–P', the United States is willing to offer O–U of wheat against O–R of cloth. At P'', the United Kingdom is willing to offer O–S of cloth for O–T of wheat. Prices cannot differ and solve the equation of trade.

The difficulty, of course, lies in the fact that when transport costs are introduced, we really move to a three-commodity diagram, in which Britain offers cloth for wheat and transport and the United States offers wheat for cloth and transport. The difference between what the United States gets in cloth for wheat at O–P' and what Britain receives in wheat for cloth at O–P'' represents the cost of transport expressed in wheat and/or cloth. It makes little sense to express transport costs in terms of these commodities, but examples can be produced which are slightly more realistic: Transport costs of oil and coal can be expressed in terms of the proportion

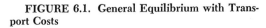

FIGURE 6.1. General Equilibrium with Transport Costs

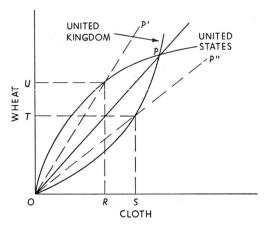

of the delivered commodity used up in transit: immediately after World War II, Silesian coal was sold by Poland in France even though the round-trip train journey required burning up one third of the original trainload of fuel. Or one can hypothesize commodities such as ice which arrive smaller than they start. In these cases, using the general-equilibrium apparatus of offer curves or production possibilities and indifference curves, transport costs will require the price lines in the two countries to differ in slope by an amount representing transport costs in terms of the two commodities.

We can show the effects of transport costs more readily, however, if we fall back on **partial-equilibrium** analysis. This shows the position before and after trade in one commodity only. The partial-equilibrium analysis, though incomplete, is useful for a variety of purposes. In particular we shall find it invaluable in the analysis of tariffs, which appears in the next chapter, and of exchange adjustments, which we will encounter in Chapter 19. The analysis is partial because it suggests the impact of trade on the demand and supply of a single commodity, priced in terms of money, without taking into account the repercussions on these demand and supply curves of changes in income, exchange rates, prices of other goods, or anything else that may be affected. A demand curve can be drawn only with a knowledge of all other demand curves in the system, and it is valid only as long as the latter remain unaltered. The offer curve analysis, as well as production possibilities and indifference curves, all get away from considerations of money and income and represent a long-run equilibrium position. The partial-equilibrium analysis, on the other hand, deals only with the immediate position after trade is begun and abstracts from secondary effects, repercussions, and adjustments.

Transport Costs in Partial Equilibrium

Figures 6.2*a* and 6.2*b* give the demand and supply of cloth in the United Kingdom and the United States before trade. Demand and supply represent quantities of cloth sought and available, respectively, against a given price per yard. The price in the United States has been converted by means of the existing exchange rate to the English unit of account, or perhaps it is the other way; it does not matter. The price of cloth in the United States is much higher, in the absence of trade, than the price in Britain.

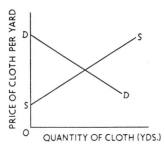

FIGURE 6.2*a*. Demand and Supply for Cloth in the United Kingdom

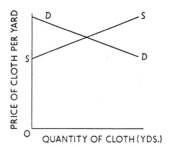

FIGURE 6.2*b*. Demand and Supply for Cloth in the United States

To indicate what will happen after trade is opened, it is necessary to get both figures on the same diagram. This can be done in either of two ways. It would be possible to construct a new curve from the quantities demanded in the United States and United Kingdom at various prices by simply adding the two demands at each price and drawing a single new curve. The same could be done for supply. The intersection of the two new curves would be the new price, after trade is begun, in the absence of transport costs (and, to issue the warning for the last time, as an initial response). This is done in Figure 6.3.

The other method is portrayed in Figure 6.4. Here the four curves are put on the same diagram with the same vertical axis. The horizontal axis, however, runs in two directions from the origin. For the United States it runs in normal fashion from left to right, and for Britain it starts from the same point as for the United States but goes from right to left. The U.S. demand and supply curves are exactly as in Figure 6.2*b*. The British curves, however, are now inverted. The demand curve is negatively sloped in proper manner, if one reads it from right to left. If one is not careful, however, it appears to be positively sloped, like a supply curve. The supply curve, on the other hand, now looks something like a demand curve.

The new price after trade in the absence of transport costs is calculated by the horizontal price line common to both curves which will balance the excess of supply in the one country with the excess of demand in the

FIGURE 6.3. Demand and Supply for Cloth in the United Kingdom and the United States

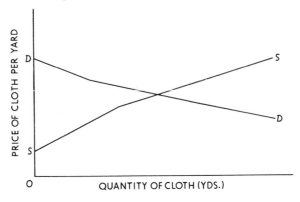

other. In Figure 6.4 the price line *a–d* settles at that level where *a–b*, the excess of supply in Britain, is equal to *c–d*, the excess of demand in the United States. Of course, *a–b* then represents exports, and *c–d*, imports. In Britain home production amounts to *a–x*, while home consumption is only *b–x*. In the United States, on the other hand, only those producers within the range *x–c* are efficient enough to compete with imports. The rest of consumption is satisfied by imports.

The partial-equilibrium diagram is useful in showing how exports raise the price of a commodity above what would have been the case without trade and how imports lower the price. This is a truth worth emphasizing. When we put aside the fancy apparatus of production possibilities and in-difference curves, there is a tendency to remember merely that a good

FIGURE 6.4. Partial-Equilibrium Price for Cloth, No Transport Costs

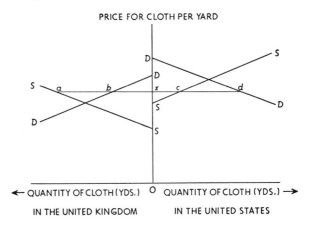

must be cheap before it can be exported from a country. This is true. But exports raise the price of the goods in which the country has a comparative advantage, as the partial-equilibrium analysis shows. The United States exports wheat because it is cheap; wheat is less cheap there than it would be without exports. The selection of the example of wheat underlines an important assumption which the student should note—that of decreasing returns. With increasing returns or decreasing costs, of course, exports cheapen commodities.

Thus far the partial-equilibrium analysis has been like that of general equilibrium—in the absence of transport costs. But transport costs can readily be included. Prices in the importing country will be higher than in the exporting country by a determinate amount: the unit costs of transport. The solution is the same as that in Figure 6.4, except that the price line must now be broken at the vertical axis and continued at a higher level. The equilibrium price is that which equalizes exports and imports and is higher in the United States than in Britain by the costs of transport. This is shown in Figure 6.5, where *a–b* equals *c–d*, and *w–t* represents the costs of transport.

FIGURE 6.5. **Partial-Equilibrium Price for Cloth, Transport Costs**

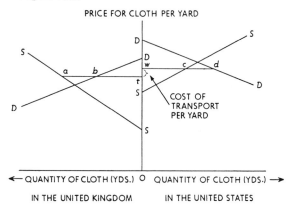

PRICE FOR CLOTH PER YARD

COST OF TRANSPORT PER YARD

← QUANTITY OF CLOTH (YDS.) O QUANTITY OF CLOTH (YDS.) →

IN THE UNITED KINGDOM   IN THE UNITED STATES

Costs of transport, the diagram shows, reduce trade below what it would otherwise be. No matter how frequently the theorist may abstract from them in his exercises, their existence means that prices in the exporting country are below what they would otherwise have been and that prices in the importing country are higher.

The notion of transport costs may be broadened to include all costs of transfer, mainly freight, but also insurance, handling, freight forwarders' commissions, etc., and even tariffs.

The Impact of Transport Costs

The existence of transport costs affects the theory of international trade in two ways. In the first place, it requires us to modify the answer given to the question of what goods are exported and imported. Price differences in two countries before trade must be wider than costs of transfer. In Figure 6.6, for example, transport costs, $w-t$, are wider than the difference in price between the United States and Britain. The result is that international trade will not take place in this commodity, no matter what the factor endowments of the countries concerned or the factor requirements for its production. If transport costs did not exist, which means that all goods and services would be transportable in costless fashion, international trade would take place in every good and service. The existence of home goods has its origin in transport costs. Some goods, such as houses, for which transport costs approach infinity, can never take part in international trade.

FIGURE 6.6. Transport Costs in Excess of Price Differences in Partial Equilibrium

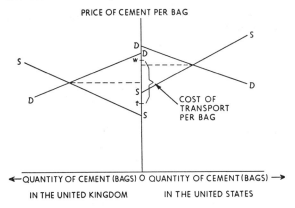

A major cause of expanded world trade after World War II has been the progressive reduction of transport costs. This is partly owing to technological improvement, which is discussed below. But a reduction of transport costs relative to production costs acts as a reduction in tariffs, expanding trade relative to output in already traded goods and bringing goods into international commerce which had previously been home goods.

Some trade between nations has little to do with a general theory of comparative advantage based on factor proportions or a technological gap. Instead, it has its origin in heavy transport costs. Such trade can even be balanced. This is particularly true of local trade that takes place across a long international boundary. With the elimination of tariffs as a result of the European Coal and Steel Community, Germany now exports steel to France in the north and imports steel from France in the south. This economizes transport. Or to take another example, Canada exports oil to the United States in the west and imports oil from Venezuela (by pipeline from Portland, Maine) in the east, so that its net comparative advantage is based on gross comparative advantage and disadvantage, which can exist simultaneously because of the importance of transfer costs. Or West Germany can export coal to the Netherlands down the Rhine while at the same time it imports coal into Hamburg from the United States.

But transport costs do more than serve as a cause of some trade and a barrier to other. With the fact that processing involves changes in weight and bulk, a knowledge of transport costs can be developed into a generalized theory of the location of industry, whether internationally or between regions, to form the link between industrial economics and industrial engineering. Location theory is a distinct and significant branch of economics. Classical trade theory tended to think of each region as a point, and all regions so close to one another that transfer could take place in costless fashion. To the location economist, distance is a cost to be met, or its opposite—access to the market is an input into the production function, along with land, labor, and capital, which makes it possible to produce a commodity cheaply. Coal in West Virginia in mines located on railroads which run downhill to the sea is a different commodity than coal in Antarctica. Oil in Texas, Oklahoma, or Louisiana is different (whatever its chemical composition) from oil on the North Slope of Alaska; and North Sea oil, adjacent to the enormous markets of Europe, has an advantage over that in the Middle East.

The theory of location of industry has validity even though the principles of location have not always been understood explicitly or followed by business entrepreneurs. Location analyses are now being made by industrial engineers in accordance with these principles. But industry follows locational principles in Darwinian or evolutionary fashion. Industry which has been well located has survived and flourished. Industry which has been badly located has tended to die through perennially low profits and business failure.

Not all evolutionary location is due to transport costs, of course. A good deal of industrial location is related to economics external to the firm—particularly in the form of a supply of trained labor—which have their origin in accidental or random occurrences and grow by agglomeration. Fichtel and Sachs, a bicycle firm, happened to locate their plant in Schweinfurt and to prosper. Various workmen split off and formed separate competing firms, staying close by in the hope of attracting other trained workers. The old firm and the new trained more workers. The result of several generations of this kind of growth was the development of one of the ballbearing capitals of the world. The location of the clock industry in

Meriden, Waterbury, Derby, and Ansonia—a cluster of towns outside New Haven in Connecticut—was also due to accidental growth of this kind. With decreasing costs, an industry may evolve in a given location through an initial success, with the choice of location based on mere chance.

The Rationale of Transport Costs

It would be simple enough to take transport costs into account in the real world if they were proportional to weight and distance. But weight is by no means the only criterion relating to the goods shipped. Weight, bulk, and value are not all positively correlated. When a commodity is relatively valuable, it can bear a higher proportional charge to its weight than when it is relatively cheap. Orchids cost more to ship per pound than sand. This is a reflection of the fact that the market for transport services is not perfectly competitive as between different commodities. Transportation services have a large element of overhead cost which may be unequally assigned to different products carried. For cheap, bulky commodities, where transport costs are very large in relation to total value, the proportion of overhead charged must be kept low in order to make it possible to move the goods at all.

But there are many other aspects of transportation rates which indicate the imperfectly competitive nature of the market. Goods must move by fixed routes, and two different routes of different distance between the same points generally charge the same rate. So-called backhaul rates, or cheap rates given for cargoes on ships which would otherwise be returning in ballast to pick up a new cargo, are another indication of the same general phenomenon. The overhead costs are assigned mainly to the outward journey, and the backhaul rate can be kept cheaper because only direct costs must be met and any return in excess of these is clear profit. Examples of backhaul rates are to be found in the rate on coal from the lower lakes to Duluth, which is far cheaper per ton than the rate on iron ore from the head of the lakes to, say, Cleveland. Conversely, in export trade, the rate on coal from Hampton Roads, Virginia, to Norway was $12 a ton when the backhaul rate on iron ore from Narvik, Norway, to Sparrow's Point in Baltimore was $4.50.

Not only do rates differ per commodity, depending upon its value or the direction of movement. The ratio of overhead to total costs will also vary, depending upon the form of transport. Once a commodity is loaded upon a barge, for example, it makes little difference whether it is hauled 10 or 500 miles. The overhead element is less significant in railroads, but still important. In trucking, it is of almost no importance, but direct operating costs are high. The result is that truck rates are cheap for short hauls

FIGURE 6.7. Cost of Hauling 100 Pounds by Different Carriers for Different Distances

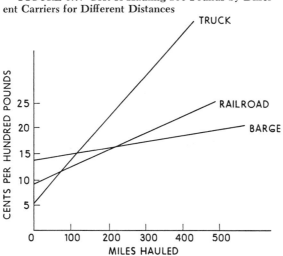

Adapted from E. M. Hoover, *The Location of Economic Activity* (New York: McGraw-Hill Book Company, 1948), p. 21.

but become increasingly expensive as the distance is increased. Figure 6.7 shows the cost per 100 pounds for carload lots of commodities by railroad, barge, and truck in 1939 and 1940, to illustrate the point.

Implicit in the data in Figure 6.7 is the high cost of handling, as contrasted with simple haulage. This is seen especially when the fixed path by which goods must move causes their transshipment from one type of transport to another. In a few cases, transport by two types of carriers is competitive with the use of a more expensive carrier for the entire journey. Part of the freight moving from Chicago to New York for export comes by rail the whole way, and part by barge to Buffalo and train (or by Erie Canal boat) thereafter. Frequently, however, transshipment from one means of transport to another involves such cost of handling that processing is undertaken at those places where transshipment is required.

Supply-Oriented Commodities

In terms of location theory, all commodities fall into one of three categories. They may be supply oriented, market oriented, or footloose.

Supply-oriented commodities are those in which the industrial processes tend to be located near the source of the major materials or fuel. These commodities are, for the most part, weight losing or weight saving in the course of processing or manufacture; or they may be products with heavy fuel consumption at a stage where the weight of the fuel (or its unique character) is important relative to the weight of the product; or they may be, particularly in agriculture, commodities which require preservation, grading, or standardization.

These industries or industrial processes will be located near the supply of the material or fuel in order to reduce procurement costs, which would otherwise include a large element for the transport of the materials. It is evidently sensible to concentrate ores near the mine, if the power or fuel can be found, in order to save on the bulk transport of waste material. It may, on the other hand, be necessary to move bauxite from Surinam to the Saguenay River in Canada, despite its bulk of unusable material, because the electric power necessary for the reduction of bauxite to alumina is unavailable in Surinam. Atomic power may change this and ultimately relocate all processes now strongly rooted to electric power. Similarly, high-voltage transmission of electricity, which extends the range which hydropower can be cheaply transported, lessens the attractions of water-power sites for electric power-intensive processes.

Cane crushing, extraction of sugar from beets, canning and freezing of vegetables and fish, and grading of fruit are all supply-oriented industries. Frequently an industry will have a historic supply orientation which is no longer valid but will continue to remain where it is, more or less. Thus the textile industry in New England was originally attracted to waterpower sites on the Merrimac, Taunton, and Blackstone rivers; the paper mills on the Connecticut River were originally constructed near a supply of pulp, long since cut over.

The iron and steel industry abundantly illustrates the intricacies of supply and fuel orientation. When charcoal was used to produce cast iron, the industry was located at the iron mines—in the Catskills, Berkshires, Adirondacks—where wood for fuel was abundant. With conversion to coal, the industry became coal oriented, particularly as 17 tons of coal were originally required for 1 ton of iron ore. Improvements in technology and the substitution of scrap for iron ore gradually reduced these proportions, but only after the industry in the United States had been historically oriented in the Pittsburgh, Cleveland, and Gary areas. With the prospect of higher prices for Mesabi iron ore toward the end of the 20th century, however, and imports of ore from Latin America, Africa, and Labrador, mills are moving toward the East Coast. In part, this is supply orientation toward iron ore and recovery scrap. To some extent, however, with new, huge, bulk carriers, the steel industry is overcoming transport costs. In part, it is market orientation, which was always important for certain steel products such as shipplate, but which now becomes stronger throughout the industry.

The steel industry in Europe and Asia is also moving from coal and iron mines to certain ports, Dunkerque in France or Taranto in Italy for example, and down the Rhine from the Ruhr to the Netherlands. Cheap ocean transport is making possible the intercontinental shipment of high-grade ores and coking coal. Italy and Japan, which used to be high-cost steelmakers because of deficiencies in natural resources in coal and iron, are now not only self-sufficient but important exporters, relying on iron ore from Morocco and Australia, respectively, and coal from the United States.

All great innovations in transport—new means of locomotion such as the steamship, railroad, pipeline, propeller airplane, jet airplane, and now the giant tankship, ore carrier, and the reinforced tanker for carrying liquid gas under pressure—have wide repercussions on the character and size of international (and domestic) trade. So do new techniques of handling cargo like the container ship or the drive-on freighter for transporting automobiles without loading them into holds with cargo slings and new routes like the Suez and Panama Canals and the St. Lawrence Seaway. Every reduction in transport costs thus brings about joined markets, opens new trade opportunities, and changes old ones. Walter Isard has expressed the view that of all the innovations in economic life, those in transport have the most pervasive consequences in stimulating economic activity and altering its location.

The sword cuts both ways, of course. Some innovations destroy old locational advantages. With the advent of the giant tankship, Britain is restricted to importing oil in bulk through only two ports which can handle the deep-draft vessels (Southampton and Bristol), which leaves the country militarily vulnerable. And the United States finds itself seriously handicapped in competing in steel with Japan because of the granite bar across San Francisco harbor at a 45-foot depth, or the Chesapeake Bay tunnel connecting the eastern shore of Maryland and Virginia with Cape Henry in Virginia at a depth of 55 feet, which bars deep ore carriers drawing as much as 70 feet from entering the bay fully laden, or the use of giant bulk carriers for exporting coal from Hampton Roads. It now makes a difference how many ports a country has capable of taking tankers and bulk carriers to a depth of 70 feet, and the United States has only one: Seattle.

Market Orientation

Some commodities such as bread have to be produced near the market because of their perishable nature (frozen bread, however, may eliminate the local bakery in the way that the automobile has led to the virtual demise of the corner grocery store). The product need not be perishable in physical terms. Other industries which are primarily service are pulled to the market where the service has to be rendered: gasoline stations, television repairs, plumbers, handymen. A major industry in international economics involves bringing the consumer to the site where the service can be consumed—the tourist industry. And this is one item in international commerce which has been strongly affected by innovation—in this instance the aircraft, first the transoceanic propeller plane, then the jet, and prospectively the supersonic transport.

Processes which add weight or bulk to the product are likely to be attracted to the market in order to minimize transport costs. Soft drink bottling is a good example. The extract may be manufactured in a single location, but the process of dilution and bottling adds so much weight and bulk that it must take place as close as possible to the point of consumption. The point may be made more generally in terms of assembled and packaged products. Assembly adds bulk. Automobile fenders, chassis, and frames pack more neatly in knocked-down form and ship more readily than the equivalent number of finished automobiles—or did so until Volkswagen devised a new drive-on freighter for speedy and efficient shipment of small cars. Accordingly, there is a strong pull of the assembly plant to the market, though parts manufacture may remain concentrated. And the same principle applies in all assembly operations, whether of radios, electrical equipment, tire making, bookbinding, or wine bottling.

In some lines of activity where the buyer is concerned to compare values and service, the market area attracts the bulk of the suppliers. This has been called the **coalescence of market areas.** It is represented in a city by the department store, theater, garment, financial, and similar districts. A new firm starting an insurance business will be unlikely to seek a new location in New York City but will try to find office space in the Williams Street–Maiden Lane area, where other insurance firms and the insurance brokers swarm. In international trade, the same effect is obtained by insurance centers such as New York, London, Munich (pre–World War II), and Zürich; style centers such as Paris, New York, and Rome; and the fur market of Leipzig. Coalescence of market areas is a phenomenon which occurs most frequently in service industries, where taste is likely to change.

In general, the early stages of production are likely to be supply oriented and the later stages pulled to the market. To locate an industry at the early stages minimizes the costs of producing the article by keeping down the cost of transport of materials. At the same time, the establishment of an industry at the market will reduce costs of distribution of the product to the ultimate consumer. The transfer costs in procurement and distribution may be added for different locations for an industry. The lowest point for the two types of costs will constitute the best location.

As the location of industry is moved from the source of material supply to the market, neither transfer costs of procurement nor those of distribution move in continuous fashion. Discontinuities occur for a variety of reasons but especially because of costs of handling due to the necessity for transshipment. Where transshipment is required both of materials on their way to processing and of finished products en route to market, there are likely to be sharp discontinuities in both curves, and a probable **nodal point** which will attract location. This is particularly true of ports, where a sea journey is transformed into a land journey. Ports as nodal points frequently attract supply-oriented industries dependent on imported materials and market-oriented industries which produce for export. Refining processes, whether of metals, oil, or sugar, are typically located at ports. Hamburg, Marseilles, and Southampton all make soap and refine petroleum. The economics of pipeline transport is changing this currently, however, as it is more economical to tranship crude oil by pipeline to the population center for refining than to carry the products there separately. And trans-Alpine pipelines save turnaround time on expensive tankers by shortening their voyages, at the same time that they deliver oil to consuming centers of Lyons or Karlsruhe. But ports retain attraction for many industries such as automobile assembly plants, whether in the export trade, as the Ford plant at Manchester, England, or in imports, as the General Motors plant in Antwerp.

Where transport is performed on a single type of carrier, the economies of the long haul mean that processing is likely to be located at one end or the other, but not in between.

Footloose Industries

A number of industries have no strong locational pull either to supply or to market. The reason may be that costs of transfer are relatively unimportant; or the changes of weight and volume in the course of processing may be small. In these cases, following the proposition just enunciated, location is likely to be at either end of the transport chain, but not in between.

The textile industry has historically been loose-footed. Originally, cotton and woolen textiles had locational advantages on either side of the Pennines in northern Britain. Cotton manufacture was concentrated in Lancashire, and especially in the city of Manchester, because of the moisture on the western side of the mountains which prevented cotton thread from breaking. Another locational attraction was the port of Liverpool, at which cotton was unloaded from the United States. Woolens, on the other hand, were mildly attracted to the supply of wool east of the Pennines and the Yorkshire coal fields which furnished fuel. But none of these forces was strong. An industry in which cotton can be bought in Syria for manufacture in Japan and the cloth resold in the Middle East is evidently one in which transfer costs are unimportant. The same verdict applies to the woolen industry, where produce from Australia and New Zealand, manufactured in Leeds and Bradford, is reexported to the Antipodes.

The refining of crude petroleum into various fractions involves little change in volume or weight. Accordingly, the question of whether a refinery is installed at tidewater near the wells or at the market depends on other considerations. Historically, some oil refineries have been located in Texas and some at the market, as in Bayonne, New Jersey, or Marcus Hook on the Delaware River in Pennsylvania. Europe used to import refined products from the Gulf of Mexico, the Caribbean, and the Middle East. Since World War II, however, refining operations have tended more and more to concentrate in Europe. In part this has been the result of commercial policy and a response to fears of expropriation. In part, however, it has followed from the fact that European consumption of petroleum products ceased to be concentrated strongly in the light fractions, especially gasoline. It made sense, in the interwar period, to refine Venezuelan crude oil in the West Indies and to export gasoline to Europe and residual fuel oil to the United States. Now that Europe consumes a more balanced set of products—tending in fact to need a higher proportion of fuel oil to gasoline than the United States—it is wasteful of transport to separate the products at a great distance from the market.

The rapid decline in transport costs since World War II has made some heavy commodities, like steel, which used to be confined to separate continents, virtually footloose like cotton and wool textiles. More shocking to older observers, however, is the new footloose character of veal. Breeding cattle on prairies in one location and fattening them in another nearer the market, where grain is abundant in rich land, is an old division of labor and basis for international trade: Live animals were exported from Ireland to Britain and from Canada to the United States. In recent years, however, as income has risen in Italy and with it the demand for meat, that country has imported both newly weaned calves, transported by airplane, and grain, to fatten the veal to the Italian taste near the market.

Since transfer costs are relatively unimportant in footloose industries, processing costs count for more. It is in these industries—textiles, matches, oil refining, etc.—that the theory of comparative costs in its undiluted form operates to determine what a country exports and imports in the absence of direct intervention by the state in the form of tariff policy. By the same token, as we shall see, it is in these footloose industries that commercial policy can be most effective in distorting the operation of the law of comparative cost. Tariffs can readily be used to attract a market-oriented industry to a market, or a loose-footed industry; they can do little with supply-oriented industry.

Location Economics

This short chapter, intended to make some amends for the unreality of international trade discussion in abstracting from transport costs, should not be taken as a full-fledged introduction to location economics, to which it does much less than justice. This rapidly growing field requires detailed study of its own and mastery of many more techniques than can be suggested in these pages.

Summary

The pure theory of trade has abstracted from a vital fact of life—the existence of transport costs. When this is reintroduced into the subject, it no longer follows that the price ratios between export and import goods are the same in the exporting and importing countries. Export goods must be lower in price to overcome transport costs; import goods higher. If transport costs are wider than price differentials in the absence of trade, trade cannot take place. This explains why many goods and services do not move in international trade.

The impact of transport costs can be illustrated with offer curves or in partial equilibrium.

Transport costs are not regular but vary according to the weight, bulk, value, perishability of the article, method of transport, and distance. Transport has to follow certain routes, and goods require handling in transport if the mode of travel changes. These characteristics make for complexity.

Three broad types of effects on the location of industry can be detected as emanating from transport costs. Supply-oriented industries are those in which weight and bulk of fuel or material are large in relation to value and production involves weight-losing processes. These are generally the early stages of manufacture. The later stages of manufacture tend to be market oriented, because assembly builds up bulk without adding weight. Goods which are valuable in relation to weight or in which weight and bulk do not change in process are likely to be loose-footed. Transport costs do less to determine their location than do the processing costs discussed in the theory of international trade.

SUGGESTED READING

Treatises, Etc.

The classical work in international economics incorporating transport costs is B. Ohlin, *Interregional and International Trade* (Cambridge, Mass.: Harvard University Press, 1933; rev. ed. 1967), especially part III. From the side of location, reference may be made to a number of studies and the literature discussed in them. A. Löch (translated by W. Woglom with the assistance of W. Stolper), *The Economics of Location* (New Haven, Conn.: Yale University Press, 1954), is a pioneering attempt to produce a general-equilibrium theory of economic location. It is uneven, brilliant in some passages and difficult in others. W. Isard's *Location and Space-Economy* (New York: The Technology Press and John Wiley & Sons, Inc., 1956) is the most comprehensive statement of the subject. See also the subject of regional economics, on which J. R. Meyer has written a survey article in "Regional Economics: A Survey," *AER,* March 1963, with a comprehensive bibliography of 130 items. E. M. Hoover's *The Location of Economic Activity* (New York: McGraw-Hill Book Co., Inc., 1948) (paperback, 1967), from which Figure 6.7 was drawn, is a long-lived item, as evidenced by its reprinting.

Points

The most careful study of transport costs within the United States is given in J. R. Meyer et al., *The Economics of Competition in the Transportation Industries* (Cambridge, Mass.: Harvard University Press, 1959). For a rather narrow discussion of the structure costs relative to value, see C. Moneta, "The Estimation of Transportation Costs in International Trade," *JPE,* February 1959.

PART II

Commercial Policy

Chapter 7

COMMERCIAL POLICY:
TARIFF AND NON-TARIFF
DISTORTIONS

Eight Effects

We now move from positive analysis to policy and to interference in trade. Such interference is generally undertaken by government, but for a wide number of reasons and at the urging or insistence of a particular interest or interests. It can be analyzed under a variety of effects, eight of which are worth our attention:

1. The protective effect.
2. The consumption effect.
3. The revenue effect.
4. The redistribution effect.
5. The terms-of-trade effect.
6. The competitive effect.
7. The income effect.
8. The balance-of-payments effect.

Not all these aspects of, say, a tariff refer to the same interest, and it is important in discussing a distortion of trade to specify the level of the interest concerned. A tariff can be analyzed from the standpoint of a plant, industry, region, factor of production, country, or the world, and one interest's meat may be another's poison. In particular, an interference is likely to alter trade, prices, output, and consumption, and to reallocate resources, change factor proportions, redistribute income, change employment, and alter the balance of payments. Results will be judged desirable or undesirable according to the interest concerned.

The Protective Effect

The protective effect can be illustrated in partial and general equilibrium, along with a number of other effects on the list. In Figure 7.1, $Q-Q_3$ represents imports at the price OP, prior to the imposition of a tariff. For

FIGURE 7.1. Protective, Consumption, Revenue, and Redistribution Effects of a Tariff in Partial Equilibrium

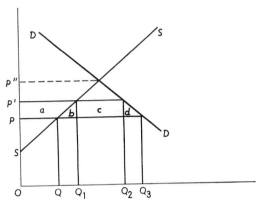

purposes of demonstration, the tariff, $P-P'$, is presumed to have no effect on the foreign offer price, because of the infinite elasticity of the supply of imports at the price OP. The protective effect is shown by the increase in domestic production, $Q-Q_1$. The consumption effect is the reduction in total consumption, Q_2-Q_3. (The protective and consumption effects sum to a **trade effect**, which is the reduction in trade, viz., $Q-Q_3 - Q_1Q_2$. It also has effects on price. These are obvious and need not be treated separately.) The revenue effect is the money amount received by the government on the new level of imports, the rectangle c, and is derived by multiplying the new level of imports, Q_1-Q_2, by the tariff, $P-P'$. The redistribution effect is the quadrilateral a, which is the additional economic rent paid to the preexisting domestic producers, plus the rent paid to new producers above their supply price. In old-fashioned economic terms it is an addition to producers' surplus derived by subtraction from consumers' surplus.

If it be assumed that the resources which are drawn into new production by the higher price were just on the margin of entry at the old price and were earning a return equal to $Q-Q_1 \cdot O-P$ in some other industry, the loss to the economy through the protection effect is limited to the area b. Similarly, if it be assumed that the expenditure diverted by the consumption effect to other products obtains a satisfaction equal to the marginal return under free trade, i.e., $Q_2-Q_3 \cdot O-P$, then the net loss in consumption is represented by d. These two areas, b and d, may be referred to as the **deadweight loss** of the tariff, all other losses in one direction being compensated for by a gain or change in another. They may also be called the cost of the tariff.

The size of the protective effect, produced by an existing tariff, is evidently determined by the elasticity of the supply curve. If the supply curve is highly elastic, the protective effect will be large; if inelastic, the effect will be small.

A tariff is prohibitive when the protective effect is sufficient to expand domestic production to the point where it will satisfy domestic demand without imports. In Figure 7.1 the minimum tariff which will keep out all imports is $P–P''$.

The protective effect can also be shown in general equilibrium, but it poses some problems of exposition. In Figure 7.2, the tariff is represented

FIGURE 7.2. Protective and Consumption Effects of a Tariff in General Equilibrium

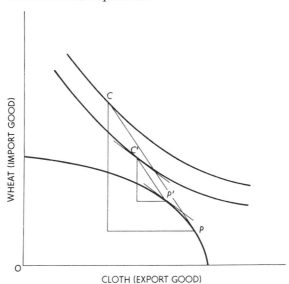

by the difference between the terms of trade and the internal prices of the goods, that is, by the difference between the slopes $P'–C'$ (the after-tariff terms of trade) and the parallel slopes, tangent both to the production possibilities curve and to the consumption indifference curve. As in partial equilibrium, the tariff raises the internal price of the import good above the external trading price. The marginal rate of substitution in consumption equals the marginal rate of transformation in production but differs from the marginal rate of transformation through trade. The tariff is the difference in the two slopes. In Figure 7.2 it is assumed, though this is not necessary, that the imposition of a tariff has left the terms of trade unchanged from the free-trade position, i.e., $P'–C'$ is parallel to $P–C$. The protective effect is the change in production, P to P', and the consumption effect is the change in consumption from C to C'. Note that if the terms of trade are unchanged, the country necessarily ends up on a lower consumption indifference curve as a result of imposing a tariff.

Note, too, that we have refrained from designating in Figure 7.2 which product is subject to a tariff. It could either be an import tariff on wheat or an export tariff on cloth, or some appropriate mixture of the two. In the case of an import tariff on wheat, the protective effect is increased production of the protected article. If the diagram represents an export tax on cloth, the "protective" effect is misnamed and should be regarded as a "destructive" effect, reducing the profitability of production of the export good. The Constitution of the United States prohibits export duties because the states in 1789 were unwilling to assign to the federal government this power to destroy export trades.

The protective effect of an import duty is almost always favorable for an industry or a region dominated by a single economic activity. The country as a whole may lose, but the particular industry whose price is raised is likely to benefit, at least in the short run. The resources engaged in an inefficient industry might do better in the long run to shift into occupations where they would be more productive. So long as they remain in the given industry, however, they gain from the tariff.

It follows that whenever a tariff is removed, an industry is hurt. A number of attempts have been made to devise methods of offsetting the injury to an industry from the removal of a tariff. But there will be times when an industry has gotten lazy and sluggish behind tariff protection, failing to take advantage of opportunities for improving productivity by introducing new methods. In these cases, removal of the tariff may actually stimulate improvements in productivity through competition.

It further follows that a program of trade liberalization, such as the Reciprocal Trade Agreements Act in the United States, which promises to reduce tariffs without hurting anybody is based on misrepresentation or stupidity. The Trade Expansion Act of 1962 finally recognized this and provided programs for alleviating injury—through extra unemployment benefits and retraining for labor, and special loans plus accelerated depreciation for industry—to meet, rather than evade, the necessity for reallocation into more efficient uses. It has proved very difficult to administer these provisions of the act: import-competing industries tend on the whole to be inefficient, and it is difficult to separate and cope with losses due to increased imports resulting from tariff reduction as distinguished from losses due to a widening of relative inefficiency.

The Consumption Effect

The consumption effect is almost always adverse. When it is adverse, total consumption is reduced, by Q_2–Q_3 in Figure 7.1, or from C to C' in Figure 7.2; and the consumer pays more for each item he continues to purchase.

A region can be adversely affected by the consumption effect. Thus the South in the United States, which sold its cotton on world markets, was obliged by the northern tariffs on manufactures to buy its textiles and other manufactured products in a protected market at high prices. Similarly industry suffered in Britain and Germany from tariffs on wheat, which raised the cost of living and wage rates.

An export tax has a favorable consumption effect. Italian city-states used to impose export taxes on wheat to lower the price of food for urban dwellers. Because export taxes are unavailable in the United States, the plywood industry asks for export quotas on peeler logs to increase the domestic supply and hold down price, and the leather industry wants restrictions on exports of hides and skins.

The Revenue Effect

Governments must raise revenue for a variety of public purposes, and from time immemorial foreign trade has been an object of taxation. In the United States 90–95 percent of all federal revenues came from the tariff in the 1850s. The less developed the country, the more likely it is that a substantial proportion of government revenues comes from tariff duties. This is less a matter of equity in taxation than of administrative convenience. Goods are easier to tax than the intellectual abstraction which is "income." And the flow of goods is constricted at ports of entry so that foreign trade is more readily taxed than domestic trade.

A tariff for revenue only is one where the protective and redistributive effects are missing. The consumption effect will be eliminated only under the limiting assumption that prices abroad fall by the full amount of the tariff, so that the tax is in effect borne by the foreign producer. A tariff for revenue only can be on goods which are not produced at home at all; or one where an equal tax is imposed on domestic production to eliminate the protective and the redistribution effects.

The Redistribution Effect

The redistribution effect shown in Figure 7.1 represents a higher price, and higher profits, for existing producers. In the real world this may be much more important than the protective effect. Interests seeking tariff protection argue the case of the marginal producer. The main drive for protection, however, is frequently the inframarginal supplier who will not be driven out of business by free trade but will make a lower profit.

The partial-equilibrium diagram shows the redistribution effect as the transfer of consumers' surplus to producers in a single commodity. More fundamentally, tariffs will redistribute income among factors engaged in different proportions in the production of different goods. Just as free trade raises the price of the abundant factor and lowers the price of the scarce, so a move away from free trade raises the price of the scarce factor and lowers the price of the abundant.[1]

In these terms, the tariff may represent an attempt by the scarce factor to reduce the trade which weakens its quasi-monopoly position. The drive to remove tariffs, on the contrary, can be equated with an attempt of the abundant factor to improve its position by widening its market. An increase in imports typically leads to an increase in exports, which raises export prices and the rate of return to the factor engaged intensively in export industry.

This analysis provides an insight into tariff history. The removal of the Corn Laws in Britain in 1846 is sometimes regarded as a response to the teaching of Adam Smith 70 years earlier. But the Corn Laws were imposed only after the Napoleonic Wars, some 40 years after *The Wealth of Nations* had appeared in 1776. And the removal of the Corn Laws was engineered after the rising industrial and commercial classes (enterprise plus capital) became plentiful. These groups asserted their political ascendance with the Reform Bill of 1832. Having achieved political power, they were able to increase their return, at the expense of the previously dominant agricultural classes who had engineered the tariff on wheat.

In Prussia, on the other hand, the landed interests were for free trade so long as they exported grain to Scandinavia and Britain, but shifted to protectionism when cheap wheat from the United States, Australia, and the Ukraine converted the comparative advantage into a disadvantage.

The internal redistribution argument in the United States is highly complex, involving separate industries, sectors, factors of production, regions, and political parties. Traditionally, the North was identified with capital, manufacturing, Republicanism and high tariffs, the South with land, agriculture (especially cotton), the Democratic party, and free trade. As manufacturing in the North split into mass-production exporting industry and labor-intensive, import-competing industry, the Republican North for a long time clung to its protective philosophy through cultural lag; while the Democrats under Franklin Roosevelt reversed the long wave of protection through the Reciprocal Trade Agreements program of Cordell Hull and other southern leaders just as the movement of the textile industry to the South changed its interest.

For a time there was a difference between the attitudes of the then separate American Federation of Labor, opposed to imports which threatened their labor-intensive industries, and the Congress of Industrial Organiza-

---

[1] A geometric demonstration in general equilibrium can be provided by the box diagram set out in Figure B.1 in Appendix B. Here the tariff shifts production away from the factor-price equalization points, R and U, and in the direction of the autarchic points, S and T. In so doing, it changes factor proportions and factor returns in both industries. This demonstration by Stolper-Samuelson reintroduced the Edgeworth-Bowley box diagram into international trade theory, as set forth in Appendix A.

tions, engaged in mass-production and export industries. With the recent wave of U.S. imports of automobiles and steel, the CIO's enthusiasm for trade expansion has been lost.

There is this much in the "cheap labor" arguments for tariffs, which, as normally put forward, is fallacious. If labor is the scarce factor, imports of labor-intensive commodities, which are those in which the country has a comparative disadvantage, will reduce the return to labor. But this is not much. The cheap-labor argument in its usual form is wrong, based on an erroneous labor theory of value and ignoring the obvious fact that countries with high wages are able nonetheless to export.

Government policy may deliberately strive to alter the distribution of income in the general interest. In Canada, it has been felt that a tariff on labor-intensive products to stimulate the demand for and raise the price of labor is a necessity in order to encourage immigration and discourage emigration to the United States. This is important politically, of course, but also helps to keep or move the population nearer some optimum level. Or a developing country could take the opposite tack and protect capital-intensive products in the interest of stimulating profits and savings. This idea, which is reminiscent of the modern (Leibenstein-Galenson) arguments for investing in industries which will produce the greatest savings (rather than the greatest output per unit of input) was expressed as early as 1908 by Alvin S. Johnson. It requires, of course, positively sloped supply curves, that is, some low-cost producers whose profits can be built up by a substantial redistribution effect. If the supply schedule is relatively flat, and the tariff is just sufficient to expand domestic production (the protective effect) without large rents to the inframarginal units, a tariff cannot produce savings. But this sort of reasoning may be operative in Mexico where business profits are encouraged for their contribution to reinvestment and growth.

Infant-Industry Argument

The consumption effect of a tariff on imports will not be adverse in the case of an infant industry, where the tariff serves to call the attention of producers to a line of production subject to increasing returns or decreasing costs based on external economies, imperfect knowledge, or learning by doing. A subsidy might be better. This would lower the price to the consumer rather than raise it, and in this way help to broaden the domestic market. It has the disadvantage of requiring revenue rather than raising it. But it must be recognized that the infant-industry argument, however much abused, is valid.

The infant-industry justification for a tariff is frequently abused. The world is full of industries with tariff protection which never have achieved sufficient scale to be able to dispense with protection. The test, of course, is whether the industry ultimately is able to function without tariff protection after the economies of scale have been achieved and the infant has "grown up." Actual removal of the tariff is not necessary. The pharmaceutical industry in the United States, for example, operates behind a wall of protection which is evidently not needed in many lines, since the industry is on an export basis. The tariffs which aided the industry in getting started, or rather helped it to stay alive after World War I, are retained through inertia or as a defense against possible dumping (discussed in Chapter 9). If a protected industry develops to the point where it can compete in world markets, as many have, it has grown up.

Typically, the infant-industry argument is used to justify the imposition of tariffs on an industry which had enjoyed the natural "protection" of trade disruption during war. The Embargo of 1807 in the United States gave the textile industry a start which the Tariff Act of 1816 was passed to defend. The same argument was used to justify the protection of machinery and chemicals in Britain after World War I and of chemicals and pharmaceuticals at the same time in the United States. The object was not the procreation of infants but the prevention of infanticide in the cold, cruel world of competition. In these cases the costs of entry had already been met: the question was whether, with time, increased efficiency could make the industry normally profitable without protection or subsidy.

No other argument for tariff protection based on efficiency is valid for the world as a whole. With decreasing returns, specialization based on comparative costs ensures maximum output.

Tariff Factories

While the infant-industry argument can be justified from a world point of view, great care must be taken, as pointed out, to apply it in individual cases. The theory of location may be helpful in this connection, as in the case of tariffs imposed on the finished product but not on parts or materials, to encourage foreign producers to establish tariff factories for final assembly or processing in the country in question. Pig iron and steel scrap may be duty free in Italy, for example, while semifinished and finished steel were subjected to high duties (before the European Coal and Steel Community). Equal encouragement can be given to factories working up raw materials for export by the imposition of export taxes on material such as jute, while the manufactured product, in this case burlap, is exported without impost.

Tariff factories pose certain problems for capital movements which are discussed in Part III, especially Chapter 16. But a tariff on a final product when the raw material is free of duty raises an important question which has been much debated in the last few years under the designation of the **effective rate of protection**.

Effective Rate of Protection

Suppose the tariff on cotton textiles is 10 percent but the value of cotton, which is imported free of duty, makes up 50 percent of the value of the final product. Since cotton is free of duty and can be imported by the textile manufacturers, the duty on cloth applies not to the entire price of cotton textiles, but only to half the total value, i.e., to the "value added" by manufacture. The nominal duty of 10 percent on the total value is really an effective duty of 20 percent on the value added.[2] For this reason schedules of nominal tariffs are said not to reflect adequately the real protective and consumption effects, which are more accurately measured by the effective rate of the tariff. Where finished goods bear high rates of duty and raw materials and components much lower rates, as is frequently the case, effective rates of protection are higher than nominal rates. They can, of course, be lower and even negative. In Italy at the end of the 19th century there was a high tariff on iron and steel and lower duties on finished machinery. Italian manufacturers in the engineering industry claimed that they were penalized rather than protected as compared with foreign manufacturers, who had access to cheap iron and steel.

The effective rate of protection is a highly useful concept in calling attention to the structure of tariffs in a world of trade in intermediate goods. The concept has proved not to be completely unambiguous because it rests, in its simplest formulations, on a fixed relationship between components and final products. Should input coefficients shift with price, as for example in iron and steel, where the inputs of iron, coal, and scrap steel alter with changes in their relative prices, the effective rate of the tariff cannot be readily computed. The effective rate of the tariff, therefore, is a partial-equilibrium concept which assumes other things equal when in fact other things change. The formula for the effective rate is one equation with two unknowns, a system which is evidently underdetermined. One needs another equation to indicate how r in the footnote reacts to changes in t.

The Terms-of-Trade Effect

The static argument in favor of tariffs at the national level is that under the appropriate circumstances a tariff will enable the country to obtain

---

[2] The formula for the effective rate of the tariff is $f = \dfrac{t - qr}{1 - r}$ where f is the effective rate of the tariff, t is the nominal rate, q is the rate of duty on components or intermediate goods, and r is the proportion of final product represented by imported or importable components. Where components are duty free, the formula reduces to $f = \dfrac{t}{1 - r}$. Where the same tariff obtains on finished goods as on components, i.e., $q = t$, then the effective rate is equal to the nominal rate, i.e., $f = t$.

its imports cheaper. In effect, the foreigner pays the duty, or some considerable part of it. This terms-of-trade argument in favor of a tariff may be demonstrated both with the partial-equilibrium analysis and, more completely, with Marshallian offer curves.

In the partial-equilibrium case, Figure 7.3*a* shows the effect of a tariff in widening the spread between prices in the exporting and importing countries. *P* is the price with trade, before the imposition of a tariff, assuming no transport costs. *P'* is the price in each market after the imposition of a tariff. In this case, where the elasticities of demand and supply are roughly the same in both countries, the tariff will partly raise the price in the importing country and partly lower the price in the exporting country. If the price in the exporting country is lowered at all, however, the importing country gets the product cheaper.

Tariffs to Improve the Terms of Trade—Partial Equilibrium

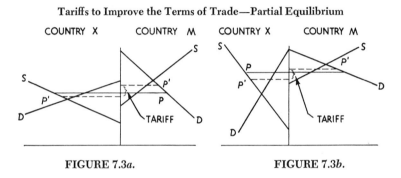

FIGURE 7.3*a*.   FIGURE 7.3*b*.

It is true that the consumer in the importing country has to pay a higher price. But this is offset, so far as imports are concerned, by the revenue effect. If the redistribution effect can be ignored, the revenue effect, which is the tariff times imports after the imposition of the tax, is levied partly on producers in the exporting country. If the supply is very inelastic in the exporting country, as in Figure 7.3*b*, and the demand fairly elastic in the importing country, the imposition of a tariff will have only a small protective effect, i.e., imports will not be much changed, but they will be obtained much more cheaply.

The reader may be reminded that if the supply in the exporting country is very elastic, close to horizontal or constant costs, then the imposition of a tariff cannot improve the terms of trade at all. This is what the classical economists, for the most part, assumed.

A similar demonstration may be made more completely with Marshallian offer curves. Figure 7.4 shows a pair of offer curves of Britain and the United States, *OB* and *OA*, respectively, which intersect at *P*. This gives a price *OP* between the two commodities, wheat and cloth. A tariff imposed by Britain on wheat from the United States may be represented by a new offer curve, *OB'*.

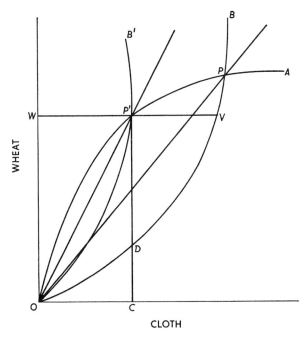

FIGURE 7.4. Tariff to Improve the Terms of Trade—
General Equilibrium

The tariff-distorted offer curve, OB', may represent either an import tax on wheat or an export tax on cloth. As an export tax, Britain is now prepared to offer less cloth for a given amount of wheat, collecting the export tax in cloth. For OW of wheat, for example, it used to offer WV of cloth but now offers only WP', collecting $P'V$ in taxes. Or it used to be prepared to offer OC of cloth for DC of wheat, whereas now it requires $P'C$ in wheat, collecting $P'D$ as tariff.

The shift of the offer curve from B to B' changes the terms of trade from OP to OP'. This is an improvement for Britain.

The improvement in the terms of trade may or may not make the country as a whole better off. In retailing, profit per item can be very high, but if sales fall way off, total profit is less than if the rate of profit had been more modest. Analogously, there is an optimum tariff at which any further gain from the improvement in the terms of trade would be more than offset by the related decline in volume. This optimum represents that tariff which cuts the opposing offer curve at the point where it is tangent to the levying country's highest trade indifference curve. Beyond this optimum, improvements in the terms of trade are still possible, but they are accompanied by a decline in the volume of trade which more than offsets the gain. Short of it, there is room for improvements in the terms of trade not completely offset by the shrinkage in trade quantities. Appendix D presents a geometric derivation of the optimum tariff.

Note here, too, that the gain in terms of trade from imposing a tariff depends on the elasticity of the foreign offer curve. If the foreign offer curve were completely elastic, a straight line from the origin with the slope of *OP*, the imposition of a tariff cuts down trade but leaves the terms of trade unchanged.

But two can play at this game. If Britain can improve its terms of trade by imposing a tariff, so probably can the United States. The original British gain will accrue only in the absence of retaliation. But if both parties retaliate, both almost certainly lose. Figure 7.5 shows such a case

FIGURE 7.5. Tariff to Improve the Terms of Trade—Retaliation

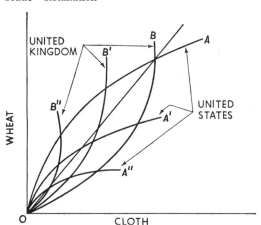

in which tariffs imposed by Britain and the United States in retaliatory sequence *B, B′, B″*, and *A, A′, A″*, and so on, leave the terms of trade unchanged at the end but greatly reduce the volume of trade. Each country would have been willing to buy and sell much more at these terms of trade if the price relationship in domestic trade were the same. The successive increases in British tariff on food and the U.S. duty on clothing, however, have resulted in a high price of the imported commodity after payment of duty in each country and the necessity to curtail consumption at these prices. The imposition of tariffs to improve the terms of trade, followed by retaliation, ensures that both countries lose. The reciprocal removal of tariffs, on the other hand, will enable both countries to gain. This is an explanation, or a rationalization, of the reciprocal nature of the Trade Agreements Program in the United States and of the General Agreement on Tariffs and Trade.

The Competitive Effect

Autarky breeds monopoly. If foreign competition is kept out by tariffs, domestic industry tends to become sluggish, fat, and lazy. Or it may start that way, and resist the change which foreign innovation threatens for it by persuading government to impose tariffs. The competitive effect of a tariff is really an anticompetitive effect; competition is stimulated by tariff removal.

The competitive effect has been important both historically and currently. The Anglo-French commercial agreement of 1860, for example, is credited by some scholars with having pushed France into the Industrial Revolution, forcing its iron forges to convert from charcoal to coal, and its textile industries from hand-driven to power spindles and looms.

While many observers hold that the main impact of the European Common Market (European Economic Community, or EEC) has been the achievement of larger markets and economics of scale, some of the most astute believe that its most significant result has been the breaking up of monopolies in such a country as France. Before the Common Market took effect, first in iron and steel and coal and then more widely, much of French industry could be described as made up of one or two large and relatively efficient companies which maintained a high price umbrella over the heads of a number of small, inefficient firms. This situation could exist because foreign competition was limited. Once the tariff walls came down, the smaller firms were forced to merge with or combine into larger, more efficient units or go bankrupt. It is true that the larger firms which survived competition with imports could always have lowered prices and forced the less efficient small ones to the wall. But among national firms, this sort of behavior was regarded as reprehensible. The same result could be achieved, with enlargement of volume and profit for the bigger firms which were efficient enough to export once tariff barriers abroad were lowered, by getting government to lower tariffs and letting the foreign firm do in the local inefficient operators.

We come to economic integration in a later chapter, but it is evident that part of the interest of the British government in joining the Common Market is to stimulate sluggish firms in the country and provide room for expansion of the lively ones. Not all British observers believe it will work. One poignant comment has been heard: "Not every kick in the pants galvanizes; some just hurt."

The Income and Balance-of-Payments Effects

The full explanation of the macroeconomic items on our list of effects must wait until the second half of the book. But enough can be said to indicate the nature of the problem. Tariffs cut spending abroad. The income not spent abroad will presumably not all be saved. Most will be spent at home. Under conditions of less than full employment, this will raise money and real incomes and employment. With full employment, however, it can only raise money income, through inflation, leaving real income worsened by the altered allocation of resources. With idle resources it remains true, tariffs raise domestic spending and national income.

But this clearly is a beggar-thy-neighbor policy. The increase in spending in the tariff-levying country is at the expense of the previously exporting nation. Its income and employment are reduced. Thus while the income effects of a tariff are recognized, they do not come in for approval. But tariff reduction as an antiinflationary device does. This is a good means of cooling off an overheated economy by mopping up the money supply with imported goods. It was used successfully by Germany in 1956. It should be used more widely, and doubtless would be, save for the unpopularity of unilateral tariff reductions with import-competing producers.

The balance-of-payments effect in the case of an import tariff comes from the reduction in import trade. This leads to an "improvement" in the balance of trade and the balance of payments in the first instance. How much of the improvement will endure depends upon a variety of factors, which we reserve for discussion in Chapter 18. Here we will only caution that the initial reduction in imports must not be regarded as the final balance-of-payments change. In partial equilibrium, with other things equal, this could be taken as the case. But partial-equilibrium analysis is peculiarly inappropriate here, with incomes changing. In classical analysis, with no money savings, the increase in domestic spending due to cutting down on spending on imports raises domestic income until it spills over into additional imports sufficient to restore the balance of payments. The shift of the curve is matched by a shift along the curve restoring the former status quo. With accelerators and similar fancy apparatus, one can even have a decline in imports through a tariff lead to an import surplus. The likelihood, as we shall see in due course, is that some portion of the impact effect of the tariff will be offset, but that tariffs will improve the balance of payments.

In today's tariff bargaining at the **General Agreement on Tariffs and Trade (GATT)**, the world organization at Geneva which is the forum for tariff negotiations, it is agreed that balance-of-payments weakness is no basis for refusing to reduce tariffs. Reductions are reciprocal, so that the increase in imports from our reductions is likely to be offset by gains in exports from theirs. More than this, however; it is understood that while tariffs have side effects on the balance of payments, their main impact is on the efficient allocation of resources, and the efficient means of handling the balance of payments lie in broad macroeconomic policies rather than in diddling with rates of protection.

One can go further and suggest that interference in trade should not be justified on balance-of-payments grounds and that balance-of-payments weakness should not give rise to interferences in trade. The balance of payments is a macroeconomic phenomenon, and its adjustment calls for macroeconomic policies. Contrariwise, the allocation of resources is a microeconomic question which should be justified in microeconomic, not macroeconomic, terms. The Canadian-American automotive agreement is good or bad depending upon what it does for the allocation of resources in the automotive industry of North America, not what it does to the balance of payments, and by the same token, the state of the balance of payments is no reason for building (or not building) a supersonic transport or cutting off tourist travel.

As a last resort, it is sometimes necessary to mix up micro and macro diagnosis and remedies in the same way that it is sometimes necessary to drive home a nail with the heel of a shoe rather than a hammer. It is not recommended.

The Reciprocal Trade Agreements Program

In 1930 the Smoot-Hawley Tariff Act raised tariffs in the United States to their all-time height. Since then, and despite the depression, the direction has been down. The Reciprocal Trade Agreement Act, first passed in 1934 and regularly renewed, had two premises: first, that reductions should be mutual, and second, that reduction accorded to one country in an agreement should be extended to other countries with which the United States exchanges **most-favored-nation treatment.** One exception to most-favored-nation treatment was recognized: agreement to enter into a cutoms union, which could take place slowly. Despite wide protest that it is illogical to permit 100 percent discrimination but not 99 percent, the customs union exception was regarded as a permanent abandonment of tariff protection vis-à-vis a given country, whereas 99 percent reduction retains the distinction between domestic and foreign firms.

After World War II, the Reciprocal Trade Agreements program was fundamentally altered by changing the bargaining from bilateral to multilateral, or rather to simultaneous bilateral bargaining, at which each "major supplier" bargaining with a partner kept an eye cocked over his shoulder at what the generalization of his concessions would mean for other countries (minor suppliers) and what their concessions on other items would mean to him. These negotiations were carried out under rules laid down by the General Agreement on Tariffs and Trade, an executive intergovernmental agreement which did not require congressional approval.

Successive renewals of the Reciprocal Trade Agreements Act culminated in the Trade Expansion Act of 1962, under which negotiations reaching agreement in 1967 provided for reductions in tariffs over a five-year period to 1972. This time, however, tariff levels were uncommonly low by historic standards, averaging little more than 10 percent in the industrialized countries. Effective rates of protection on finished goods were higher than that, but nontariff barriers were beginning to dominate the field. The General Agreement on Tariffs and Trade and the Williams Commission on International Trade and Investment Policy urged that the United States and the world should expand trade negotiations to include nontariff barriers.

Nontariff Barriers

Apart from tariffs, there are myriad ways to interfere with trade. Among the oldest are sanitary regulations—the British six-month quarantine of imported dogs to prevent rabies from spreading to the British Isles and the U.S. prohibition of meat imports from countries where hoof-and-mouth disease is endemic. Among the newest are antipollution regulations, such as the requirement that all automobiles sold in the United States meet a certain standard for emission of exhaust fumes. Both examples relate to legitimate regulatory functions which interfere with trade. But not all intervention is designed for broader purposes. Many are barriers to trade in less recognizable or more readily legislated form.

Tariff levels have always been bound by treaties. In order to evade the limitation on national sovereignty coming from such treaties, the world went in for nontariff barriers, notably during the depression of the 1930s. Quotas on imports were one device.

Import quotas can be analyzed in terms of the eight effects already specified for tariffs. The import quota fixes imports in terms of quantities, rather than a tax of so much per unit or such-and-such percentage of value. For every quota there is an "**equivalent tariff**" if one has a reasonable idea of the shape of the demand and supply curves. The protective, consumption, and redistribution effects of a quota and its equivalent tariff are the same, as Figure 7.6 makes clear.

There is, however, one considerable difference between a tariff and a quota, even where conditions underlying the market are known. This is in the revenue effect. Under a tariff, the area *abcd* in Figure 7.6 would be collected as governmental revenue in the importing country. If a quota of 100,000 tons is laid down, the price of imports is greater than before. Who will capture this increase cannot be determined in advance. If the importers have a monopoly of the trade and exporters are unorganized, the importers may succeed in obtaining it. If the exporters are effectively organized and the importers are not, the terms of trade may swing against the country as the foreign exporters hold up the price. Or the government may issue import licenses to anyone it chooses; when the U.S. system of issuing oil import licenses was shifted, under the Eisenhower administration, from previous importers to oil refineries, it made little difference for

FIGURE 7.6. Tariffs versus Quotas in Partial
Equilibrium

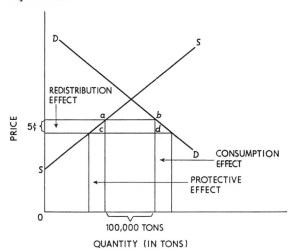

QUANTITY (IN TONS)

some companies which both imported and refined, but the difference for
others could be reckoned in large amounts of money approaching or sur-
passing a hundred million dollars a year. Inland refineries which had never
used imported oil gained and coastal refineries built to use imported crude
oil lost, as the latter had to acquire the license to buy oil at the world price,
which was about a dollar a barrel below the domestic price. These licences
turned out to be worth just about the difference between the world and
the domestic prices.

Or the government of the importing country, by auctioning off import
licenses, may succeed in obtaining for itself this increase in value due to
scarcity, which economists sometimes call a "rent." This would make the
quota the exact equivalent of the tariff, down to and including the revenue
effect. The auction of import licenses is not used widely, however, so that
the scarcity value inherent in the limited imports may accrue to either exporter or importer, depending upon the proximate conditions in the market.
The greater likelihood is that importers will capture this rent. In any event,
if the government does not auction off licenses to import, it must decide
who imports on some basis: first come, first served (a rather messy system);
traditional importers (which confers a monopoly on them unless room is
left for new entrants); or some even more arbitrary system. The invisible
hand of the competitive market must become visible.

In terms of offer curves, the situation can be set forth along the lines
of Figure 7.7. If Britain, with the offer curve OB, limits its imports of wheat
to OD, the terms of trade between clothing and wheat may be OP' or OP''
or any price between. As in the case of bilateral monopoly—with a monop-

FIGURE 7.7. Effects of a Quota on the Terms of Trade

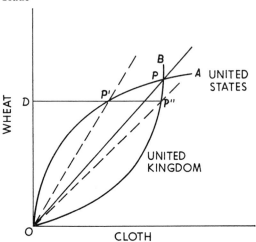

oly buyer and a monopoly seller—the outcome is theoretically indeterminate. The new terms of trade, it will be observed, are either more or less favorable to the country imposing the quota. If the importers capture it, as has been suggested is likely, the terms of trade are improved by a quota, to the extent that the foreign offer curve has an elasticity of less than infinity.

Export Quotas Abroad

A particular nontariff barrier of the past decade is the substitution of export quotas for import tariffs. The United States, for example, unhappy at imports of textiles, shoes, steel, or similar products and jealous of its leadership in the struggle for lower tariffs, has been unwilling to raise tariffs directly or to impose import quotas, but twists the arm of the foreign exporter until it imposes export quotas. (A further reason for requiring the foreigner to take action is that if the Congress were asked to raise tariffs or impose quotas in one industry, logrolling might get out of hand and lead to widespread restrictions.) The disadvantages of this technique lie first in the assurance that the terms of trade turn against the restricting country, and second in the fact that the increase in prices in the restricting country tempts new foreign suppliers into the market, thus requiring successive negotiations to restrict until all potential candidates are bound. With import rather than export restrictions, one determination of the amount must be made, although the decision as to who provides it remains open.

Nontariff barriers other than quotas and trading restrictions abound. A famous example is the **American Selling Price** provisions of U.S. tariff legislation relating to chemicals. Ad valorem tariffs are normally applied to the wholesale export value. In the tariff regulations of the United States, chemicals are taxed on the basis of the American selling price, which is the price including transport, retailer's profit, and tariff. Foreign countries have long objected to the anomaly, and the U.S. government has tried to alter the system while keeping the same level of protection. Since a tariff amounting to say 25 percent on the American selling price might have to be raised to 100 percent ad valorem on the foreign export value to provide equal protection, the chemical industry has resisted the change for the sake of appearances. It has been politically strong enough to do so.

An ancient device is to require imported goods to carry **marks of origin.** Labeling and container regulations are among the measures which may have legitimate regulatory purposes but also can be perverted to restrictive purposes.

Barriers to Trade in Agriculture

Tariffs, quotas, and other nontariff barriers are numerous in the field of agriculture. The reasons are the incapacity of the sector to adjust supply to demand rapidly so as to sustain prices; the strength of the power of agricultural forces in most countries, where farmers are overrepresented because of the lag of shifts of political behind economic power; Engel's law, which means that with economic growth food is an increasingly smaller part of total consumption; and the sentimental view that the countryside somehow sustains national virtues better than the town or the city. The quota was developed in agriculture in France as tariffs proved insufficient to hold up grain prices. A barrier to trade which takes the form of a tariff but is contrary to the spirit, under which tariffs are set but thereafter competition proceeds between domestic and foreign forces, is the sliding-scale tariff. This adjusts the tariff as the domestic price falls below or rises above some target level judged desirable. The device goes back to the Corn Laws of 1819 and is reproduced in the Common Market's special regime for agriculture, a treatment altogether different from that for manufactures. The European Free Trade Area (EFTA) dealt solely with manufactures and ignored agriculture as too difficult. If one moves from nontariff barriers to "distortions," a wider term, export subsidies which expand trade rather than restrict it are much more abundant in agricultural commodities than in manufactures.

Coal is sometimes called "underground agriculture" to emphasize the difficulties of allowing market competition to settle the pattern of trade in the area, because of the demands of national defense (the need to have energy supplies to some degree within one's border), inelastic supplies, and a specialized class of worker who until recently was unwilling or unable to shift to other occupations. In some countries, the government wants to maintain oil prices high when none is produced at home, in order to maintain coal income and employment. In both coal and agriculture, the academic economist is ready to urge more adjustment to the uninhibited forces of supply and demand than governments and legislatures are able to countenance.

Noneconomic Arguments

The difficult problems of agriculture and coal lead to consideration of the limits of economics and what might be called "noneconomic arguments," which are presumably excluded from the present discussion. In each case, the tariff involves a national loss which must be weighed against the gain in the other field.

Adam Smith admitted one such case, saying, "Defense is of much more importance than opulence." Clearly it is better for a country to continue as a going concern in the long run than to live at a higher standard in the short run. But while the economist is prepared to admit the validity of this argument, he is forced by his common sense to suspect that many of the defense arguments put forward by special interests are rationalizations of positions which are really based on industrial interests. It is too much to say in this connection that "patriotism is the last refuge of a scoundrel," but it is easy for everyone concerned with the production of a given item to exaggerate its importance to the national interest, and easy for politicians who want to "do something" for a given area to do so under the national defense label. In total war, everything is involved in defense. An inefficient watch firm, woolen manufacturers, the candle industry, and independent oil producers will all plead the need for tariffs in the national interest. The economist who has not thoroughly examined each case may nonetheless suspect special pleading.

One other noneconomic argument is concerned with both national defense and sociology. German writers of the 19th century argued for protection for agriculture to maintain the peasantry. In part this was to furnish a supply of soldiers for the army, since rural families were more reproductive than their urban counterparts, and in part it was a desire to maintain agriculture and the rural way of life—as has been the case recently in Britain. In France, protection against wheat imports provided in the 1880s and 1890s appears to have had its origin in the urge to preserve the family and the family farm. The argument for maintaining the price of an import commodity in the face of a decline in price abroad—due to inelasticity of supply where factors cannot be shifted readily into other occupations—is both social and economic. We shall later discuss its counterpart in resources engaged in exporting which cannot be shifted into other occupations. This is the primary argument for **intergovernmental commodity agreements** in basic foodstuffs and raw materials, particularly minerals.

Summary

The only valid argument for a tariff from the world point of view is the infant-industry argument. For a nation, a variety of valid cases can be made: a tariff may be needed for defense or other noneconomic reasons—to raise revenue, improve the terms of trade, expand income, or improve the balance of payments. The last three of these are beggar-thy-neighbor policies in that the gain for the country creates problems or losses for foreign countries. Their success assumes no retaliation.

Within a country redistribution of income can result from a tariff: Between producers and consumers of a given product, between producing and consuming regions, or between the scarce and the abundant factor of production.

Anything that a tariff can do, some other weapon of economic policy can do better.

With the decline in the use of tariffs brought about by negotiations in reciprocal reductions, attention has shifted to nontariff barriers. Ancient barriers are attracting more attention as the tariff problem is reduced, but there are also new and different restrictions on trade through quotas, export quotas demanded by importers, and discrimination in government procurement. Nontariff distortions to trade are especially strong in agriculture and coal because of inelasticities of supply and (except for coal) of demand, because of the political strength of the constituencies in those occupations, and because of national defense needs. In agriculture, lingering sentiments of Physiocracy, the notion that the real strength of the economy is in farming, also are influential.

SUGGESTED READING

Texts

For an elementary but good treatment, see L. B. Yeager and D. G. Tuerck, *Trade Policy and the Price System* (Scranton, Pa.: International Textbook Co., 1966) (paperback). See Södersten, chaps. 19–22.

Treatises

For basic articles, see the papers by Stolper and Samuelson, and Scitovsky in American Economic Association, *Readings in the Theory of International Trade;* Metzler, Lerner, and Bhagwati and Ramaswami in American Economic Association, *Readings in International Economics;* Bhagwati (No. 11) and Corden in Bhagwati, *International Trade.* A useful monograph is H. G. Johnson, *Aspects of the Theory of Tariffs* (London: George Allen & Unwin, 1971). J. Bhagwati's *Trade, Tariffs and Growth* (Cambridge, Mass.: The M.I.T. Press, 1969), part III contains some of the author's essays anthologized above, but more. A useful survey of the literature is contained in R. M. Stern, "Tariffs and Other Measures of Trade Control: A Survey of Recent Developments," *Journal of Economic Literature,* March 1973.

Points

A wealth of empirical data is contained in part II, "Major Issues," in the Williams report, *United States International Economic Policy in an Interdependent World, Papers Submitted to the Commission on International Trade and Investment Policy,* Vol. I. For studies of effective protection, see B. Balassa and Associates, *The Structure of Protection in Developing Countries* (Baltimore, Md.: The Johns Hopkins Press, 1971). R. E. Baldwin, *Nontariff Distortions of International Trade* (Washington, D.C.: The Brookings Institution, 1970), contains an extended treatment of the subject concisely handled by the same author in *Papers* to the Williams Commission cited above.

| Chapter 8 | OTHER NATIONAL POLICIES AFFECTING TRADE |

The treatment of nontariff distortions and noneconomic arguments for tariffs and quotas in the preceding chapter opened up but did not pursue a wide area for discussion. The present chapter is intended to expand that discussion by dealing with:

1. National policies which incidentally affect trade.
2. Trade policies unrelated to the usual purpose of trade, such as maximizing income or wealth.
3. Trade policies of countries interested in maximizing income or wealth but not using market or price signals.

Under the first heading we will discuss especially the impact of tax systems on trade; under the second, state trading for sumptuary purposes and economic warfare to limit the gains to a potential enemy rather than to increase a country's own gain; and under the third, socialist trade, especially in the Eastern bloc of states with so-called "planned" economies, and East-West trade between market and planned economies.

Elements of Public Finance

From at least the time of Adam Smith, the recognized task of public finance has been to raise the revenue necessary to pay for government expenditures with a minimum of distortion of resource allocation and in ways that conform to the community's standards of equity. These revenue, allocation, and equity considerations, which are not always readily harmonized, correspond to five of the eight effects we have treated under tariffs. The revenue effect is identical. The impact on resource allocation is the protective effect on production and consumption. Equity is represented by the redistribution effect within a country and the terms-of-trade changes between countries. Much more recently, since John Maynard Keynes, economists have occupied themselves further with the impact of taxation and government expenditure on total output and income. This corresponds to the income or employment effect of tariffs. The effects of taxation on competition are highly complex and lie outside the scope of this chapter, which refers only to the other seven effects.

The question cannot be dealt with thoroughly because we have not yet acquired the equipment to analyze exchange rates and balance-of-payments effects, and we shall not have time or space later to return to these aspects of the problem. The student should have little difficulty in extending the analysis himself. It is useful at this stage to say, however, that we proceed with partial-equilibrium analysis when evidently the need is for a treatment in general equilibrium, to specify what else beside the tax system changes—especially the exchange rate—before coming to final conclusions.

The analysis is incomplete in another respect, since taxes affect much more than trade, notably international factor movements and especially foreign direct investment. These questions are touched upon in later chapters.

Our interest is in international economics rather than public finance. Accordingly we make very simple assumptions regarding the incidence of taxation, having in mind that alternative assumptions would change many of our results. It is assumed, for example, that turnover and value-added tax (VAT) are passed forward to consumers, rather than falling on factors of production or entrepreneurs. This rests on an assumption of inelastic demand and elastic supply. Alternative elasticity assumptions would produce different results, of course, but would render the analysis altogether too complex. It is further arbitrarily assumed that social security taxes on employment rest on labor income.

Government Activity and Comparative Advantage

The mere existence of government distorts comparative advantage. Assume country A without government of any kind, and country B with. Both government expenditure and taxation in B are virtually certain to alter the basis for comparative advantage that would have existed without them. On the expenditure side, it might be assumed that government takes factors off the market in exactly existing proportions, so that the Heckscher-Ohlin basis for trade is unaltered; and that expenditure affects no demand or supply schedules through complementarities or substitution effects. These are hard assumptions to swallow. But on the tax side there is virtually certain to be distortion. Excise taxes clearly distort, except under the most extreme assumptions; and even progressive income taxes which leave price proportional to marginal social cost distort the input of effort by making leisure more attractive relative to work. Public finance experts have devised the theoretical device of a lump-sum progressive income tax which leaves marginal rates of return unchanged and thus is not distortionary in terms of effort. Unfortunately, this tax is universally recognized as impossible to apply and remains an intellectual curiosity.

We thus start from the proposition that governmental activity distorts comparative advantage, and this would be true if all the countries of the world had the same philosophies of government expenditure and taxation. But where there are differences in governmental systems of taxation—to limit ourselves to one side of the coin—the effects on international economic behavior can be far-reaching.

Differences in Rates of Tax

Domestic excise taxes are like tariffs in their effect on consumption, revenue, the terms of trade, internal income distribution, the balance of payments, and national income. Since they apply at home as well as to imports, however, they do not have protective effects. The six effects they have are not without importance at home and abroad, which is why the coffee- and oil-producing countries want the members of the European Common Market to lower their excise taxes on coffee and gasoline.[1]

Our concern is less with the impact of domestic excise rates than with differences in their rates between countries. There will be instances where the consumer can escape the payment of any excise tax at all: he has left one tax sovereignty, and, in transit by ship or airplane, or pausing in the customs-free portion of an international airport, he has not yet entered another. When he does, he will typically have a tourist's exemption from customs duty which enables him to escape taxes in both countries. But this loophole is not likely to be very large. Where the tourist exemption is large, the quantities of articles subject to excise tax—liquor, tobacco, and so on—which may be imported by tourists are typically limited. We refer rather to the distortion induced by differences in excise rates between countries, much like the distortion along state lines in the United States with different states imposing different taxes on gasoline, cigarettes, and alcoholic beverages.

Where rates are low and the excise tax is levied at the retail level, the distortions in trade introduced by differences in rates are relatively unimportant. They are limited to the border and to what the individual consumer finds it worthwhile to transport. Where the tax applies at a higher stage of production or distribution, however, say on the gasoline refiner

---

[1] Note that the oil-producing countries' claim that they are "entitled" to the consuming countries' taxes on oil (or to taxes on profits at later stages of production after the oil leaves their borders) represents a departure from normal standards of commerce and taxation. After goods are sold and title to them passes into other hands, a seller normally has no more rights to them or over them. The exception is for copyrights and patents, where the law preserves for the seller a right against others reproducing his work.

or the coffee roaster, it is necessary to apply excise duties along with tariffs at the border. Thus far no problem. But, as will be seen in Chapter 11, when two countries form a customs union, the fact of differences in excise taxes above the retail level does pose a choice: either submit to the tax-induced and distorted trade, with consumers individually buying in the low-tax country, or maintain customs inspectors at the border for the sole purpose of collecting domestic excise taxes. To escape the dilemma there has arisen strong pressure to harmonize excise taxes. Such **harmonization** generally takes the form of equalization and evidently has revenue, equity, and allocational effects in those countries where rates are changed.

If one looks just at the tax side, there is an important gain in simplicity from harmonization. But it is by no means clear that this gain is a net one. To do the job completely it may be necessary to harmonize benefits as well. Assume two countries with two different tax systems: one has public schools financed by a tax on alcoholic beverages and cigarettes; the other private schools without the taxes. To harmonize the tax systems without doing something about the benefits will evidently be awkward, giving rise to budget and allocation problems in one country or both.

Different Tax Systems

The difficulties posed by differences in rates become enhanced when we consider different systems. Assume two countries of roughly the same size, government revenue, and allocation of public benefits. If these assumptions cannot be granted there is evident distortion. But if one taxes goods and services and the other incomes of factors, even with equal size revenue and allocation of expenditure, there is almost certain to be distortion. There must be some distortion of effort in the income-taxing country and of consumption in the nation taxing goods and service. It is virtually unthinkable that these distortions would be offsetting. Hence comparative advantage would be altered.

So much is highly academic. The more lively issues turn on the administration of turnover taxes, the question of turnover taxes versus the value-added tax, and social security taxes. The first two pose problems of **border adjustment**, as one jurisdiction responds to the need for fitting internationally traded goods to the fiscal requirements of another.

When a trading country taxes goods through a levy on sales, or turnover, a decision must be made whether the tax is applied on the **origin** or the **destination** principle. In autarky, they come to the same thing. With foreign trade, however, the question is how to handle the taxes on exports and imports. Under the origin principle, there is no need to tax exports, since these are already taxed at the factory (let us say), nor to tax imports, since these are presumably taxed when produced abroad. Under the destination principle, however, a turnover tax at some level is applied to imports, and the turnover taxes already collected on goods produced for export must be refunded.

The level of taxation under the destination principle is awkward, as it should depend on how many stages of production the goods have gone through, paying taxes at each stage as they turn over. Most countries apply a so-called "cascaded" tax, which assumes a certain number of vertical stages. If the turnover tax were at 4 percent, for example, and it was assumed that the average number of stages of production before foreign shipment was three, then the cascaded tax would be fixed at 12 percent, which would be applied to imports and remitted for exports. Where a good was produced by a vertically integrated company which paid only one tax on final product, the cascaded turnover tax remitted on exports would be larger than the tax actually paid, equivalent to a subsidy. And the same tax levied on imports produced by a vertically integrated firm abroad would be an added penalty to trade. A turnover tax based on the destination principle is thus clearly distortionary.

The turnover tax is disliked by public finance experts because it provides an incentive to vertical integration which may not be economically desirable. (We ignore whether it is or is not.) To meet this objection, French experts devised the administratively tricky but analytically elegant device of a value-added tax. Each stage of production pays a tax only on the value added by the stage, or rather, pays a tax on the total value sold but claims a rebate for taxes paid on components or materials bought from earlier stages. There is thus no incentive to integrate vertically and no need for a cascaded tax. The rate of tax for border-tax adjustment is the same as the tax actually paid.

Assume that country A applies the VAT on the origin principle, and country B has a VAT of the same level but uses the principle of destination. A's goods going to B are taxed as exports by A and as imports by B. B's goods shipped to A are not taxed by A, and the taxes already paid by producers in B are refunded to the last processor. Goods going the first way are subjected to double taxation; those going the other are not taxed at all, net, and there may be some distortion between early and late stages of production and the exporting stage.

When the problem first presented itself in the European Coal and Steel Community (ECSC) formed in 1950, it was thought to be serious. A distinguished committee of economists was appointed under the chairmanship of Professor Jan Tinbergen of the Netherlands to examine it and make recommendations. The French, in particular, thought that the Germans should adopt their system as a matter of harmonization. But the economists observed that so long as the bilateral balance of payments between the two countries was appropriately balanced in the long run, it made no difference. Any tax distortion in favor of France, which taxed on the destination principle, and against Germany, which used origin, was balanced out by a somewhat higher exchange rate. The balance-of-payments, terms-of-trade, production, consumption, and so on effects of the taxes could be offset by equal and opposite influences on the side of the exchange rate. Like other distortions between social and private marginal values, the tax system had already been absorbed into the general-equilibrium system. The experts recommended that the problem be ignored.

This recommendation is no longer universally supported by economists, on the ground that exchange-rate changes are much more general than even the very general VAT. Depreciation which will correct the distortion in the current account between these two countries will produce new distortions in capital items between them, and in all payments and receipts with third countries. Exchange-rate changes are a meat ax when a surgeon's scalpel is needed. The Common Market countries chose not to settle the problem by ignoring the tax difference and adjusting the exchange rate.

Harmonization of excise taxes without harmonization of the total fiscal system (including benefits) produces new distortions. To take just revenue, it reduces the revenue of the government whose tax system had relied most on excise taxes and increases the revenue of the one that had used such taxes least. Pressure to harmonize any one aspect of the economy seems to lead to new pressures to harmonize further. The end is the merging of fiscal sovereignties, which in the European Economic Community still lies some distance ahead.

French pressure to harmonize social security taxes seems to have as its basis less a broad integrative purpose than the wish to impose on the other members of the Common Market the same disabilities under which France labors. It is paralleled by French insistence on equal pay for men and women in the rest of the Common Market as well as in France. This legislation distorts resource allocation and trade in France. If applied through the Common Market it would eliminate relative distortion among the Common Market countries at the expense of increasing it between such countries and the outside world. The question of social security arises in particularly significant form for Britain joining the Common Market. British social security is paid for to a considerable extent by general taxation on incomes at progressive rates, rather than entirely by employer and exployee taxes on employment. For Britain to adopt the French or Continental system would alter the distribution of income in Britain against the worker and in favor of the well-to-do, who are most affected by general taxation. If, on the other hand, each country retains its own internal system, the differences in their own social security financing would make labor costs higher in France relative to Britain and thus would distort comparative advantage.

State Trading

Closely related to the fiscal motive is the case where the state takes over trading in order to maintain a monopoly in a product it wants to control for the sake of sumptuary regulation. Alcohol and tobacco are the classic examples of goods in which a number of states established monopolies for the sake of earning high returns on the basis of inelastic demands. The rules of GATT sought to ensure that where the state went into the buying and selling of goods across national boundaries it should not act as a discriminating monopolist but behave like a competitive market. In particular it should not afford disguised protection to domestic industry by buying at home at a higher cost than it could have done abroad, or subsidize exports by selling abroad below costs of production, nor should it discriminate in prices among foreign suppliers or purchasers of the same commodity.

For a time after World War II, there was much interest in so-called **bulk-buying agreements** among countries to replace the private international market with government purchases and sales. The thought was that with assured markets, the seller could concentrate on output and lower costs through economies of scale, sharing these economies with the buyer through lower prices. In addition it was believed that bulk-buying agreements would provide stability to prices, supplies, and output, with any possible loss in profit maximization being more than made up in stability. In actuality, governments found it difficult to achieve stability except within contract periods. When a contract expired, there was an inevitable tendency to compare the contract price with the open-market quotation: if the open-market price was lower, the buyer was unwilling to renew on the old basis; if it was higher, the reluctance was on the side of the seller. It fairly quickly proved to be the case that state trading through bulk-buying agreements produced more contention than stability. The result was that the free-market economies ultimately gave up the device.

There is one area, however, where states do as they like. This is in purchasing for their own use. Here there are no international rules nor any standard of conduct. All governments tend to buy at home. The tendency was accentuated during the 1930s depression, when "Buy British," "Buy French," and "Buy American" campaigns were urged on the public to expand employment. In the United States, the Buy American criterion for government purchases, which was laboriously reduced from 25 percent as a normal rate in the 1930s to 10 percent in the 1950s, was raised to 50 percent in the balance-of-payments weakness of the 1960s.

Governments pay no tariffs, so that perhaps some nominal preference for domestic supplies such as 10 percent is understandable. Buy-local campaigns, like putting up a tariff during a depression, are clearly a beggar-thy-neighbor policy. And to jam up the rate to 50 percent, as the United States did in the early 1960s, is clearly to set up a double standard—no balance-of-payments tariffs or quotas for the private sector, because of international commitments, and near autarky for the government. For the United States to buy dairy products in Wisconsin for its troops in Germany, next door to Denmark, is evidently uneconomic—wasteful of real resources and causing the Department of Defense budget to run out faster than it otherwise would, thereby raising appropriations and the need for tax revenues.

Governments tend to buy at home under most normal circumstances. Larger governments are unwilling, for example, to buy arms from any country that is not a certain ally. And considerations of prestige require that government officials ride in American limousines rather than Daimler-Benzes and fly on American airlines. Many of these considerations are not even articulated. But the economic rule remains the presumptively correct one: one should buy in the cheapest market and sell in the dearest, whether household, firm, or government sector.

Economic Warfare

In economic warfare the problem is not so much to maximize the country's gain but to limit the gain of another country or one regarded as an enemy or as a potential enemy. It is even possible to take offensive action against the well-being of another country. Orators tend to emphasize that trade is a path to peace, just as Marxists claim that the need for trade outlets leads to war. The most tenable position between these two is that trade has in few cases led to hostilities or prevented their breaking out. Trade is, however, a possible means of conducting a sort of warfare. A state, for example, may attempt to limit the output of another country, particularly of materials of war; or a state may attempt to depress markets in foreign countries for the sake of encouraging world revolution. Sometimes it is difficult to tell whether a country is selling abroad to depress world prices and thus wage economic warfare against capitalist countries, or to pursue a comparative advantage, including, on occasion, getting rid of surplus production. Thus the Soviet Union has been accused of attempting to wreck the West by dumping wheat (in 1932) and, since World War II on various occasions, tin, aluminum, and oil. While it is natural for Western competitors in these products to regard the Soviet sales as politically motivated, careful observers have in each case found an economic reason for selling which carried more conviction. Nonetheless, while improbable, the possibility exists that one country could use its powers of purchase and sale in international markets to achieve nonmilitary political designs on another.

Economic warfare is unhappily a much more usual phenomenon. Here the entire purpose of trade changes. In economic warfare conducted parallel with military operations, such as that waged by the Allies against Germany and Japan during World War II, the weapons included blockade, preclusive buying, and agreements with neutrals to cut off trade beyond the range of blockade. Preclusive buying is perhaps the most interesting, since here the purpose of state trading is not to acquire what a country wants but to prevent the enemy from getting access to it. In frequent cases, as in the rival attempts to buy tungsten and tungsten ore (wolfram) in Spain and Portugal, or chrome in Turkey prior to Turkey's entry into World War II, the effect of the rival preclusive buying is to divide supplies much as before, to raise the price many times above its original relative value, and to expand output. In some cases, such as Swedish ball bearings, purchases were made to keep supplies away from the enemy, and the goods were mainly stored. Blockade-running British Mosquito aircraft could carry only a few tons of goods per trip in addition to their diplomatic traffic.

Short of "hot" economic warfare, there should perhaps be a stage of "cold" economic warfare. Here there is no military blockade imposed by force of arms, but one country will attempt to deny to its potential enemy those goods which are of extraordinary strategic interest to the latter's armament needs. The gain in slowing down the rate of armament of the potential enemy country, however, should be measured against its cost. Where no credit is extended, trade is a two-way balanced affair, and the restriction of exports involves a restriction of imports. Success in the denial of exports should therefore be weighed against the impact of the loss in imported goods.

It is important to calculate in sober fashion the effectiveness of economic warfare on specific industries and specific programs. The impact of the economic blockade of Germany in World War I was exaggerated by the German General Staff to excuse its own shortcomings. Even with aerial bombardment, the blockade of World War II had a supporting rather than a leading role in the defeat of the German armies. The difference between what a country needs to survive comfortably and what it can get along with at a minimum is substantial, as the oil sanctions of Rhodesia in 1967 and against Italy in 1935 amply demonstrate. There is first the task of making sure that sanctions are effective, and that small shippers in great number do not replace the large suppliers whose operations can be overseen. Next, even if total supplies are cut down, there is much fat to be cut through before one gets to muscle. For instance, much of the Rhodesian oil imports is normally used for nonessential purposes, which can be eliminated without basic harm to the economy.

Moreover, a modern industrial nation is capable of shifting and adapting resources among industries, substituting one material for another with only a limited loss of efficiency. In consequence, except in the relatively short run, the denial to an enemy or potential enemy of materials for a particular industry results in diversion of other resources to this industry.

If the country is industrialized on a fairly broad front and moderately adaptable, economic warfare will deprive it of resources in general rather than final weapons in particular. Viewed in this light, it is particularly important, in hot or cold war, to weigh the potential gain in minimizing the position of the other country against the cost to one's own.

Where the country is not highly industrialized, such as the Soviet Union or even more Red China, a further consideration enters. To deprive these countries of industrial products in the short run stimulates them to increase their industrial capacity in the long run. Much depends upon the most probable time of trouble. To an economist, it might even make sense to sell war material to a potential enemy, if trouble were far away, in order to reduce his incentive to develop his own weapons and to lull him, if possible, into obsolescence.

Much of the appeal of economic warfare is emotional, based on a social reluctance to trade "with the enemy." Its efficacy as a weapon is dubious. In particular, its enthusiasts fall into the now-familiar trap of reasoning in partial-equilibrium terms in a general-equilibrium situation, assuming other things equal when they in fact will change. It is one thing to deprive the "enemy" of shot or shell if he has no capacity to tighten his belt or reallocate resources from other purposes—if, that is, other things remain unchanged. But as a rule other things can and will change, and the effect of economic warfare becomes marginal.

Trade among Socialist Countries

When we move from market to nonmarket countries, the question is how trading states go about deciding what goods to buy and sell. Initially, after World War I, when the Soviet Union was the only "socialist" country in the world, it chose to use foreign trade as a device to achieve autarky. Not without reason, it feared dependence on imported supplies and pushed its traditional exports—wheat, timber, furs, manganese and so on, largely primary materials—to buy the machinery which would make the country independent of foreign supplies. Its success in certain commodities like steel was impressive, and in all but a few primary commodities such as rubber and wool and in most basic manufactures, the Soviet Union did well. Especially did it build up heavy industry.

When after World War II there were other socialist countries, in China and Eastern Europe, the notion of using foreign trade to get rid of foreign trade made less sense. The Soviet Union, for one, was planning for the **socialist division of labor,** a concept which never has become clear. Other countries such as China and Romania thought it useful to follow the Soviet path and build their own heavy industry. But even if it had been agreed that it was useful to specialize and exchange, the question presented itself (with a series of national plans, independent prices, and inconvertible currencies) of how to go about it.

Soviet planning, with its emphasis on materials balances, is regarded as biased against balanced foreign trade. Plan fulfillment as a prime target of administrative purpose means holding back on exports and speeding up imports to make good the gaps in the plan. But foreign trade in independent plans in seven countries becomes even more difficult to regulate. The trade organization of the Soviet bloc, COMECON, has been searching for a fundamental way to organize the foreign trade of its members, without great success. Meanwhile, trade continues on an ad hoc basis, and even that gives rise to serious problems of deciding what countries export and import what commodities, at what price, and of balancing the national value of exports against the value of imports on a multilateral basis. In particular, there was no effective way of deciding whether, say, Hungary should sell shoes to Romania or Czechoslovakia should sell it shoe machinery so the Romanians could ultimately produce shoes for their own market.

Since the Soviet Union traded at world prices in the interwar period, one solution for the pricing problem in principle was to value trade among the bloc countries at world prices. This has proved difficult in practice. For bulky commodities, it is not clear what the world price of a commodity is in Eastern Europe, until a decision is made as to whether the Eastern bloc would export or import that commodity to the West. The price in North America or Western Europe is clearly inappropriate because of transport costs, but the question whether transport costs should be added or subtracted cannot be decided until it is clear which way the trade would go. For differentiated products, moreover, the question of quality can be decided only on an arbitrary basis: Is the Moskvich more like the Renault, the Volkswagen, or the Cortina? Studies of the prices actually used in Eastern trade suggest that the Eastern countries frequently trade with each other at higher prices than those at which they trade with the West. Various explanations have been used to account for this phenomenon, including trade discrimination, a "custom union effect" which has produced an island of higher bloc prices than those in the outside world, and rather arbitrary adjustment of prices after trade to help balance exports and imports.

But the more important problem is what goods to trade. Part of the difficulty lies in the lack of an efficient price system at home in each country. Real prices used in consumption and production differ widely because of heavy turnover taxes, which are added to imports and subtracted from exports to make it possible to trade abroad at all at arbitrary exchange rates. But even after prices are adjusted for taxation, they fail to reflect economic values. If capital is not regarded as a factor of production, capital-intensive goods tend to be relatively cheap, overproduced, and exported, which is inefficient for the system as a whole. Planning techniques without prices, or with only implicit shadow prices, became too complex, even with computers, when seven systems have to be meshed, subject to the constraint that excess demand in one commodity in one country is matched by an excess supply in another, and that the value of all exports equals the value of all imports for each country, on a multilateral basis. These issues are solved in the West with prices and money. The Soviet bloc tries to operate without explicit prices reflecting scarcity values, and with a monetary system which is unsatisfactory so that its countries are unwilling to hold ruble balances. Thus far it is making slow work of it. COMECON has organized trade in ways variously described as "absolute advantage" or "empiricism" and resolved conflicts at the "highest political level," all the time seeking and failing to find an objective, scientific basis for international socialist specialization.

The suggestion has been put forward by a Hungarian economist that trade in the Eastern bloc needs convertible currencies and international corporations to make effective price comparisons so as to see where comparative advantage and disadvantage lie. Along with effective goods prices and international money in which to compare them, the bloc needs at least a notional set of factor prices (sometimes called "shadow prices") to calculate the desirability of investing capital to take advantage of foreign-trade opportunities. Without such pricing, the bloc remains condemned in its internal trade to traditional, empirical, ad hoc, or arbitrary trade, on which it is impossible to be sure of gains.

East-West Trade

Trade between the private enterprise economies of the West and the state trading organizations of the Soviet bloc poses a variety of difficult institutional and organizational problems. But it has not been possible for the United States to tackle many of these because of its restrictions on trading with the East: an absolute prohibition on trading with Communist China and Cuba, and a restricted list of products which cannot be sold to the Soviet Union and the Eastern bloc. The position has eased somewhat since the passage of the rigid Battle Act of 1951 at the height of the Korean War. After long, unsuccessful efforts at detente on the part of President Johnson, President Nixon, the business community, and some limited portions of the Congress (interrupted when the Vietnam War intensified), the visits of President Nixon to Communist China and the Soviet Union in 1972 started a movement toward resolution. But the problems abound. They include concern for political independence, one-sided economic advantages, the Eastern need for credit, the problem of what the East should sell to the West, and the problem of making two different systems function in tandem.

Fear of dependence on, say, Soviet trade on political grounds finds support in its sudden cutting of purchases of Icelandic fish in 1948 and of sales of oil to Israel in 1956. But in its turn the United States abruptly reduced the Cuban sugar quota in 1960. There is risk of great dependence on any supplier or outlet, and Western governments may have to exert pressure, when they do, more overtly and publicly. The fact that Socialist trade organizations are governmental may enable them to squeeze a customer or a supplier more gradually. But the difference between East and West is probably small, since the trading organization in Eastern countries is different from the Politburo.

The one-sided economic advantage concerns Eastern-bloc sales of primary products to Western developed countries, while purchasing products of high technological content. At the same time it seeks to buy primary products from the less developed countries and sell them arms, machinery, and machine tools. The West would like to buy output of the sophisticated Soviet space organization, particularly rocketry. The dissatisfaction rests on the contention that the Western price system does not in fact appropriately reflect relative scarcities as between primary and more advanced products. If we leave aside the military and space equipment which neither side sells to the other, it can happen that the economic prices at which various goods are traded in the West give large gains from trade to the East. This is the way competitive market economies work: sellers get the going price even though they would have been willing to accept less, and demanders pay the going price even though they gain a large consumers' surplus therefrom. The less developed countries get large gains from trade in this fashion, as pointed out earlier. This does not bother us. We are interested only in maximizing our own income and disregard, or react benignly to, the gains of our trading partners. Such is the normal trading utility function. But it can happen that a country's utility function is more complex and includes not only its own income, positively, but the gains of trade of its partner, negatively. In this case, the West, for example, would be willing to trade with the East and enjoy gains from trade only if the gains of trade of the East were taken into account. If the West has such a utility function—as seems evident by its unwillingness to accord most-favored-nation tariff treatment to the East, though this involves some technical problems—it may be an argument for restricting trade on the grounds that the East gains too large an advantage from it.

The problem of credit and what the East should sell to the West run into one another, since if the East had plenty to sell to the West there would be no need for credit. As it is, however, the Soviet Union has bought $750 million of wheat from the United States, largely on credit, and the question is how the latter is going to be repaid. To obviate the possibility that Western nations would overextend credit to the East or compete too avidly for sales by loose credit terms, a Berne convention signed in the 1930s set a five-year limit on credits. Recent competition has broken this barrier, and the Organization for Economic Cooperation and Development (OECD) is seeking to provide at least exchanges of information in the West so that the separate lenders can make a judgment as to the extent to which safe limits of credit extension are being approached. The Soviet Union has some uncertain amount of gold (and an excellent record on repaying the few commercial credits it has received in the past). Communist China earns a substantial amount of sterling from trade with Hong Kong. Most Communist countries are jealous of their credit standing. But there is some limit on the amount of credit which can safely be extended, a limit dependent upon Eastern success in selling in Western markets. Thus far East-West trade has been limited less by Western regulations, especially those of the United States, than by the lack of goods for the East to sell.

In discussing goods availability, one must distinguish between standardized products traded in organized markets—wheat, copper, timber, etc.—and differentiated products, which, as noted in Chapter 4, must be marketed. If the Eastern bloc is prepared to limit trade to standardized goods sold in organized markets, the prospects for trade are not bright. Investment by the Soviet Union in oil and gas drilling and pipelines will provide energy for Europe—in welcome competition for the West with the Middle East. Extension of railroads to the North and East in the Soviet Union would render more forests accessible to Baltic ports and provide Europe with an important scarce natural resource in timber. The prospect for selling manufactures is not good: Soviet products are on the whole poor in quality, except in the forbidden space and military fields. Marketing is poor. Spare parts and repairs facilities do not exist. The most likely path is for Western companies to buy Eastern products which they market under their own name—a U.S. electrical company selling Hungarian light bulbs of quality under its label, for example, or Fiat producing its own cars and trucks in Yugoslavia and the Soviet Union and being paid in kind, i.e., transferring its fees in components, spare parts, or finished assemblies.

The fundamental awkwardness is to mesh two entirely different systems. Should the Eastern bloc belong to GATT? The concept of a tariff means little when all trade is conducted for the account of the state. Can Western firms take the risk of selling their copyrighted and patented products in the East? In the Soviet Union and China, at least, as well as in many parts of the so-called free world, there are different rules for patents and copyrights; royalties are paid, if at all, in inconvertible currencies, and patent infringements must be pursued in the local courts, which may be overcome by myopia when it comes to recognizing the rights of foreigners. Multilateral trade would run safely in only one direction until the Eastern bloc developed multilateral trade of its own and a currency, provided by all, that was convertible into Western monies. By this is meant that any Eastern country could run an export surplus (first) with one Western country, acquire a balance in hard currency, and convert it into another Western money used to buy net imports from another country; but any Western country that accepted an Eastern currency for later use in another

Eastern country would be taking (under present conditions) a heroic risk. There is much that can be done to improve East-West trade: limiting the provision of the Battle Act to narrowly military items; extending most-favored-nation treatment to the Eastern countries in the matter of tariffs, especially in the United States; and understanding, in matters like the blockade of Cuba, that bygones are bygones after 10 years or so, and blockades may well be counterproductive. The prospect for a lively expansion of trade between East and West to a meaningful level is dim, although percentage gains from low numbers are readily achieved. Despite the difficulties, the pursuit of expansion is probably worthwhile for peace, and possibly for the sake of the trade itself.

Summary

Governments affect comparative advantage, especially the existence of different tax rates, different tax systems, and differences in governmental benefits. Among the more significant problems in the field are those concerning whether the excise taxes of integrating countries should be harmonized and how border taxes can be adjusted when turnover or value-added taxes are applied on the "destination" principle.

State trading was undertaken in monopoly products, restricted for sumptuary purposes and exploited for revenue. There is a question how to provide rules for nondiscriminatory trading by states. Bulk purchases by states, however, were designed to improve on the market. They were abandoned on the ground that the improvement, if any, was not equal to the trouble involved and the decline in international amity.

In economic warfare, the task is not to maximize a country's gain but to maximize another country's loss or to weaken its capacity to conduct warfare, subject to some limitations on the cost to the warring country.

Trade among socialist countries which lack identical pricing practices and convertible currency to make price comparisons suffers from the inability of planners to calculate relative scarcities and comparative advantage and disadvantage.

East-West trade compounds the difficulties by confrontation between two different systems. The East should be free to trade, except in military equipment, with the West. Even if restrictions are removed, however, the likelihood for a significant level of trade is not bright because of the difference in the systems and the difficulty of finding abundant supplies of goods and services for the East to provide to the West.

SUGGESTED READING

On the wide range of issues covered in this chapter, the student is directed to the William report, *United States International Economic Policy in an Inter-*

dependent World, especially the *Papers.* Volume I of the *Papers* has three studies on tax adjustment, two on East-West trade.

Treatises

On Eastern-bloc trade see especially P. J. D. Wiles, *Communist International Economics* (New York: Frederick A. Praeger, Inc., 1969) and S. Pisar, *Co-existence and Commerce: Guidelines for Transactions between East and West* (New York: McGraw-Hill Book Company, 1970). G. Adler-Karlsson, *Western Economic Warfare, 1947–1967: A Case Study in Foreign Economic Policy* (Stockholm: Almqvist & Wiksell, 1968) is good on analysis and history.

Points

There is an extensive literature on harmonization. See, for example, H. G. Johnson, P. Wonnacott, and H. Shibata, *Harmonization of National Economic Policies under Free Trade* (Toronto: University of Toronto Press, 1969).

For government nontrading, see especially R. E. Baldwin, *Nontariff Distortions of International Trade* (Washington, D.C.: The Brookings Institution, 1970), chap. 3, "Restrictions on Governmental Expenditure."

The work of the Tinbergen Committee was entitled: High Authority of the European Coal and Steel Community, "Report on the Problems Raised by Different Turnover Taxes Applied within the Common Market" (Luxembourg, 1953).

I. Vajda, in P. A. Samuelson, ed., *International Economic Relations* (New York: St. Martin's Press, 1969), is the source of the suggestion that Comecon needs a convertible currency and international corporations.

Chapter 9

MONOPOLY, CARTELS, AND

PRICE DISCRIMINATION

Competitive Trade?

The two previous chapters dealing with tariffs, quotas, and other policies affecting trade may convey the impression that only governments are responsible for distortions of trade which differ from what comparative advantage would dictate if there were perfectly competitive markets. Not so. Firms also intervene in ways that affect quantity and price, and occasionally government and enterprise combine—the temptation is to say "conspire"—to alter the competitive outcome. Some examples of this action are:

1. In Canada a Royal Commission on Farm Machinery Prices was established when Ontario farmers found that they were unable to purchase for import certain types of farm machinery in Britain, where they were on sale cheaper than in Canada even after payment of transport and duty, because British dealers had been forbidden by a Canadian company with a subsidiary in England to allow any sales back to Canada.
2. The U.S. Treasury Department has been bringing a series of actions against importing firms, threatening the application of countervailing duties designed to compensate for dumping. Prominent among them was SONY, Japanese producer of color television sets.
3. When in 1971 the German deutsche mark was revalued upward, the prices of Volkswagens in the United States and Germany remained unchanged.
4. At the meeting of the United Nations Conference on Trade and Development (UNCTAD) in Santiago, Chile, in April 1972, a Secretariat paper dealt with the way in which exports of manufactures of the developing countries were limited by "restrictive business practices."
5. The action of the countries belonging to the Organization of Petroleum Exporting Countries (OPEC) in taxing "profits" on a notional rather than a transaction price for oil sales holds up the price of oil, restricts

output, gouges consumers, with the tacit approval of international oil companies and consuming-country governments.

6. Whereas traditionally under the Sherman and Clayton antitrust acts, the United States has reacted vigorously to the possibility of foreign restraint on trade with the United States (albeit tolerating restraint by U.S. exporters under the Webb-Pomerene Act), the position today is that foreign cartels in textiles and steel, specifically for the purpose of limiting sales to the United States, are organized and directed by the Department of State.

One might almost say that competition in international trade is more honored in the breach than in the observance.

This is a tricky subject because so much of the rhetoric is pejorative rather than clinical and because under certain conditions it is necessary to choose between modes of behavior, each of which is traditionally approved. The economist and the businessman fail to understand one another on a semantic basis. Monopolistic competition and price discrimination have a technical meaning for the economist, and the fair price has none, whereas the first two terms are opprobrious to the practitioner, while a fair price sounds fine to him. Businessmen are urged by economists to maximize profit and to sell to all comers at the same price. When demand curves in different markets have different elasticities, the two slogans come into conflict, and the businessman tends to charge different prices in each market. This is called price discrimination by the economist and sounds like criticism.

In what follows we employ the reasoning and terminology of the economist and hope that the reader used to thinking in business terms will withhold judgment until he understands what is intended.

Monopoly and Monopsony

Under perfect competition, as every student of economics past the introductory course knows, no individual seller or buyer has control over price. The demand curve facing the firm is infinitely elastic, even though the demand for the product may be inelastic; and the supply curve facing the individual buyer is infinitely elastic. Firms are numerous and enter and leave industry easily. Marginal revenue equals marginal cost equals price. It does not pay a firm to restrict its sales, since its place will be taken by others, nor to restrict its purchases, since other demanders will take up the slack.

In monopolistic competition, the position is otherwise. The curves facing an individual trader are no longer flat but sloped. This may be because of a natural monopoly, as in nickel, diamonds, or patented products, so that the inelastic demand curve for the product is that for the firm. Or because of collusion among "competitors" who agree to restrict output, maintain price and quality, and limit conditions of sale. Or because all competitors understand one another and realize that any attempt at vigorous competition through price reductions or aggressive selling would be matched by others, so that without express collusion, sellers maintain price above marginal cost and forgo the opportunity to expand output and make extra profits because they know these would be ephemeral. The significant point is that entry is limited for monopoly, so that the super profits are available only to the monopolistic competitor. In monopsony, the buyer gets the product below the seller's long-run average costs because the latter is unable to exit from the business and continues producing even when he cannot cover more than his average variable cost.

Cartels

Monopolies are few, except for patented products, and even there competition is such that imperfect substitutes are likely to be plentiful. I.B.M. computers held the field for a while, and Xerox in copiers, but imitation overtakes such firms with a fair degree of speed—though not always with success.

Business agreements and **unconscious parallel action** to follow **restrictive business practices** are more frequent. They tend to take place in standardized products costly to transport, with limited numbers of sellers— as in iron and steel, nonferrous metals, oil, coal, etc.; in some complex chemicals such as rayon, nylon, synthetic rubber, dyestuffs, and pharmaceuticals (though there is some product differentiation in the last two); and in industries dominated by patents, such as dyes, photographic equipment, optical supplies, and electronic equipment. The history of these agreements or understandings is one of cutthroat competition followed by understanding, which breaks down when there is excess capacity. In numerous cases in industry, as in primary products (especially agriculture), governments support the business understandings to maintain price when private industry by itself proves inacapable of so doing.

The history of the oil industry is particularly edifying in this connection. In the 1920s there was a formal international agreement, to which the Soviet Union—a rhetorical opponent of cartels—belonged. This broke down in the 1930s depression. An international agreement restricted Middle East exploration: the British above a "red line," the American companies below it. In the immediate postwar period, the U.S. government sought to prevent price discrimination, particularly through "basing point" arrangements, under which oil was delivered to Western Europe from the Middle East but charged at the Gulf of Mexico price plus freight from the Gulf (phantom freight). Its interest was that it was paying for European oil under the European Recovery Program.

With the end of the Marshall Plan and the withdrawal of U.S. interest in policing oil prices, the price structure of oil first firmed and then began to erode under the influence of new entrants into the world market. The big two of the 1920s—the Standard Oil Company of New Jersey and Royal Dutch Shell—became five, seven, ten, and ultimately many more as concessions were made available to new companies in Latin America, the Middle East, Asia, and Africa. To prevent price reductions, the OPEC kept raising its tax rates, but not on actual income so much as on income based on a hypothetical price. The effect was that of an export tax of something on the order of $1.50 on a product which cost 30 cents to produce. Middle East income taxes on oil rose from $1 billion in 1960 to an estimated $9.2 billions in 1972, with the governmental cartel substituting for the crumbling private tacit understanding.

Cartel Policy

A number of interesting questions respecting cartels present themselves in international trade. It is argued by some that cartels cannot endure without government support; the case of the British governmental tariff action in behalf of the Iron and Steel Federation in its dispute with the European iron and steel cartel in the 1930s is cited. Some think that private cartels are superior to intergovernmental agreements or bulk-buying contracts because private cartels dissolve under the impact of diverse interests of individual producers. There is a body of American opinion which holds that international cartels are subversive of the national interest in self-preservation and that the member of a cartel somehow loses his patriotism—but this is difficult, if not impossible, to sustain.

What interests us primarily is the question of public policy toward international (and, if you like, national) cartels. Three possible lines of action present themselves: One may ignore them, attempt to break them up, or work out a way of living with them in which their worst features are softened or eliminated.

The policy of ignoring cartels attracts a wide body of conservative opinion. **Laissez-faire,** a rule derived from competitive conditions with freedom of entry and exit, becomes perpetuated into a rule with validity after the underlying conditions which justified it have changed. There are those who are unable to make intermediate distinctions between monopoly and perfect competition, but the tenor of this chapter may have persuaded the reader that there are many shadings. If regulation is appropriate to monopolies such as public utilities, then the principle of laissez-faire— hands off business under any and all circumstances—has been breached.

The notion that it is possible to restore perfect competition by breaking up cartels, insisting upon the disintegration of combines and trusts, and enforcing arm's-length bargaining between separate stages of production in vertically integrated industries is perhaps more idealistic as a policy, but at the same time more naïve. Economies of large-scale production, especially in highly capitalized industries, may be in some part irreversible. The third alternative has the drawback of being much less clear-cut than the other two. In part, it requires publicity for written agreements among firms and certain limitations on the content of such agreements, such as forbidding the division of markets and restriction on entry. In addition, it requires the instilling of restraint in pricing and of approximating, to the maximum degree consonant with the long-run interests of the owners of the business, the behavior of the trade under competition, including flat pricing. This involves restraint in the exercise of monopoly and oligopoly power. It is this third alternative which the European Economic Community is trying to develop. Prohibitions against cartels are combined with provision for the registration of industrial agreements for clearance, in much the same way as the British special courts on restrictive business practices distinguish between good and bad business agreements and approve of the former.

The difficulty with the pursuit of this third line, however, is the absence of objective criteria. How high should profits be in oligopolistic industry? What is a fair price, a fair share, a fair profit? In part, the basic difficulty occurs in the period of transition. Under perfect competition, with freedom of entry and exit, maximization of the short-run interest, i.e., of short-run profit, is a satisfactory rule and accords with the national interest. With its use, resources will be properly allocated among industries. Under imperfect competition, where a company is attentive to its long-run interest and long-run profit and is prepared to ignore short-run opportunities to increase profits, there may also be a satisfactory outcome. Companies will then abjure exploitation of monopoly positions because of fear of reprisal and will limit short-run profit maximization in favor of more security. The intermediate period is where the troubles press. Here companies have power but continue to exercise it in accordance with the rules applicable to the time when the private firm was impotent.

Market Separation

In international trade, monopolistic competition through monopolies, monopsonies, and cartels increasingly takes the form of price discrimination. Trade takes place in separate markets. In a single market, only one price prevails. This is true by definition—the **law of one price,** which says that only one price can obtain in one market. Where price discrimination is practiced, there must be more than one market which can be distinguished. This can occur in a fairly limited geographic area—see the different prices charged for first-run, second-run, and country movie houses; for professional services of doctors, lawyers, and others, depending on the patient's or client's income; and for the same article in the convenient corner store as opposed to the serve-yourself giant at a shopping center some distance away from residential areas. In international trade, however, markets are already differentiated at a minimum by space and may be further separated by differences of custom, habit, language, etc., even though other factors common in the domestic market—such as product advertising, snob appeal, or professional ethics—are absent.

If a seller has access to two separate markets and can exercise some control over price in one or both, it will pay him to sell at different prices if the elasticities of demand in the two markets differ. The general rule for the maximization of profit then holds: profit will be maximized where marginal revenue equals marginal cost. But the marginal cost of his output will be identical for sales in all markets, since we abstract from transfer costs. (The price we are discussing is the price f.o.b. the factory. Transfer costs are eliminated from calculations of price, revenue and cost.) The crux of the matter then becomes the difference in marginal revenue in the two markets.

The seller may ignore the difference between the markets. In this case he will add average revenue curves and marginal revenue curves. The point where the marginal cost curve intersects the combined marginal revenue curve will be the production point of maximum profit. In Figure 9.1, with average and marginal revenue curves added for markets A and B, the quantity *OQ* will be produced and sold in the two markets, at the same price, *OP*. The quantity *OQ* will be made up of *OQa* sold in market A and *OQb* sold in market B. But observe that the sale of *OQa* units in market A produces a marginal revenue of *OMa*, while *OQb* sold in market B gives a higher return, *OMb*. A policy of identical or flat pricing in two markets with different elasticities means that a higher marginal re-

FIGURE 9.1. Aggregated Demand Curves—No Price Discrimination and Inequality of Marginal Revenue

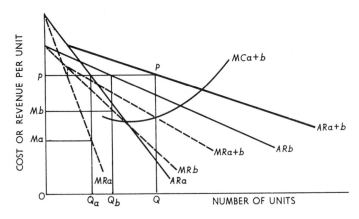

turn is earned per unit sold in one market than in the other. The profit of the seller could be increased by shifting sales from the less elastic to the more elastic market.

Price Discrimination

This can be made clear by putting the two sets of revenue curves on different sides of the vertical axis, as is done in Figure 9.2. This diagram, which omits the marginal cost curve, shows the same marginal and average revenue curves in markets A and B, but no totals. The A curves are to the left of the vertical axis and run from right to left. The B curves perform in the usual manner. The quantity QQ is the same as OQ in Figure 9.1 and is also the same amount as $Q'Q'$. In this diagram, however, we can see that a shift of QQ' from market A to market B will equate marginal revenues ($Q'U = Q'W$). This will result in price discrimination, a higher price (OP_a) in A, the market with the less elastic demand, and a lower price (OP_b) in B, with the more elastic demand.

The fact that price discrimination can take place at all is due to the quasi-monopoly position of the seller and the fact that he can fix his price, whether because of monopoly, because the other few competitors in the business will follow his leadership, or because of a cartel agreement.

It will be noticed that the higher price is charged by the discriminating seller in the market with the less elastic demand curve, and the lower where demand is more elastic. This underscores the monopolistic nature of discriminatory pricing. A maximum return is reached when the seller exploits to the full through price discrimination the inelasticity existing in each

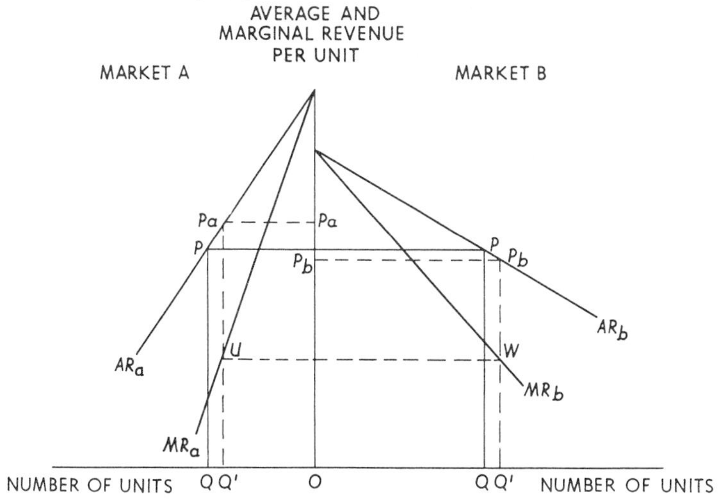

FIGURE 9.2. Discriminatory Pricing by a Seller—Equating Marginal Revenue in Two Markets

separate market. The limiting case is reached where the seller singles out in a separate market each potential buyer and charges him what he is willing to pay as a maximum for each unit. In these circumstances, the seller captures for himself the whole area under the demand curve. Under perfect competition the average revenue curve is completely elastic, or horizontal, and marginal revenue equals average revenue. If one market is highly competitive, the discriminatory price solution comes to simply selling at a monopoly price in one market. In the other the discriminating seller has no power over price and has to sell at the market. Here average and marginal revenue are identical, and marginal cost equals price, which is the competitive solution. Marginal revenue in the other market is the same as in this market, but the monopoly price charged is higher.

Notice that the difference in delivered prices between two markets cannot exceed the costs of transport between them. If the difference were wider than this amount, it would pay others to undertake arbitrage, buying in the cheaper market and selling in the dearer. On this account, price discrimination is much more prevalent in heavy products than in light.

Discriminating Monopsony

Less frequent in international trade is the discriminating buyer, or monopsonist, who is sufficiently big to take account of the effect of his purchase on price (see Figure 9.3). The monopsonist may be a big company, such as the De Beers syndicate which dominates the market for uncut diamonds, or a state trading organization which goes in for bulk buying. It is an organization big enough to take account of the effect of its pur-

FIGURE 9.3. Discriminatory Pricing by a Buyer—Equating Marginal Cost in Two Markets

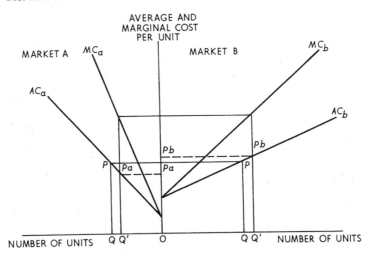

chases in raising the prices it pays for goods. Accordingly, it will shift purchases from the less elastic source of supply to the more elastic and pay a lower price in the former than the latter, in order to reduce its over-all cost. It will equate the marginal cost of supplies in the two markets.

Note that the competitive buyer equalizes the delivered cost of his purchases, not the cost f.o.b. from different destinations, while the discriminating monopsonist equalizes marginal cost on a delivered basis. The return to the seller excludes the cost of transport, but the cost to the buyer most definitely includes it.

Dumping and Reverse Dumping

Charging different prices in different markets is called, in international trade, "dumping." The word is unfortunate. Its origin goes back to the case of the manufacturer with an unsold supply who "dumps" the excess abroad in a market in which he does not normally sell in order to avoid breaking the price in his own market. By default more than anything else, the practice of sale at different prices in two markets has become "dumping." The height of absurdity in nomenclature is reached when the manufacturer sells abroad at a higher price than at home. This is called "reverse dumping" to designate the notion that he is then dumping in the domestic market.

Dumping is simply price discrimination. It takes place when the demand abroad is more elastic than the demand at home and arises only because of the monopolistic element in the home market. In reverse dumping, the demand abroad is less elastic than the home demand, whether because competition abroad is less keen than at home or for any other reason. In this case it is possible to exploit the inelasticity of demand of the foreign market by higher prices abroad than at home, balancing marginal revenue in the two markets.

In some cases, such as the steel industry, foreign and domestic prices will go separate ways, and the U.S. industry dumps or reverse dumps as the occasion calls for. Prices outside the United States expressed in dollars tend to fluctuate in a wider range than prices in the United States. At times they are above those in the United States, and reverse dumping takes place; at times below, and market positions are maintained only by dumping.

Various kinds of dumping have been distinguished, including mainly **sporadic, predatory,** and **persistent.** Sporadic dumping is the sort which occurs when a company finds itself with distress goods on its hands that it wants to dispose of without harming its normal markets. It is engaged in by companies that typically stay clear of foreign markets and only occasionally find themselves with more inventory than they can hope to dispose of in orderly fashion through their normal outlets. For such companies, the demand abroad is more elastic than it is at home, where they want to preserve their quasi-monopolistic position. Or it may regard the cost of the goods as already sunk (i.e., marginal costs ex transport costs as zero) and cut its losses abroad by selling the goods for anything that can be realized.

Predatory dumping is selling at a loss (as measured by average but not marginal costs) in order to gain access to a market, to drive out competition, or for any other short-run purpose. Predatory dumping is followed by an increase in prices after the market has been established or the competition overcome. Foreigners are frequently accused of this sort of price conduct by U.S. producers. It is difficult to establish cases. American textile producers after the removal of the embargo in 1814 charged that British exporters were dumping in the American market to drive them out of business. However valid, the argument was a powerful factor in the passage of the Tariff Act of 1816. The British iron industry was also accused of dumping in Germany in the 1840s and in Italy in the 1860s and 1870s to prevent the establishment of new firms in that industry in those countries.

But if these allegations are true, dumping is not only undertaken to stop the rise of new competitors. It may be practiced by newcomers as a device to break into a certain market. The reduction of price to marginal cost is one way to get a foot in the door. Others are to engage in extra costs, to advertise, to establish a distribution system, or to indulge in the marketing expenses discussed in Chapter 4. It is curious that the harsh public view of dumping to break into a market—such as the Japanese are accused of doing for some years in the United States and more recently, after yen revaluation, in Europe—is not applied to extra selling costs, with which they are strictly comparable.

Persistent dumping occurs when a producer consistently sells at a lower price in one market than in another. As a rule, this occurs when the firm regards two markets differently from the point of view of overhead costs. Suppose, for example, that average variable costs are low relative to average total costs and that average fixed costs can be covered in the domestic market. Additional sales at any price above marginal costs in the foreign market will increase the profits of the firm. It may then pay a firm to dump persistently. An example of this is the motion-picture industry, in which, prior to 1948, the cost of many motion pictures was covered by exhibition rentals in the United States, where marginal costs were low, especially if no new sound track were required, and where foreign sales at almost any price would increase profits. Overhead costs are not prorated between markets on the basis of quantity sold, and persistent dumping may be profitable to the firm. Most economists regard persistent dumping as beneficial to the importing country and harmful to the exporting country, in which consumers are charged a monopoly price. The analogy in domestic trade with which some students will be familiar is the well-known Filene's basement in Boston, where the department store puts on sale at rock-bottom prices distressed goods bought up all over the country which other merchandisers are anxious to prevent from being sold and reducing local prices in their areas.

If the argument is made that persistent dumping is good for the buyer (and there are exceptions), it is usually harmful to domestic consumer interests, whose prices are raised. In Japan there is evidence that like producer groups in the United States, consumers are growing restive, in the Japanese instance at the high prices they pay for automobiles, radios, cameras, and television sets in order to absorb the overhead costs which are remitted for export sales.

Most economists regard dumping as a vicious policy, much more to be condemned than tariffs. Unconsciously, these writers hold that while it is legitimate for a government to make distinctions between its citizens and foreigners (so long as it does not make invidious distinctions among foreigners), it is inadmissible for a firm to do so. The intervention of the government is charged with the general good—even though it may be used to advance a private interest. The producer in a position to discriminate, on the other hand, is a monopolist, in whole or in part, working for his own profit.

Trade Restrictions against Dumping

A wide number of countries impose penalty tariffs or quotas against goods which they believe are being dumped within their borders from abroad. For this purpose dumping is usually defined not in terms of f.o.b. price discrimination but as sale below average costs of production. The facts are always difficult to establish, and, in addition, the theory is questionable. The economist's defense of persistent dumping has just been made. Sporadic dumping which pushes distress goods into a foreign market can evidently be upsetting to businessmen in the same way that any competition is, but it, too, evidently benefits the consumer. Most feared presumably is predatory dumping, with the argument being that the foreign seller drives out the local competitor and then raises prices higher than ever before and mulcts the consumer.

A question arises, however, as to why, when the price is raised again, the former local competitor who has been driven out does not effect a reentry into the now-profitable business. If he can, the possibility of pillage is eliminated. If he cannot, why not? It may be that the predatory dumper achieves economies of scale and can keep the price permanently lower. This shifts the argument back to persistent dumping and is presumably a gain. It is conceivable that there is an irreversibility in the system, so that producers driven out cannot effect a reentry when the price is subsequently raised, but it is not self-evident.

The subconscious producers' bias which most of us have, and which makes us mercantilists in instinct, operates here to make us typically applaud antidumping measures. Thus a measure of poetic justice appears in the European Economic Community retaliating against the U.S. escape-clause withdrawal of tariff concessions on Wilton carpets and flat glass by imposing tariffs on polyethelyene (plastic), which the American chemical industry had been accused of dumping in Europe.

But the international trade theorist must beware of succumbing too quickly to instinct. Countervailing measures against alleged dumping are obnoxious because they reduce the flexibility and elasticity of international markets and reduce the potential gain from trade. From 1846 to 1913, when Britain followed a free-trade policy, distress goods in any part of the world could be disposed of in London, which was the Filene's basement of the world, to the benefit of the British consumer and of the overseas producer. With antidumping tariffs everywhere, adjustment after miscalculations which result in overproduction is much less readily effected. Price discrimination serves an economic purpose in effecting transitions from one pattern of production to another after, say, the entry of a new source of production, and for cleaning up mistakes.

The Dilemma of Policy

The basic dilemma, as noted earlier, is how to reconcile rules of conduct which are approved separately when taken in partial equilibrium but may conflict under particular circumstances. We want nondiscrimination and profit maximization, but under certain circumstances profit maximization requires discrimination.

We confer monopolies on producers through a patent system to encourage research into new products, but once a product has been developed, continued monopoly restricts output and reduces welfare below its potential maximum.

An efficiency maximum calls for price equal to marginal cost, as in perfect competition, but in industries with high overhead costs, society must find some way to bear such costs.

The economist thus objects to monopolies, cartels, and price discrimination but increasingly recognizes that in a world of imperfectly elastic demand curves which differ in different markets, limited entry and exit, heavy overhead costs, and oligopolistic industry, the rules of perfect competition cannot prevail. He is therefore prepared to settle for something such as **workable competition.** By workable competition is meant, of course, competition in which price cannot get too high because new entrants will be encouraged to come into the industry and may do so unhindered by capital costs, patent restrictions, lack of access to raw materials, or other barriers, and in which price cannot get too low because existing firms will be encouraged to quit and shift their efforts into other more profitable lines.

The role of the state is to limit monopoly and monopsony by encouraging entry and exist, to prevent mergers and takeovers which reduce firms in an industry below some reasonable number such as eight, or six—or is four enough? But of course countries want it both ways: monopolies for exports, no monopolies abroad in imports, and even monopsonies. Or dumping by us in wheat, but not by them in color television.

Summary

Interference in trade takes place not only through government action but by the restrictive business practices of monopolies, monopsony (a monopoly buyer), and cartels. Cartels are international business agreements to regulate price, division of markets, or other aspects of competition. They occur in industries with less than perfect competition. If the cartel is eliminated by some action, imperfect competition will still exist. This fact argues against the policies of either ignoring cartels or eliminating them by fiat, and in favor of a policy of regulation and publicity. In the present state of economic theory, however, no consensus exists as to how cartels should be regulated.

Perfect competition means that no individual buyer or seller has control over price, i.e., that the demand and supply curves facing the individual firm or consumer are infinitely elastic. In the real world of international trade, however, firms in many industries are of such a size that they can affect price.

When demand curves in different markets have different elasticities, a profit maximum is reached by charging discriminatory prices. The higher price is charged in the market with less elasticity. Or, looked at in different terms, a disproportionately high share of overhead costs may be allocated to the market with the less elastic demand curve.

Dumping is merely price discrimination. Sporadic, predatory, and persistent dumping have been distinguished in theory. While governmental action to prevent predatory dumping may be justified when its existence is clearly established (a difficult matter), sporadic dumping performs a highly useful service for the seller, and persistent dumping is a benefit to the buyer.

SUGGESTED READING

Texts

See D. A. Snider *Introduction to International Economics,* 5th ed. (Homewood, Ill.: Richard D. Irwin, Inc., 1971), chap. 12.

Treatises

E. S. Mason, *Controlling World Trade* (New York: McGraw-Hill Book Co., Inc., 1946) and J. Viner, *Dumping* (Chicago: University of Chicago Press, 1923;

reprinted by Augustus M. Kelley, Publishers, 1967) are out of date in terms of examples and later theory, but still useful.

See C. Edwards, *Control of Cartels and Monopolies: An International Comparison* (Dobbs Ferry, N.Y.: Oceana Publications, Inc., 1966).

On oil, see M. A. Adelman, *The World Petroleum Market* (Baltimore, Md.: Johns Hopkins Press, 1973); for competition in the Common Market, D. L. McLachlan and D. Swann, *Competition Policy in the European Community* (London: Oxford University Press, 1967).

Points

The *Special Report on Prices* of the Royal Canadian Commission on Farm Machinery was published by The Canadian Queen's Printer in Ottawa, in December 1969.

The UNCTAD Secretariat Report on Restrictive Business Practices of developed countries will appear in the Conference's papers.

| Chapter | COMMERCIAL POLICY AND |
| 10 | DEVELOPING COUNTRIES |

The 75 or so developing countries of the world—or those apart from the Soviet bloc and the developed West (Western Europe, North America, the British Dominions and, on an honorary basis, Japan)— are unhappy about the conditions of world trade within which they pursue economic development and actively seek to change them, as was pointed out in Chapter 5. In particular, they believe that the development of world trade is unfavorable to their growth; that the markets in which they sell primary products are unstable, with adverse repercussions on sustained development efforts; that the terms of trade are evolving systematically against them; and they are discriminated against in trade in manufactures. For the most part they blame the fact that trade is not a positive factor in assisting growth on the world trade environment and the policies of the developed countries. The developed countries, on the other hand, while sympathetic with the ambitions of those that are less developed, assert that the difficulty lies in the inability or unwillingness of these countries to take advantage of the opportunities available to them. The crux, they believe, is not weakness of world demand but rigidity of supply in the less developed countries. The latter blame much of their trouble on the protectionist policies of the developed countries, which reserve their markets for domestic producers in competitive primary products as in simple manufactures. The developed countries retort that the developing countries have brought on their own troubles by pushing import substitution policies in manufacturing to the point where they lower agricultural product prices and raise the prices of agricultural inputs.

There is this much agreement: the less developed countries are caught in a dilemma. To achieve greater stability of primary product prices and an improving trend, they need economic development and the capacity to reallocate resources into other activities; to pursue programs of economic development, which cost foreign exchange, they need stability and a better trend of prices.

This chapter discusses first the commodity problems of developing countries and then their policies in manufactures, including import substitution (already touched upon in Chapter 5) and their demand for preferences for their manufactured exports in the developed countries. The potentialities of regional preferential arrangements among developing countries will be held until the next chapter, "Economic Integration."

Commodity Price Stabilization

The less developed country case about commodity prices, as just noted, has two main aspects. One concern is with short-run instability, the other with trend. The basic case about instability was made as long ago as 1952 in a United Nations study which pointed out that from 1900 to 1952 primary-product prices rose or fell on the average of 14 percent a year. Price changes do not necessarily imply changes in export proceeds, of course, since the volume of exports can change in the opposite direction, but the data showed that the volume of exports tended to move less than price, and often in the same direction, to compound the instability.

It has been widely agreed, without much evidence until the studies of Joseph D. Coppock and Alistair I. MacBean, that instability of export proceeds complicates the problem of economic development by interrupting the flow of imports, and hence of domestic investment. Case studies by MacBean, however, cast doubt on this conclusion. Investment in the less developed countries seems to have been well insulated from instability in export prices by a number of factors: offsetting volume changes, expenditure for imports out of foreign exchange reserves, and restrictions on imports of consumers' goods. But instability, or at least excessive instability, is clearly undesirable. Some movement of price around the long-run equilibrium trend is useful to pay speculators to hold the crop, in the case of agricultural commodities, which are harvested in a few months and consumed over the year. But there is generally more, and almost certainly too much.

The causes of instability in primary products can be summarized as changes in demand or supply reacting against inelastic supply or demand curves. In the case of agricultural crops, supply moves in response to weather. Moreover, planting can take place in response to one set of price signals, and the harvest can occur under different circumstances. With products of long gestation, such as tree crops, especially coffee, cocoa, and rubber, there are strong cobweb or lagged responses. When the price rises today, planting cannot affect supply for five years or more. This may mean five years of high prices and high planting before a large volume of supplies presses on the market and drives prices down. (This cobweb excessive response is found in manufactured lines with long periods of gestation, most notably perhaps in tanker shipbuilding.)

In minerals, the instability tends to arise from variation in demand which is subject to cyclical swings and from speculation, both of which run demand up and down against a relatively inelastic supply.

In some commodities, particularly sugar, much of world output is traded under preferential arrangements outside the world market, so that the spillover of changes in national demands and supplies impinges on a relatively small world market, which exaggerates price fluctuations.

A wide variety of remedies for price instability has been offered. There are schemes for fixing maximum and minimum prices, as in the International Wheat Agreement; buffer stock plans, as in tin; export quotas, as in coffee; and various financial measures, ranging from International Monetary Fund assistance to countries experiencing export price declines to varied export taxation.

The International Wheat Agreement fixes maximum prices at which the exporting countries guarantee to make stipulated amounts of wheat available to the importing countries, and minimum prices at which the importing countries agree to purchase fixed amounts of wheat from the exporters. The range between is left for the price system to operate in, to encourage output when crops are short, and to discourage them in periods of glut. The system can work only if governments intervene when a limit is reached, to make available exports at the maximum price or to purchase imports at the minimum. In fact, prices under the Wheat Agreement have been almost continuously at the maximum, so that the U.S. and Canadian governments have been obliged to make wheat available for export below domestic prices in the United States. The narrower the range between maximum and minimum prices, of course, the more nearly the system approaches a system of export and import quotas; on the other hand, the wider the range, the more nearly the scheme resembles the free market. The object of the exercise is to forecast and agree on a range within which price will fluctuate most of the time, with the limits coming into operation occasionally to moderate extreme swings. This objective, however, has not been achieved.

Buffer stock arrangements call for an international authority to set a range of prices and to buy the commodity at the minimum and sell at the maximum. If the authority's funds are too small, and the price rests long at the minimum, it will, of course, be unable to hold the price up. If its stocks of the commodity are limited, and the price stays long at the ceiling, it will be unable to hold the price down after it runs out of supplies. The larger its resources, the more effectively it can carry out its task. The tin scheme ceased to stabilize when it ran out of tin and was obliged to let the price go up.

Export quotas are perhaps more a device for holding up the trend of prices than for stabilizing variation around an equilibrium level. In coffee, agreement among major producers of Latin America and Africa limits the amount that can be exported, although if the price were to move up, the enlargement of quotas would be quickly accomplished in view of the heavy burden of accumulated stocks. The need for an international agreement arose because export restriction by the major supplier, Brazil, encouraged expansion of output and even new entry on the part of other Latin-American countries and, largely, East African producers. The central feature of the agreement is that quotas are policed by the importing countries, most significantly the United States, since the smaller exporting countries tended to exceed quotas and inch into the Brazilian export position. The West African Cocoa Marketing Board, which marketed the cocoa of Ghana and Nigeria when they were colonies of Britain, acted largely as an export quota scheme, feeding supplies to the market in an effort to stabilize the price. The attempt to replace the marketing board with a commodity agreement in cocoa proved very difficult, since the cocoa-growing countries were for many months unable to agree on relative quotas and the consumer countries, mainly the United States, objected to the minimum price as too high.

Inability to reach agreement easily—which has been a notable feature also of the International Coffee Agreement—is a widespread phenomenon in bargaining situations of all sorts, including the oligopoly markets discussed in the last chapter, alliances, trade-union negotiations, and generational clashes. The country (or element) that has the most to lose is likely to bear a disproportionate share of the burden. In bargaining situations of the sort known as non-zero-sum games, there is usually no scientific way of determining what is "fair." In consequence, commodity agreements like industrial cartels, as well as industrial and international peace, tend to break down.

Maximum-minimum price schemes and buffer stock and export quota agreements together pose the critical questions for a stabilizing commodity plan: How much room is left for the price mechanism to guide the market itself? How far should the scheme be automatic or discretionary? Should there be consumer representation? Who finances the holding of stocks? Is room left for new entry? Is there a mechanism for restricting output as well as exports in export quota plans, so as to prevent the buildup of unsold supplies? Should programs be permanent or designed only to overcome a particular imbalance? Should the plan deal with one commodity at a time or a wide range? The implications of many of these questions are obvious and need no gloss. But a few points may be less than self-evident.

Who holds or finances stocks has a substantial impact on balances of payments. If buffer stocks are held in the importing countries, for example, exports are stabilized during, say, a business cycle, whereas if the stocks are held by the exporting countries, price may be stablilized, but exports are not.

Export quotas are designed to hold up price. But does the benefit accrue to the grower or to the country? If the grower gets a high price, he has an incentive to go on producing at a high level. Production quotas may be introduced but are not always effective, as illustrated by U.S. acreage restrictions which led to closer planting and heavier applications of fertilizer. The ideal scheme economically is to have a high price for export but a low price to the grower to hold down production. This gives a substantial revenue to the government. If the scheme is one for stabilization rather than merely to raise prices, the funds should be kept intact for a period of low prices, when growers may be given a higher domestic price than the export price. But the economically desirable solution is not always politically or administratively feasible. Producers of export crops are often important politically and are unwilling to submit to what is in effect heavy export taxation; even if they do so, governments in prosperity seldom have the restraint to set aside foreign exchange reserves from large export taxes. The West African Cocoa Marketing Board piled up a large surplus in sterling but then yielded to pressures from the growers to raise prices and dissipate the reserve.

Automaticity, it was felt, would have helped with the last problem. Peter T. Bauer and Frank W. Paish recommended that the West African Cocoa Marketing Board pay the farmers in effect a moving average price, paying, for example, one half of the current price plus on third of the retained proceeds of the previous three years. Managers of a buffer stock scheme may be given set limits at which to buy and sell, or they may be allowed discretion to respond to market forces.

The question of whether commodity plans should be temporary or permanent cuts across whether they are wanted to change the long-run price or merely to stabilize around it. The U.S. government was initially entirely opposed to commodity agreements. In the 1948 Havana conference which produced the draft charter of the International Trade Organization, the position was loosened to provide for temporary agreements, limited to five years with a possible renewal for another five years, to meet a situation of particular imbalance such as a burdensome surplus in a commodity, after which it was expected to be left on its own. By the time of the so-called Haberler report of 1958 under the auspices of the General Agreement on Tariffs and Trade (GATT), permanent agreements were respectable. The difficulty was that they were still not workable.

Finally, the question continuously brought up by the less developed countries was: Why was it necessary to deal with commodity agreements one at a time, whereas there were apparently economies of scale, and room for bargaining, in dealing with more than one, and even with all major commodities in international trade? A number of experts, including staff members of the Food and Agriculture Organization (FAO), have talked of "planning" the flow of primary products in international trade. Most of this discussion is vague and amorphous, without specific plan. One concrete but unacceptable version is to establish commodity backing for international money, either for its own sake or as part of monetary reform.

It is difficult to the point of impossibility to make commodity agreements function effectively in a single commodity. As Harry G. Johnson says, the whole trick is to estimate the long-run equilibrium price. A United Nations group of commodity experts pronounced that the adequate, fair, and equitable price sought by the less developed countries was in fact the long-run equilibrium price (although the representatives of the less developed countries seemed uneasy about the admission). The theoretical conclusion is one thing; to estimate the equilibrium price and to plot its future course is something else again. But the difficulties extend beyond the technical. Producer pressures have been universally more effective in pushing for a high price than consumer or governmental representatives in holding price to the equilibrium level. Thus there are strong incentives to expand, to violate the restrictions, or to undertake new production in new areas outside the agreement. The result in the long run is overproduction and breakdown.

The rationale of dealing with many prices at once is that each country will be willing to agree to price supports for the other fellow if he is getting his share. Presumably it is easier to negotiate the whole network of primary-product prices than to take them on one at a time. This is a most dubious proposition.

In some formulations, the "planning" of commodity prices reduces itself to providing commodity markets, producers, and buyers with better information on the present and future state of production and consumption. This is always desirable. So-called study groups under the authority of the commodity wing of the United Nations, however, seem invariably to lead to attempts to raise prices, not merely to provide market information.

Financial Devices

Rather than operate directly on commodity prices, one line of attack is to work with the financial consequences of price instability. One of the successful fruits of the United Nations Conference on Trade and Development (UNCTAD) at Geneva in 1964 was the agreement of the International Monetary Fund (IMF) to make credits available more automatically to countries that suffer a fall in export proceeds because of the decline in export prices. One fifth of a country's IMF quota was the so-called commodity tranche (a French word for "slice" which has wide usage in international finance) to which different rules and more automatic access applied than to the so-called credit tranches.

If a country had tremendous discipline, it could stabilize its economy itself over cyclical rises and falls of prices. Start first with the rising portion of the cycle to get off on the right foot. Export taxes skim off rising prices from producers' incomes, and these permit the authorities to accumulate foreign exchange which they "sterilize," i.e., hold idle and prevent from enlarging the domestic money base. When prices turn, export taxes are removed, the foreign exchange is sold to permit imports to continue, and the local currency is used to pay exporters more than their prices at existing exchange rates in international markets.

The late Ragnar Nurkse thought it undesirable to use export taxation for this purpose, as it distorted relative prices among export, import-competing, and domestic lines of output. He wanted to use general taxation to run a domestic and foreign exchange surplus in the boom to be disbursed in balance-of-payments and budget deficits in depression. This would minimize the distortion of relative prices.

But this calls for a standard of fiscal management which is beyond the powers of the developed, much less the less developed countries. As the West African Cocoa Marketing Board's experience demonstrates, large sums of foreign exchange held for the uncertain future are scarcely proof against the political urge to spend. The advantages of the IMF commodity tranche are that one can start from a fall in prices, rather than have to wait for an initial rise, and the repayment is a requirement. Many of us force ourselves to save in contractual ways—through insurance, pension plans, and even Christmas clubs, because it is so hard to summon up the self-discipline to pay ourselves back when we borrow from our savings.

Another device which has not been accepted is to make financial assistance, or perhaps insurance based on premiums paid by all trading countries, available to countries that suffer adverse shifts of a certain magnitude in their terms of trade. Under one scheme, a country with a 10 percent gain in its terms of trade over the base year would have to pay part of its gains over to a pool which would be distributed to countries suffering losses of 10 percent or more. Under the insurance plan, all countries pay a small proportion of exports as a premium and countries that suffer poor price experience are accorded the proceeds. Since the developed countries are expected to have relatively stable prices, this amounts to more aid from them than insurance for them. But the technical details of these international schemes proved impossible to overcome: Are the net barter terms of trade really a valid measure of the gains from trade? (Chapter 5 argues that they are not.) How is it possible to match contributions into the pool with the demands on it, under various postulated conditions? It proved difficult if not impossible with pencil and paper to find past periods when these schemes would not break down, unless the initial period were chosen with great skill or luck.

"Commodity" dollar proposals, which go back to Benjamin Graham some years ago, have been supported by Frank D. Graham and by

J. Goudriaan of the United Nations commodity experts. A variant of the idea embodying international monetary reform was proposed to the Geneva 1964 conference of UNCTAD by three distinguished economists, Nicholas Kaldor, Albert Hart, and Jan Tinbergen. In essence the schemes provide that national or, in the latter instance, world, monetary authorities attempt to stabilize a (world) price index of primary commodities by buying a fixed bundle of commodities when the price index fell below the agreed range and selling it when the index rose above that range. There would be no attempt to fix the price of any single commodity. The whole bundle would be bought and sold whenever commodities were traded. Provision would have to be made, on infrequent occasions, to change the proportions of a bundle when some commodity or other became too scarce or too abundant. But the effort would be to stabilize the index, not particular commodities, by issuing new money when the index fell and redeeming it when prices rose substantially.

The monetary features of the plan take us a little ahead of our plotted course, though we shall have to deal with them briefly. But note some interesting features. First, many commodities which are not readily stored— petroleum products, meat, eggs, coal, many fats and oils, fruit, and fish— would have to be left out of the scheme altogether, and the cost of storing and turning over stocks of others would be a substantial expense. Second, the incidence of the system is highly arbitrary and, if it were extended to primary commodities generally, would benefit the developed more than the developing countries. Consider wheat, cotton, wool, corn, bacon, butter, and so on. It would perhaps be possible to order the list so as to eliminate the major commodities produced by the temperate zones. But commodities do not regulate themselves between the developed and the developing countries without overlapping, and it would be difficult to exclude the former while covering the main less developed countries. Third, the occasions for changing the commodity bundle to accommodate underlying changes in the demand and supply situation, which would go beyond the power of the price system to settle within the stable average, would pose tough bargaining sessions at best.

The main issue, however, is the monetary one, and the question is whether one stabilizes the terms of trade of primary products by fixing their average in money terms. The answer is almost certainly no. If the long-run position of primary commodities deteriorates as a result of adverse relative shifts in demand or supply, with demand growing more slowly and supply, or ease of entry, more rapidly, the terms of trade are going to turn against the less developed countries. This is a real phenomenon. If an index of money prices of these commodities is stabilized, this means inflation of the prices of manufactured goods. More and more primary products will be offered to the monetary authorities; increasing supplies of new money will be created, and they will be spent in greater relative amounts for manufactures, to drive their prices up. Like so many ideas in the monetary field, what appears to be an ingenious device to stabilize turns out on second thought to be an engine of inflation.

Developed-Country Protection in Primary Products

The developing countries could be aided to some degree—but hardly dramatically—if the developed countries were to reduce their import restrictions on primary products. Of exports of $16.2 billions of commodities from developing countries in 1963–65, excluding petroleum, only one third represented commodities subject to substantial barriers; notably sugar, vegetable oils and oil seeds, cereals including rice, and wood. Sugar is perhaps the most disgraceful commodity in the world, with virtually every country in the world, developed and developing, stimulating domestic production, and the world pattern of production and consumption a caricature of what it would be under free trade unaffected by political intervention. The crops of Cuba are bought up in the Soviet Union and Eastern Europe as foreign aid, where they produce a sort of "import diabetes." The United States awards limited quotas to special foreign countries—and takes them away—on the basis of foreign policy, not economics. In Europe, the price level is twice that of the tropical world, and through subsidies, there are even exports. Sugar beets, however, fit into the mixed-farming pattern of production favored by peasant farmers, since the pulp of the beets is utilized as cattle feed. In the same way, the soybeans produced by U.S. farmers are partly for vegetable oil and partly for high-protein cattle feed, which makes it difficult for developing countries producing, say, palm nuts solely for the oil.

The opportunities for expanding primary-product exports to the developed countries, with or without reduction of trade restrictions, are probably less bright than the dangers of loss of existing markets through competition from substitutes. Cotton, rubber, wool, hard fibers, hides and skins, and jute, which accounted for a fifth of the developing countries' exports of commodities in the mid-1960s, are threatened by synthetics. A chemical preparation which would taste like coffee is not outside the realm of possibilities.

There are some primary commodities, notably meat and dairy products, including eggs, which are produced mainly in the developed countries. Argentina and Uruguay used to have substantial exports of beef to Europe but allowed them to collapse through failure to maintain supply. On the other hand, Australia and New Zealand, which have expanded output, increasingly face trade barriers, especially in their attempts to sell to the United States. The opportunities for the developing countries in this field critically depend upon developed-country commercial policy. In 1972 President Nixon allowed import quotas to be raised in an attempt to hold down prices. This temporary action in the interest of price stability was very different, however, from the sort of action which would let the developing countries develop primary-product exports over the long run.

Import Substitution

Given the inelasticities and restrictions facing primary products, the developing countries have for some time been substituting domestic manufactures for imports, as mentioned in Chapter 5. The question is with what success; the answer is not much.

Import-competing industries are the place where capital and labor should be allocated when the return is higher, at the margin, than in exports. If there are externalities, they may even pay a little less than export or sheltered industries and be worthwhile for their growth potential: as a generator of capital, teacher of skills, signaler of investment opportunities, etc. But import substitution that transfers resources out of efficient export primary-product lines into inefficient industries which permanently require effective rates of protection of 100 percent and higher is a simple waste of resources. It is not development but consumption when Argentina builds an automobile industry which produces cars at a cost of $5,000 when they can be imported for $2,000. The critical questions are how much protection will the industry need and for how long.

How much protection must of course be addressed in terms of effective rates, since nominal rates may seriously understate the extent of restriction. In research in a few countries for *The Structure of Protection in Developing Countries,* Professor Balassa and his associates found that the "cost" of protection went as high as 6.2 percent of gross national product (in Pakistan and Chile) and 9.5 percent (in Brazil), largely through raising the costs of industries that would have become competitive under free trade. (The study did not cover Argentina, which is generally regarded as the country which has carried import substitution to the extreme.) In other countries studied—Malaya, Norway, Mexico, and the Philippines—the cost of protection ranged from −0.4 percent to 3.7 percent. In Mexico, for example, a country which has been highly successful in industrializing both along the border of the United States and in the interior, it was 2.5 percent.

The countries with the least cost had the lowest levels of effective tariff. Balassa's group concluded that it is better to impose flat-rate tariffs on finished goods averaging about 10 percent effective, than to try to pick and choose. Even in infant-industry cases, effective rates of 20 percent can hardly be justified. Unless great restraint is applied, import substitution leads to great waste by fostering inefficient investments and may even waste foreign exchange by stimulating imports of components and drawing resources away from export industries.

How long protection should be provided is a question less frequently asked. The difficulty is that once investment in inefficient industry is undertaken there is a vested interest in keeping it going. Few experiments have been conducted in which protection is afforded for a fixed period of time in the future, after which the level of protection declines on schedule. If exports result in the industry which was initially import competing without subsidy, it is clear in the usual case that protection can be dropped. It may be that economic calculation can never be sufficiently precise to enable a manufacturer to decide whether he would be able to invest profitably in an import-competing activity if the tariff ultimately disappeared. Yet some means is needed to ensure that the patient does not become addicted to the stimulant and survive only so long as it is applied.

Preferences for Manufactures from Developing Countries

One of the demands of the less developed countries at UNCTAD in Geneva in 1964 was for preferences in the developed countries in manufactured goods. It was thought too much to ask for free trade in such products; the developed countries were presumably entitled to discriminate in favor of domestic producers against foreigners. But within the totality of foreigners, the less developed countries wanted to be given a preference over other developed countries.

The United States rejected this demand at Geneva. It was strongly opposed to discrimination and preferences of all sorts. The arguments against preferences have been given by H. G. Johnson—they would generate friction, involve government surveillance and control, build new vested interests, open Pandora's box for other discrimination by countries, and lead to wrangles as the countries of the world sought to discriminate in a "fair" way. Nonetheless he urged that the idea be given serious consideration on political grounds. The developing countries believed that they had a grievance: they were discriminated against in the tariff reductions in manufactures in GATT, which were concentrated in highly developed manufactures, and in textiles, where they had reason to hope for manufactured exports, they were restricted by being forced to impose export quotas. The claim that tariffs on manufactures were low is false: in textiles for example nominal rates of 24 and 21 percent in the United States and the Common Market are really effective rates of protection of 51 and 52 percent. The low-wage manufactures that the less developed countries are able to produce impinge on the sensitive, vote-conscious, labor-intensive, import-competing sectors of the developed countries, where it is politically very difficult to welcome the competition of imports. Reduced barriers and free trade are achieved in commodities produced by other developed countries—products made by the rich for the rich, the less developed countries would say—but a poor man who wants to break into the game is fenced off with quotas or even made to impose them himself.

The developed countries maintain that things are not as bad as the less developed countries paint them. Tariffs in the developed countries are low. The Textile Agreement provides for a 5 percent expansion in quotas each year, which over time will permit a very considerable expansion of imports from the less developed countries. And the less developed countries were given a handsome present at the Kennedy Round of GATT in having the mutual concessions of the developed countries extended to them under the most-favored-nation clause, without being asked for reciprocal concessions. But these professions of goodwill can be refuted. If one moves from nominal to effective rates of tariff, the duties of the developed countries do not seem low. The 5 percent expansion in the Textile Agreement is more than used up by new quotas which are imposed as soon as new supplies come to the United States from countries previously uncovered. The benefit of uncompensated reductions in tariffs under the Kennedy Round is of scant value to the less developed countries, since the bulk of the manufactured products which concern them are covered by quotas or were held out of the developed-country bargaining by the exceptions procedure.

All this, it should be recalled, is on top of the accusation by the developing countries that the developed countries use restrictive business practices to limit their manufactured exports, protecting their own markets by copyrights and patents and making technology available to the developing countries only with prohibitions against export to third markets.

There can be no doubt but that the developing countries have a case of discrimination against them. And the answer has been to attempt to remove the discrimination, not to swing to positive discrimination in their favor. But the United States and the developed countries could not stand the political heat. Shortly after the New Delhi meeting of UNCTAD, led by Australia, they caved in and agreed to preferences for developing-country manufactures. The United States insisted that this should be accompanied by abandonment of "**reverse preferences**," i.e., preferences for French manufactures in the *Communauté* in Africa, for Britain in its former colonies, and even for the United States (until 1974) in the Philippines. It further insisted that the preferences should not be limited to specific countries, i.e., in France to the *Communauté*, etc., but should be "**generalized**." And so it went. But not far. Generalized preferences were granted with quota limits beyond which the general tariff applied. These quotas were on the whole so limited that most students of the subject regard them as shadow but not substance.

Where the preferences are not narrowly circumscribed, they may well benefit the countries that are already well along the road to industrialization: Taiwan, Hong Kong, Singapore, Korea, Israel, Mexico, and the like. Or at some stage these countries should be dropped from the preference list, as has Japan—the once-undeveloped country with the greatest success in growing through exports of manufactures. This creates the same sort of incentive problems found in relief: at some level the marginal return to growth is sharply negative as the welfare recipient or country passes a milestone at which its former assistance or preference is removed.

Export Incentives and Subsidies

Countries like Taiwan and Korea have been aided in expanding manufacturing exports by such devices as refunding customs duties on the import content of exports (a familiar process known as **"drawback"**) and remitting commodity taxes on exports (**border tax adjustment**). Beyond these devices, their firms have been exempted from income and business taxes on export proceeds, foreign exchange has been advanced for imported materials, and preferences have been given for licensing under foreign exchange control. None of these last-named devices is permitted under GATT. The United States, however, is exploring various devices for itself, such as special corporations called "Disc" (Domestic International Sales Corporation) which are permitted to defer income tax on export sales, in the same way that a foreign subsidiary might be able to do so. The arguments pro and con on this sort of device are complex. GATT is opposed to export subsidies. Two points can be made: (1) it is inequitable for poor countries to subsidize the imports of the rich unless in the long run it pays them via the infant-industry argument, and even then it would be more equitable for the subsidy to come from the importing country; and (2) if developed and developing countries both subsidize exports, the latter have a better chance of getting away with it, given the asymmetrical application of the rules of international trade.

Asymmetric Rules

The division of the countries of the world between GATT and UNCTAD, with many countries represented in both but having a decisive role only in one, suggests the difficulty of concocting a series of rules for world trade which all will adhere to. Nondiscrimination is a key provision of GATT. Generalized preferences are an exception of barn-door width. Even where the same rules apply, as in export subsidies, enforcement is likely to be different in the two cases. The rich countries have little objection to enforcing the rules on each other; they are less willing to protect the principle, and even to defend their interest, against the poor.

This, of course, is not the way the poorer countries see it. In their view, past exploitation has meant that the gains from trade have been skewed against them. If the pendulum swings the other way (as most would deny), the reaction is overdue. Optimum tariffs among developed countries are not likely to succeed because of retaliation. If the countries of the Middle East succeed in raising the price of oil, as they have, or Brazil and East Africa raise the price of coffee, as they have done, not very effectively, retaliation will not be forthcoming even if it would be effective. While all nations claim to be equal in sovereignty, they do not act identically with one another.

When do the countries which emerge from the "developing" class take their place with full application of the rules of trading among the developed? First the Dominions and then Japan have made the transition. It had been expected 30 years ago that Argentina, Brazil, and Chile would be next, but too much import substitution has slowed them down. Mexico is perhaps almost ready. Meanwhile, separate chapters for the commercial policy problems of developed and developing countries are in order.

Summary

The trade problems of developing countries are considered (at least by them) to be sufficiently different in degree and kind to require special treatment. For primary commodities they want stabilization policies, or, as a substitute, financial transfers to compensate them for declines in prices. They rightfully resent the developed-country protection in a limited number of primary products—notably sugar, which is worth study as an example of pathological tissue in the corpus of international trade, vegetable oils and seeds, meat and the like. Most of their primary production is not protected, however. A greater danger may be synthetic substitutes.

Import substitution policies in the developing countries have been pursued in many instances well beyond the point of positive returns.

The demand of developing countries for preferences in manufactures has been met after a wrangle, but circumscribed by tariff quotas to the point where they are not worth much. The developing countries have a persuasive case that they are discriminated against, rather than for, insofar as tariff reductions among developed countries have avoided the labor-intensive goods which interest them.

Some use may be made of export incentives. On the whole they are disapproved of by GATT. They are being explored by the United States.

The fundamental problem lies in the belief among developing countries that they have always been exploited by the developed world, in a neoimperialistic or neocolonial way, and the belief on the side of the developed countries that much of their problem is of their own making. Whatever the historic truth of these allegations, it seems likely that the two groups of countries cannot function under the same set of nondiscriminatory rules.

SUGGESTED READING

Texts

As a substitute for a textbook, see H. B. Malmgren, "Trade for Development," *Overseas Development Council Monograph No. 4* (Washington, D.C., 1971) (paperback) which furnishes a neat statement of the issues in 75 pages.

Treatises, Etc.

For a thorough treatment, see H. G. Johnson, *Economic Policies toward Less Developed Countries* (Washington, D.C.: The Brookings Institution, 1967) (paperback, Frederick A. Praeger, Inc.). On commodity agreements, see J. W. F. Rowe, *Primary Commodities in International Trade* (Cambridge, England: Cambridge University Press, 1965) (paperback). See also A. I. MacBean, *Export Instability and Economic Development* (London: George Allen & Unwin, Ltd., 1966) and J. D. Coppock, *International Economic Instability* (New York: McGraw-Hill Book Co., Inc., 1962). On trade preferences see S. Weintraub, *Trade Preferences for Less-Developed Countries* (New York: Frederick A. Praeger, Inc., 1967). A thorough factual exploration of the position of seven countries and of desirable industrial protection policy is furnished in B. Balassa and Associates, *The Structure of Protection in Developing Countries* (Baltimore, Md.: Johns Hopkins Press, 1971).

Foreign-trade policies of particular developing countries are worth study. See, for example, T. King, Mexico: *Industrialization and Trade Policies since 1940* (London: Oxford University Press, 1970); J. Bergsman, *Brazil—Industrialization and Trade Policies* (London: Oxford University Press, 1970); and J. N. Bhagwati and P. Desai, *India: Planning for Industrialization* (London: Oxford University Press, 1970). The general themes of these volumes written for the Development Center of the OECD are treated by I. Little, T. Scitovsky, and M. FG. Scott in *Industry and Trade in Some Developing Countries* (London: Oxford University Press, 1970).

The International Coffee Agreement is discussed from different points of view in T. Geer, *An Oligopoly: The World Coffee Economy and Stabilization Schemes* (New York: The Dunellen Co., 1971), and P. Streeten and D. Elson, *Diversification and Development: The Case of Coffee* (New York: Praeger Special Studies, 1971).

Points

The estimate of the average nominal and effective rates on textile fabrics in the United States is from B. Balassa, *Trade Liberalization among Industrial Countries* (New York: McGraw-Hill Book Co., Inc., 1967), Appendix, Table 3.1, p. 180.

The experience of the West African Cocoa Marketing Board is discussed in P. T. Bauer and F. W. Paish, "The Reduction of Fluctuations in the Incomes of Primary Producers," *EJ*, December 1952.

Chapter 11
ECONOMIC INTEGRATION

Customs Unions and Free-Trade Areas

We will start our analysis of economic integration (which will not be completed until we consider monetary unification in Part V) with a discussion of customs unions and free-trade areas—the elimination of trade barriers between two or more countries while maintaining them against the rest of the world. The difference between a customs union and a free-trade area is that in a customs union it is necessary to agree on a common tariff nomenclature or schedule and identical tariff rates, whereas the countries in a free-trade area maintain their own tariffs against outsiders while scrapping duties among themselves.

The Theory of Customs Unions

Our interest is in the theory of customs unions and in the paradox that not every step toward freer trade is desirable in welfare terms even when free trade is a welfare optimum. This is an example of the **theory of the second best,** which we discuss in greater generality in the next chapter. One example has been suggested in connection with the effective rate of the tariff: a tariff increase on the raw material may reduce the effective rate of the tariff on the finished good and add to welfare rather than reduce it. In the same way, as we shall see, reducing trade barriers between two partners may worsen rather than improve welfare.

The welfare effects of eliminating trade barriers between partners can be illustrated both in partial and general equilibrium. The position in partial equilibrium is shown for a single commodity in Figure 11.1. Assume that $D-D$ and $S-S$ are the demand and supply curves of a "home" country which imports $M-M$ of a product with a tariff WH. The world price OW is assumed to represent an infinitely elastic supply schedule, which eliminates adverse terms of trade effects on the rest of the world after the formation of the customs union. In short, the world price is fixed no matter

174

FIGURE 11.1. Trade Creation and Trade Diversion in Partial Equilibrium

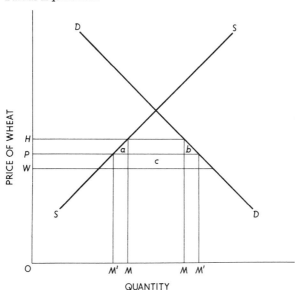

what happens. The partner's supply is also assumed to be infinitely elastic at the price OP. Before customs union the prospective "partner," facing the same tariff as the rest of the "world," is out of the market, since its pretariff price is higher than that in the outside world. After the union, with no tariffs against partner and the tariff WH still applying to imports from the rest of the world, all imports come from partner and none from the rest of the world.

Forming the customs union affects trade and welfare in two opposing ways. First, it brings **trade creation** by raising total imports from MM to $M'M'$. The world welfare gain associated with this trade creation equals the triangle a and b, which correspond to the net production and consumption effects discussed in Chapter 7. Second, it diverts MM of imports from the low-cost foreign supplier to the high-cost partner. This **trade diversion** brings a deadweight loss of c, measured by the increased cost of getting MM produced. In addition to these net deadweight gains and losses, there is a variety of gross shifts which the student may profitably consider. For example, what happens to the tariff revenue that the home country used to receive? Part of it goes to reduce prices to domestic consumers and is therefore not an element of national or world loss; the rest is paid to producers in the partner country.

In this one-commodity case, trade creation and the gains from the customs union are evidently greater, the greater the elasticities of demand and supply in the home country (or the flatter the demand and supply curves in the figure), the wider the cost differences between home country and partner, and the smaller these differences between partner and the world. On the other hand, the trade diversion loss is greater, the less elastic the demand and supply curves in the home country, and the smaller the cost differences between home and partner, and the wider they are between partner and the world.

In this simple case of fixed world and partner prices, it happens that the net welfare effect for the home country—area *a* plus *b* minus *c*—is also the net static welfare effect for the world. The welfare results are more complicated when the present simplifying assumptions are relaxed, but the rule remains that the world's gains are tied to trade creation and its losses to trade diversion.

In general equilibrium it is not so easy to portray customs unions, and the geometric results with three countries and two commodities are unsatisfactory. Assume that countries A, B, and C used to trade multilaterally in two commodities, X and Y, each country exporting one commodity and importing the other, subject to a tariff. If A and B form a customs union, removing the tariffs between them but maintaining tariffs against C, and if A and B were both exporting, say, X to C and importing Y and continue to trade in the same direction, the customs union will make no difference. A and B will not trade with each other before or after the customs union. If A had been selling X to B and C, and B and C selling Y to A, the customs union has elements of trade creation and trade diversion. The increased trade between A and B is trade creation, the reduced trade between A and C is trade diversion. Note that in this case there was no trade between B and C, since both were exporting and importing the same goods. Whether the trade diversion is greater than the trade creation is impossible to say a priori and without a great deal of information on elasticities of demand and supply.

The most important case of trade diversion, however, comes when one country shifts its commodity composition of trade. Suppose both A and B had been trading X to C for Y, with tariffs all around. Enter customs union between A and B. Now B switches from importing Y and produces it for itself and for sale to A. A diverts some or all of its purchases of Y from C to B. B also stops exporting X and imports it from A.

All this can be shown with tariff-distorted offer curves, netted and summed, but all but the most intrepid student is advised not to consider doing so. For the excepted *rara avis*, an attempt at geometric exposition was attempted in the fourth edition of this book. It is best ignored. Three countries and two commodities make for expositional difficulties.

Jacob Viner, whose *Customs Union Issue* focused attention on the paradox that steps in the direction of freer trade may reduce rather than increase welfare, stated that trade creation was more likely to result when the countries forming the customs union were competitive, and trade diversion was likely if they were complementary. This is somewhat ambiguous (until one defines terms) and fails to put the matter in its full complexity. Customs union between industrial countries can be trade diverting, if one country subsequently buys its food from the other instead of from low-cost producers abroad; and union between countries that are competitive in the sense that they buy and sell the same sorts of commodities from the rest of the world can be trivial if they have little trade with each other. The issue is whether customs union stimulates or discourages tariff-protected activities. To the extent that tariff-protected industries in the union are encouraged, there is trade diversion; to the extent that they face the competition of imports, trade creation results.

The Real World

Trade creation and trade diversion are not purely hypothetical concepts. In U.S. history the foremost example is the customs union between the plantation agriculture of the South and the nascent manufacturing of the North. These were not separate countries, but they were different regions in terms of factor proportions, factor prices, and comparative advantage. Before World War I, in fact, trade between the North and the South was conducted much like international trade and unlike internal trade. Little capital moved south or labor, north. With factor immobility, factor prices failed to equalize, and it paid to employ different factor proportions. The South had a labor- and land-intensive agriculture; the North a capital-intensive manufacturing industry.

The inclusion of the agricultural South in the customs area of the North, which is what a common customs meant, required the South to buy in a protected market while it was selling in a free market. Like country A in the general-equilibrium discussion, it was required to buy its Y from the high-cost producer B, instead of on the cheaper world market represented by C. The price of its imports increased, and its terms of trade were reduced. This economic exploitation of the South by the North is generally regarded as a factor contributing to the War between the States.

A further example can be given from the history of Germany, in which the Zollverein, or customs union, actually preceded political union by many years. The Zollverein was formed in 1834; Bismarck united Germany under the leadership of Prussia in 1870. In 1879 the first of the increases took place in the tariff on grain. This was combined with a tariff on steel; but Germany was in the business of exporting steel, so that the tariff was useful only in widening its scope for dumping. The tariff on rye, on the other hand, raised the cost of living of the worker in western Germany well above what it would have been had Germany bought its grain on the world market. Customs union thus involved the exploitation of the working classes by the Prussian Junkers, who were both soldiers and managers of estates which grew rye. After World War II unsophisticated observers thought that West Germany would be harmed by being cut off from its traditional source of food in the east. As it turned out, however, West Germany gained by being able to obtain its food abroad at low world prices, rather than from protected high-cost farms in the east.

The net welfare impact of trade creation and trade diversion effects of the European Economic Community (EEC, or Common Market) is difficult to weigh. The gains in trade in manufactures within the union have been substantial, and there has been some relative loss in the trade of the United States. In 1958 50 percent of manufactured products of the EEC countries were bought from other members, whereas in 1968, 10 years later, the percentage was 60. Most of the diversion was from the other countries of Europe that had originally declined to join. Lawrence Krause estimates that U.S. manufactures exported to the Community fell $275 millions as a result of the customs union, but that 40 percent of this was made up as a result of faster growth in the Community resulting from the union. Such gains and losses in trade must be distinguished from welfare gains and losses, however, because they do not take into account the alternative uses of the resources absorbed in the one case or released in the other.

Trade diversion is much more substantial in agriculture and is being substantially increased as Britain becomes a full member of the EEC. France has long been protectionist in farming and continues so. Germany and Britain, which used to protect and subsidize agriculture but import what they needed additionally from the cheapest sources overseas, now import from high-cost France and divert some purchases of tropical products from Latin America and the independent African states, generally to former French colonies in Africa.

The trade diversion effect may not be serious for the world because of the narrowness of the difference in cost between the excluded outside seller and the favored inside one. It is still painful to the outside seller. This is why the Norwegians (until they decided against it), British, and Danes were so anxious to join, and the neutrals (Austria, Sweden, and Switzerland) and the underdeveloped countries (Greece and Turkey) were so concerned to find a basis of association. Trade diversion also adversely affected the United States, which, however, was able to mitigate the economic hurt of discrimination in industrial products by establishing facilities to manufacture inside the Common Market boundaries. The United States was in any event prepared to pay the economic price of European integration to obtain the political benefits in the form of strengthening the Free World. But the other outsiders—Japan (where cost differences in manufactures were substantial), the Commonwealth, and the producers of tropical products which were discriminated against by the preferential position in the Common Market given to former colonies—were adversely affected. The U.S. Trade Expansion Act of 1962 attempted to reduce the damage by providing for mutual lowering of tariffs. If the tariff, WH in Figure 11.1, is reduced below WP, the home country will buy nothing in the partner which, in its turn, will buy for the first time in the world market. The more countries join the customs union, and the lower the common external tariff, the less will be the extent of trade diversion and the more nearly will the customs union approach the free-trade ideal.

The Dynamic Effects of Customs Union

Trade creation and trade diversion are static effects of customs union or trade integration. There is some doubt as to their importance. A number of scholars have sought to measure the effects of tariff reductions, both total and partial, and the impact on national income usually turns out to be exiguous, to use a fancy word, or very small. Imports, say, are 20 percent of national income. Elimination of a 10 percent tariff may expand trade to 22 or 24 percent of income. But the change is not a clear gain for national income, as partial-equilibrium diagrams such as Figure 11.1 remind us. The protective effect and the consumption effect are represented, not by the total change in trade, which includes resources, but by the increment in trade times the change in price made possible by the new arrangements—in the case of trade creation, the higher price for exports and the lower price for imports. Even if this is substantial, we end up with a small measure of the static gain.

Not all the gains are static, however. Dynamic gains include economics of scale, the stimulus of competition, and the stimulus to investment. Economies of scale were touched upon in Chapter 2. As specialization takes place, costs may fall for a number of reasons: through learning to make the product more effectively through repetition, developing a higher skilled pool of available labor, spreading a number of capital items of a lumpy character more thinly per unit of output, and so on. These matters are discussed more thoroughly in courses in intermediate theory. Economies of scale are the great hope of customs unions among less developed countries, and they are much debated. They may occur in customs union among manufacturing countries through product specialization which enables manufacturers in two countries to concentrate on particular sizes or models of a product, rather than to make a full line (this is even sometimes the result of a business agreement). Many Europeans assert that the advantage of the United States is that it has a large internal market which enables its manufacturers to achieve economies of scale. The opponents point to the efficiency of many small companies and the sluggishness of some large ones and note that countries like Sweden and Switzerland have efficient manufacturing where the market extends beyond the national boundaries.

The importance of economies of scale cannot be demonstrated. This gives us students of international economics much to argue about.

The competitive effect has been touched on in Chapter 7. Tibor Scitovsky believes that this was the most important impact of the EEC. As suggested in the earlier discussion, high tariffs foster monopoly in which one or two large companies preside over a larger aggregation of small, inefficient producers. The big companies like the quiet life and prefer high prices to substantial volume, which they could achieve to drive out the little firms if they chose. With lower tariffs, the big companies are forced to compete and the little ones to merge, combine, become efficient, or go under. This effect has been particularly observed in France. It may be a function of lower tariffs within the EEC, or their anticipation.

Finally among the dynamic effects, the change in relative prices and the prod to competition stimulate investment. This may be domestic investment, to take advantage of new trading opportunities or under the spur of competition attacking from abroad. One important aspect of the change in domestic investment is the pull of market-oriented industry to the frontier nearer markets in the trading partner. This is hard on such regions as southern Italy, southwest France or southeast Germany, which lie far from the markets in the union partners. New investment to take advantage of opportunities is accompanied by disinvestment in industries adversely affected by trade creation, i.e., the import-competing industries which are no longer able to make a go of it. The investment stimulus of new industries is likely to be greater than the disinvestment discouragement in old industries, unless substantial excess capacity is available. On this score, customs union may be said to be inflationary.

The possibility that investment will decline in the remote and backward portions of a newly integrated area has led to special measures to assist them. Thus the EEC established a European Investment Bank to undertake new ventures in the adversely affected portions of the Six (the original members of the EEC). This constitutes explicit acknowledgment that in the absence of policy certain parts of the integrated area will suffer.

In addition to the dynamic stimulus to domestic investment, however, there is the possibility of inducing investment from abroad. This is of two kinds. There may be rearrangement of existing foreign capacity in the community to take advantage of the new conditions. This effect is identical to the pull to the border in the market-oriented industries, with this difference, that domestic firms are not likely to cross the border and foreign firms, without roots in the particular country, may be drawn across. Or the trade-diverting effect of the customs union may induce foreigners who have served the various national markets by exports and now are discriminated against to substitute tariff factories for trade. American firms undertook massive investment in Europe after about 1955 for a variety of reasons (or excuses), and the EEC may have been one or the other. To a considerable extent, in the judgment of more than one writer, the effect of the EEC was not so much that it provided the marginal conditions under which a close calculation revealed that it was better now to invest in Europe than to provide that market from the United States. Rather it called the attention of manufacturers who had neglected to notice investment opportunities in Europe to the fact that here was a growing, vigorous market from which outsiders might be expelled and which it was useful to join.

Beyond Customs Union

Ascending (so to speak) from a free-trade area and customs union are common market, economic union, and complete economic integration. In the usual definitions, a **common market** goes beyond the customs union for goods by removing all restrictions on the movement of factors of production, labor, and capital. **Economic union** goes further and provides for harmonization of national economic policies. **Economic integration** is still more intimate and requires some common policies in the macroeconomic field, especially monetary and fiscal.

We cannot explore this institutional framework fully until we get to Parts IV and V, but there is merit in analyzing a number of definitions of economic integration which have been put forth by economists.

In his *International Economic Integration,* Jan Tinbergen suggests that economic integration is free trade. Removal of tariffs, however, is insufficient to provide for free movement of all goods. It is necessary first to get rid of the border guards, who are still required so long as excise taxes are not harmonized in the trading countries.

Bela Balassa's definition of integration goes beyond Tinbergen's to encompass the absence of all government discrimination against movements of goods or factors. This evidently includes harmonization of excise taxes and freedom for migration and may involve, for the movement of capital, parallel or identical policies in the regulation of capital markets, interest rates, foreign exchange, and the like. It may require comparable programs in such things as agriculture and wages. Is this still enough?

The absence of government discrimination is perhaps not the ultimate definition of economic integration. Suppose Iceland and New Zealand were to adopt regulations granting each other's nationals not most-favored-nation treatment, but **national treatment**, i.e., treatment identical with each country's own nationals over a wide area. There might be customs union, harmonization of tax policy, and even parallel policies in other fields. Would this result in economic integration? Evidently not.

The reason an Iceland–New Zealand customs union of this sort would not result in economic integration is that whether or not governments discriminate between the two countries, Nature does. By putting them in separate hemispheres, both East-West and North-South, Nature has reduced the economic contacts between Iceland and New Zealand to what one may presume, without being burdened by the facts, is virtually zero. So it is not government discrimination alone that counts.

This brings us to a definition of economic integration which makes it a standard of measurement, but one which, like absolute zero in low-temperature physics, is never reached. Economic integration is factor-price equalization. This can be produced by trade, without factor movements, by factor movement without trade, or by some combination of the two. But any interference with trade, whether by tariffs or transport costs, prevents goods prices, and therefore factor prices, from being equalized. And discrimination can be carried on by governments or by the public.

Take first transport costs. The reason that an Iceland–New Zealand customs union would fail to produce economic integration is that distance would prevent an equalization of goods prices. In addition to distance, moreover, two such widely different countries are almost certain to be completely specialized, thus eliminating another of the significant assumptions of the factor-price equalization theorem. Both points make clear why the EEC was a much more serious step in the direction of integration than was the European Free Trade Association (EFTA) among Britain, the three Scandinavian countries, Austria, Switzerland, and Portugal. The Six— France, Belgium, the Netherlands, Germany, and Italy—share common frontiers, across which transfer costs, after the removal of tariffs, are zero. The countries of the EFTA are spread out in an enormous circle around the EEC, with long distances between many of them, whether physical, as between Portugal and Sweden, or economic, as between Austria and Switzerland, where the economically important areas are divided by mile after mile of Alps. The issue is of prime importance also in the Latin-American Free Trade Area (LAFTA), where countries which are contiguous are not necessarily close economically. Argentina and Chile, with a long common border, find it cheaper to ship steel around by sea than to lug it up over the passes of the Andes. In economic terms, therefore, Buenos Aires is not much nearer Valparaiso than the Sparrows Point plant of the Bethlehem Steel Company in Baltimore.

Next is the possibility of private discrimination, even when governmental discrimination has been eliminated. When Benelux (the economic union among Belgium, the Netherlands, and Luxembourg which preceded the EEC and was absorbed into it) finally lifted the barriers to the movement of capital and labor between the countries, nothing happened. The Dutch preferred to keep their capital in Holland, and the Belgian workers preferred to live and work in Belgium, both despite the possibility of higher monetary rewards from the newly permitted migration. Thus private discrimination prevents economic integration.

Under the factor-price equalization definition, economic integration is likely never to be fully achieved. The definition is useful, however, as a standard. The content of integration then becomes one price, as in the law of one price. In one market there is one price, and if there are transactions and one price, there is, in effect, one market. By this definition the labor market in the United States is not integrated, since wages are not the same everywhere, and the market for blacks and whites is still not integrated, despite governmental prohibition of discrimination, because blacks earn less than whites even when they have entry to the same jobs. The test of whether customs union works toward integration is whether it narrows factor-price differences.

One quibble with this definition of economic integration may be worth raising: Suppose factor-price equalization is achieved not through direct dealings in goods, factors, and policies between the two countries, but through third markets and factors in third countries. If these third-party dealings produce factor-price equalization, have they produced integration? Goods prices in countries A and B can be equalized through their separate trade with C, without any trade between A and B. This is hardly integration in the ordinary sense of the word. It happens that wages within the Common Market have been narrowed by the readiness of outside labor—from Portugal, Spain, southern Italy (inside the market to be sure), Greece, and Turkey—to move from one country to another among the Six in search of higher pay. Interest rates can be brought into line by lending to and borrowing from the external Euro-currency market (about which more below) without direct capital movements among the participating countries. American international corporations (again, more later) act to foster factor-price equalization by moving from high- to low-cost locations, or contracting in the one and expanding in the latter. The outside factors may be less rooted in any one country of the Six and hence more ready to move. Local forces do nothing, outside forces do it all: is this economic integration?

This is of course pretty much a pure quibble. In the European Common Market the internal forces of trade, factor movement, and harmonization are at work, assisted by the external connections of the separate European markets with southern labor, Euro-currency markets, and American multinational corporations. All push in the same direction, working toward integration. So long as this happens, the question posed does not arise. But the reliance to a degree on outside factors suggests how strongly national factors of production tend to discriminate, whatever the attitude of government: the foreign laborer, dollar, or corporation, belonging to no member country, can feel as much at home in one as another. This increases elasticity of supply, competitiveness, and economic integration.

Some Lesser Problems of Customs Unions and Free-Trade Areas

The development of a single tariff schedule in a customs union is a difficult task. First, there is the problem of arriving at a common tariff nomenclature. There is no unique way to classify goods. Most countries have their own systems, and when two or more systems are joined, the task is to develop a new one which is agreeable to all. Like all classification systems in a world of change, moreover, there are different rewards and penalties for retaining an old system and for altering it frequently in the light of new conditions. The one gives comparability in time; the other best suits current problems. The experts of the EEC spent several years working out a common tariff nomenclature, even before it was time to set the rates.

Rates come next. GATT rules, which authorize customs unions, state that the common tariff must be no higher than the average tariffs of the countries which go to make it up. There are problems both in measuring the height of a tariff and in choosing a suitable average of more than one. The simplest system of measuring the height of a tariff is to average separate ad valorem tariff rates. This is misleading, as there should be a weighted average. What weights? To weigh by actual trade is likely to give a biased result, since the higher the tariff, the more it keeps out trade and the lower its impact. A prohibitive tariff would get no weight, which is absurd. The correct system of weighting is the values which would be achieved under free trade. There is no way of knowing these without an enormous amount of information on elasticities. A proxy for free-trade weights is domestic consumption; here goods which enjoy a prohibitive tariff (a strong protective effect) enter the index.

Belgian, French, and Italian tariffs were reduced in the EEC averaging, and the Dutch and German tariffs were raised. Observe that this means more trade creation for the first group and more trade diversion for the second. The discussion of trade creation and trade diversion earlier in this chapter assumed a constant and uniform rate of tariff. But if any country raises its tariff, trade diversion is evidently accentuated, and for those that lower theirs, the reverse occurs.

Once given the common tariff, what happens to the financial proceeds? They evidently must be divided among the members. How? A simple system is to have each country keep the proceeds it collects, but this is more practical than equitable. Should the Netherlands keep the duties on goods for Germany which enter at Rotterdam on their way up the Rhine, or Italy keep those for goods transshipped across the Alps from the Mediterranean? But to trace goods to the country of consumption and assign it the duties requires more organization than is desirable. In the Zollverein, Prussia bought the adherence of a large number of the smaller, poorer states by offering to share customs proceeds on a per capita basis. This was expensive for Prussia, with more trade per capita, but it accomplished the political objective of winning adherence. The Rome Treaty of 1957 turned the question over to be resolved by the commission.

In a free-trade area, there is no problem about dividing customs receipts: to each his own. But differences among tariff schedules give rise to a problem because of the possibility of arbitrage, that is, entering the goods into the free-trade area in the country with the lowest duty and then reshipping them to another country with a higher duty. This problem may not be serious when the countries are far apart, as in Portugal and Norway, or Switzerland and the United Kingdom in EFTA: the saving in tariffs is likely to be less than the added transport costs. But the problem is sufficiently significant to require control. This is provided by certificates of origin. Goods going from one member of a free-trade area to another are accompanied by a certificate of origin, issued to attest that the goods originated in the member country and not in a third country. The process of issuing such certificates and verifying the facts is tiresome, but inescapable.

EEC's Special Regime for Agriculture

The Rome Treaty of 1957, which created the EEC after the partial "functional integration" in iron and steel and coal of the European Coal and Steel Community, proposed a special regime for agriculture. This sector is a problem in virtually every country and was supported by subsidies and restrictions on trade in particular ways in each member country. No country except the Netherlands was willing to let its farmers compete in world markets. But most countries were unwilling to apply simple tariffs because of uncertainty as to the shape of the foreign excess supply curves and, therefore, as to what the protective and redistribution effects of the tariff might be.

The negotiations on agriculture proved to be difficult politically. There was initially the question of the system and then that of details under the system. The system adopted was one of a sliding tariff of the sort that Britain used at one time under the Corn Laws. First a domestic support price for separate commodities in the Common Market is determined. The sliding tariff is the difference between this support price and the world price. If domestic supplies are short and the price tends to rise above the support price, the world price plus tariff (equal to the support price) will bring it down. If, on the other hand, the crop is heavy, the domestic price will sag, and the tariff will become a prohibitive one. The student should have no trouble figuring out the partial-equilibrium diagrams. The tariffs on agriculture, incidentally, are paid into a special fund designed to modernize EEC agriculture.

The system was one thing. To agree on support prices proved much more difficult. Germany, where the Christian Democrat party depended on farmer support, wanted a high price for wheat. France, where agricultural efficiency was rising rapidly, was afraid that a high price would keep too many men on the land and produce a larger surplus than Germany could absorb. These negotiations were complicated by U.S. insistence in the

Kennedy Round negotiations that provision be made for quota minimums representing amounts of wheat, cotton, soybeans, and so on, that the Common Market would continue to import despite the sliding tariff.

The British application to join the Common Market was made the first time, and subsequently, on political grounds, but their very different agricultural system poses serious problems. The British start with world prices of foodstuffs and add subsidies for farmers. To move to the EEC system requires a large increase in the price of foodstuffs, and the difference between the world price and the new high prices will in effect be paid to modernize French, German, and Italian farms, since the British are already efficient.

The British swallowed their irritation at moving from a good to a poor system of agricultural subsidy and entered the Common Market despite limited success in modifying the terms of the agricultural agreement. Perhaps they hope to modify them when they have become a full member. Membership, however, does imply, along with trade diversion for the Commonwealth (the most importantly affected country being New Zealand), a sharp rise in the cost of living in Britain, which may create new problems.

Regional Integration among Developing Countries

The most successful case of economic integration thus far is the European Economic Community. Regional integration is a device often recommended for the developed countries, however. Some have come to fruition, such as the Central American Common Market (CACM), or are struggling to make the grade, such as LAFTA. Others have broken up already, such as the West Indian Federation or the arrangements on the East Coast of Africa among Kenya, Uganda, and Tanganyika. Some have been for years in the talking stage—the Arab League. Others are now being talked about for the first time, among the Maghreb countries of Tunisia, Algeria, and Morocco, and the Asian countries of the Philippines, Malaya, and Thailand. That with the most current momentum is the Andes pact formed as a subgroup of LAFTA in August 1966 among Chile, Colombia, Ecuador, Peru, and Venezuela. Bolivia joined later and Venezuela refused to accept the final treaty.

The purpose of regional integration in all cases is to industrialize. National markets are thought to be too narrow; a regional market may be able to support modern industry. There is much less interest in trade creation through destroying inefficient producing units existing in the member countries than in trade diversion—shifting purchases from the rest of the world to member countries, and more constructively, the achievement of economies of scale. If the countries are going to industrialize anyway, it is best to do so with minimum inefficiency.

But the difficulties are great. On the economic side, the lagging country becomes frightened that by giving its partners free access to its market, it will never be able to start any industry. Thus Bolivia refuses to join LAFTA on the ground that it would impede its development rather than assist it. It regards LAFTA as a device to speed up the development of Mexico, Argentina, and Brazil—now leading in industry in the area—at the expense of the slower countries. In the Andes pact it is recognized that unless Bolivia and Ecuador gain in the sense of catching up to some degree with Chile, Colombia, and Peru, the arrangement will not have succeeded.

Various devices are being developed to meet this objection. The lagging country may be given special treatment. This may consist of investment assistance, as in Europe, or the obligations of the less developed countries to the others may be reduced. In the EEC, the association agreement covering Greece and Turkey provided for access to the markets of the Six, but the reciprocal reduction of their duties were delayed for five years. Similar asymmetric treatment of the laggards is promised in LAFTA.

One device for which support is still strong is industrial planning. This would assign certain industries to certain countries in the union, and forbid them to others. The Central American Common Market tried this with little success: inevitably each country was pleased with the monopoly it was granted but sought to chisel on that granted the other countries. Industrial planning with assigned industries broke down even before the collapse of the CACM over the "soccer war" between Honduras and El Salvador.

The fact is that despite their geographic proximity, the less developed countries are not economically unified. They are typically more competitive than complementary, and their competitive interests make it hard for them to form a community. Forming a single landmass with good communication, as they do, the EEC members for the most part have an economic advantage over the outside world in the markets of the community. In the developing countries, many of them with only exterior lines of communication (as noted for Argentina and Chile), there is no natural unity, and the artificial unity of political resolve is difficult to sustain. The fact that benefits for one member are costs for the others is divisive.

If the political difficulties can be overcome, however, there can be little doubt that industrialization in large units is better than industrialization at the same levels of protection in five times that number. The question may be raised, however, whether economic integration into the world market may not be more efficient, because it is trade creating, than regional integration of a trade-diverting sort would be.

Summary

The welfare effects of discrimination are shown by analysis of customs union. As an example of the theory of the second best, not every step toward freer trade increases welfare. In addition to trade creation, there is trade diversion, the expansion of high-cost production at the expense of low cost. The analysis is presented in partial and general equilibrium.

Beyond customs union (and free trade areas), there are common markets, economic union, and economic integration. Economic integration is defined as factor-price equalization, achieved through joined goods markets, joined factor markets, or a combination of the two. It is noted that third-country markets and factors can serve to equalize factor prices between two countries that are not in a strict sense integrated.

Attention is called to problems of the height of tariffs, to the division of the proceeds of customs unions, to special regimes for agriculture, and to the difficulties faced by regional integration of developing countries, including their attempts to solve them by industrial planning.

SUGGESTED READING

Texts

See B. Balassa (ed.), *Changing Patterns of Foreign Trade and Payments* (New York: W. W. Norton & Co., Inc., 1964) (paperback), Part II.

Treatises

On a theoretical level, see B. Balassa, *The Theory of Economic Integration* (Homewood, Ill.: Richard D. Irwin, Inc., 1961); R. G. Lipsey, *The Theory of Customs Union: A General Equilibrium Analysis* (London: Weidenfeld & Nicholson, 1970). See also the latter's survey article in American Economic Association, *Readings in International Economics*, with its citations of the vast literature.

The student is left to find his way around in the rest of the abundant literature. He might start, however, for Europe with L. B. Krause's *European Economic Integration and the United States* (Washington, D.C.: The Brookings Institution, 1968) and J. Gruenwald, M. S. Wionczek, and M. Carnoy, *Latin American Economic Integration and U.S. Policy* (Washington, D.C.: The Brookings Institution, 1972).

Points

The works of Viner, Scitovsky, and Tinbergen cited in the text are:

J. Viner, *The Customs Union Issue* (New York: Carnegie Endowment for International Peace, 1953).

T. Scitovsky, *Economic Theory and Western European Integration* (London: Unwin University Books; reprinted with a new introduction, 1962) (paperback).

J. Tinbergen, *International Economic Integration* (Amsterdam: Elsevier Publishing Co., 1965).

Useful material on integration of Europe and the developing countries can be found in the Williams Commission, *Papers Submitted to the Commission on International Trade and Investment Policy*, Vol. II.

Chapter 12 | THE CASE FOR FREE MULTILATERAL TRADE

The last few chapters have suggested that there are many cases where tariffs or subsidies are justified and many circumstances in the real world when countries in fact interfere with foreign trade. Modern theorists, moreover, make a very weak case for free trade, arguing only that free trade is better than no trade, and even some trade better than no trade, but being unwilling to say anything as strong as that free trade is better than restricted trade. How then can economists, with a weak basic case, and recognizing so many exceptions, go on uniformly recommending free trade as the best commercial policy? We have saved the case for free multilateral trade for this last chapter in Part II on commercial policy to see how much of the classic doctrine of free trade is left or can be salvaged after modern economic theory has chipped or hacked away at it with qualifications. We will proceed by discussing efficiency conditions with two and then more countries, and then the distribution of welfare between countries. Thereafter we will recur to the theory of the second best, which suggests that even if free trade is best, not every step toward free trade should be taken. Finally, in the light of all the possible violations of efficiency conditions, the possible desirability of altering the distribution of welfare, and the dangers of moving toward free trade piecemeal, we get back into line with most economists in arguing for free multilateral trade as a general presumption.

Merits of the Price System

The case for free trade rests at basis on efficiency. Provided certain conditions are met, the invisible hand operating under free trade will produce a maximum of world output for a given distribution of income or welfare. Resources will be allocated among various activities and goods will be distributed among consumers so as to produce the greatest possible volume of satisfaction for the distribution of welfare. It will be impossible to make any one person or group better off without making some other person or

189

group worse off. This is called (after the great Italian economist) Pareto optimality.

We will come to the conditions and assumptions shortly. Assuming these conditions, however, and within the limitations of the assumptions, free trade works to equate goods prices everywhere (abstracting from transport costs). These prices are equivalent to the marginal rate of substitution, which optimizes consumption, and to the marginal rate of transformation in output, which optimizes production. Being the same between the two countries, they eliminate any further gain from trading. Moreover, competition ensures that factors earn the same in every industry in each country (and possibly in several countries), which assures an optimum allocation of resources. If social and private marginal value are everywhere equal to social and private marginal cost, society has reached an optimum of efficiency in the allocation of resources, the production of goods, and the distribution of goods. This may not be an optimum welfare position, because the distribution of income may leave differences in the significance of income for different income recipients. But for the moment we are discussing efficiency rather than equity.

The case for free trade rests on the view that it is the most direct approach to Pareto optimality, and the distributional arguments can be taken care of in ways which do not distort efficient allocation of resources. But the conditions are far-reaching. There must be no marked divergence between social values and market prices, either for goods or factors. Such divergences, as the last chapters have shown, do in fact occur. Market prices may differ from social values—apart from governmental interference for redistributional purposes—because of scale economies and diseconomies, monopoly and monopsony, and nonoptimal taxation. Divergences at the factor level may be the result of rigidities and other distortions of factor prices from social marginal products. Rigid factor prices may result in unemployment. While we have discussed most of these at some stage during the past few chapters, it is well to recapitulate.

Demerits of the Price System

When external economies or diseconomies exist, social marginal value diverges from the private marginal value given by the market. Private costs may overstate long-run social costs, as in the infant-industry case: a tariff on imports, or better a subsidy on domestic production, is needed to develop for producers the new cost conditions that enable them to reduce price.

Internal economies of scale, which may persist due to lack of competition arising from ignorance or lack of access to complementary factors such as land or capital, similarly produce a divergence between social and private value and reduce economic efficiency below the optimum.

External diseconomies formerly received less attention but are rapidly coming to the forefront of the discussion. Private costs may understate social costs because they fail to take account of erosion, depletion, the stripping of forests without provision for reforestation, or pollution of the air or water. Here the remedy is to require replaceable resouces to be replaced (in farming and lumbering) or precautions to be taken to limit pollution. These add expense, of course, but they are socially necessary and assist in bringing private costs up to social costs. Where the resources are irreplaceable, as in mining, there is much to be said for taxation—not on imports but on domestic production, where the country is on an import basis, or on exports if the country sells abroad. The heavy taxes on oil profits in countries such as Venezuela and Iraq have as their justification the replacement of wasting natural resources by man-made capital assets in order to maintain the productivity of the economy. (Note that as land is depleted and capital built up, the transformation schedule must change, and with it comparative advantage.) The external economies or diseconomies may be dynamic, as well as static. It is, for example, sometimes argued that primary-product exports may yield a higher return than import-competing manufactures, but that manufacturing has training effects, through a learning process, which lead to increased productivity over time, while the gains from specialization in export products are once and for all.

Where competition is imperfect, the results achieved by free trade again fall short of the efficiency optimum. Monopoly unduly restricts production and raises private above social value. Monopsony unduly restricts consumption and holds private below social value. In goods markets, these results flow from the existence of market power, along with the existence of overhead costs. They can also stem from ignorance, habit, and tradition. Consumers purchase in the expensive rather than in the cheaper market for any of these reasons or because they lack the capital to act in economical fashion. Producers may fail to foresee how permanent a shift in demand is against their product.

It is not only firms which have overhead costs and which act with imperfect foresight. The same is true of factors. Factors may be badly allocated, with crowding of factors in some lines and scarcity in others, through lack of awareness of opportunities, inability to forecast their duration, or costs of moving. Labor has difficulty in transferring between occupations, except insofar as the alternative employments exist side by side in the same locality. There are costs of changing jobs—of selling one house and buying another in a different locality or of merely moving and starting a new home. Labor is mobile over a generation; young people hesitate to enter a shrinking industry unless family and local traditions are very strong, and the overhead costs of moving for young people fresh from schools and colleges are low or nonexistent. The fact is that there are depressed areas of immobile and often specialized resources in most countries: the miners of Appalachia and the Ruhr; the black farmers of the Delta and the dark ones of the Mezzogiorno in southern Italy; the shipyard workers of the Fore River in Quincy, Massachusetts, and the Clyde in Scotland. Immobility of labor may be assumed away, but it exists.

Real, as opposed to financial, capital, of course, is even more immobile, although less so than land. Capital is completely mobile only over the long run as it wears out in one location and is replaced in another through the investment of depreciation allowances. This takes time, which may run as long as 20 years. In the short run, an individual may be able to move his capital, if he can sell his textile mill in New Hampshire, let us say. But this is not mobility of economic capital, since the buyer puts in what the seller takes out. In economic terms, the equipment may have some mobility, if it can be transported or sold as secondhand machinery or as salvage or scrap steel. The building, however, is unlikely to be movable, and the capital it represents can be shifted only in the long run.

If firms and factors are frequently unresponsive to price signals in the market, and so fail to bring about equality of social and private value, they sometimes actively produce divergence by responding excessively to price change. The cobweb theorem mentioned in Chapter 10 is illustrative of this phenomenon. A higher price for potatoes this year produces too many next year, which leads to a low price then and a shortage the year after. Each rise in price elicits too large an increase in output to bring about equilibrium; each decline too large a decrease.

How far the price system can serve as a guide to investment in new capacity remains a debated point. There are economists who attach great significance to the time lag which supervenes between the recognition of the need for new capacity—during which the supply of consumers' goods is inelastic with response to price increases—and the time when the new capacity is completed and goes into production. If this period is long, as it will be in capital-intensive processes, there is danger that the persistence of scarcity and high prices during the period of capital formation will lead to the establishment of what ultimately proves to be excess capacity. The inability of the price system to guide investment decisions adequately in this regard is charged with much of the responsibility for the business cycle.

Alternatives to the Price System

This book is concerned with international trade and not with comparative economic systems. It may nonetheless be worth mentioning that the possible weaknesses of the price system to which reference has been made do not imply that any alternative system—whether cartel or government planning or state ownership—is superior or, for that matter, worse. What appears to be important is the size of the decision-making unit and the scale on which decisions are taken. Monopoly industry, governmental planning, and competitive industry, in which all entrepreneurs are culturally identical and respond in the same way to the same stimuli, are likely to react in the same direction to a change in demand or supply. There may be differences in the speed with which they recognize errors of judgment—this is an advantage claimed for private enterprise. But all will differ from a situation in which tradition decrees what is produced and how, or in which production is carried on by a large number of small firms whose views are arrived at independently. Mistakes will be made by the small firms, but they will be small, and there will also be some fortuitous breakthroughs.

It is of some interest that in market economies, governments simulate planning with the use of "shadow prices," which represent an approximation of social values for the calculations of costs, while the socialist countries, as we have seen in Chapter 8, search for means to organize international trade among countries which have plans and arbitrary prices but no way to compare prices, since they vary rather widely from real scarcities. Neither overcome the disability of a centralized system that its errors are more devastating because they affect a much wider proportion of total resources.

It does not help to have many small firms if they all think alike and behave alike, responding to the same news and the same interpretations of the news. Formally decentralized, such a system is centralized.

Efficiency and Welfare

The optimum in terms of efficiency would also be the optimum welfare position under either of two circumstances: first, that it made no difference what the distribution of income was, because a dollar of income produced the same amount of welfare no matter who received it; or, second, that the distribution of welfare did not change as one moved toward the efficiency optimum. Unfortunately neither of these assumptions is tenable. Accordingly, even if the price system worked well enough to produce an efficiency optimum, it is by no means certain that this would maximize world welfare.

The classical economists of course recognized that the marginal utility of income was different for rich and poor, so that it was inappropriate to assume that a dollar of income was a dollar of welfare for every income recipient; they also understood that a change toward freer trade redistributed income so that one cannot claim that free trade produces more welfare than protection even if free trade produces more goods at less cost than protection. They nonetheless held that free trade, like honesty, was the best policy.

Modern welfare economists have two hypotheses by which they attempt to say something about free trade and welfare. One device is to assign weights. If country A's income is worth one for every $1 of income, and country B's, one half, then it would be possible to calculate whether free trade produced more welfare than a given position of protection by deriving a weighted result. If free trade turned the terms of trade in B's favor, and lost A 10 but gained 18 for B, this would reduce welfare on the weights indicated: A's weighted loss of 10 is greater than B's weighted gain of 9. But, on the basis of equal weights, free trade would produce gain for the world of A and B. If equal weights are assigned to income recipients in all countries, free trade produces an optimum of welfare. If A's weight is one and B's zero, on the other hand (a highly nationalist point of view), the welfare optimum is the optimum tariff which will improve A's terms of trade to the maximum possible without a counterbalancing decrease in quantity.

The system of weights, which is one form of international social welfare function, could be extended to income recipients within each country. Free trade will distribute income in A against the scarce factor and in favor of the abundant one. If the abundant factor is rich, and the scarce poor, free trade may be a worse position in terms of welfare than the protected position. But of course it would be possible to adopt free trade and redistribute income through fiscal policy.

The other hypothesis is the so-called compensation principle. Situation 1 is better in terms of welfare than situation 2 if the gainers in welfare in moving from 2 to 1 gain enough to be in position to compensate the losers and still have something over. This reduces welfare comparisons to those in efficiency: any time there is an increase in the value of total output, it follows that the gross gainers would be in position to compensate the gross losers. But of course such compensation rarely occurs. The progressive income tax and transfer payments to the needy who may become unemployed go a short part of the way to provide compensation. But for the rest, the compensation principle remains a pure hypothesis.

Provided that the price system worked efficiently to produce a material optimum, there is no doubt that free trade produces a welfare optimum, either with equal weights for countries and income recipients within countries or with the compensation principle, also between and within countries. But this is a trivial truth. Every country has rich and poor, and some countries are richer than others. From the free-trade position, then, it would be possible to impose tariff barriers and other interferences with trade which would improve welfare within and between countries. This is far different, however, from saying that any interference with free trade improves welfare. Some trade barriers transfer income from the poor in the protecting countries to the rich within their borders, and internationally from impoverished countries to wealthy. Unless one knows the distribution of income, there is just as much reason to believe that a movement away from free trade will worsen the welfare position as that it will improve it. Nay, there is more; and for two reasons.

First, the free-trade position tends to produce overall more income. For any given distribution, more is better than less; for any random distribution, moreover, more is better than less. Since there is no presumption that free trade worsens the distribution, there is a presumption that the total welfare position is superior when efficiency is higher than when it is lower. Second, the rich are more likely to have political power and to exercise it than the poor. In consequence, tariffs are likely to favor the rich, and the removal of tariffs, the poor. If the internal welfare function calls for shifts of income from rich to poor, there is a second presumption in favor of freeing trade. The sum total of these two presumptions, however, is not sufficiently high to make an overwhelming case.

Part of the difficulty is that the price system both allocates resources and distributes income. It used to be thought that within an economy the price system and the tax system specialized and divided functions: the price system was used to create an efficiency optimum, the tax system to redistribute income and welfare. This is no longer true even within a closed economy; the existence of cartels, monopolies, price-parity formulas, cost-of-living clauses in wage contracts, and so on, demonstrates the extent to which the price system has been used to affect the distribution of welfare. Perhaps the division of function never really existed except in the minds of economists. Internationally, however, no such division of function is possible, because the countries of the world are not bound together in a common budget and so are not linked through taxes. The price system is responsible both for efficiency in the allocation of resources and for the distribution of income and welfare internationally. The price system then tends to produce a maximum of efficiency, to the extent that it operates effectively and achieves a distribution of income and welfare between countries. This welfare distribution is not necessarily the optimum. For the same distribution of welfare, however, free multilateral trade produces more welfare all round than autarchy. (Note, however, that if one moves away from free multilateral trade, one inevitably changes the distribution of welfare.)

One important feature of the price system when it operated with a considerable degree of competition was that its decisions were accepted as the impersonal judgments of a sort of fate. The market in a competitive society represents a collective judgment, different from the arbitrary or quixotic decisions of government, monopoly, or a foreign country. An adverse decision administered by the market gives less ground for retaliation through market forces or through extra-market action. Adam Smith regarded the market's actions as those of an "invisible hand." One of the strongest arguments for free multilateral trade with any considerable degree of competition is that it gives an objective basis for the allocation of resources and the distribution of income, both nationally and internationally.

One possible qualification must be admitted. Free trade is both the optimum material position for all countries for its given distribution of welfare and the possible welfare optimum for the abundant factor in the economically more advanced country. If all countries are of equal size and power and income is distributed relatively evenly among them, the first consideration is relevant. If one country is more advanced technologically than the others and of greater economic (and political) power, then free trade may represent an optimum position for the existing distribution of income, but welfare may be capable of increase through a redistribution of income brought about by trade barriers.

If tariffs are justified by the international redistribution of income from a rich country to a poor, the Free Trader has still one more string to his bow. His alternative: adopt free trade and international income transfers. Or to put it another way, if it agrees that welfare should be transferred to the tariff-imposing poor country, let the rich country that has a tariff applied against its products adopt an offsetting subsidy. The price distortion produced by the tariff will be corrected by the subsidy. One country taxing imports and the other country subsidizing them is equivalent to a subsidy from the second to the first country, or an international transfer.[1]

This seems a fairly unrealistic suggestion for dealing with international trade, but there is one relevant case: At the UNCTAD Geneva meeting in 1964 the developing countries suggested that the European nations that maintain high taxes on coffee, tea, and chocolate should eliminate them. It was originally thought that this would expand consumption and developing country exports. But the idea occurred to a number of people that if these import, tariff-for-revenue-only (since there is no local European production) taxes were removed in Europe, the developing countries could replace them with export taxes. Europe would lose revenue, and the developing countries would gain revenue. Production and consumption would still be inefficient, but the shift of tax revenues from the

---

[1] For the student who has studied the appendices, especially C and D, it should be observed that it is not enough for A to counter B's optimum tariff with an optimum subsidy. What is required is a reduction in B's tariff plus A's subsidy, which will in combination keep B on the same indifference curve attainable by the optimum tariff but make A much better off. In Figure 12.1, B's original optimum tariff displaced the B offer curve to B', which enabled B to reach the trade indifference curve i_b. A subsidy on exports by A, displacing its offer curve from A to A', combined with a reduction in B's tariff so that the offer curve is displaced from B' to B'', keeps B on indifference curve i (moving from T to W) but enables A to advance from indifference curve I (at T) to indifference curve II at W. This exercise underlies the truth that the contract curve, K–K, is an optimum locus along which one country cannot benefit without another country losing.

FIGURE 12.1. Replacing the Optimum Tariff by an International Transfer

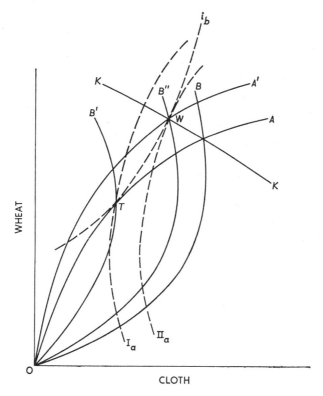

importers to the exporters would be equivalent to foreign aid (and would require the same budgetary steps). In short, intergovernmental economic assistance is superior to the optimum tariff, as it accomplishes the sought-after transfer of welfare without distorting production and consumption. The Free Trader repeats: There is nothing a tariff can do that something else cannot do better.

The German School has consistently regarded free trade as the ideological weapon of the dominant country. A number of economists have considered the attempts of the United States to achieve a multilateral convertible world of lower tariffs in the same category. There can be no doubt that the distribution of income internationally will be different and possibly improved with trade barriers than with free trade, but the total material level will be lower. If the social welfare function or set of value judgments called for a shift of income from export interests to import-competing industry in the United States, or if the terms of trade could be turned against the United States by tariffs abroad and the international social welfare function required a shift of income from the United States to other countries, the free-trade optimum position in material terms would not represent the desirable position in terms of welfare. Peter Wiles has put it: "Free trade is the mercantilism of the strongest power."

Free trade is necessarily nondiscriminatory trade. And the case against discrimination is a solid one, despite the demand of the less developed countries for preferences in manufactures. If the less developed countries require help to get a start to achieve economies of scale, subsidies are better than tariffs that are relaxed in a discriminatory fashion. Perhaps even better than export or manufacturing subsidies by the developing countries would be import subsidies by the developed countries, having the international distribution of welfare in mind. This is perhaps perfectionism. But nondiscriminatory trade in which imports are bought in the cheapest market and sold in the dearest to the extent needed to equalize prices (adjusted for transport costs) is the efficient ideal, and transfers are the optimal means of achieving desired welfare distributions. The slogan "**trade not aid**" has it wrong, especially because it means distorted and discriminatory trade. Trade and aid are complements, not substitutes. The economist's answer should be "Free trade and equitable aid."

The Case for Multilateral Trade

In a world of more than two countries the case for free trade becomes a case for multilateral trade and convertible currencies. If free trade takes place only between pairs of countries and, because of inconvertibility, each segment of paired trade must be in balance, the overall criterion for a free-trade maximum of efficiency is breached. Goods will be bought in markets other than the cheapest and will be sold for less than the dearest price. This follows because of the necessity to balance. If a single pair of countries shows an export surplus for A and an import surplus for B, with all buyers and sellers maximizing their gain, balance will require the redirection of A purchases from a cheap source to B, or a shift of A sales to a less profitable market than B.

Multilateralism requires convertibility. The export surplus earned by A in B's currency must be convertible into C's exchange to require the gross deficit incurred by A in trade with C. The difficulty in a world of interconnected trade balances is that the maintenance of convertibility of a country's currency is not solely within its capacity. The currency of the countries with which it has export surpluses must be convertible if it is going to meet its gross deficits. In a system of interlocked export and import gross balances, convertibility requires that each country maintain overall balance simultaneously or that any country with a net deficit have reserves which it is prepared to spend, in a medium of exchange acceptable to the country or countries with which it has gross deficits.

The Conditions Needed for Free Trade

The presumption in favor of free trade comes down partly to the argument that interference in trade has a comparative disadvantage in meeting the economic or social condition which is said to call for tariffs. Thus if the problem is that wages in manufacturing are too high in a less developed country, the remedy is not to put a tax on the good but to subsidize manufacturing employment. This hits at the source of distortion, rather than producing an offsetting one which incidentally results in misallocations elsewhere in the system. Similarly the alternative to a tariff in the case of external economies is a subsidy, this time not on the employment of the factor, but on the output of the good.

Where monopoly prevents the realization of Pareto optimality, it must be remembered that freeing up trade helps to destroy monopoly and to assist competition. The general argument against free trade because its conditions are not met backfires, and free trade helps.

The argument to achieve a socially desirable distribution of income through transfer of aid rather than interference in trade is more difficult. Aid has not developed very far, nor the sort of tax cum subsidy that, as we have just seen, can substitute for aid. In the long run, the international community needs to build the common objects of expenditure, such as budgets for the United Nations and its specialized agencies, to permit international transfers as a regular matter by unequal incidence of costs and benefits. A market is different from a budget. Markets are used for efficient allocation; budgets for income redistribution. Until international budgets are substantial in relation to national money incomes, the scope for automatic income redistribution through international spending and taxation will be limited. Redistribution of income through national budgets helps make the income distribution decreed by the national market more tolerable although such groups as farmers refuse to accept it even then and insist on efficiency-distorting price supports. In the long run, readiness to submit to the dictates of the market is assisted by the existence of devices for sharing income which exist alongside the market and mitigate its most severe consequences on income distribution.

The Theory of the Second Best

We have already explicitly encountered the theory of the second best in two forms: because of the difference between nominal and effective rates of protection, it may be better to raise a duty on raw materials rather than lower it in order to move toward efficiency; and in customs unions, lowering duties in some circumstances produces trade diversion, encouraging tariff-protected activities at the expense of efficient production. The move away from freer trade is a second-best policy in both cases, because the first-best policy of lowering the duty on the manufactured good in the first instance, or lowering tariffs on a nondiscriminatory multilateral basis, was regarded as politically or institutionally impossible. The general statement is that when the best policy of expanding trade all around is excluded, a second-best policy may involve lowering tariffs but may require raising one or more.

Suppose, for example, that the best policy for an equitable distribution of welfare—taxing the rich to aid the poor through aid transfers—is politically impossible. It may be second best in terms of this objective for the poor to raise taxes on the goods they sell the rich—like the Organization of Petroleum Exporting Countries (OPEC) and oil. This is not first best, because the efficient set of prices is distorted, and with it production, consumption, and trade. But one cannot use the best way. Use the next best.

The infant-industry argument for the tariff is another example of second-best reasoning. Under competitive markets with perfect foresight, the future declining costs or increasing returns would be evident, and prospective profits would be so clear that entrepreneurs would be willing to lose money now to earn more later. Moreover they would be able to borrow from all-wise banks which understand the facts regarding present and future. With less than perfect markets and foresight, the first-best solution, it may be useful to put a tariff up, to attract attenion to the opportunity, to make profits to encourage the bankers, etc. Or perhaps in this case the tariff is third best and a subsidy second best, as contrasted with the first-best but unattainable solution of perfect markets.

Or—another example—factor prices do not reflect factor scarcities. Labor is overpaid, or capital paid too little. Comparative advantage under free trade would be distorted. The first-best solution is to improve the functioning of factor markets. The second-best solution is optimal subsidies and taxes on overpaid and underpaid factors, or on the goods in which they are embodied, to restore market to social values.

In a world of second best, all rules of thumb are suspect. Complete free trade may be undesirable because of divergences of social from private values through externalities and market failures. Or even if complete free trade will help, it is not clear whether every action in the direction of free trade will move the economy in the right direction. As James E. Meade put it, not every step upward helps to climb the highest hill. If one is on a foothill, it may be necessary to descend for a bit and cross to the main slope.

Professor Meade has gone further and devised a notional system of comparing social marginal value with social marginal cost and measuring the **divergence**. Divergence is measured initially per unit and then weighted by output (and trade). A tariff removal will improve welfare if it on balance reduces total divergence in the system. This it may do. But it may not. The reduction of a tariff in one commodity will narrow the divergence in this commodity but may give rise to an increase in production or trade in another commodity in which the divergence is large. The system requires adding algebraically the weighted divergences across affected items. A net reduction in divergences is an improvement; an increase is a setback.

Suppose Britain reduces the tariff on wine from France. This narrows the divergence between the social marginal value of wine and the social cost in Britain and increases its consumption. This much is a gain in welfare. But many additional effects may occur. The increase in wine consumption in Britain may lead to increased consumption of a complementary product with a large divergence, or decreased production of a competitive product with a small or no divergence. Similar distortion may take place in the country expanding exports. If the tariff reduction is discriminatory, it is necessary to take into account the effect on, say Germany, which may or may not be able to sell its wine elsewhere or may cease its production. Until one has a view of the total effects on consumption and production in all the affected countries, weighted in each case by the divergence between social value and social cost, one cannot really judge whether a given tariff reduction improves or worsens the welfare position.

This sounds highly overintellectualized, and admittedly economists lack the information and the techniques to make the calculations called for by the system. It is, nonetheless, a generalization of the system of the second best, which we have seen in action in a number of particular problems—effective protection, customs union, infant industry, factor distortions. And by extension, the rule of second best breaks all other rules. If one cannot correct balance-of-payments disequilibrium easily by macroeconomic measures, then by all means help yourself to tariffs or quotas or restrictions on particular expenditures like tourism—it's a second-best solution, you know. But here it is useful to note Harry G. Johnson's warning: Application of second-best rules requires a first-best economist to provide the theoretical and empirical investigation of the conditions under which such a policy will actually improve welfare, whereas "policy is generally formulated by fourth-best economists and administered by third-best economists."

The Burden of Proof

There is something of a temptation at this stage to say that no holds are barred and anything goes. The efficiency conditions for a Pareto optimum are not usually met; the international and domestic distribution of income are rarely satisfactory; and from a condition of divergences between social and private marginal values, any particular reduction in trade barriers may lead toward or away from an optimum of efficiency and welfare. But one can say more.

In the first place, there are some strong presumptions. Since tariffs improve the terms of trade, the richer countries should take off tariffs first.

In taking off tariffs, a country should take off tariffs on substantial amounts of trade, so that the reduction of the discrepancy between private cost and social value will be as wide as possible.

A country should reduce tariffs more on goods with a high divergence between private and social marginal value than on goods with a low divergence. Where the divergence is the result of the tariff, it should reduce high tariffs before low tariffs.

In multilateral trade, a country should equalize the severity of import restrictions by lowering restrictions on goods of high divergence and raising them on goods of low divergence, if necessary to maintain balance-of-payments equilibrium, both on all goods from any one country and as between countries.

The fact is that while specific interference with trade to correct a departure from the assumptions for Pareto optimality or to achieve a particular redistribution of income may be justified on second-best grounds (because the first-best method of dealing with the difficulty was ruled out for some reason), this is a far different thing than arguing that since economists as a rule don't know whether tariffs help or hurt, you might just as well put them on as take them off. The presumption lies in favor of freer trade, even though not all steps toward freer trade are desirable. Professor Haberler suggests that tariffs and quotas are like poison, helpful in small doses for particular ills, but poison nonetheless, to be kept on an upper shelf of the bathroom closet and used with great discretion. Or perhaps free trade should be likened to honesty which is the best policy, as is well known (particularly because it is not then necessary to remember what you said), but must be held in check on limited occasions. Or as Mr. Churchill said about democracy, a very poor system of government, but better than any alternative. The difficulty with removing the strong presumption against interference with trade is that tariffs and quantitative restrictions are unlikely to be used correctly to meet ills which are correctly diagnosed. If we may recur to democracy, it is well known that benevolent despotism is the optimum form of government, just as optimum trade interventions are the best way to handle trade. The task with despotism is to keep it benevolent, and with interventions, to keep them optimal. In the long run it is better to try to improve the workings of democracy and to correct the ignorance, monopoly, rigidity, and other divergences which would justify exceptions in the case for free trade.

Social versus Economic Goals

Gottfried Haberler's summary of international trade policy says that it calls for not only keen analysis but also historical, political, and social judgment, and that economic history may have more to offer than economic theory. The point is apt. When social goals and efficiency fall out, the tradeoff between them is not immediately obvious. To the economist, it was evident that when the price of wheat fell in the 19th century, because of the expansion of settlement onto the rich lands of North America, Argentina, and Australia, the European farmer was doomed. Social policy, however, insisted that it was impossible economically to wipe out such a large class of the community, particularly one which embodied national virtues (France) or which provided foot soldiers (Germany). Karl Polanyi stood aghast that in Britain it was possible for a tradition of laissez-faire to permit a social class to be destroyed in the interest of efficiency.

But French experience in high protection for an agriculture which felt no pressure to modernize until the 1950s was not a happy one. Some tradeoff between social protection and economic efficiency is required which will slow down the rate of social change to a tolerable pace but ensure that it is accomplished. Today's equivalent are the miners everywhere in Europe who must be reallocated to higher earning occupations as quickly as can socially be done to allow the Continent to depend primarily on oil for its fuel (with stored supplies if need be for protection against the danger of Arab blockade) and U.S. coal for those uses in steel where it serves as a chemical rather than as a fuel. How long is long for coal miners? For wheat farmers, it seems likely that 15 years was too short in Britain, and 80 years too long in France.

By the same token, however, the comparative advantage of a year or two should not be allowed to decide the issue for all time. In the famous chicken war of the late 1950s, the Common Market sought to limit imports of chicken from the United States to give Dutch, Belgian, and German farmers a chance to catch up with the head start of a few years which the broiler houses of Maine and Delmarva (Delaware, Maryland, and Virginia) had staked out. (France bought no American chicken on a sanitary pretext, alleging that its treatment with hormones somehow corrupted it.) American farmers, the U.S. Department of Agriculture, and the U.S. Department of State resisted any attempt to restrain imports on the high moral ground of laissez-faire and the small head start. But here was a footloose industry, using farms literally as factories, with no real comparative advantage in the United States. A couple of years of protection would suffice to overcome the industry's teething troubles. It is hard not to feel great sympathy with this case for restricting trade.

It is thus reasonable to believe in the doctrine of free trade but unreasonable to be doctrinaire about it. Perhaps we may give the last word to the economic historian, as Haberler suggests, and quote from William Woodruff's *Impact of Western Man:*

Especially important in England was the ideal of "Free Trade." "Free Trade" was identified with civilization; out of greater international coordination would come the economic cosmos of the world; "Free Trade" was peace and progress;

"Free Trade" would provide a natural harmony and order in human affairs. . . . Britain in its trade policy was by no means altruistic; it was not regard for great economic truths or high moral purpose that led Britain to abandon the protection of its agriculture, industry and shipping; it was the hope of economic gain. Yet some of the noblest and ablest minds in Britain believed in the dream of "Free Trade" . . . and not for pecuniary reasons alone.

"Free Trade" proved to be an illusion. Its fault was the overwhelming importance it gave to economics; especially in its attempt to apply to the world something that was built up on premises specifically English. But it was never a mean illusion, and it helped to strengthen the commercial ties binding nation and nation. . . .

Summary

The case for free trade depends on the fulfillment of certain conditions for efficiency—no monopoly, external economies, distortions of market price from social values, and so on—and an acceptance of the income distribution it provides. But free trade plus other action to correct the distortion is better as a rule than trade intervention. Where the international distribution of income should be altered, trade and aid may be better than "trade not aid," which distorts efficient resource allocation.

The theory of the second best states that when the conditions for free trade cannot be achieved, not every move toward free trade takes an economy to a more efficient or more equitable solution. In fact, it justifies raising tariff barriers under certain conditions.

While particular measures to interfere with trade may advance national and international welfare, the presumption lies in favor of freer trade and against intervention. Intervention must be used with restraint. Whenever social and economic objectives seem to clash in the short run, the efficient solution is likely to be the socially desirable one in the long run.

SUGGESTED READING

Texts

Heller, chap. 11.

Treatises

See Meade, *Trade and Welfare*, Part IV; R. E. Caves, *Trade and Economic Structure* (Cambridge, Mass.: Harvard University Press, 1960), chap. 7; G. Haberler, "A Survey of International Trade Theory," SPIE, July 1961; papers by Paldwin, and Bhagwati and Ramaswami in American Economic Association, *Readings in the Theory of International Economics;* J. Bhagwati, *Trade, Tariffs and Growth* (Cambridge, Mass: M.I.T. Press, 1969), pp. 68–96; and Bhagwati,

"The Generalized Theory of Distortions and Welfare," in Bhagwati et al., *Trade, Balance of Payments, and Growth.*

Points

The quotations from and references to Wiles, Johnson, Polanyi, and Woodruff are:

P. J. D. Wiles, *Communist International Economics* (New York: Frederick A. Praeger, Inc., 1968), p. 555.

H. G. Johnson, "The Efficiency and Welfare Implications of the International Corporation," in C. P. Kindleberger, ed., *The International Corporation* (Cambridge, Mass.: The M.I.T. Press, 1970), p. 56.

K. Polanyi, *The Great Transformation* (New York: Farrar & Rinehart, 1944).

W. Woodruff, *Impact of Western Man* (New York: St. Martin's Press, 1966), p. 12.

PART III

Factor Movements

Chapter	THE INTERNATIONAL
13	MOVEMENT OF LABOR

Part I dealt with the economics of the international movement of goods, and Part II with commercial policy affecting such movement. In Part III we deal with the international movement of factors of production—or at least of the mobile factors, labor and capital, including capital with technology in the form of direct investment. But the division between analysis and policy in trade that was made in Parts I and II will not be followed symmetrically. Such little policy as arises in the migration of labor (mostly social rather than economic) is included in this chapter. Intervention in the movement of finance capital is part of the theory of foreign exchange control, which we reserve to Part V. Only in the case of direct investment will there be two chapters, one on analysis, a second on policy.

Labor Migration

Most textbooks on international economics, and most courses, steer clear of the question of migration. This is probably only partly due to the pious classical assumption of factor immobility between countries; capital movements have been accommodated into the corpus of the subject. In part, migration may be thought to have been overwhelmed in importance by trade; the fact that Europe exported 60 million people overseas between 1851 and 1970 and that today approximately 4 million migrants in Europe are working outside their native countries, however, suggests that migration is not small. President Roosevelt once addressed the Daughters of the American Revolution, it will be remembered, as "fellow immigrants." The more likely reason is that the subject is thought to belong rather to sociology or demography than to economics. More recently, however; the reduction in transport costs brought renewed interest in the economics of international migration and national migration policy. The latter may lie largely in the social field, but the economic questions are neither uninteresting nor unimportant.

The International Labor Market

There has always been a limited international market for labor. Workers commute to jobs across frontiers in Europe; between Windsor, Ontario, and Detroit, Michigan; and between Brownsville, Texas, and Matamoros, Mexico. Casual workers journey from country to country in search of work, particularly moving northward with the harvest or in the construction season, whether they are Mexicans in North America or Italians, Greeks, and Spaniards in Europe. Government administrators in colonies, businessmen managing foreign subsidiaries, planters, Peace Corps recruits, and, increasingly, professional and technical consultants spend varying amounts of time in economic roles outside the country of their permanent residence. And long-term or permanent migration is a familiar phenomenon, as masses of people have been driven abroad by one or another kind of trouble or attracted abroad by economic opportunity.

An international market for labor may be said then to exist. But classical economists were right to the extent that it is a most imperfect one. The return to common labor is not equalized around the world. And even within specialized noncompeting groups the equalization is far from complete. Indeed, equalization of wages does not take place within a country, except in broad terms and for some professional and technical classes; some labor economists make a lot (too much) of the fact that there is variability in wages for equal skills in the same town. Between continents, the returns to labor differ persistently, despite the fact that labor can move to a limited extent in overseas migration, and despite the tendency for international trade to bring about some equalization of factor prices, as discussed in Chapter 2.

In Europe, since about 1955, however, the international labor market has become more efficient. There is some increased movement across the borders of the developed countries in the Common Market, especially from the Netherlands to the Ruhr, from southeast France to southwest Germany, and from Belgium into the Netherlands and France. But the major change has been a northward movement, especially to Switzerland, Belgium, France, and Germany, first by Italians and then by Greeks, Spaniards, Portuguese, Turks, and more recently, once they had overcome their ideological reluctance, Yugoslavs. Foreign workers comprised as much as 30 percent of the Swiss labor force before restrictions were imposed in the 1960s and early 1970s, much higher than in Belgium, 10 percent; France, 9 percent; and Germany, 4½ percent. But their importance is greater than these numbers, as the student of marginal analysis knows. As noted in Chapter 11, "Economic Integration," since the foreign worker is without strong ties to any one location away from his native heath, his mobility makes a vital contribution to the improvement of the European labor market at the margin. European wage rates have converged sensibly in the period since 1955, with emigration raising wages along the Mediterranean and immigration holding them down relatively in the north. Factor-price equalization, however, has not been achieved either for worldwide professional and technical labor or for common labor in Europe, much less for common labor between continents.

There is doubt that the factor-price equalization model is relevant for intercontinental migration. This migration, as we shall see also in the case of capital, follows well-worn grooves rather than spreading evenly over the world in response to economic signals. The design of many flows is political and related to noneconomic or quasi-economic considerations. Thus as subjects of the Queen, West Indians had the right to migrate to Britain, until that right was modified and virtually destroyed by the requirement that they line up a job in Britain before they arrive. Algerians and members of the French *Communauté* had strong cultural ties to France and legal discrimination in their favor from that country. The British emigrate largely to the English-speaking dominions or the United States. Even when cultural and political considerations are not initially present, moreover, migration is a positive feedback process which follows a learning pattern. The movement is initially small and slow, as the early migrants overcome inertia. Once the channel is opened up, however, institutions are built which make it possible to move large numbers.

The Patterns of Labor Movement

Of particular interest among the world patterns of labor movement are the waves of immigration to the United States in the period up to 1914 that brought in large numbers of English, German, Scandinavian, Irish, Italian, and eastern European immigrants. Each wave had a pattern of cumulative growth. After small numbers of pioneer emigrants made a successful start, they sent for their relatives and friends, and the movement snowballed until the wave died down for one reason or another. Economic historians have debated whether the pull of opportunity was greater than the push of economic difficulty. In any case, however, it seems clear that these forces acted only against the background of a long-run migration cycle, which may or may not have had its origin in economic circumstances. In the burst of emigration from Ireland in the 1840s, the potato famine provided the push. Conversely, in the large-scale movement from Italy and eastern Europe which had its beginnings in the collapse of the European wheat price in the early 1880s, the size of the annual flow was affected by conditions in the United States, slowing down as a consequence of the panic of 1907 and picking up with the subsequent revival.

Whether push or pull starts a movement, the history of the 19th century reveals a crystal-clear instance of forces in the home country stopping one. The rapid growth of the German economy in the 1850s cut off sharply (in

1854) the previously snowballing movement of distressed peasants and artisans to the United States. With continued growth in Germany, emigration died away. Incidentally, recent historical research makes clear that the flow of the late 1840s and early 1850s was by no means the ideological movement stemming from the unsuccessful Revolution of 1848 which the tradition of Carl Schurz in New York City would have us believe. All but two or three hundred political refugees of the wave of German migration were seeking to improve their lot economically.

Brinley Thomas has detected a broad pattern in the Atlantic community in which long cycles connected with construction were counterposed in Europe and North America to produce rhythmical movements in migration. Large numbers of people were left stranded in rural occupations in Europe by the improvement in agricultural productivity in the first half of the 19th century and in the second half by the technological advance in transport, which made possible grain imports from the rich plains of North and South America, Australia, and the Ukraine. The Industrial Revolution created opportunities for work in European cities. In the upswing of the long construction cycle, the rural exodus was directed internally to the industrial cities. In depression, however, when it was necessary to pause and consolidate the domestic economic position, the rural reserve went abroad. One regulator of the movement that directed the Scandinavian, German, and British peasant now to the city and now to North America and (for the British) the Antipodes was the terms of trade. When they favored Europe, economic opportunity at home was high in textiles, coal, and steel, and ultimately engineering trades and the chemical industry. In the slump, the terms of trade turned against Europe, and capital and labor went abroad.

This pattern is sketched in broad strokes, of course, and does not fit parts of the picture. In southern Italy, Hungary, Poland, and Russia, there was little industry to attract the rural surplus. For a long time it stayed put. When it moved, it headed almost entirely abroad. It has been said that the southern Italian was regarded as socially and culturally inferior by the inhabitants of the industrial cities of Milan or Turin and was more at home in New York or San Francisco—once, that is, the movement got under way. It is interesting, too, to note that the migrants upon their arrival in the United States found their way into limited occupations and limited places of residence. Much of this was largely accidental. It is claimed that the Irish settled in Boston in greater numbers than in New York because the transatlantic fare to the former port was five shillings cheaper. Communities of Germans in Milwaukee and St. Louis, Swedes in Minnesota, Norwegians in the Dakotas, Poles in Baltimore and Buffalo, and Polish and Russian Jews in New York emphasize that the migrants were seeking their own kind, in the beginning, to provide a transition to life in the new world. Construction attracted Irish and Italian labor, Germans and Scandinavians went in for mixed and grain farming, northern Italians took to truck gardening, and Polish, German, and Russian Jews went into the garment industry.

The imposition of immigration quotas by the United States in 1921 and 1924 is explained largely on social grounds. The cumulative flow of migrants from southern and eastern Europe, cut off by the war, showed signs of sharp revival. The check to cumulative emigration provided in Britain, Germany, and Scandinavia in the 19th century by industrial development and rising real incomes had never taken hold elsewhere, and the natural rate of increase had shown no signs of diminishing. Potential immigration was accordingly large. Its restriction posed grave social and economic problems for the affected areas, but its continuance would have done so for the United States and other receiving areas as they filled up.

Equally in Switzerland, the movement to restrict immigration had economic aspects (discussed below) but the basis was largely cultural and political. After a certain point, the Swiss felt their "Swissness" threatened by a large and indigestible lump of foreigners.

The growing consciousness of international differences in levels of living has led to significant streams of immigrants to Britain from the poorer portions of the Commonwealth, especially Malta, the Indian subcontinent, and the West Indies. This influx created economic and social problems which led in the sixties to a change from completely free immigration, by people in search of work, to immigration limited to workers already in possession of jobs.

There is no need to outline the tragic story of the role played in international migration by the movement of refugees uprooted by war and political and religious persecution or fundamental differences. Miami, Florida, Thailand, Jordan, and India are full of refugees waiting to go back to Cuba, Vietnam, Israel, and East Pakistan (Bangladesh), respectively, to name only a few.

The European Labor Market

Not every country in Europe welcomes foreign labor. In some, such as Britain, trade-union opposition keeps down readiness to import workers. In Scandinavia, there is a Common Market for Labor limited to Scandinavians, with the largest movement having been from Finland to Sweden, but all the countries are reluctant to admit workers from the Mediterranean area, and justify this by saying that the southern laborer would find the northern climate dark and cold. As a member of the European Economic Community, the Netherlands has subscribed to the Rome Treaty providing for freedom of movement of labor within the Community; it is not, however, aggressive in recruiting labor in Italy. The other northern members of the EEC not only have welcomed the movement of labor within the Community, to the point of sending recruiting agencies abroad, but have extended the same generous provisions for national treatment (not most-favored nation) to Spain, Portugal, Greece, and Turkey. Until their labor shortages became so acute in the first half of the 1960s that foreigners with limited skills could not meet them, these countries depended on foreign labor for a significant contribution to growth, measured not by the proportion they constituted of total labor but by their contribution to holding wages down and thereby profits up, at the margin.

Once inflation hit, costs rose, profits were squeezed, and the long upswing from the early 1950s to the mid-1960's in Europe was over. The pressure to hire more foreign workers was relieved, and the regular turnover of workers who had filled their contracts and were returning home with their accumulated "target" savings reduced the numbers of foreign workers in northern Europe. Again in the recession of the early 1970s, countries like Germany let old contracts of foreign labor run out without replacing the workers until the recession corrected itself. In one sense, this could be thought of as exporting unemployment; a more generous way of looking at it was that the country had exported its peak labor demand. But in any case, the position was very different from the 1930s, when the French forced the Poles and Italians in their country to return home by canceling their police permits, rounding them up, and shipping them out.

The return movement is due to more than just contracts running out, however. In depression, migrants generally tend to return to their native countries. Net migration in Britain was inward during the 1930s from all over the world, following the outward movement of the 1920s. Scientists who were attracted to the United States in the boom of the late 1960s returned on balance to Europe in 1970–72.

The returning foreign worker runs the risk of being disenchanted with life at home. Australia, which used to recruit in Britain the white immigrants it insisted on, now extends its search and finds that Mediterranean workers who have been to northern Europe and returned south make excellent prospects. The experience of higher standards of living and better working conditions abroad makes them intolerant of life at home. But then Australians assert that the immigrant from Britain does not become a real Australian until he has taken his first trip "home" to Britain.

One complex pattern of migration is found in Canada, where immigrants come from the United Kingdom and emigrants leave for the United States. Among the latter are young people who go to the United States for an education and decide to stay on, as many students from other countries would do if the student visa did not require them to leave the country for at least two years. Recently education has been equated with investment in human capital, which has led to attempts to estimate whether Canada gains or loses on balance on capital account, i.e., in terms of the education which it contributes to emigrants and gains from immigrants.

Only about 10 percent of the immigrants entering Canada represent a net gain in numbers. But it was found the gain in education is much higher than this, since trained Britons immigrate, and relatively young and less educated Canadians emigrate.

Does Emigration Benefit the Sending Country?

If we leave out convulsive population movements, an interesting question which has received some discussion from economists is whether emigration is a good thing. It has been argued against it that sending grown people abroad permanently is a form of capital export: the country of emigration raises them from birth, feeds, clothes, and educates them through an unproductive period, and then loses them as they begin to reach a productive stage. This loss of a productive worker is comparable to the export of productive capital, except that the exporting country does not in all cases get a return on the net marginal productivity of the labor, over and above the maintenance and replacement costs (subsistence).

If the workers were slaves, sent abroad to produce a higher return than at home, and if their net product above subsistence were returned to the capital-exporting country, the capital-exporting analogy would be appropriate, provided that the slaves were raised for the purpose of earning a return. As a rule, however, population growth is independent of the opportunities for emigration, at least in the short run; the choice is not between investing resources in productive workers for migration abroad or in more productive domestic lines. It is rather whether labor stays home in unemployment or underemployment or seeks a job abroad. The resources invested in raising the labor to working age can be regarded as sunk. It is then a question whether a positive return on these resources is possible or, to put it otherwise, whether it is possible to relieve the pressure of the unemployed on the domestic labor market through emigration.

Broadly speaking, this is a general-equilibrium problem, and, as in all of them, the question is, Compared with what?—or, What would have been the likely course of events if the emigration had not taken place?

If, in fact, emigration means escape from the long-run check to population growth, it may be wasteful in terms of real income per head. The ideal policy would be not to allow emigration until the Malthusian barrier has been broken and family limitation is used to maintain per capita income.

Even with rapid population growth, large-scale emigration may add to disposable income for the remaining population and contribute foreign exchange to the balance of payments, if the rate of remittance home is high. Italy recovered rapidly from the depression of 1907 because the flow of remittances from the western hemisphere was so buoyant. Greece and, to a lesser extent, Turkey find their balances of payments today very much eased by emigrant remittances. It was necessary for Turkey to adopt appropriate policies. For a time, with a seriously overvalued exchange rate for the Turkish lira, Turkish workers in Europe would bring back goods—second-hand automobiles, television sets, or household appliances—rather than sending money, which would have accumulated foreign exchange for the economy. When a special and slightly undervalued rate was adopted and special interest rates were devised for emigrant deposits in Turkish lira, these remittances were transformed into foreign exchange of wider benefit for the total economy.

How long a worker will send remittances home depends on his personal circumstances and the length of time he has been away. Temporary workers remit heavily to their dependents, especially because they tend to be **target workers,** saving for a particular purpose. Permanent emigrants, including those who are temporary *ex ante* but become permanent *ex post,* cut remittances drastically when they marry abroad or are joined by an existing family initially left behind. They may send further moneys to parents and other relatives for a time, but these decline through time. Finally, as a generation passes, remittances dwindle to a trickle. Cultural change has altered the pattern as well as the time profile. In the 30 years before World War I, immigrants into the United States lived in ethnocentric groups in this country and moved only slowly to acquire the standard of living of the second- and third-generation families in the country as a whole. Today, the cultural hold of the immigrant group is virtually nonexistent, since numbers are so small, and the pressure is strong on the occasional immigrant, such as the Hungarian refugees, to adjust quickly to the American standard. Even if it were easy and convenient to remit to relatives abroad behind the iron curtain (which it is not), social pressures to be assimilated to the new level of consumption reduce the capacity.

But there are more elements in the calculation of the benefit of the emigrant to the country. The emigrant remits home. His relatives spend part of the money, and he or they save part. The part of the money spent leads to increases in imports, offsetting part of the foreign exchange gain. The savings belong to individuals, not to the state or to the country as a whole. They may gain; what about the country? This raises the question about the external effects of the remittances—their impact on taxes, capital formation, factor prices, and factor combinations.

If there were no external effects of any kind, it could be argued that what a man did was entirely his business. If he earned more in one country or another, he consumed or saved more, and in either case the savings accrued to him. If all factors were paid their marginal product, changes in factor endowments brought about by migration have these impacts on taxes and other factor prices, but that's all. The concern that many people feel about the **brain drain** of talented professional youth leaving the less developed countries is overdone, according to this calculation. The main effects cancel out. If a scientist leaves Britain, he takes his production with him, but he also takes his income representing a claim on goods equal to his marginal product. Much of the analysis of migration, according to this way of looking at it, stresses the loss in output, but not the equal reduction in his claim on the output of others.

The external effects cannot be overlooked, however. Abundant and therefore cheap scientists and engineers, doctors, or even economists are an external benefit for other factors in the nation, and a scarcity of technical and professional personnel is a diseconomy. Above a certain minimum these effects are relatively unimportant. Thus the Netherlands and the Scandinavian countries, for example, export professional personnel because they cannot employ all their educated nationals at socially acceptable levels of remuneration. But larger countries can benefit from large numbers of scientists, to limit ourselves to one category, and small and poor countries may be dangerously close to the minimum needed as a fixed input critical to other activities. Emigration which pulls the numbers below these minimum levels is harmful to output in general.

These external effects are, for the most part, incalculable. This is especially true of the highest quality of scientist—the Fermis, Von Neumanns, Von Brauns—who change the course of scientific and technological history.

By no means is all emigration deleterious. A case can be made that when there is open or disguised unemployment, a distortion of factor prices in the language of Chapters 10 and 12, emigration helps to get rid of it. The point is limited to unskilled labor. If disguised unemployment means that the marginal product is zero or close to zero, this inhibits investment. Why install machinery when there is in effect free labor, or rather family labor which must be paid anyhow? When enough labor is drawn off so that marginal product rises to the wage, it pays to calculate the returns on investment. Emigration thus stimulates investment, technological advance, and growth. In these cases, as the experience of the Mediterranean countries shows, high emigration rates were accompanied by high rates of growth.

But it must not go too far. Below some optimum population, the economy has trouble supporting the variety of activities it needs, as Goldsmith's *Deserted Village* and the ghost towns of the West remind us.

Does Immigration Benefit the Receiving Country?

Whether immigration will benefit or hurt a country depends upon the country's resources of capital and land, relative to population, and the dynamic effects of the movements in question. Australia, Canada, Brazil, and similar large, underpopulated countries are interested in immigration of selected types of workers—young, farmers, skilled factory workers, and so on—because their resources are large relative to labor supply and because the social overhead capital in countries of vast expanse typically produces increasing returns. Broadly the same investment in interurban roads, railroads, and harbors, for example, is required for a large population as for a small one, and a given population may be well below the optimum.

It is nonetheless likely that capital expenditure will be needed as a consequence of immigration, at least in the later stages. At the beginning, excess capacity exists in many lines of infrastructure, although in housing, where the indivisibilities inherent in a transport network should not exist, the increase in population without additional investment in housing often results in crowding in slums. The new immigrants in some countries, moreover, may get few public services. But this is less and less the case. Typically today, as immigration takes place, sooner or later the receiving country must provide housing, schools, hospitals, streets, and intraurban transport. One of the economic as opposed to cultural reasons for Switzerland cutting down on immigration was that its social infrastructure was fully extended, thus limiting the potential gains from adding workers. A considerable volume of investment in Australia today is linked to immigration requirements.

In Israel and West Germany, the large-scale inward movement cannot be said to have hurt these countries in the long run, despite the fact that they were well above the optimum population at the beginning of the movement in terms of social overhead capital. The reasons lie in the dynamic aspects of the movement. Israel's readiness to receive all Jewish refugees who were able to leave the countries where they constituted minorities contributed substantially to the spirit of dedication which evoked long hours of work and acceptance of low levels of consumption. These were extramarket phenomena which the economist has difficulty in explaining in terms of marginal productivity. In Germany, the dynamism lay partly, but only partly, in the evocation of a national effort. In large measure it operated through short-run pressure on wages which held profits high and out of which a compulsive and even neurotic drive to work and invest by entrepreneurs rebuilt German capital at a rapid rate.

But immigration does not always bring one's co-religionists or co-nationalists, and even when it does, as in the case of the Palestinian Arab refugees in the Sinai peninsula and Jordan, there is no necessary dynamic result. (In these cases, the receiving countries discouraged efforts of the refugees to improve their economic conditions, since this might have implied an acceptance of the view that they were not entitled to return to their land in Israel.) The return of the European settlers from Algiers to France in the 1960s had an effect halfway between the stimulation of the East German refugees for West Germany and the deadening impact of the Jordanian Arabs.

Apart from external economies in social overhead capital and dynamic forces, immigration has effects on total output and on income distribution.

It has been suggested by Abba Lerner that where diminishing returns exist, and where on that account marginal product is below average product, it might be possible for the receiving country to alter the market distribution of income after immigration in order to bribe existing workers to accept an inflow of labor. Immigration lowers the marginal product of labor and hence wage rates and raises the rent of unchanged factors such as land and capital. Government, however, could pay new workers their marginal product, but old workers their old wages, using part of the increase in rent in the system to make up the difference between the new and old marginal product. Since the marginal product in the new country is higher than in the old, everyone benefits from this operation.

To a certain extent this happens automatically, at least in the short run. Immigrants form a noncompeting group which takes on the dirty jobs that no one in the rest of the economy wants, such as the Italians who move into farm, hotel, and other service jobs, plus some in heavy industry, and free the Swiss to transfer to skilled work and offices. The immigrants may be sought because native labor is not available for particular tasks which would be remunerative with cheaper labor available from abroad: the slaves needed to make cotton planting pay in the 1830s and 1840s kept down wage rates in cotton-farming areas. Similarly, the importation of Mexican wetbacks and Puerto Rican truck-farm workers lowers wage rates at the margin. The pressure to halt immigration was primarily social but partly economic, the latter stemming from the newly powerful trade unions that emerged from the war.

Or the immigration may be needed to keep down wages in general, as in Germany. In part this may be the net effect of separate plants looking for workers, which ends up in the government establishing recruiting agencies overseas. Or it may be conscious. An authoritative writer on Latin America asserts that support for immigration into these countries comes from employer groups who are anxious to hold down wage rates and maintain rates of profit. As we have had occasion to observe in discussing tariff policy, one policy may recommend itself from an overall point of view, but another be adopted for distributional reasons where the factor or group which benefits wields political power. In this instance, however, it seems likely, as in the support given for free trade by Manchester liberals in the 1840s and Detroit manufacturers in the 1950s, that the distributional argument and the total efficiency argument overlap. While population is growing rapidly in many of these countries, such as Brazil and Venezuela, they have been underpopulated relative to resources and possess a fairly efficient network of social capital.

Apart from its economic merits, however, the proposal is highly academic for social reasons. In the long run, the immigrants will want to be assimilated in the receiving country and to end discrimination against them in wages. Social and cultural conditions, including the color of their skins, will affect how rapidly this comes about. But the pressure will be ineluctable.

Cosmopolitan Migration Policy

From a strictly economic point of view, which we are not warranted in taking in this discussion, the optimum policy for the world with respect to migration would be freedom of movement to equalize wages among those countries where the rate of population growth had shown some check. If there were no social and political inhibitions to movement, countries of immigration would experience a decline in wages, while wages would rise in countries of emigration. If the overpopulated country has not experienced the Malthusian revolution, however, unlimited migration can only equalize wages by reducing them abroad, as the reduction in the surplus population through emigration is replaced by natural increase.

This position is not fundamentally altered by the recent demographic counterrevolution in North America and in some countries of western Europe under which the large family was sought, despite its effect on the level of material income per capita, because large families were regarded as good in themselves. The enlarged family should be counted as part of real income. Income increases at a fixed income of $6,000 per family as family numbers rise from four to six, despite the decrease in income per capita from $1,500 to $1,000.

A special problem is posed by migration from a country where family limitation prevails to one where it is not needed, with the consequence of a return to much larger families. Ireland in the last half of the 19th century limited the rate of population increase by late marriages. Emigrants from Ireland to the United States were able to obtain incomes and marry at a much earlier age, with the result that the birthrate of the immigrants from Ireland was very much higher than that of the society they left. This case should probably be counted as one in which the Malthusian revolution had not been accomplished.

Technical Assistance

Current interest in economic development of underdeveloped areas, with its emphasis on technical assistance, suggests that the international transmission of technology through personal visits is a new phenomenon. This is not so. Flemish weavers taught their secrets to the British woolen industry in the 13th and 14th centuries. Somewhat later Lombardy merchants and bankers led the commercial revolution in London. After the Industrial Revolution, British engineers built the railroads of the Continent, and British textile and steel workers communicated their skills to French, German, and Italian factories and mills. Up to about 1830 it was illegal in Great Britain to export machinery, for fear of competition; but master workers coming to the United States or going to Belgium, France, Germany, and Italy smuggled it out or reproduced it upon arrival from drawings.

There are, to be sure, differences in the extent and character of international diffusion of technical capacity now as compared, say, to the 19th century. International organizations, national governments, and international corporations provide new institutions for this transmission which are evidently more efficient than the single worker or engineer or the limited colony of workers. The result is that international travel and foreign residence of skilled personnel, professional and manual, have reached new heights each year since World War II. Crews of Texas oil drillers can be encountered anywhere; teams from Morrison-Knudson, Krupp, and similar construction enterprises are found from Afghanistan to Zanzibar; economists from Scandinavia and the British dominions—which produce impressive surpluses for export—are found advising central banks, planning boards, and treasuries in Asia, Latin America, and Africa. A special kind of technical assistance, not always of a very high technical caliber but certain to spread an awareness of modern economic life and of the capacity of man to improve it, is the Peace Corps of the United States and its smaller European and British equivalents.

The impacts are not always on the receiving country. In the Europe of the 19th century it was normal for sons of merchants to spend six months or a year working in a foreign country or countries to acquire languages, learn bookkeeping, and acquire a knowledge of markets. Today it is reported that the Italian communists who went with the Fiat organization to Togliattigrad in the Soviet Union to build an automobile plant returned with a new understanding of economic and political issues in Italy, as well as those in the Soviet Union.

Freedom of Movement and Social Integration

Reduction in transport costs relative to income means that the populations of the world can mix with one another on an increasing scale. They become more aware of each other in other ways than travel—through motion pictures, magazines, radio, and television, including live overseas television by Telstar. But there is a significant difference between the interest of the outsider and the familiarity of the habitué who feels at home in what was once a strange environment. The social barriers against outsiders begin to be overcome when there have been so many trips that the traveler stops counting them. In some occupations persons have now stopped counting trips to Europe and Asia, as they once stopped counting trips between the East and West Coasts, and before that trips from Washington to New York or Los Angeles to San Francisco.

Much of the world is still far from mobile. Some of it is in the stage of first trips. But increasingly people are beginning to feel at home over wider areas. The Harvard Business School graduate of the 1930s probably had strong preferences for work in a region of the United States—East, South, Middle West, Far West; the graduate of the 1950s was usually content to work anywhere in the United States. Today's graduate is willing to be hired for work (for an American company and at an American salary) anywhere in the world. The parentheses in the last sentence indicate the room left to go. By the end of the century it seems inevitable that factor-price equalization will have taken care of the salary part, and social integration of the need to work with fellow countrymen.

The trend is clearly in this direction, to extend freedom of movement, on a scale which leads to social integration, to more and more groups and classes in societies in more and more countries. The mobility poses problems for countries with few facilities which are or feel threatened by the loss of particularly intelligent, well-trained, and energetic individuals. Love of country (and difficulties in learning foreign languages) will retain some. Interest in the different and narrower differential returns will attract similar people from abroad. That the movement of peoples will become an increasingly important aspect of international economics, however, there can be no doubt.

Summary

Labor moves across international boundaries in limited amounts, and generally in structured paths. Some movement is daily, seasonal, and institutionalized through companies and government bodies, and some is permanent. The pattern of migration in the 19th century tended to be synchronized with alternating long cycles in Europe and abroad. Waves of emigration from Britain, Ireland, Germany, and Scandinavia initially built up in cumulative fashion and then came to a halt as the difference in wage rates narrowed between Europe and the areas of settlement. From Italy and eastern Europe, however, the migration built up cumulatively until cut off by war and immigration quotas. Birthrates remained high, and there was no substantial domestic industry to assist in absorbing the rural surplus.

Large-scale European movements, mainly from the Mediterranean countries to Switzerland, Belgium, France, and Germany, have helped to create a European labor market. The Common Market for Scandinavia, and Britain and the Netherlands stand largely aloof from this movement.

Emigration benefits the sending country through remittances, improvement in the terms of trade as a result of expanding production abroad, and relief for structural unemployment. In one sense, however, the raising and education of able-bodied workers constitutes a capital investment when it is not clear that overpopulated countries should export capital. Emigration may also attract the most vigorous elements in a society. Immigration is desirable for a country, provided the process of social assimilation is not serious, if its population is below optimal. In addition, immigration may be undertaken for structural and distributional reasons. Immigration, however, may have dynamic effects in other circumstances which outweigh adverse economic considerations.

Technical assistance is provided partly by the written word, but most effectively through the international movement of people. Increased mobility is leading to wider intermingling on social and economic bases.

SUGGESTED READING

Texts

S. Enke and V. Salera, *International Economics*, 3d ed. (Englewood Cliffs, N.J.: Prentice-Hall, Inc., 1957), chap. 16; Kemp, chap. 9.

Treatises, Etc.

B. Thomas, *Migration and Economic Growth* (Cambridge, England: Cambridge University Press, 1954, revised and expanded, 1972), studies the experience of the Atlantic migration and contains a detailed bibliography. On migration in Europe and the creation of an international labor market, see C. P. Kindleberger, *Europe's Postwar Growth: The Role of Labor Supply* (Cambridge, Mass.: Harvard University Press, 1967), especially chaps. 9 and 10.

Papers by A. Scott and H. Rieben discuss respectively "Transatlantic and North American International Migration" and the "Intra-European Migration of Labour and Migration of High-level Manpower from Europe to North America" in C. P. Kindleberger and A. Shonfield, eds., *North American and Western European Economic Policies* Proceedings of a Conference held by the International Economic Association (New York: St. Martin's Press, 1971). The former has a bibliography. See also Walter Adams, ed., *The Brain Drain* (New York: The Macmillan Company, 1968).

H. Jerome, *Migration and Business Cycles* (New York: National Bureau of Economic Research, 1926), examines whether the push of depression is more significant than the pull of prosperity abroad. Meade, *Trade and Welfare*, chap. 27, studies the effects of factor movements.

Points

On the emigration from Germany to the United States, largely social but with some economic analysis, see M. Walker, *Germany and the Emigration, 1816–1885* (Cambridge, Mass.: Harvard University Press, 1964).

Chapter 14

LONG-TERM PORTFOLIO CAPITAL

Forms of Long-Term Capital

Long-term capital movements take place through instruments of longer than one-year maturity; short-term capital movements, through currency, demand deposits, bills of exchange, commercial paper, time deposits, and the like, up to a year. The distinction between portfolio capital and direct investment is that the latter carries with it control of a business; the former does not. Long-term capital is typically embodied in bonds and stocks but can be in notes, convertible debenture bonds, term loans (made by banks), and the like. A significant distinction is between governments and private lenders, although this is occasionally muddied when private loans receive a government guarantee. Governments borrow as well as lend, of course, but if governments borrow from the private market, without a guarantee by another government, they must meet the market test, just like private borrowers.

Long-term capital flows can take place through the flotation of new securities, typically bonds, or by trading in outstanding securities. A considerable international flow of capital, for example, takes the form of purchases and sales of existing securities on the New York Stock Exchange. Foreigners trade substantially in the leading American stocks, just as American investors trade in Royal Dutch/Shell, Pechiney, Rhône-Poulenc, British Petroleum, Imperial Chemical Industries, and many more European and Japanese stocks. In what follows we will deal primarily, however, with the movement of capital through new bond issues.

The first part of the chapter deals with long-term lending among relatively developed countries. Thereafter we focus on some particular problems and points of view raised by foreign borrowing by developing countries.

New Bond Issues

The traditional form of long-term lending is the bond. For 100 years, up to 1914, the sterling bond dominated world financial markets. For a period from 1919 to 1930, the New York bond market assumed the role previously played by London. But this interlude was brief. Excessive lending, international disequilibrium, depression, the collapse of export markets, the notoriety given to certain questionable practices by bond promoters, all combined to turn the investor away from foreign bonds, except for those of Canada, which have never really been regarded as foreign. With few, but perhaps gradually increasing, exceptions, moreover, borrowers no longer liked fixed obligations in an uncertain world. The foreign bond fell on evil days.

After World War II, with the reestablishment of convertibility of European currencies, the New York bond market experienced a revival. European capital markets were compartmentalized. Those like the Swiss and Dutch which had low rates of interest limited issues to relatively small amounts. Others that could handle larger sums had high rates. The New York long-term market gradually overcame its antipathy to foreign issues and undertook new issues of bonds not only for Canada and Israel (the latter with a large element of charity about them), but also for European, Dominion, and Japanese borrowers. The net was smaller than the gross, since European investors, impressed with the breadth and liquidity of the New York market, bought dollar bonds issued by European borrowers, even though the rate of interest on New York issues was below that obtainable in Europe. So substantial was the expansion of the market that, given the weakness of the U.S. balance of payments, the Treasury authorities in July 1963 imposed a prohibitive tariff on new securities, the Interest Equalization Tax (IET). The market then moved to Europe, where Euro-dollar bonds, i.e., bonds denominated in dollars, were issued and bought, by borrowers and lenders, outside the United States. Although such a market was smaller than the dollar bond market located in New York, with the strength of U.S. investors behind it, it remained at close to $1 billion of new issues a year, an amount well in excess of the foreign bond markets—both national and international—available in Europe.

The eclipse of the bond after 1928 or 1929 led to new forms of foreign lending. Some was private banking, some government lending at long term, some government banking. From 1930 to 1950 some private long-term lending by banks had been limited to advances against gilt-edged security, such as gold, or to loans made with governmental guarantees. In the 1950s there was renewed banking interest in medium-term financing of international trade, in part under the provisions of the little-used Edge Act of 1919 and in part with the help of an Export-Import Bank program of credits and guarantees. After the IET European borrowers switched to long-term bank loans from the United States until the Gore amendment to the IET made the tax apply also to bank loans of more than one year. Governmental lending has been carried on partly through banking institutions such as the Export-Import Bank in the United States and, since 1946, partly through international agencies such as the International Bank for Reconstruction and Development (IBRD), the Inter-American Development Bank, the European Investment Bank, and the Asian Development Bank. Other governmental lending has taken place through specially created institutions such as the Lend-Lease Administration, the Economic Cooperation Administration, the Mutual Security Agency, the International Cooperation Agency, and the Agency for International Development, or has been arranged for particular purposes such as ship disposal or disposal of surplus commodities.

We may restrict ourselves, therefore, to private lending through the bond market and government lending in its many long-term forms. The flow of capital through bank loans can be neglected on the grounds that it conforms largely to the principles of one or the other.

Foreign and Domestic Investment

Foreign investment is similar to domestic investment in that it increases income and employment in the process of capital formation and ultimately enlarges capacity for higher income after the capital has been formed. On the first score, loans lead to increased employment and income when the proceeds are spent on exports to obtain command over real resources either by the borrower himself or by the party who bought the foreign exchange from the borrower. On the second, foreign capital increases income through time in the same way that domestic investment does, although one needs to make a distinction between "national income" and "geographic product." If country A lends to country B, which adds to its productive capital, A's receipt of interest from B increases its national income received but not its net national product. Not all of B's increase in geographic product can increase its national income, since, under the terms of the loan, interest (which is part of geographic product) must be subtracted and paid to A. Hence such interest is counted in A's, not B's, national income.

The foreign lending alters factor proportions in the two countries from what they would have been without foreign investment. Foreign investment leaves domestic factor proportions unchanged and forestalls an increase in the capital/labor ratio, which would have raised the marginal product of labor and lowered that of capital had the capital been invested domestically. One should accordingly expect labor to oppose foreign lending, in the same fashion that it has in the past approved of tariffs on labor-intensive imports. In recent years such concern has begun to be expressed by labor, but primarily in the direct investment field, where the connection between the foreign investment and local jobs can be clearly seen.

One old distinction made by Keynes turned on the location of the physical assets. The private investor runs risks whether he invests at home or abroad. If he makes a mistake in judgment and his investment proves worthless in the case of domestic investment, the physical assets at least are within the national boundaries, but if the unsuccessful investment is foreign, the physical assets accrue to foreigners. This distinction is an appropriate one if the risk he incorrectly judges is that of confiscation by government authority without adequate compensation. But it cannot be made for economic risks. A worthless factory or railroad is worthless whether at home or abroad; and an asset with some salvage value can be sold for that value, again whether at home or abroad.

With perfect international capital markets, there would be one interest rate all over the world. But of course such perfect capital markets are far from achieved. There are risks of default and confiscation, which require a subjective risk premium, different for each country, before capital will flow from a safe home market to countries abroad. Moreover, most investors and borrowers are myopic in that their horizons are restricted to the home territory, both for investments and for loans. (This is not necessarily irrational, as there is a cost to obtaining information on investments and opportunities for loans abroad.)

Economists like to play with the idea that it would pay a country to limit the movement of capital abroad, if the unrestricted movement of capital lowered the interest rate abroad. The domestic price of capital under optimum lending should be equal to the marginal rate of return on foreign capital, not the average rate, if the two differed, as would be the case if the lending country were a price maker in the world capital market. The analogy with the optimum tariff is exact. Under an optimum tariff strategy it pays to limit exports and/or imports and, if the nation's trade has an impact on world prices, to equate relative prices at home to marginal rates of transformation abroad, not average rates. So with lending. There is even a small literature which combines the optimum tariff with the optimum level of foreign lending. This literature contributes to theoretical elegance more than to practical relevance.

Foreign bond markets tend, on the whole, to be competitive. Where there is private intervention organized by the bond buyers, as in the case of Switzerland, its purpose is to provide the lenders with a wide choice of investment issues, rather than with the highest possible return. By limiting the size of foreign issues to SF 60 million (about $14 million) the oligopolistically organized market optimizes the spread of risk, not the rate of return.

Institutional Pattern of Lending

The imperfection of the international capital market may have been diminishing prior to the IET, as a consequence of better communication and transport in the modern age, but it is still marked. Well-established attitudes of investors, practices of investment banking houses, governmental intervention, and controls have all contributed to confining capital movements to well-worn paths. To use a hydrological analogy, capital flows not as in broad rivers which equalize levels over a vast area, but as in irrigation canals and ditches which bring moisture to some areas and not to others, even though they may be on a lower level and need it more. In these circumstances, the understanding of capital movements calls more for the techniques of the historian, who can explain where the channels of capital flow were dug, than the analysis of the economist, who merely describes the supply and demand for capital in separate markets without indicating how, and to what extent, they are connected.

From about 1825 to 1850, British foreign lending was largely to Continental borrowers, with the largest amounts sought for railroads and the associated supplying industries. With the revolutions of 1848, however, British investors turned away from European loans to lending to the Empire, the United States, and, gradually, the Middle East and Latin America. The emphasis continued on railroads, although the fact that colonial issues qualified as trustee investments, i.e., as approved for investors requiring very safe securities, helped sell the bonds of colonial governments at rates approaching British government yields. The movement of capital to specific countries would follow a learning-process growth pattern: loans to Argentina, for example, started slowly in the 1880s and spurted from 1885 until the crash of Baring Brothers in 1890.

After getting its railroads started with British help, France turned to lending elsewhere on the Continent, largely for railroads and industrial banks, rather than developing capital issues for other French industries. French financiers and engineers contributed importantly to the development of Germany, Italy, Spain, and Austria. The high commissions received by French banking houses and the corruption of the press by foreign borrowers led to the flotation of numerous dubious issues. The czarist government, for example, managed to issue in Paris loans which it could not sell or refund in London or Berlin.

It is a still open question whether British and French foreign lending diverted abroad capital which could have been profitably employed at home. The city of London and the Paris bourse were widely accused at home of having slowed down the growth of Britain and France prior to World War I by lending abroad for purposes of lower economic utility than loans refused at home.

In the interwar period, the demands of capital for reconstruction took London and Paris out of international lending, except for a continued flow of British loans to the Empire, then in process of becoming the Commonwealth. New York took over as the world's financial center and went in for an orgy of foreign bond issues, particularly those for Germany and Latin America. Big underwriting commissions led to abuses, including the high-pressure selling of bonds by investment banking subsidiaries of New York banks at times when they had private knowledge of the borrower's default. New York also took the place of London as the provider of investment capital to Canada, with U.S. insurance companies, which deny that they buy foreign bonds, ready to admit in the next breath that of course they buy Canadian.

The revival of the New York bond market in the late 1950s until it was hit over the head with the IET was largely for European borrowers, the Dominions, and Japan (apart from the IBRD and Israel). Most of the developing countries needed still to establish their credit worthiness. Mexico was one that did. The IET did not apply to Canada, to the less developed countries, or to Japan up to a limit of $100 million a year. Despite its exemption, however, Mexico chose to borrow in the Euro-dollar bond market, at higher interest rates, in an effort to maintain its good credit standing in the New York market.

Government Control

The effect of qualifying colonial issues for trustee investment in Britain has been mentioned. In France in the 19th century, the Foreign Office attempted to foster loans for its allies and restrain them for others. In the United States in the 1920s, the State Department asked the financial community to advise it of contemplated loans, so that it might enter an objection to a loan whose purposes were contrary to U.S. foreign policy. The basis for possible objection was purely political and had nothing to do with the soundness of the loan in question. Later, when the Securities and Exchange Commission was established, foreign borrowers, including foreign governments, were required by law to file a registration statement with the commission, prior to the issuance of new obligations, setting forth a host of financial data by which the soundness of the loan might be judged. These data included balance-of-payments statements as well as material on the national income, government expenditure and receipts, and so forth. The SEC passed no judgment on the merits of a particular loan but was concerned solely to ensure that the borrower made full disclosure of information which would enable a purchaser of the bonds to judge these merits for himself.

Diplomatic representations are also made by governments in connection with default on obligations to their nationals by foreign governments. In another day not long ago, U.S. Marines were used to protect U.S. property abroad and to assist countries in the recognition of obligations to American investors. Today, questions of default are regarded as primarily the concern of private groups, such as the Council of Foreign Bondholders in the United States. These groups are entitled to and receive the support of their governments in presenting their cases, to such an extent in Britain that the United Kingdom council is regarded as a quasi-official body. This concern and assistance of government, however, are far from "control."

Government has been associated with international lending in other ways. The Johnson Act of 1934, for example, prohibited borrowing from the public by foreign governments which were in default on obligations to the U.S. government. This act, passed at the peak of isolationist sentiment in the United States, did not have to be repealed to enable the United States to lend to Britain in the early stages of World War II. It did not apply to the government itself or to its subsidiaries as the Reconstruction Finance Corporation. Even if it had, there might still have been room for the United States to lease or give equipment to other nations, under some authority as that of the Lend-Lease Act of 1941, so long as it did not lend money.

The major governmental intervention in long-term lending, however, has been for two reasons: (1) the protectionist purpose of reserving the local capital market for domestic borrowers, and notably for the government itself, and (2) to safeguard the balance of payments. In the European Common Market it was agreed more or less without thinking about it that integrating the European capital market would be a good thing. When the EEC appointed a group to investigate the problems of so doing, it was found that virtually all of the Six had discriminatory regulations which favored domestic over foreign borrowers, most of them designed to assist the local government in borrowing cheaply to meet its capital needs and any possible deficit. The Experts' Committee recommended that these discriminatory regulations be removed. So much inertia is involved, however, that almost nothing has been accomplished.

The balance-of-payments issue must be postponed in its entirety until a later point in our analysis. This much can now be said. A group of experts discussing adjustment in the balance of payments stated rather blandly that if balance-of-payments difficulties arose because of "excessive capital movements," the remedy was to impose capital controls. This raises the question whether there is any presumption in favor of freedom of capital movements, comparable to the weak presumption in favor of free trade discussed in Chapter 12.

Capital Movements and Welfare

Factor-price equalization is an efficiency optimum and, with normal assumptions about distribution (e.g., that a dollar for one is equal to a dollar for another), a welfare optimum. If freedom of capital movements helps to move in the direction of equalization of the return to capital worldwide, it helps move toward a welfare optimum.

But first we must face the question whether freedom of capital movement does work toward equalization of capital returns. Where domestic capital goes abroad to evade taxes, it may move from jurisdictions where capital is scarce to those where it is abundant. Such a movement does not promote welfare. Where capital moves from poor to rich countries, for lack of complementary factors, it may again be contrary to Pareto optimality. Where market returns do not reflect social return because of distortions, there is another reason for inhibiting freedom of movement. Still another reason would be destabilizing speculation, a wave of capital seeking refuge, say, in Germany for fear of devaluation of the U.S. dollar, the British pound, or the Italian lira. The West German government adopted exchange controls in 1972 at the behest of the governors of the Bundesbank, and over the objection of Karl Schiller, the Finance Minister, who resigned. The possibilities that national interest rates may not reflect social values of abundance and scarcity and that private capital movements may not respond to market rates when they do are so pervasive that a number of economists believe that the presumption in favor of freedom of capital movement is very small indeed.

But thus far we have made only the negative case. The argument in favor of a national capital market in the United States is strong. Regions that have abundant savings can earn a higher return on them; regions with sizable capital needs can have them met more cheaply. Even if there were no net movement of savings, a single capital market would be useful, since there are economies of scale in joined capital markets. The wider number of borrowers and lenders provides the former with lower rates and the latter with greater liquidity, through trading on a broader market. This is why both California savers and borrowers move their operations to the New York capital market instead of just borrowing the net deficit— as is the case for net imports of goods.

When one region or country borrows and lends through different securities, again with no net capital movement, there is a gain in welfare through the reduction in risk from diversification. This was realized when it was proposed in Canada that the country mobilize its citizens' holdings of U.S. securities and exchange them for U.S. holdings of Canadian securities, including, to be sure, companies owned through direct investment. The reduction in number of securities the Canadian investor could buy was recognized instantly as a loss in welfare.

The argument for controlling capital flows rests then on second-best grounds. If capital movements flow in directions contrary to welfare, i.e., from capital-poor to capital-rich countries, without a gain in liquidity or diversification, it may be necessary to control them on second-best grounds, that is, because it is impossible to correct the underlying situation giving rise to the undesirable movement. The question still presents itself, however, whether it is possible.

The Feasibility of Controlling Capital Movements

When most investors and borrowers were myopic and scanned investment and borrowing opportunities limited largely to the domestic capital market and a few organized foreign securities, it was fairly easy to control international capital movements. Today, however, with much more mobility of persons and money, the question arises whether control of capital movements is technically possible. Much depends upon the discipline of a society. What might work well in a Scandinavian society accustomed to following governmental directives in an orderly fashion will not succeed in a Latin country emerging from foreign occupation in which civic virtue consisted of black-market operations. But there are technical as well as sociological aspects.

In July 1963, the U.S. government came to the conclusion that too much capital was flowing abroad through the foreign bond market for balance-of-payments comfort. It applied the IET to stop the flow, implicitly adhering to a partial-equilibrium view of the balance of payments. If $500 million of foreign lending were halted, the theory seemed to imply, the balance of payments would improve by $500 million.

The balance of payments, however, as we shall see in Chapter 18, is a macroeconomic phenomenon, which means that microeconomic remedies work badly, if at all; and it responds to general-equilibrium, not partial-equilibrium, reasoning. In 1963, interest rates were low in the United States, high in Europe. There were many individuals, firms, and banks, moreover, who were interested in maximizing by lending in the dearer market and borrowing in the cheaper. When one form of borrowing was halted, others were set in motion.

The first response was an increase in long-term bank lending. This was halted through the Gore amendment, applying the IET to bank-term loans. Secondly, international firms found they could earn more on Euro-dollar deposits in Europe than they could on liquid funds in the United States. Time money started to move to Europe through firms. This was halted for 400 firms in January 1965 through the so-called Voluntary Credit Restraint Program. The number of firms was raised to 700, to 900. In January 1968 the program was made mandatory—the so-called Mandatory Credit Program (MCP). Then American firms not permitted to send funds to Europe would go there and raise funds locally. If General Motors borrowed $100 million in Belgium to build a plant at Antwerp, this would raise interest rates in Belgium, shift local borrowers from Brussels and Antwerp to the Euro-dollar market in London, raise interest rates in London, and stimulate movements to London from Canada and from New York to Canada. Through the inefficient chain, some considerable amount of the moneys that General Motors was not allowed to bring to Belgium from New York got there from New York anyway, via the Canadian gap. Or an international firm would raise money in the Euro-dollar market by selling convertible debenture bonds. These would pay higher returns than securities of the same company issued in the United States. Foreign holders of the American securities would sell them, repatriate the proceeds, and use them to buy the Euro-dollar bonds. The foreign securities gap remained opened.

If two reservoirs are connected by a dozen pipes of some considerable size, cutting off a few pipes does not separate the levels of water. Foreign exchange control has never been efficient, even in the Nazi period in the 1930s, when violations carried the death penalty. In today's world, with hundreds of thousands of communications across national lines and with a commodity so fungible and easy to hide as money or securities, foreign exchange control is not likely to function effectively. To be sure of isolating the capital market of a country, one has to have censorship of mail, border searches of tourists, control of the credit terms of trade transactions, freezing not only of one's own nationals' dealings in foreign exchange but also foreigners' dealings in national assets—actions which civilized countries abhor, except in wartime. A sloppy control is inequitable, as large companies can find their way through the labyrinth of regulation fairly easily.

We are left then with something of an impasse. Capital controls are difficult, unaesthetic, but possibly necessary if one cannot work out the first-best policies of serene coordination of national monetary and capital-market policies. We will return to this issue later. First, however, we have to address a few issues of foreign bond lending of particular relevance to the developing countries. Some of them have a counterpart in the lending country.

Borrowing to Finance Imports

Prior to 1913, and to a lesser degree up to 1929, foreign borrowing had as its purpose the acquisition of resources in general, cheaply. Interest rates were lower abroad than at home. A country in need of purchasing power in order to undertake investment or even to make up a budget deficit borrowed abroad when the risk premium demanded by foreign investors was less than the difference in the rates of interest at home and abroad. In Dutch experience, for example, a company would borrow abroad one year, when interest rates were lower abroad than at home. The next year, when the position had reversed itself, Dutch investors would go abroad and buy back the whole issue.

During the depression, risk premiums rose, and domestic interest rates in the money markets of the developing countries tended to decline under cheap money policies. Purchasing power in general could be obtained at home. Foreign loans were sought to meet deficits in the balance of payments.

In today's world of development, another element has been added to the analysis. When a country can reallocate resources and faces a sufficient elastic demand for exports so that it can readily convert domestic resources into imports via exports, its only need for foreign loans for growth is to add to total resources for investment, i.e., to make up for any deficiency in savings. But not all countries are capable of such transformation. Imports may be a bottleneck to growth because of fixed ratios of foreign equipment in investment and the need for intermediate goods to utilize existing capacity. The stock of automobiles and trucks may need imported petroleum products to operate, or steel may need imported coal or iron ore. If domestic resources cannot be readily transformed into imports, either because of difficulties of reallocating resources internally at the existing level of output, or because of inelasticity of the demand for exports, foreign loans may be needed for imports.

Ronald McKinnon has suggested that in a simple growth model, in which growth depends on capital, the capital may be divided into foreign and domestic elements, each with different capital/output ratio, or a different relationship between the rate of growth and capital. It could happen that with abundant capacity to transform domestic resources and relatively elastic demand for exports, the bottleneck to growth which foreign loans are needed to break is merely domestic savings. Or foreign loans may be needed to buy bottleneck imports until capacity to produce exports or import substitutes is sufficiently enlarged. Or one bottleneck may bind for a while, and later the other. In Figure 14.1*a*, the relationship between the

The Contribution of Foreign Loans to Domestic Growth under Differing Assumptions about the Capacity to Transform Resources into Imports

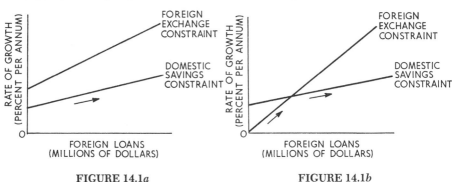

FIGURE 14.1*a*   FIGURE 14.1*b*

domestic savings and the foreign exchange constraints on growth is drawn so that it is the former that binds. In this case foreign loans are needed for general purchasing power, not to purchase specific imports. But in Figure 14.1*b*, the foreign exchange constraint is the binding one for a certain distance, until productive capacity has been sufficiently expanded. After that the limit is total savings. Attempts have been made to apply this analysis in more elaborate form to particular developing countries in connection with programming international aid.

Tied Loans

The incapacity of borrowing countries to transform gives rise to the necessity to borrow specifically for purchasing imports. The difficulties of lenders have led to the device of tying loans to the purchase of specific exports.

During the 1930s depression, loans were frequently made for the purpose of stimulating exports. The Export-Import Bank in the United States, for example, the Export Credit Guarantee Department in Britain, and similar organizations in other countries selling capital equipment found it necessary to provide governmental credit to continue to export machinery during the depression when the private international long-term market for capital collapsed. Here the purpose of the loan was to sell the exports. In some countries, such as Germany, moreover, there was never any thought of separating the finance from the sale of goods. But the problem posed by tied loans today is otherwise. Foreign loans or other forms of assistance are sought by the developing country. In order to prevent these loans from weakening the balance of payments of the United States, as the most notorious example, the loans are tied to expenditure in the United States.

Such tying of course violates the principle of Pareto optimality in which one should always purchase in the cheapest market. It would only happen by the rarest coincidence—at least in peacetime—that the cheapest market for the capital was also the cheapest market for the various imports to be bought with the proceeds of the loan. To the extent that tying is effective, it raises the cost of goods or reduces the value of the loan. The International Bank for Reconstruction and Development has estimated that the price level on which tied loans are spent is some 30 percent higher than the cheapest sources.

But tying is not always effective. Money is fungible, as we have indicated, and accountants over time achieve a certain low cunning. In partial equilibrium, with other things equal, a new loan which is tied will achieve its purpose. But other things have a habit of refusing to stay equal. Contemplate tied aid, for example. If military aid is available but economic aid is not, a country can switch its own resources from military to economic expenditure and, in effect, maintain the old level of military effort and expand the economic level. Or vice versa. It can shift a development project it was planning to undertake with the proceeds of exports to the lending country to a loan basis, and use the free exchange from exports for other purposes. Especially if it can transform its resources, a country can minimize the cost of tied loans (or tied aid) by using the loans (or aid) for inframarginal purposes, freeing up untied exchange for use at the margin.

In many countries, however, such capacity to transform is limited. Suppose such a country is interested in a domestic investment. In this circumstance, tying loans to the foreign exchange content of an investment can present a considerable obstacle.

Let us assume that a country wants to undertake the construction of a railroad as part of a program of economic development. The total cost of the project amounts to $100 million. Of this total, $50 million, we may say, represent the foreign exchange value of materials and equipment which must be bought from abroad; the remaining $50 million constitute costs to be incurred in local currency.

Under a system of tied loans, only $50 million could be borrowed in the United States, since the borrower must specify what U.S. goods are to be purchased with the loan. The United States may or may not be the cheapest place to buy the goods, but the loan is tied to U.S. goods. The remaining $50 million expended locally are likely to give rise to a foreign exchange requirement. Whether they will or not will depend upon how the local funds are obtained. If they are acquired through new savings or through taxation which reduces consumption, then the expenditure is not inflationary, i.e., it does not increase national money income or imports. If, on the other hand, as is frequently the case, some part or all of the local expenditure is financed through credit creation or deficit spending, the domestic expenditure will spill over into new imports. How large an increase in imports will occur depends on how much of the new spending goes for domestic resources and how much for imports, in the first instance and in successive rounds of spending. But there is no foreign exchange from the loan to finance these incremental imports. The exchange available was all used up on the first round of spending. Any increase from subsequent rounds of spending will have to be paid for out of reserves, or, if these are inadequate, it will lead to depreciation or foreign exchange control.

The Project Basis for Loans

The International Bank for Reconstruction and Development started out to make what were essentially tied loans, although the officials of the bank deny that they can properly be called such. Loans were made on a project basis, i.e., a borrowing country had to indicate the purpose for which the loan was sought, and this could not be so vague as "to fill the deficit in the budget." Moreover, the borrower originally was required to specify what new imports were needed for the project, and where these would be bought. If it approved the project and regarded the imports as reasonable, the bank was then prepared to lend the moneys needed to finance the imports.

This procedure, which the bank has now altered, was objectionable on two scores. It was "discriminatory," and it was likely to increase rather than mitigate the foreign exchange difficulties of the borrowing country. The discriminatory feature is found in the fact that the bank loaned currency which the country expected to spend, rather than loaning purchasing power in general. In a completely nondiscriminatory system, loans would be provided from the cheapest source—that is, the money market with the lowest interest rates—and the proceeds of these loans would be spent where the goods sought were cheapest. Dollars might be borrowed and spent in Britain, or, as during the 19th century, pounds might be borrowed and spent on the Continent. To lend only the currencies to be spent is to require the borrower either to borrow in a dearer market for loans or to buy in the dearer market for goods, unless the cheapest markets for goods and loans are the same. This objection was not perhaps important in practice up to 1950, because goods as well as loans were cheaper in the United States. But the principle of tying the currency of the loan to the currency of the projected import is discriminatory.

In the second place, a loan limited to the cost of imports needed for a project is insufficient to balance the international accounts except in the limiting case where all the local expenditure is raised in a deflationary fashion. Any inflationary financing of local expenditures of the project will raise income and imports and unbalance the international accounts. Purchasing power in general is neglected in favor of a limited amount of foreign purchasing power in particular. These loans and projects worsened rather than improved the country's balance of payments.

Capacity to Absorb Capital

The International Bank, which we will discuss at greater length below, has argued that the problem it faces is not lack of funds but lack of projects. The capacity to absorb foreign loans, it holds, is limited. What determines the capacity to absorb loans?

The earlier analysis in terms of alternative bottlenecks—foreign exchange or total savings—is relevant here. If there is no bottleneck, the capacity to absorb capital is a function of the cutoff point at which projects of diminishing productivity cease to be interesting. The payoff which indicates the limit may be a rate of productivity of 20 percent a year, or 10 percent or 5 or zero. But the view that the capacity to absorb capital is limited, or kinked, supposes there are more bottlenecks such as administrative capacity, skilled labor needed in fixed proportions, or the engineering talent to prepare project proposals for submission to the IBRD. Many of these bottlenecks could be broken by more foreign loans used to hire specific talent from abroad, although the concept may implicitly assume that the country uses its own administrative or engineering talent. When it is recognized that the notion of a limited capacity to absorb capital rests on the existence of bottlenecks, it would seem sensible not to accept the limit, but to break the bottleneck.

Cumulative Lending

If foreign investment is broadly similar to domestic investment, it follows that a country with a deficiency of investment opportunities at home relative to savings should lend abroad, and one with a deficiency of savings at home relative to investment opportunities should borrow abroad. But there are those who worry about the necessity of continuing to lend or borrow. It is objected, for example, that foreign loans cannot long offset a deficiency of domestic investment opportunities because of interest and possible amortization. Suppose, it is argued, a country wants to maintain an export surplus on current account of $1 billion annually. The first year it can lend $1 billion abroad. The subsequent year, however, it will have to lend $1 billion more, plus enough to enable the foreign borrowers to pay interest on the first year's loan and amortization, if the loan contract calls for regular repayments. The higher the rates of interest and amortization, the more rapidly will the rate of lending increase to sustain the stipulated export surplus. Table 14.1, taken from an article by Randall Hinshaw,

TABLE 14.1. Annual Amount of 20-Year Loans Required at Various Interest Rates, to Maintain an Annual Export Surplus of $1,000,000,000* (billions of dollars)

| | Percent | | | | |
Year	2	3	4	5	6
5th	1.35	1.38	1.43	1.47	1.52
10th	1.81	1.92	2.03	2.16	2.31
15th	2.44	2.65	2.90	3.18	3.50
20th	3.28	3.67	4.14	4.68	5.32
25th	4.41	5.08	5.90	6.88	8.09

* It is assumed that the sum of interest plus amortization on each loan is paid in equal installments.

shows the effect of interest at various rates with amortization. In another table which we do not reproduce, the compound interest arithmetic is carried still further; $46.90 billion would have to be invested as a perpetual loan without amortization if one assumes 8 percent interest and calculates the requirement for the 50th year.

This analysis is applicable to amortization, which is an abnormal capital movement involving difficulties of repayment unless offset by new capital lending. The Export-Import Bank, and increasingly the International Bank for Reconstruction and Development, must undertake each year a substantial amount of new loans if they are to avoid the contractual repayments on old loans producing an inward movement of capital to the dollar area from weaker currencies. To help equalize marginal efficiencies of capital, movement of capital from capital-rich to capital-poor countries should involve perpetual loans, such as fixed assets which are kept intact, or British consols. In fact, however, the loans are made for short periods and involve periodic repayments of principal.

The requirement of amortization is a further illustration of the fallacy of composition: useful in the case of an individual loan, it complicates foreign lending as a whole by constituting an uphill movement of capital unless offset by new loans.

Leaving aside amortization, the changing of interest on old loans seems to raise a problem. If lending stops, the payment of contractual interest turns the balance of trade against the lending country. The rate of increase in foreign loans outstanding must equal the rate of interest received on foreign loans to prevent such a shift. If the productivity and income of a country grow at the same rate as the level of the rate of interest at which it lends abroad, and it, on this account, lends abroad at the same rate, the balance of trade, other things equal, will remain constant.

But this analysis is uninteresting. It is partial equilibrium in character when it should not be, holding other things equal when in the nature of events they must alter. It makes no sense to cling to the objective of maintaining a constant export surplus as the only way of offsetting an existing excess of savings over investment opportunities, if in fact the receipt of income from abroad raises spending for consumption and gives employment to the resources involved. Nor is the borrowing country condemned to borrow in order to pay interest, if in fact the original loan is invested productively and yields an income out of which interest can be paid. The problem of a geometric growth of lending to stay in the same place would be a real one only if all income from loans were saved, on the one hand, and all loans were consumed rather than invested in capital formation, on the other.

Take first the lending country. It lends and receives an income in the first year. This income has a multiplier effect just like, or almost just like, an increase in exports. The moneys from abroad will be partly spent on domestic goods, partly spent on imports, and partly saved. The amount saved in the first round of income creation reduces the multiplier below that for normal exports, so that the foreign interest multiplier may be somewhat smaller than the foreign-trade multiplier. It is analogous to the balanced budget theorem known to students with a knowledge of the finer points of income analysis. That portion spent at home in the first round and respent in subsequent rounds of spending, however, will employ part of the resources previously engaged in foreign investment. The need to maintain an export surplus will progressively diminish.

The Need to Borrow Interest

In the borrowing country, the notion that a country must borrow to pay interest on old loans is unacceptable. Latin-American observers are continuously comparing debt service on old loans with new loans, often making statements such as, "The United States is taking more out of Latin America in profits and interest than it is putting back in new investments." Evsey Domar, in an article, worked out that the balance of payments of a borrowing country would turn adverse unless the rate of growth of total lending was equal to the rate of interest on outstanding loans. Put into a formula,

$$R = \frac{a+i}{a+r},$$

where R is the borrowing country's balance of payments (the ratio of debits to credits), a is the rate of amortization, i is the rate of interest on outstanding loans, and r is the rate of growth of new loans. So long as i is less than r, R is less than 1, and the balance of payments remains favorable.

But this analysis is far from complete. It is appropriate, perhaps, to lending for consumption to people at the subsistence level. As loan sharks know, if a poor man falls behind and has to borrow, his borrowing has to increase geometrically. But when loans are contracted for productive purposes, each loan should pay its own way, producing new exports or saving on old imports, sufficient to pay its debt service. Under the Domar–Latin-American analysis, it would be impossible to borrow for a single project without going increasingly into debt through eternity, which is absurd. What should be compared is not new lending with old interest, but new lending with new imports for capital investment, and old interest with the increase in exports and decrease in imports arising from the productivity of old investment. If subscripts 0, 1, 2, and so on, indicate time, L stands for loans, X and M for exports and imports, and i for interest, the balance of payments at the several stages (amortization being left out) should look like this:

Stage I

$$\frac{M_0 + dM_{cap_0}}{X_0 + L_0},$$

where $L_0 = dM_{cap_0}$ is the transfer process.

Stage II

$$\frac{M_0 + iL_0 - dM_{L_0} + dM_{cap_1}}{X_0 + dX_{L_0} + L_1}, \text{ etc.}$$

Thus iL_0 (the interest on the original loan) should not be matched against L_1 (the borrowing of the next period) but with $+ dX_{L_0}$ and $- dM_{L_0}$ (the increase in exports and decrease in imports made possible by the productivity of L_0). This is done in the line encircling them. And new loans, if any, should be used for transfers of new goods ($L_1 = dM_{\text{cap}_0}$), not to pay interest on old debt.

The reasoning must be qualified in some cases: where a project has a long period of gestation, its productivity does not produce exports or import substitutes immediately. Here it is necessary to borrow the interest until production gets under way. But this merely says that the real amount of capital borrowed is more than the face amount by the accumulated interest to the period of production. The High Dam at Aswan, for example, for which it took 10 years to get production under way, cost $1 billion or so in face amount of capital, plus 10 years' interest. Or the borrowing is for domestic projects and the country is facing an exchange bottleneck as in Figure 14.1b or is unable to transform resources. In this case, it must be expected that the country will ultimately be able to achieve increased productivity which it can direct into export-increasing or import-reducing activities, or the case is similar to a consumption loan. And consumption should be financed by aid, rather than lending.

If the borrowing country does not need to borrow the interest, neither does the lending country have to lend it. Britain at the end of the 19th century did lend roughly each year about as much as it received as interest on its outstanding debt, but there is no analytical connection between the two items in the balance of payments. Individual recipients of income from overseas investment mingled that income with income from domestic sources and then divided disposable income between consumption and savings, and the latter into savings invested at home and savings invested abroad. Some corporations directly reinvested foreign earnings abroad (as well as remitting dividends to Britain). But there was and is no necessary condition between overseas earnings and overseas investment.

Debt Service Ratio

The increase in postwar borrowing by developing countries has recently excited interest that some countries may have borrowed too much and be on the verge of default. The shorthand measure for the extent of a country's involvement is the ratio of its debt service—interest and amortization—to the current value of exports. This ratio on the average was under 5 percent on public debt for the developing countries after World War II until about 1955. Thereafter it rose to more than 10 percent in 1965. A number of countries have defaulted in this period—Argentina, Brazil, Chile, Turkey, and so on. Others have been rescued by international consortia. Still others, such as Indonesia and Ghana, which contracted debt for military operations and spectacular but impractical development projects, face very high debt service ratios and a strong possibility of the need to readjust external commitments.

The debt service ratio is hardly the neatest possible concept. As the ratios on the previous page indicate, interest should be related to the increase in exports and the decrease in imports. Equally or more important in the background are the capacity to transform resources from one sector to another, the productivity of new investment, and the marginal propensity to save out of increased income. Where a country maintains an overvalued exchange rate, with domestic inflation in excess of external depreciation, the outlook for its ability to maintain service on its debt is dim. The tendency to single out a particular ratio as critical in analysis is understandable, but the message of this chapter is that the economist must have his eye on a wide variety of aspects of international borrowing. Particularly critical points are that loans should be invested productively; that some considerable portion of the productivity should be skimmed off, part to pay debt service and part to save for new projects; that the economy must be able to reallocate resources from domestic to export and import-competing activities, to transfer the productivity subtracted for debt service abroad; and that the economy must not be otherwise mismanaged. These are perhaps rigorous conditions in today's world, but their fulfillment would make it possible to abandon a whole service of illogical views and expedients in the field of foreign lending from tied loans to insistence on the lending of the interest on past loans.

Summary

There are many forms of foreign capital movement, but the traditional one, which had virtually died out but is now coming back, is the foreign bond. Foreign investment is like domestic investment insofar as multiplier and growth effects on national income are concerned. There are differences in effects on factor proportions.

Capital flows internationally in deep channels dictated by institutional considerations as well as by differences in the marginal productivity of capital. Government control has been an important influence. Government also has developed into an important international lender, making stabilization loans and loans to finance particular projects or particular exports or imports.

Free movement of capital may not contribute to Pareto optimality if market prices diverge from private values, but the presumption of some economists that capital controls are generally justified flies in the face of external economies from joined capital markets, gains through diversification, and gains from moving capital from where it is abundant to where it is scarce. Foreign exchange control is difficult to apply except in highly disciplined countries.

There is general objection to tied loans, on the ground that they depart from the welfare-maximizing principle which calls for borrowing in the cheapest market for capital and buying in the cheapest market for goods. The project basis for loans is analytically unacceptable because of its tied feature, and in addition because borrowing countries typically need help in financing their general balance-of-payments deficits created by investment projects, not merely the projects' foreign exchange content.

The debt service ratio, which relates interest and amortization on outstanding foreign debt to the value of exports, is a crude measure of a country's capacity to borrow abroad, invest productively at home, and service its debt.

SUGGESTED READING

Texts

Kemp, chaps. 11, 12 and 13. For a good account of 19th-century lending, with tables and references to the literature, see W. Woodruff, *Impact of Western Man* (New York: St. Martin's Press, 1966), chap. 4, including notes to tables and bibliography. See also R. F. Mikesell, *Public International Lending for Development* (New York: Random House, Inc., 1966) (paperback).

Treatises, Etc.

For a modern rounded treatment, partly historical, partly descriptive, and partly analytical, see J. H. Adler, ed., *Capital Movements and Economic Development*, Proceedings of a Conference held by the International Economic Association (New York: St. Martin's Press, 1967). An international capital market among the developed countries is criticized in essays by R. N. Cooper and A. Lamfalussy in C. P. Kindleberger and A. Shonfield, eds., *North American and Western European Economic Policies* (New York: St. Martin's Press, 1971), but held necessary by R. N. Cooper and E. M. Truman in "An Analysis of the Role of International Capital Markets in Providing Funds to Developing Countries," *Weltwirtschaftliches Archiv* (June 1971) (in English).

For accounts of 19th-century lending by Britain, see L. H. Jenks, *The Migration of British Capital to 1875* (New York: Alfred A. Knopf, Inc., 1927); H. Feis, *Europe: The World's Banker, 1870–1913* (New Haven, Conn.: Yale University Press, 1931) (paperback, W. W. Norton & Co., Inc., 1966); C. K. Hobson, *The Export of Capital* (London: Constable & Co., Ltd., 1914); A. K. Cairncross, *Home and Foreign Investment, 1870–1913* (Cambridge, England: Cambridge University Press, 1953); and R. E. Cameron, *France and the Economic Development of Europe, 1800–1913* (Princeton, N.J.: Princeton University Press, 1960).

On the pure theory, see R. A. Mundell, "International Trade and Factor Mobility," in American Economic Association, *Readings in International Economics;* R. W. Jones, "International Capital Movements and the Theory of Tariffs and Trade," *QJE*, February 1967; and M. C. Kemp, "Foreign Investment and the National Advantage," in *Economic Record,* March 1961. An attempt to measure the welfare effects of U.S. capital controls is provided by N. S. Fieleke, "The Welfare Effects of Controls over Capital Exports from the United States," *EIF*, January 1971.

Points

The distinction between the foreign exchange and the savings bottleneck to growth is made in R. I. McKinnon, "Foreign Exchange Constraints in Economic Development and Efficient Aid Allocation," *EJ*, June 1964.

On the capacity to absorb capital, see J. H. Adler, *Absorptive Capacity* (Washington, D.C.: The Brookings Institution, 1965).

The compound interest problem is discussed in R. Hinshaw, "Foreign Investment and American Employment," *AER*, May 1946; W. S. Salant, "The Domestic Effects of Capital Export under the Point Four Program," *AER*, May 1950; and E. D. Domar, "Foreign Investment and the Balance of Payments" *AER*, December 1950.

The debt service ratio is analyzed in a series of books by D. Avramovic and others of the Economics Division of the IBRD, the latest of which is D. Avramovic et al., *Economic Growth and External Debt* (Baltimore, Md.: The Johns Hopkins Press, 1964).

An excellent institutional discussion of the requirements of an integrated capital market is given in European Economic Community, *The Development of a European Capital Market* (Brussels, 1967).

Chapter 15

THE THEORY OF DIRECT INVESTMENT

Perhaps the most sensitive area in international economics today is direct investment. The United States and Britain try to restrain direct investment by companies domiciled within their borders, in order to limit the pressure on their balances of payments. Canada, European countries, and Japan seek to limit foreign investment within their borders lest their control over domestic resources be diluted by foreign ownership. Developing countries worry both that foreigners will invest in them and that they won't, fearing exploitation on the one hand and inadequate access to foreign capital and technology on the other. Prohibitions and restrictions are laid down against investment in certain lines of activity which are regarded as peculiarly vulnerable to foreign influence or particularly wasteful—natural resources, banking, newspapers, retail trade, soft drinks. Conditions are laid down that there must be local participation, foreign exchange brought from abroad, training, components purchased locally, domestic research, exports, and so on. And still the trend toward internationalization of the firm continues.

This chapter explores the theory of direct investment, how it differs from the movement of portfolio capital, and its impacts on efficiency, welfare, and the balance of payments of home (investing) and host (in which the investment takes place) countries. In the next chapter we will discuss policies toward direct investment from the host-country and cosmopolitan points of view. The student is reminded that the subject evokes strong emotions. He should be wary of any alleged objectivity on the part of the author, but should also be prepared to acknowledge any bias of his own.

Direct Investment as Capital Movement

It used to be thought that the major difference between portfolio and direct investment was that direct investment involved control, whereas portfolio investment did not. Control was a legal concept and rested on

245

100, 98, 51, or 48 percent ownership of the equity of a foreign corporation. Or control was thought of in decision-theory terms, which meant that the head office made decisions respecting foreign operations, within a clearly laid-out scheme, on such questions as choice of top personnel, new products, capital budgeting, research and development, and dividend policy. But direct investment was a capital movement combined with control and perhaps other elements, such as technology.

It was observed, however, that direct investment often did not involve a capital movement. A firm would undertake investment abroad with funds borrowed in the local country. It might provide the equity in foreign exchange, but if it were going into a joint venture, this equity investment might take the form of patents, machinery, technology, or other real considerations. Once the investment became profitable, moreover, it grew from local borrowing and reinvested profits. Direct investment represented not so much an international capital movement as capital formation undertaken abroad.

Other theories were not lacking. In one view direct investment was akin to gambling. A firm undertook a small investment abroad and tried to pyramid it into a large stake, much as a gambler leaves his winnings on the table. It was noticed that 50 percent of profits on direct investment was reinvested on balance, so the rule of thumb developed that direct investment withdrew half its earnings and pyramided the other half. Or direct investment was the last stage in a technological cycle, along lines touched on in Chapter 4. First comes domestic production, then exports, and when imitation abroad is about to take over, the company undertakes production abroad. This is akin to the **"defensive investment"** concept of Alexander Lamfalussy. Some investment, he asserted, with reference to domestic capital formation, is motivated not by the desire to make profits but in order to avoid losses. The marginal rate of return on this investment is equal to any other, measuring from the expected loss to the low profit. But the average is low. It is better to enter a market with a low expected profit than to get pushed out of it altogether. This theory is related to a business view: direct investment is undertaken where there are large and growing markets. It is markets, not profits, which guide it. Where markets exist, profits will be found in the long run.

Monopolistic Competition

While each of these explanations has a piece of the truth, none has the power and the generality of that of Stephen Hymer in his M.I.T. thesis on "The International Operations of National Firms." In this view, direct investment belongs to the theory of monopolistic competition rather than that of international capital movements. A local company has an advantage over a foreign company, other things being equal. It is expensive to operate at a distance, expensive in travel, communication, and especially in mis-understanding. To overcome the inherent native advantage of being on the ground, the firm entering from abroad must have some other advantage not shared with its local competitor. The advantage typically lies in technology or patents. It may inhere in special access to very large amounts of capital, amounts far larger than the ordinary national firm can command. It may have better access to markets in foreign countries merely by reason of its international status. Or the company, as in petroleum refining or metal processing, may coordinate operations and invested capital requirements at various stages in a vertical production process and, because of its knowl-edge of requirements at each stage and the heavy cost of inventories, be able to economize through synchronizing operations. It may merely have differentiated products built on advertising. Or it may have truly superior management. But some special advantage is necessary if the firm is going to be able to overcome the disadvantage of operating at a distance.

The firm must be able not only to make higher profits abroad than it could at home, but it must also be able to earn higher profits abroad than local firms can earn in their own markets. For all its imperfections, the international capital market would be expected to be able to transfer mere capital from one country to another better than a firm whose major pre-occupations lie in production and marketing.

The implications of this theory of direct investment are many. For one, direct investment will not occur in industries with pure competition. Few farmers operate overseas, nor do retail distributors other than Sears Roe-buck, or many representatives of the textile, clothing, leather and so forth, industries. Second, a company is not interested in acquiring local partners in a joint venture, seeking to keep the good thing for itself; at the same time, the local investors naturally resist the suggestion that they should buy the shares of the parent company: the return on the overall stock is diluted as compared with the profitability of the local situation which they observe. Third, direct investment takes place in two directions in the same industry, which would not be the case if the movement were based on general levels of profit. In part this is because of differing advantages resulting from differentiation and specialization. But in part it is a peculiar phenomenon of oligopolistic competition: each firm must do as the others to prevent another from getting an unanticipated advantage. Thus with soap, Lever Brothers operates in the United States and Proctor and Gamble in Britain; with oil, Shell in the United States and Esso (now Exxon) in its various markets, and similarly for Knorr and Heinz with soup, Agfa and Kodak with photographic supplies, and so on. When one automobile com-pany builds a small and inefficient plant in Brazil, 15 more follow. Like the leader in a sailboat race, one must not let the second boat split tacks, but cover it to protect one's lead. This is "defensive investment" in which the return is not positive but the prevention of a possible loss.

The oligopolistic character of direct investment is easily misunderstood. To the local inefficient competitor, the difficulty is that the foreign invader competes too vigorously. As in the case of the chain stores in the 1920s and 1930s, the local monopolist decries the large firm from outside the district because it competes, although he accuses it of monopoly. And firms which teamed up with foreign firms, such as R.C.A. briefly with Siemens of Germany in the computer field, or General Electric (later Honeywell) with Machines Bull of France, did so not to extend a monopoly but to gather strength to challenge the industry lead of International Business Machines. This increases international competition. The contrary example is furnished by the 1967 purchase from the Norwegian government by Alcan Aluminium Ltd. of Canada of a 50 percent interest in the Aardal Og Sunndal Verk, an aluminum smelter that had been "a source of price competition that had vexed the entire industry." Buying up a competitor tends to restrain trade. But one cannot judge whether any particular takeover or investment increases or reduces competition without examination of the particular facts.

Firms maximize profits within a horizon which extends in time and space. Horizons change. Prior to about 1950, the Campbell Soup Company had few if any foreign branches outside Canada, whereas the Heinz company had almost 57. The former was preoccupied with its domestic operations; the latter, finding domestic competition stiff, had expanded especially abroad. After 1950, however, the Campbell company put on a drive to expand overseas. In the same way the chemical and pharmaceutical industries in the United States had been so busy prior to World War II fending off foreign competition that they had not contemplated foreign operations. In the depression of 1954, after fulfilling the bulk of their planned postwar domestic investments, they lifted their eyes to the world horizon and started to invest abroad. As indicated in Chapter 11, the Rome Treaty of 1957 perhaps stimulated U.S. foreign investment more through calling attention to existing profit opportunities than it did by creating new ones. Up to the beginnings of the Common Market, rapid and sustained European growth had passed unnoticed over the horizon of many large firms that would have been capable of investing there. With the formation of the EEC, the horizon suddenly was enlarged to encompass Europe, and investment in Europe as a whole soared.

This theory of direct investment can be summarized with reference to a simple formula used in elementary economics for capitalizing a perpetual flow of income:

$$C = \frac{I}{r},$$

where C is the value of an asset or obligation, I is the stream of income it produces, and r is the market rate of interest or profit. Thus, the student will remember, a perpetual bond with a face value of $1,000 bearing a 4 percent coupon (an income of $40 per year, or I) will sell for $1,333 ($C$) when the market rate of interest (r) stands at 3 percent. Hymer's theory of direct investment states that foreigners can pay more for an earning asset, such as a business, in country A than residents of country A would, not because they are content with a lower r, but because they can earn a higher I. It will happen, to be sure, that international capital markets are less than perfect, and that differences in r contribute to the flow of capital. But the behavior of direct investment—the readiness of investors to borrow in the host country at the same r as residents face, its concentration in oligopolistic industries, its movement in two directions, and the insistence on complete ownership—indicate that it is I, not r, that dominates.

This view of direct investment clashes head on with one expressed by Irving Brecher and S. S. Reisman. Things equal to the same thing, they said, are equal to each other. A firm located in Canada will try to maximize profits whether it is a Canadian or a foreign firm, say one whose head office is located in the United States. If both face the same conditions in Canada and abroad, both earn the same I and both capitalize it as the same r. The Canadian enterprise is thus worth the same capital value to Canadians and to citizens of the United States.

The analysis of this chapter, however, suggests that a larger international firm and a smaller Canadian firm will probably behave differently, owing to differences in the horizon within which they maximize. The Canadian firm expands within its borders, pays taxes only to the Canadian government, purchases components and equipment largely in Canada, recruits Canadians for empty positions, and so forth. The international firm faces a wider range of alternatives on many fronts. Typically its actions will be dictated by efficiency considerations, and its wider range of opportunity will result in greater efficiency. But it may not. It may respond to its ownership-country citizenship against the dictates of efficiency, sending capital or profits home when they could usefully be invested in the host country or maintaining high-cost production in the home country in depression times in preference to low-cost production in the host country because of "patriotic" concern for employment in the country where its head office is located. Or it may, at the urging of the host-country government, or even without it, seek to be a good citizen of the host country, which in some cases may involve departure from the efficiency standard and from the short-run interest of the owner country.

Bilateral Monopoly: Direct Investment in Resource Industries in Developing Countries

A particularly sensitive issue is the investment of large international companies in primary products—oil, copper, aluminum or bauxite, iron ore, and the like—in less developed countries. The true believers of the left insist that the international companies "exploit" the developing countries in some sense, obtaining primary products cheaply and with great profits for themselves. Those at the other extreme maintain, on the contrary, that the international companies confer great benefits on the developing countries, providing them with capital, technology, markets, and so forth, that they would otherwise lack and furnishing a source of large gain through taxation. The difference in view arises because each critic compares the existing situation with a different alternative. To the Marxist, the alternative is the same oil wells, copper mines, refineries, ships, and so forth, but in local government ownership. To the staunch defender of the status quo, if the foreign direct investment were to be eliminated, the developing country territory would revert to desert or jungle.

The fact is that both company and host country have advantages to bring to the bargaining table. The company has an advantage to exploit: technology, preferred access to capital markets, efficient management, market outlets, and the like, and the host country has natural resources, the known or suspected existence of oil or minerals. This is a bilateral-monopoly situation, for which there is no determinant solution. Moreover, there is so much room between the minimum reserve price at which the country chooses to keep the company out and that at which the company chooses to stay out that the term "exploitation," confuses more than it clarifies.

Bargaining between the company and the country in this situation calls for the analysis of non-zero-sum game theory, akin to love and war, where the range of possible solutions runs from both happy (peace); to one happy, the other unhappy (victory); to both unhappy (devastating war). A more fruitful mode of analysis is to observe how the relative bargaining strengths of some hypothetical country and company change through time and as a consequence of policies. Initially, the advantage lies entirely on the side of the company. The underdeveloped country lacks markets, technology, capital, and management skills, which the company brings to the bargain. All the country has is the natural resource. Unless it can induce a great many companies to bid against one another for the concession, unrestricted by cartel divisions of territory, it has to take what is offered. If there is a gunboat in the harbor during the negotiations, its room for negotiation is still further restricted.

With the passage of time, however, the balance of bargaining strength shifts. The company is committed for a large investment. It may no longer have all the skills on its side, because native personnel has been technologically trained by the company, at the country's insistence, and government personnel has acquired economic sophistication about the industry. With proven reserves, the risks for new entrants are much reduced, which increases the readiness of competitors to enter. As the old agreement comes to an end, or if it can be abrogated, new terms much more favorable to the country replace the original arrangement. The companies make an attempt to "hold the line," as for a while was done in the petroleum industry with the 50–50 agreements under which the company and the local tax authorities divided equally profits plus royalties. But the bargaining position fails to come to rest. The country tends to enact new conditions: an overvalued exchange rate at which the company must buy its local currency, for example, or a requirement that taxes be paid on the posted price rather than the sales price, which includes discount. New concessions provide for a 40–60 division, or a 25–75, and the old concessions have gradually to be brought into line. The original bilateral bargain approaches the competitive solution. In the end the country may "exploit" the company by forcing it to accept less-than-normal profits, maintained just high enough to prevent it from withdrawing. And in many cases, of course, the countries go farther, and the companies do withdraw.

Direct Investment and Welfare

Where direct investment transfers capital, technology, and management from countries where they are abundant to countries where they are scarce, it is evident that efficiency has been increased and Pareto optimality approached. Whether world welfare has been increased depends on the observer's international social welfare function. Labor in the home country will be worse off, having to be combined with less capital, technology, and management and hence receiving lower returns, and perhaps even experiencing unemployment. The gain for the investing country may include special benefits for capital and losses for labor which are regarded as unattractive; on the other hand, in the host country there are likely to be gains for labor and losses for capital, as well as the world cosmopolitan gain.

Apart from the static improvement through moving in the direction of equalizing factor prices internationally, there are also possibilities of dynamic gains: of training workers, or stimulating savings and capital formation through private and governmental increases in income.

There are also chances of blocking growth. The foreign firms may all be content to lose a little each year in defensive investment for the comfort of ensuring that no other company in the same field steals a march. All companies are of inefficient size. None can break out of the mold and start a process of growth. The seven refrigerator companies in the United States reproduce themselves in Canada, which has one tenth the population of the home country. In Latin America, there are too many, too small, high-cost companies in the automobile field in Argentina, Brazil, and Chile.

The technology that the foreign firm brings to the host country may be suitable for the home country, with one set of factor proportions, but not for the host country, with cheaper labor and more expensive capital. Nonetheless, economies of scale may make it economical for the international company to adopt one technology worldwide rather than to adjust its technology and factor proportions from country to country to varying factor endowments and prices.

Research and development may be retained in the home office and confined largely to the needs of the home country, rather than each country having its own independent technology, competitive with those of other countries. The large economies of scale in standardization in manufactured goods confer a sizable advantage on the first in the field and may frustrate later superior innovations which cannot break through the stranglehold of the international corporation.

While the international corporation is often accused of exploiting foreign labor through paying it too little (less than its marginal product?), it may equally, or even more widely, contribute to dual markets in labor by overpaying its staff in terms of the conditions of the local labor market and by diverting bank credit, skilled workers, and growing firms from tasks needed for the domestic economy through its superior purchasing power. In some oil countries it is said that many workers would rather wait in line for a high-paying job with the foreign firm than go to work immediately in the domestic economy, thus depriving the domestic sector of some of its potentially most energetic workers.

It is sometimes claimed that foreign firms distort efficient resource allocation by importing too much into the developing countries and exporting too little. This assumes either that the firm is not a maximizing unit or that the prices it faces do not reflect social values. On the latter score, it is evident that where firms (occasionally) import components at high prices from tax-shelter subsidiaries in third jurisdictions, there is distortion from an efficient solution. Here the remedy is to eliminate tax evasion—as discussed in the next chapter. The suggestion that international firms restrict the exports of developing countries is one we have already encountered in Chapter 10 and which we also deal with in the chapter that follows. It may now be noted, however, that to be valid, this suggestion presupposes that the international firm is not a maximizing entity.

The International Corporation

It is an interesting question of economics whether markets or corporations are better devices for allocating resources among competing uses. The imperfections of markets have been discussed in Chapter 12. The possibility that international corporations may not maximize the efficient use of given resources has been touched upon in this chapter. But a case can be made that the development of the large international corporation in the 20th century will prove in the long run to be a more effective device for equalizing wages, rents, and interest rates throughout the world than trade conducted in competitive markets by small merchants. The analogy is with the national corporation, which in the United States after about 1890 helped to equalize wages, interest rates, and rents within the country's borders by borrowing in the cheapest market (New York) and investing where it was most productive in terms of cost and markets. The resultant movement of capital and shift in demand for labor was probably more effective in, say, raising wages in the South and lowering interest rates there than either trade by local companies or the limited direct movement of factors.

Today more and more companies are lifting their horizons from the national to the international scene, contemplating a wider geographical range of alternatives on where to borrow, build, sell, undertake research, or buy. The giant oil, chemical, automobile, tire, food-processing, and similar firms cover the world. Companies with subsidiaries in 40 or 50 countries are no longer rare, and those with 5 to 10 are common. To the extent that these companies coordinate the operations of firms in different markets with a view to achieving monopoly profits and succeed in preventing new entry through imitation, it is not clear that they maximize welfare. To the extent that these companies buy in the cheapest market and sell in the dearest—with reference both to factors and goods—they provide an institutional network which may go farther than trade flows or the movement of labor or portfolio capital to equalize factor returns and improve welfare throughout the world.

It is not clear that international corporations do act in a nondiscriminatory way. Donald T. Brash observes that General Motors–Holden started out in Australia with a rule which said that purchases would be made in the United States unless the products concerned could be obtained 10 percent cheaper in Australia, and shifted over time to a criterion which said that products would be bought in Australia unless they were 10 percent cheaper elsewhere. Neither rule is justified. There is something to be said, to be sure, for rules of thumb which minimize the cost of decision making and do not require a purchasing agent to get quotations from all over the world before he buys tacks. Costs of information are high, and some implicit rule for small amounts and differences as small as 10 percent may be justified on this account. If the General Motors regulations meant no more than this, they are understandable. If the discrimination is deliberate, however, and runs contrary to the rule of profit maximization when the facts are known, it suggests that corporations feel the need to have a citizenship, and that discrimination in favor of the country of citizenship can be the enemy of efficiency.

The international corporation is not truly international in another respect, despite the accusations of the Marxists. Each one has a home office and a home unit of account in which it keeps its liquid assets as well as calculates its maximization of profits. The truly cosmopolitan corporation which is prepared to move head office and liquid assets out of any country whose currency is weak is yet to arrive. Few have reached the position of even those U.S. corporations such as General Motors that have two offices, one for production (in Detroit) and one for finance (in New York). More and more corporations are organizing themselves worldwide with regional offices in Europe, Latin America, and the Far East. In the long run more companies may organize like the Arabian American Oil Company, with production in Saudi Arabia, marketing through its owning oil companies, and accounting in the Hague. It is a sign of the times, however, that the Saudi Arabian government wants the head office moved from New York to Dhahran.

That the large international corporation has not yet developed to its ultimate extent can be seen by looking at the balance sheet of any large American corporation which separates out earnings and assets and possibly sales in the United States and abroad. It will be seen that earnings are higher on foreign investment and on foreign sales than in the United States, whether for Otis Elevator, Du Pont, Gillette, Corn Products Refining, Standard Oil Company of New Jersey, or whatever. This trend would be much greater were it not for the existence of defensive investments in which the return is less than the average at home. It is also partly a function of higher risks abroad than at home. But even if we had data on earnings per share and per dollar of sales in countries where the risks are little if any higher than in the United States, say for Canada, Australia, or the United Kingdom, the returns are still going to be higher abroad for the U.S. corporation (and higher in the United States for the foreign corporation with investments here) because the companies feel that they belong somewhere in particular and go afield only for a higher than ordinary return. When it earns an equal return (after risk) on every dollar and dollar equivalent invested everywhere in the world, the large corporation can be said to be truly international.

The truly international corporation would probably also behave differently from existing corporations, with their strong national base in recruitment, research and development, introduction of new products, reinvestment of earnings, and the like. The strongly nationalist company, for example, will hire its own nationals in all key jobs. The company which is trying to be a good citizen everywhere will hire local personnel. The truly international company will try to hire the best man for the job no matter what country he comes from or what country he is going to. If there were such truly international corporations—and the trend is in this direction—it is evident that they would assist the pressure for factor-price equalization. The student may interest himself in comparing the behavior of national corporations with foreign operations, multinational firms which try to act as good citizens everywhere, and truly international corporations which maximize profits worldwide on a variety of other dimensions: capital budgeting, exchange risk both for holding cash and for borrowing credit, research and development, new products, marketing, and the like.

Direct Investment and the Balance of Payments

There is an apparent paradox that both home and host country are worried about the impact of direct investment on the balance of payments. The home country is worried that the initial investment supplies the home currency to world exchange markets; the host country puts it that once the investment has built up and becomes profitable, the annual drain on the balance of payments is likely to be serious. The resolution of the apparent conflict, of course, is that the home country's worries are largely short run, the host country's long run.

In the Home Country

The Voluntary Credit Restraint Program of February 1965, replaced by the Mandatory Control Program of January 1968, was designed to limit the outflow of capital from the United States through direct investment and to increase remittance of dividends. Corporations were asked to produce a 5 percent improvement in the balance-of-payments impact of the enterprise, counting increases in goods exports and dividends repatriated plus reductions in funds transmitted abroad as "improvements." Attention was focused not on restraining direct investment but on limiting its impact on the balance of payments.

The initial naïve notion was highly partial equilibrium in nature. It was thought, for example, that a reduction of $100 in direct investment would improve the balance of payments by $100 through reducing debits. It quickly became clear, however, that such a partial-equilibrium model was inappropriate. Other items in the balance of payments were affected by the change in direct investment. The general-equilibrium task was to see what the total effect of a change in direct investment might be, counting repercussions and feedbacks throughout the system. The issue then became, what was the appropriate general-equilibrium model? If a given item of direct investment were reduced, what were the appropriate assumptions to make throughout the rest of the model as to the consequences that followed?

It was agreed, for example, that direct investment stimulates direct exports of equipment, especially where it takes place in developing countries without machinery industries of their own and also stimulates exports of components and inventories. A decline in direct investment would thus imply a decline in exports, at least in the first year. Direct investment also stimulated exports of other products in a company's line beyond that being manufactured abroad, since there was likely to be some excess marketing capacity along with that created for the new production. Here again was an offset loss to match part of the gain to the balance of payments from reduced investment. Other positive help to the balance of payments from direct investment consisted in rents and royalties from the use of the firm's technology, the flow of interest and dividends after operations were under way—although not all profits were remitted home. On the negative side were the displacement of exports by new production abroad, some imports of foreign output for the domestic market (such as components for the compact-car assemblies brought in by Ford, Chrysler, and General Motors), and, of course, the initial financial investment. The estimates for the various parameters were derived from balance-of-payments experience.

In his early formulation of the problem, Philip Bell used only a few variables, broken down as follows:

Balance-of-Payments Improving		*Balance-of-Payments Worsening*	
Export stimulus and fees	19	Capital	100
Remitted earnings	6		
Total (annual)	25		100

The earnings took place year after year, beginning with the second period. The question turned, however, on what was the appropriate assumption to make about the capital outflow. On the basis of a single investment, the balance of payments turned adverse in the first year by $100 but improved each year thereafter, with the cumulative total zero by the end of the fifth year and everything thereafter gravy. But Bell considered this model to be naïve. If one shifted the foreign investment schedule up by $100 and had $100 newly invested each year, the cumulative deficit would grow to $250 at the end of the fourth year, would decline annually thereafter, but would not reach zero until the ninth year. Even this may not be the most realistic model. Between 1957 and 1961, U.S. direct investment grew at 25 percent a year. Extrapolating this percentage, each $100 of direct investment pays for itself in five years but the cumulative adverse effect of the total on the balance of payments rises forever.

The business community argued hotly against the models for the schedule shift and constant rate of increase, in favor of that for single injection. Of course. But there really is no ideal answer as to which is the appropriate model. It depends on the question asked. The geometric progression model is silly, to be sure, for anything but a relatively short period of time. Trees never reach the sky, and babies who double their birth weight in five months and triple it in a year end up weighing positive and not infinite numbers of pounds, stone, or kilograms. But as between the single injection, schedule shift, or spurts of geometric growth, there can be no scientific answer as to the best model.

One business group, the National Industrial Conference Board (NICB), sought to make a distinction between the "incremental" and the "organic" approaches to direct investment. The former singles out one investment at the margin and tries to work out its implications. The NICB understands the logic of this approach but rejects it as unrealistic. In its view, foreign investment is all of a piece. To maintain the profitability of old investments, it is necessary to undertake new ones. To halt the outflow is not only to cut off future returns but to undermine the continuation of the present stream of dividends. A firm operating abroad must move with the market as the latter grows; to stand still is to lose market position, which is to begin to die. It is hard to judge the merits of the biological argument, which has overtones of mysticism about it. If the foreign investment is profitable, it is possible to reinvest profits; if it is not, there may be doubt whether expansion is warranted. The economist tends to be skeptical in the face of such argument, but it is easy to understand how businessmen feel this way.

If progress on the proper choice of a model is difficult, it has been possible to refine the variables. A Brookings study divides the effects into:

Balance-of-Payments Improving		Balance-of-Payments Worsening	
Export stimulus	10.6	Capital	100
Remitted dividends	8.1	Import stimulus	6.5
Royalties and fees	2.3	Loss of exports	(none)

With these numbers one injection pays off in the 6th year, a steady flow in the 11th year, and a flow growing at the rate of 22 percent a year never pays off. The annual investment under the last approach reaches numbers such as $53 billion in the 20th year, with the export stimulus $37 billion and so forth.

One observer raises a still further question: Suppose a new investment of $100 is undertaken with no money transfer, the equity consisting of goods and other valuable considerations transferred in kind, and the remaining capital raised through local borrowing or through reinvestment of profits on existing investment. In this case the positive effects of investment start immediately and grow. The model which starts out with a negative impact of $100 is by no means the only possible one. The reply to this, however, is that the coefficients used in the various models were derived from balance-of-payments statistics. If one poses a different problem, one needs to work out a different set of coefficients. If you eliminate the $100 initial investment, you must change the other positive and negative numbers.

The most careful study for the United States, however, was that undertaken by Gary Hufbauer and Michael Adler, which produced a series of different models, depending upon what one expected to happen in case a particular direct investment was not carried out. In the developing countries, for example, the alternative to a given direct investment might be that no other investment would be made in its place and that the market would continue to be supplied by exports from the United States (which had no foreign exchange content). In this case, direct investment produces serious losses in exports year after year and hurts the balance of payments. In Europe or Canada, on the other hand, a direct investment made at the right stage of the product cycle might be the alternative to a similar investment made by local enterprise. The exports displaced by the investment were lost in any event, so that the export loss was not an appropriate charge against direct investment. In this model, the balance-of-payments effects of direct investment are much less negative.

A similar study in Britain by W. B. Reddaway and his associates at the Cambridge Institute of Statistics came to the same conclusion: The impact of direct investment on the balance of payments on the home country depends upon what is assumed as the alternative, in case the investment is not made. A crucial assumption is what would happen to exports in the absence of the investment.

It is premature before we get to the chapter on the balance of payments to draw any very general conclusions, but in line with what has been said earlier about the unsuitability of microeconomic measures to address macroeconomic problems (p. 121 above), there is something to the view that the whole issue was blown up out of all proportion to its importance. A number of countries were concerned about direct investment, largely on noneconomic grounds. In the next chapter we conclude that this is fine so long as they recognize the economic consequences of intervention in the process. On the balance-of-payments question for the home country, the presumption is that the investor gets a fair return for his money, so that the present discounted value of the stream of net benefits is equal to or greater than the present value of the investment. If the country cannot afford to invest abroad, this suggests that the private rate of discount used by the investor in making his calculations is wrong, i.e. too low, or that the investor has overestimated the value of I. There is something to this last possibility: direct investment can become a fad, just like any other activity of an economic, social, or cultural character. Business can become bemused by the fact that other firms are going abroad, and firms then go abroad without seriously calculating the payoffs from so doing. The wave of direct investment abroad by American firms after about 1955 has been revealed to have included some poor decisions which have resulted in losses. In these cases, of course, the initial pressure on the balance of payments is not later offset by a flow of dividends.

The Impact on the Balance of Payments of the Host Country

Direct investment can be regarded as negative for the balance of payments of both the investing and the host country if the one concentrates on the short run and the other on the long. And so they do. The host country regards direct investment as "expensive." A small investment with little balance-of-payments impact in its early years will develop through reinvestment into a company with a sizable remittance of dividends abroad. In not-infrequent cases, a comparison is made of the initial investment and the annual flow of dividends years later. In an early and notorious case, the Australian public became agitated in the early 1950s when it learned that one year's profits of General Motors–Holden Proprietary, Ltd., ran 14 percent of sales, 24 percent of funds employed, 39 percent of shareholders' equity, and 560 percent of General Motors' original investment. Dividends paid from these profits amounted to 11 percent of funds employed, 18 percent of shareholders' equity, 260 percent of the original investment, and 8 percent of the Australian dollar export receipts for the year. All this occurred despite the fact that the company had priced the Holden car—occasionally held to be the forerunner of the Corvair—at a level which failed to clear the market. There was a six-months' waiting list.

The General Motors–Holden case has been explained by one scholar as an example of the gambling-money thesis: direct investments grow at rapid rates because the companies plow back profits on the basis of some rule of thumb. The consequence is that the original investment pyramids rapidly and ultimately returns a stream of income which is large in relation to the original investment. Possibly. But this will only work if the product makes money, if, that is, the direct investor produces and sells a product the public wants. Not all direct investment can make profits to reinvest, and no direct investor will plow back profits unless the prospect for further profit is bright. Instead of being expensive, the direct investment may be regarded as efficient, in that it provided at limited cost an automobile the Australian public wanted very much.

On this score it is not legitimate to compare the subsequent rates of profits or dividends with the original investment. They are appropriately compared to total funds employed and with the foreign equity. Reinvestment each year must count as a separate and additional investment, so long as the investor had the option of taking his profits out. Reinvestment and pyramiding are not inevitable. In the last chapter we saw that investors don't have to lend the interest on past debts, nor do borrowers have to borrow it. Similarly, an initial direct investment does not always grow exponentially; such reinvestment as does take place is entitled to a return of its own.

One small point may be made about how Holden sales were financed. The introduction of a new product may produce a shift in demand to it. If total demand is unchanged, an increase in purchases of the Holden will involve decreases in purchases of other goods, which will cut back imports directly in part, and for the rest release resources which can be transferred into export-increasing or import-decreasing occupations. If, howevre, purchases of the Holden are all financed on credit—say installment loans—there will be an increase in total spending and an increased strain on total resources, leading to an import surplus. But the strain on the balance of payments should be blamed not on the direct investment so much as on the credit expansion.

A third point of considerable importance is that General Motors–Holden made its large profits behind substantial tariff protection. In July of 1966, when the Japanese Toyota automobile managed to take over 7½ percent of the total market with imports into Australia, the Tariff Board raised the tariff from 35 to 45 percent ad valorem to ensure that the market was supplied by domestic manufactures instead of imports. The higher the tariff needed to maintain the marginal inefficient producer, the larger the profits of the inframarginal efficient producer. It is impossible to know what the General Motors–Holden profits were in the 1960s because so great was the outcry in the 1950s that General Motors bought up the minority stockholdings and transformed itself into a private company with a single owner under no obligation to publish its accounts. But to the extent that the Australian Tariff Board maintains high tariffs on imports, the General Motors–Holden profits (the redistribution effect in Figure 7.1) is the result of Australian, not foreign company action.

More fundamentally, when direct investment makes large profits, it is a sign that supply is very small in relation to demand and that new entry is called for to expand supply to the point where only normal profits are made. It would be desirable from the national point of view for a domestic producer to take advantage of the opportunity. But the high profits are there for the foreign investor because domestic enterprise is incapable of filling the vacuum. In the General Motors–Holden case, the high profits performed the function that they are supposed to do under the capitalist system; the success of General Motors–Holden was followed by the establishment of Australian subsidiaries of other world automobile companies such as Ford and Daimler-Benz which would have restored profits to normal levels had it not been for the tariff. The high profits were needed as a signal of where output should be expanded. The monopoly power of the direct investor may preclude new entry. But where it is based on efficiency and skill, as in the General Motors case, imitation, not suppression, is called for.

It is of some considerable interest that the rate of profits on U.S. direct investment in Australia went down sharply after 1960, when import controls were relaxed. Of all the points made about the expensive character of direct investment and its impact on the balance of payments then, it appears that the protection afforded to the foreigner through trade controls may be the most important. Monopolies and oligopolies make higher-than-normal profits. Tariffs and quotas protect monopoly positions. Governments which raise tariffs to give more monopoly protection have the capacity to reduce rates of profits on direct investment.

Note the possibility of a clash between the home and host country over the impact of direct investment on the balances of payments of the two. The home country may attempt to require the parent company to remit home profits earned abroad. The host country may impose foreign exchange control which prevents subsidiaries of foreign companies located within its borders (and hence squarely in its legal jurisdiction) from remitting dividends to parent companies. The conflict of interest is evident. We postpone its discussion, however, to the next chapter on policies toward direct investment.

Summary

The foreign operations of domestic corporations, or direct investment, belong to the theory of monopolistic competition rather than to that of international capital movements. This theory explains better than any other the industries in which direct investment takes place, the cross currents, and the borrowing abroad.

Direct investment by developed countries in less developed countries cannot properly be regarded as exploitation without defining the terms. Typically the advantage in a bilateral monopoly situation starts out all on the side of the investing company and gradually shifts to the host country.

The international corporation is likely in the future to become an important vehicle for equalizing the returns to factors of production and spreading technology internationally, as the national corporation has done domestically. Where the international corporation is faced by national jurisdictions with conflicting interests, it may slide between them, or it may be penalized by double penalties or conflicting commands. Harmonization of tax, antitrust, and balance-of-payments policies will help, especially if such policies put efficiency above citizenship as criteria for corporate behavior.

The impact of direct investment on the balance of payments of the investing country is adverse in the short run, helpful in the long. The question as to what is the appropriate model for a balanced judgment remains open. Conversely the balance of payments of the host country is helped in the short run and may be hurt in the long. This is especially the case if profits on direct investment are helped by loose credit policies and high tariffs.

SUGGESTED READING

Texts

C. P. Kindleberger, *American Business Abroad* (New Haven, Conn.: Yale University Press, 1969).

Treatises, Etc.

The Harvard Business School has a substantial program of research and publication under way on the international corporation. See especially R. Vernon, *Sovereignty at Bay* (New York: Basic Books, 1971). A useful collection of essays on various functional aspects of the subject is C. P. Kindleberger, ed., *The International Corporation* (Cambridge, Mass.: The M.I.T. Press, 1970).

Among the periodical literature, see H. W. Singer, "The Distribution of Gains between Investing and Borrowing Countries," in American Economic Association, *Readings in International Economics;* and E. T. Penrose, "Foreign Investment and the Growth of the Firm," *EJ,* June 1956, and "Profit Sharing between Producing Countries and Oil Companies in the Middle East," *EJ,* June 1959.

The major monographs on the balance of payments are G. C. Hufbauer and F. M. Adler, *Overseas Manufacturing Investment and the Balance of Payments,* Tax Policy Research Study No. 1 (Washington, D.C.: U.S. Treasury Department, 1968) and W. B. Reddaway, J. O. N. Perkins, S. J. Potter, and C. T. Taylor, *Effects of U.K. Direct Investment Overseas* (Cambridge, England: Cambridge University Press, 1967).

Points

The other references for the discussion of the impact of direct investment on the U.S. balance of payments are P. W. Bell, "Private Capital Movements and the U.S. Balance-of-Payments Position," in *Factors Affecting the United States Balance of Payments* prepared for the Subcommittee on International Exchange and Payments, Joint Economic Committee, 87th Cong., 2nd sess. (Washington, D.C.: U.S. Government Printing Office, 1962); and J. W. Polk, I. W. Meister, and L. A. Veit, *U.S. Production Abroad and the Balance of Payments: A Survey of Corporate Investment Experience* (New York: National Industrial Conference Board, 1966).

The concept of defensive investment mentioned in this chapter is from A. Lamfalussy, *Investment and Growth in Mature Economics* (Oxford: Basil Blackwell & Mott, Ltd., 1961).

The view that national firms and international firms behave identically is set out in I. Brecher and S. S. Reisman, *Canadian-American Economic Relations* (Ottawa: The Government Printer, 1957), chap. 7.

Chapter	POLICIES TOWARD
16	DIRECT INVESTMENT

In dealing with policies toward direct investment in the host country, the home country, and the world as a whole, greatest attention is given to the first in this chapter. Host-country discontent with foreign control of local enterprise is an important factor in policies of direct investment. Some attention is paid to the labor case against foreign investment in the United States, as represented by the Burke-Hartke bill, which would change the basis of taxation of direct investment in an effort to prevent the "export of jobs." The desirability of some international regulation of the multinational corporation is also explored, with a view to alleviating the politicoeconomic problems raised by direct investment.

No attention is given to balance-of-payments questions raised in the previous chapter. Interference with direct investment to improve the balance of payments is clearly a second-best policy. The best attack is through macroeconomic tools, as we will indicate in Part V.

Instinctive Reactions

It is only a slight exaggeration to suggest that the normal individual has certain instincts which come into play in discussing foreign investment, irrational instincts which the study of economics is perhaps designed to eradicate. Social man tends to some considerable degree to be a **peasant** with a territorial instinct which leads him to object to foreign ownership of national natural resources; a **Populist**, which makes him suspicious of banks; a **mercantilist**, which makes him favor exports over imports; a **xenophobe**, which leads him to fear those from outside the tribe; a **monopolist** who reacts strongly against competition; and an infant, to the extent that he **wants to eat his cake and have it too.** It is overstating the case to suggest that these instincts, which we recognize as on the whole unworthy of rational man, are at the basis of three quarters of the objections to foreign investment, but the proportion cannot be much below two thirds, or five eighths, or three fifths.

The **peasant instinct** appears more clearly in the reaction to foreign ownership of our land, or natural resources. The thought is that Nature or God gave the land to "us" and intended us to have it. It is all right, perhaps, for foreigners to build factories within our borders, but it goes contrary to nature to have them own our mines, forests, waterfalls, petroleum reserves, farms, or grazing land. To an economist, this is an example of the fallacy of misplaced concreteness. Natural resources, like man-made plant and equipment, are capital assets. If the asset is worth more to a foreigner than to a citizen of the country, it adds to natural wealth and income for the citizen to sell the natural resources to the foreigner and use the financial capital gained from the sale in lines of greater productivity. There is no difference between "natural" and man-made capital in this regard. Some natural resources, like farmland and forests, are replaceable. These are exactly like man-made capital. Where they are not replaceable, as in the case of mines, the capital values can be maintained through depletion allowances which are invested in exploration and discovery of new natural resources, or maintained as other kinds of productive capital, earning an equivalent income.

One sound economic reason might militate against the sale of a natural resource or any other asset to a foreigner. This is that while the foreigner may earn a higher return today on, say, the petroleum deposits, the day is coming when the local resident can earn a still higher profit. The time profiles of the streams of income look like those shown in Figure 16.1, with I_f the return on the petroleum deposits in foreign ownership and I_h the return in local hands. In a world of perfect markets and perfect knowledge,

FIGURE 16.1. Different Time Profiles of Income Earned on an Investment in Natural Resources by Foreign and Home Investors

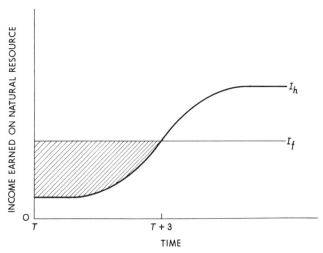

TIME

the foreigner would not be able to outbid the local resident for the asset at period T, assuming that the amount by which I_h exceeded I_f after $T + 3$ was sufficient to pay interest on the shaded area by which I_h had initially been below I_f. But without perfect knowledge or perfect markets, or with a high degree of uncertainty attaching to the long-run shape of I_h, the foreigner may outbid the local investor. This is the infant-industry argument for restricting foreign investment, and of course it is a second-best argument. First best is to improve the perfection of knowledge and markets; second best is to save the asset from the clutches of the foreigner until the local resident can develop its full earning power. As in the case of tariffs, the infant-industry argument is a valid basis for interference with the market in the absence of optimal intervention.

We may recognize another argument against foreign ownership of, say, land—the national defense argument. A country might be nervous having all its oil wells, or all its coal mines, or strategic defense areas along its borders in foreign ownership. The national defense argument, like the infant-industry argument, is a valid basis for interference with the international market for assets within a country's borders. One can say more: Like the valid arguments for a tariff, **noneconomic and second-best arguments are the only valid arguments for restricting foreign investment by the host country.**

Norway and Sweden limit foreign ownership of natural resources. Canada, Australia, and Germany object to foreign ownership of banks. In the German case, the basis is simple concern that the local monopoly might be adversely affected by competition. Like most industries that assert a transcendental reason for restricting imports of competitive goods, so local industry, including banking, is likely to produce high-minded rationales for limiting foreign bankers. Lenin, for example, suggested that banks are the "commanding heights of the economy." It is sometimes hinted that foreign banks can serve an industrial espionage function, learning the financial strengths and especially the weaknesses of domestic industry and feeding the information to foreign competitors. But the main objection to foreign bankers is the instinct of **Populism,** which has such a strong hold in the South and West of the United States. Fear of Wall Street and its malign schemes is endemic among farmers, small merchants, and such informed Populists as Representative Wright Patman and former President Lyndon B. Johnson. That Populism merges into simple **xenophobia** or dislike of foreigners was indicated when the Canadian government decided against the First National City Bank's application to buy the Mercantile Bank on the ground that it was opposed to foreign ownership of banks, only to discover that the Mercantile Bank was already foreign owned—by Dutch interests. As in Australia, where British-owned banks are tolerated but American attempts to acquire ownership of banks is resisted, it may be less the fact of foreign ownership than the nationality of it.

Foreign Enterprise and Exports

The restrictive business practice involved in parent companies forbidding subsidiaries to export except as directed from the home country has been mentioned in Chapter 10. This applies, of course, primarily to manufactures, since direct investment in primary production is generally for the explicit purpose of exporting; in fact, the complaint often expressed in this area is that the foreign company is too ready to export, rather than to process goods within the national borders. Several points can be made relative to this essentially **mercantilist** criticism, which rests on the notion that exports are good, whereas import-competing industry is somehow not so worthy.

First, where the company is rational, it will export from the cheapest source. If a company does not export from a given country, there is a presumption, though perhaps not a very powerful one, that the subsidiary is high cost.

Second, where the country in question resists foreign investment and some resident enterprise enters into agreement to employ foreign technology, it is likely to obtain the patent or copyright only for the home market. It thus is unable to export patented products without permission. This is not meant to condone the restrictive practice, but rather to recognize that in awarding rights, the patent system avowedly monopolizes markets for the sake of encouraging invention.

Third, even if it maximizes profits by producing in the cheapest source, the investing enterprise is not disposed to invite surprises by encouraging all its subsidiaries to compete with one another in all markets. Supplying of third markets tends to be directed from the head office to avert surprise, in particular "dumping" or low-profit sales by one branch at the expense of another.

Fourth, the record of foreign enterprises in exporting manufactures from investments in developed countries is a good one. In Britain, for example, there is no complaint.

Fifth and last, the initial complaints in Canada over the poor export record of U.S. companies investing in manufacturing north of the border was based upon a tyro's error in economic reasoning. Most of the investments were in tariff factories, import-competing industry which was able to survive only because of high tariffs. An import-competing industry has a comparative disadvantage. To export, a company needs a comparative advantage. If it has a comparative disadvantage, it cannot have a comparative advantage. Therefore, it cannot export.

It is true, however, that occasionally an import-competing industry which needs a tariff to get started achieves low costs through economies of scale, learning by doing, and the like, and converts a comparative disadvantage into an advantage. This is the infant-industry argument, which, as an example of the second best, is valid. In the usual case, however, the criticism of foreign industry for its failure to export is made without recognition of the conditions necessary to give it validity. It is usually based on instinctual mercantilism.

Foreign Control

To a considerable degree host countries object primarily to having foreigners control their enterprises. This **nationalist** sentiment is understandable and normal, but it is noneconomic. The economist has no basis for objecting if a country chooses to exclude foreign enterprise on the ground that it wants to preserve its national identity, or worries about being overwhelmed by goods made to foreign designs and specifications. Nationalism can be regarded as a public good, like national parks, paid for not by taxation but through foregoing opportunities for increases in national income. All the economist can rightly do is to ask the decision makers to recognize that nationalism has a cost, and they should be prepared to decide how much they want at what cost.

What is unacceptable is to want to have your cake and eat it too. The Watkins and Gray reports in Canada are surely within proper bounds when they urge the limitation of new foreign investment. Where they give rise to doubts is in their implications that policies of restriction are at the same time the ones that will maximize Canadian national income.

There is one possibility that the Watkins and Gray analysis is correct. This is the **optimum restriction** argument, exactly comparable to the optimum tariff line of reasoning. If a country restricts foreign investment, it might get it cheaper, giving up nothing in the way of economic gains from foreign investment and achieving a measure of freedom from foreign control. Some observers claim that Japanese policy has been an adroit one of this kind. But the optimum tariff increases the welfare of a country only on the assumption of no retaliation. The non-zero-sum game of restricting foreign investment may readily evoke retaliatory measures. In this case it loses. And it seems unlikely that a country like Canada, with so few of the assets that the Japanese brought to their policy of restriction—cheap labor, a high marginal rate of savings, effective capacity for imitation and innovation—could gain from optimum restriction even without retaliation. Foreign enterprise on the whole is not that anxious to invest in Canada and, if restricted, will go away rather than beg to be let in on less favorable terms.

The choice for Canada and for countries like France is thus whether or not to keep out or keep down the foreigners, at some cost to national income but a gain for cultural independence. It is not without interest that the same issue is being faced within Canada by the French Canadians and within France by the Bretons. It is not an easy choice.

Market Failure

A strong case can be made for restricting foreign investment when markets function badly. When markets are evidently not working, it is a mistake to follow their dictates. In 1898 after the Spanish-American war, American carpetbaggers (like those of the North in the South in 1864 after the Civil War) went into Cuba and bought up much of the good sugar land. With the dislocation of war, it was not clear what such lands were worth. The prices at which they were sold did not represent the values that would have been achieved by orderly markets. It was a mistake for the newly independent Cuba to permit such purchases, and especially for the United States not to restrain its citizens. In Germany after World War II, a moratorium on new foreign investment was imposed in the three Western zones, largely at the instance of the United States, until monetary reform and a reparations settlement had been achieved and market prices came closer to representing economic scarcities.

Less dramatic but the same sort of market failure occurred in Brazil in a short, sharp deflation which was produced by a Brazilian government attempt to adopt the recommendations of the International Monetary Fund. Stock market values were hard hit by the loss of liquidity. American and other foreign firms bought up Brazilian shares. To the Brazilians it looked like a plot to deprive them of the ownership of their enterprise. A strong second-best argument against permitting markets to operate when they are in a pathological state would have condoned orders by the Brazilian government forbidding the transfer of shares to foreigners in liquidity panics.

A still more difficult question is posed in the early 1970s in Italy. Italian capital markets perform badly. Italian entrepreneurs with large losses are unable to raise capital in the private capital market. They can liquidate their holdings, if at all, only by selling them to the government equivalents of the Reconstruction Finance Corporation or to foreign firms. The first-best policy is to repair and reform the Italian capital market. That Herculean task being impossible, the question presents itself whether foreign purchases of Italian firms should be forbidden as second best.

Restricting Nonessentials

Foreign investments are often thought to bring products that are not wanted—cosmetics, breakfast foods, soft drinks, or commodities like ink—which local manufacturers can make (at least after a fashion). Steel, machinery, export products would be welcome; breakfast foods should stay home.

This is an excellent example of implicit market failure. What the critics are saying is that private values represented by market prices do not reflect social values, with the result that even if a foreigner could make a large profit in producing, say, Coca-Cola, which the market wants (as evidenced by profits available), the market is wrong, and its indications must be ignored. Consumer sovereignty is rejected.

This again is a second-best argument, and within its assumptions it is entirely valid. If the market is wrong, don't follow the market. It is unlikely, however, that the market is wrong for all "nonessentials" produced by foreigners, and right on everything produced at home. If a foreigner can make a profit producing ink, for example, it suggests that locally produced ink is a poor product or is wastefully made, so that a gain in resources is available to the community by shifting out of existing ways of making ink into different ones. If this were to mean unemployment for the labor currently engaged in ink that was not offset by increased employment in the foreign plants, there is another second-best argument that factor prices do not reflect factor scarcities. Again it is valid within its assumptions, and assuming that it is impossible to tackle the problem with first-best methods.

Mitigating the Effects of Foreign Investment

The agonizing character of national decisions over these issues is illustrated by the on-again–off-again quality of many decisions regarding foreign investment. Even before J.-J. Servan-Schreiber wrote *The American Challenge,* the French government changed its mind three times in five years, veering between encouragement and restriction. Many other countries (with and without changes of governments) confiscate foreign enterprise one year and pass new legislation to attract it the next. In the case of Peru, the nationalization of the International Petroleum Company's property, with a tangled legal history, and of some farm properties of the W. R. Grace Company, along with indigenous holdings, as part of land reform was accompanied in a matter of days by an advertisement in *The New York Times* welcoming foreign investment.

When they are not restricting foreign investment altogether, a number of countries have tried to develop solutions which would gain them more or most of the benefits of foreign investment—capital, technology, management, access to markets, training, and the like—without incurring the costs of loss of national control. In particular, countries have tried insisting on joint ventures; being selective as to the types of enterprises they will admit; limiting takeovers as contrasted with new enterprises; excluding foreigners in whole or part from the local capital market; entering into contracts separately for management, technology, and patents, and borrowing through portfolio securities; and forming "cartels" with neighboring countries to limit tax concessions granted to foreigners. It may be useful to say a word on each.

Joint Ventures

The insistence by many countries that they will welcome foreign enterprise in joint ventures with their own nationals, but not by themselves, seems, offhand, to be designed to provide training effects to domestic capitalists, at some cost in reducing total capital formation by excluding the import from abroad of the capital furnished locally. It is often vaguer in purpose. In Canada, for example, there is talk of the desirability of a "Canadian presence" in ownership, direction, management, and upper staff to ensure that "Canadian interests" will be taken care of. Some simpleminded observers fear that foreign enterprise will dominate government circles; a more sophisticated view is that wholly- and jointly-owned foreign enterprises rather reduce the vitality of local politics by subtracting the political influence of a large share of Canadian business, as the foreigners stand aside rather than mix in.

The enterprises themselves appear to detest joint ventures, not, so far as one can tell from what they say (if this can be believed), because of the "national presence," but because of the built-in conflict of interest. The local shareowners may want dividends, while the foreigners want capital gains. Or the time may come when the enterprise needs more capital and the local capitalists are unable to provide their pro rata share.

In a rational world, of course, any owner would be willing to sell off any proportion of his ownership of an enterprise "if the price were right." The view of many firms that they are willing to enter into joint ventures where the local partner contributes something "in kind," but not money, is irrational, since with an adequate pricing system any contribution in kind can be valued in money. But the market for direct investment is not a perfect market, as our oligopoly theory asserts. Joint ventures in Japan are usually welcomed by investors because the culture is so strange to Western ways that Caucasians need an indigenous partner to interpret market and government to them. In Latin countries with peculiar systems of negotiating over corporate income taxes, the local partner makes a contribution in serving as a cultural filter between foreigner and tax authorities.

But partners frequently fall out. The general record of joint ventures is that one ultimately has to buy out the other. An oil company wants its profits in producing areas. Its marketing partner is unhappy unless profits are made in marketing. In this regard, of course, every taxing authority is a joint partner of all firms, including those that appear to be 100 percent owned. To redistribute profits nationally so as to minimize taxes is certain to get the company into trouble with this particular partner.

Selectivity

Selectivity is choosing among industries in permitting foreign investment, with limitations for nonessentials, banks, newspapers, natural resource industries, and the like. It may be an optimum restriction strategy or a second-best policy in a world of market failure. It is likely to be played badly, from instinct rather than careful economic reasoning, in which case it will lose national income.

Limiting Take-overs

There is a strong argument for encouraging new enterprises and prohibiting the purchase of existing firms. It rests on opposition to monopoly. In an industry of six firms in a country, a take-over keeps the number at six; new entry moves it to seven, and perhaps nearer "workable competition."

The argument, as we have said, is strong. But the policy is recommended as well in cases where it is weak, where there is already plenty of competition, and where a country instinctively feels that buying out an old firm is somehow very different from building a new one. The thought verges on the fallacy of misplaced concreteness.

Assume that in an industry with 20 firms there is one which makes no profit because its technology is old, its management moribund. The plant and equipment will be worth more to a foreign firm than to the existing owners. If the assets are sold to a foreigner through a take-over, some of the difference will be shared with the old owners. They are better off. The foreigner is better off for having bought the assets below their value to him. There is net gain all around. A policy of requiring the foreigner to build a new plant and the existing owner to scrap his plant is clearly wasteful.

Excluding Foreigners from the Local Capital Market

It was noted in the previous chapter that foreign enterprise can adversely affect local markets for labor and capital by dominating them, drawing off skilled workers and young managers, or siphoning off savings which might otherwise be invested in mascent indigenous firms. Because of training effects, the host country typically requires foreign firms to hire certain percentages of its labor at all levels of skill on the local market. It may be desirable in the capital market, however, to deny foreign enterprise access to local banks and investment bankers.

The restriction has a balance-of-payments aspect. The foreign exchange authorities are suspicious of firms that enter a country without bringing in foreign exchange, tendering technology or management or similar investment in kind as their share of the equity and expecting to raise the funds for bricks and mortar in the local market. With growth and reinvestment, the ultimate strain on a country's foreign exchange earnings may be substantial on a trivial investment in foreign exchange. This, however, is an inadequate way of analyzing the problem, since the postponement of repatriation of profits at all stages has been the equivalent of an investment in foreign exchange.

Where capital markets function poorly, however, there is a second-best argument for requiring foreign investors to bring money and to furnish none locally. It must be used gingerly, however, because if the screw is tightened too hard, the investor may be driven off. The matter is one for bargaining, not doctrine.

Taking the Package Apart

The success of the Japanese in resisting foreign investment while hiring technology and borrowing capital to the extent they were needed has led a number of observers to urge "taking the foreign investment package apart"—buying technology, management, and capital separately, as required, rather than acquiring them gift-wrapped in a foreign enterprise. The notion is a useful one to analyze. It is strongly possible, however, that it lends itself much better to the Japanese, with their skill in imitating foreign technology and adapting it to their requirements, than it would to the ordinary run of developing or even developed countries.

The basis for foreign investment is that the corporation can earn more on its management, technology, capacity to coordinate operations in different vertical stages, and the like, than it can by selling its skills separately. It earns, that is, a rent, rather than an ordinary return on marginal product. Sometimes it is a close decision whether to sell the technology under a royalty contract or to invest oneself. In these cases, strong insistence of the host country in favor of a royalty arrangement may tip the balance. But as a rule the decision is not close. Technology leased abroad is quickly dispersed; one keeps control of it best by using it oneself in a direct investment.

Creating new products through hiring research firms is said to be expensive. This is possible. Advice is also expensive. It may be possible to improve local management permanently under contracts with Peat-Marwick, Booz-Allen, or McKinsey for a short period, rather than to pay for management through infinity by permitting direct investment. In this case, the local management must be quick learners.

Surely it is desirable for the host country to explore the potential for taking the package apart and buying only those parts of it needed, in the right quantities. The opportunities for doing so are probably limited so long as the host country is relatively undeveloped.

Cartels

It was suggested in the last chapter that direct investment is a conflict, bargaining game in which the locus of bargaining strength shifts through time from the parent company to the host country. In some cases, however, potential host countries worry that they may be giving away too much of their bargaining power initially and would be well advised to consort with potential competitors to limit concessions. This is especially the case where a number of countries in the same area—in the Andes pact in western Latin America, or in the eastern Pacific—find themselves offering larger and larger tax concessions to foreign enterprises in an effort to woo investments away from their neighbors. In this instance, parent companies gain at the expense of host countries as a whole, while no host country is likely to attract more than its share of total investment, because any concession will be matched.

But the interests of the competing host countries are opposed. Any country which sees a chance of attracting a particular investment through a timely concession has to be very high-minded, or group-minded, to resist it.

A significant reason why the French ultimately gave up their resistance to foreign investment was that the other members of the EEC were unwilling to adopt a common policy regarding external investment. In these circumstances, it was idle for the French to oppose specific foreign investments, since the firm in question could always locate in Belgium, the Netherlands, Luxembourg, Germany, or Italy and have access to the French market from a neighboring site.

The cartel technique has been brought to its pinnacle of success in the Organization of Petroleum Exporting Countries (OPEC), which has found a successful device for levering up the price of oil and their share of profits. Each new producer stays outside of OPEC until its place in the market has been established. First Libya, then Algiers, then Nigeria have to be allowed to bite off a market share before they are willing to join the club. There is danger that the club will continue to grow and eventually become unwieldy, like the dinosaur, and collapse.

Disinvestment and Disappearing Investment

Albert Hirschman has made a point that portfolio investment is superior to direct investment in that it can be repatriated in small increments, bond by bond, whereas the repatriation of direct investment is all or nothing, and convulsive. He would provide for government policies of disinvestment, the host country undertaking bit by bit over time to pay off the capital investment. P. N. Rosenstein-Rodan wants to provide in initial investment contracts that after a certain period of time the ownership reverts to the country, at a price agreed upon in advance.

There is much to think about in these proposals, but they suffer from the same weakness as long-term commodity contracts—the inability to find the right price long in advance. Suppose company A invests in mining in country X in the year T, with a provision in the contract that at $T + 15$

the property will revert from company A to country X, or the company it designates, at a price of $1 million. For the next 14 years, but especially the last four or five, company A is trying to make sure that it does not have more than $1 million of assets in its investment, and country X is equally engaged in ensuring that the amount does not go below $1 million. How best to employ the assets so as to maximize the present discounted value of the firm—the efficient solution—is lost to sight. What is implied by long-term future arrangements is revealed by the action of the government of Venezuela in 1971 in imposing conservators for certain oil companies whose concessions run out in 1984, on the ground that the companies' interest was to leave as little as possible of plant and equipment or oil in the ground, whereas Venezuela wanted to inherit going concerns. The price in this case was zero, but the principle is the same: to agree on a price long in advance is to distort incentives. It might be possible to agree in advance that the company would remain a going concern and to agree on a technique for appraising its value. Even this is likely to be fraught with controversy.

The Burke-Hartke Bill

If the world and the United States gain from foreign investment, as suggested in the last chapter, it is by no means clear that American labor gains. In fact, the case can be made that direct investment is the export of jobs, and that plants going abroad to serve the foreign market better or to produce components or finished goods for the United States are "runaway plants," like the firms in the garment industry in the first quarter of the century that ran to nonunion towns as the needle trades were organized into unions. In the late 1960s and early 1970s, the AFL-CIO altered its traditional benevolent attitude toward world trade and investment and called for a change in taxes on international income, supervision of foreign investments, U.S. government regulation of U.S.-based international firms, "fair labor" standards worldwide, and, as a stopgap measure pending the adoption of these policies, regulation of the flow of imports into the United States. In due course, the labor movement got behind the Burke-Hartke bill introduced into the Congress in 1972. This bill proposed to "close tax loopholes" which favored foreign investment and in particular to shift from the principle of "crediting" income taxes paid abroad against corporate income taxes due in the United States to the practice of deducting such taxes from income, and imposing taxes on foreign income when it is earned, rather than when it is repatriated to the United States.

The significance of these provisions can be illustrated by a simple example. Suppose a U.S. firm with a subsidiary in Canada earns $100 there, pays a tax of $50 in Canada, and repatriates $50 to the United States. Its income for U.S. tax purposes would be $100. Assuming the U.S. corporate tax rate were the same as the Canadian, its tax liability would be $50, but the payment made to Canada would count as a tax credit, and it would pay nothing in the United States. Shifting from crediting foreign taxes to deducting them as an expense would mean that income for U.S. tax purposes would be $50 ($100 less $50 of taxes paid in Canada). At a 50 percent rate, the U.S. tax on this amount would be $25. Total taxes on the $100 would thus be $75.

A change from taxing on the basis of repatriated profits to profits when earned is best illustrated by an example where tax rates abroad are lower than those in the United States. Assume that the $100 of profits is earned abroad in a jurisdiction with a corporate tax rate of 25 percent and that the $75 remaining after paying foreign corporate taxes was reinvested abroad. No U.S. tax liability would accrue. In a sense, the U.S. government would be granting the corporation an interest-free loan of the U.S. tax liability ($25 with the tax credit, or $37.50, with foreign taxes a deduction rather than a credit) until the funds were ultimately repatriated, which might be never. The Eisenhower administration proposed a shift from repatriated profits to earned profits in the legislation which ultimately resulted in the Revenue Act of 1962. It was rejected by the Congress after the vigorous protests of business. The argument for taxing earnings is equity with U.S. taxpayers. The argument against is that the double taxation, or the higher rate of taxation of the United States, distorts competition against the local companies. It is also insisted that until the funds are repatriated, the parent company has nothing to pay with.

It is impossible in this space to discuss adequately the efficiency, equity, and administrative features of the two systems of taxation. A case of sorts can be made for or against almost any principle. To change from the tax credit to deducting foreign taxes where tax rates are roughly equivalent is to submit foreign investment to double taxation, as against domestic investment. On the other hand, the application of taxation on the basis of repatriated profits rather than earnings where taxes abroad are lower than U.S. rates is to subsidize foreign investment at the expense of domestic investment. **Tax neutrality** would appear to call for the tax credit and taxation on earnings rather than remittances. But the AFL–CIO, in supporting the Burke-Hartke bill, is perhaps not concerned with tax neutrality. Protection for domestic industry is admittedly discriminatory. The optimal policy would seem to be to maintain full employment in the United States by macroeconomic means and to allow capital to be invested where it can earn the highest return in the world, without reference to taxes (or assuming rates of income tax are harmonized). This is a Pareto optimal solution under certain conditions. Since it would reduce its monopoly position, it would be too much to expect labor to embrace it.

Government Guarantees and Insurance

The case for tax neutrality has a corollary that the United States may have made a mistake in the postwar period in seeking to stimulate foreign investment by insurance and guarantees against expropriation in the developing countries. The theory was that foreign economic development could be assisted by private investment, which would relieve the government of the necessity of making loans directly. To the extent that private investment was inhibited by fear of expropriation, there was a case to be made for insuring the investor against political, but not economic, risks. The difficulty has been that it has injected the U.S. government into the middle of investment disputes which are doubtless better settled without it.

The home country is a partner in any foreign investment to the extent that it earns a tax on the profits and permits losses to be written off against other corporate taxes due. This may be enough. Where the investor is sophisticated and the host country is learning gradually that it cannot have it both ways—nationalizing old properties without compensation and expecting to continue to get new capital, technology, and management assistance from abroad—it is sufficient to leave the complex issues of foreign investment to the private market on the one hand and the host country on the other. The home country's intrusion—through the application, say, of the Hickenlooper amendment, which requires cutting off foreign assistance to countries which nationalize U.S.–owned property—is frequently counterproductive.

The fact that Chile's expropriation of U.S. copper companies exhausts the reserves of the U.S. government insurance entities and requires Congressional appropriations raises the awkward specter of not-always-informed Congressmen debating Chilean economic policies. This seems calculated to exacerbate international misunderstanding. While some aspects of direct investment should be internationalized, as we suggest in the next section, the delicate relationships between private investors and the developing countries might well be left to the competitive forces of the market.

A Forum for Resolving Conflicts over Direct Investment

Much of the difficulty over direct investment is political. A corporation with assets in two jurisdictions may well be a vehicle for the intrusion of one sovereign power into the jurisdiction of another. The United States tells corporations in its midst not to allow their foreign subsidiaries, located in the jurisdictions of other governments, to trade with the enemy, to provide sophisticated equipment which would assist a country to become a nuclear power, or to act in restraint of trade. It urges them to bring home profits, and the like. Thus the corporation may be subject both to double taxation and to conflicting directives. A useful device might be a forum to discuss such issues.

If the corporation is sometimes subject to double taxation, it frequently threads its way between tax systems, or systems of regulation, so as to escape any or all of the controls governments have found it useful to impose. It may divert profits from one jurisdiction to another by charging arbitrary "transfer prices" on materials or components. It may establish financial subsidiaries in the Bahamas, Panama, Liechtenstein, or Luxembourg to escape financial regulation. In due course, with national regulations on such issues as pollution not everywhere uniform, corporations may evade the restraint of the best regulation by establishing themselves where it is weak or nonexistent.

It has been claimed that the rise of the national corporation in the United States weakened the power of the states, counties, and cities and required a corresponding rise in the power of the national government and of national unions. Today the rise of the international corporation has produced a corresponding loss of sovereignty on the part of nation-states, calling for the beginnings of international regulation in the fields of taxation, trading-with-the-enemy acts, and antitrust and financial regulations. The process is necessarily conducted case by case, rather than by writing a code with rules and exceptions. The developing countries would undoubtedly be suspicious of rules agreed upon by the developed countries, and, while invited, should not be pressured into joining. If they were to choose to do so, they could stand aside, as in the trade field from GATT, and even organize on their own, as in UNCTAD.

The rise of neomercantilism in the world in the past few years may be a reflection of the weakening of sovereign states in a world of mobility of capital, skilled labor, and corporate management. As the world gets smaller, it becomes more and more necessary to harmonize tax rates, economic policies, and attitudes toward forces like the multinational corporation, which implies a loss of national sovereignty. One reaction is to try to suppress the mobility and the international forces. Another is to seek to contain them with international institutions.

Summary

Host-country restrictions on foreign investment are generally motivated by instinctive feelings of the peasant, the Populist, the mercantilist, the xenophobe, the monopolist, and those who want to have their cake and eat it too. The only valid arguments for restricting direct investment in the host country are noneconomic or second best. When markets fail to work, it makes little sense to accept the dictates of the market.

Many countries concerned about direct investment seek to restrain it by requiring joint ventures, selectively refusing certain types of investment, refusing permission for takeovers of existing companies, or limiting access to the local capital market. They may also seek to get the benefits of foreign investment without foreign control by hiring capital, technology, management, and so forth, separately. Agreements among potential host countries to limit tax concessions are useful but difficult to achieve. To restrict investments to a particular period of years poses a problem of determining in advance what the investment will be worth in future, or at a minimum agreeing to procedures for establishing such values.

The opposition to direct investment in the United States seems to be largely in the interest of a single factor—labor. This opposition poses a complex issue of keeping the tax system neutral. Early postwar attempts to stimulate investment in developing countries may now be ready for the scrap heap.

In the long run, it is desirable to develop a body of international regulations to prevent companies from sliding between national regulatory and tax systems and to guard them against double jeopardy, with two jurisdictions taxing a given profit or pulling a corporation in diverging directions.

SUGGESTED READING

Texts

V. Salera, *Multinational Business* (Boston: Houghton Mifflin Company, 1969).

Treatises, Etc.

The issues faced by host countries are raised for the most part in the monographic literature, e.g.:

D. T. Brash, *United States Investment in Australian Manufacturing Industry* (Cambridge, Mass.: Harvard University Press, 1966).

J. H. Dunning, *American Investment in British Manufacturing Industry* (London: George Allen & Unwin, Ltd., 1958).

H. Hughes and Y. P. Seng, *Foreign Investment and Industrialization in Singapore* (Canberra: Australian National University, 1969).

M. Kidron, *Foreign Investment in India* (London: Oxford University Press, 1965).

A. E. Safarian, *Foreign Ownership of Canadian Industry* (Toronto: McGraw-Hill Book Company of Canada, 1966).

A. Stonehill, *Foreign Ownership in Norwegian Enterprises* (Oslo: Central Bureau of Statistics, 1965).

Policy-oriented statements are found especially in the so-called Watkins report in Canada: "Foreign Ownership and the Structure of Canadian Industry," *Report of the Task Force on the Structure of Canadian Industry,* prepared for the Privy Council (Ottawa: Queen's Printer, January 1968); and the so-called

Gray report: *Foreign Direct Investment in Canada,* Published by the Government of Canada, Ottawa, 1972.

Points

Worth reading for its political points, if not its economic analysis, is J.–J. Servan-Schreiber, *The American Challenge* (New York: Atheneum Publishers, 1968). A Marxist view is set forth by Harry Magdoff in *The Age of Imperialism* (New York: Modern Reader Paperbacks, 1969) (paperback).

The Hirschman proposal for disinvestment is found in his "How to Divest in Latin America and Why" *EIF,* November 1969. The Rosenstein-Rodan proposal is published in Inter-American Development Bank, *Multinational Investment in the Economic Development and Integration of Latin America* (Bogota, Colombia: Round Table, April 1968).

L. B. Krause and K. W. Dam, *Federal Tax Treatment of Foreign Income* (Washington, D.C.: The Brookings Institution, 1964) was written long before the Burke-Hartke bill was proposed but explores the complex tax issues. M. v. N. Whitman's thesis explores guarantees and insurance in *Government Risk-Staring in Foreign Investment* (Princeton, N.J.: Princeton University Press, 1965).

A strong statement of the AFL–CIO objections to foreign investment by American companies is contained in Volume I of *Papers Submitted to the Commission on International Trade and Investment Policy,* in N. Goldfinger's "A Labor View of Foreign Investment and Trade Issues."

PART IV

The Adjustment Process

Chapter 17

THE FOREIGN EXCHANGE MARKET

A foreign exchange transaction is a purchase or sale of one national money against another. Prior to 1913, the instruments traded in the foreign exchange market were bills of exchange, largely bankers' acceptances, drawn by exporters on importers and accepted by the importers' banks. These were near-money, rather than money. Today, transactions are almost entirely in demand deposits, which are money. There is thus no need to quibble about the word "money" in the foregoing definition.

More significance should be attached to the word "national." There is a temptation to say that a foreign exchange transaction involves the purchase or sale of a domestic money for a foreign money. This temptation must be resisted. "Domestic" implies residence, which is a proper concept for the balance of payments in the next chapter, but misleading for the foreign exchange market. Economic literature is full of references to the New York foreign exchange market, or the London, Paris, or Frankfurt markets. In economic terms, these are imprecise. We should instead refer to the foreign exchange market for the dollar, pound, French franc or deutsche mark, wherever they may be traded.

Perhaps a better illustration of the importance of the nationality of money and the unimportance of residence is to point out that the demand and supply of foreign exchange need not clear the market in New York. If there is an excess supply of pounds, it can be sold for dollars in London, or if there is an excess demand for pounds, it can be satisfied by selling dollars for pounds in London. The foreign exchange market is the market for a national currency anywhere in the world, as the financial centers of the world are united in a single market. This unity has not been a permanent feature, however, since there have been periods of political and economic upheaval, as in the 1930s and 1940s, when exchange controls and other devices effectively segregated national exchange markets. Since the late 1950s, however, national markets for the major currencies have been effectively joined by arbitrage, which we will discuss presently, so that the price of Swiss francs in terms of dollars will be the same all over the world.[1]

Functions of the Foreign Exchange Market

The three functions of the foreign exchange market are to effect transfers of purchasing power, to provide credit for foreign trade, and to furnish facilities for hedging foreign exchange risks. Of these by far the most important is the transfer of purchasing power—from one country to another and from one currency to another. The means of effecting these transfers is identical in broad outline with that used in domestic trade, through the clearing of payments in opposite directions.

International Clearing

The foreign exchange market effects transfers of purchasing power through a clearing process which is the international analogue of the domestic clearing that takes place informally between banks of the same community, in city clearinghouses, within a Federal Reserve district, and in the Interdistrict Settlement Fund. Exporters in one country have claims abroad, and importers have payments to make abroad. Goods move between countries, but payments take place within countries by means of the clearing mechanism, except for the settlement of net balances.

In what follows we leave aside the possibility that international trade will take place in a single internationally acceptable money, for example, that European firms are willing to hold dollars and buy and sell goods to each other and with U.S. traders against dollars. But assume that national and domestic money are identical. A country pays for its imports with its exports. Exporters in a given country receive payment in domestic currency from the country's importers, who thereby pay domestic currency for their purchases from abroad. Goods and credit instruments move across the border, but payments in domestic currency take place within the country as part of the clearing process. The exporter in the United States ships goods to the importer in Britain; and the importer in the United States acquires goods from the exporter in Britain. The U.S. exporter is presumably paid by the British importer, and the British exporter by the U.S. importer. But in an ultimate sense of the U.S. importer pays the U.S. exporter and the British importer the British exporter. The detailed way in

---

[1] The price of Swiss francs three months from a given date in terms of Swiss francs on that date, i.e., the rate of interest on Swiss franc time deposits, may not be identical in different locations, however. This is a subtlety of Euro-currency markets still under investigation.

which this is done will depend upon the way in which the transactions are organized.

Suppose the British importer buys dollars to pay his obligation to the U.S. exporter. How are dollars produced in the London market? Evidently by British exports to the United States for dollars. Dollars paid by the U.S. importer to the British exporter are bought by the British importer and paid to the U.S. exporter.

Or the transaction can proceed in sterling through the medium of the New York exchange market. The U.S. exporter draws a sterling bill on his British customer and discounts it with his bank. The bank then sends it to London for rediscount, selling the resulting sterling to the U.S. importer, who needs it to discharge his debts for goods bought in Britain.

If we omit the case where the British importer starts off with a supply of dollars and the U.S. exporter accepts payment in them, the variety of possible combinations which will clear the market can be summarized as follows:

Foreign Exchange Transaction	Payment by British Importer to U.S. Exporter	Payment by U.S. Importer to British Exporter
U.S. exporter sells £ in New York to U.S. importer	Payment in £	Payment in £
British exporter sells $ in London to British importer	Payment in $	Payment in $
U.S. exporter sells £ to (buys $ from) British exporter	Payment in £	Payment in $
U.S. importer buys £ from (sells $ to) British importer	Payment in $	Payment in £

The international character of the exchange market is evident from the fact that the third and fourth of these transactions between the two exporters or the two importers can take place in London or New York.

This limited example, in which one export is paid for by one import, evidently requires that the separate transactions involve identical amounts of money. Clearing on a more substantial scale, such as is involved in domestic clearings and in the actual foreign exchange market, occurs for instruments ranging over an almost infinite variety of amounts, with large sums on each side canceling out and leaving only small net balances to be settled. But the essence remains simple. Like any other clearing arrangement, the foreign exchange market carries out payments, in this case internationally, by simultaneously clearing debts owed in both directions.

The clearing need not be bilateral. In fact, trade thrives best when the clearing takes place on a multilateral basis. Malaya earns dollars from its sales of rubber and tin to the United States, which it pays to Britain for chemicals, enabling Britain to pay dollars for its purchases of machinery in the United States. Or Canada, by means of the exchange market and multilateral clearing, exchanges wheat and bacon sold to Britain for automobiles and coal bought from the United States. The clearing function of the foreign exchange market applied multilaterally enables countries to effect exchanges of goods far too intricate to negotiate by barter or clearing organized on an ad hoc basis.

In fact, the more multilateral the system, the more it becomes necessary to increase the efficiency of the foreign exchange market through the development of a **vehicle currency** or currencies. With, say, 100 countries trading with each other, there would have to be 4,950 quotations for separate currencies ($n[n-1]/2$) as each country traded with each of the others, but one must not count the same pair twice. With a *numéraire* or vehicle currency, there need only be 99 quotations in terms of the 100th chosen as the *numéraire*. The pound sterling served as the vehicle currency up to 1913, and to a lesser degree to 1931. The dollar has filled the role in the postwar period after 1945. Thus a German importer may buy dollars with which to buy francs to pay for French goods. The dollar market against both DM and French francs is so much broader than the direct DM–French franc market that the transaction may be cheaper in the roundabout way. In this manner, the dollar becomes a part of many transactions in which U.S. residents are not direct participants.

The Eastern trading bloc organized by COMECON suffers from the fact that the ruble is not sufficiently hard for the trading countries to be willing to hold it. In consequence, clearing is inefficient because it is bilateral rather than multilateral.

When a country's claims arising from foreign transactions differ from its payments, there is a balance which must be handled—an excess demand or supply of foreign exchange (supply or demand for the national currency). This may be taken off the market by speculators, short-term capital movements, the monetary authorities, or gold movements. It may be repressed by foreign exchange control which refuses to satisfy certain demands for foreign exchange. Or the price of foreign exchange must change. The possibility of imbalance at the margin complicates the foreign exchange market and opens up a variety of possible outcomes. But the basic function of the market is discharged in dealing with the inframarginal transactions, that is, in clearing payments against receipts in transactions with foreign countries.

Credit Function

In addition to its primary function of clearing payments, the foreign exchange market is also called upon to provide credit. We do not propose to discuss this matter in great detail. This is more properly a subject belonging in books on the techniques of foreign trade and involves detailed discussion of the credit instruments used in the foreign exchange market. In this section we ignore the domestic credit aspect between the traders and their banks and focus on the international extension of credit.

That international trade requires credit follows from the fact that all trade does. It takes time to move goods from seller to purchaser. Someone must finance the transaction for this period, and possibly for longer. In the normal case, credit will be needed as well by the exporting firm during the period required to manufacture the goods and by the importer for the time between his payment for the goods and his receipt of payment after selling them in their original or processed form. But if the exporter can finance manufacture and the importer can finance marketing, credit is necessary for the transit of the goods. If the importer pays cash, he may be said to finance the transaction. If the exporter holds the accepted bill of exchange for his own account or finances the export through an open-book credit to the importing house, the exporter undertakes the financing. In general, however, when the special credit facilities of the foreign exchange market are used, the foreign department of a bank or the bill market of one country or the other will be called upon to extend the credit.

In the 19th century the world financed its trade in sterling. Exporters to London drew bills of exchange on London. The London discount rate was below that in other centers. Foreign banks therefore discounted their sterling bills and repatriated the proceeds to their own money markets. A New York bank, for example, which could earn 8 percent on its money at home and only 4 percent in London would be foolish to hold sterling bills. In discounting for its local exporter it used the New York interest rate, but it rediscounted in London at the lower rate. This meant that a three-month bill for which it has paid 98 (8 percent a year is 2 percent for three months) could be rediscounted for 99. With the London rate typically lower than rates abroad, there was a strong incentive to draw bills in sterling and to discount them in London. In this way, London financed its own import trade.

London, however, also financed its export trade. London banks could have earned a higher return by encouraging their exporting customers to draw bills in foreign currencies which the banks would hold to maturity. But this would have involved taking an exchange risk that these banks were unwilling to undertake. During the period the bills ran, the foreign currencies might change in value. Accordingly, the London banks were resigned to earning the lower rate of interest available in their own market. British exporters drew their bills in sterling, and these were discounted and held to maturity in London. This involved an exchange risk for the foreign importers, who received goods for which they had to pay in foreign currency in three months. But since sterling provided the world's standard of value, exchange risks in sterling were taken unhesitatingly. In this manner, London financed its imports and exports, representing a substantial part of the rest of the world's exports and imports, respectively. In addition, London financed a considerable amount of trade which did not touch British shores, by discounting sterling bills drawn by exporters in second countries on importers in a third.

Note that in such a system London extends short-term credit for a long period, assuming that its trade is steady or growing. Each transaction gets paid off, but the volume of short-term credit remains the same or grows. To the extent that changes in interest rates altered the incentive of foreigners to finance their imports in London and to discount the bills drawn on London for their exports, the short-term credit form gave rise to short-term capital movements. An increase in the London discount rate led foreign exporters to hold more of their claims on London and to finance more of their imports at home rather than in London. The result was a large flow of capital to London (the old bills being paid, not being replaced with new bills drawn). Thus there was a normal position, but the possibility of swings around it by virtue of changes in discount rates.

The decline of the sterling bill and the rise of the dollar as a vehicle currency and a means of financing world trade somewhat altered the mechanics. U.S. trade, exports and imports, was financed in dollars but with less switching of bills between countries. As world trade grew, the export of credit from the United States in short-term form grew on a regular basis. Initially, however, and unlike London, U.S. banks instinctively "tied" their credits to U.S. trade. After 1958, and with the restoration of currency convertibility in Europe, however, there grew up, partly accidentally, a complex institution called the Euro-dollar market by which the United States and many other countries provided credit in dollars to the world.

The Euro-Dollar Market

A major factor which gave rise to the Euro-dollar market was Regulation Q of the Federal Reserve System, which fixed the rates of interest paid on time deposits but did not apply to time deposits owned by foreign accounts. Competition of New York banks led returns on such deposits in 1958 and 1959 to rise one fourth of 1 percent above the Regulation Q ceilings. This in turn induced banks in London to bid for dollar deposits, which they in turn relent to New York. Moreover, some depositors, such as the official agencies of the Soviet Union, found it convenient to hold their dollar accounts in Europe, largely London, out of the jurisdiction of American authorities. European lenders and borrowers in dollars also found it convenient to trade in dollars in London, rather than New York, because of the identity of the time zones, without the need to limit trading to the few hours a day when European and U.S. banks were open simultaneously.

Through the 1960s, the Euro-dollar market grew rapidly. Other currencies than dollars were traded outside their domestic markets. By 1971, bank liabilities in Euro-currencies of eight European countries were $70.8 billion in dollars and $27.1 billion equivalent in other Euro-currencies. (Additional Euro-currencies are held in Canada and Japan.) The major location of the market is London. Depositors consisted of European central banks, firms, and individuals and banks, firms, and individuals in the United States and in third countries outside Europe.

Many transactions in Euro-dollars involve no foreign exchange component. Where U.S. depositors hold dollars in London and U.S. banks or firms borrow dollars in London to be used in the United States, the Euro-dollar market is a simple extension of New York. The balance of payments of the United States is affected, the way the figures are compiled, but there is no foreign exchange transaction. Where, however, the deposits are owned by a European account, there usually has been a past foreign exchange transaction by which the dollars were acquired; and where the funds are borrowed for use in Europe, it is usually necessary to convert them to local currencies before they can be used. The depositor has a **long speculative position** in foreign exchange (dollars), and the borrower a **short** position.

The Euro-currency market poses a number of difficult questions for the international monetary system, which will be dealt with fully only in Chapter 25, but it may be useful to consider some of them here. In the first place, there is a considerable debate whether the Euro-dollar market creates dollars. Those who claim that it does not insist that dollars are created only in the United States. Behind every Euro-dollar liability is a Euro-dollar bank claim on the United States in dollars. When a European business or merchant borrows Euro-dollars, he can only be paid by the transfer to him of the claim on the United States. The opposition, led by Milton Friedman, insists that Euro-dollar banks create money, and primarily dollars, in the same way that ordinary commercial banks do, by making loans which are redeposited in the same banking system. If the first-generation banks (to use the Samuelson textbook phrase) lend to borrowers who spend dollars in the United States, there can be no money creation. But many of those who receive these dollars redeposit them in, say, London in a second-generation bank, which can relend. Initially the resolution of this dispute was found in the thought that very little was redeposited in the Euro-currency market, so that while that market created money, it did so on a modest scale, with modest gearing, like savings and loan associations in the United States. Later, however, it became evident that the dollars were often spent for local currencies in Europe, which meant they were sold to central banks, which redeposited them in the Euro-dollar market. This meant that the expansion rate was higher. In June 1971, however, major European central banks agreed to redeposit dollars in New

York, which cut the connection. The Euro-currency market can create money, then, but not much.

Note here that total deposits of the Euro-currency market include interbank deposits, which on the usual definition are not money. Money is currency and demand deposits in the hands of spenders, not banks.

Another issue was whether the Euro-currency market should be regulated. In September 1968 the Federal Reserve Board required U.S. banks to maintain reserves against borrowings from the Euro-currency market in excess of the amounts outstanding on the previous May. This constituted a sort of reserve requirement. In 1970, the Export-Import Bank sold some debentures for dollars in London in an effort to mop up excess dollars in the market. This represented something like open-market operations. In 1966, a number of central banks, including the Swiss National Bank and the Federal Reserve Bank of New York, undertook to deposit more dollars in London at the year end, to avert a squeeze when banks tried to improve their December 31 statements of condition. This came close to internationally coordinated open-market operations. Despite these rudimentary beginnings, however, the Euro-currency market on the whole has not been regulated but has constituted a pool of funds available now for lending to Italy when it suffers a credit squeeze, now to the United States in the "crunch" of August 1966. It is of great interest as a market falling outside the jurisdiction and responsibility of any one country, which has behaved flexibly and without undue strain—so far. The question is whether the international monetary system and the foreign exchange markets can support such a mass of relatively nervous funds, ready to move from one currency to another.

Hedging

The third function of the foreign exchange market, in addition to clearing and credit, is to provide hedging facilities. An importer with foreign currency to pay abroad in the future runs the risk that the price of the currency will rise between the time the obligation arises and the time it must be discarged. To cover himself against this risk, the importer can deposit funds abroad now equal to the prospective debt, or he can buy forward foreign exchange. By the same token, an exporter with funds coming due in foreign exchange runs the risk that the rate of exchange will fall between the time he enters his contract and the payment date. For cover, he can borrow abroad, sell the foreign exchange for domestic currency, and use the proceeds of his exports when received to pay off the debt, or he can sell his expected foreign exchange forward. Covering an exchange risk is called hedging. Hedging can be done through the spot market, if the trader has cash or credit facilities, including credit facilities abroad. A forward contract is simpler.

A forward contract is a contract to buy or sell foreign exchange against another currency at some fixed date in the future at a price agreed upon now. No money passes at the time of the contract. But the contract makes it possible to ignore what happens to the exchange rate, or almost to ignore it. There is no way the trader can protect himself against what changes in the exchange rate will do to or for his competition. An importer establishes the rate at which he buys foreign exchange and the foreign prices of the goods. But if the foreign exchange depreciates (and the prices of goods do not change *pari passu*), his competitor will get a bargain which will affect the importer's transaction.

The existence of a forward market makes it possible to hedge an exchange position. It also makes it possible to speculate without possessing domestic funds or having a credit standing abroad, provided that one has a sufficient credit standing to be regarded by one's bank as a suitable customer for forward exchange. What constitutes an exchange position which should be hedged by one who is unwilling to hold a speculative position is a complex question. Contracts to buy and sell goods at fixed prices should be hedged. The average commercial trader has enough to worry about in his own product line without concerning himself additionally with forecasting the course of the foreign exchange market. But the possession of cotton in London is not equivalent to a position in sterling: if sterling changes price, the cotton also changes in price and in the opposite direction, since its price is determined in dollars. On this account, the cotton does not involve an exchange risk, and it should not be hedged. On the other hand, if a trader possesses goods in Britain which are specially produced for the British market or costly to transport, so that they have to be sold against sterling, this is equivalent to an open position in sterling.

Financial assets pose even more complex questions. Demand and time deposits in a foreign currency imply a foreign exchange risk and should be hedged through a forward sale unless one deliberately welcomes the exchange risk (assuming, of course, that there is no future liability against which the deposit is held). Equities, such as land or shares, should not be covered, since they may be expected to change in price oppositely to the exchange rate. Especially difficult are the installment paper obtained for sales of durable consumers goods, fixed in local currency but running sometimes as long as five years, and contracts to buy raw materials at a fixed price in a foreign currency at an agreed rate over 5 or 10 years. These contracts might well be written in an international money, since one of the functions of money is to serve as a standard of deferred payment (for contracts). Because of the lack of an agreed international money and since the weakness of the dollar, there is need for hedging facilities for such transactions, but they do not exist. One can hedge particular amounts for one, three, six or nine months—even a year, but the market has not developed five-year contracts, or those which cover a stream of payments as opposed to a single sum.

The most interesting question relates to long-term, fixed-money claims, such as bonds. Here is clearly an exchange risk, but nearly all forward markets are very thin for contracts beyond 6 months or a year, and it makes little sense to try to cover a 10-year asset in dollars with a 3-months' forward sale. In the world of risk averters, the international long-term capital market is likely to dry up when exchange rates change frequently. On the other hand, the movement of long-term capital between the United States and Canada did not cease when the exchange rate was flexible, largely, this writer thinks, because the market took the view that the Canadian dollar would be somewhere near the U.S. dollar in the long run, near enough, in any event, to compensate for the wide difference in interest rates.

An important question is whether the existence of a forward market fundamentally changes the character of the exchange market. The short answer is no. A longer and dustier response is given in Appendix F. The short answer can be expanded here beyond the single word already given. At the opening of this section, it was indicated that hedging can take place through the spot market—holding funds abroad against future requirements, or borrowing funds abroad and transferring them through the spot market. Assuming adequate facilities, the cost will be the same whether one goes through the spot or the forward market. Take the case of an exporter who either borrows abroad and sells the proceeds through the spot market (ultimately paying off the debt through the payment for exports), or sells his exchange forward. In the first instance, he pays interest on the foreign loan but earns interest on the proceeds of the spot sale deposited in his bank at home. If the interest rate abroad is 6 percent and that at home 4 percent, he pays a net of 2 percent interest per annum for the benefit of having his exchange risk covered. If he operates through the forward market, it will also cost him 2 percent per annum. With interest rates at 6 percent abroad and at 4 percent at home, forward foreign exchange will sell at a discount of 2 percent per annum. If it were higher than this, it would pay financial houses to put funds abroad at 6 percent and sell them forward at less than the 2 percent per annum discount. By this means they would earn more than the 4 percent interest rate available at home. Or if the discount on foreign exchange (premium on our exchange) were greater than 2 percent, it would pay foreigners to put their funds here, earning 4 percent, plus the premium of more than 2 percent, which would be a return greater than the 6 percent available on domestic loans. In the real world, the forward exchange rate, calculated in terms of percent per annum, discount or premium, departs from the difference between the two interest rates, or **interest differential,** up to 0.5 percent either side under normal conditions. **Interest arbitrage,** the process of moving spot funds and covering them forward, is unwilling to operate for a return less than 0.5 percent per annum above the return available at home. Over the years, however, the number of people satisfied with smaller margins, down one-eighth of 1 percent, has increased.

In time of stress, interest arbitrage considerations may be overwhelmed by speculators using the forward market to take exchange positions rather than to avoid them. When this occurs and the amount of arbitrage funds is overwhelmed by the volume of speculation, or even reduced by official restrictions, the forward market may not clear itself through offsetting interest arbitrage funds. On such occasions the forward rate can diverge widely from the interest parity, and the forward market can become an expensive facility for hedging.

Arbitrage

To discuss interest arbitrage before arbitrage in general is to get ahead of our story. In interest arbitrage, a position in the spot is cancelled against a position in the forward market. In ordinary arbitrage, a foreign exchange trader will move in and out of a single currency at the same time. It is arbitrage which keeps the market for a given currency unified all over the world.

Suppose a change in demand for pounds occurs in New York. The increase in the dollar rate on pounds will be practically instantaneously communicated from New York to London by arbitrage. The rate for the pound cannot exist at $2.4010 in New York with the rate for the dollar at $2.40 in London, because it would be profitable for arbitragers to buy pounds at $2.40 in London and sell them at $2.4010 in New York. This would increase the demand for sterling in London and the supply in New York and would continue until the prices became the same or differed by no more than the cost of telegrams and interest. Arbitragers are not speculators. Except for a matter of moments, they have no open position in foreign currency. They make their profit from buying *and* selling foreign currencies, in the course of which they end in the same currency in which they started.

Two-point arbitrage is that in which the arbitrager finds a spread in the price of his own currency in two markets, generally his own and one abroad. Three-point arbitrage might involve the purchase of francs in New York, their sale in Paris against pounds, and the sale of pounds for dollars in either London or New York. In this case it is assumed that the rates are identical for the franc in Paris and New York, and for the pound in London and New York, but not for the pound and franc in London and Paris. A three-point deal by an arbitrager in New York would then accomplish simply what two-point arbitrage in francs and pounds would do from either London or Paris. Three-point arbitrage occurs only when exchange dealers in the local market are unaware of the opportunities or forbidden to take advantage of them. It is rare.

Arbitrage is the mechanism which makes two markets that are physically separate a single market in an economic sense. A single market is defined as the place where buyers and sellers of an article trade it at an identical price. In the same market only one price exists. Where the same price exists continuously for the same commodity, there is one market. Where there are two markets and the costs of buying in one and selling in the other are small, arbitrage will produce essentially one price and one market. Where arbitrage cannot take place for one reason or another—for lack of knowledge of the facts of the other prices, because of inadequate communication, or because of prohibitions—prices between markets will differ. In the last case, when arbitrage is prohibited, large price differences will encourage covert trading because the rewards for operating contrary to the law are great.

In the absence of exchange controls, the foreign exchange market for a currency, including all countries where it is traded and with which arbitrage takes place, is among the most nearly perfect markets of the world. This is because money is the most homogeneous of articles, and it can be transferred instantaneously. The wheat markets in Chicago and Liverpool were closely linked in normal times, but not so closely as foreign exchange markets. The international gold market on the gold standard represented a series of markets separated within certain limits by the costs of transferring gold from one country to another. But, for foreign exchange, the cost of the telegrams and the loss of interest on the money for the period of time it is tied up in arbitrage are very small in relation to the amounts of money which may be transferred. The time element is practically eliminated. Accordingly, the price of sterling in New York cannot differ by much or for long from the reciprocal of the price of the dollar in London. Arbitrage is the force which prevents the single market from separating into two markets.

The Foreign Exchange Rate

The supply and demand for foreign exchange determine the foreign exchange rate within certain constraints imposed by the nature of the foreign exchange system under which the country operates. Assuming no foreign exchange controls, traders, banks, and speculators will trade in the market under any system. Under the gold standard there were gold arbitragers. Under the fixed-exchange standard short of gold, there are the monetary authorities. And these monetary authorities may also operate under the flexible exchange rate standard or the gold standard.

The simplest system, though not necessarily the best, is the flexible exchange standard without intervention by the authorities. The price of foreign exchange is determined by the demand and supply for foreign exchange, which are in turn determined by domestic and foreign prices of goods and services, domestic and foreign awareness of trading opportunities, international capital movements, the anticipations of speculators as to the future course of exchange rates, and so forth. The market clears itself through the price mechanism. Some academic authorities insist that such a market will be stable, with speculation acting to hold the market down in the short run when demand exceeds the supply at the old price or to hold it up under the opposite circumstances. We will postpone discussion on the flexible exchange standard until later.

Under other arrangements, however, the movement of the exchange rate is bounded. Under the gold standard, the limits were set by the costs of moving gold from one market to another, the costs including not only transport, insurance, and handling charges but also interest during the time gold arbitragers have their funds tied up. The **mint parity** in Figure 17.1 has no effect except to set the limits of the gold export and gold import

FIGURE 17.1. Establishing an Exchange Rate between the Gold Points under the Gold Standard

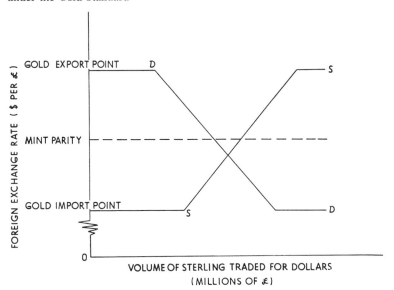

points. It is calculated by dividing the price of a given amount of gold in one currency by the price of the same amount in another. If an ounce of gold costs $35 in the United States and 292s. in London, the mint parity is $2.40 ($35 ÷ 292s. = $2.40 ÷ 20s.). Gold arbitragers then see to it that the two currencies do not depart from the mint parity by more than the cost of moving gold. In Figure 17.2a, demand and supply were equated within the gold points (but with no pull to the mint parity), with the demand and supply curves equal to D–D and S–S, respectively. A change in demand to D'–D' leads to gold exports. In Figure 17.2b, a shift in supply from S–S to S'–S' leads to gold imports.

FIGURE 17.2*a*. Demand for Foreign Exchange Partially Satisfied by Gold Exports

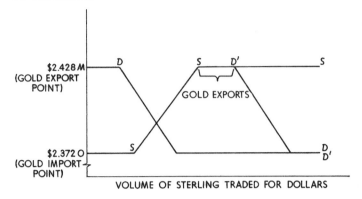

VOLUME OF STERLING TRADED FOR DOLLARS

The role taken by gold in these illustrations can be assumed by speculators, if they believe that the exchange will stay within the gold points in the long run and that it pays to buy foreign exchange when the rate approaches the gold export point. Here short-term capital movements sub-

FIGURE 17.2*b*. Supply of Foreign Exchange (Demand for Local Currency) Partially Satisfied by Gold Imports

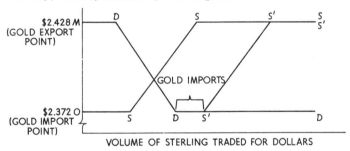

VOLUME OF STERLING TRADED FOR DOLLARS

stitute for gold movements. Or the monetary authorities can intervene in the market. The British authorities, for example, support sterling or hold it down, within a range narrower than that dictated by the cost of transporting gold.[2]

---

[2] The operations of the Bank of England and the Exchange Equalization Account in sterling are more complex than suggested by these paragraphs because there is no fixed gold price, but the London price of gold can change. The British authorities can therefore affect the pound sterling by operating either in the foreign exchange rate for the pound or in the London gold market. Selling gold for sterling in London supports the pound by lowering the London gold price and encouraging gold arbitragers to buy sterling with foreign currencies and gold with sterling. In recent years, however, the Bank of England's management of the London gold pool has been passive, rather than active, supplying gold to the market when demand is brisk and mopping it up when it is abundant.

Note that under the ordinary exchange standard, such as the International Monetary Fund system of Bretton Woods (to be discussed more fully below), parity is fixed not by gold content of currencies but by national decision. Each country is required to choose a **par value** of its currency. Moreover, the width of the range within which the currency fluctuates is again a matter of national or international decision—assuming that the country's currency is fixed and not floating. The Bretton Woods agreement called for support levels, equivalent to the gold export points in the diagrams, that were 1.25 percent away from the par value. At the upper end of the range, equivalent to a gold import point, a country would supply its currency to the market against foreign exchange—sterling prior to 1913 and for the sterling area afterwards, and mostly dollars since and otherwise. The sum of the 1.25 percents on both sides constituted a **band** of fluctuation. One of the proposals for reform of the international monetary system is for a wider band, such as 2¼ percent each side of parity, or 4½ percent altogether adopted at the Smithsonian meeting in December 1971.

Types of Intervention

The defense of the foreign exchange rate may be undertaken for monetary authorities by speculators who intervene before the gold points are reached, by gold arbitragers, or by the monetary authorities themselves. When the monetary authorities intervene, there are the questions of, first, which set of authorities does so, and second, how. On the first score, for example, assume that there is an excess supply of country A's currency or an excess demand for country B's. To keep the A–B exchange rate from changing, the monetary authorities in B may intervene to buy up the A currency, supplying B currency to the market, or the A authorities may be required to sell off gold or B currency or to obtain B currency by one or another of various devices, such as swaps, loans, and selling B currency forward. Where B buys up the excess supply of A's currency automatically, the total reserve bank credit in the system is expanded. Where A draws on existing balances of B's currency, total monetary reserves of the system are reduced (A's reserves are reduced, and B's are not increased). Where A pays gold to B, total reserves in the system are unchanged.

Most of the implications of intervention by the authorities in the foreign exchange market must be left for later discussion. Here we should provide the technical details, however, of three techniques: **forward operations, swaps,** and **"Roosa bonds."**

A country's currency is under attack, let us say, and it has to support it by selling off gold and foreign exchange. When these come to an end, it may, if it chooses, sell forward exchange. In the middle 1960s, the British ran out of dollars. Instead of providing dollars to the market, they provided forward dollars. This had the effect of depressing the forward dollar and encouraging **interest arbitrageurs** to sell spot dollars and buy them forward. The market demand for spot dollars was met by the arbitrageurs, who ended up with contracts to receive dollars again from the authorities after a stated interval.

The notion of intervening in support of an exchange in the forward rather than the spot market was put forward years ago by John Maynard Keynes and has been undertaken from time to time. Some economists have taken the view that it can be undertaken without difficulty, since maturing contracts can be swapped forward (see below). If this were so, a country could defend its currency forever with promises to deliver in the future— sometime.

The British, as indicated, tried this ploy in the 1960s and found it did not work well. By the time its forward sale of dollars amounted to several times its holdings of gold and dollars, the market refused to renew its old contracts and insisted on delivery. The devaluation which had been postponed from 1964 became inescapable in 1967, and the forward contracts for dollars at $2.40 had to be fulfilled with dollars acquired at $2.67— a hard way to make money.

Swaps are a means whereby two sets of monetary authorities can acquire claims on each other. Assume that the Bank of England seeks a short-term credit in dollars to meet pressures in the sterling market. Under its agreement with the Federal Reserve System, it would credit the Federal Reserve with say £100 million and would itself receive $240 million credited to its account with the Federal Reserve Bank of New York. There is no net short-term capital movement, but the Bank of England is better placed to meet an excess demand for dollars. (Likewise the Federal Reserve could be the one seeking credit; the initial phase of the swap is the same.) Such swaps could be irreversible, i.e., final transactions. In actuality, they have been almost entirely temporary transactions which are reversed after a fixed period of time under the terms of the original contract. Indeed, the term "swap" in the foreign exchange market means that a forward contract is involved. Thus the central bank swaps include a spot exchange of currencies with a contract to reverse the exchange at a specified future date.

Market swaps are also common, either by individual traders or by central banks. The Italian authorities use swaps with Italian commercial banks as a means of domestic monetary control, or to limit the volume of dollars held overtly in official reserves. The Italian authorities will sell dollars to banks under repurchase agreements (i.e., forward contract to buy dollars back at a fixed lira price). The spot and future rates are set so as to make the investment attractive to the Italian banks, with a forward rate on the dollar better than that generally available in the market. Since banks pay in spot lira under the swaps, local bank reserves are drawn down and lira credit is tightened. At the same time, the published foreign exchange reserves of Italy are reduced, as spot exchange is transferred to private holders against forward purchases.

The Federal Reserve System has constructed a network of swap or mutual credit agreements with foreign central banks which amounted to $13 billion by 1972. Any credits drawn under the agreements were limited in time, so that they were less useful to defend the foreign exchange rate than foreign exchange or gold owned outright would have been. For temporary pressure against the currency, however, like the forward contracts with which they have many similarities, they serve well. It is because they are useful in the short run while more basic adjustment measures are getting under way that they are called perimeter rather than main defenses.

"Roosa" bonds are less a device to meet current pressure than one to relieve potential future strain. Where the excess supply of A's currency is met by B purchasing it, B has a demand claim on A. Such a claim, which may be used to purchase gold, may be funded into a long-term claim, denominated in A's currency. But, it may be given additional attractiveness to B by a funding which provides a guarantee of its value in B's currency, against the possibility of a devaluation in A's money. This device, named after the then Undersecretary of the Treasury, Robert V. Roosa, has been extensively with foreign currency bonds issued to the authorities in Austria, Belgium, Germany, Italy, and Switzerland. In effect, they substituted future liabilities against current ones, much like the swaps or forward contracts.

The Foreign Exchange Market and the Balance of Payments

As an introduction to the discussion of the balance of payments in the next chapter, it is useful to ask how a record of foreign exchange transactions differs from the balance of payments. These differences will occur in valuation, timing, and coverage.

The differences in valuation between a record of foreign exchange transactions and the balance of payments are that the former mirrors what happens in the world, while the latter records transactions on a consistent basis, perhaps f.o.b. (free on board) or f.a.s. (free alongside ship) for exports and imports, or f.o.b or f.a.s. for exports and c.i.f. (cost, insurance, freight) for imports. The importer may take delivery from the exporter at the factory, at the dock, at the customhouse in the importing country, or at the warehouse in the importing country, and pay for such freight and insurance as may be involved. The balance of payments, on the other hand, must treat the merchandise trade consistently and put in the necessary offsetting items for freight and insurance to accord with what has actually transpired.

Timing is concerned with when transactions are recorded, and the choice of time is among orders, deliveries, receipts, or payments. The foreign exchange record evidently deals with payments: the balance of payments with shipments for exports and receipts for imports (these may differ by a few days, which means that this month's or year's exports from country A may be recorded as next month's or next year's imports in country B). But the relationship of payments to deliveries (to take only one) is by no means uniform. If all goods are consistently sold on three-months' credit, there would be the problem of having a portion of this year's exports for balance-of-payments purposes count in next year's record of foreign exchange transactions. But the relationship varies. Some goods normally are prepaid, some paid at the time of shipment, and some paid with a lag. Bent Hansen recorded the surprising fact that, at a given point in time, close to 10 percent of Swedish exports were prepaid. And the relationship can change as expectations about a national currency change. When there is a likelihood that a given currency will be devalued, foreign importers slow down payments and foreign exporters speed up collections, to give rise to a **leads-and-lags** problem. Normally the question is of little or no importance: payments lag or lead deliveries by a small and constant margin. But if, in any one year, as a result of a change in the speculators' view of a currency the imports of a country which had been sold on 3-months' credit shift to a cash basis, and its exports move from a 3-months' basis to 6-months' credit, the balance of payments (exports and imports) may remain unchanged, but the country receives 9 months' payments for exports in its foreign exchange transactions and is required to pay for 15 months of imports.

The most interesting aspect of the question today is coverage. The balance of payments covers transactions between residents of a country and foreign residents. The summary of foreign exchange transactions is limited to exchanges of the national currency for a foreign one. The balance of payments includes, and the record of foreign exchange transactions excludes, the following: barter; private compensation (where credits and debits in a single currency are cleared within an international firm, or between firms which clear outside the foreign exchange market); and transactions in Euro-dollars, where the dollars come back to the United States and are held here. On the other hand, a foreign exchange record includes, and the balance of payments excludes (since it deals only in net capital movements), gross capital transactions in foreign exchange. But this question is less interesting for a discussion of the foreign exchange market than it is for the balance of payments, to which we turn next.

Summary

A foreign exchange transaction is a purchase or sale of one national money against another. The functions of the foreign exchange market are three: to clear payments between countries; to provide credit for the foreign-trade sector, both within and between countries; and to provide hedging against exchange risks. The credit function of the foreign exchange market has been developed in recent times in new ways by the Euro-dollar market. The forward market used for hedging does not fundamentally alter the behavior of the foreign exchange market.

Arbitrage is the practice of buying and selling a currency simultaneously to take advantage of spreads in the price for it in separate locations, or as between the spot and forward market, for different time periods. The arbitrager takes no exchange risk. Arbitrage makes one market of two, whether it be the market for sterling in New York or for the dollar in London, or the market for spot and forward sterling against dollars. With freely available and plentiful arbitrage funds, the forward rate will tend to the interest differential.

The foreign exchange rate is determined by the foreign exchange market in ways which are affected by different monetary institutions. Under the freely flexible exchange rate without government intervention, changes in price clear the market. Under the gold standard, gold arbitrage at the gold points offset an excess demand or excess supply for foreign exchange. Speculation near the limits of exchange rate fluctuations cleared the market. Or the authorities may buy up the excess supply or satisfy the excess demand, with the aid of various devices to acquire foreign exchange.

A record of foreign exchange transactions differs from a balance of payments in valuation, timing, and coverage.

SUGGESTED READING

Texts

See Yeager, chap. 2; Södersten, chap. 13; Kemp, chap. 14.

Treatises, Etc.

See A. Holmes and F. H. Schott, *The New York Foreign Exchange Market*, 2d ed. (New York: Federal Reserve Bank of New York, 1965); and R. Z. Aliber, ed., *The International Market for Foreign Exchange* (New York: Frederick A. Praeger, Inc., 1969). On the Euro-dollar market, see H. V. Prochnow, ed., *The Eurodollar* (Chicago: Rand McNally & Co., 1970), which includes the paper by M. Friedman on the creation of money by the Euro-dollar market.

On exchange risks, see B. A. Lietaer, *Financial Management of Foreign Exchange* (Cambridge, Mass.: The M.I.T. Press, 1971).

A good discussion of forward rates is in E. Sohmen, *Flexible Exchange Rates*, rev. ed. (Chicago: University of Chicago Press, 1969).

Points

The difference between the balance of payments and a record of foreign exchange transactions is set out in the International Monetary Funds first *Bal-*

lance of Payments Yearbook for the years 1938, 1946, and 1947, issued in 1949.

The best discussion of leads and lags, but an advanced one, is B. Hansen's *Foreign Trade Credits and Exchange Reserves* (Amsterdam: North-Holland Publishing Co., 1961.)

The definitive work on the gold standard is W. A. Brown, Jr., *The Gold Standard Re-Interpreted, 1914–34* (New York: National Bureau of Economic Research, 1934), 2 vols.

Chapter 18

THE BALANCE OF PAYMENTS

Purposes

The balance of payments of a country is a systematic record of all economic transactions between the residents of the reporting country and residents of foreign countries during a given period of time. Such a record may be useful for a variety of reasons, large and small. The major purpose of keeping the c records is to inform governmental authorities of the international position of the country, to aid them in reaching decisions on monetary and fiscal policy on the one hand and trade and payments questions on the other.

The distinction between monetary and fiscal policy and trade and payments emphasizes the manyfold nature of the balance of payments. First came the statistics for trade, which were kept primarily to measure the **resource flows** between one country and another. To these records of goods and, ultimately, services there was added information on other payments and receipts in foreign exchange, to constitute a **foreign exchange budget,** to assure monetary authorities that the country could go on buying foreign goods and meeting payments in foreign currency when they became due. More recently, with the development of national income accounting and the depression of the 1930s, the balance of payments has been used to measure the influence of foreign transactions on **national income.**

Each of these three approaches to the balance of payments can be thought of as linked to a separate system of domestic accounts: the resource approach to the input-output table; the foreign exchange budget approach to the sources and uses of funds statements of the economy; and the national income approach, of course, to the national income accounts. As all three domestic sets of accounts are interrelated, the differences among the separate approaches do not lead to very wide differences in balance-of-payments accounting, as explained below.

Balance-of-payments statistics are being increasingly refined to serve these broad purposes, with quarterly, regional, and detailed breakdowns. They also throw light on particular problems of international commerce.

Definition

The balance of payments of a country is "a systematic record of all economic transactions between the residents of the reporting country and residents of foreign countries." This seems straightforward enough. But it also raises questions. For example, who is a resident? What is an economic transaction?

Tourists, diplomats, military personnel, temporary migratory workers, and branches of domestic companies are regarded as residents of the countries from which they come, rather than the country where they are. These decisions are arbitrary, but since the rest of the accounting is adjusted to them, that fact makes little difference. Some of these decisions which make sense from one way of looking at the balance of payments make little from another. Thus the Italian balance of payments, adjusted to fit national income categories, treats permanent and temporary migrants entirely differently, although there is very little difference between them (i.e., some workers who regard themselves as temporary *ex ante* turn out to be permanent *ex post*, and vice versa). The earnings of permanent workers are part of national income abroad, and all that enters into the balance of payments is their remittances to Italy as a "transfer." The earnings of temporary workers abroad, however, are sales of services which form part of Italian national income and go into the foreign accounts as exports; their local expenditures for room, board, and so on, are imports, and *their* remittances, as an internal Italian transaction, are excluded from the balance of payments. Whichever way it is done makes no difference for the total balance; but the national income approach in this case is the enemy of the foreign exchange budget approach, which would be interested in knowing directly how much is remitted from abroad by emigrants.

Economic Transactions

An economic transaction is an exchange of value, typically an act in which there is transfer of title to an economic good, the rendering of an economic service, or the transfer of title to assets from one party to another. An international economic transaction evidently involves such transfer of title or rendering of service from residents of one country to residents of another.

Normally an economic transaction will involve a payment and a receipt of money in exchange for the economic good, the service, or the asset. But it need not. In barter, goods are exchanged for goods, and in private compensation, assets against assets. Moreover, some goods are transferred to other ownership as a gift, without expectation of payment. In each case, there is an international economic transaction, and the necessity to make an entry in the balance of payments. But some entries are made where there is no international "transaction" in the sense of an international payment: the foreign subsidiary of an American corporation earns a profit in its foreign operations and reinvests it in the country where it operates, without paying a dividend to the parent company. There are those who insist that this should go into the balance of payments as a credit on current account, receipt of profits, and debit on capital account, new investment, even though no international payment takes place. Or a contra item may be required to offset some overstatement elsewhere in the balance of payments, as we shall see below in the treatment of the transport accounts. Here is the necessity for an entry even though the transaction may be purely domestic.

Balance-of-Payments Accounting

In theory, the balance of payments is kept in standard double-entry bookkeeping under which each international transaction undertaken by residents of a country results in a debit and a credit of equal size. An export is a credit for the movement of goods; the means of payment for that export would show up as a debit—the new claim on a foreign company, or bank, the purchase of a foreign security (capital outflow), the acquisition of gold, and so on. Conversely, imports (a debit) might be paid for out of an increase in liabilities to foreigners or by reduced claims on foreigners (both recorded as credits). In actuality, the Department of Commerce measures only one side of physical transactions and the net of the changes in assets and liabilities. Where one side of the transaction is caught by the accountants, say a CARE package sent abroad which results in an export but no balancing claim on foreigners, it is necessary to put in a contra item, in this case "donations" (a debit). It is not always possible to have sufficient knowledge of transactions to effect a complete record of international transactions. Some items can only be estimated. Others are carried out by individuals who, unlike bankers, brokers, security dealers, and large corporations, do not report regularly on their foreign operations. The result is that it is necessary, after summing total credits and total debits, to put in an item for "Errors and Omissions" in order to strike a balance between the two sides of the accounts. Where nonrecorded transactions are large and tend to all be in one direction, the residual "Errors and Omissions" item may be sizable in comparison with other items in the accounts.

Balances within the Total

While total credits equal total debits, by definition, policy questions often call for an analysis of various groups of items within the total. At least five separate types of balance have been distinguished—the merchandise balance, current-account balance, basic balance, the balance on regular transactions (or liquidity balance), and the balance settled by official transactions (or overall balance). Each one matches up selected credits with selected debits and assets that the net of these is significant, presumably in sign and amount. A surplus occurs when credits exceed debits; a deficit, when debits are greater than credits. Since total credits and debits are equal by definition, or would be in a perfect recording system where errors and omissions were zero (as we shall assume), the balance of some items of the balance of payments implies a corresponding balance (with reverse sign) of all other items as well. The student is warned that some tabulations are made on the "reverse sign" basis and that a surplus can show up with a minus sign.

The Merchandise-Trade Balance

The most usual, and the least interesting, balance is the merchandise balance:

$$X_{\text{merch}} + M_{\text{merch}} = 0, \tag{1}$$

where X_{merch} is exports of merchandist (a credit, or plus) and M_{merch} is imports of merchandise (a debit, or minus). This balance has some resources significance, but services belong in the input-output table along with goods. It made more sense in the days of the mercantilists when services played only a minor part in balances of payments. It has less point today. A large merchandise import surplus may be balanced by shipping, interest and dividends, and tourist and other service income, quite apart from the capital account. It is useless from the foreign exchange budget and the national income approaches. There is a temptation to excoriate the attention given to the merchandise balance as evidence of the fallacy of misplaced concreteness—thinking a concept to have analytical significance because it refers to objects with bulk and solidity. One aspect of the merchandise balance, however, can justify the attention it gets in the press. The data are among the earliest received on the balance of payments for a recent period. As such, X_{merch} and M_{merch} serve as proxies for exports and imports of total goods and services, X and M, respectively. But it is correct that the merchandise balance receives too much attention.

The Current-Account Balance

The current-account balance, including services with goods, allows us to set out the other principal items in the balance of payments along with exports and imports of goods and services:

$$X + M = 0 = LTC + STC + G, \qquad (2)$$

where LTC is a long-term capital ($+$ or credit for inflows; $-$ or debit for outflows), STC is a short-term capital (with the same signs) and G is gold ($+$ or credit for exports; $-$ or debit for imports). Errors and omissions, transfers and similar complications are omitted.

When exports consist of newly produced goods and imports go into final use, the current-account balance has interest for national income accounting. As we shall see in the next chapter, when we analyze the impact of foreign trade on national income, $X - M^1$ is a foreign investment, positive or negative:

$$X + M = Y - (C + I_d + G). \qquad (3)$$

When $X + M$ is positive, the country is gaining net claims on the rest of the world, and foreign transactions are a stimulus to national income. It is solvent, even if it is borrowing funds from the rest of the world to buy long-term securities, so long as $X + M > 0$, and the assets it acquires are worth what has been paid for them. With net domestic investment also positive, the net worth of the country is increased. This current-account balance is thus like the break-even or zero-profit position in a profit and loss statement. Obviously, this analogy should not be carried too far. An economist who asks firms to maximize their profits would be calling for a strict mercantilist policy if he asked nations to do the same, that is, to maximize their current-account surpluses.

But the current-account balance says nothing about the foreign exchange budget. For this it is necessary to know how the current-account budget matches with the foreign investment decisions the market makes. This leads to the so-called basic balance.

Basic Balance

The basic balance shifts long-term capital to the left-hand side of equation (2).

$$X + M + LTC = 0 = STC + G. \qquad (4)$$

It assumes that long-term capital movements are autonomous, and short-term capital movements, transitory. It summarizes what is called the transfer problem. With $X + M + LTC = 0$, the long-term capital outflow is exactly offset by a positive current-account balance (or the long-term capital inflow is matched by an import surplus of goods or services), and the capital movement is transferred in real goods and services. If $X + M$ is

---

[1] $X - M$ in national income accounting is the same as $X + M$ in balance-of-payments accounting, since the former concept uses only absolute amounts, without implicit signs.

positive, then LTC is negative, or an outflow. If $M > X$, then LTC must be positive, or an inflow.

If the two sides of equation (4) differ from zero, they must have opposite signs. When the left-hand side is positive because the export surplus exceeds the capital outflow, the country is accumulating short-term claims or gold from the rest of the world, which are minus, or debits. When the two sides of the equation differ from zero, with opposite signs, the economy has not achieved basic balance, capital flows are not being transferred, and the balance of payments is said to be in disequilibrium by those who uphold basic balance as the correct concept of balance-of-payments equilibrium.

Equilibrium is a state of the balance of payments which can be sustained without intervention. It is, of course, unnecessary to have equation (4) hold each hour, day, week, month, season, year, or part of a cycle so long as over the relevant period, whatever it be, the balance of payments will adjust itself with or without the help of regular seasonal or cyclical policy actions. In the start of the transfer process, long-term capital is balanced by short-term capital, and the current account remains unchanged. But if the transfer process has been set in motion, this transitional state is not disequilibrium.

Notice that on this definition, a country that is lending at long term more than its export surplus and borrowing abroad at short term to make up the difference is regarded as in deficit:

$$X + M + LTC = STC + G \neq 0. \qquad (4a)$$

In (4a) assume that the left-hand side is negative and the balancing right-hand side positive, making clear that at least part of the long-term capital outflow is matched by a short-term inflow. The country is lending long and borrowing short. On basic balance this is a deficit. Contrariwise, a country that borrows abroad at long term more than it is able to transfer inward through an import surplus would be said to experience a surplus in its basic balance.

To call equation (4) the "basic" balance does not make it *the* equilibrium concept. It is widely regarded as such. The late Ragnar Nurkse used this concept as his definition of equilibrium (though in prose, not symbols). The U.S. Brookings Report of 1963 also regarded it as the central equilibrium concept, and the British authorities tend to discuss their payments problems in terms of basic balance. Others regard it as insufficient. Basic balance may be satisfactory from the point of view of resources (foreign investments are being transferred in real goods and sevices); or national income (the excess of intended savings over intended domestic investment is equal to intended foreign investment); or the foreign exchange budget (the demand for foreign exchange for foreign investment is equal to the supply created by the export surplus). But it may not account for all the international monetary possibilities.

Suppose, for example, that the right-hand side of the equation ($STC +$ G) is equal to zero, but both STC and G are large and increasing. Foreign deposits in the country are being converted into gold (i.e., a short-term capital outflow, a debit, is offset by gold exports, a credit). It could happen that if foreign claims on the country exceeded its gold stock it could ultimately run out of gold and have to depreciate its exchange rate. The state of the balance of payments may therefore not be capable of being sustained. It is not in equilibrium. Accordingly, the concept of the balance on regular transactions was devised by the Department of Commerce to add a further constraint to the equilibrium position of equation (4).

The Balance on Regular Transactions

The Department of Commerce's definition of balance-of-payments equilibrium has been:

$$X + M + LTC + STC_d = 0 = STC_f + G \,, \qquad (5)$$

where short-term capital (STC) is broken down into domestic (STC_d) and foreign (STC_f) components.

This criterion of equilibrium is sometimes called the **liquidity** definition. Its purpose was to ensure that foreign claims on the country did not mount to a point where the country would be unable to meet them if they were suddenly presented for payment. Concern is really with the stock position, i.e., the balance of indebtedness discussed below, rather than the balance of payments, which is a flow concept. It goes beyond basic balance to focus upon changes in the country's international liquidity position.

Note the sharp asymmetry in the treatment of domestic and foreign short-term capital. This was justified by the Department of Commerce on the ground that the United States cannot be certain of being able to liquidate its claims on foreigners, whereas it must be in a position to make good if foreigners decide to liquidate their claims on the United States. U.S. short-term claims on the rest of the world were treated as unavailable; foreign claims on the United States were regarded as liable to be presented *in toto* at any instant in time.

This asymmetric treatment is not completely proof against criticism. It separates some items which in fact are joined. If a domestic corporation deposits funds in a Canadian bank in New York which are invested in the call-money market which finances the New York Stock Exchange—a balance-of-payments item, since the Canadian bank is treated as a nonresident, but not a foreign exchange transaction—the United States is recorded as in deficit on the overall basis. The short-term liability to the Canadian bank—the call-money loan—is regarded as on the right-hand side of the equation—"**below the line**" in the usual expression—whereas the U.S. deposit in the Canadian bank is "**above the line**" Or Japanese deposits in the United States are below the line, whereas U.S. banking loans to Japan—

an offsetting amount—are above the line. Or U.S. claims on European financial centers—often in dollars, and proved liquid in the summer of 1966—are regarded as frozen, whereas the counterpart deposit in New York is thought to be a highly volatile and nervous sum.

There is, to be sure, the possibility that funds deposited with Canadian banks or invested in the Euro-dollar market could all be reloaned abroad and be unavailable for recall or repayment when and as needed. But the assumption that this will happen is a strong one, and experience proves it does not hold. This is not to say that STC_d and STC_f belong on the same side of the line. A special committee appointed by the Bureau of the Budget to review balance-of-payments statistics, under the chairmanship of Edward M. Bernstein, proposed a new concept which separated official from private foreign short-term capital.

The Balance Settled by Official Transactions

The balance of payments settled by official transactions puts private foreign short-term capital on the left-hand side of the equation (above the line):

$$X + M + LTC + STC_d + STC_{f_p} = 0 = STC_{f_o} + G \qquad (6)$$

where STC_{f_p} are short-term capital movements attributable to private foreigners and STC_{f_o} are those of foreign monetary authorities or officials. Since U.S. official short-term capital movements are treated along with gold reserves, below the line, it is simpler to transform (6) into:

$$X + M + LTC + STC_p = 0 = STC_o + G \qquad (7)$$

where STC_p is all private short-term capital and belongs above the line, and STC_o is official short-term capital and goes below the line. Foreign holdings of U.S. securities of more than one-year's maturity—ordinary U.S. goverments, and special transactions in Roosa bonds, should go in STC_o, not in LTC. So should foreign obligations paid to the U.S. government in advance to hold down the U.S. deficit.

This formulation makes perhaps too sharp a distinction between private and official short-term capital movements. The practice of the Bank of Italy selling off its dollars to commercial banks under a repurchase agreement was mentioned in the last chapter. Swiss and German private banks tend to dump their foreign exchange holdings on the respective central banks each June and December, as they undertake "window-dressing," i.e., prepare for the half-year bank statement of condition in which they presumably like to show large domestic balances and small holdings of foreign exchange—as if they fooled anyone.

The balance on official transactions, sometimes called the "**overall balance**," presents changes in a country's net reserve position (apart from newly mined gold or new issues of Special Drawing Rights [SDRs]). The word "net" is critical. Changes in the country's gross reserves are supplemented by changes in foreign official claims on the country. Where a currency is not held in central-bank reserves, gross and net reserves for the country come to the same thing. For a reserve currency, however, overall balance (or the balance on official transactions) presupposes that any change in gross reserves is offset by an appropriate change in foreign claims.

A word may be useful about newly minted gold and SDRs, which are an artificially created international reserve asset akin to paper gold and represent a vague, long-run claim on the issuing countries. Typically countries count the SDRs received as reserves, but the remote liability as no offset. When SDRs are issued, all countries gain gross and net reserves. The question is whether the SDRs should be put through the balance of payments, to connect up the balance on official transactions with the change in reserves, or whether it is sufficient to leave the connection between the balance of payments and the change in reserves loose. One school wants, for example, to regard newly issued SDRs as exports (for which there are no countervailing imports) so that all countries have an export surplus at the same time. To purist statisticians this is unattractive, since they like symmetry under which all surpluses and deficits in the system add to zero. The issue is trivial. But it underlines a danger about accounting, that men may use it to fool themselves rather than to remind themselves exactly who did what to whom and who got paid for it.

Autonomous versus Compensatory Items

Equation (7), which puts all private operations above the line and official transactions plus gold below the line, recalls a distinction made by the International Monetary Fund in its first *Balance of Payments Yearbook,* issued in 1949, between autonomous and private transactions on the one hand, and official or compensatory items on the other. The distinction between autonomous and compensatory movements is valid: when autonomous movements cancel out over some appropriate time period and there is no need for compensatory movements, the balance of payments is in equilibrium. But to identify private movements with the autonomous and official ones with the compensatory may be carrying the analysis farther than it is appropriate to go. Fritz Machlup, for example, attacked the IMF when it included the official transfers under the Marshall Plan as compensatory payments. He said it was just as (or even more) accurate to say that official transfers under the Marshall Plan made possible the current-account deficits of Europe as it was that the Marshall Plan transfers compensated for the current-account deficits.

This is the nub of the difficulty. It is entirely correct to put autonomous movements above the line and compensatory movements below it, but there is no unique and unchanging way to designate which movements are which. Foreign aid may start out as compensatory and subtly evolve as autonomous. When the sea change occurs, it is impossible to say. And any rule of thumb which argues that such and such kind of transactions is always autonomous and such and such always compensatory will find itself on occasion in difficulty.

Banker versus Trader

Equations (5), (6), and (7) all put a considerable amount of short-term private capital above the line, or on the left-hand side of the equation. This is because some short-term capital, especially domestic, is regarded as moving in response to deep-seated forces such as trends in the quantity of trade, and hence as in no way responsive to short-term swings in payments. But it is too much to say that all domestic private short-term capital is impervious to short-run stimuli. The proof is that tight money in the United States in 1966 and again in 1968–70 drew funds to the United States from the Euro-dollar market. To the extent that private short-term capital flows are subject to monetary policy, which is controlled by the monetary authorities, they, as well as official funds, can be regarded as compensatory.

Hal B. Lary of the National Bureau of Economic Research thought it useful to separate those private capital movements which were responsive to monetary policy from others which were slow moving and influenced by such factors as the growth of trade, putting the latter above the line and the former, along with gold and official holdings of foreign exchange, below. The difficulty, however, is that there is no clear basis for distinguishing between the two types of capital by instrument or character. How to tell the sheep from the goats?

If Lary's reorganization of the balance-of-payments equation is non-operational because of the difficulty of separating out short-term capital movements that respond to interest rates from those that do not, his distinction between a trader and a banker is a suggestive one. What it suggests is this: that the rules of thumb appropriate to a trader may not apply to a banker, and that the Department of Commerce's definition of equilibrium may fit a country which is essentially a trader, but leaves something to be desired for the United States, which is in the international banking business.

Take an ordinary business. It likes to have a quick asset or current ratio of 2 to 1; that is, for every dollar of its quick or current liabilities it likes to have two dollars of cash or other quick assets. This provides a safety margin against the sudden presentation of claims against it and possible difficulties in speedily liquidating inventories or collecting accounts receivable. The current ratio is a liquidity, not a solvency measure. In its calculation, all demand liabilities are regarded as dangerous and not all current assets as cashable.

A bank, on the other hand, operates with a ratio of roughly 1 to 6 or 8 between its vault cash and reserves with the Federal Reserve System and demand liabilities. It knows from experience that not all its liabilities are going to be presented for conversion into the ultimate reserve. These liabilities are used as money and pass from hand to hand. The bank must be alive to the possibility of a run, against which it may have to encash its secondary reserves and seek support from rediscounting agencies as the Federal Reserve System and the FDIC. But its solvency depends upon its capacity to match a flow of cash from new deposits and maturing loans and investments against withdrawals of existing deposits. To claim that a bank is in deficit every time its deposits and loans and investments rise, or its quick-asset ratio falls below 2, would be to apply the wrong analysis.

The United States is both a firm and a bank, of course, but its liquidity is more akin to that of a bank than of a firm. As all good elementary economics textbooks explain, bank reserves present a paradox. When no one mistrusts the bank, they are not needed (apart from a mismatch in the normal flow of payments and receipts). When no one trusts the bank, 100 percent reserves are hardly sufficient. Moreover, while it is true that banks grow, expanding assets and liabilities, without being regarded as in deficit as would be the case if the increase in liabilities were counted against them without the increase in assets counting in their behalf, the assets normally grow proportionately. In the case of the United States, the primary asset, gold, has declined from $23 billion to $10.5 billion over the postwar period, other reserve assets have recorded gains of $2.0 billion for Special Drawing Rights, $500 million for convertible foreign exchange, and a loss of $1.5 billion in the IMF position, but liabilities to foreigners have risen from $5 billion in 1947 to more than $68 billion in 1972. $50 billion are owed to foreign central banks, and the rest largely to banks. There is a question as to how much of this last figure is a temporary peak from short speculation, which will be drawn down when bear speculators ultimately reverse their positions. But the 1947 reserve ratio, which was generously high, has shrunk to painfully low levels.

The distinction between official and private deposits implicit in the balance settled by official transactions assumes that private holders of dollars are willing holders, and official holders are not. There is something to this, at least beyond a certain point reached some time ago. The French converted dollars into gold in 1965, and even the Belgian National Bank undertook some conversions in 1971, despite the understanding after 1968 (not contractually spelled out) that foreign central banks would hold dollars and not seek to convert them to gold in the United States. From the **two-tier gold system** of March 1968, which meant that gold in the central-bank pool sold at $35 an ounce and gold outside at whatever the private market chose, convertibility was on the books, but it was generally understood that it would not be used. When an attempt was made to use it in August 1971, it was abandoned. The bank had ceased to pay off its liabilities in high-powered money. But dollars (at least half of the supply in circulation) were useful as international money in world trade.

A bank is "in deficit" when it is acquiring dubious assets against its undoubted liabilities, which raises the question of solvency discussed in connection with equation (3).[2] It is also in deficit when its portfolio is unbalanced and includes a shrinking proportion of quick assets. But lending long and borrowing short is not *ipso facto* a deficit, so long as reserve ratios are maintained. Lending long and borrowing short is what financial houses, including banks, do. It can be overdone: portfolios must be balanced among quick, secondary, and long-term assets, and deposits must be watched for their nervousness. But rules of thumb which say that this and this asset does not count for, and this and this liability counts against, are too mechanistic.

Here, then, are five concepts of balance-of-payments equilibrium. For trading countries, basic balance is sufficient. And for the trader role in the United States, it is equally cogent. When it comes to banking, however, rules of thumb mislead rather than inform. A statistical or stochastic approach could measure the mean of the probability distribution and its variance, that each asset could be turned into cash when it was needed and that each deposit would be withdrawn. This is the exercise which good bankers perform instinctively rather than with mathematics.

But the student is reminded that he should not say that a country's balance of payments is in deficit without specifying what concept he has in mind and giving some indication why that is the appropriate concept. Politicians, editorial writers, and the man in the street all insist that they don't want analysis: "Just give me a number." But there is no number which is fully informative. In recent years there have been occasions when a deficit on the liquidity balance has been accompanied by a surplus on overall balance—as U.S. banks borrowing Euro-dollars have drawn down foreign central-bank dollar holdings in the United States. From time to time governmental authorities have diddled the numbers by selling foreign holders securities of one-year-and-a-day maturity to convert short-term capital to long-term capital and improve the statistics. It is of some interest that the Department of Commerce publishes an analysis of these "special" transactions which enables the careful student to unscramble the omelette. But in general, be wary of the numbers. What counts is anal-

---

[2] If $X + M = 0 = LTC + STC$ where $LTC < 0$, $STC > 0$, it is assumed that the long-term capital assets are worth what they cost. Otherwise $X + M = LTC + STC \neq 0$, with the left-hand side negative and the right positive, which is a deficit position.

ysis and even "feel": How solid is the underlying statistical position and how much confidence does the market, including foreign central banks, have in the currency?

The Figures

Table 18.1 gives averages of the balance-of-payments entries for 1953–55 and 1958–60 from the Brookings report. This emphasizes the basic bal-

TABLE 18.1. Major Changes in U.S. Basic and Total Net Balances of Payments, Averages for 1953–55 and 1958–60 (billions of dollars)

Item	1953–55 Average	1958–60 Average	Change
Goods and services:			
Merchandise exports	13.1	17.3	+4.2
Merchandise imports	−10.9	−14.3	−3.4
Trade balance	2.2	3.0	+.8
Military expenditures	−2.7	−3.2	−.5
Net investment income	1.7	2.2	+.5
Other services, net	−.2	−.5	−.3
Net goods and services	.9	1.5	+.6
Aid and long-term capital:			
Government aid	−2.1	−2.7	−.7
U.S. private long-term capital	−.9	−2.5	−1.6
Foreign long-term capital	.3	.4	+.1
Net aid and long-term capital	−2.6	−4.9	−2.2
Basic balance	−1.7	−3.4	−1.7
Prepayments of foreign debts	...	.1	+.1
Recorded movements of U.S. short-term capital and net errors and omissions ...	.1	−.5	−.6
Total net balance	−1.6	−3.7	−2.1

Source: W. S. Salant and Associates, *The United States Balance of Payments in 1968*, Washington, D.C.: The Brookings Institution, 1963.

ance and the balance on regular transactions or liquidity balance (here called the total net balance). Table 18.2 presents extracts from a condensed summary table from the Bernstein Committee report, reconciling the balance settled by official transactions and the balance on regular transactions. The tables are presented to show the arbitrary relationships between the various concepts, although the official balance is always smaller than the balance on regular transactions.

The tables suggest one point worth great emphasis. It is analytically wrong to connect up two items in the balance of payments unless there is independent evidence of their functional connection, as in the case of

TABLE 18.2. Condensed Summary of U.S. Balance of Payments, 1958–66, with Reconciliation Items (billions of dollars)

	1958	1959	1960	1961	1962	1963	1964	1965	1966
Goods, services, and remittances	1.5	− 0.7	3.2	4.9	4.3	4.9	7.6	5.8	4.2
Merchandise exports	16.3	16.3	19.5	19.9	20.6	22.0	25.3	26.2	29.2
Merchandise imports	−13.0	−15.3	−14.7	−14.5	−16.1	−17.0	−18.6	−21.5	−25.5
Services and remittances (net)	1.4	1.2	1.1	2.0	2.2	2.1	3.0	3.2	3.3
Military payments and receipts	− 3.1	− 2.8	− 2.7	− 2.6	− 2.3	− 2.2	− 2.1	− 2.1	− 2.8
U.S. government grants and capital (net)*	− 2.6	− 2.4	− 2.8	− 3.5	− 3.7	− 3.9	− 3.7	− 3.6	− 3.9
Long-term private capital (net)	− 2.6	− 1.4	− 2.1	− 2.2	− 2.7	− 3.3	− 4.3	− 4.6	− 1.5
Short-term claims of foreign banks (net)	0.0	1.1	0.1	0.6	0.1	0.4	1.5	0.1	2.7
Other short-term private capital (net)	− 0.2	− 0.1	− 1.6	− 1.3	− 0.5	− 0.3	− 1.7	1.2	0.1
Foreign official capital, except claims of monetary institutions	0.3	0.4	0.6	0.4	0.4	0.3	0.0	0.2	− 1.0
Net errors and omissions	0.5	0.4	− 0.8	− 1.0	− 1.1	− 0.3	− 0.9	− 0.4	− 0.4
Balance settled by official transactions	− 3.0	− 2.5	− 3.5	− 2.0	− 3.3	− 2.3	− 1.5	− 1.3	+ 0.2
Less: Selected inflows of foreign capital short-term claims of foreign banks	0.0	1.1	0.1	0.6	0.1	0.4	1.5	0.1	2.7
Other liquid foreign private claims	0.2	− 0.0	− 0.2	0.1	0.1	0.4	0.3	0.3	0.2
Foreign official capital, as above	0.3	0.4	0.6	0.4	0.4	0.3	0.0	0.2	1.0
Plus: Other adjustments, including rounding	0.0	− 0.2	0.1	0.0	0.1	0.1	0.5	0.6	0.3
Balance on regular transactions	− 3.5	− 4.2	− 3.9	− 3.1	− 3.6	− 3.3	− 2.8	− 1.3	− 1.4

* Excludes debt prepayments.

Source: *Report of the Review Committee for Balance of Payments Statistics to the Bureau of the Budget*, Washington, D.C. April 1965; plus various *Surveys of Current Business*.

the funds deposited in the New York branch of the Canadian bank reinvested in the United States, or the dollar deposits in London which were laid off in New York. We have seen in Chapter 14 the error of comparing interest and dividends with new investments in Latin America. The point is worth making more generally. All the debits determine all the credits in the balance of payments, and vice versa, and it is analytically wrong to say that the imbalance between some collected debits and some credits is the result of a change in any one or more debits and credits. There is a temptation to ascribe the worsening of the basic and overall balance in Table 18.1 to the private capital outflow of the same order of magnitude, but it must be resisted. Or Table 18.2 suggests a villain in U.S. government grants and capital lending. Occasionally we have information that interest and dividends are partly reinvested abroad, so that the items are linked, or foreign aid is tied, so that exports are connected to aid. Lacking such information, we can only say that the system is a general-equilibrium one, with all determining all, through links which takes them to domestic and foreign prices and incomes, and behind them tastes, resources, technology, domestic and foreign economic policies, and so on. A strong case in fact can be made against comparing merchandise exports with merchandise imports, as in equation (1), despite the long tradition of so doing, since merchandise exports are linked with all other credits to imports and all other debits, and no more to one class of debits than to another (except where we have direct knowledge of barter).

If the merchandise balance is a concept of dubious value, so much more is the tourist balance, the interest and dividend balance, or the technology gap, as measured by payments for patents and technology netted out against credits. These are perhaps useful measures of comparative advantage, or specialization, but they seem to imply that zero balance has some validity or that a surplus should be sought. A particularly offensive form of this balancing is the U.S. insistence that Germany should buy as much from the United States in military equipment as it costs the United States to maintain an army (for its own protection) in Germany. That it is futile for the United States to focus on the tourist gap is illustrated by the possibility that foreign countries might in turn seek to narrow the interest and dividend gap. An economist friend of the author attacks the concept sarcastically by bemoaning the U.S. banana gap.

Table 18.3 presents a somewhat different breakdown of the details, along with the change in reserves. The original table, by L. B. Krause for the Williams Committee, gave figures only for 1969 and a forecast for 1975. Insertion of the data available for 1971 suggests how quickly the exercise at forecasting runs into trouble. The student might learn a great deal by comparing the figures on the balance of payments forecast by the Brookings Institution in 1963 for 1968 with the 1968 actuals and trying to figure out where and why the Brookings estimates went wrong. The in-

TABLE 18.3. The U.S. Balance of Payments, 1969, 1971 and 1975 Projected (billions of dollars)

Balances	1969*	1971†	1975
Trade	0.7	—2.9	0
Travel	—1.3	—2.2	—1.5
Military expenditures	—3.4	—2.9	—2.0
Investment income and fees	5.8	8.0	10.3
Other services	0.3	—	0.3
Goods and services	2.1	0.7	7.1
Private transfers (net)	—1.2	—1.5	—1.2
Private U.S. capital			
Direct	—3.0	—4.5	—3.0
Other private	—2.0	—5.1	—4.8
Foreign private capital			
Direct	0.7	—0.2	0.3
Other private‡	9.2	—15.6	4.7
Net private capital‡	4.9	—25.4	—2.8
U.S. government grants and loans	—3.2	—3.7	—3.2
Overall balance	2.7	29.8	0
SDR allocation	0	0.7	1.0
Net reserve§	—2.7	2.3	—1.0

* *Survey of Current Business,* March 1970.
† *Survey of Current Business,* March 1972.
‡ Includes errors and omissions.
§ Negative figure indicates an increase.

clusion of Krause's estimate for 1975 in these pages will in due course provide another opportunity for such an exercise—or it may not.

The Balance of Indebtedness

Table 18.4 sets out the balance of indebtedness of the United States for selected years from 1914 to 1955, and Table 18.5 shows the somewhat altered form of the same statement for 1960 and 1970, emphasizing the liquidity or nonliquidity of claims and liabilities. In the previous editions of this book, the balance of indebtedness was gently derided as a less significant statement than the balance of payments because of the difficulties encountered in valuing various assets and, indeed, in obtaining complete coverage. Direct investments abroad are included at book value, i.e., initial investment plus or minus successive annual investment or disinvestment. This is an inaccurate measure of market value or their value as going concerns. Some of the government loans, moreover, have little value as repayment runs in foreign currencies with limited likelihood of collection in hard cash.

Nonetheless, despite its weakness as a statement, the balance of indebtedness has increased in interest, as the concept of the United States as

TABLE 18.4. International Investment Position of the United States in Selected Years, 1914–55 (billions of dollars)

	1914	1919	1930	1939	1946	1955
U.S. investments abroad	3.5	7.0	17.2	11.4	18.7	44.9
Private	3.5	7.0	17.2	11.4	13.5	29.0
Long-term	3.5	6.5	15.2	10.8	12.3	26.7
Direct	2.6	3.9	8.0	7.0	7.2	19.3
Portfolio	0.9	2.6	7.2	3.8	5.1	7.4
Short-term		0.5	2.0	0.6	1.3	2.4
U.S. government					5.2	15.9
Long-term					5.0	15.2
Short-term					0.2	0.7
Foreign investments in the U.S. ...	7.2	4.0	8.4	9.6	15.9	29.6
Long-term	6.7	3.2	5.7	6.3	7.0	12.6
Direct	1.3	0.9	1.4	2.0	2.5	4.3
Portfolio	5.4	2.3	4.3	4.3	4.5	8.3
Short-term*	0.5	0.8	2.7	3.3	8.9	17.0
U.S. net creditor position	−3.7	3.0	8.8	1.8	2.8	15.3
Net long-term	−3.2	3.3	9.5	4.5	10.3	29.3
Net short-term	−0.5	−0.3	− 0.7	− 2.7	− 7.4	−13.9

* Includes U.S. government securities.

a bank has come to the fore. The balance sheet of a bank may be less than 100 percent communicative because of some assets which should have been written down and have not been, and of other hidden assets which do not appear at all. Judging how solvent and liquid the bank is, is an art for the depositor and bank inspector, as it is for the banker himself.

Summary

The balance of payments of a country is a systematic record of all economic transactions between the residents of the reporting country and residents of all foreign countries. Certain problems must be settled in determining who is a resident and what is a transaction. But any consistent scheme of reporting is adequate for the purpose, so long as it is organized in such a way as to serve the uses to which it is put. The most important use of the balance of payments of most countries is to describe in a concise fashion the state of international economic relationships of the country as a guide to monetary, fiscal, exchange, and other policies. The balance of payments was originally estimated to reveal the sources and uses of foreign exchange and then was thought of in terms of the contribution, positive, or negative, of international transactions to domestic income determination. At the current time in the United States, interest is reverting to foreign exchange, and in particular to the international liquidity position of the United States.

While total credits equal total debits in the balance of payments, a num-

TABLE 18.5. International Investment Position of the
United States, 1960, 1970 (billions of dollars)

	1960	1970
U.S. assets abroad	85.6	166.6
Nonliquid assets	66.2	149.7
U.S. government	16.9	32.2
Private long-term	44.5	104.7
Direct investment	31.9	78.1
Stocks and bonds	9.6	19.6
Other nonliquid	3.0	7.0
Liquid assets	19.4	16.9
U.S. liabilities to foreigners	40.0	97.5
Nonliquid liabilities to other than		
official agencies	19.8	50.5
U.S. government	0.8	2.0
Private long-term	18.4	44.8
Direct investment	6.9	13.2
Stocks and corporate bonds	10.0	25.6
Other nonliquid liabilities	1.5	6.0
Liquid liabilities and nonliquid liabilities		
to foreign official agencies	21.0	47.0
Private	9.1	22.6
Official	11.9	24.4
U.S. net creditor position	44.7	69.1
Nonliquid	46.4	99.2
Liquid	− 1.6	− 30.1

ber of partial balances have been devised to indicate the degree of approach to equilibrium. The merchandise-trade and the current-account balances are not highly useful for this purpose. Basic balance or the current account less long-term capital exports (or plus capital imports) indicates whether long-term capital is transferred. Balance on regular transactions is designed to measure liquidity, rather than solvency, and assumes that demand liabilities will have to be paid, whereas quick assets are not available to meet them. The balance of payments on official transactions assumes that private capital inflows from broad are voluntary, but official inflows are unwilling and are undertaken only to compensate the accounts. All these concepts apply more fully to a trader country than to one which acts as a banker.

It is a mistake to match up a debit with a credit item in the balance of payments, or to attribute a deficit or surplus to a single item with opposite sign, unless one has specific information that the items are functionally associated.

The balance of indebtedness is a statement of outstanding claims and liabilities of dubious accuracy, given the difficulties of measurement, but of increasing interest as the liquidity status of a banker country attracts attention.

SUGGESTED READING

Texts

Stevens, chaps. 2–6, 13, and 14; Yeager, chap. 3; Södersten, chap. 14; Kemp, chap. 14.

Treatises, Etc.

See Report of the Review Committee for Balance of Payments Statistics to the Bureau of the Budget, *The Balance of Payments Statistics of the United States*, A Review and Appraisal (Bernstein report) (Washington, D.C.: U.S. Government Printing Office, 1965); W. S. Salant et al., *The United States Balance of Payments in 1968* (Brookings report) (Washington, D.C.: The Brookings Institution, 1964) (paperback); H. B. Lary, *Problems of the United States as World Trader and Banker* (Princeton, N.J.: Princeton University Press, 1963).

In the periodical literature, see the essay by R. Nurkse in American Economic Association, *Readings in the Theory of International Trade;* W. Lederer, *The Balance on Foreign Transactions: Problems of Definition and Measurement*, Special Papers in International Economics (Princeton, N.J., September 1963); C. P. Kindleberger, "Balance-of-Payments Deficits and the International Market for Liquidity," *EIF*, May 1965; and R. Triffin, "The Balance of Payments and the Foreign Investment Position of the United States," *EIF*, September 1966.

Points

Table 18.3 by L. B. Krause is from his article in *Papers Submitted to the Commission on International Trade and Investment*, Vol. I, p. 64. The other papers in Part II of Volume I of the *Papers* are also worth attention. Tables 18.4 and 18.5 are from the *Survey of Current Business* annual article of indebtedness, which usually appears in the October issue.

Professor Machlup's attack on the IMF's concept of compensatory finance is presented in "Three Concepts of the Balance of Payments and the So-called Dollar Shortage," *EJ*, March 1950, reprinted in F. Machlup, *International Payments, Debts and Gold* (New York: Charles Scribner's Sons, 1964).

| Chapter 19 | DISEQUILIBRIUM AND ADJUSTMENT: THE ROLE OF PRICE |

Having explored the foreign exchange market and the balance of payments, we now come to questions of disequilibrium and adjustment. The issues are complex. To simplify them, we will deal with price, income, and money in three separate chapters on a partial-equilibrium basis—varying the exchange rate (price), for example, while making *ceteris paribus* assumptions about incomes and money. A fourth chapter will suggest how the mechanism can work in general equilibrium by allowing several variables to change at once.

If the foreign exchange market gets out of equilibrium, equality of demand and supply can be restored in one of a number of ways:

1. Through buying up excess supply, or supplying excess demand, by the authorities for a period and waiting for the disequilibrium to reverse itself. This is financing the deficit or surplus in the balance of payments. Persistent deficits cannot be financed, of course, since the country in question runs out of reserves and credit; and persistent surpluses, while possible to finance, are uncomfortable. But within limits, disequilibriums can be financed.
2. By shifting the demands for foreign goods and the supply of goods for export by altering domestic national income.
3. Through rationing the supply of foreign exchange among competing uses or restricting the demand, i.e., foreign exchange control.
4. By allowing the exchange rate to change.

This chapter examines the last alternative. The analysis applies to freely fluctuating exchange rates, changes in pegged rates, and movements within bands. To a limited degree and with necessary modifications, it applies to cases where the domestic price level changes but the exchange rate remains fixed. By and large, however, we assume the exact contrary: a set of goods prices fixed in local currency and a varying exchange rate. The question is how changing exchange rates affect the demand and supply for exports and imports, and through them the demand for and supply of foreign exchange.

The Fluctuating Exchange Rate

When the demand for foreign exchange differs from the supply, the market can be cleared by altering the rate. This change in the rate not only clears the market in the short run. It changes the relationship between the prices of internationally traded goods—goods exported and imported, and goods produced domestically which are close competitors of imports—and the prices of domestic goods which do not enter into international trade. An increase in the prices of internationally traded goods will expand the production of exports and of import-competing goods that are now more profitable and will curtail expenditure on imports. A decrease in the prices of internationally traded goods, relative to domestic goods, on the other hand, would increase imports and lead to a contraction of exports.

Depreciation of a currency will increase the domestic price of internationally traded goods if we assume that world prices are unchanged. Suppose that the world prices of cotton textiles and wheat are represented by their New York prices and stand at 50 cents a yard and $2 a bushel, respectively. Leaving out of consideration costs of transportation, with the French franc at 20 cents (five to the dollar), the Paris prices of these commodities will be 2½ francs per yard for cotton textiles and 10 francs per bushel for wheat. If the value of the French franc is changed by the foreign exchange market, still assuming world prices unchanged, the franc prices of these commodities will be affected. A depreciation of the franc to 15 cents will raise the price of cotton textiles to 3⅓ francs per yard and that of wheat to 13⅓ francs per bushel. Cotton textile manufacturers will be disposed to expand their production and sales abroad, which increases exports; domestic producers will raise more wheat at the higher price, which will enable millers to limit imports.

An appreciation of the franc from 20 cents to 25 cents (from 5 to the dollar to 4 to the dollar) would lower the prices of textiles and wheat to 2 francs and 8 francs, respectively, which would discourage exports and encourage imports.

Even if we abandon the assumption that the world price remains unchanged, the first effects of depreciation will be to encourage exports and discourage imports, while the converse will be true of appreciation. Suppose that the French franc depreciates from 20 cents to 15 cents U.S. but that instead of franc prices of cotton textiles and wheat rising to 3⅓ and 13⅓ francs, respectively, world prices fall in New York to 37½ cents for cloth and $1.50 for wheat. In Paris the price of cotton textiles is still 2½ francs a yard, and of wheat, 10 francs a bushel. There may be no incentive to alter trade in France with prices unchanged, but there will be in the rest of the world. It is less profitable to produce wheat for export to France at the lower price, so that French imports will decline; and since the goods bought from France are cheaper than before, it pays to buy more. French exports will increase.

A change in the exchange rate alters the relationship between prices of internationally traded goods in two countries. At one limit and the other, the price change will occur all in one country, while the price in the other remains unaffected. In the normal case with only two countries, prices will change somewhat in both and will alter the relationship of internationally traded to domestic goods in both countries.

There will be secondary effects operating through income, if only those which are brought about by the initial repercussions on foreign trade. These will work in the opposite direction from the foreign exchange rate change. A depreciation of the exchange rate, for example, will expand exports and reduce imports. But both the expansion of exports and the reduction of imports will increase national income, and this will tend to decrease exports and expand imports. These secondary effects may be offset through action of the monetary or fiscal system; or they may be exaggerated through policy decisions or mistaken action. Price is then not the whole story in adjustments brought about through exchange rates. But it bears the initial impact.

The complications of the income movements set off by exchange rate changes are left for Chapter 22. At this stage the task is to go into how much exports and imports are affected by changes in exchange rates. This involves a discussion of elasticities of demand and supply in foreign trade.

Excess Demand and Supply Curves

The elasticity of demand for imports is higher than the elasticity of demand for the product as a whole if there is any elasticity to the domestic supply schedule. Similarly, the elasticity of the supply of exports is higher than the elasticity of the supply curve as a whole if there is any domestic consumption of the export product and the domestic demand curve has elasticity greater than zero. These propositions may best be illustrated by the process of consolidating domestic demand and supply curves into a single curve representing excess demand or excess supply. It is this last excess-demand or excess-supply curve which is the operational schedule in international trade.

Figure 19.1*a* shows an ordinary set of curves representing the domestic demand and supply of a given commodity, say wheat, expressed in terms of money prices. Without international trade, the market would be in equilibrium at the price P. At a higher price, supply would exceed demand; at a lower price, demand would exceed supply. These amounts of excess supply and excess demand, derived by subtracting the demand curve from

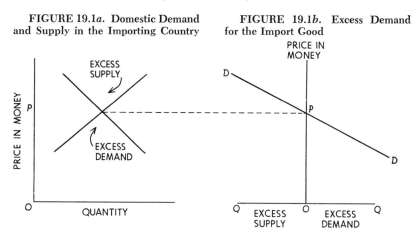

FIGURE 19.1a. Domestic Demand and Supply in the Importing Country

FIGURE 19.1b. Excess Demand for the Import Good

the supply curve at prices above *OP* and the supply curve from the demand curve at prices below it, can be transferred in a single curve to another diagram, such as Figure 19.1b. This is a curve representing excess demand. Above the price *OP*, the excess demand is negative (or excess supply). Note that the excess-demand curve has greater elasticity than the domestic demand curve. If domestic production were nonexistent or had zero elasticity, i.e., were a fixed amount, the slopes of the two curves would be identical. If domestic production were infinitely elastic, the excess-demand curve would be infinitely elastic at the same price.

The position in the exporting country is shown in Figure 19.1c, and the excess supply available to the importing country is derived in Figure 19.1d. Notice that this is calculated in the currency of the importing country. This means that the two curves can be put together on the same diagram

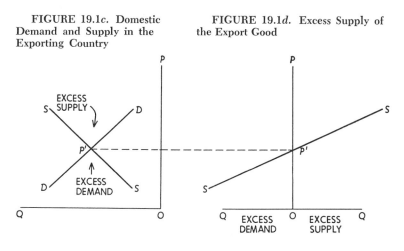

FIGURE 19.1c. Domestic Demand and Supply in the Exporting Country

FIGURE 19.1d. Excess Supply of the Export Good

and used to indicate the equilibrium of the international market in the single commodity, expressed in the currency of the importing country. This is done in Figure 19.1e. We can use this simple variation on the usual demand and supply, partial-equilibrium diagram to study exchange depreciation.

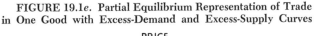

FIGURE 19.1e. Partial Equilibrium Representation of Trade in One Good with Excess-Demand and Excess-Supply Curves

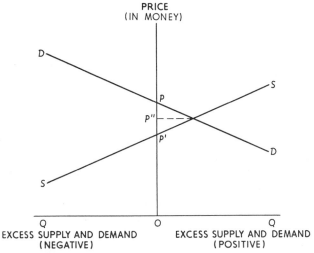

Exchange Depreciation

Our task is now to translate the excess-demand and excess-supply curves for a given commodity in two countries into demand and supply curves for foreign exchange. To do so we need a number of simplifying assumptions. We assume that there is, in the country we are studying, only one export good (perhaps a composite good representing a wide variety of separate commodities, which, however, all behave exactly the same way). And the same for imports. The excess demand at home for the import good and the excess supply of it abroad, in combination, will indicate what happens to the demand for foreign exchange. Similarly, the excess supply at home of the export good and the excess demand of it abroad represent the factors determining the supply of foreign exchange.

We must decide whether to calculate in local currency or foreign exchange. For many purposes, one is better than the other. On the foreign-exchange budget approach to the balance of payments, we need to know what happens in foreign exchange. If we are interested in a national income analysis, local currency is better. For expositional purposes we use both.

There are four diagrams in Figure 19.2, two for the depreciating country's exports (supply of foreign exchange), two for imports (demand for

Excess Demand and Excess Supply of Exports and Imports, in Local
Currency and in Foreign Exchange, before and after Foreign Exchange
Depreciation

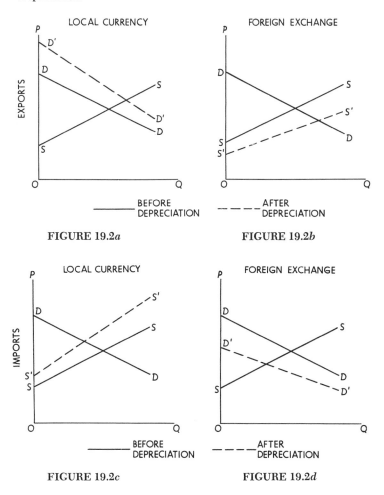

FIGURE 19.2*a*   FIGURE 19.2*b*

FIGURE 19.2*c*   FIGURE 19.2*d*

foreign exchange). Figures 19.2*a* and 19.2*c* show the positions of exports
and imports in local currency; Figures 19.2*b* and 19.2*d* represent the same
variables in foreign exchange. The position before depreciation is identical
in the two cases because we choose units of currency at home and abroad
equal to each other, i.e., an initial exchange rate of 1.

What is the effect of a change in the exchange rate? Let us concentrate
only on the local-currency diagrams. The impact of a depreciation, let us
say, on exports is to shift upward the demand curve, which is fixed in foreign exchange. Every unit of foreign currency exchanges for more units
of local currency, so that depreciation shifts the foreign demand curve

upward, appreciation downward. The shift is not a parallel one, since it is a constant percentage. The dashed-line demand curve in Figure 19.2*a* represents the new demand curve for exports after a depreciation of 20 percent.

The upward shift of the demand curve for exports, expressed in local currency, raises the local-currency value of exports. The value of exports is, of course, expressed in price times quantity (PQ) and is represented by the area of the rectangle formed by their product. With exchange depreciation, the local-currency value of exports cannot fall. At the worst, if the demand curve is completely inelastic, i.e., straight up and down so that an upward shift could not be seen, the value of exports in local currency would remain unchanged.

Depreciation may, however, expand, reduce, or leave unchanged the local-currency value of imports. Depreciation involves an upward shift in the supply curve, which is fixed in foreign exchange as shown in Figure 19.2*c*. Whether the value of imports will rise, fall, or remain unchanged depends upon the elasticity of demand for imports. If this elasticity is unity, the value of imports will remain unchanged. If it is less than one, it will increase. If it is greater than one, it will fall.

The Marshall-Lerner Condition

It is now time to combine the effects of depreciation on exports and imports to see whether depreciation will improve the balance of trade (or payments) of a country, or worsen it. Wh_t happens to the value of exports, what happens to the value of imports, and what happens to the net? The authorities of a country need to know the answer to this question before they can use exchange policy, appreciating or depreciating the rate of exchange or adopting a floating exchange rate. The answer is given by the Marshall-Lerner condition which states, in effect, that depreciation will improve the balance of payments of a country and appreciation will worsen it if the sum of the elasticities of demand for a country's exports and of its demand for imports is greater than 1. Take first the case where the elasticity of demand for exports is zero. Exports in local currency are now no smaller than before. If the sum of the elasticities is greater than 1, this must mean that the elasticity of demand for imports is greater than one, so that the value of imports falls. With no decline in the value of exports and a decline in the value of imports, the balance of payments has improved. At the other extreme, if the demand for imports has zero elasticity, the value of imports will rise in local currency by the full percentage of the depreciation; but if the demand for exports is greater than unity, as it must be if the sum of the elasticities of demand is going to be greater than one, the value of exports will expand by more than the percentage of depreciation, and the balance of payments will be improved.

If each elasticity of demand is less than one, but the sum is greater than one, this will improve the balance of payments expressed in local currency, because it means that expansion in exports in local currency exceeds the expansion in the value of imports.

These same relationships can also be found in the values of exports and imports worked out in foreign exchange. Here depreciation leaves the demand curve for exports unaffected, as in Figure 19.2*b*, since this is fixed in foreign exchange, but lowers the supply curve. For imports expressed in foreign exchange, depreciation of the local currency (appreciation of the foreign exchange) lowers the demand curve.

The Marshall-Lerner condition continues to operate. Depreciation can lower, leave unchanged, or raise the foreign exchange value of exports as the elasticity of the foreign demand curve is less than, equal to, or greater than unity. At the limit, where its elasticity is zero, the foreign exchange value of exports will decline by the full percentage of depreciation. The balance of payments will still be improved, however, if the sum of the elasticities is greater than one, since the elasticity of demand for imports must now be greater than one. This means that the value of imports will be reduced by more than the percentage of depreciation. Depreciation can leave imports unchanged in foreign exchange or reduce them; it cannot serve to increase them. With zero elasticity of demand for imports, the foreign exchange value of imports will be unchanged; but if the demand for exports has an elasticity greater than one, the foreign exchange value of exports will rise and the balance of payments will be improved.

The Marshall-Lerner condition, which is derived algebraically in Appendix G, is broadly correct if supply elasticities are relatively large and if the balance of trade is in equilibrium to begin with. But the supply elasticities may be relatively low, as was the case, for example, with Scotch whiskey in Britain at the time of the 1949 devaluation, or as is likely to be true under conditions of full employment. In this circumstance, the Marshall-Lerner condition is sufficient for balance-of-trade improvement, but not necessary. With low supply elasticity, the price of exports will not fall so low in foreign exchange, and foreign exchange earnings will not decline to the same extent with a low elasticity of demand as would have been true with infinite supply elasticity. Compare, in Figure 19.3, points *a* and *b*. Since the slope of the demand curve between *a* and *b* has an elasticity of less than 1, the higher price at *b* more than makes up for the decline in volume. Accordingly the sum of demand elasticities can be less than one (but not much less) and still improve balance of payments when supply elasticities are low.

The condition that the imbalance of trade must not be large to begin with is grounded in the characteristics of percentages. If the sum of the elasticities is greater than one, the percentage increase in exports will always be greater than the percentage increase in imports, or the percentage

FIGURE 19.3. The Market for Exports in Foreign Exchange before and after Devaluation, with Infinite and Low Supply Elasticities

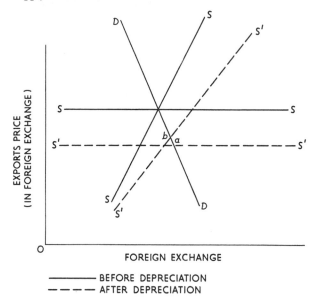

FOREIGN EXCHANGE

――――― BEFORE DEPRECIATION
― ― ― ― AFTER DEPRECIATION

decrease in foreign exchange will be smaller. But if imports are very large relative to exports, the absolute increase in imports may be larger in local currency, or the absolute decrease in imports smaller in foreign exchange. This worsening of the arithmetic $(P_xQ_x - P_mQ_m)$ balance of payments is accompanied by an improvement in the geometric balance $\left(\dfrac{P_xQ_x}{P_mQ_m}\right)$.

The Marshall-Lerner condition emphasizes the critical nature of unity for the sum of the elasticities. But for substantial improvement in the balance of payments from exchange depreciation, the sum should clearly be much higher, nearer four, or five, or six. The smaller the elasticities, the larger the price changes needed to effect a given balance-of-payments change. The larger the elasticities, on the other hand, the smaller the price change needed to obtain a given balance-of-payments improvement, or the larger the balance-of-payments effect from a given price change.

Unstable Equilibrium

The Marshall-Lerner condition can be shown on a single diagram by netting the demand for foreign exchange, from imports, and the supply, from exports, and putting them together. The technique is not the same as that used in deriving the excess demand and supply curves in the Figures 19.1. In this case we take rather the area (PQ) for various exchange rates in Figures 19.2—either 19.2*a* and 19.2*c* in local currency or 19.2*b* and 19.2*d* in foreign exchange—and plot the value of foreign exchange against the price. This is done in Figures 19.4*a* and 19.4*b*. We have

The Marshall-Lerner Condition with Demand and Supply Curves (rather than Local and Foreign Demand Curves)

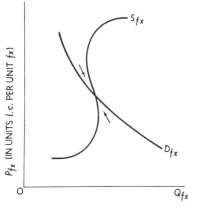 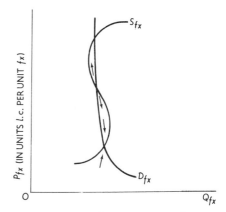

FIGURE 19.4*a*. Stable Equilibrium **FIGURE 19.4*b*.** Unstable Equilibrium Bounded by Two Stable Equilibria

fx = foreign exchange
l.c. = local currency

chosen to set the diagrams forth in foreign exchange, rather than local currency, but this choice is arbitrary. Note that the demand for foreign exchange comes from imports and the supply from exports. In Figure 19.4*a* the intersection of supply and demand is a stable one. A depreciation of the exchange rate—a larger number of units of local currency per unit of foreign exchange, or an upward movement of P_{fx}—will produce a supply of foreign exchange in excess of the demand, which will lead to appreciation of the local currency. As the arrows show, the fact that the demand curve crosses the supply curve from above means that depreciation improves the balance of trade and appreciation worsens it. The intersection of the demand and supply curves is stable.

The Marshall-Lerner condition here is that the elasticity of demand for foreign exchange, less the elasticity of the supply of foreign exchange, must be less than zero. It is necessary to be careful of signs. When we deal with the sum of the elasticities of demand we use absolute values, disregarding signs. (It would be more accurate to say that the algebraic sum of the elasticities of demand must be less than -1.) But with demand and supply curves, the relevant criterion is zero. This is identical with the sum of the elasticities of demand as one as is evident when we recall that the supply of foreign exchange is really the foreign demand for local currency, and that converting a demand curve to a supply curve reduces the elasticity by 1. (A demand curve with unit elasticity means that the demander is willing to pay the same amount of money for any quantity of the good. As a supply curve of money against the good, it has zero elasticity.)

In Figure 19.4b the middle intersection is unstable. A higher price for foreign exchange in local currency, i.e., depreciation, leads to excess demand for foreign exchange and more depreciation. At this point the demand curve crosses the supply curve from below. As drawn, the demand curve has zero elasticity, and the supply curve elasticity is negative. Subtracting the latter from the former gives us a result greater than zero.

It is argued that even if there is a local unstable equilibrium, the market by and large is stable. At some very high price for the country's exchange (fewer units of local currency per unit of foreign exchange—a downward movement on the diagram) the demand for foreign goods and hence foreign currency must exceed the supply. No one will want to earn the relatively worthless foreign exchange, and foreign goods are so cheap that everyone will want to buy them. There is thus a stable equilibrium intersection below the unstable one. By the same reasoning, the unstable equilibrium is bounded by a stable one at very depreciated levels of the currency, where the incentive to earn foreign exchange through exports rises and the opportunity to spend foreign exchange through imports declines. The demand curve converges to the vertical axis somewhere higher up. Every unstable equilibrium is logically bounded by two stable equilibriums.

The fact that unstable equilibriums are bounded by two stable intersections does not dispose of the problem of an unstable exchange market. One country may prefer one stable point, while another country may prefer the other. In Figure 19.4b, one country might prefer the lower stable intersection with high prices for its produce, while the other prefers the one high on the diagram. Moreover the unstable area gives trouble. If there is a deficit and the sum of the elasticities is less than 1 (with large supply elasticities, as in a depression), the balance of trade cannot be improved by depreciation, but appreciation will improve it. Because of the inelasticity of the demand abroad for the country's exports, increased exports would reduce foreign exchange earnings, but a higher exchange rate and smaller exports will raise them. By the same token, cheaper imports will expand quantity less than the decline in price and reduce the value of imports. Some economists have used the unwillingness of countries to try appreciation as a remedy for a balance-of-payments deficit as a *reductio ad absurdum* of the position that elasticities are low in the real world. But where elasticities are high in the long run, even though low in the short run, appreciation is a dangerous device to use to remedy a deficit. The short-run advantage from the monopoly position in exports and the monopsony in imports quickly melts away.

Elasticity Optimism and Pessimism

During the depression of the 1930s, there was considerable doubt whether depreciation would improve the balance of payments, and a whole school of thought grew up which became known as elasticity pessimism. In the post–World War II period, on the other hand, apart from the developing countries where pessimism still prevails, most economists have turned into elasticity optimists. The change is often thought of as due to improvements in reasoning and measurement. Much of it, however, seems better explained as the result of changed conditions.

Elasticities vary with many circumstances: with the number of sellers and the size of a particular seller in relation to the size of the market; the amount of domestic production or consumption; the size of price changes; expectations; the time allowed for reaction; and, especially, market conditions and alternative outlets or sources. A few words on each point may be useful.

It is well known that the demand for the product is less elastic than the demand for the output of an individual seller. At the extreme, the demand for wheat is price inelastic; the individual farmer can sell all he can produce at a constant price. On a moderated scale, the same is true in international economics. A country small in relation to the market will have higher elasticities than one which is large. The very large country may have only the same elasticity as the elasticity of the product. It is a price maker, rather than a price taker, to use the phrase of Metzler. Brazil in coffee, Ghana in cocoa, Malaya in rubber and tin face inelastic demand curves and cannot expand the value of exports through price reduction, or (the same thing with unchanged domestic prices) exchange depreciation.

Earlier in this chapter, a demonstration was offered that excess-demand and excess-supply curves of a country have higher elasticities than national product demand and supply curves. The excess-demand curve includes the product demand curve plus the elasticity of domestic supply; the excess-supply curve includes the product supply curve plus the elasticity of domestic demand. These effects are larger for manufactured products than for some primary products, particularly that class known as "colonial" products. If consumption of coffee, cocoa, or bananas in a producing country is of low elasticity, adding the demand elasticity to the product supply elasticity does not change it much. Since there is also no production of these commodities in the developed world, the product demand elasticity and the import elasticity abroad are identical.

Size, expectations, and time can all be dealt with together. The outcome depends on consumer reactions in demand elasticity and on producer reactions in supply. For price changes which are small and not expected to last, and which do not last, it is not worthwhile to make adjustments in production and consumption. When the price change is large, is expected to continue, and has lasted for a time, however, it pays to adapt.

But the major question is what the alternatives are, and particularly whether the world is depressed or prosperous. In depression, demand and supply elasticities are low for price decreases, and depreciation fails to work well. Appreciation, however, is likely to be effective in producing an adverse balance of trade, since there is extra capacity to produce supply, and marginal demanders drop off when the price is raised. Conversely in periods of prosperity, demand and supply elasticities are high for price decreases: in a seller's market, people turn avidly to the country that cuts prices, and adjustment is easy in declining lines because of alternative opportunities. (Conversely for price increases.) Accordingly it is not surprising that the econometricians, for all their inability to agree exactly how to go about measuring elasticities in international trade, find higher elasticities now than in the 1930s, with a rise in the optimism felt about the effectiveness of exchange depreciation.

Terms of Trade and Depreciation

What will happen to the terms of trade with depreciation? We avoid the temptation to say that they decline because the price of exports falls in foreign exchange and the price of imports rises in local currency. It is now evident that the comparison must be made in the same *numéraire*. Having avoided one temptation, we succumb to another. The answer, like our answer to most questions in economics, is "It depends." And when the matter is advanced one stage, the usual reply is again called for: "It depends on the elasticities."

Three main positions have been staked out. To the ultraclassicists such as Frank D. Graham and his students, the terms of trade are likely to be unchanged because a country typically deals at world prices, on which it has no effect. Depreciation raises domestic prices of both exports and imports by the full percentage of depreciation, since the ordinary country faces an infinite demand elasticity for its exports and an infinite supply elasticity for its imports. The foreign offer curve is a straight line. The terms of trade are given.

The classic, as opposed to the ultraclassic, position is that depreciation worsens the terms of trade and appreciation improves them because a country specializes in exports but not in imports. It has an effect on the price of its exports, that is, but none on imports. The classic assumption has been tested and found to be correct as a general rule. It is particularly true of the large developing countries.

But the classic assumptions do not hold in all cases. A country can specialize in imports and generalize in exports, i.e., have a larger monopsonist position in imports than its monopoly position, if any, in exports. The outstanding example here is Britain, whose terms of trade improved with depreciation in 1931. Partly this was the result of dynamic effects, but largely it was because the world depended on the British import market to sell its foodstuffs and materials, so that world prices of British imports fell more than world prices of British exports.

Partial versus Complete Elasticities

As stated with tiresome but useful repetition, the elasticity approach is based on partial-equilibrium analysis. Exchange depreciation produces changes in exports and imports which can be calculated from elasticities because we assume other things equal. But while it is satisfactory to regard other things as equal for all intents and purposes in microeconomic analysis of the demand and supply for one commodity, the exchange rate is something different. A change in this price produces changes which reverberate throughout the economy, altering incomes and goods prices over a wide range, so that other things cannot be taken as equal. At the very least, if exports rise and imports fall, there will be an increase in domestic spending which changes domestic money income. We need then not partial elasticities, which assume other things equal, but total elasticities, which take all effects into account. The elasticity optimists are not disposed to regard the difference between partial and complete elasticities as a serious problem. The elasticity pessimists fear that total elasticities are lower than partial elasticities, or even that the repercussions of exchange devaluation within the economy may produce a rise in nontraded goods prices and all incomes, which would mean that nothing happened. If the exchange rate falls, and all prices and incomes rise by a like amount, the system is homogeneous, and the only change that has occurred is in the unit of account.

Changing Prices and Fixed Exchange Rates

This analysis can be applied to the situation when the exchange rate is fixed, but the price level moves. Domestic inflation, as appreciation, worsens the balance of payments through price effects. The inflated country is a better place in which to sell at the old exchange rate, and a poorer place from which to buy. Deflation of prices, if it could be produced, would improve the balance of payments. This is the mechanism by which the gold standard was supposed to have worked, the so-called **price-specie-flow mechanism,** which more logically would have been called the specie-flow-price mechanism. If a country gained gold (specie), this added to the money supply, its prices rose, and the balance of payments turned adverse. If it lost gold, it was assumed to deflate its money supply, reduce prices, and improve the balance.

Note one important assumption in this reasoning. There are assumed to be continuous full employment and no relation between money income and imports or exports, apart from the changes produced by the price elasticities. But if real income does change, or if changes in money income, apart from changes in real income, do have an effect on spending on imports for any reason, the changes will be in the same direction. Inflation raises prices, increases money income, and may lead to some increase in real income. All three work in the direction of more imports.

The Marshall-Lerner condition still obtains with fixed exchange rates and moving price levels. For price inflation to worsen the balance of trade, the sum of the elasticities of demand must exceed one (or the sum of the elasticities of demand and supply be less than zero). If the Marshall-Lerner conditions are not met, the higher local price of exports improves the balance.

Finally note that inflation which worsens the balance of payments, followed by an equivalent depreciation which improves it, will restore the original position of prices, money income, and trade, apart from a dimensional change. This is a widespread pattern among developing countries. The question of particular interest is whether the sequence works the other way and has causal significance; i.e., whether depreciation leads to inflation which offsets its impact on the balance of payments. But first we need to discuss the impact of income changes on the balance of payments, assuming prices constant.

Summary

How effectively the price mechanism will work in international trade depends upon the elasticities of demand and supply. If these elasticities are high, as they would be if the classical assumptions of perfect competition, factor mobility, and constant factor proportions were realized, small price changes would produce large changes in exports and imports. This means that a deficit in the balance of payments could be corrected by a small price change or that the terms of trade would not have to move much.

Elasticities of demand and supply, however, are difficult to deal with in the real world. The elasticity for a given good will change through time and with different degrees of price change. In addition, methods of measurement leave much to be desired. Despite these handicaps to conclusive statements, it is probably true that elasticities in international trade are less now than they were 50 years ago.

The Marshall-Lerner condition requires that the sum of the elasticities of demand—the demand at home for a country's imports and the demand abroad for its exports—be greater than one if depreciation is to improve its balance of payments. This is true whether one deals in the foreign currency or the domestic currency balance. The condition assumes that supply elasticities are high and that the deficit in the balance of payments is not large. If the sum of the elasticities is less than 1, currency appreciation will improve the balance.

Price changes cannot be isolated from income changes. It is also necessary to take into account the money supply.

SUGGESTED READING

Texts

Yeager, chaps. 6 and 8.

Treatises

See Meade, *The Balance of Payments*, Part IV; and essays by Robinson and Machlup in American Economic Association, *Readings in the Theory of International Trade*, Nos. 4 and 5. See also E. Sohmen, *Flexible Exchange Rates: Theory and Controversy* (Chicago: University of Chicago Press, revised edition, 1969) and, on a mathematical level, G. Stuvel, *The Exchange Stability Problem* (Leiden: Stenfert Kruese, 1950).

A. Marshall, *Money, Credit, and Commerce* (New York: The Macmillan Company, 1924), Appendix J; and A. P. Lerner, *The Economics of Control* (New York: The Macmillan Company, 1944), are the original references for the Marshall-Lerner condition. Modern citation may be made of L. A. Metzler, "The Theory of International Trade," in American Economic Association, *A Survey of Contemporary Economics* (Philadelphia: The Blakiston Co., 1948), and A. O. Hirschman, "Devaluation and the Trade Balance," *RE & S*, February 1949.

Points

The long econometric discussion after World War II on the size of the elasticities in international trade is summarized by A. C. Harberger in "Some Evidence on the International Price Mechanism," *JPE*, December 1957. Harberger is an elasticity optimist.

M. Michaely presents evidence in support of the classical presumption that depreciation will worsen the terms of trade because a demand for a country's exports is less elastic than its demand for imports (i.e., it specializes in production and generalizes in consumption) in *Concentration in International Trade* (Amsterdam: North-Holland Publishing Co., 1962). For a discussion of one-commodity exporting countries, 1913 and 1953, see P. L. Yates, *Forty Years of Foreign Trade* (London: George Allen & Unwin, Ltd., 1959), Table 121 and Appendix Tables 37–45, which present shares of different commodity export markets.

Chapter 20

INCOME CHANGES AND INTERNATIONAL TRADE

The Assumptions

We now turn from the world in which prices changed and incomes were fixed to a world of constant prices and changing income. This is an analytically interesting world, but it may be no more realistic than the one we have left. And it behooves us, before we enter, to have clearly in mind the various assumptions under which it operates. A few of the major ones are set out here by way of introduction. Others, among them some no less important, will be encountered as we go along.

In the first place, if prices are constant, any change in money income is a change in real income and output. In Chapter 22, which will discuss situations in which income and prices both change, we shall have to worry whether imports should be related to real or to money income. The requirement that prices are constant implies that there are unused resources ready to be taken up into production with an increase in spending, or factors ready to be withdrawn from current employment if spending falls. Full employment is excluded by assumption.

Second, we assume away time by using a simultaneous multiplier. Changes in income take time, and it is possible to divide time into spending periods and trace through who pays what to whom at each stage of the process. But the simultaneous multiplier shows the end result of a smoothly operating period analysis. It is neat in exposition. We use it.

Third, all balance-of-payments deficits and surpluses are assumed to be financed in some fashion or other by gold movements, short-term capital, or other means. At this stage the means do not interest us.

Fourth, we ignore the money supply and the rate of interest. This is an assumption of *ceteris paribus*, or other things equal, with a vengeance, since we do not specify at this stage which is equal—the money supply or the rate of interest.

As we proceed, other important assumptions will be introduced and

338

explained. A few may be listed here for convenience: functions are linear and constant; imports are for consumption or investment but not for re-export; exports are sold exclusively out of current production. There is no government expenditure nor any taxes.

The Import Function

The relationship between imports and national income is expressed in a variety of ways. The **average propensity to import** is the dollar value of imports as a percentage of total national income (M/Y), or the proportion of national income spent on imports. The average propensity to import may vary from low values of 2 or 3 percent, as in the Soviet Union, to 20 to 40 percent in small, highly specialized countries such as Norway, Belgium, or New Zealand. Too much significance should not be attached to differences in average propensities to import; much will depend upon the size of a country as well as the degree of specialization. Each community in the United States may be as specialized as each community in, say, Britain; but if the United States includes within its borders areas as economically diverse as Maine, Texas, Florida, and Wyoming, the sum total of its communities will find it less necessary to import than those of Britain. Divide a country in two without disturbing trade patterns, for example, and you very much increase the average propensity of each part to import.

More important than the average propensity for many purposes is the **marginal propensity** to import. This is the *change* in imports associated with a given change in income. In algebraic terms it is dM/dY, where d stands for "the change in." If imports rise by $100 million when income increases by $1 billion, then the marginal propensity to import will be 0.10.

The marginal propensity to import is likely to differ from the average propensity to import. Two typical cases may be cited. Brazil, for example, supplies most of its basic needs and is close to the subsistence level. A rising standard of living leads to imports of new types of goods not available at home. In this case the average propensity to import is low, but the marginal propensity may be high. Contrast with this Britain, which imports a number of necessities such as wheat and tobacco and produces luxury products at home. In this case, the average propensity to import is high, the marginal propensity low.

The relation between the average propensity to import and the marginal propensity is expressed by the ratio called "income elasticity." This is more usually thought of as the percentage change in imports associated with a given percentage change in national income. Expressed in algebraic terms, income elasticity is measured by $(dM/M)/(dY/Y)$, which is the percentage change in imports associated with a given percentage change in national income. Since

$$\frac{dM/M}{dY/Y} = \frac{dM/dY}{M/Y},$$

income elasticity can be computed by dividing the marginal propensity to import by the average propensity. If these are the same value, the income elasticity of imports is unitary, or, in other words, a given percentage change in national income will produce a change of equal percentage in imports.

The average propensity to import at various levels of national income is the import schedule or propensity to import. This is shown in Figure 20.1, where $M(Y)$—in mathematical language, imports as a function of national income—is the propensity to import of the economy. It does not pass through the origin at 0, because at zero national income some imports may still be bought from abroad out of reserves. The marginal propensity to import is the slope of $M(Y)$. The assumption that $M(Y)$ is a straight line is, of course, an unreal simplifying aid to analysis.

FIGURE 20.1. The Propensity to Import

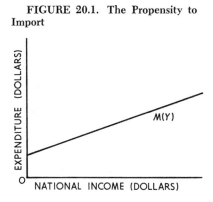

Propensities of the United States

The average propensity of the United States is 6.2 percent for goods and services and approximately 4.5 percent for merchandise trade alone. National income in 1971 was $1,050 billion, imports of goods and services $65 billion, and merchandise imports $46 billion (all figures moderately rounded). Note that with constant 1958 dollars, the average propensity to import merchandise—to stick to one measure, and the most widely used one—was somewhat higher at 5 percent, because the price deflator for imports had a somewhat different course from the national income deflator. The average propensity for merchandise in current dollars had been declining slowly over the years, but turned during the 1950s and 1960s. Early in the 19th century it stood at 10 percent. After World War I, it fell to 7 percent, and after World War II to 3 percent. Since full European recovery, however, the trend has turned, and imports have risen relatively to national income. Such a reversal had been anticipated because of depletion of raw materials, which was expected to lead to more complete reliance on imports. In actuality, the substantial increases in imports in the period after World War II occurred in manufactures as the American consumer became more conscious of the variety of products available throughout the world. In 1960–64 merchandise imports constituted 2.9 percent of GNP. By 1965–69 the proportion had risen to 3.5 percent, and by 1971 to 4.4.

The marginal propensity to import (for merchandise) reached 8 percent in 1971. This means that 8 cents out of every additional dollar of income, measured in current dollars, was spent on imports. But this marginal propensity to import can change, depending upon the circumstances of the period. In the 1950s it tended to be 4 percent or identical with the average propensity of about 4 percent. In the middle of the 1960s, with the U.S. economy reaching full employment, more of national income spilled over into imports than was true when unemployment was substantial.

With the average propensity to import at 4.4 percent in current dollars and the marginal propensity to import at 8.0 percent, the income of elasticity of demand for imports amounts to 1.8.

Exports and National Income

As already noted, we assume that exports take place out of current production rather than from past production, such as disinvestment of inventories or transfers of existing assets, such as antiques and rare paintings. This means that exports increase income.

Exports, moreover, are assumed to be a constant at every level of national income rather than a positive or negative function of income. Figure 20.2 shows this relationship. Implicit in it is the assumption that the country exports commodities which it either does not consume at all or for which its demand is income inelastic. This assumption is appropriate for a primary producing country—Surinam exporting bauxite but consuming none of it, or Australia exporting wheat and wool. But it is unrealistic for those countries that export manufactured products, particularly consumers' goods. In Britain, exports and consumption, and exports and investment are both competitive rather than independent, as we show them. An increase in income under this circumstance will lower exports, and exports may be taken as a falling function of income. In what follows, this complication is ignored.

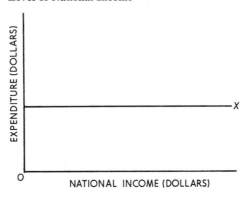

FIGURE 20.2. Exports Constant at Every Level of National Income

The Multiplier in a Closed Economy

We propose to construct the foreign-trade multiplier by analogy with the domestic. This means representing the simplest kind of system in which there are savings and investment schedules (but no government expenditure, taxes, transfers, or similar complications). Savings are a rising function of national income with a negative vertical intercept (i.e., dissaving occurs at zero national income), as in Figure 20.3a. Investment is a constant at every level of national income, as in Figure 20.3b. Superimposing the investment on the savings schedule in Figure 20.3c gives us the equilibrium level of national income, Y, where

Income produced = Income received = Income spent.

Income produced is the sum of consumption goods and services and investment goods ($C + I$); income received equals consumption plus savings ($C + S$). We define investment goods to include any goods originally intended for consumption and not sold. On this definition the value of consumption goods produced equals the value of consumption goods consumed. From this,

$$C + I = C + S$$
$$C = C.$$

Therefore

$$I = S.$$

The equilibrium level of national income, therefore, is that level where the investment and the savings schedules intersect.

If now there is an autonomous change in the investment schedule, from I to I' in Figure 20.3c, national income is increased. The amount of the increase is determined by the increase in investment and the domestic

FIGURE 20.3a. The Savings Schedule

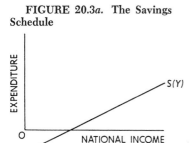

FIGURE 20.3b. The Investment Schedule

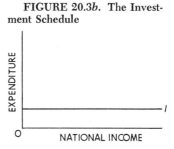

multiplier. Using the symbol d for "the change in," we want to find dY from dI. This is done either geometrically from the characteristics of the triangle combining them in Figure 20.3c or by simple algebra. In Figure 20.3c, dY is dI times the reciprocal of the slope of $S(Y)$. The slope of $S(Y)$ is dS/dY, so that the multiplier, by which we have to multiply dI to get dY, is $1/dS/dY$ or $1/MPS$, where MPS is the marginal propensity to save.

FIGURE 20.3c. The Multiplier in a Closed Economy

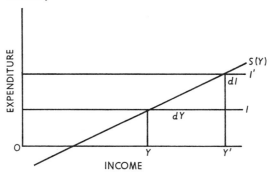

Algebraically, $I = S$ at equilibrium levels of national income. Therefore in equilibrium,

$$dI = dS.$$

Dividing both sides into dY, we get

$$\frac{dY}{dI} = \frac{dY}{dS} \quad \text{or} \quad \frac{1}{\dfrac{dS}{dY}} \quad \text{or} \quad \frac{1}{MPS}.$$

This is the domestic multiplier in a closed economy. The change in income equals the change in investment times the multiplier,

$$dY = \frac{dI}{MPS} \; .$$

The question now presents itself, what is the foreign-trade multiplier? Assume a change in exports, dX, what is dY? Or dY/dX, the foreign-trade multiplier, equals what?

The Foreign-Trade Multiplier—No Savings, No Investment

In an open economy with foreign trade, goods produced (Y) plus imports (M) are equal to goods bought $(C + I)$ plus goods exported (X). It is assumed, still, that there is no government. If there are no savings and no investment, all income is spent on consumption and Y must equal C.

Since
$$Y + M = C + I + X$$
and
$$I = O, Y = C \; ,$$
therefore
$$X = M$$

and exports are equal to imports at equilibrium levels of income. Given the schedules of exports and imports, as in Figures 20.1 and 20.2, one can determine the level of national income. This is done in Figure 20.4, which

FIGURE 20.4. The Foreign-Trade Multiplier, No Savings

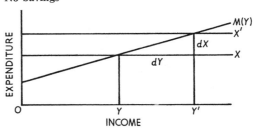

combines the two early schedules exactly as Figure 20.3*c* combined 20.3*a* and 20.3*b*.

By comparable steps, we can derive the foreign-trade multiplier for this simple economy. If exports shift from X to X', the change in income, from Y to Y', is the change in exports multiplied by the reciprocal of the slope of the import schedule, or the reciprocal of the marginal propensity to import. In algebra,

$$X = M$$

at equilibrium levels of national income.

Therefore in equilibrium,

$$dX = dM .$$

Dividing both sides into dY, we get

$$\frac{dY}{dX} = \frac{dY}{dM} \quad \text{or} \quad \frac{1}{\frac{dM}{dY}} \quad \text{or} \quad \frac{1}{MPM} .$$

Any continuing increase in exports in an open economy without domestic savings or investment will raise the equilibrium level of national income to the point where the increment of new exports is matched by an equal increase in imports. With no savings, the increased spending injected into the system by the increased exports can be spent on consumption (which increases income) or spent on imports. In a period multiplier, at each round of spending current income is divided between consumption and imports, and every increase in income is also divided between them (though perhaps on a different basis if the marginal propensity differs from the average). Income will continue to grow because of increases in consumption until the cumulative increase in imports offsets the autonomous injection of new spending from exports.

A shift in the import schedule will also affect national income, as Figure 20.5 illustrates. Here exports remain unchanged, but imports are assumed

FIGURE 20.5. The Foreign-Trade Multiplier, Shift in the Propensity to Import

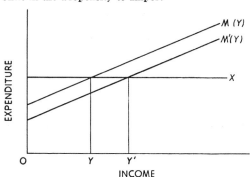

to be reduced at each level of income from what they would have been. Such a shift in the import function may occur because of a change in tastes, or an internal shift in the distribution of income, or any one of a number of possible causes. It might have been caused by a rise in prices brought about by foreign inflation or by a tariff, except that we have excluded price changes from our analysis by assumption. It should be noted that the actual level of imports does not change. Under the conditions assumed, the reduction in the readiness to import at the old national income leads to such an increase in income that imports are built up again to their original level. The shift *of* the schedule, that is, is matched by a movement *along* the schedule. If the propensity to import were changed by an increase in tariffs, for example, the defenders of the tariff might argue that the tariff had no effect because the level of imports was unchanged. This would not be true. There would be no balance-of-payments effect because the shift *of* the import schedule would give rise to a change in income sufficient to produce an equivalent shift *along* the import schedule in the new position. The income effect, that is, would wipe out any balance-of-payments effect. (This is the discussion of the income effect and the first installment of that on the balance-of-payments effect of a tariff, which we have owed the reader since Chapter 7).

The Foreign-Trade Multiplier—Savings

With savings and investment present, the equilibrium condition of national income is still

$$I = S,$$

but investment (I) breaks down into two parts, domestic (I_d) and foreign (I_f):

$$I_d + I_f = S.$$

Foreign investment is the difference between exports of goods and services and imports of goods and services:

$$I_f = X - M.$$

Substituting this in the previous equation we get

$$I_d + X - M = S,$$

or

$$I_d + X = S + M,$$

which is the basic equilibrium condition of national income in an open economy.

This is readily diagrammed by adding the domestic investment schedule in Figure 20.3b and the export schedule in Figure 20.2 on the one hand and the import and savings functions in Figures 20.1 and 20.3a, respectively, on the other. This is done in Figure 20.6.

The multiplier is now the reciprocal of the slope of the sum of the two functions $M(Y)$ and $S(Y)$, and will be the same for an increase in exports or an increase in investment. To take the former only, in algebraic terms, with domestic investment constant at all levels of national income and

$$X + I_d = S + M,$$

the change in exports must be equal to the change in savings plus the change in imports. Expressing this as

FIGURE 20.6. The Foreign-Trade Multiplier with Savings and Domestic Investment

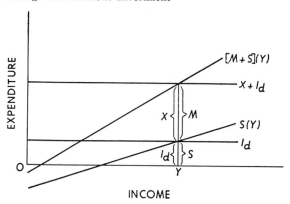

$$dX = dS + dM,$$

we can divide both sides of the equation into dY and derive

$$\frac{dY}{dX} = \frac{dY}{dS + dM},$$

where

$\dfrac{dY}{dX}$ is k (the multiplier), and

$$k = \frac{dY}{dS + dM} \quad \text{or} \quad \frac{1}{(dS/dY) + (dM/dY)} \quad \text{or} \quad \frac{1}{MPS + MPM}.$$

The diagram has been drawn in Figure 20.6 so that $I_d = S$ and $X = M$, at the equilibrium level of national income, Y. This is not necessarily the case. If long-term lending takes place, X can exceed M, provided that S exceeds I_d by an equal amount sufficient to maintain the equation $I_d + X = S + M$. With a higher level of exports than X, say X' in Figure 20.7a, ex-

The Foreign-Trade Multiplier with Changes in Exports

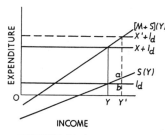

FIGURE 20.7a. Increase in Exports

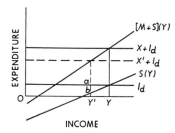

FIGURE 20.7b. Decrease in Exports

ports will exceed imports by the amount *ab*, the amount by which savings will exceed domestic investment. If exports were to fall to X' in Figure 20.7*b*, however, imports would exceed exports, and domestic investment would exceed savings. The export surplus in the first case can be regarded as a deduction from savings; generally, however, it is thought of as positive foreign investment. In the second case the import surplus may be regarded either as a supplement to savings or as negative investment to be subtracted from I_d.

The new equilibrium of national income where savings differ from domestic investment by the amount by which exports differ from imports (care being taken to get the signs right) emphasizes that we have been talking about national income equilibrium, not balance-of-payments equilibrium. Any leakage, whether into imports or savings, is good enough to offset the factors tending to raise income. And the student will recall that we abstracted from balance-of-payments difficulties, at an early stage in this chapter, by assuming that any foreign-trade balance could be financed.

It will be appreciated that the leverage working to change national income at each stage is the change in consumption based on the increase in income in the previous period. On this basis, the analysis can be broadened to include other leakages, such as taxes and corporation profits.

Income Changes and the Balance of Payments

Figures 20.7*a* and 20.7*b* are appropriate enough for illustrating the equilibrium condition for national income. They fail, however, to show very clearly the effect on the balance of payments. For this purpose it is useful to express the equilibrium conditions of national income in another way. Instead of

$$X + I_d = S + M ,$$

we can transpose I_d and M, and get

$$X - M = S - I_d ,$$

which is to say that the balance of payments on current account equals the difference between savings and domestic investment. This can equally be diagrammed. It requires only that we subtract the import from the export schedule on the one hand (Figure 20.1 from Figure 20.2), and the domestic investment from the saving schedule on the other (Figure 20.3*b* from Figure 20.3*a*). This is done in Figure 20.8. The combined X–M schedule is downward sloping because the upward-sloping import schedule is subtracted from a constant level of exports. This indicates that the balance of payments is positive at low levels of national income and declines as income rises. The S–I_d schedule is upward sloping because savings

FIGURE 20.8. The Balance-of-Payments Effect of a Change in Investment

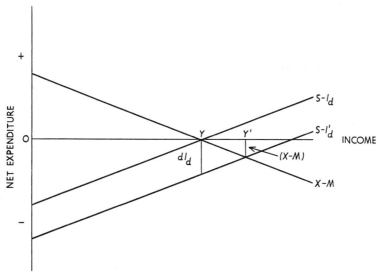

increase with increasing income and have a positive sign, while investment is constant. The intersection of the two schedules gives the equilibrium level of national income and the balance-of-payments position. In Figure 20.8 as drawn, the two schedules intersect with zero balance of payments. But as already indicated at some length, this is not necessary.

This diagram is not well suited for showing the multiplier, but it can indicate what happens to the balance of payments, as well as to the national income, as a result of a change in any of the four schedules. An increase in domestic investment will displace the $S-I_d$ schedule downward to $S-I'_d$ because the negative term is increased. This will raise national income from Y to Y' and open up a balance-of-payments deficit. The deficit $(X-M)$ is less than the amount of the increase in investment (dI_d) because the movement along the schedule, represented by increased savings, partly offsets the shift of the schedule, represented by additional investment.

One can as readily explore the impact of changes in the other schedules—an increase or decrease in exports, which would move the $X-M$ schedule up or down, respectively; a change in the import schedule down or up, which would have the same effects on the $X-M$ as a whole; or a change in the propensity to save. Increases in exports, decreases in imports, decreases in investment, and increases in savings all help the balance of payments. And movements in the opposite direction hurt it.

We can see from this diagram what it would mean if exports declined with increased income because of the competition between exports and consumption or investment such as occurs in a number of countries selling manufactures, like Britain. The negative slope of the $X-M$ curve would be steeper; the balance-of-payments effect of a given shift in any of the schedules would be greater; and the income effect would be reduced.

Foreign Repercussion

An important extension of this analysis may be introduced by the foreign repercussion, which is the effect of the change in exports and/or imports on national income abroad and the backwash effect this has on foreign trade and national income at home. If the country we are considering is small in relation to the outside world, the foreign repercussion can be neglected. An increase in such a country's imports will not stimulate income abroad by significant amounts. And even if there were a noticeable effect on income abroad, the repercussion may still be small if the marginal propensity of the countries affected to import from the original country is small. An increase in income in New Zealand may be sufficient to raise income in Britain (through the resultant increase in British exports to New Zealand and the multiplier), but it is unlikely to have any further repercussion in New Zealand because the British marginal propensity to import from New Zealand, let us say by way of illustration, is so small.

With large countries, however, the foreign repercussion is likely to be significant. The United States accounts for virtually 40 percent of world money income. An expansion in U.S. income increases its imports from the world, the world's money income, and in turn the world's imports from the United States. This feedback raises U.S. income still further. Where the system will come to rest depends upon the marginal propensities to save and import in the United States, and those in the rest of the world as well.

The interaction can be set out in a series of stages, as in Figure 20.9. At stage 1, the United States increases its domestic investment (to Id'), which spills over into imports from the rest of the world, i.e., the movement along the import schedule from the position at Y to that at Y'. To the rest of the world this appears at stage 2 as a shift of its export schedule. Exports rise, and with them, by means of the multiplier, income, and in turn imports. This last shift feeds back to the United States as an increase in exports, which helps to dampen the original import surplus but raises income still further, inducing still another increase in imports. Back to the rest of the world: exports rise, income and imports ditto. And so on. Successive stages of smaller and smaller changes could be diagrammed until the system came to rest.

A simultaneous geometric representation of the foreign repercussion has been worked out in which national income in each of two countries is

FIGURE 20.9. The National Income Multiplier, with Foreign Repercussion, by Stages

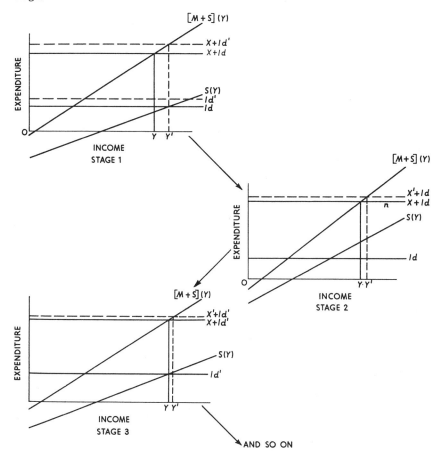

expressed as a function of national income in the other. In Figure 20.10, for example, national income in country A is expressed as a function of national income in country B. Even if B's income is zero, A's income will be what it is from consumption, investment expenditure, and government expenditure in A, which are entirely independent of what is taking place in B. This independence is shown by the fact that the sum $Ca + Ida + Ga$ is a horizontal line, which means that it is constant at all levels of B's income.

Exports in A create income, however, whose size is not independent of the level of income in B. In Figure 20.10, B is assumed to import from A even at no income. This creates some income directly (Xa at the vertical axis) and, through the foreign-trade multiplier in A, induces some further increases in consumption (dCa). As B's income increases, A's exports in-

FIGURE 20.10. Income in Country A as a Function of Income in Country B

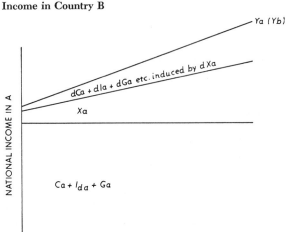

crease and, with them, the induced increase in spending dependent on exports.

The total of the three lines indicates the level of income in A at various levels of national income in B.

A similar representation of income in B as a function of income in A can be drawn on the same diagram. This is done in Figure 20.11, where line A reflects income in A as a function of income in B, and line B, income in B as a function of A. If these two lines intersect in a stable system, the interaction between the national incomes of the two countries is indicated. Now, if national income in B rises because of a change of any sort—let us say, in this case, because of an increase in investment in B— the line representing B's income as a function of income of A will be displaced to the right, since B's national income will be higher even if national income in A is zero. In Figure 20.11, line B is displaced to B'. This will raise national income in A from Y to Y'. Notice that national income in B has increased by more than the displacement of income, i.e., that the distance between Y and Y' along the B axis is greater than the amount by which the B function was displaced. This is because the increase in investment in B raised national income in B, imports from A, and hence national income in A, imports from B (or B's exports), and national income in B again.

This analysis can be used to demonstrate the interaction of national incomes in two countries (or in one country and the rest of the world taken as a whole) under a variety of circumstances. A change in the marginal propensities in B, whether to save, to import, to tax, or for any other

FIGURE 20.11. Simultaneous Representation of the Foreign Repercussion

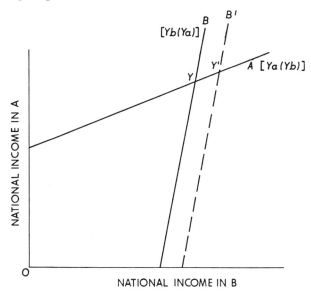

reason, will alter the slope of the curve of B's income as a function of income in A. This will produce a change in national income in both countries. A change in tastes in B which decreases domestic consumption in B and increases imports from A will displace both curves simultaneously but will lead to a unique new equilibrium, so long as the two curves continue to intersect. This diagrammatic analysis, which is needed where the foreign repercussion is important, is capable of handling all the various foreign-trade multipliers.

The derivation of these multipliers is given in an appendix to this chapter (Appendix H). Here it is sufficient to give a pair of formulas, one for a change in foreign trade and one for a change in domestic investment. The foreign-trade multipliers depend, of course, on the marginal propensities to save and import at home, which determine how much of the original increase in exports will be spent on consumption at home, in the first instance, and on the marginal propensities to save and spend abroad, which determine, first, how much of a change in income abroad is brought about by the original decrease in consumption and, second, how much of this is communicated through imports back again to A. The formula for the multiplier for an autonomous change in exports is

$$k = \frac{1}{MPSa + MPMa + MPMb(MPSa/MPSb)} .$$

This multiplier in A will be larger as

the marginal propensity to import in A is smaller,
the marginal propensity to save in A is smaller,
the marginal propensity to import in B is smaller,

and

the marginal propensity to save in B is larger.

The first two propensities cut down the leakage of income in A and ensure that the first and successive doses of expenditure arising from the increase in exports will be larger than otherwise. The effect of a small marginal propensity to import in B is to increase the multiplier in A, since it limits the induced decline in A's exports resulting from any decline in income in B. Finally, the larger the marginal propensity to save in B, the smaller will be the decline in income and the smaller, in turn, the induced decline in A's exports.

All these relationships can be expressed inversely, of course, but we may limit ourselves to one. If the propensity to import abroad is large, the multiplier in A will be small because the decrease in income abroad will be quickly translated into decreased imports as an offset to the original increase in A's exports.

The multiplier for an autonomous change in home investment is

$$k = \frac{1 + (MPMb/MPSb)}{MPSa + MPMa + MPMb(MPSa/MPSb)} .$$

This value is larger than the multiplier for an autonomous change in exports, because the foreign repercussion is working in the same direction as the increase in domestic investment, rather than against it, as in the case of the change in exports.

One reminder may be useful before we leave the foreign-trade multiplier and the foreign repercussion. If the rest of the world (country B in our illustration) is large relative to country A and consists of many countries, the foreign repercussion can be neglected. Each country may have a large propensity to import overall, but its marginal propensity to import from country A is likely to be small. The foreign repercussion is a negligible element, that is, in the foreign-trade multiplier for Guatemala and New Zealand and Egypt. It can, however, be neglected only with great peril in a discussion of the foreign trade of the United States or of Western Europe.

The student must once again be warned that the discussion in this chapter, though complicated, has relied upon a wide range of simplifying assumptions which serve to clarify the exposition of basic principles. In light of present (and still unsettled) discussion on income determination, it is worth pausing to pay tribute to some of the important qualifications to the basic model.

Adding Realism

Mainly through empirical studies in the postwar period, it has been realized that the multiplier relationship described here, though valid as a tendency, is far from an adequate description of reality. The consumption (or savings) function may not be a straight line, for, as incomes increase, the marginal propensity to save may increase. Indeed, as with the permanent income hypothesis, increments in income that are considered windfalls may be entirely saved. Variables other than current income show significant effects upon consumption and savings behavior, including past income and consumption levels and past savings now embodied in wealth held as real property, stocks, bonds, and savings deposits. And, of course, price changes occur over time.

With the admission of time into the system, we run into the problem of lags and the possibility of accelerators, which operate in a dynamic world lying beyond the static model outlined above. The investment functions employed have been linear and horizontal, unchanging with respect to income changes. But changes in income, say through increased consumption, may induce changes in the level of investment. As production of consumption goods increases to meet higher final demand, especially as full capacity of the system is approached, investment is increased to provide new machinery and equipment for further expansion of output. As long as the rate of increase of consumer demand is itself increasing, there will be a growing demand for investment goods. Once the rate of increase falls off, investment demand will fall absolutely. With less investment, the multiplier will work to decrease income, hence also to decrease consumption. With this line of causality in mind, accelerator-multiplier models have been developed to describe business cycles and fluctuations around a long-term growth trend.

In foreign trade there may on occasion be an effect comparable to the domestic accelerator. We may call it the "foreign-trade accelerator." An increase in exports leads through increases in investment to an import surplus. The increase in investment may take place in the export industries themselves: an increase in American tourist expenditure in London may lead to the construction of more hotels. Or the general propensity created by expanded exports may lead to new investment in industries producing for home consumption.

This accelerator effect may be also demonstrated in successive steps. In the first period there will be an increase in exports. This will raise national income and consumption in the second. The increase in exports and induced consumption requires an enlargement in capacity, so that the third period produces an increase in investment, which in turn stimulates income and consumption. And so on.

The simple accelerator itself has fallen into disrepute in theoretical and empirical literature due to its restrictive assumptions. And since most national income theorists work with closed economies, the trade economist must wait while the complex arguments over closed systems are settled before applying the results to a many-country world. But just as accelerators exist in domestic economies and produce the business cycle, so may they, from time to time and under particular circumstances, be found in international economics. And when they are, an increase in exports, starting from a balanced position, will produce an import surplus, or a decline in exports, an export surplus.

Summary

Under Keynesian assumptions national income is intimately related to foreign trade, being stimulated by exports and extinguished by imports. In the absence of savings, an increase in exports will increase income to the point where sufficient additional imports are created to offset exports. The amount by which national income will increase is the increase in exports times a multiplier equal to $1/MPM$. But if savings take place, the increase in exports will be balanced by increases in imports and in savings, provided that investment is unchanged. In this case the multiplier is $1/(MPM + MPS)$.

The foreign-trade multiplier expresses the change in income caused by a change in exports or in investment in an open economy in which income spills over into imports.

If the effect of the change in imports on income abroad is significant and if the effect of income changes abroad on a country's exports is again appreciable, there is a foreign repercussion. More complex formulas are now necessary to express the relationships among savings and import propensities in the countries involved.

If an accelerator is at work so that an increase in income due to a rise in exports leads to an increase in investment, the increase in exports may produce a larger increase in imports and turn the balance of trade unfavorably.

SUGGESTED READING

Texts

See Yeager, chap. 5. An old but complete treatment is given by D. B. Marsh in *World Trade and Investment* (New York: Harcourt, Brace & Co., Inc., 1951).

Treatises

Meade, *The Balance of Payments*, Parts II and III, gives a simultaneous analysis based on a generalized technique for solving problems. F. Machlup, *Inter-*

national Trade and the National Income Multiplier (Philadelphia: The Blakiston Co., 1943, reprinted by Augustus M. Kelley, Publishers, 1965), is an early work but uses a period analysis. Some teachers swear by L. A. Metzler, "Underemployment Equilibrium in International Trade," *Econometrica*, 1942. Among the pioneer writing, see J. M. Keynes, *The General Theory of Employment, Interest, and Money* (New York: Harcourt, Brace & Co., Inc., 1936), chap. 21.

The refined treatment of the foreign repercussion used in the chapter is taken from R. Robinson's interesting "A Graphical Analysis of the Foreign Trade Multiplier," *EJ*, September 1952.

Another graphical analysis which the student may enjoy is J. Black, "A Geometrical Analysis of the Foreign-Trade Multiplier," *EJ*, June 1957.

Points

Modern econometric model building relying on this sort of income analysis is found in chapters in L. Klein and A. Goldberger, *An Econometric Model of the United States, 1929–1952* (Amsterdam: North-Holland Publishing Co., 1955), and by R. Rhomberg and L. Boissonneault in J. Duesenberry, G. Fromm, L. Klein, and E. Kuh (eds.), *Brookings Quarterly Econometric Model of the United States* (Chicago: Rand McNally & Co., 1965). The latter includes price, has exports dependent on world income, and disaggregates imports.

Chapter

21

MONEY IN THE

ADJUSTMENT PROCESS

Price-Specie-Flow Mechanism

After considering price and income, we come to the role of money in the adjustment mechanism. It is ironic that we deal with money last, since in the historical development of the theory of adjustment, money was the first factor to be pointed to. David Hume, the 18th-century Scottish philosopher and economist, developed the price-specie-flow mechanism to answer the Mercantilists, who believed it useful to accumulate gold in a country as a war chest. He argued that it was a vain undertaking, since the additional money would lead via the quantity theory of money to higher prices, which would make the country a poor place to buy and a good place to which to sell. Exports would fall, imports would rise, and the negative balance of trade would require shipping the gold abroad again.

Several points should be made about the price-specie-flow mechanism. Note first that the law of one price means that the same good cannot rise in price in the country gaining gold and decline in the country losing gold. One must be careful in stating the theory so as not to fall into this error. There are many ways around it. Under classical assumptions, in which a country is a price taker for imports but a price maker for exports, the gold-gaining country's terms of trade improve. Export prices rise and import prices fall, but the balance of trade worsens, since imports are cheap and exports to the gold-losing country expensive. Or the prices that rise in the one country and fall in the other are domestic prices and costs in the foreign-trade sector so that profits in exporting are squeezed in the gold gainer and enlarged in the gold loser, thus stimulating the necessary quantity changes.

Second, the simple-minded quantity theory of the 18th century can be modernized by saying that spending is proportional to money supply, and, with full employment, prices are proportional to spending. The **full-**

358

employment assumption, or something close to it, is critical to the analysis. One need not, however, reply on an archaic version of the quantity theory.

Third, in the Hume version the initial gain in gold is exactly eliminated. More or less will not do. This is akin to the exact offset in imports to the increase in exports in the income analysis with less than full employment and an MPS of zero, which we encountered in the last chaper.

The reintroduction of money into the analysis of balance-of-payments adjustment is the result not of new piety toward Hume and his successors. It derives from the rediscovery of money in the postwar period and the prevalence in most parts of the world of full employment, rather than the widespread unemployment of the 1930s which gave rise to the Keynesian income analysis. But instead of relying on the quantity theory of money, modern monetarists place great emphasis on real balances.

Real Balances

Under real-balance theory, it is believed (or perhaps only assumed) that households and firms strive to maintain a certain level of real balances in money. The balances are real because their holders lack all **money illusion,** i.e., the mistaken belief that a given amount of money is unchanged in value when the price level changes. The amount of real balances that firms and households want to hold may be related to wealth, through portfolio decisions, or to income, through transactions and other demands for money. But when the money supply corrected for changes in the price level declines, households and firms save to build back real balances. When the real money supply increases, on the other hand, spending units increase their spending to bring real balances down to the desired level. In the Keynesian analysis, spending is a function of income; in the monetarist analysis, exemplified by Pigou, Patinkin, Friedman et al., it is a function of real balances.

Note that when the price level changes but the amount of money is unaltered, real balances have changed, with the consequence that spending alters. In the theory of exchange-rate variation, for example, the major engine of adjustment is not the response of spending units with unchanged incomes to changes in prices, as in Chapter 19. It is rather the change in the price level as a consequence of the adjustment of the exchange rate. Appreciation lowers the prices of foreign-trade goods (both exports and imports), and depreciation raises them. The change in prices in the foreign trade sector affects the price level as a whole and the value of real balances. It therefore leads to a change in spending, which in turn affects income, imports and exports. We return to this issue in the next chapter.

The Rate of Interest

Real balances are one mechanism of adjustment. The rate of interest is another. The chief criticism of the foreign-trade multiplier leveled, for example, by S. C. Tsiang is that it presupposes a fixed rate of interest. This implies either that the economy is in the **liquidity trap,** in which the rate of interest cannot be raised or lowered because open-market operations involve nothing more than the infinitely elastic exchange of bonds against money; or that the monetary authorities take pains to stabilize the interest rate by adjusting the money supply in such a way as to keep it level. If the economy is not in the liquidity trap, and if monetary authorities permit export surpluses to increase the money supply and import surpluses to reduce them, the rate of interest will move and may induce changes in spending. As we shall see, this assumes that capital movements are limited. The monetary authorities may even accentuate the change in interest rates called forth by the trade balance, raising the discount rate when the balance is adverse and lowering it when it is in surplus.

The impact of interest-rate changes back on the foreign-trade sector may run through holdings of inventories and prices, or through decisions to save and spend. Sir Ralph Hawtrey, a British Treasury official for many years, was the economist who emphasized inventories and prices. In *Currency and Credit,* written in 1919, he asserted that an increase in the Bank of England discount rate had its primary effect in making it more costly to hold inventories, both of internationally traded and domestic goods. Merchants would get squeezed and sell off their holdings of goods, and this would reduce prices. More goods would be sold abroad as exports, and less would be bought, both directly by the merchants and through the reduction in prices. Reductions in interest rates, of course, would produce additions to inventories which would add to imports and reduce the supply of exportables.

Changes in interest rates, of course, may have effects in changing spending which go beyond those of the merchants holding inventories. An import surplus which reduces the money supply and raises interest rates may lead to cutbacks in investment programs on the part of firms and to a lower level of house construction. This reduced spending lowers income, reduces imports, and frees up goods for exports which would otherwise have been used for domestic investment or consumption.

IS-LM Analysis with Foreign Trade

The wide range of possible roles for money in the adjustment process can best be illustrated with the help of the *IS–LM* analysis, familiar to many students of elementary economics, as a means of compromising between the purely monetary and purely Keynesian views of inflation and employment in a closed economy. (Warning: *LM* in this case means liquidity and money, so that we cannot use *M* for imports, as is our normal wont.) In an open economy there are three markets to be cleared: for foreign exchange, for money (and other financial assets such as bonds), and for domestic goods and services. We can plot equilibrium loci of these three markets in interest-rate and national income space. This is done in Figures 21.1*a*, 21.1*b* and 21.1*c*.

Market Equilibriums Plotted in Interest Rate and National Income Space

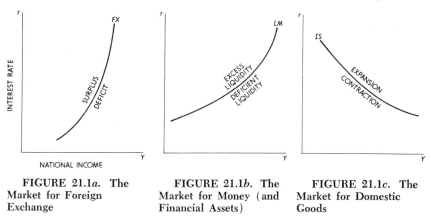

FIGURE 21.1*a*. The Market for Foreign Exchange

FIGURE 21.1*b*. The Market for Money (and Financial Assets)

FIGURE 21.1*c*. The Market for Domestic Goods

The *FX* curve in Figure 21.1*a* traces out those combinations of interest rate and national income that will produce equilibrium in the balance of payments. The exact shape of the curve depends upon a number of factors in the economy, particularly the mobility of capital. As drawn, the curve shows that a higher rate of interest and a lower level of national income tend to produce surplus in the balance of payments, while lower rates of interest and higher national income lead to deficit. In a pure Keynesian analysis, in which the balance of payments was a function of national income alone (as in the last chapter) and capital was immobile, the *FX* curve would be vertical. The more impact the rate of interest has on the balance of payments, the flatter it is. If capital were completely mobile between the country in question and the rest of the world (and the latter was large in relation to the former), the curve would be flat. The interest rate would be determined by the world interest rate, and any attempt to raise or lower it would produce a surplus of foreign exchange (through capital imports) or a deficit (through capital exports), respectively.

The *LM* curve in Figure 21.1*b* shows the amount of money which is appropriate to various combinations of the rate of interest and national income. Above and to the left of the curve, money is excessive, which leads spending and lending units either to spend more (to reduce real balances), which increases national income, moving rightward back to the curve, or to lend more vigorously, which lowers the rate of interest and returns to the curve in a downward direction. The slope of the curve is critical. In the liquidity trap it is horizontal: the authorities cannot raise or lower the rate of interest. To the quantity theorists, it tends to be vertical: the amount of money in circulation determines national income and has little impact on the rate of interest. As drawn, the *LM* curve represents a compromise between the two positions, being fairly horizontal (though positively sloped) up to some level close to full employment, when it becomes vertical.

The *IS* curve represents the locus of points in *r* and *Y* space which produce a stable level of national equilibrium because $I = S$. It is negatively sloped because of the marginal propensity to save: with higher incomes, savings rise, and it is necessary to lower interest rates to stimulate investment to keep $I = S$. In Keynesian analysis, the curve is vertical at some given level of *Y* determined by *I*, itself unresponsive to the rate of interest. To monetarists, the curve is relatively flat, since investment and savings are highly responsive to the rate of interest and the relationship between savings and national income is minimized.

Equilibrium in Three Markets

If we superimpose the three curves, as drawn, they show equilibrium levels of the balance of payments, the money supply, and the savings and investment, or domestic goods. In 21.2*b* all three markets are in equilibrium. In Figure 21.2*a*, however, we start at *a* with an export surplus. $I = S$ because the surplus of domestic savings over domestic investment is offset by foreign investment ($S - I_d = X - M$). But the export surplus increases

FIGURE 21.2*a*. Export Surplus Expands Money Supply and Restores Equilibrium

FIGURE 21.2*b*. Equilibrium in Three Markets

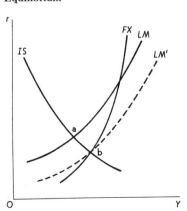

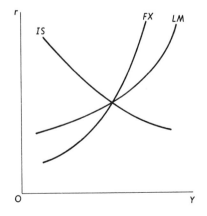

the supply of money in the system, which ultimately shifts the *LM* curve to the *LM'* position, intersecting the *FX* and *IS* curves at *b*.

Exchange-rate changes can be worked into the analysis: they shift the *FX* curve. Appreciation shifts it to the left, reducing the surplus area and enlarging the deficit. Contrariwise, depreciation moves it to the right. These results assume, of course, that the Marshall-Lerner condition holds.

Monetary policy alters the position of the *LM* curve, and fiscal policy shifts *IS*.

Keynesianism versus Monetarism

The previous diagrams have fudged the issue whether the world is Keynesian or monetarist, and so does everything that follows. It may assist analysis, however, if we indicate in Figures 21.3a and 21.3b the polar

FIGURE 21.3a. Keynesian Equilibrium

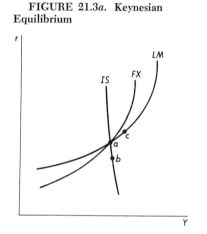

FIGURE 21.3b. Monetarist Equilibrium

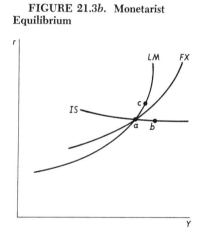

Keynesian and monetarist cases. In the former, spending in equilibrium determines national income, and the money supply determines the rate of interest. In the latter, the *IS* curve sets the rate of interest and the money supply the level of income. In both cases we refer to point *a*.

Monetary and fiscal policy produce different results in the two cases. This is illustrated by points *b* and *c*, representing new intersections of *LM* and *IS* curves, respectively. The new curves are not drawn, to keep the diagram from becoming messy. Expanding the money supply, however, gives new intersections of the *IS* and *LM* curves at *b* in both cases. In the Keynesian analysis, the interest rate falls, national income remains unchanged, and a small deficit occurs. Under the monetarist analysis, there is only a small decline in interest rates, along with a substantial increase in money income and a large deficit.

If we use fiscal policy to shift the *IS* curve to the right and up, the results are reversed, as point *c* in the two diagrams illustrates. Under the Keynesian analysis, there is a moderate, if any, increase in interest rates, a substantial increase in national income, and a sizable deficit, which will ultimately produce a change in the *LM* curve. In the monetarist way of looking at the matter, however, not much happens. Interest rates rise, to be sure, but national income remains virtually unchanged, and the balance of payments may even improve because of the inflow of capital occasioned by the increase in the interest rate.

Capital Mobility

If capital is immobile between countries, the *FX* curve is nearly vertical. Monetary and fiscal policy can be used in combination to find an appropriate level of the interest rate and national income, and the *FX* rate can be adjusted through exchange appreciation or depreciation to suit it. This is not worth illustrating in a separate diagram.

If capital is perfectly mobile between countries, the *FX* curve is horizontal. The interest rate is fixed. Any change in spending or taxation via fiscal policy will automatically produce a change in money supply: an increase in spending will produce an increase in money through capital imports, a decrease vice versa, *mutatis mutandis*. But an increase in money unaccompanied by expanded spending will have no effect on the interest rate or national income: it will all spill over into capital outflow. The student who likes to see for himself will be able to visualize these results in Figure 21.4. A shift of the *IS* curve to intersect the *FX* curve at *b* will pro-

FIGURE 21.4. Foreign Exchange, Money, and Domestic-Goods Equilibrium with Complete Mobility of Capital

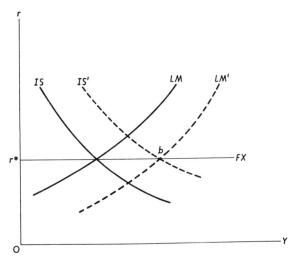

duce an inflow of capital, expanding the money supply to LM'. If the country tried to add to internal money creation by the difference between LM and LM', however, it would all spill abroad if the IS curve holds steady, since it is impossible for the interest rate to fall below r^*.

The Identification Problem

In his *Europe and the Money Muddle*, written some years ago, Robert Triffin of Yale indicated that he was about to explore the relationships among the surplus or deficit in the balance of payments, the creation of credit, and the money supply. He started with a simple identity,

$$dM = dC + BP,$$

where dM is the increase in the money supply, dC is credit creation, and BP is the balance-of-payments surplus. All variables can have implicit negative signs: the money supply can shrink, credit may be extinguished, and the balance of payments can show a deficit. If there are both a deficit and credit extinction, the money supply will decline by their sum. Or one can be positive and the other negative.

It is possible to ring the changes on this identity by rearranging the variables:

$$dC = dM - BP$$

and

$$BP = dM - dC$$

but the exercise turns out to yield little fruit. One hoped to be able to conclude, for example, that credit creation leads to a balance-of-payments deficit. This turns out to be true only when $dM = 0$, for then $dC = -BP$. Or that changes in the money supply are the result of surpluses or deficits in the balance of payments: true only when there is no possibility of credit creation. The difficulty with these identities is that it is impossible to generate any rules about what happens among money, credit creation and the balance of payments without more information. One needs to be able to identify which is the independent variable or variables, and which the dependent. It greatly helps to constrain the problem by setting one variable to zero.

The Pure Gold Standard

In the pure gold standard, where gold is used both for internal and external transactions—before the days of sophisticated goldsmiths—dC could be set at zero. The money supply changed with the balance of payments, and by the same amount. Increases in money for domestic use had to be earned by an export surplus. A deficit in the balance of payments reduced the domestic supply. All these relationships were one-for-one and automatic.

The Pure Dollar Standard

The pure gold standard had its replica in Cuba before 1936, when that country was on the dollar standard. Cuban pesos existed, but most of the money in circulation in Cuba in that period consisted of dollar currency, issued by the Federal Reserve Bank of Boston. A good sugar crop enlarged money in circulation, a poor one contracted it. The fact that dollars circulated in Cuba seemed to relieve the country of balance-of-payments problems, as the adjustment mechanism through changes in the money supply was automatic. *LM* in our earlier diagrams moved only when the economy diverged from the *FX* equilibrium line.

Colonial Currency Standards

Similar, though not identical, was the system used in British colonies prior to independence in which the local currency board issued money for domestic use which was 100 percent backed up by sterling deposits in London. Any change in the balance of payments produced an increase or decrease in both the local money supply and sterling balances. Local credit creation was impossible. But the colonies could borrow in London and add to sterling reserves, thereby creating money for local use. If borrowing in London is identified with changes in the balance of payments,

$$dM = BP$$

because

$$dC = 0 \, .$$

Inside Money and Outside Money

In domestic monetary theory, a distinction is made between money assets that are the liabilities of other actors in the system (but not the government) and those that are not. The first are called "inside," the latter "outside" money. Inside money represents primarily bank deposits and can vary widely up and down, depending upon whether credit in the system is being expanded or contracted. Outside money is backed by an asset like gold, or in a domestic context represents the liability of the government which is not expected to be paid down. In international terms it is gold under the pure gold standard, dollars under the Cuban pre-1936 dollar standard, and the local issue backed 100 percent by sterling under the colonial standard. Outside money changed with the balance of payments.

The development of domestic banking and credit creation under the gold standard probably assisted in the functioning of the adjustment mechanism so long as the **rules of the gold standard game** caused central banks to vary their monetary policy in ways dictated exclusively by the balance-of-payments position. This meant that dC and BP always had the same sign. When BP was positive—a surplus in the balance of payments—credit was enlarged; when it was a deficit, credit was contracted. The supply of inside money varied with the supply of outside money, and the total money supply varied so as to reinforce the effects of the outside-money change.

With monetary policy independent of the balance of payments, however, and directed rather to questions of full employment and growth, credit creation and the balance of payments may go separate ways. In particular, if monetary policy is tied in with domestic policy objectives, a decline in outside money brought about by the balance of payments may lead not to a reinforcing decline in inside money but rather to an offsetting expansion. BP and dC are not linked together positively, but are independent or opposed. In this circumstance, monetary policy's role in adjustment may be to disturb it.

Borrowing Money

When one identifies changes in the money supply with the balance of payments, one is tempted to think that countries can increase their supply of (outside) money only by earning it through an export surplus. Such was the system by which new gold production was distributed throughout the world. Spain in the 16th century, California in 1849, Australia in 1851, and South Africa in the 1890s would produce (or steal) gold and spend it abroad. To obtain and retain a share of the injection of new gold a country had to enjoy an export surplus. In the discussion of colonial balances after World War II, a number of observers concluded that the only way that the colonies could expand their money supply under the currency-board system was to run an export surplus.

This view is incomplete, however. It is possible to borrow money abroad. In booms in the 19th century, the United States borrowed cyclically in Europe, largely in London, and brought in largely goods, but partly gold to shore up the banking system with outside money. In depressions, loans would be repaid, partly in gold and partly with exports. As Jeffrey Williamson interpreted it, the gold was not a mechanism for transferring the loan in goods and services, but was itself in a modest degree the object of the exercise.

When colonial governments wanted to invest in public works, they would borrow in London, acquire local currency against sterling, and spend the local currency. In some considerable degree the income created would spill over into imports and use up the sterling—the transfer mechanism. But to the extent that local savers added to their holdings of local money as their incomes and wealth rose, permanent increases in colonial borrowing from and lending to London were recorded. The difference in the rates of interest paid by the colonial goverment and earned by the currency board represented a payment to London by the colony for the provision of liquidity. The colony borrowed long and lent short; London lent long and borrowed short, serving as a **financial intermediary.**

Adjustment in the Reserve Center

When gold is dug up and spreads through the system, there is an increase in the world supply of outside money. Under the pure exchange standard, the position is not clear. We need to distinguish two cases: the first, when the "colony" earns the increase in money through an export surplus in goods and services, with no capital movements; the second, when the increase in money comes from borrowing long and lending short. The position is broadly the same in the country expanding its money. The issue turns on what happens in the reserve center.

Assume that country A has an export surplus which it uses to expand its holdings of foreign exchange on country B, and that B had an import surplus of goods and services. A's money is increased. B's money supply may be decreased or not, depending upon where the A central bank or currency board holds its reserves and how country B regards its balance of payments. If the reserves are held with the central bank in B, the shift of deposits from residents of B to the central bank or currency board of A reduces money in B. If, on the other hand, the funds are held in money-market instruments such as bills of exchange, Treasury bills, or even long-term government bonds, there is no immediate contraction in B's money supply. If country B believes that it ought to regard its international reserves on a gross basis and these have not changed, it will take no policy steps to contract money. There is no adjustment in the reserve center. If, on the other hand, B is aware of the current-account deficit which gave rise to the increase in liabilities or nets its assets against quick (or total) liabilities to foreigners, it may or may not operate to tighten monetary policy. If its monetary policy is regarded as an instrument for operating on the balance of payments, it will. If it uses monetary policy mainly for domestic goals, it will not.

Where the A "surplus" and B "deficit" are borrowed, however, through B lending long and borrowing short and A lending short and borrowing long, there is no signal of disequilibrium in B from the current account. B may think of itself as a banker, regarding itself as in the business of providing financial intermediation, and stay relaxed. Or it may adopt something more nearly like a "liquidity" definition of its balance of payments, net its reserves, and consider itself in deficit. The conduct of A, the trading country, is straightforward and clear-cut. The line to be followed in B, the banker, is less evident.

Jacques Rueff, Robert Triffin, and a number of other economists believe that the exchange standard inevitably leads to disequilibrium because the reserve center ignores increases in its liabilities. Conduct is asymmetric: the country gaining exchange reserves expands; the country that acts as a reserve center ignores the increase in its liabilities and does not contract. This may be so. It seems in the recent history of the United States, however, that the country was acutely aware of its "deficit"—perhaps more than it should have been up to 1968, since the gain in foreign reserves came from borrowing long and lending short rather than U.S. current-account deficits. The problem seems to have been rather than monetary policy was directed to domestic goals, not balance-of-payments considerations. If this be the case, the exchange standard is not so responsible for our balance-of-payments difficulties as is sometimes claimed.

Balance-of-Payments Adjustment through Long-Term Assets

Dean James Ingram of the University of North Carolina has made the point that adjustment in the balance of payments need not be confined to gold and short-term claims on a reserve center. He sees no reason why countries should not have portfolios of long-term bonds which they add to or sell off as their balances of payments become more or less favorable, respectively. Instead of adding or subtracting from its stock of international money, a country could trade in near money.

The point is an interesting one. Dean Ingram came upon it in studying the balance-of-payments adjustment mechanism in Puerto Rico, which, though an island and not an integral part of the United States, operates in effect as part of the U.S. banking system. Puerto Rican banks, like American banks in general, adjust their positions vis-à-vis the rest of the country by changing their reserve position at the Federal Reserve System, their interbank deposit claims on New York, and their holdings of U.S. government bonds. It is not just any old long-term asset that is bought and sold, but a particular one with a broad market of great liquidity. The balance of payments can be adjusted by changes in holdings of international money—gold or deposits on a reserve center—or in near-money. These must be internationally traded bonds, with markets which extend beyond the confines of a single country. European holdings of dollars are by no means limited to demand deposits but extend into U.S. government bills, notes, and bonds. Some part of U.S. financial intermediation consists not of lending long and borrowing short, but of lending long and borrowing long—lending long through private corporate entities and borrowing long by the U.S. government from central banks and other monetary authorities.

Such a system is feasible, as long as it is believed in. Money backed by U.S. government bonds is outside money inside the United States because it is understood that there is no need to pay it off. Government can discharge it debts internally by issuing more debt, and this holds true for

Puerto Rico as well as the banks of the Second Federal Reserve district in New York. For the rest of the world outside the United States, however, United States liabilities, short and long, are inside money. For some years the supply has been rising. Both holder and issuer want the amounts to decline.

The role of money in the adjustment process, therefore, is complicated by the question of the money or near-money that is used, and how it is regarded by holders and issuer.

Summary

Money used to be regarded as the major force making for balance-of-payments adjustment under the price-specie-flow mechanism. How large its role is or should be today is a matter of debate at a profound level. The quantity theory has been replaced by real-balance effects. Some monetary theorists assign an important role to the rate of interest.

The role of money can be illustrated with *LM–IS* curves, which, for an open economy, also include a curve of foreign-exchange balance. The Keynesian and monetarist views can be illustrated with polar positions (vertical and horizontal) of the *LM* and *IS* curves. The shape of the *FX* curve depends on the mobility of capital.

The relationships among credit creation, money supply, and the balance of payments can be expressed through identities, but it is impossible to identify the model in a general way to distinguish the independent from the dependent variables.

The role of international money and near-money is affected by its character, as outside or inside money. Money can be earned or borrowed. The behavior of the reserve center, when international money consists of claims on a financial center, is not readily predictable from fixed rules.

SUGGESTED READING

Texts

Stevens, chaps 7, 9, 10; Officer and Willett, passim; Grubel, chaps 5, 7.

Treatises, Etc.

R. A. Mundell, *International Economics* (New York: The Macmillan Company, 1968), part III; R. I. McKinnon, "Portfolio Balance and International Payments Adjustment," in R. A. Mundell and A. K. Swoboda, eds., *Monetary Problems of the International Economy* (Chicago: University of Chicago Press, 1969); and S. C. Tsiang, "The Role of Money in Trade Balance Stability: Synthesis of the Elasticity and Absorption Approaches," in American Economic Association, *Readings in International Economics*.

Points

The Triffin references are *Europe and the Money Muddle* (New Haven, Conn.: Yale University Press, 1957) and *Gold and the Dollar Crisis* (New Haven, Conn.: Yale University Press, 1960) (paperback).

For a study of the Cuban monetary system prior to the introduction of a central bank, see H. C. Wallich, *Monetary Problems of an Export Economy* (Cambridge, Mass.: Harvard University Press, 1950).

The role of money changes in 19th-century United States borrowing is discussed in J. G. Williamson's *American Growth and the Balance of Payments, 1820–1913, A Study of the Long Swing* (Chapel Hill, N.C.: University of North Carolina Press, 1963).

J. C. Ingram's study of Puerto Rico is contained in "State and Regional Payments Mechanisms," *QJE*, 1959.

Chapter
22

INTERACTIONS OF PRICE,
INCOME, AND MONEY

Partial versus General Equilibrium

In our discussion of price we assumed income constant and ignored money. In treating income, we ignored both price and money. The preceding chapter, in bringing money into the discussion, was not so cavalier in leaving aside price and income. But it is time to move from the partial-equilibrium world of other things equal to that of general equilibrium, where other things can change. Such a world is highly complex. For the most part we can deal only with particular problems posed in particular ways; to try to be more general lets the discussion get completely out of hand.

One general point of importance can be made, however. There is something of a tendency for the system to be **homogeneous:** i.e., for the variables all to change in ways that offset one another. If the exchange rate is halved, and prices, money, and money incomes all double, nothing has happened.[1] Real exports, imports, income, income distribution, etc., are unchanged. It is important throughout the chapter to see what is altered to ensure that homogeneity is escaped, if it is, or what variables resist change in the ways that homogeneity would call for. In some cases the need is to alter some resistant variables in order to achieve homogeneity and avoid undesirable effects.

The discussion runs in terms of:

1. The income effects of devaluation.
2. Depreciation under full employment.
3. Structural inflation.
4. Different tradeoffs between employment and inflation.
5. Flexible exchange rates with balanced trade.

---

[1] This is not entirely true. Creditor-debtor relationships have changed, unless existing contracts are all rewritten, as are all money claims and liabilities.

372

The Income Effects of Devaluation

We may start by reviewing the simple fact that the balance-of-payments and the income effects of devaluation are closely linked. In Figure 22.1, assume that depreciation shifts the $X-M$ schedule upward[2] because the

FIGURE 22.1. The Balance-of-Payments Effect of Depreciation

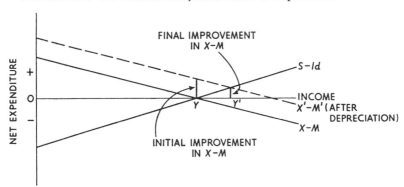

sum of the elasticities is greater than 1. The net improvement in the balance of payments will be less than the amount by which the schedule is displaced, because the initial balance-of-payments effect produces an income effect, that is the shift from Y to Y' consequent upon the shift of the $X-M$ schedule to $X'-M'$.

What determines how much the initial impact of depreciation will be cut down? The answer is obvious: it is the slope of the $S-I_d$ schedule. If this is very steep, so that the multiplier is very small, the final balance-of-payments effect will be very much like the initial impact. But if the $S-I_d$ schedule is relatively flat, the income effect will greatly modify the balance-of-payments effect in the long run.

This emphasis on the income effect of exchange depreciation leads us to make the further point that some exchange-rate changes are undertaken not for their influence on the balance of payments but to promote income expansion or to hold it down. This was the point of the Canadian effort in 1961 to get the Canadian dollar down from $1.05 in terms of U.S. dollars. Or upward revaluation of the exchange can be adopted as a counterinflationary move: witness the New Zealand revaluation of 1948. Similarly,

---

[2] Observe that we have to be careful in using the income diagram for cases where prices change. In this diagram, money and real income are identical, and since prices are constant under all circumstances, a change in the $X-M$ schedule can be independent of changes in $S-I_d$. Not so when prices change. Strictly speaking we should stay away from the income diagram; but we propose to use it circumspectly.

the upward revaluations of the German deutsche mark in 1961, 1969, and 1971 all had their origin in the effort to damped down the overheating of the economy and slow down inflation. Balance-of-payments effects were not sought except as a transitional deflationary device. It was intended that the system would be homogeneous, with price levels reduced to the extent that the exchange rate was raised.

Whether the income or the balance-of-payments effect will be the more pronounced depends, of course, on the slope of the $S–I_d$ schedule. When this schedule is flat, depreciation produces pure inflation as in Figure 22.2

FIGURE 22.2. Failure of Depreciation to Improve the Balance of Payments in Absence of "Money Illusion," Etc.

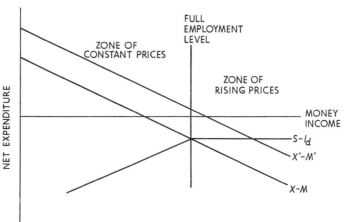

and the balance-of-payments effect is nil. When it is steeply sloped upward, the balance-of-payments effect will be large and the income effect small. Without knowing what is going to happen to savings, the monetary authorities can get fooled, adopting exchange-rate change for balance-of-payments reasons and getting an income effect (if the marginal propensity to save is much lower—and the multiplier much higher—than estimated), or seeking an income effect and achieving a change in the balance of payments.

Depreciation under Full Employment

So much follows on the Keynesian analysis, which requires that the supplies of other factors be elastic, i.e., that land, labor, and capital are available in abundance at constant prices and that changes in money income are equivalent to changes in real income. The literature which produced the Marshall-Lerner condition was for the most part fashioned during the Great Depression of the 1930s, when this was broadly true. But does it apply under conditions of full employment?

Note that the final improvement in the balance of payments in Figure 22.1 can be regarded either as the initial improvement in the balance of payments, less the increase in real income times the marginal propensity to import, or as the marginal propensity to save times the increase in real income. The net improvement in the balance of payments is matched by an increase in savings.

The point may be put algebraically. The equilibrium condition of national income is

$$Y = C + I_d + G + X - M .$$

If we transpose a bit and change signs, we get

$$X - M = Y - (C + I_d + G) .$$

The balance of payments on current account is equal to Income Produced less Expenditure.

Sidney Alexander has introduced into the literature the term **absorption** to cover the expenditure terms $C + I_d + G$. Using A for absorption and B for the balance of payments, he puts it

$$B = Y - A .$$

This also holds for changes from a given position. Using small letters to designate changes in variables,

$$b = y - a .$$

The change in the balance of payments equals the change in output less the change in expenditure.

With less than full employment, the balance of payments can be improved by increasing output more than absorption, or by sliding along an $S-I_d$ schedule which is positively sloped. But under conditions of full employment such as obtained in underdeveloped countries and have applied in developed countries for most of the period since World War II, it is by no means clear that Y can be increased. In these circumstances, the possibilities of improving the balance of payments by depreciation, Alexander insists, turn on whether absorption can be reduced. What is the mechanism by which exchange depreciation can increase savings or decrease absorption?

One possibility is "money illusion." Suppose savings are a positively rising function of money income rather than of real income. This implies "**money illusion,**" i.e., that spending habits respond to money incomes without reference to the level of prices. Under exchange depreciation, people would reduce the proportion of income spent if money incomes rose, despite the fact that prices were rising along with them and real incomes were constant. It would in fact leave us in the position indicated by Figure 22.1 above, provided the horizontal axis represented "money income" and not "real income" as well. An upward shift in the $X–M$ schedule would intercept the $S–I_d$ schedule at a higher money income and identical national output, but real savings would increase and the balance of payments would improve.

Alexander does not put much credence in money illusion, and neither do many economists. After the series of inflations since World War I, the public is too sophisticated to be fooled when all prices rise in the full-employment zone. Money illusion in these circumstances is possible but unlikely.

There is even doubt that the public will be misled by the increase in import prices from depreciation under conditions of less than full employment. When the terms of trade turn against a country, real income declines because of the rise in import prices.

$$Y = C + I_d + G + X - \frac{M}{T},$$

where T is the terms of trade. When import prices rise, real income declines. Whether households and firms experience what may be called "**exchange illusion**" (believe that their money incomes determine real income and ignore import price changes) will depend upon the size of the average propensity to import (M/Y) and the country's recent experience with inflation. The larger the M/Y and the more severe and recent the country's inflations, the less chance will there be of exchange illusion.

Another possibility is the **real-balances effect**. With a constant money supply, the increase in prices will produce an increase in savings (or so monetarists think) as spending units try to build back the real value of their cash balances. This is the opposite of money illusion. Households and firms have a clear idea of the real value of their cash balances, and a firm resolve to maintain it. They therefore cut absorption, which improves the balance of trade.

Or money can have an impact in a somewhat different way. The rise in prices and money incomes against a constant money supply will raise **interest rates** provided that there is a positive slope to the LM curve discussed in the previous chapter and that this will decrease absorption.

Alexander is not disposed to rate the real-balances effect or the interest-rate effect very highly, whereas monetarists think of them as the main mechanisms for adjustment. Even the price rise from the change in the terms of trade, leaving aside the general inflationary price rise from full employment, has been singled out in a University of Chicago thesis as the main engine of change in the balance-of-trade change. In this model, the improvement in the balance of trade is not permanent. When real balances have been built back by the savings and the export surplus (which adds to the money supply), expenditure rises again and restores the old trade balance at the new exchange rate. The system is homogeneous after a transitional improvement while the real-balances effect is working. But to non-monetarists, the model seems contrived and hardly realistic.

In addition to money illusion, real balances, and interest-rate changes, there is still another mechanism for reducing absorption under full-employment depreciation of the exchange rate—**redistribution of income** from small to large income recipients, i.e., from small to large savers. If imports bulk large in ordinary consumption, there may be no exchange illusion, but the real incomes of workers, civil servants, teachers, pensioners, and the like are cut without their being able to do anything about it, and profits in the foreign-trade sector (exports and businesses competing with imports) increase. Alexander was inclined to dismiss this source of reduced absorption as uninteresting, on the ground that the foreign-trade sector with higher profits and savings would be likely to expand its investment as well. This is clearly a possibility. Another force which would negate the effects of income redistribution in cutting absorption is the resistance of the workers, civil servants, etc., to the redistribution itself. We will touch on this presently in the discussion of structural inflation. In these cases the system reverts to homogeneity. But history is replete with cases of both sorts, those where depreciation failed to improve the balance of trade because of homogeneity, and those where improvement was achieved.

Much depends here on institutional forces: the political strength of labor, or the readiness of various income groups to use every weapon at their command to resist any decrease in their share of the total income. Where wage rates are tied to the cost of living, as in the Scandinavian countries, there is almost no prospect of effecting substantial income redistribution, and increased savings, through depreciation. Or where, as in France, the separate income groups—peasants, workers, civil servants, veterans, industrialists—use every means, including strikes and violence, to prevent any reduction in the real income of the group, depreciation is unlikely to work in this way. It was only with the advent of strong government under de Gaulle in 1958 that French devaluation was successful— a devaluation which reduced the real income of labor and agriculture in favor of the business sector. In the long run, it may be noted, economic growth offsets the losses of these sectors, but in the short run there can be no doubt that the balance of payments was improved at their expense.

Unless one can count on income redistribution, money illusion, the real-balances effect, or some other means of increasing savings as a function of a given real income, according to Alexander's view exchange depreciation is unlikely by itself, with full employment, to improve the balance of payments. If real output cannot be expanded, there must be a decrease in absorption: a decline in consumption, or a decline in investment. If depreciation does not decrease absorption, prices will rise internally with depreciation, and the change in the exchange rate works like a change in dimensions from yards to feet, which alters the length of nothing.

But economists now agree that Alexander leaves out one important step: the possibility of expanding real income by means of depreciation through resource reallocation. Assume a balance-of-payments deficit with full employment. The exchange rate is overvalued. This means that resources have been drawn out of exports and import-competing goods into domestic lines. Correcting the exchange rate leads to resource reallocation, which improves real income. The extent of the improvement is ambiguous, quite apart from any particular case, because the change in prices gives rise to an index-number problem. Measured in terms of before-devaluation prices (the Laspeyres index), the income change will read differently from the measurement in terms of postdevaluation (Paasche index) prices. But despite the measurement difficulty, the improvement exists. And if absorption can be held down while income expands, there will be room for improvement in the balance of payments, even without a cut in absorption. Various writers attach greater and less importance to this effect, with Fritz Machlup and Egon Sohmen regarding it as central. Whatever the relative weights attaching to absorption and reallocation under full employment, it remains true that neither can be neglected.

Structural Inflation

In Alexander's analysis, equal (and limited) importance is attached to money illusion, the real-balances effect, and income redistribution. But there can be little doubt that the redistribution effect is at the core of the explanation of much Latin-American devaluation, along with what is called in that area "structural inflation." Take Argentina, or Brazil, or Chile. The pattern runs something like this: Rising labor costs and a fixed exchange rate result in a cost and profits squeeze for exporters, and, together with freedom of city workers to import, a balance-of-payments deficit. The fixed exchange rate with full employment redistributes real income in favor of the urban workers. The real income of this group is improved still more by the increase in imports, at the expense of the national reserves.

When it becomes necessary to halt the deficit, devaluation effects a shift of real income from urban workers to rural export interests, as the cost of living rises along with export prices. Profits that go into savings rise at the expense of real wages, which depresses total consumption and cuts back absorption. In some extreme forms, this Latin-American thesis about devaluation holds that the income redistribution effect of depreciation is more important than any balance-of-payments effect, and in fact that devaluation is sought by exporters as a measure of income redistribution to offset the wage rises of the laboring classes. In this analysis, both groups save little and consume a lot, so that there is not much improvement in the balance of payments from devaluation. Or the point can be made differently. It is the failure to achieve an effective redistribution of income in favor of saving classes, including the government which taxes profits, that prevents depreciation from improving the balance of payments. Each group which feels its real income being cut raises prices, withholds product, or goes on strike until its money income rises to offset the increased cost of living owing to the higher prices of imports. The end result is that domestic prices and money incomes rise by the full percentage of depreciation, and the system is homogeneous. Structural inflationists claim, with what reason it is hard to judge, that exchange depreciation cannot help the balance of payments.

This concept of structural inflation is anathema to the monetarists, who properly point out that in the form given above it neglects all mention of the money supply. Inflation cannot proceed through the shifting of the burden of excess demand under full employment from one income group to another, and from time to time meeting it through a trade deficit, unless extra money is being created in the system. In fact, for absorption to exceed income, giving rise to a deficit, there must be credit creation. Where strong men dig in and block the expansion of money—Poincaré in 1926, Erhard after 1948, de Gaulle in 1958—the structural inflation stops. In their view the only source of inflation is money, and the expression "structural inflation" is a feeble apology by poor economists and weak central bankers who fail to guard the gates of the central bank.

The issue, however, is not one of technical economics but of practical politics. So-called structural inflation in Latin America differs from what might be called pure inflation, first in the fact that it stems from the clash of conflicting claims for income and not initially from foolish issues of excess money, and second in that, with prices already raised, the validating issue of new money cannot be blocked except with enormous political force. Any central banker who tried to resist on purely technical grounds would be swept away by the imperious demands for credit of government on the one hand and business on the other. There is a money aspect to structural inflation; it lags rather than leads, and it rests not on economic ignorance but political impotence.

Different Tradeoffs between Employment and Inflation

A strong argument for flexible exchange rates, or at least frequent changes in exchange rates (topics which we address more squarely below) is that different countries are comfortable at different places on their Phillips curves. The Phillips curve, as most students will know, is the tradeoff between price inflation and full employment. Sample curves are illustrated in Figure 22.3. The more nearly a country at a given instant in

FIGURE 22.3. Phillips Curves Representing Tradeoff between Inflation and Unemployment

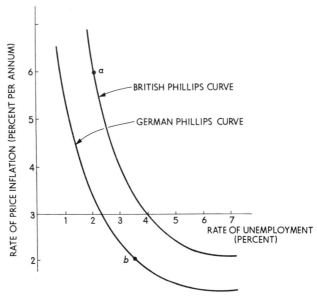

time moves toward full employment, the higher is likely to be the rate of price inflation. The closer it moves to zero price inflation, the more it will have to experience unemployment. The monetarists detest the Phillips curve. All inflation is monetary, in their view, and the Keynesian model of fixed prices and varying employment is accepted only with qualification and grumbles. (Friedman has said, "We are all Keynesians now.") The monetarists want flexible exchange rates, but not for the purpose of harmonizing different choices along Phillips curves.

The Phillips curve is also under attack from econometricians, who find little evidence of a single Phillips curve for a given country stable through time. The answer may well lie in the fact that the public learns through experience, like learning by doing, so that continued inflation makes the Phillips curve drift out and to the right, raising the level of price inflation for a given level of unemployment—until the process is reversed, when it may drift in and to the left. The basic argument for the price and wage controls that the Nixon administration adopted in August 1971 when the dollar was devalued was that they would reverse the outward drift of the Phillips curve.

Assume that a country, such as Britain, has a record of severe unemployment, and another country, like Germany, has a record of severe inflation. On the basis of past experience, their Phillips curves take different positions. Their past experience is also likely to make them choose different positions on their respective curves. Britain will prefer a position such as a in Figure 22.3, with less unemployment and more inflation; Germany will find itself politically more comfortable at home with a position nearer b. With 6 percent per year inflation in Britain and 2 percent per year inflation in Germany, the pound sterling must depreciate roughly 4 percent a year against the deutsche mark to keep the system homogeneous.

Successful maintenance of a fixed exchange rate requires the two Phillips curves to move toward each other and the two countries to adopt broadly the same position on their Phillips curves. Contrasting experience—more inflation in Germany and more deflation in Britain—would gradually push the Phillips curves toward each other. It might, however, lead them to draw further apart on the same Phillips curve.

Note that the analysis assumes that monetary and fiscal policy are dominated by domestic, not international, considerations. When countries go their separate ways in macroeconomic policy, it is virtually impossible to maintain the balance of payments in equilibrium at a fixed rate.

Flexible Exchange Rates with Balanced Trade

The interaction between the price and income effects of exchange-rate changes can be seen in a different perspective. Suppose a country adopts a flexible exchange-rate system so that the balance of payments is always in balance. Will this enable the economy to maintain an independent monetary and fiscal policy so as to stabilize domestic money income without repercussions from foreign influences? Many economists have thought so. In a pathbreaking article, Sven Laursen and Lloyd A. Metzler concluded that it will not.

Let us set the stage by noting the balance-of-payments behavior of the economy. When changes in the demand for exports or supply of imports occur, the economy adjusts to them readily and smoothly by means of changes in the exchange rate and costless and speedy reallocations of domestic resources. If, for example, the demand for exports falls off, the exchange rate will depreciate to the point where newly induced exports, or reduced imports, automatically offset the original change. If the demand for exports increases, exchange appreciation leads to displacement of incremental exports, or the stimulation of incremental imports, to match the initial change. The balance of payments is always in balance. The amount of spending on domestic resources is constant, as a first approximation, because the change in foreign spending on exports is matched either by other changes in spending on exports, as a result of depreciation, or by other changes in spending on the domestic output of import substitutes, as imports change. If exports fall, for example, and imports fall to match, the decline in foreign spending for exports is counterbalanced by an increase in domestic spending on import substitutes. This calls for a smooth and frictionless transfer of domestic resources from the export sector to the import-competing sector. Assuming that this can be achieved, will not domestic income be stabilized?

Laursen and Metzler put the issue as one of the impact of changes in the terms of trade on domestic total expenditure. The balance of payments may be left unaffected by the change in foreign demand or supply, but the terms of trade will be affected. How will changes in the terms of trade affect national income and expenditure?

In the two-country, two-commodity model, there can be no employment effects because this barter model implicitly uses Say's law of markets: All income is spent. Changes in real income cannot affect savings, because the model has no room for savings. But if savings are allowed, there is a question, and there may be a problem.

In order to answer this question, we need to provide further assumptions about the economy. We need to know, in particular, how the rate of saving is related to changes in the terms of trade. A variety of such assumptions has been provided by a variety of economists.

Laursen and Metzler took as their assumption that savings are a function of real income, and an improvement in real income from an improvement in the terms of trade will increase savings, a worsening, reduce them. This led them to conclude that a favorable shift in the terms of trade will reduce national income by raising real income and increasing savings. An improvement in the terms of trade, they concluded, is deflationary. Conversely, a worsening of the terms of trade through depreciation was regarded as inflationary through its effect in increasing expenditure (reducing savings) because of a reduction in real income.

Wolfgang Stolper worked from import prices (rather than the terms of trade) directly to savings, using the assumption that savings and imports were competitors for the consumers' dollar. In this circumstance, an increase in import prices (worsening of the terms of trade) led to a reduction in spending on imports (elasticity greater than 1) and an increase in savings. Total spending declined, and income fell. When imports were cheaper, on the other hand, savings were drawn down to buy more goods from abroad, which led to an expansion of spending.

According to Laursen and Metzler then, an improvement in the terms of trade was deflationary; according to Stolper, inflationary; and vice versa for a worsening of the terms of trade.

The Laursen-Metzler assumptions can be criticized as highly limiting. A large change in the terms of trade—say 10 percent—will produce a much smaller change in real income. If the average propensity to import is 20 percent, this change in the terms of trade will affect real income by 2 percent. Under no circumstance can a 2 percent change in real income produce a very large shift in savings or expenditure.

More fundamental, an increase in real income arising from lower import prices cannot be very deflationary, since any considerable deflation would reduce real income and restore the level of real expenditure to its level before import prices fell. It seems likely, rather, on the Laursen-Metzler assumptions, that the country will end up with some small decline in money income but a small increase in real income and real expenditure.

The Stolper assumption, in its turn, has been criticized as unrealistic. There is less justification for assuming that imports and savings are alternatives than the opposite, i.e., assuming that cheaper imports mean more saving.

What will happen to imports, savings, and domestic expenditure as a result of changes in the price of imports depends on the structure of a country's trade. If price elasticity is high, the substitution effect will be substantial but the income effect will be small. There will be a substantial increase in imports; a necessity to shift the resources released from the import-competing sector into exports to balance trade; but very little change in overall spending or saving. No substantial change in income arises from the model as it exists. Dynamic changes can occur, however, because of the failure of adjustment to be that smooth. Thus, for example, the expansion in exports may require more investment in export industry than is provided by the savings released from the import-competing sector.

If the price elasticity of demand for imports is low, the substitution effect will be small but the income effect will be large. Some part of the increase in income will be saved, and money income may fall to some extent. But much will be spent. At higher real income, more is consumed as well as more saved. Resources will be released from the export sector and transferred to domestic occupations.

The classic example offered by the real world is that of Britain in the early 1930s, when a rise in the terms of trade increased real income substantially, because of the inelastic nature of the demand for foodstuffs and raw materials, and provided real income which spilled into domestic house building (investment rather than consumption).

It is, in short, difficult to generalize about the interactions between the terms of trade and domestic spending. The nature of the income effect and the substitutability between imports and domestic goods will differ from country to country and circumstance to circumstance.

Elasticities versus Absorption versus Monetarism

The quarrels among academic economists do not go very deeply into these separate issues. All recognize that the system is one of general equilibrium in which the approaches through prices, spending, and money supply must ultimately converge. The issue is which is the best handle to grasp to begin with.

The elasticity optimists start out by calculating price elasticities. If these add to more than 1 they assume that changes in the exchange rate will improve the current account (we leave for later the response of capital movements). The elasticities involved should be general, not partial, and take account of the reactions of changes in spending and changes, if any, in the money supply.

The absorptionists approach the problem rather through spending and saving in the home market. If at home there is an excess of spending at the given exchange rate, there will be a deficit; if an excess of saving, a surplus. But as full employment is approached, the absorptionists must take account of the reaction of spenders to price changes as well as the changes in their money incomes. They must also be aware of what is happening to money.

Finally the monetarists tend to take the view that deficits are the consequence of excessive issues of money, surpluses to relative shortfalls. Most of them choose to regulate the money supply by domestic criteria and let the exchange rate and the balance of payments take care of themselves. But all must contemplate price changes and the response to them and the paths of spending.

Which is the most productive approach will depend upon a given situation. Is the Japanese balance of payments in current-account surplus because the Japanese are so productive and make goods cheaply in a world where the sum of the elasticities is much greater than one. Or is the surplus a consequence of the high marginal propensity to save, deriving from the system of payment which pays out a large proportion of annual income in bonuses, which are readily saved? Is Japanese monetary policy a major factor? This writer's predilection here is for the absorption approach, but the others cannot be excluded.

Or take the change in the merchandise balance of the balance of payments of the United States after the middle of 1970. Up to that period, according to the econometricians, the development of exports and imports followed closely the experience of the previous decade in responding to price and income changes. After the middle of 1970, however, imports rose more rapidly, especially from Japan and Canada, and exports rose more slowly than one could have predicted. An absorption or money model would have adjusted for any change in comparative advantage. An elasticities model would not.

Or regard the sharp improvement of the balance of payments of Brazil when the rates of money creation and inflation were slowed down after 1969. In this case the cutting edge would seem to have been control of the money supply, though the identity that the improvement in the balance of payments on current account was matched by an increase in net savings still holds, as always.

It is disturbing to the student to insist on eclecticism. It is nonetheless the most intellectually respectable and the safest ground on which to stand.

Summary

Interactions of price, spending, and money supply require economists to move from partial to general equilibrium. With so many degrees of freedom, it is necessary to constrain the problem before much that is useful or pointed can be said. The income effects of depreciation constitute a partial offset to the impact effect. If they go far enough and spending pressures force the expansion of the money supply, the system may be homogeneous, i.e., ending up with the same real values for all variables but the money variables of incomes, prices, money supply, and exchange rate all altered in the appropriate direction by similar percentages (or their reciprocal).

Depreciation requires an increase in savings (relative decrease in absorption) if the balance of payments is to improve. With idle resources, production may outstrip spending, and the change in saving is the change in the balance of payments on current account. Under full employment, an increase in saving may be achieved through money illusion, the real-balances effect, an interest-rate rise, or income redistribution.

Further general-equilibrium exercises are undertaken for structural inflation, different tradeoffs between employment and inflation, and flexible exchange rates with balanced trade.

Fully elaborated, the elasticities, absorption, and money supply effects merge into one another. For particular problems, however, one or another may produce the most mileage. The skill of the economist is in making the right choice.

SUGGESTED READING

Treatises, Etc.

The absorption approach was introduced by S. S. Alexander in "Effect of a Devaluation on a Trade Balance," American Economics Association, *Readings in International Economics*, and has been attacked by F. Machlup in "Relative Prices and Aggregate Spending in the Analysis of Devaluation," *AER*, June 1955, and "The Terms-of-Trade Effects of Devaluation upon Real Income and the Balance of Trade," *Kyklos*, No. 4 (Bern), 1956. Alexander revised his first view in "Effects of a Devaluation: A Simplified Synthesis of Elasticities and Absorption Approaches," *AER*, March 1959.

One of the earliest attempts to incorporate income and price analysis into the same framework was A. C. Harberger's "Currency Depreciation, Income and the Balance of Trade," *JPE*, February 1950. Only a few months behind were the papers by S. Laursen and L. A. Metzler, "Flexible Exchange Rates and the Theory of Employment," *RE & S*, November 1950, and W. F. Stolper, "The Multiplier, Flexible Exchange Rates and International Equilibrium," *QJE*, November 1950.

Points

For a case study of the redistribution effect, see Carlos F. Diaz-Alejandro, *Exchange-Rate Devaluation in a Semi-Industrial Country: The Experience of Argentina, 1955–1961* (Cambridge, Mass.: The M.I.T. Press, 1966).

The University of Chicago thesis elaborating the theory of depreciation in terms of real-balances effects is by R. Dornbusch.

PART V

Balance-of-Payments Adjustment and International Monetary Arrangements

Chapter
23

NATIONAL ADJUSTMENT POLICIES

Adjustment, Confidence, and Liquidity

A group of 32 economists examining international macro-economic issues broke them down into those of adjustment, confidence, and liquidity. We examined the adjustment process in detail in Part IV, and this chapter summarizes the issues at the national level. In the following chapter we will deal with means of financing disequilibriums while waiting for adjustment to take place and the role of stabilizing and destablizing short-term capital movements. This embraces the question of confidence. Chapter 25 deals with the international monetary system, considering whether international money exists, who issues it, and in what amounts. This poses the issue of liquidity. A penultimate chapter deals with foreign aid, only partly connected, to be sure, with the issues of adjustment and issuing international money, before the final chapter discusses the international economic system more broadly.

Equilibrium

As we saw in Chapter 18, equilibrium in the balance of payments is an elusive concept. For a trading country which is not a reserve center, acting like a bank to issue money held by other countries, basic balance is the appropriate concept. For a financial center the currency of which is held abroad as reserves, a somewhat different concept may be required—though not the liquidity, official transactions, or any other readily measurable one. Under any concept, however, the current account, the long-term capital account, and perhaps some international exchanges of claims are all adjusted to one another. Behind the current account lie tastes, resources, production functions, including technology, and the money supply, which bespeak levels of prices at home and abroad appropriately related to one another through an exchange rate. If prices in one country are too high relative to those abroad, the current account is likely to be adverse, or insufficiently positive, relative to the long-run capital movement, and the exchange rate is said to be **overvalued**. If, on the other hand, prices are low relative to prices abroad, the current account tends to be insufficiently adverse, or excessively positive, and the exchange rate is said to be **undervalued**.

The Purchasing-Power Parity Doctrine

At the end of World War I, a Swedish economist, Gustav Cassel, devised a means of measuring departures from "equilibrium." During the war, trade had been interrupted, monetary conditions in various countries had gone separate ways, and the problem, when foreign trade was resumed, was to choose a new exchange rate which would balance the accounts. Cassel suggested the purchasing-power parity as the appropriate level at which to set the exchange rate. This was calculated by measuring relative departures of price levels from some base period when the balance of payments had been in satisfactory adjustment. Two countries, A and B, whose payments were in reasonable adjustment in period 0, should choose an exchange rate (R) which reflected the changes in their prices between period 0 and a later period 1:

$$R_1 : R_0 = \frac{P_{a1}}{P_{b1}} : \frac{P_{a0}}{P_{b0}}$$

or

$$R_1 : R_0 = \frac{P_{a1}}{P_{a0}} : \frac{P_{b1}}{P_{b0}}$$

If prices (P) in A doubled relative to prices in B, from period 0 to period 1, the exchange rate (R) should fall in half (or the price of foreign exchange expressed in local currency should double). This is the **relative** version of the purchasing-power parity doctrine. Another and **absolute** doctrine rests on the assumption that goods prices should be equalized by trade everywhere in the world. Where goods cost more in A than in B, when A's prices are converted into B's currency at the existing exchange rate, A's currency is overvalued by the percentage of the higher cost.

The absolute version of the purchasing-power parity theory cannot, of course, depend on the equalization of goods prices by trade. This is because of transport costs. Transport costs bring it about that not all goods are traded, as we have seen, and that goods are more expensive in the importing country than in the exporting country by the amount of transport costs. Hendrik Houthakker, who upholds the absolute version of the theory, relied on more complex reasoning. Trade brings about something approaching factor-price equalization. With factor-price equalization and identical production functions for nontraded goods, nontraded goods prices will be the same in countries joined by trade, despite the impossibility of joining such markets through goods movement.

The purchasing-power parity doctrine assumes that the balance of payments was in equilibrium in the base period, and further that there have not been **structural changes** in the factors underlying this equilibrium, i.e., changes in technology, resources, and tastes, including the attitudes toward foreign investments affecting portfolio decisions. In 1926, the French chose an exchange rate with great care on the assumption that capital already abroad would stay abroad. In fact French investors decided to repatriate their holdings of sterling and dollar assets, which called for an import surplus to bring back the capital in real form. The exchange rate chosen was undervalued. Similar structural changes have been frequent in the postwar period as capital started out immobile and became more and more mobile, with international firms based in the United States ending up scanning investment opportunities all over the world. The purchasing-power parity suited to zero-capital movements is structurally unsuited to a heavy flow of savings abroad. Or the change may be merely one in tastes affecting merchandise: in an example furnished by P. A. Samuelson, with constant costs and three commodities, where previously country A exported commodity X and imported commodities Y and Z, a change in tastes now requires A to export X and Y and import Z. No change in costs or prices takes place, but the exchange rate must alter to shift good Y from imports to exports.

These theoretical qualifications to the purchasing-power parity are supported by an empirical assault by Bela Balassa, who directs his fire to Houthakker's use of consumer price indices. Houthakker claimed that the U.S. dollar was overvalued by 22.2 percent relative to the deutsche mark in March 1962, measured by the consumer price indices calculated by the *Statistisches Bundesamt* of the West German government. Many governments calculate the cost of living in various places so that they can adjust the living allowances of their foreign service personnel. The German statistical authorities are particularly careful, and their results are published. Calculated by a Fisher Ideal formula, U.S. prices turned out to be 22.2 percent higher than German prices. The dollar, said Houthakker, was therefore 22.2 percent overvalued in absolute terms.

The choice of what price index to use in calculating purchasing-power parities has been a vexing one. If one takes the prices of internationally traded goods for which transport costs are unimportant, the law of one price makes the doctrine a tautology. Such goods are traded in a single market, and in a single market there can be but one price. Consumer price indices contain nontraded goods. They, therefore, get away from the tautological content of the doctrine.

But consumer price indices, Balassa points out, contain a lot of personal services which are not only not traded, but the prices of which diverge with economic growth. The reason is a complex one. With improved efficiency, wages in efficient industries rise. Wages can rise and goods prices remain unchanged in these industries because of technological improvement. But wages have to rise as well in the industries with little or no technological change in order for them to retain their labor. With constant efficiency and rising wages, their prices have to rise. To the extent that personal services— in barber shops, beauty parlors, lawyers' and doctors' services, teaching, and so on—rise in price, they affect the consumer price index without impinging on the balance of payments. In a world of one-sided technological progress, absolute and relative departures from purchasing-power parity cannot be measured by the cost of living.

The point can be made more generally. There are differences in the purchasing-power parity, and in the implicit exchange rate, for different types of goods. When the Organization for Economic Cooperation and Development (OECD) undertook to compare real incomes between countries with money incomes converted at the market exchange rate, it found a wide range of differences. Exchange rates of the more productive countries were found to be increasingly overvalued as one moved from commodities to services. It is thoroughly misleading to compare real incomes per capita between countries by converting money incomes at going rates of exchange. Happily for the employment of economists, it is necessary to compare actual outputs for fairly narrow categories of national income. From the resulting estimates, one can compute separate purchasing-power parities for different classes of expenditure.

The absolute version of the purchasing-power parity thus has to be rejected because of transport costs, domestic goods, and structural changes, and the relative version must be carefully policed because of difficulties of choosing the appropriate base equilibrium year, selecting the appropriate price indexes, and again structural changes. But there is something to the theory. It furnishes a first approximation of the appropriate exchange rate when international economic intercourse is resumed after an interruption such as a war, and it helps suggest what changes are necessary in the exchange rate (or in price levels) when inflation is proceeding at different rates in different countries. It is not, however, an infallible measure of disequilibrium, particularly where capital movements are subject to arbitrary changes because of shifts of confidence.

Fundamental Disequilibrium

The Articles of Agreement of the International Monetary Fund, signed at Bretton Woods in 1944, permitted exchange-rate adjustment within limitations: 5 percent from the par value agreed to by the Fund at any time; 10 percent upon notification to the Fund, and any amount, with the consent of the Fund's directors, in the case of a fundamental disequilibrium. Nowhere in the Articles of Agreement, however, is fundamental disequilibrium defined, nor have the deliberations of the directors over close to 30 years since the Fund opened its door produced further enlightenment. The previous section has shown the difficulty of measuring disequilibrium through comparing price levels. It is equally difficult to ascribe a fundamental quality to any one particular equilibrium. Fundamental may refer to the size of the disturbance, and to its obduracy. Economic analysis, however, has been unable to single out any one kind of disequilibrium as more fundamental than any other.

Kinds of Disequilibriums

A later official body, Working Party No. 3 of the Economic Policy Committee of the OECD, found it useful in 1966 to make "a broad distinction between cases where an imbalance is due to an inappropriate level of internal demand in the country concerned, to excessive or deficient competitive strength in world markets, or to excessive capital movements." The report of the Working Party goes on to qualify the analysis by saying that multiple causes of disequilibrium can occur. In some cases, however, the origin of a payments imbalance is comparatively straightforward, as is its cure. An inappropriate level of demand should be corrected by a change in internal demand, excessive or deficient competitive strength by exchange-rate adjustment, and excessive capital movements by control of capital movements.

This is too simple by half. It fails to go behind the inappropriate level of domestic demand or the excessive or deficient competitive strength. It makes no allowance for an inadequate flow of capital. There is no recognition that automatic forces of adjustment through, say, changes in the money supply may be sufficient to correct the disequilibrium—a topic we will treat, along with capital movements, in the next chapter. Nevertheless, the distinction between changes in levels of demand and changes in competitive capacity is a useful one, following closely the distinction between income and price in Chapters 19 and 20. It also parallels a broad distinction between principal categories of adjustment measures. But first it is useful to observe that not all disequilibriums are attacked head on. The temptation is always to temporize in the hope that it will go away. While waiting for this to happen, governments often seek to repress the disequilibrium.

Quasi-Adjustment Measures

Basic adjustment policies correct disequilibrium; quasi adjustment represses it. This useful terminological contribution comes from John Williamson. Quasi adjustment may be called for because deep-seated corrective measures are at work but slowly, and the means of financing the transitional deficit have been stretched. Or they may be applied as a second-best policy because the appropriate corrective measures are politically unacceptable, or the monetary and trade authorities lack an adequate diagnosis of the problem.

Quasi adjustment takes the form of a number of policies discussed in the preceding pages. Imports may be reduced temporarily through an import surcharge, like the 10 percent levy imposed by the United States in August 1971 (and lifted under the Smithsonian agreement of December of the same year), or through cuts in government foreign spending, tying of foreign aid, restrictions on foreign travel, or raising the cutoff point for buying at home instead of abroad. Raising interest rates to attract short-term capital to finance a deficit is a quasi-adjustment measure—on the Bernstein definition of a deficit which regards private foreign funds as autonomous and above the line rather than as compensatory and below the line. The most extreme form of quasi adjustment is foreign exchange control, in which demand and supply are matched administratively rather than through the price system, and in which exchange-rate prices and national incomes at home and abroad are not linked in appropriate relations to one another. This leads not to correction of disequilibrium, but to the **disequilibrium system** under which price, demand, and supply are maintained at nonequilibrium values by administrative action.

Most economists disapprove thoroughly of quasi adjustments. They prefer to operate with more basic measures and to finance transitional deficits while they are working out. A defense of these measures can be made under certain circumstances, however. In the major structural recovery from World War II, foreign exchange control limited the size of the transitional deficit to be financed by European liquidation of foreign assets or U.S. aid. Ultimate recovery required abandonment of quota restrictions and the reallocation of resources into lines of comparative advantage. To attempt to achieve free international markets before the gaps in the productive structure had been repaired, however, would have entailed either a much larger volume of financing or acceptance of a lower level of income and substantial unemployment as the recovery standard.

Internal and External Balance

The broad policies of adjusting internal demand or changing the exchange rate have been characterized by Harry G. Johnson as **expenditure changing** and **expenditure switching**. Expenditure changing, of course, comes from varying the level of national income. Expenditure switching uses the exchange rate to divert domestic (and foreign) expenditure between home and foreign goods.

The impact of expenditure-switching and expenditure-changing policies

on the balance of payments and the level of employment can be demonstrated with the aid of a diagram worked out by Trevor Swan, much along
the lines of those in Chapter 21, but substituting a proxy for the exchange
rate for the interest rates used in the *LM–IS* diagrams. On the vertical axis
in Figure 23.1 is a cost ratio (*R*) which represents the ratio of international

FIGURE 23.1. Internal and External Balance Determined by
Real Domestic Expenditure and the Cost Ratio

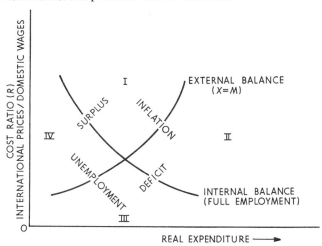

to domestic prices, or to domestic wages. This is an index of the country's
competitive position. The higher one moves up this scale, the larger are
exports and the smaller are imports, because the exchange rate is increasingly undervalued, foreign prices are rising relative to domestic prices, or,
less likely, domestic prices are falling relative to foreign prices. On the
horizontal axis is real domestic expenditure, which increases from left to
right.

Two curves are shown in the figure, one for internal balance or full employment, and one for external balance, representing a particular current-
account balance appropriate to a given autonomous level of long-term
capital. There is, of course, a separate external-balance curve for each possible level of capital movements. The internal-balance curve moves down
from left to right, indicating that the lower the cost ratio which limits exports and import-competing production, the higher must be real domestic
expenditure to maintain full employment. Positions to the right and above
the curve represent inflation, with domestic real expenditure too high relative to exports and import-competing production, or the other way round.
Below and to the left of the curve there is unemployment because domestic
expenditure plus production for exports and import replacements are too
low to occupy domestic resources fully.

Let us choose one external-balance curve, perhaps where long-term capital movements are zero and $X = M$. This is positively sloped: as one moves north, the balance of payments improves because of the more favorable cost ratio; as one moves east, on the other hand, the balance of payments worsens because of the spillover of expenditure onto imports (and perhaps what were, at lower levels of expenditure, exports). Moving to the northeast, therefore, balances the two forces and gives external balance. Above and to the left of the curve, the balance of payments is in surplus; below and to the right, it is in deficit. The figure can thus be divided into four quadrants, I with inflation and a balance-of-payments surplus; II with inflation and a deficit; III with unemployment and a deficit; IV with unemployment and a balance-of-payments surplus.

There is, of course, only one point, where the curves intersect, where the country is in complete equilibrium. In zones II and IV, with a deficit and inflation, and a surplus and unemployment, respectively, the country should alter real expenditure, contracting it for zone II and expanding it for zone IV. In zones I and III, on the other hand, the major tool of policy should be to alter the cost ratio, using switching policies, such as exchange-rate depreciation and appreciation. But these pure policies apply best to positions on the horizontal and vertical lines through the intersection of the two curves (not drawn in Figure 23.1). To each side of the horizontal and vertical lines, the separate policies must be combined with an admixture of the other therapy. To the right of the vertical line through the intersection, in zone I, for example, appreciation to lower international relative to domestic prices should be combined with contraction of spending to help move toward internal balance; and below the horizontal line through the intersection, in zone II, contraction of expenditure should be combined with depreciation to move toward external balance. Since each zone in the graph is divided by the horizontal or vertical line through it, there are eight possible combinations of policies.

The limits of this analysis, and of the simple division of therapies into expenditure switching and expenditure changing, are found in the fact that the internal-balance curve assumes only general unemployment because of deficient demand and makes no allowance for structural unemployment. The curve is displaced to the right by capital formation and additions to the labor force. It is shifted to the left by capital destruction. As mentioned, there is a separate external-balance curve for each level of autonomous capital movements, for a given level of productive capacity. Changes in productive capacity will also displace the external-balance curve representing a given capital movement. Thus the $X + M$ curve will be displaced leftward and up by capital destruction, and rightward and down by capital formation and additions to the labor force. Additional capacity makes it possible to maintain external balance with increased expenditure, at the same exchange rate or a higher exchange rate (lower cost ratio) with a given level of expenditure.

We indicate the relations of the curves to productive capacity to illustrate the problem of major structural disequilibrium brought about by war. The destruction of the war, and neglected depreciation, shifted the internal-balance curve to the left and down, and the external-balance curve to the left and up. Figure 23.2 shows the curves after displacement by war. The postwar position is marked by the dot at *B*, which shows a position of inflation and substantial deficit.

FIGURE 23.2. Internal and External Balance Curves Shifted by Wartime Destruction

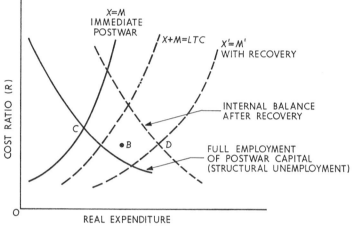

Monetarists tend to think that the great bulk of balance-of-payments difficulties come from inflation. After World War II, there were many classical economists who called for **halting the inflation and adjusting the exchange rate.** In the most specific formulation, put forward by the isolationist Senator Joseph Ball of Minnesota, the call was for European countries to "balance their budgets and adjust their exchange rates to the purchasing power parity." In the terms of Figure 23.2, this requires a movement from *B* to *C*. But the displaced curves which intersect at *C* reflect a far-reaching structural disequilibrium which would leave structural unemployment and a permanently reduced level of real expenditure. The Marshall Plan, which involved moving from the immediate postwar $X = M$ curve to the postwar $X + M = LTC$ curve to finance a large capital inflow, gradually restored productivity and shifted the internal- and external-balance $(X = M)$ curves out to where they intersected at a point such as *D*.

Monetary and Fiscal Policy

Expenditure-changing policies can be divided further into monetary and fiscal policy. Fiscal policy can be represented by the national budget, whether surplus or deficit, and has effects on both internal and external balance, through changes in spending by government, households, or business, as noted in Figure 23.1. Monetary policy has two effects. In the first place, changes in the interest rate affect business investment, and through the multiplier, consumer spending. Secondly, however, they give rise to short-term capital movements, assuming that the financial sector is willing to undertake exchange risks. External balance in this formulation is $X + M + LTC + STC = 0$, which differs from the equations given in Chapter 18. In Figure 23.3, internal and external balance are plotted against the na-

FIGURE 23.3. **Monetary and Fiscal Policy Used in Pursuit of Internal and External Balance**

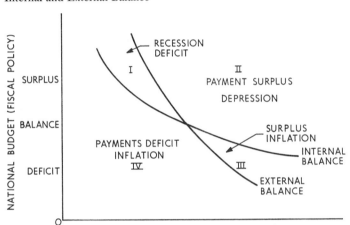

tional budget and the interest rate, representing fiscal and monetary policy, respectively; the steeper slope of the external-balance curve indicates that it is more responsive to monetary policy, with internal balance more responsive to fiscal policy. The curves are drawn for a given cost ratio of domestic wages to international prices, as measured along the vertical axis in Figure 23.1. A change in the exchange rate would displace both of them. An increase in domestic costs relative to foreign prices, from currency appreciation, for example, would shift the external balance curve to the right, requiring a higher interest rate to achieve balance at a given government surplus or deficit. At the same time the internal balance curve would be shifted downward and to the left. This follows from the fact that a reduction in spending on exports and import substitutes requires a higher budget deficit at a given interest rate to maintain full employment.

Robert A. Mundell, who devised this analysis, uses it to address what he calls the **assignment problem**. In zones II and IV, no assignment problem exists. At a given cost ratio, with stable prices and a fixed exchange rate, monetary and fiscal policy should both be expansionary in zone II and contracting in zone IV. The problems arise in I and III. In the former, with recession and deficit, monetary policy should be assigned to external balance and tightened, and the fiscal policy should be assigned to internal balance and shifted to less surplus or more deficit. To use both in the same direction would be to move in a northeast or southwest direction, parallel to the equilibrium intersection without approaching it, while easier money combined with tighter fiscal policy moves away from equilibrium to the northwest. Since the slope of the external-balance curve is steeper than that for internal balance, monetary policy has a comparative advantage in working on external balance, and fiscal policy on internal.

Objection has been raised to Mundell's view of this analysis as adjustment. It is rather, some economists claim, quasi adjustment. The capital movements produced by capital flows in response to monetary policy are arbitrary, as is the definition of external balance. The capital flows, in particular, may move in the wrong direction from a long-run normative point of view—to the capital-rich country, for example, away from countries needing capital for economic development. This raises a "welfare problem" along with the assignment problem and detracts from the merits of the analysis except for the short run.

The Costs of Adjustment and Financing

There are costs of disequilibriums and costs of repressing, correcting or financing them. The costs of disequilibrium have an offsetting benefit. In the deficit country, the benefit is absorption in excess of output; the cost is the loss of reserves, the short-term borrowing, or the unintended foreign aid if the country defaults on its credits—in the last instance, a cost borne abroad rather than by the deficit country. There is also likely, however, to be a cost in the loss of credit standing. In the surplus country, the cost is the unintended reduction in absorption below output, whereas the offsetting benefit is the accumulation of claims to future consumption, except where unintended foreign aid offsets the unintended abstinence.

The costs of adjustment have been divided into continuing and transitional. Continuing costs reflect the loss of the benefit from the disequilibrium on the part of the deficit country. But this neglects the offsetting cost of disequilibrium. The real issue is the transitional costs from disequilibrium to equilibrium.

Quasi adjustments have costs in distorting resource allocation and in operating the system. There is great dispute over the size of these costs. Liberals regard them as high; interventionists as trivial. The latter insist that monopoly, taxation, and producer and consumer ignorance are already so great that a little more misallocation through tariffs, quotas, capital restrictions, and foreign exchange control fails to hurt. The liberal worries that if a government starts off to intervene by trying to reshape deep-seated forces, it will only make things worse, requiring more and more bureaucrats in time to do a poorer and poorer job. This book is no place to try to resolve these issues, though it is perhaps useful to point both to government success in the area of maintaining employment and its persistent failure to diagnose and cure balance-of-payments disequilibriums successfully.

The costs of basic adjustment are on the whole well understood. Adjustment through deflation in the deficit country has a cost of unemployment when wages are sticky and when world demand is not particularly buoyant. Adjustment through price inflation in the surplus country has a cost in the distortion of debtor-creditor and fixed income–variable income relationships. Adjustment through changing the exchange rate, so frequently that in the limit it approaches the flexible exchange rate system, has the disabilities of possible encouraging destabilizing speculation, a moot point reserved for the next chapter, and further of disintegrating the world economy to the extent that traders and investors are risk averters and would choose under these circumstances to abandon foreign trade and investment, another debated question to be dealt with in Chapter 25. To anticipate briefly, the argument is made that the risks of change are as great with fixed exchange rates and merely take a different form: tariffs, surcharges, exchange controls, and the like. With fixed exchange rates, however, there is a commitment to adjustment and equilibrium about the existing rate which encourages traders and investors to maximize by trading and investing beyond the national borders. With flexible exchange rates, goods and capital markets are less likely to remain integrated. And flexible exchange rates produce some changes in rates, leading to reallocation of resources (e.g., in the business cycle) which later must be reversed.

Dividing the Costs and the Responsibility for Disequilibriums between Deficit and Surplus Countries

In his proposed International Clearing Union circulated before Bretton Woods, Lord Keynes proposed that interest be charged on balances at the clearing union, whether they were positive or negative. The point was to penalize surpluses as well as deficits in international payments and to provide surplus countries with an incentive to correct their imbalances, parallel to that existing for deficit countries with their cost of deficit. During and after the war, other suggestions were put forward for putting all the burden of adjustment in the surplus country, including some which would have required surplus countries to spend their credit balances within a specified period of time or have them written off. This would have meant that they would give away their export surplus.

The point is well taken that under existing arrangements the cost of disequilibrium falls almost entirely on the deficit country, and that this is not necessarily equitable. It is clearly inequitable where a country permits itself to go into recession and runs a surplus. In this circumstance, the deflating country is responsible for the payments imbalance and has its internal imbalance (unemployment) moderated by the external imbalance (payments surplus), but the cost falls on the innocent party or parties abroad. On the other hand, when the deficit is owing to inflation at home rather than deflation abroad, the deficit country is responsible for the imbalance and has its rise of prices dampened by the availability of goods from abroad. In this circumstance it is entirely appropriate that it bear the burden of correcting the imbalance and of financing it.

The answer as to how the costs of financing and correcting payments disequilibria should be distributed thus depends upon the state of world resource use. In depression, the surplus country is exporting unemployment to the rest of the world and fairly may be asked to take a major share of these costs. This and the memory of the depressed 1930s accounts for the proposals to shift part of the costs to the surplus country. In prosperity, on the other hand, the deficit country is exporting inflation. Responsibility for the imbalance belongs to it, and so should the costs of financing and correcting.

Whose Exchange-Rate Change?

The question whether the surplus or the deficit country should adjust became particularly acute in the 1970s when the U.S. balance of payments slipped. It has two aspects. First, in a multilateral world, the counterpart of a deficit in a single country may be broadly spread around the world, or it may be concentrated in a few countries. The counterpart of the U.S. current-account deficit was, in fact, surpluses which were very large on the part of Japan, Canada, and Germany. For the United States alone to depreciate its currency would perhaps wipe out its deficit, but a general improvement against all the countries of the world would have left somewhat reduced surpluses for Japan, Canada, and Germany, perhaps, but deficits for all other countries. It was necessary, therefore, to adjust the exchange rates of both deficit and surplus countries. In a two-country world there is a choice as to which country adjusts. In a multilateral world, both surplus and deficit countries must act.

Second, there is an aspect connected with the use of the dollar as international money—one which perhaps should wait until we discuss international monetary arrangements but which can conveniently be disposed of here. U.S. reserves include few foreign currencies; other countries' reserves consist to a great extent of dollars. In this circumstance, it is hard for the United States to change the value of its currency and easy for other countries to adjust their buying and selling prices for dollars. If the United

States were to change the value of the dollar against gold, other countries could maintain their old buying and selling prices for dollars; the price of gold would have risen but the exchange value of the dollar would not have fallen. In a domestic context the price of money is the reciprocal of the prices of all commodities and services. In the international system, with the dollar used as international money, the value of the dollar was the reciprocal of the exchange rates of the other countries of the world. The United States could change the price of gold, but not the value of the dollar. Other countries could change the value of their currency, but not the price of gold. In these circumstances, if the foreign exchange value of the dollar was to change after August 1971, the U.S. monetary authorities had to obtain the agreement of the rest of the world.

This was done in Washington in the Smithsonian agreement of December 1971. Secretary of the Treasury John Connally imposed the 10 percent surtax in August as a bargaining weapon to obtain the consent of other countries to a devaluation of the dollar. On multilateral grounds, and because the largest surpluses were in Japan and Germany, the yen and the deutsche mark were raised in value.

All this emphasizes that the question whether the surplus or the deficit country should adjust its exchange rate in a two-country world using the gold standard becomes more complex with many countries, and especially for the particular country whose money is used as international money.

Summary

Payments disequilibriums can be repressed, corrected, or financed. Quasi adjustments which repress disequilibria distort resource allocation and in the limit, under foreign exchange control, represent the disequilibrium system. Correction involves basic adjustments, typically of either the expenditure-switching or expenditure-changing type. Expenditure switching involves altering the ratio of international prices to domestic prices or wages by exchange-rate changes or by relative inflation or deflation with a fixed rate. Expenditure changes may come about through fiscal or monetary policy. Fiscal policy has a comparative advantage on internal balance in the economy, while monetary policy has an advantage in external balance because of its effect on capital movements.

Repression and correction of disequilibriums have costs. How these costs are shared between surplus and deficit country is a complex issue. In world inflation, the deficit countries should bear the largest burden. In depression, the burden should shift to the surplus countries. Institutional arrangements, however, make it easier to sustain a persistent surplus than a persistent deficit.

In a multilateral world, it may be necessary to have both surplus and deficit countries share the costs, when the counterpart of any surplus or deficit is not evenly spread among all countries. When one country's currency is used as international money, moreover, it is difficult for it to change the value of its currency, which is the reciprocal of the price of all of the others.

SUGGESTED READING

Texts

Yeager, chaps. 6, 7, and 8.

Treatises

A general discussion of adjustment by a number of experts is contained in R. Hinshaw, ed., *The Economics of International Adjustment* (Baltimore, Md., Johns Hopkins Press, 1971).

See also OECD, *The Balance of Payments Adjustment Process,* a report by Working Party No. 3 of the Economic Policy Committee (Paris, August 1966).

On the purchasing-power parity doctrine, see G. Cassel, *Money and Foreign Exchange after 1914* (New York: The Macmillan Company, 1923); L. A. Metzler in *International Monetary Policies* (Washington, D.C.: Federal Reserve System, October 1947); P. A. Samuelson, "Theoretical Notes on Trade Problems," *RE & S*, May 1964; and B. Balassa, "The Purchasing-Power-Parity Doctrine: A Reappraisal," *JPE*, December 1964, the latter two criticized H. S. Houthakker's "Exchange Rate Adjustment," in Joint Economic Committee, *Factors Affecting the Balance of Payments of the United States,* 87th Cong., 2nd sess. (Washington, D.C.: U.S. Government Printing Office, 1962).

For the mix of expenditure-switching and expenditure-changing policies, see essays by Swan, "Longer-run Problems of the Balance of Payments," Johnson, "Toward a General Theory of the Balance of Payments," and Metzler, "The Process of International Adjustment under Conditions of Full Employment: A Keynesian View," in American Economic Association, *Readings in International Economics;* R. A. Mundell's "The Appropriate Use of Monetary and Fiscal Policy for Internal and External Stability," *SP*, April 1962, and W. Fellner, F. Machlup, and R. Triffin (eds.), *Maintaining and Restoring Balance in International Payments* (Princeton, N.J.: Princeton University Press, 1966).

Points

Comparisons of real national income from which purchasing-power parities for different classes of expenditure can be derived will be found in M. Gilbert and Associates, *Comparative National Products and Price Levels: A Study of Western Europe and the United States* (Paris: OECD, 1958).

For the distinction between quasi and basic adjustments, see J. H. Williamson, "The Crawling Peg," *EIF*, 1965. That between continuing and adjustment costs in adjustment is made by B. J. Cohen in *Adjustment Costs and the Distribution of New Reserves, PSIF,* No. 18, 1966.

Chapter 24

SHORT-TERM

CAPITAL MOVEMENTS

AND EQUILIBRIUM

Financing Disequilibrium

"What can't be cured must be endured," and whatever disequilibrium cannot be repressed or corrected must be financed. Financing is required, moreover, when the policies of repression or adjustment take time, or while the automatic forces working for correction produce their results. In the last case, financing may be the best therapy.

If the balance of payments varies regularly around the equilibrium, balanced position, now on one side, now on the other, it may be desirable not to repress or correct the fluctuations about the equilibrium mean but to finance them. The balance of payments has no need to be in equilibrium every second, minute, hour, day, week, month, season, year, or phase of the business cycle. Perhaps the cycle furnishes an apposite example. To balance international payments in every phase of a business cycle originating at home is to deprive the country of the stabilizing forces of surplus in depression and deficit in prosperity. The payments imbalance will be reduced at the cost of exacerbating domestic imbalance. And to balance international payments in every phase of business cycles originating abroad is to force the country to trace out the foreign cyclical pattern, in greater or lesser degree depending on income elasticities. A system for automatic and immediate payments balance, such as a flexible exchange rate, is thus mistakenly taken to deal with cyclical disequilibrium. It is better to finance the imbalance through the cycle, accumulating foreign exchange reserves through foreign boom or domestic depression, and spending them in foreign slump or domestic expansion. When the disequilibriums are self-correcting, with or without the aid of built-in stabilizers and regular anti-cyclical policies, it is better to finance than to suppress or correct, assuming that the financial means are at hand.

Adjustment takes time, and while the adjustment policies are performing their mission, there is need for financing. How much time adjustment takes is likely to be a function of the determination with which the policies are applied, and this may be related to their costs, discussed below. Financing also has a cost. There is a tradeoff between speed of adjustment and readiness to finance the deficit which is related to the relative costs. But it should also be noted that financing may be undertaken unwisely, as a result of failure to diagnose accurately the nature of the disequilibrium. "If we ignore it, it may go away." The art of government is to know what and what not to ignore in this fashion, and not all administrations have the art.

The Means of Finance

Finance can be provided by national monetary reserves in the form of gold and/or foreign exchange, by short-term capital movements responding automatically to movements of exchange rates, possibly within gold points or similar limits, or by loans from national or international monetary authorities. The use of national reserves presupposes their existence at the start of the trouble. If a primary-producing country, subject to cyclical fluctuations in the price of its exports, adopts a policy of countercyclical financing of the balance of payments at the right moment, at the trough of the cycle, it can accumulate reserves in prosperity and spend them in depression, provided it accurately forecasts the course of prices, incomes, exports and imports, capital movements, and so on, and has the courage not to change its mind as reserves first build up and then dwindle. For the most part, however, it is difficult to start from zero. A country has to have a normal level of reserves as protection against the unexpected and must seek to operate a cyclical policy from that standard.

International Monetary Fund

Each country can maintain an international reserve provided that there are no persistent deficits (with their accompanying surpluses), which run reserves down for some countries. But this condition was not met in the 1930s, and international monetary reserves became badly skewed. For a fresh postwar start, therefore, the International Monetary Fund was established at Bretton Woods in 1944 to make it possible for countries with limited reserves to finance short-run and transitional deficits. The Fund was established as a pool of central-bank reserves and national currencies, available to its members under certain conditions to finance deficits which are likely to be corrected automatically or, in the course of time, with policies already adopted. It could not be used to finance persistent deficits and continue viable, however, so that its operations are undertaken only after a careful examination of a country's conditions and policies.

The Fund differs from an international central bank in that it operates not with its own liabilities but with national moneys. Each member country was originally given a quota, and these quotas have been enlarged from time to time. Twenty-five percent of a country's quota is paid in in gold, and 75 percent in national currency. The gold and national currencies thus accumulated are available for purchase by individual member countries against national currencies, with a limit of 200 percent of the national quota which the Fund can hold in the currency of any country. Since it starts with 75 percent in national currency, this means that a country can purchase foreign exchange up to 125 percent of its quota. The first 25 percent, or "gold tranche," is automatically made available to the country on its request. A further "commodity tranche" is made available quasi automatically, as noted in Chapter 10, when commodity prices of less developed countries fall. Other 25 percent tranches are dealt in at higher rates of interest and under more stringent conditions as the Fund's holding of a national currency increases, in order to ensure that the reserves are used for temporary and not permanent financing of deficits.

There are limits to the extent of financing of imbalances. The limit of financing by the International Monetary Fund is fixed by Fund policies and a country's quota. How far a surplus country's currency can be used by the Fund depends upon the original quota, 75 percent of which is available in national money. Thereafter the Fund can only acquire the currency with gold. A deficit country using its own gold and foreign exchange reserves is limited by their size. Of course, a country's surplus can be financed much longer, because, while there is a finite amount of gold in the world, foreign exchange reserves can be manufactured indefinitely. But the surplus country may be expected to have qualms about exchanging goods with a real cost for claims which may not be convertible in the future into real values. While pressure on the surplus country to bring its financing of balance-of-payments surpluses to a halt is much less than that on the deficit countries, under present institutional arrangements, it nonetheless exists.

Seasonal Adjustment through Short-Term Capital Movements

Prior to the IMF and prior to frequent intervention by exchange authorities through the use of national reserves, temporary changes about long-run equilibrium were financed primarily by gold flows or by short-term capital movements. Up to World War I, for example, the United States had a strong seasonal behavior in its merchandise-trade balance. Exports of wheat and cotton moved abroad heavily from August to January. During this period the dollar was strong. When the movement came to an end, the currency was weak. Short-term capital inflows financed the seasonal weakness of the currency and were reversed during the period of strength. Two major mechanisms, both seasonal variations, were involved: in the New York short-term interest rate and in the exchange value of the dollar.

With zero mobility of short-term capital, the seasonal deficit could still be financed by gold flows. The dollar would be weak in the spring and fall to the gold export point. Gold arbitrageurs or the money authorities would then provide foreign currencies wanted in the United States by selling gold against foreign currencies, which would be converted into dollars. In the fall, the dollar would rise to the gold import point, and arbitrageurs (or theoretically, the authorities) could acquire gold against excess foreign currencies and restore the position.

With mobility, short-term capital can substitute for gold movements in the balance of payments. Again the movement may be private or official. Private financial interests might be moved to borrow in London and lend in New York in the spring, when the New York money market was squeezed by the decline in money supply arising from the import surplus, and pay off their loans in the fall, when the New York money market eased as a result of the seasonal surplus of exports. Or the motivating force might be movements of the exchange rate within the gold points. Private speculators would buy foreign exchange in the fall when it was cheap and sell it in the spring when it was dear, furnishing dollars to the market in the fall and soaking up the excess in the spring. Or if private speculators were unavailable in sufficient numbers for the purpose, the monetary authorities could accumulate foreign exchange in the fall and furnish it to the market in the spring.

Speculation

"Speculation" is a word with many overtones, but in this context it has a purely technical meaning. A speculator is someone with an open exchange position, an imbalance between short-term claims and liabilities denominated in foreign exchange. It is not speculation to hold one's own currency, or to borrow it. It is speculation to be **long** or **short** of foreign exchange, that is, with an excess of claims over liabilities or liabilities over claims in a foreign currency.

There are two reasons why a speculative position might be taken in foreign exchange: either because the foreign exchange risk was ignored, or because its existence was recognized and embraced. During the 19th century, when the whole world traded in sterling, traders outside of London "speculated" in sterling because they ignored the exchange risk. Similarly in the period from 1945 to about 1963, dollars were bought and sold freely by foreigners who took positions in dollars without being conscious of the risk of a change in the value of the dollar. In these instances, the existence of exchange risk does not impede capital movements, because the risk is overlooked.

Often the risk is recognized and assumed. A man who bought sterling when it was weak in the fall and who sold it in the spring when it was strong was a speculator who counted on earning a higher return on his funds than he could in the New York money market from the fluctuations in the exchange rate (between the gold points). Buying cheap and selling dear is **stabilizing speculation.** There are many definitions of **destabilizing speculation,** and much controversy, but one of them is selling when a currency is weak, in the expectation that it will be weaker, or buying it when it rises in price, believing that it will rise still more. We will return to destabilizing speculation presently.

One important fact: Assuming no change in trade or other payments, no speculation means no capital movement. It is sometimes erroneously believed that a holder of dollars can move his capital into sterling in London and bring about a capital movement, without speculating, by selling forward the sterling he bought spot. It is true that the individual can move his capital and not take an exchange risk. What is true of the individual, however, is not true of the totality. The forward sale of sterling has to have, as a counterpart, a forward purchase. If the forward sale drives the price down far enough, a speculator will buy sterling forward. In this case the speculation by the forward purchaser is what makes the capital movement by the hedger or arbitrageur possible. Or the price of forward sterling can go so low as to induce incremental imports from Britain. This violates our assumption of no change in trade. Perhaps the forward sterling is bought by the Bank of England. Then the Bank is speculating by going short of dollars, providing forward rather than spot dollars to the market. The point is a difficult and tricky one, but vital: for a net capital movement to occur, someone must take a speculative position or there must be a change in trade. There can be many instances of gross capital movements but no net movement, as when a New York corporation transfers funds from New York to the Euro-dollar market in London. There is a gross capital movement, but the corporation, with dollars, does not have a speculative position. On the other hand, the Euro-dollar bank would normally match its dollar liability to the depositor by holding dollars in New York. This is a gross movement in the other direction. Two gross movements, no exchange position, no net capital transfer.

Mobile Short-Term Capital and Monetary Policy

Assume that exchange speculation is not a problem because everyone is willing to speculate. Exchange-rate stability is believed in, and the risk is ignored. The volume of funds willing to move is large, let us assume, and the incentive that money needs to move from one currency to another is minimal. In this case national money markets become joined. In one market there is only one price. Interest rates become identical. National monetary policy—at least for the smaller countries—loses its independence. We visited this sort of world in Chapter 21, where in the *LM–IS–FX* analysis we found the *FX* curve completely horizontal.

In a world of many countries of equal size, with highly mobile capital, no country can use monetary policy. All could cooperate and determine a joint monetary policy, which would suit some countries better than others if they were at different stages in the business cycle or had different preferences on the same, or different, Phillips curves.

Where some countries were larger than others, however, and especially if there were one dominant country, its independence in monetary policy would not be altogether lost, whereas that of the smaller countries might be. It could set the level of world interest rates. Other countries could stimulate capital movements, trying to set an interest rate different from that in the major financial center. A flow of capital in or out would bring the intended rate down or up to the level in the major center.

In the real world, from about 1958 and lasting to broadly 1968, New York was the dominant financial center of the world and set monetary policy for all countries to which U.S. capital was mobile. In Britain, where foreign capitalists were unwilling to take long positions in sterling and capital was mobile only to the extent that the Bank of England was willing to furnish the forward cover, the money market remained largely separate. To a lesser degree, the French market, too, stood aside as foreign exchange controls (never very complete or effective) and a certain myopia on the part of French lenders and borrowers reduced capital mobility below that between New York and the Euro-currency market, and the Euro-currency market and Frankfurt, Rome, Brussels, Amsterdam, etc.

The trouble with this world of the 1960s, in this writer's judgement, was that it was not understood by the authorities. Germany, Italy, France, the Netherlands, Belgium, and the United States tried to operate their monetary policies independently when their money markets were more or less joined, and rather more than less for the most important one, that of West Germany. Fearful of inflation, the Bundesbank would raise interest rates. Wary of the political response to unemployment, the United States would expand its money supply. U.S. lower rates would communicate themselves to the Euro-dollar market. U.S. firms in Europe would borrow dollars in the Euro-dollar market and pay off loans to banks in Germany, France, the Netherlands Gradually the horizons of the local firms extended so that they too found it tolerable to borrow dollars in London at, say, 7 percent to pay off DM loans in Germany at 10 percent, accepting the exchange risk. As more dollars poured out of the United States and the dollar became weaker in exchange markets, the risk of going short of dollars became positively attractive, rather than merely tolerable. The speculation which had started out by ignoring the exchange risk ended up in embracing it.

Destabilizing Speculation

There is no agreement on what constitutes destabilizing speculation. Earlier in this chapter it was suggested that on one definition, speculation is destabilizing when it buys when the price rises and sells when it declines. In both cases, it drives the rate further in the direction it is going and accentuates the movement. In a discussion of destabilizing speculation in the 1920s, however, Milton Friedman pointed out that if an exchange rate were highly overvalued or undervalued, speculation which drove it toward equilibrium might properly be regarded as stabilizing even if it reinforced market movements.

A further technical definition ran in terms of the directions of change of spot and forward exchange rates. Robert Aliber of the University of Chicago believes that if speculation drives the spot and forward markets in the same direction rather than in opposite directions, it is destabilizing. The normal swap, buying spot and selling forward, for example, moves the two rates in opposite directions. When both rates move together, speculation is accentuating the rate movement.

A more general view, less linked to market phenomena, runs in terms of reversibilities. If speculation drives a rate past some critical turning point from which return is impossible, or very difficult, it may be regarded as destabilizing. In 1963 when speculators sold lire for dollars and DM because of political difficulties in Rome, it could be said to be destabilizing, for if the rate had broken from 625 to the dollar, exchange depreciation, leading to a rise in prices and wages in Italy, would have become irreversible, given the downward stickiness in prices and wages. On this showing speculation in the direction of the inevitable is stabilizing. That which snaps brittle systems which might otherwise have been expected to hold is destabilizing. But this evidently requires the observer characterizing the speculation to defend his view of what would have happened had the course of history been otherwise.

Those who believe in flexible exchange rates (a subject addressed more fully in the next chapter) are reluctant to admit that destabilizing speculation exists. Some have difficulty in finding even a single historical example of destabilizing speculation. Others dismiss it on a priori grounds. A priori one reason for disbelieving in the existence of destabilizing speculation is that destabilizers buy when the rate is rising and sell when it is falling. To make a profit, one must sell when it is high and buy when it is low. For speculators as a whole to survive, they must make a profit. Since speculators appear to survive, they must buy when a rate is low, sell when it is high. Therefore on the market view, they must be stabilizing. Ergo, there is no destabilizing speculation.

The trouble with this, of course, is that, as in the stock market, there are two bodies of speculators, the inside professionals and the outside amateurs. The insiders sell a weak currency and buy a strong one, driving the rate further in the direction it is moving and destabilizing. At the top they sell out a strong currency, and the outsiders buy it. At the bottom, the insiders buy a weak currency, and the outsiders sell it. The insiders are destabilizing in the range of movement, and stabilize at the limits. The outsiders—the sheep who get shorn in the stock market as well—destabilize and as a body lose.

The other a priori argument against destabilizing speculation converts the definition from *ex post* to *ex ante*, from what actually happened to what might have happened before the situation unfolded. This suggests that speculation is destabilizing if, at the time the exchange position was taken, it did not appear as a reasonable bet on the basis of the information available to the speculator. But this begs the entire question. On this showing, everyone who speculates and is half-way rational is a stabilizing speculator, and only the few idiots who find their way into the exchange market can be characterized as destabilizing.

Speculation and the Equilibrium Rate

We have spent so much time on this issue because it is critical to the question of flexible exchange rates. If there is no speculation, then the monetary authorities must intervene in the exchange market to ensure that the rate does not move to balance out the minute-by-minute, hourly, daily, weekly, etc. failure of supply and demand to equate exactly. Typically this can be left to speculators, banks that close their positions once a day and take care of the transitional disequilibrium shorter than a day, or speculators who concern themselves with weekly, monthly, seasonal, or cyclical movements. If all speculation is stabilizing in the sense of buying when the rate is weak and selling when it is strong, or moving the rate toward its long-run level, the flexible-exchange-rate system can be relied upon to produce balance-of-payments adjustment without disturbing macroeconomic factors. If, on the other hand, there is the possibility of destabilizing speculation (not continually, of course, for under normal circumstances speculation tends to be stabilizing, but from time to time), to rely on speculation may be dangerous. It may on occasion drive the exchange rate in an exaggerated track, giving rise now and then to overvalued and undervalued rates which put pressure on income, employment, prices, and wages rather than help the balance of payments to adjust to them as they are. In this case the authorities must take pains to curb the destabilizing speculation or offset it.

Moral Suasion

Where the authorities know something that the speculators don't know, it has been suggested that the authorities inform the speculators. This is the foreign exchange equivalent of "moral suasion" in monetary policy, sometimes known as "body English" or "jawbone regulation." The market tends to be cynical and to believe that the authorities are motivated less by love of truth than by the hope that they can seduce the market into favorable action. Frequently the market's cynicism is justified.

Discount Policy

The normal technique for reversing short-term capital movements has been to adjust monetary policy so as to alter interest rates. Higher interest rates will attract inflows and make it more expensive to borrow for outflows. Lower interest rates will repel foreigners who choose to bring funds to earn a higher return and marginally discourage those who are escaping from another jurisdiction for any one of a number of reasons, including fear of exchange depreciation. Lower rates will also assist those who might borrow to put funds abroad. Such capital movements require speculation which ignores the exchange risk or which happens to be going in the right direction as dictated by interest rates. When a currency is weak and there is much destabilizing speculation, raising the discount rate may be interpreted as a sign of weakness and constitute a signal for moving funds out of a given currency rather than into it.

Domestic Offsets

It can happen, however, either that destabilizing speculation is impervious to reason or interest rate motivations, or that a country is unwilling for any reason to submit to the monetary policy dictated by the balance of payments. If destabilizing speculation is producing inflows of funds and interest rates are already low enough, for example, it may be useful to sterlilize the incoming capital. Especially is this the case if the capital is thought to be temporary and likely to be withdrawn shortly. In this case, it would be a mistake to expand monetary policy, raise money incomes, and produce the import surplus necessary to transfer the capital in real goods and services, only to be obliged to reverse the process at a later date. To meet this problem in the 1930s, and to gain control of its exchange rate, the British government devised the **Exchange Equalization Account (EEA)**.

The principle was simple. French capital, fearful of domestic political developments, fled to Britain. The British wanted neither their exchange rate bid up nor their monetary base enlarged. They therefore bought the francs, converted them to gold, and held the gold outside the monetary system in the Exchange Equalization Account. To obtain the pounds sterling to furnish the French, the EEA borrowed sterling in the market, by issuing government bills. Frequently it issued the bills to the French capitalists and took their gold. Later when the French wanted to sell their sterling and buy francs, the process was reversed.

Notice that a stabilization fund of this sort, equipped originally with the privilege of selling sterling bills, could cope with an inflow of capital but not with an outflow. If foreigners wanted gold, it had none. Conversely the U.S. Stabilization Fund had only gold and was unable to provide dollars to foreigners who wanted them against foreign currencies (and gold). In consequence the U.S. Treasury had to borrow dollars from the market and sell them to foreigners against gold. If there had been an outflow from the United States, the Stabilization Fund could have offset it by selling gold and buying dollars.

The IMF and Speculation

While the EEA could assist Britain with an inflow, the French, suffering the outflow and lacking a large fund in gold, had nothing to help them. In the 1930s, they relied on foreign exchange control or currency depreciation. The Bretton Woods rules of the IMF provided that a country could impose foreign exchange controls but allowed exchange depreciation only within narrow limits (5 percent without prior permission, 10 percent with), except in the case of "fundamental disequilibrium," which, as noted in the last chapter, was not defined. But the amounts of financing provided by the IMF were limited in size to those likely from current-account disequilibriums alone. There was no provision for financing speculative capital flows. And, in the postwar period, it gradually came to be realized that capital controls were difficult to enforce and that temporary financing might be needed from time to time to finance destabilizing capital flows.

The Basle Agreement

In the 1950s, when sterling was under speculative attack, the IMF was stretched to a degree by allowing one year's financing to be used on one day, and another's in the year following a day later, thereby permitting half, instead of one quarter, of a country's quota to be used in a two-day period. This was insufficient. In 1961, when the deutsche mark and Dutch guilder were revalued upward by 5 percent, speculators became persuaded that this was merely the first of a series of steps of appreciation and moved funds heavily out of sterling and dollars into DM and guilders. The amounts were more than the Fund could cope with. Almost spontaneously at the Bank for International Settlements in Basle, Switzerland, a consortium of central banks agreed in March 1961 to buy the pounds and dollars offered on the market and to hold them until the speculation quieted down. This was discounting in a crisis, of the sort that Walter Bagehot called for in a domestic financial crisis in his classic *Lombard Street*, written in 1870. Later in June, when the crisis had died away and most of the funds had returned to their normal habitat (to use a word from domestic monetary theory associated with the maturity of an investment rather than its home currency), the residue which had not been reversed was funded through the IMF. The world had learned how to handle financial crises of short-term destabilizing speculation, for which the IMF had made no provision.

The General Arrangements to Borrow and Enlarging the Fund's Quotas

With economic growth, inflation, and the rise in world trade, the Fund's quotas would have had to grow in any event as the world moved on after 1947. The Basle agreement, however, called attention to the fact that quotas based on trade were insufficient to cope with the need for financing disequilibriums. In the fall of 1961, the Fund's Articles of Agreement were amended by General Arrangements to Borrow (GAB), under which 10 leading financing countries pledged special amounts to be made available through the Fund in case of perverse movements of short-term capital which could not be handled by a country's reserves and its IMF quota. The ten were Belgium, Canada, France, Germany, Italy, Japan, the Netherlands, Sweden, United Kingdom, and the United States,[1] and the initial amount was $6 billion on top of the quotas, which had started at $7.8 billion and risen in June 1960 to $14.4 billion. The **Group of Ten,** so constituted, formed an inner core of financial leaders with more cohesion than the much more numerous IMF membership.

Even with enlarged quotas and the GAB, however, it was still necessary to keep the Basle agreement going. Speculative attacks on the Canadian dollar, the Italian lira, and the pound sterling for the second time elicited fairly spontaneous central-bank support for the currency under attack. In the early efforts, the leadership was typically assumed by the United States. Late in the 1960s and in the early 1970s, as the dollar came under attack, the United States adopted a policy of **benign neglect,** leaving to others in the Group of Ten the choices whether to continue to accumulate dollars, to allow their exchange rates to appreciate against the dollar, or to apply foreign exchange controls.

An effort was made in 1968, as noted earlier, to impose reserve requirements on borrowing from the Euro-dollar market, for the purpose of slowing down capital movements from Europe to the United States. Central banks also agreed, also noted earlier, to refrain from recycling dollars back into the Euro-dollar market, where they might again be lent to non–U.S., borrowers who would use them to buy foreign currencies and raise further dollar holdings of central banks outside the United States. A number of countries adopted foreign exchange controls. Belgium and, later, France tried to separate the **financial franc** from the **commercial franc** in a sort of two-tier system, with separate exchange rates for each, to limit the capital inflow, but the difficulty of separating the markets meant that

---

[1] Switzerland stayed aloof from the formal arrangements but always cooperated closely.

there was no difference in price between the commercial and the financial Belgian franc, and a very small one between the two rates in France. In Germany, Japan, and Switzerland, local banks were instructed not to accept foreign deposits; foreign holdings of domestic securities were subject to special taxation. As in the case of U.S. foreign exchange control, however, money is so fungible that there is great difficulty in keeping it out, especially when local residents borrow abroad to repay debts owed internally.

Confidence

"A good reputation is worth more than money." Confidence in a currency ensures that when its balance of payments is temporarily weak, speculation will be stabilizing. (If speculation is destabilizing when it is strong, this is no bad thing for the currency, though it is awkward for the monetary system.) The Swiss franc remains strong in the exchange market through thick and thin for the balance of payments on current account because it has an enviable reputation for strength which gives the world confidence in it.

The Gold-Exchange Standard

In terms of the international macroeconomic trilogy—adjustment, confidence, and stability—confidence is associated with an inherent weakness of the gold-exchange standard. In Robert Triffin's analysis, a currency starts strong, finds itself becoming a reserve center, and issues too much of its currency to the world, whereupon foreign central banks and private holders become restless and find the currency weak and redundant. There is a crisis of confidence. The gold-exchange standard breaks down.

There can be no doubt that the gold-exchange standard is subject to Gresham's law that bad money drives out good. Jacques Rueff's critique of the gold-exchange standard—that if his tailor would let him issue money for his suits he would buy more of them—is probably not a felicitous analogy. M. Rueff's credit with his tailor is doubtless excellent, and he merely limits the number of suits he buys to some function of his wardrobe space, willingness to change his clothes, and so forth. The U.S. overissue of dollars in the world market was connected less with the overvaluation of the dollar on current account (until the middle of 1970) or with the instability between gold and dollars. Even after the adoption of the **two-tier system for gold** in March 1968, when the world was on a pure dollar standard rather than a gold-exchange standard, the problem persisted. Failure to coordinate monetary policy in the world's leading nations—either to reduce interest rates in Europe and Japan or to raise them in the United States— meant that dollars moved abroad in spite of U.S. foreign exchange control through the Interest Equalization Tax, the Voluntary Credit Restraint Program of February 1965, and the Mandatory Control Program of 1968. Large amounts of dollars were accumulated in the Euro-dollar market, partly by multinational corporations; partly in the hands of Middle East oil-producing countries which were unable to adjust their imports of goods and services rapidly enough to the rising flow of dollars from income taxes on exports of oil valued at notional prices; and partly in the hands of central banks, as international European and Japanese businesses borrowed dollars and paid off local loans. In these circumstances, the world lost confidence in the dollar. International corporations, Middle East sheikdoms and central banks (in moderation) tried to get out of dollars and to slow down accumulations. Willingness to rediscount in a crisis on the part of central banks was eroded by the concern that the process was not temporary and about to be reversed, but persistent.

Flexible Exchange Rates and the Movement of Short-Term Capital

The Bretton Woods system, with fixed exchange rates altered from time to time, was devised in a period of limited capital movements and allowed for capital controls. When capital mobility becomes considerable, the question arises whether the fixed-exchange-rate system can properly function. In particular it is asked by economists whether, if exchange control cannot be made to work, it is not time to adopt flexible exchange rates, perhaps within a wider band around a parity, as a means of discouraging short-term destabilizing capital movements. Under a fixed-rate system, a weak currency, at the floor of its trading limits, offers speculators a **one-way option**. A narrow band around the par level prevents the currency from rising significantly. If speculators can force the country to abandon parity, the amount by which the currency can decline is substantial. The speculator is protected from large losses and offered an opportunity of large profits. Especially is this the case for international corporations whose accounting practices encourage destabilizing speculation by typically charging as expense (and therefore to be ignored) any higher interest charges which come from speculating but penalizing a subsidiary or treasury that has to write off any capital sum caught in a devaluation. With flexible exchange rates or a wider band, rates could go up as much as they could go down, eliminating the one-way option; with no par values subject to discrete changes, accounting rules might be modified either to provide reserves against exchange depreciation or to reckon all foreign investments in the home currency, regardless of their nature.

The issue is whether speculation with flexible exchange rates or a wider band would decline, become stabilizing, or continue to be destabilizing, as with the one-way option. We will tackle in the next chapter the larger question of the costs and benefits of fixed and flexible exchange rates and the optimal compromise between the two systems. The issue here is limited to the nature of speculation, if any, under the two systems.

It is important to compare like and like. It is unfair, for example, to compare an idealized fixed-exchange-rate standard and coordinated monetary policies in the major financial countries with a disorderly system of flexible exchange rates such as obtained in the 1920s and 1930s. By the same token, however, it is important not to compare the present disorderly fixed-exchange-rate system with a large **overhang** of dollars abroad accumulated during a period of uncoordinated monetary policies with an idealized system of flexible rates and stabilizing speculation.

There is no way in which to be sure about the outcome of such comparisons (though most economists claim to be). With a limited overhang, an initial appropriate set of rates, moderate monetary and other macroeconomic policies, and few structural changes in the system, speculation is likely to be stabilizing under flexible exchange rates, and the exchange rates will not fluctuate over wide ranges. These are exactly the conditions, however, under which a fixed-exchange-rate system will work.

Contrariwise, given a large overhang with no particular habitat to which it gravitates, highly independent macroeconomic policies, and significant and frequent structural changes, neither a fixed- nor a flexible-exchange-rate system is likely to prevent destabilizing capital movements. The flexible-exchange-rate system does not offer speculators the one-way option. Nonetheless, when the time comes for a change in exchange rate, speculation may easily carry it to excessive heights or depths, as speculators misjudge the force of events—exactly as they do from time to time in the stock market. When this happens, the disequilibrium exchange rate puts pressure on the system in the same degree that forced discounting or gains and losses of reserves do under the fixed system.

In short, the question of whether speculation is stabilizing, destabilizing, or nonexistent under flexible exchange rates is critical for the success of the system, but one which does not afford an easy answer. It is likely that the outcome depends on other parameters which themselves are only loosely connected to the nature of the exchange system.

Summary

Disequilibriums which correct themselves may need financing, and so do transitional disequilibriums which take time to find adjustment. Such financing may be afforded by national or international reserves. The International Monetary Fund was established at Bretton Woods to provide financing for countries that lacked their own reserves. The IMF, however, assumed that capital movements would either be benign or controlled.

Speculation may arise from ignoring the exchange rate or being acutely conscious of the possibility that it will change. Stabilizing and destabilizing speculation can be defined in terms of market movements of prices, long-term equilibrium rates of exchange, setting in train irreversible changes in the system, and so forth. With highly mobile capital and speculation which ignores exchange rates (or speculates against the currency with the looser monetary policy), monetary policies are joined. If this is not recognized, large flows of capital may move from the low- to the high-interest-rate countries, to accumulate a substantial overhang of mobile funds abroad.

Short-term capital can be dealt with by monetary policy, domestic offsets (provided that the country of inflow has enough domestic debt capacity, and the country of outflow enough reserves). The IMF was late in coping with these movements, which called into being the General Agreements to Borrow of the Group of Ten and the Basle agreement for getting funds to return to their original habitats for rediscounting. When confidence is lost in a currency, the problem of correcting the overhang becomes difficult.

Whether short-term capital moves less and in a more stabilizing fashion under fixed or flexible exchange rates is a conundrum for which it is difficult to have a conclusive answer.

SUGGESTED READING

Texts

Grubel, chaps. 2 and 3.

Treatises, Etc.

For an out-of-date discussion of short-term capital movements see C. P. Kindleberger, *International Short-term Capital Movements* (New York: Columbia University Press, 1937; reprinted by A. M. Kelley, 1966). Modern econometric discussions are given in W. H. Branson, *Financial Capital Flows in the U.S. Balance of Payments* (Amsterdam: North-Holland Publishing Co., 1968) and R. C. Marston, "The Structure of the Euro-Currency System," unpublished doctoral dissertation, Massachusetts Institute of Technology, 1972.

M. Friedman's discussion of stabilizing and destablizing speculation is contained in "The Case for Flexible Exchange Rates," in American Economic Association, *Readings in International Economics*. See also his comments on C. P. Kindleberger's "The Case for Fixed Exchange Rates," in the Federal Reserve Bank of Boston's *The International Adjustment Mechanism* (Boston, 1970).

Points

R. Aliber's definition of destabilizing speculation is found in "Speculation in the Foreign Exchanges: The European Experience, 1919–1926," *Yale Economic Essays* (Spring 1962).

The Exchange Equalization Account is the subject of a book of that name by N. F. Hall (London: Macmillan & Co., Ltd., 1937).

R. Triffin's criticism of the gold-exchange standard is in his *Gold and the Dollar Crisis* (New Haven, Conn.: Yale University Press, 1969).

J. Rueff's views on the gold-exchange standard can be found in J. Rueff and F. Hirsch, "The Rule and Role of Gold: An Argument," *EIF*, June 1965.

Chapter
25

INTERNATIONAL MONETARY
ARRANGEMENTS

The Issues

With the adjustment and confidence problems out of the way, or at least analyzed in part, we come to the last of the trilogy of economic issues, **liquidity**. The issue of international monetary arrangements goes well beyond liquidity. In essence it is whether it is desirable to have international money. If there is to be an international money, there must be decisions as to how it is issued, in what amounts, and to whose benefit. A decision against any and all international money, with amounts of money to be determined solely by national monetary policy, implies fully flexible exchange rates. Between the two extremes lies a series of graded compromises. With one way of looking at it, the issue is what area by size, political characteristics, or economic behavior should have a single money, issued under a fixed set of rules by a single authority. In jargon, the question is what is the **optimum currency area**. With another, the question can be put in terms of exchange-rate arrangements, with a variety of compromises possible between the fixed-rate system and the fully flexible rate. The most widely discussed of these are the **wide band**, flexible within the limits, but prevented from going outside them; **the adjustable peg**, in which the par of exchange is altered from time to time as required by overvaluation or undervaluation, and the **crawling peg**, in which adjustment is minimal at any point in time but is continuous.

With flexible exchange rates, moreover, questions present themselves as to how much the monetary authorities should intervene in the determination of the rate. Under **clean floating**, there is no intervention, and the rate is left to the determination of the market. By analogy, central-bank intervention in the market to move the rate or prevent its moving has been pejoratively associated with **dirty floating**. Mixed systems are possible under which there is one international money, say, the dollar, the value of which is left to the determination of the market and the intervention of other authorities. This raises the issue of **symmetry**, or whether the rights and duties, benefits and costs of the international monetary arrangements are the same for all countries in the system.

International Money

If international money is adopted, it may be a commodity such as gold, a national currency such as the dollar or pound sterling, or a specially created unit adopted by sovereign nations as a political act of will. As this is written, the world has all three, **gold**, the **dollar**, and **Special Drawing Rights**, or SDRs. None is functioning well, and there is little agreement as to how this functioning might be improved. Gold is traded at different prices—as money, at $38 an ounce, raised from $35 by the U.S. Congress pursuant to the Smithsonian agreement in Washington, D.C., in December 1971, and as a commodity, with a fluctuating price in the free market. The dollar bulks large in the exchange reserves of major central banks of the world, so much so that they are anxious to reduce their holdings of dollars and to find substitutes. Since August 1971, moreover, the dollar is inconvertible into gold by central banks, making *de jure* a condition which had taken effect, it was thought, with the adoption of the two-tier system in March 1968, but which the small central banks of Belgium, the Netherlands, and Switzerland ignored in the summer of 1971 to push the dollar off gold. The United States wants new and substantial issues of SDRs, without changing the volume of dollars in circulation; the European monetary authorities and the Japanese are interested in exploring the substitution of SDRs for the dollar but agree to no large issue until the question of the dollar overhang or redundancy is settled.

With any money, the questions are who issues it, in what amounts, to whom. The commodity, gold, won out as money over clam shells, beads, tin, copper, and silver because its ore deposits were spread rather thinly in the world. Annual production today is roughly 40 million ounces, worth at $38 an ounce $1.5 billion. Much of this is needed in industry. Much is also hoarded or bought in the free market for speculation. The price of gold is central to the question of liquidity. Many economists want to raise the price of gold substantially, revalue gold holdings in central banks, and increase the value of current production. The increase in price from $35 to $38 agreed at the Smithsonian Institution in December 1971 has a purely technical reason, to offset the decline in the local-currency value of dollar reserves when the dollar was devalued. Some economists, like Jacques Rueff, want to revalue gold and use the enlarged amount to replace the dollar as international money. Others such as Sir Roy Harrod and Milton Gilbert of the Bank for International Settlements staff are interested primarily in balancing the amounts of gold and dollars to escape from the clutches of **Gresham's law** (that excessively issued money drives scarce money into hoarding). At the depth of the Great Depression the price of gold was raised from $20.67 an ounce to $35 in February 1934. Subsequent inflation of prices and costs reduced the profitability of mining. The industry insists that a rise in the gold price would be "fair," a word that does not belong in the economist's lexicon. The United States strongly resists an increase in the price of gold (and France pushes for it, for Rueff-like reasons). The argument is bound up with two issues—whether the dollar should remain an international money, and how much liquidity is appropriate for the world.

The distribution of gold as international money is determined by who earns it by export surpluses. Gold producers run import surpluses, balanced by new gold production, which may properly be regarded as commodity exports. When it leaves their shores it is monetary gold, available to the countries that provide goods in exchange.

The dollar is issued by the United States. How much goes abroad, however, is determined by two major forces: the overvaluation or undervaluation of the dollar on current account, and the relationship of interest and profit rates in the United States and abroad. It is easy to see the nature of the debate here. On current account, the argument is over whether the dollar is overvalued or the DM, yen, Canadian dollar, and so forth, are undervalued. In the capital area, an excess flow into foreign hands can be stimulated by too easy a monetary policy in the United States or policies in Europe and Japan that are too tight. The failure of monetary policies to be coordinated has been far more responsible for the volume of dollars in foreign hands than the current-account imbalance, which began only in the middle of 1970 and was attacked in 1971 by the 10 percent surtax on imports of August and the devaluation of the dollar by 7.9 percent in December at the Smithsonian Institution. If the dollar is going to survive as international money it seems clear that monetary policies in the United States and the other major financial centers of the world must be coordinated to produce agreed amounts of liquidity.

The distribution of dollar reserves is determined partly by what countries earn them on current account and partly by what countries acquire them in **international financial intermediation,** through holding their interest rates temporarily above world levels and encouraging foreign investors to acquire their earning assets and local borrowers or asset sellers to seek liquidity abroad. With coordinated monetary policies, the distribution of dollars worldwide under a dollar standard would be determined by liquidity preferences and capital market imperfections. Any country where liquidity preference was high or where capital markets functioned badly would borrow or sell assets abroad in more than ordinary proportions.

Special Drawing Rights were introduced in 1968 as a supplement to gold and dollars. The U.S. concern was to add to its reserves so as to strengthen the dollar. In its view, SDRs were paper gold. Abroad the hope was that the availability of SDRs would make it possible to reduce reliance on the dollar. In July of 1972, at a European Economic Community meeting of finance ministers, Anthony Barber called for the use of SDRs as international money instead of the dollar.

The volume of SDRs issued, and their distribution, has been determined by international agreement. At their issue, the SDR represents a claim on the world and a liability to the world. If the liability could be postponed to eternity, the SDR could be viewed as outside money, an asset which did not need to be repaid, a permanent addition to international money. If, on the other hand, it was necessary to keep open the possibility of repayment, the SDR was inside money, a credit, rather than an eternal asset like gold. In the agreement, this issue was compromised. Each country was required to maintain at least 40 percent of its quota as a partial offset to its share of the liabilities, and no country could be forced to take more than three times its original quota, to prevent dumping the worthless claims on a few countries.

National Money

We leave aside the issue of what constitutes the appropriate international money, who should issue it, in what amounts and to whom in order to explore the opposite solution—reliance on national moneys alone, with each country adopting an independent monetary policy by itself and flexible exchange rates between them. The argument for this system rests on substantial benefits (or avoidance of other costs) and low costs. In particular it is contended that a flexible-exchange-rate system obviates the necessity for countries to adjust monetary policies to the balance of payments, gaining an extra degree of freedom for domestic policies. It is also claimed that the costs in foreign trade and investment are minimal, since they can be maintained through the foreign exchange market, buttressed if need be by an expansion of forward dealings.

The second law of thermodynamics makes one suspicious that an extra degree of freedom for domestic policies is available by adopting a technical solution to a problem. Economists know that perpetual motion is unlikely, and that there is no free lunch. And so on examination it proves to be with flexible exchange rates, although their more doctrinaire adherents will agree with reluctance. Any one country can gain an extra degree of freedom for monetary policy by adopting a floating exchange rate. Either the authorities intervene in the exchange market, or they do not. If they intervene, they can prevent destabilizing speculation from moving the rate (on occasion, from time to time) to levels which add to the problems of domestic monetary management rather than ease them—a depreciated rate in a period of inflation, or an appreciated rate during deflation. Control of the rate adds exchange policy to monetary and fiscal policy. With three policies, one can attack three targets (according to Jan Tinbergen's theory of economic policy): balance-of-payments equilibrium, price stability, and full employment. But the weapon of exchange policy is not obtained out of thin air, but granted by the other countries with which the one country has trade and financial relations. If they too intervene, they may want to do so at cross-purposes. Just as in international money it is necessary to coordinate monetary policies, so in flexible exchange rates and intervention it is necessary, with more than one country floating and intervening, to coordinate exchange policies. Independence is either granted by other countries, or it is not obtained. The fallacy of composition remains on top. What one country can do with impunity (perhaps Canada, which has experimented from time to time with floating exchange rates) cannot be generalized into a system.

The purists among flexible-exchange-rate advocates (or the doctrinaire) push for freely flexible rates without intervention. If speculation is stabilizing, this will work very well. If speculation is occasionally destabilizing, in the sense of moving the rate away from equilibrium rather than toward it, and threatening to produce irreversibilities in levels of prices, wages, costs, and the like, it seems inevitable that intervention will be resumed. Monetary authorities cannot lock the door and throw away the key.

Under flexible exchange rates, therefore, the choice is among all but the major financial centers managing their exchange rates independently, with passivity at the major centers; countries managing exchange rates cooperatively; or, less tolerable, leaving exchange rates free without intervention.

Optimum Currency Area

Between a single world money (or the near equivalent), a permanently fixed set of exchange rates, and a world of separate nations with freely fluctuating exchange rates, how finely divided should the world be? Why stop at countries rather than groups of countries on the way to larger units, or why not go below countries to regions, states, cities, families, even people? If my balance of payments is in surplus, should I appreciate my rate of exchange on the world and be willing to work only for $1.10 dollars; or if I need work should I depreciate my exchange and offer my services at 90-cent dollars? Between the world as a whole and the single individual, the issue may make more sense for countries, aggregations of countries above them, and regions within individual countries. The questions can be merged into one: What is the optimum currency area?

Robert Mundell was the first to pose the question, and he answered it in classical fashion by reference to factor mobility. A region is an area within which factors are mobile, while factors are not mobile between regions. Lacking factor mobility as a means of adjustment, one needs another degree of freedom such as exchange-rate variability provides. The region, in his view, should have a separate currency, a region which would sometimes be larger than a country, as in the European Economic Community, but sometimes smaller than a country, as in the Maritime Provinces of Canada or Appalachia in the United States. Changing money is costly, to be sure, and in terms of convenience one should have as large as possible a currency area. But against this gain is the cost of having to endure unemployment as a means of balancing interregional accounts when the rate is fixed and emigration is limited.

A critic of Mundell, Ronald McKinnon, argues that factor mobility is not the essence of the optimum currency area. In his view, the need is for a closed economy, that is an economy which has a large volume of internal transactions and a small volume of external ones, so that when exchange-rate changes occur, the impact of the change in foreign prices on the level of living of the community is not noticed. The need is for what we called in Chapter 22 exchange illusion, after the analogy of money illusion, which disregards changes in prices arising from exchange-rate variation. An economy which is open in the sense that it trades widely with the outside world is unlikely to have exchange illusion. If its exchange rate is altered, various groups within the total are likely to alter wages, prices, costs, or income distribution so as to render the system homogeneous. Small open regions, cities, families, or individuals cannot kid themselves when they change their exchange rate.

The Mundell and McKinnon criteria for an optimum currency area point in somewhat different directions: Mundell to areas smaller than a country, or at least smaller than a big country such as Canada, and McKinnon to bigger units than a country, for example bigger than Canada, which trades to a great extent with the United States. Both criteria are economic. A very different criterion is political. In this view, the requirement of a currency area is coherent economic policies; the optimum currency area is a country. Regions lack the tools of economic policy in the fields of money, taxation, and governmental expenditure. Aggregations of sovereign countries may succeed in cooperating for a time in having their macroeconomic policies converge, but the fact of multiple sovereignty continually threatens the breakdown of coherence and a reversion to independence and divergence.

There can be little doubt that money and political sovereignty are intimately associated. Switzerland has three (or four) languages but one money. The attempt to extend the West German monetary reform of June 1948 to the three western sectors of Berlin led to the Berlin blockade and the split of Germany between what became the Federal Republic and the Peoples Republic, Western and Eastern Germany, respectively. Colonies and highly dependent independent political units may have currencies that are joined, but no single political unit has two moneys. Perhaps the best illustration, however, is the role of monetary unification in European integration. Most observers believe that monetary unification is impossible without merging central banks and coordinating macroeconomic policies in the fields of taxation, expenditure, capital markets, trade, foreign exchange, agriculture, and so on. This requires giving up most of national economic sovereignty. On one showing the problem is to calculate what policies must be coordinated to achieve monetary unification. In another light, the issue is whether, given limits on the willingness of a number of countries to yield sovereignty, it is possible for Europe to achieve monetary integration.

Europe of the Nine as an Optimum Currency Area

It seems evident that the crux of the issue for Europe is not the economic questions whether Europe has factor mobility or is a closed economy. The crux is whether the countries of Europe, and especially France, are prepared to merge their sovereignties in the fields of macroeconomic policy.

Europe of the Six—Belgium, France, Italy, Luxembourg, the Netherlands, and West Germany—made a start on a solution to the problem by appointing a committee under the direction of the Prime Minister of Luxembourg, Pierre Werner, to produce a report on "The Realization by Stages of Economic and Monetary Union in the Community." The Werner report, which appeared in the fall of 1970, called for adoption of the goal of monetary union or irreversible convertibility, the irrevocable fixing of parity rates, the complete liberation of capital movements within the Community, and, if possible, the adoption of a single currency. Margins of fluctuations about parity were to be reduced in stages and ultimately eliminated. The balance of payments within the Community would ultimately be ignored, as within a single country, owing to the mobility of factors and "financial transfers by the public and private sectors" (meaning stabilizing capital movements and rediscounting by monetary authorities). It was recognized that responsibility would have to be transferred from the national to the Community level in some spheres, and that in other areas, policies would have to be coordinated. Especially would exchange, monetary, fiscal, and commercial policy have to be managed from a central place—for example, a committee of central-bank governors, or even a new single central bank for the area.

The report laid out a series of stages for the realization of full monetary union in various functional areas. The first, to cover three years, called for consultation procedures, three surveys each year of economic policy, and Community directives to lay down guidelines in the monetary and fiscal field. The second stage, beginning in January 1974, called for tighter coordination of monetary and credit measures, but the details were left for future agreement. It was expected that complete monetary integration would be achieved by the end of the 1970s.

A number of technical issues interest economists. One turned on the width of exchange-rate variation, which was expected to widen between Europe and the rest of the world but progressively to narrow within the Community. As an example, the range of fluctuation, as agreed later, could widen to 2.25 percent each side of par against the outside world, while the range of fluctuation was to decline from .75 actual (narrower than the 1.5 percent allowed by the IMF) to .6 and then to .45 before declining to zero. If all the currencies of the Community are equally strong or equally weak against the outside world, there is no problem; all can move together within the wider band permitted for fluctuations with the outside world. But if some currencies within the Community are strong and some weak vis-à-vis one another, and they move against one another by the limit, there is the question as to where the group finds itself in the band against the outside. The smaller band may move about within the wider band, giving rise to the expression **"The Snake in the Tunnel,"** a sobriquet whose origin is illustrated in Figure 25.1.

FIGURE 25.1. "The Snake in the Tunnel": Narrowing the Range of Fluctuation among European Currencies While Widening It with Outside Exchanges

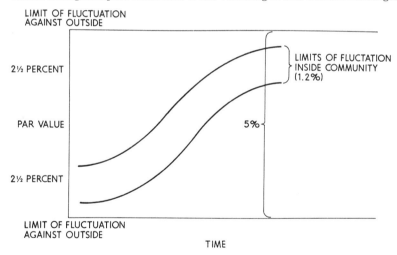

LIMIT OF FLUCTUATION
AGAINST OUTSIDE

2½ PERCENT

PAR VALUE

2½ PERCENT

LIMIT OF FLUCTUATION
AGAINST OUTSIDE

TIME

LIMITS OF FLUCTATION
INSIDE COMMUNITY
(1.2%)

5%

The Costs and Benefits of a Single Money

If we leave aside the technicalities and the modalities or means of achieving a single money, the question remains whether it is a good idea. As changes in tastes, production functions, technology, factor proportions, levels of income, and so forth occur, countries must adjust without independent monetary, fiscal, exchange, or commercial policies and must rely on coordinated action by others. The political loss in sovereignty is painful. The economic costs may be high. Is the game worth the candle? Are the benefits economic or political?

The argument for a larger currency area is largely the argument for money in general. Money serves as a medium of exchange, unit of account, store of value, and standard of deferred payment. The foreign exchange market can discharge the function of money as a medium of exchange, as Chapter 17 noted at length. But if foreign exchange rates fluctuate, it is difficult without a stable unit of account to calculate costs and prices abroad. Foreign exchange cannot function properly as a store of value to bridge temporary gaps between the receipt of income from abroad and its expenditure, and there is no standard of deferred payment for the making of long-term contracts for lending or long-term purchase and sale of commodities. Money is a public good, which makes it possible to obviate barter. When no money is provided, foreign trade and investment are not eliminated but the functions of money must be discharged privately, at private cost, with the result that trade and investment must decline (in the long run).

This writer with a predilection for international economic intercourse believes that the economic benefits of international money are substantial. The political benefits probably alter as the countries making up the currency area change. Europe wants a single currency in part because it wants to build a monetary rival to the dollar—a political purpose, though not necessarily an unworthy one. (Since the French are politically the touchiest of the countries of Europe, one suggestion has been to call the single money the European Currency Unit, or ECU, which was also the name of an ancient French silver coin worth three pounds). The political benefits of a world money, however, would be more questionable.

The political costs and benefits, moreover, are associated with the nature of the system adopted. There are strong economic reasons for believing that it is difficult to create a single world money or to reinstall gold as world money, which is different from the moneys used in at least one important country or area. Gold or SDRs, for example, would be less acceptable to international markets than national or monetary-union currencies like the pound sterling of 1913, the dollar of 1960 or, possibly, the ECU of 1978. The reason is found in the fact that markets like to avoid excessive transactions, and in the idea, debated in classical monetary theory, that market acceptance rather than government fiat determines what is money. But much as the economist may deplore it, there are evidently overtones, positive and negative, to which national currency is adopted as world money. In particular, the **dollar standard,** so-called, evokes strong xenophobic reactions outside the United States, as well as jingoist feelings within.

Compromise Solutions

In these circumstances, there has developed a certain measure of agreement among economists that the world should find a compromise between a world money, or fixed-exchange-rate system, on the one hand and fully flexible exchange rates on the other. Three broad categories of compromise may be distinguished, all involving exchange-rate movement: the adjustable peg, which is basically the IMF system of changing rates whenever there is fundamental disequilibrium, but doing so for changes of more than 5 or 10 percent only with the agreement of the Fund; the crawling peg, which is changing the par of exchange but continuously by small amounts, perhaps as little as one half of 1 percent per month, which amounts (if all the changes are in the same direction) only to 6 percent a year; and the wider band, which in some versions provides for flexible movements 5 percent either side of par, or a total band of 10 percent.

The adjustable peg is generally believed to be discredited. For one thing, it is unclear what constitutes fundamental disequilibrium. For another, countries tend not to adjust the peg until the last minute, when speculators have been furnished a one-way option (see p. 416). Third, in a crisis there is never time to undertake the mutual consultations called for by the Articles of Agreement—and if there were, the rumors of such consultations would make the foreign exchange market intensely nervous and heighten short speculation. A few economists would like to introduce more frequent discrete changes, sped up in time so as to avoid the one-way option, but most regard the system as impractical.

The crawling peg and the band are both designed to discourage speculation. The crawling peg is intended to adjust the exchange rate slowly over time to correct for overvaluation and undervaluation. The changes through time are kept small to persuade speculators that adjustment is underway but it doesn't pay to take positions for a rise or decline in the rate, because the change won't occur rapidly and the investor will do better to earn high rates of interest. The wide band, on the other hand, is intended to balance the one-way option by giving more room for the exchange rate to move against the speculator in case he guesses wrong. While both compromises are addressed to containing speculation, they do so in different ways—the crawling peg focuses on long-run adjustment, whereas the wider band around a fixed parity permits some adjustment from movements of the exchange rate within the band but is not primarily dedicated to exchange-rate changes. But of course the two can be combined—a crawling peg with a wide band.

It remains to be seen, however if the question of whether to have the benefits (and costs) of international money can be compromised. The adjustable peg, the crawling peg, and the wide band all mean that the exchange rate moves—which means that its usefulness as a unit of account, store of value, and standard of deferred payment is gone. The problem for an international investor of estimating the value of a 15-year investment in another currency is altered from what it would be under freely flexible exchange rates, but it is still different from what it is with a single money, or fixed rates, with policies devoted to their maintenance. To debate the respective merits of flexible rates, the adjustable peg, and so on, is to work on the ranking of the second-, third-, fourth- and fifth-best systems, perhaps, but all seem a long way from the best. The costs of the best may be too high: admitted. And if one cannot buy a new Cadillac (or Mercedes, Citroën, or Rover) it is worthwhile discussing various second-hand models of less well-built makes and considering whether they have been in a wreck (and if so, in how many). The metaphor is grossly unfair, of course: The best is the enemy of the good. On occasion, however, the good is the enemy of the best.

Regional Compromise

The suggestion is frequently made that compromise should run along regional rather than institutional lines. Let there be a dollar area, a European currency area, perhaps a yen area, and let the countries of the world choose up sides, joining one or another bloc. Within the bloc there should be fixed rates with narrow bands, between blocs, flexible exchange rates (whether freely flexible or guided, deponent generally sayeth not). This proposal fits into the monetary integration of the European Economic Community and emerges from somewhat larger "optimum currency areas"— but not so large that they cover the whole world. The benefits of specialization and exchange are kept by regions. Political independence is retained by the major power blocs.

It is perhaps inappropriate for an economist to comment on such a highly political notion, but this one finds it unattractive. Presumably within each bloc there would be a dominant power or powers and those that were followers. Political sovereignty would be gained for the former but more thoroughly lost for the latter. African trade would run to Europe, and Canadian and Latin-American trade to the United States, regardless of the Argentine and Uruguayan market for meat in Europe or the interest of the United States in African chrome.

In the writer's judgment, the political hypothesis on which this proposal rests has it exactly backwards. It is desirable, in my judgment, to have fixed rates among the major blocs, which gives unity and coherence to major economic policies worldwide, and to give freedom to the smaller powers to vary their macroeconomic policies within their desires and capabilities more freely. It is relatively unimportant to the world that Canada has a fluctuating dollar with which it can, if it desires, reduce its integration with the United States. What is important is to keep alternative markets open for the smaller and the developing powers, or those like Australia, New Zealand, Japan, and Israel that do not easily fit into a bloc. Political developments seem to be breaking the world into regional blocs, and economic alignments may follow. The result, if it occurs, should be deplored rather than applauded.

Symmetry

With national moneys and flexible exchange rates which were guided by the intervention of the monetary authorities, the power of various countries to set their own exchange rates, in case they disagreed, would probably be proportional to their size as measured by some weighted average of national income and national capital market. If Canada wanted a depreciated exchange rate, for example, and the United States was determined to resist such an outcome, it seems clear that the United States could buy up Canadian dollars as fast as the Bank of Canada could issue them.

Under the gold standard, where all countries have pious faith in the rules of the gold standard game and are committed to follow them, no country has much more power than another. The other two forms of international money, however, are otherwise. Under, say, the dollar standard, power is distributed asymmetrically in the system. With something like the SDRs as international money and no tendency of markets to shift to a national money, power would be distributed in accordance with the weighted voting system.

If responsibility and power go together, an asymmetric distribution of power may not be altogether a bad thing for the international monetary system. Weighted voting often turns out to produce stalemates, as it has now done in the International Monetary Fund as well as the Security Council of the United Nations. The United States started out in the IMF with a size of quota and a weighted vote that enabled it to veto any proposal of which it did not approve. The United States had somewhat over 23 percent of the votes, and 85 percent of the votes were needed to carry a proposal. Later with the enlargement of quotas and the General Arrangements to Borrow, the Europe of the Six acquired 20 percent of the votes, and a veto. The IMF could not act unless the EEC and the United States agreed.

Under the dollar system, or the sterling system before 1913, power with responsibility is not only tolerable; it may be desirable. Without leadership, little gets done. For the world monetary system to be stable, moreover, the world needs a stabilizer, some country or aggregation of countries not bound by vetos or stalemate which will move in crises. The needs are to keep markets for distress goods open, fix a set of exchange rates which are not too far from equilibrium, maintain capital flows stable, and discount in a crisis. Britain performed these functions in the late 19th century up to 1913. The United States took over the task in the period from World War II to about 1968. The depression of 1929, in the opinion of the writer, was so wide, so deep, and so long because Britain couldn't and the United States wouldn't act as a stabilizer. The fallacy of composition reigned supreme as each country in turn tried to use its national sovereign powers to cut imports, restrict capital exports, and depreciate the exchange rate.

As this is written there is some suggestion that we are again approaching in the world a period of stalemate in world monetary reform. So long as the only possible national system is for a dollar standard, Europe is for gold or SDRs. The United States is prepared to continue with the dollar standard, but only so long as it can depreciate its rate some appropriate amount and set monetary policy independently of the rest of the world. More and more it seems likely that the United States can no longer act as a stabilizer and the European Economic Community won't—or not yet. The prospects for solid international monetary reform are thus dim.

Seigniorage

Seigniorage is a technical term in monetary economics which means the profits from issuing money. The term comes, of course, from the right of the king, or "seigneur," to issue money (like another and different *droit de Seigneur*) and represents the difference between the cost of producing money and its value in exchange. With flexible exchange rates there is no international money and no seignorage. Under the gold standard, the international money is produced at cost, and there is no seignorage. Under the dollar standard or with SDRs, international money is costless to produce. The question is whether there is seigniorage, and what to do with any seigniorage which exists under SDRs. We will save this last issue of the link between the issuance of SDRs and aid for developing countries for the next chapter, "Foreign Aid."

In the eyes of many, the United States has been exploiting the rest of the world through extracting seigniorage, issuing dollars which the rest of the world holds in exchange for goods and services on the one hand and securities and direct investments on the other. It was claimed by President de Gaulle of France, for example, that the dollar standard required France to finance U.S. intervention in the war in Vietnam.

On one showing, there is no seigniorage when the foreign holder of dollars is paid interest. Non-interest-bearing currency yields seigniorage, as do demand deposits. But time deposits which pay interest have a cost to the issuer of the liability, representing the present discounted value of the stream of income paid out to the holder.

This view is disputed. It is said in Europe, for example, that the deposits held in dollars are involuntary, in the sense that the European central banks would rather have gold or domestic assets or would rather see their bank statements reduced both by claims on the United States and liabilities to domestic depositors. Under this circumstance, interest paid to a depositor is "like meals served to a kidnap victim, hardly an offset to the loss of liberty." The counter to this view is that the European countries that are experiencing a capital inflow do not have to hold the offsetting dollars. They could lower their interest rates and expand the money supply, which would partly repel the inflow of capital and partly assist in its real transfer in goods and services. European central banks acquire dollars because they have high **liquidity preference**, preferring liquidity to real assets. The difference between what the United States earns by lending long and pays out by borrowing short is its net return for financial intermediation and the European markets' payment for staying liquid with malfunctioning capital markets.

The beauty of the gold standard (if countries were willing to follow the "rules of the gold-standard game") is that, like the rule of free trade, it defuses this sort of highly political debate. The world finds itself in a transitional state, where it can no longer believe the claptrap that "gold is immutable, eternal, impartial," as President de Gaulle claimed, and is no longer willing to let a vestigial remnant of an ancient dogma dictate economic behavior. It has not yet achieved the state of grace, however, in which it can fashion new rules for optimum world money and count on all nations carrying them out under any and all circumstances.

Summary

There are three types of international money—gold, a national currency such as the dollar, and created assets, such as Special Drawing Rights. A monetary system with no international money has flexible exchange rates. With any money, the questions are who issues it, how much, and to whom.

Flexible exchange rates, or the nonexistence of international money, are thought to add another policy instrument to a nation's armory. This they do, if at all, only by subtracting it from elsewhere in the system or by converting the need to consult on monetary policy to the need to consult on exchange policy. Like domestic money, international money has benefits as well as costs.

A searching question is what is the optimum currency area within which there should be a single money. Two economic answers are given, one based on factor mobility, the other on exchange illusion. A political answer is that the optimum currency area is the one with sufficient macroeconomic powers to manage its affairs. It is an open question whether the European Economic Community will prove to be an effectively integrated currency area.

Various compromises between fixed and flexible rates include the adjustable peg, the crawling peg, and the wider band, plus a regional compromise.

In any national exchange standard, questions of symmetry arise, including that of seigniorage.

SUGGESTED READING

Texts

Stevens, chaps. 16 to 20; Grubel, part II.

Treatises, Etc.

An excellent monograph on the question of interdependence or independence is R. N. Cooper, *The Economics of Interdependence: Economic policy in the Atlantic Community* (New York: McGraw-Hill Book Company, 1968).

The separate issues in international monetary arrangements are discussed in an enormous variety of articles, books, and monographs. Among the best collections are R. A. Mundell and A. K. Swoboda, eds., *Monetary Problems of the International Economy* (Chicago: University of Chicago Press, 1969); Officer and Willett, *The International Monetary Systems: Problems and Proposals; The International Adjustment Mechanism,* Monetary Conference, Federal Reserve Bank of Boston, 1970; G. N. Halm, ed., *Approaches to Greater Flexibility of Exchange Rates: The Bürgenstock Papers,* arranged by C. F. Bergsten and others (Princeton, N.J.: Princeton University Press, 1970); *The International Monetary System in Transition,* A symposium (Chicago: Federal Reserve Bank of Chicago, 1972), and a special issue of the *Journal of International Economics,* September 1972.

Points

The articles by Mundell and McKinnon on the optimum currency area are in the *AER* for September 1961 and September 1963. The latter is reproduced in R. N. Cooper, ed., *International Finance, Selected Readings.*

For a useful study emphasizing the political aspects of monetary problems, see S. Strange, *Sterling and British Policy: A Political Study of an International Currency in Decline* (New York: Oxford University Press, 1971).

The text of the "Werner Report," i.e. the *Report to the Council and the Commission on the Realization by Stages of Economic and Monetary Union,* is given in the *Supplement to Bulletin 11–1970* of the European Communities.

FOREIGN AID

Foreign Aid and Equilibrium

It is highly arbitrary to discuss foreign aid at this late stage of a rounded treatment of international economics and under the heading of "Balance-of-Payments Adjustment and International Monetary Arrangements." The subject could just as well have been treated in Part III with factor movements, or Part IV with the adjustment process. Foreign aid does transfer resources; and, as mentioned in Chapter 1, a major difference between the intranational and international adjustment mechanisms is the automatic sharing in the former but not in the latter which operates through progressive taxation and expenditure based on need and helps to balance payments between regions.

In this chapter we must touch upon foreign aid both as balance-of-payments adjustment and as international monetary arrangements. One feeble excuse for treating foreign aid under international monetary arrangements is the seigniorage issue and the possibility seen by many economists that the issuance of international money affords an opportunity to provide real resources to the developing countries. Another is the debate during the Marshall Plan as to whether U.S. aid to the European recovery program should be based on balance-of-payments deficits or the balance-of-payments deficits should be based on aid: Which was the autonomous and which the dependent variable? Primarily, however, the justification for coming to foreign aid so late is that it did not fit in neatly anywhere else, it must be discussed for completeness, and it serves as a useful introduction to the broad philosophical cast of the wind-up chapter which follows.

Automatic Sharing versus Charity

Markets differ from budgets. Budgets have something of the market mechanism in them, to the extent that taxes are based on the provision of services to users. To the extent that the tax system is progressive, however, and to the extent that expenditures are based on need rather than provided in return for tax payments, the budget is a mechanism for sharing. Rich, childless couples with large estates pay for much of the education of poor families who have numerous children, and rich regions contribute to the welfare of the poor. When a region's income changes, up or down, the mechanism of the central budget helps balance payments. The region gaining in income will pay more in taxes and receive less in benefits, and the opposite will hold for the region losing income.

On occasion, voices will be lifted to assert that a region is paying more in taxes to the national government than it is receiving in benefits of federal expenditure. The facts are usually beyond dispute. The philosophy underlying the assertion, however, is that the several regions do not belong in a sharing community but should rather be joined in a market arrangement where you pay for what you get. Communities share. Transactions in markets are between impersonal units which keep one another at arm's length. The insistence, for example, that New England pays more in taxes than it gets in federal benefits is subversive of the national community of the United States. New England is richer than many other regions. In a communal arrangement, it should pay more.

Taxes are levied as a matter of law. Charity is given by the donor as an act of grace. The distinction is hard to maintain. In communities with a United Fund, for example, great social pressure is applied to the well-to-do to contribute substantially to organized charity, with a highly organized mechanism for distributing the yield among different agencies on the basis of social need. In some large companies, so-called "fair share plans" are developed in which executives and employees are informed as to what a fair share of their salary or wage would be as a contribution to the United Fund. This comes perilously close to taxation in the name of charity. In the Development Assistance Committee (DAC) of the Organization for Economic Cooperation and Development, a standard of 1 percent of national income (and ultimately 1 percent of gross national product) has been set as a fair share. The coefficient is proportional, not progressive, and has much less force than that in a fair-share plan in a corporation, where the amount a man or woman gives may be known to his superior. It approaches international taxation but little.

International Sharing

International sharing does takes place, however. Libya joined with Egypt in a federation in 1972, an arrangement in which the Libyan contribution consists overwhelmingly of its oil revenues. French "aid" has been the largest of any country, well above the DAC 1 percent standard, but mainly given to the *Communauté*, or French Community of former colonies in Africa. The European Economic Community organized a European

Investment Bank and a European Social Fund, the former to take on investments in areas adversely affected by the economic integration so that they could not earn the support of the market—"**soft loans**" in jargon; the latter to make grants to such areas as southern Italy, southwest France, or southeast Bavaria that are far from the center of the EEC and adversely hurt by the pull to the center.

The whole United Nations apparatus, with its substantial budgets, is a limited device for sharing. Two principles conflict when it comes to distributing the costs of these agencies. Sovereign powers pay a share which is not derisory; therefore, each member must pay a minimum "ante." Capacity to pay means that the richer nations pay proportionately more than the poor. The first principle holds up the shares in the groups' benefits of the poor, newly independent, small countries of, say, Africa, and in some cases limits the number of UN organizations they can afford to join. The second principle raises the contribution of the richer countries to heights which threaten they will dominate the international organizations. The United States started paying 50 percent of the costs of the United Nations, and then cut its share to 31 percent. In 1972, the United Nations agreed to cut the U.S. share once again.

Sharing in Defense

Opportunities for sharing are somewhat wider among military projects than with peacekeeping and civilian activities, because they are more expensive. A political principle has been detected that the larger members of an alliance—those with the most to lose—tend to pay a disproportionate share of the expense. In payments for infrastructure or overhead investments such as airfields, pipelines, and the like, the local government that will acquire title to the asset tends to pay the greater share. Nonlocalized expenses in NATO, however, have fallen disproportionately on the major powers.

European countries have undertaken a number of joint military and technological projects which offer an opportunity for sharing internationally—in nuclear energy, rocket launchers, the supersonic transport, and the like. Sharing calls for raising the funds based on capacity to contribute. Economic efficiency then requires spending the money where it can buy the most in the way of research and hardware. This means that some countries would have a balance-of-payments drain, if they were rich and paid heavily but were relatively inefficient at science and technology, so that the funds are not spent within their borders. To resist this outcome, the antieconomic principle of *juste retour* (fair return) was developed, calling for spending in each country the amount that had been contributed by it. The justification was partly perhaps balance of payments, but partly as well the view that scientific and technological expenditure conveyed a benefit on a country. The opportunity for sharing in this field was not grasped where the *juste retour* obtained.

Defining Foreign Aid

If DAC is going to measure foreign aid as a percentage of national income and compare the shares of various donors, it is necessary to agree on a definition. Does one count donations that get rid of unwanted surpluses, such as agricultural surpluses given away by the United States or sold partly against local currencies under P.L. 480? If there is no cost to the donor (though benefit to the receiver), is it aid? Or is it aid if the donor contributes valuable economic goods and services but receives in return political favors—support for its position in war, in the United Nations, the maintenance of cultural ties which keep its language flourishing (French)? Is it aid when the donor would lose prestige and allies if it did not support a client—as the Soviet Union and Cuba? What if the transaction is not a grant, with no economic return, but, say, a loan at less than private market terms, for an unusual term such as 40 years, or with payment of interest and principal in local currency, or at levels of interest well below market levels? How should one value foreign aid which is tied to purchases in the donor country when prices for the goods sought are 30 percent higher in the donor country than in the most advantageous supplier?

The subject is full of philosophical riddles. It would be possible to break down a given transaction into part aid, part commercial transaction, depending upon the nature of the consideration obtained in return for aid or the true value received by the recipient. In fact, however, DAC, which keeps score, is highly permissive, as it has to be, counting as aid anything that a donor chooses to regard as aid, from contributions to the UN Special Fund—which is perhaps aid in its purest form—to short-term export credits tied to sales and at commercial rates, which West Germany insists fall into the category of aid.

Multilateral versus National Aid

A series of issues arises in the transfer of economic assistance from one nation to another. Many of them are highly political; none can be examined in any depth. These and many others were addressed by a blue-ribbon international commission headed by the former Canadian Price Minister, Lester B. ("Mike") Pearson, which produced a report in 1969 entitled *Partners in Development.*

First is the question whether aid should be multilateral or national. Immediately after the war it was planned to give aid through the United Nations Relief and Rehabilitation Agency (UNRRA). The United States contributed 72 percent of the first tranche and 78 percent of the second. With one vote in 17 on the UNRRA Council, however, it found itself, in the absence of agreed principles, being taxed by logrolling among the other countries. Canada withdrew after the first tranche to give its aid entirely to Britain. Britain insisted as a condition of continuing that Italy and Austria be shifted from military relief, to which it contrbuted 50 percent, to UNRRA, where its share was 12 percent. The Soviet Union, with 4 percent, required shares for the independent countries of Byelorussia and the Ukraine. Multilateral aid required a community of agreed principles, which was lacking. The United States shifted strongly to bilateral aid. In the Marshall Plan the 14 recipients of aid produced a joint plan for aid, but each recipient signed a separate bilateral agreement with the United States.

Bilateral aid gives the donor control over the use of aid, subjects him to temptation to use aid for unduly short-run political advantages, and exposes him to political pressures. With time, the aid becomes established; continuing it offers no political benefits; halting it is regarded as positively unfriendly. Multilateral agencies afford protection behind which the donor can limit his political involvement and, if needed, reduce his painful involvement with the recipients. At the same time, it earns him less gratitude, if that is what he wants.

Multilateral agencies also suffer from overspecialization along professional lines. This is not true of the International Bank for Reconstruction and Development (IBRD) or the International Development Association (IDA)—its soft-loan counterpart—but it does affect such specialized agencies as UNESCO, FAO, ICAO, ILO, WHO, and so on—a collection of international agencies whose names, spelled out, would take an undue amount of space.

The multilateral agencies have a further problem—as at a children's party, every country must get a prize. Criteria for assistance have to be adjusted so that no one is omitted. The IBRD, determined to keep its record of default to a minimum, finally stopped making hard loans to countries with poor or rapidly declining credit standings but felt obliged to go on providing aid to them through IDA. The pressure of the claimants on the multilateral agencies mounted. It was finally necessary to create regional banks in Latin America, Asia, and Africa with their own capital, lest adding the same amounts to the world agencies risk the diversion of aid from one continent to another. Bilateralism has problems, but multilateralism is not without them.

Conditions of Aid

Political scientists insist that it is absurdly idealistic for a donor nation to be required to eliminate from aid all considerations of its foreign policy.

The subject is one which we have no competence to discuss. The other political conditions and the economic conditions of aid are difficult enough. Do the benefits of aid go largely to one class inside a country; and does action by this class block economic development, or recovery, in a significant measure? Does the country oppose private enterprise and drive away foreign capital which could lessen its requirement for foreign assistance? Does foreign aid enable the internal political forces to escape the necessity to face hard decisions, (such as how the burdens of recovery or economic development shall be shared) and thus to postpone effective domestic action? Or can the conditions of aid be used by the constructive forces within the aided country to persuade other domestic interests to follow the policies which will most speed development? In the Alliance for Progress, the United States wanted tax and agricultural reforms first as a condition of aid. The Latin-American countries insisted that only if they received aid would they be in a position to achieve reform. The same deadlock was met in the question of whether economic integration among the Latin-American countries could be made a condition of aid, or whether integration waited on recovery, which waited on aid.

One method devised in the European Recovery Program and extended in some of the development assistance programs, such as those involving surplus agricultural products, has been to require U.S. agreement to the disposition of the local currency counterpart of U.S. aid. Commodities representing U.S. aid are not given to consumers and firms but are sold for local currency. The use of these **counterpart funds** has important consequences. If they are saved, i.e., used to retire public debt, and particularly central-bank loans to the national treasury, the deflationary impact of the assistance is evident. They may, however, be used for capital formation or even for regular expenses, which would maintain or increase the level of national income and give rise to increased imports.

The requirement that the United States approve the disposition of these funds involves this country's representatives in a discussion of the financial aspects of the recovery or the development program. The significance of this involvement may vary widely. At one limit, as in Britain in the European Recovery Program, the deflationary impact of the piling up of counterpart funds can be fully offset by other Treasury and central-bank operations. The British went for several years without making any proposals regarding the use of counterpart funds, leaving it obvious that they resented the necessity to obtain U.S. permission. At the other extreme, however, a country such as Turkey built much of its financial policy around the use of counterpart funds and sought U.S. advice on this policy in its total aspects. When inflation in a country has deep political roots, to withhold counterpart funds sought to pay normal governmental expenses may overthrow the government in a financial crisis. The limits of the technique are thus evident. But in other cases, the requirement that the United States approve the disposition of counterpart funds gave useful leverage to a finance minister or central banker fighting a political battle against internal forces of inflation by enabling him to appeal to necessity from without.

There are some who believe that aid should be given without strings of any kind. This may be appropriate in a few cases, such as between Britain and the Dominions, where the aiding country and the aided operate at the same level of political and economic sophistication and understand one another fairly completely. But it is otherwise naïve. At the minimum, the aiding country should know how the country being assisted proposes to use the help and have some idea of whether it is capable of carrying out its intentions. And if it approves of the goals, all other conditions should be directed to their efficient achievement. On the political side, this suggests that short-run objectives should be minimized as irrelevant or even capable of interfering with the long-run political goal of political and economic independence. In economic terms, it means merely that the country use its resources as efficiently as it can.

One condition which the United States attached to most of its assistance programs—Lend-Lease, the postwar settlements, the Anglo-American Financial Agreement, and the Marshall Plan—was that the recipients dedicate themselves with the United States to the construction of a world trade and payments system of a multilateral, nondiscriminatory character. It was relatively easy for the recipients to provide an affirmation of faith which lacked operational significance (except for the disastrous requirement of convertibility in the British loan). They were doubtless, too, sincere in this affirmation at the time it was given. Some observers object to the requirement of subscribing to long-run principles. Not every country can afford to ignore its short-run for its longer run interests, and there is a danger, when repeated professions of faith are sought, that they may come to mean little more than the hymns intoned by those about to be fed by the Salvation Army.

Loans versus Grants

The religious objection to interest on loans, in pre-Reformation Europe and in much of the Muslim world today, was based on the ethical injunction not to take advantage of the distress of others. In economic conditions where the harvest was variable, borrowing took place in times of distress, and for consumption. To charge interest was to exploit a brother's bad luck.

When lending became predominantly for capital formation rather than for consumption, the Christian church modified its opposition to interest. Since the borrower was going to benefit from the loan, he could afford to pay for the use of the capital that the lender was temporarily giving up.

Similar ethical considerations seem to dominate the question of whether international economic assistance should take the form of loans or grants. Military assistance and defense support take the form of grants because the *quid pro quo* is the contribution of the recipient to the joint military effort. For the rest, disaster rehabilitation and reconstruction assistance are largely on a grant basis, while economic development or reconstruction assistance which enlarges capacity is regarded as suitable for loans. The failure to recognize the ethical aspect of reconstruction assistance was responsible for evoking the moral outcry against the collection of the war loans after World War I and against the precipitous halting of Lend-Lease after World War II.

Some observers try to make a distinction between assistance for social overhead capital—roads, ports, schools, hospitals, and so on—which it is felt should be given on a grant basis, and that for industrial capital, which is appropriate for loans. Others believe that assistance which increases the capacity of a country to export or to replace existing imports can be appropriately charged on a loan basis, whereas assistance to a mainly internal project which does not directly help the balance-of-payments position should be granted. Still a third point of view in favor of grants rather than loans would select for grants those projects with a long delay between the start of the investment and the payoff in increased productivity.

None of these points of view has much validity. If social overhead capital is productive, that productivity shows up somewhere in the economy, and a portion of it can be captured by the government and used for repayment if the governmental fiscal machinery is adequate. If it is not adequate, or if great uncertainty attaches to the question whether the investment will be productive, then a case for grants rather than loans exists. The fallacy of insisting that each project provide for its own repayment has been dealt with earlier. What is needed is capacity to subtract the necessary part of the increase in productivity from consumption and to reallocate a sufficient amount of the economy's resources, at the margin, into export- or import-competing lines. If resources cannot be reallocated, then again there is a case for a grant (but not much prospect for growth). Finally, the existence of a long delay between the start of a project and the payoff means only that the capital cost of the project is larger than the aggregated annual costs by the interest on the amounts expended in the earlier years prior to completion. If the productivity of the projects is justified after the capital has been calculated at a higher amount in this fashion, then the larger loan which would be needed to pay interest in the interval to completion is also justified.

The social ethic need not limit grants to cases of distress, or for maintaining consumption, while loans are exacted for increased productivity capacity or increased consumption. An international social welfare function could call for grants to countries with per capita incomes less than a given level, whether they used the assistance for consumption or capital formation, and loans to countries above that level. It makes a curious kind of logic to give billions to the United Kingdom to maintain its consumption above $750 per capita, say, while insisting on lending capital to India to get its income per capita up from $60.

The point to be emphasized is that the issue of loans or grants is not an economic one but moral, ethical, and social. One shares within the circle of family and friends, and deals on a business basis outside it. And some relationships change between friendship and business in complex and unpredictable ways.

Projects versus Plans

Initially the United States programmed its aid on the basis of particular projects. Like a banker, it wanted to be sure that the aid was used for the capital projects agreed upon. In the Marshall Plan it traced the steel or equipment through from the ship to the construction site to be sure that it was used in the project as agreed.

The approach was partial equilibrium. It makes no sense to follow through a particular piece of steel to see that it is used efficiently. What is called for is the efficient use of all steel. Moreover, it is misguided to limit aid to certain projects if the recipient country diverts resources it would otherwise have used for the project to other purposes. The issue arises in the distinction frequently made between economic and military assistance. Economic assistance for investments the country would have undertaken anyhow permits the recipient to divert its own resources to an enlarged military program; or contrariwise, to make assistance available only for military purposes will enable a country to switch its own resources to capital investment of a peacetime nature. What matters is the total use of resources. When it finally thoroughly understood this point, the U.S., aid agencies converted from a project to a program approach.

Under programs, the total effort of a country would be examined to see how effectively its resources were being used. Assistance could be provided not only for particular projects within a program but for balance-of-payments and even budget support, both highly general in character.

Albert Hirschman and Richard Bird have called for a return to projects from programs, on the grounds that programs require too much interference in the total life of the aid recipient. Projects, in their view, can be taken or left. Some program must be adopted by the developing country, and for the U.S. aid agency to second-guess the local government down the line is paternalistic. The argument for programs is economic; the argument against them is political.

An extension of Hirschman's and Bird's argument would lead to complete withdrawal from the assistance to economic development, leaving the question of additional resources for development to the private investor on both direct and portfolio account. The private market is not available to countries which cannot establish their credit worthiness. Those that can may submit their projects to the impersonal judgment of the capital market rather than the "visible hand" of another government. Countries that get well started on the development path, like Mexico, graduate from aid altogether and move to acquire real resources on world capital markets.

Aid and the Balance of Payments

Under the Marshall Plan, estimates of need were first produced by calculating prospective balance-of-payments deficits under European recovery programs and providing the exchange—or rather the goods equivalent of the exchange—to fill the gap. This represents an absorption approach, in which aid was thought of as compensatory. It was pointed out by Fritz Machlup, however, as noted above (p. 311) that the aid determined the program rather than the program the aid. The aid was autonomous, the program derived.

One corollary is that recovery incentives are skewed. The more a country recovers, the less aid it is entitled to claim. As in poor relief or housing for low-income families, benefits for the disadvantaged may have a tendency to make them reluctant to overcome the disadvantage. The point should not be exaggerated into the conservative diatribe against relief, but it was of sufficient importance in the early days of the Marshall Plan that in dividing aid the second year, the recipient countries decided to keep the identical first-year percentage distribution, distributing the aid made available as a lump-sum subsidy. Under this system any gains benefit the country earning them rather than cutting down its share of assistance.

Balance-of-payments problems of donors raise a familiar issue: the theory of the second best. On first-best principles, the level of aid should be related to income rather than to liquidity. A wealthy man whose bank balance was low would not be allowed by the community to claim exemption from contribution to the United Fund: his task is to fulfill his civic obligation normally and to adjust his bank balance to his obligations, rather than the other way around. By the same token, a country with balance-of-payments difficulties should not regard cuts in aid as a solution to them. Macroeconomic difficulties call for macroeconomic policies, not a change in expenditure patterns.

However invalid, the excuse is nevertheless used in the charitable behavior both of individuals and of countries. To cut foreign aid to help the balance of payments is perhaps tenth best or first worst. In the realm of second best, a more usual remedy is tied aid, discussed earlier in Chapter 14 in connection with loans. Tied aid, of course, is the requirement that the assistance be taken in goods and services bought in the donor country.

Where the aid is made available only in kind, the tying is automatic. Where a country has received resources from the U.S. Development Loan Fund, however, it is required that they be spent only in the United States, and on U.S. goods and services. Often the goods must be carried in U.S.-flag ships, usually not the cheapest mode of transport, but in any event made more expensive by the increase in demand from this source. Tied aid reduces the amount of aid made available. It may minimize the balance-of-payments deficit for a given volume of aid (partly by cutting down the value of the aid) or maximize the aid that can be granted with a given balance-of-payments deficit. It is widely practiced. Economists nonetheless object to it as a departure from optimality.

The Link between SDRs and Assistance to Developing Countries

The appeal of the link between the issuance of new credit money for the world and aid to developing countries is that such aid is multilateral, unconditional, grant rather than loan, untied, and available in foreign exchange. The developing countries reason that the issuance of new world money in the form of credit offers the world an opportunity to use the seigniorage for economic development of the poor countries, thus increasing world welfare and equity. The seigniorage is there. It would be inequitable for the developed rich countries to capture it. Hence the desirability of a program for making some or all of it available for the developing world.

Earlier plans for monetary reform made provision for distributing seigniorage to the developing countries. In 1962 the Stamp plan (a reform scheme produced by Max Stamp) called for issuing new international money directly to the developing countries for them to spend. The developed countries would have agreed in advance to accept and use it as international money when they acquire it as a result of developing country deficits.

Robert Triffin's plan for the creation of an international bank to take over the world's reserves of gold and foreign exchange in return for a new world monetary unit provided for open-market operations. These would be undertaken with the developed countries as a rule, but room was left for the new world central bank to buy IBRD bonds with its deposit money, which the world bank would lend to developing countries. Loans were subject to repayment, of course. Some might be made available through the soft-loan window, however, and if the amount grew continuously through time, the repayment would be gross but not net.

The original design of the SDRs had assumed that they would be guaranteed by and issued to the General Arrangements to Borrow, the leading 10 financial countries of the world. At this there was an outcry on the part of the developing countries. If they could not have all or most of the gains from issuing international money, at least they wanted their share. In the end the Group of Ten was obliged to adopt the IMF quotas as a formula for the distribution of SDRs, giving the developing countries 23 percent of the $9.3 billion of SDRs created through 1972 (compared with their 18 percent of world trade).

The argument for making the new money available exclusively to the developing countries is that seigniorage is available, and they are needy. The argument against it is that the SDRs are created to enhance liquidity— to provide money for holding, not money for spending; and the developing countries on the whole are after real, not financial assets. To base world money on the long-term liabilities of the developing countries would be to undermine confidence in it. No country counts its counterpart funds in developing-country currencies as valid international reserves; no more would they count SDRs issued by the developing countries. If the developed countries accept liability for the SDRs, they should accept the asset they represent. To give the SDRs to the developing countries is like giving real money. The device for giving real money is foreign aid, not issuance of international money.

Rebuttal consists in denying the contention that the liabilities assumed in the issuance of money are proper liabilities that need to be taken seriously. They are, that is, outside money, not inside money. Rerebuttal: To ignore the liabilities for the new money is irresponsible. The system might one day be liquidated; in any event, if all the assets end up in the hands of a few developed countries with persistent surpluses, and the rest of the world has become accustomed to persistent deficits, the system clearly breaks down. What looks like outside money today can turn into inside money.

A key issue is whether the world as a whole has serious unemployment with which it is not coping by international means. In this instance, issuing new money to the developing countries to spend on capital equipment bought in the developed countries is a form of international public works which is relatively costless. If, on the other hand, world employment is relatively tight, to create new money for spending rather than holding on balance is costly in world inflation.

Whether one believes in the link or opposes it depends in part on how bankerish or humanitarian one is. The technical arguments depend heavily on the surrounding circumstances. And the extent of bankerishness or humanitarianism may be related to the extent that the world is one community or a series of separate ones. In separate communities, for example, it is unlikely that a country that is unable to create money at home for employment will be willing to do so by a scheme in which the real assets end up in foreign hands. In a sharing world, such an outcome is not at all unthinkable.

Summary

A community which taxes itself progressively for common objects of expenditure that benefit the poor over the rich both shares through its budget and assists regional balance-of-payments equilibrium. The world functions this way to only a limited extent, which helps account (along with factor immobility internationally) for the differences in the smoothness of the adjustment mechanism interregionally within a country and internationally. Automatic sharing differs from voluntary charity. Foreign aid that is charity represents international sharing only to a limited extent.

The Development Assistance Committee's definition of aid is permissive and broad. Little attempt is made to eliminate items which have no cost for the donor or have something of a return. Nor is aid marked down when restrictions reduce its value to the recipient. The foremost of these is tying.

Issues in the field of aid include the questions whether aid should be multilateral or bilateral, how detailed the conditions should be, loans versus grants, whether aid should be based on projects or programs, and whether it should be made available in budgetary or balance-of-payments support.

Arguments are made for and against a link between the issuance of new credit money for the world and aid to developing countries.

SUGGESTED READING

Texts

The most detailed discussion of the theory of aid is in an old textbook, T. C. Schelling, *International Economics* (Boston: Allyn & Bacon, Inc., 1958), chaps. 26, 27, and 28.

Treatises, Etc.

Perhaps the best survey of the subject is in L. B. Pearson, *Partners in Development*, Report of the Commission on International Development (New York: Frederick A. Praeger, Inc., 1969) (paperback). It is strongly sympathetic to the provision of aid, and general rather than technical. More technical and detailed are:

J. A. Pincus, *Trade, Aid and Development: The Rich and Poor Nations* (New York: McGraw-Hill Book Company, 1967).

R. E. Asher, *Development Assistance in the Seventies: Alternatives for the United States* (Washington, D.C.: The Brookings Institution, 1971).

A. O. Hirschman, *Development Projects Observed* (Washington, D.C.: The Brookings Institution, 1967).

The link is analyzed by the UNCTAD Group of Experts on International

Monetary issues in *International Monetary Issues and the Developing Countries* (New York: United Nations, 1966).

Points

The reference to Hirschman and Bird's argument is to A. O. Hirschman and R. M. Bird, "Foreign Aid—A Critique and a proposal," *EIF*, July 1968.

An interesting case study is C. F. Diaz-Alejandro, "Some Aspects of the Brazilian Experience with Foreign Aid," in Bhagwati et al., *Trade, Balance of Payments and Growth*.

The annual reports of the Development Advisory Committee (DAC) of OECD should be consulted for recent material and current analysis.

The Stamp plan is presented in "The Stamp Plan—1962 Version," in *Moorgate and Wall Street*, Autumn 1962; the Triffin plan in R. Triffin, *Gold and the Dollar Crisis* (New Haven, Conn.: Yale University Press, 1969). Both are summarized in H. G. Grubel, *International Monetary Reform: Plans and Issues* (Stanford, Calif.: Stanford University Press, 1963).

Chapter 27

THE INTERNATIONAL ECONOMIC SYSTEM

The Classical System

The classical international economic system comprises three institutions: free trade, the annually balanced budget, and the gold standard. With the assistance of pure competition, free trade produced efficient allocation of resources in each country. The annually balanced budget was not an explicit prescription, but full employment, maintained by the inelasticity of factor supply and Say's law of markets, left no need to vary expenditure. The gold standard brought about adjustment through varying the volume of money in separate countries, raising prices in surplus, and reducing prices in deficit countries.

Free trade and the benevolent rule of Say's law left no work for a government to do. Government was called upon to play the "rules of the gold standard game," never thoroughly expounded. It is partly for this reason that ultraclassicists today want to shift from the fixed exchange rate to the more "liberal" market mechanism of freely flexible exchange rates without government intervention. If the gold standard is replaced by the flexible exchange rate, it is thought, government can lock up the international economic system and throw the key away.

Very few people would be prepared to adopt laissez-faire to this extent today. National governments are committed to maintaining full employment through the use of monetary and fiscal policies. Membership in the world economic community means that countries are unwilling on the whole to adopt a system of flexible exchange rates which reduces international economic intercourse through increasing their risks. The gold standard must be modified for full employment, and free trade may have to be diluted when altered foreign conditions call for sudden and far-reaching changes in domestic resource allocation which would effect domestic hardship. But to replace laissez-faire government with a decision-making maximizer requires government to decide what to maximize.

Maximizing National Income

A government engaged in maximizing income in the short run presumably adopts policies for optimum tariffs and optimum capital movements, provided the benefits exceed the probability of retaliation times its cost. In the macroeconomic field, it will stay clear of the flexible exchange rate, which would deprive it of the dampening effect of foreign trade on business cycles of both domestic and foreign origin. Changes in the exchange rate may be used from time to time to produce domestic-income effects and to redistribute domestic income between the domestic and foreign-trade sectors. The monetary authorities will shift back and forth between gold and interest-bearing foreign exchange, depending upon the outlook for changes in the gold price, exercising the one-way option which speculation in gold offers.

There is some doubt, however, whether a world of countries with short-run market power, all determined to exercise it, would in fact be viable. If most countries, and particularly the powerful countries, take a long-run view of the international economic machinery, one or two governments can exercise their short-run market power and get away with it. Optimum tariffs will improve their terms of trade because there will not be retaliation. Destabilizing speculation between gold and foreign exchange will be offset by the stabilizing counteraction of other governments. The system is weakened by these short-run maximizing actions, but if they are limited, it can survive them.

When all governments apply optimum tariffs and optimum capital movements, all use the foreign market actively for national income stabilization, and all speculate to protect the national position, however, the system may not work. The larger governments, unlike the average firm, have market power. One country applies an optimum tariff and others will retaliate, since this will frequently make them better off. In time, the object of the exercise may change from maximizing national income to preventing other, stronger countries from gaining from their attempts at the expense of the rest of the world. Police action may be undertaken regardless of cost. When no country or countries is willing to hold foreign exchange and all rush for gold, the price of gold rises, exchange rates bounce around chaotically, and risk averters withdraw from foreign trade and lending, turning inward to domestic transactions. Similarly, when the international monetary system breaks down, as it did in the 1930s, countries must operate (as did Germany under Dr. Hjalmar Schacht) with a disequilibrium system of foreign exchange control that permits limited barter and clearing transactions with the outside world and concentrates the major economic thrust of policy on the home front.

Building the International Economic System

All firms, and all the smaller and less developed countries, have a duty to maximize in the short run. But the larger and more powerful countries, or most of them, must be careful not to follow that lead. The fallacy of composition operates here. The world of Adam Smith does not obtain. The question is how to run the system.

One possibility is for every country to operate in the general rather than the national interest. The categorical imperative of Immanuel Kant calls for individuals acting only in ways that can be generalized. Actions which are possible if only one person or country tries them are to be abhorred. Like the central bank, which is not supposed to make money as do commercial or savings banks but is designed to act only in the interest of the banking system, highly enlightened governments might be enjoined to operate in the interest of the international economic system. This means avoiding optimum tariffs and optimum rates of lending and supporting the system against destabilizing speculation. In a world of sovereign national governments, this is a hard line to follow. When the short run is the enemy of the long run, it may be hard to justify or explain why a government passed up an opportunity to advance the country in the concrete short run in the interest of the nebulous long.

International agreement is a useful device. Countries may bind themselves against short-run gains at the expense of the system if other countries are equally bound. Agreements to lower tariffs, as in the Kennedy Round, or to improve the international system make possible action by one because of favorable action of others. Multilateral surveillance in Working Party No. 2 of the OECD subjects the monetary and fiscal policy of each country to the scrutiny of the group and limits the possibility that any one country can for long benefit at the expense of others.

The U.S. Department of State frequently complains that it has no constituents, no body of voters who will raise their voices in the Congress and apply pressure to get measures of general interest passed. Unlike the Departments of Commerce, Labor, Interior, Treasury, and so on, it represents the country as a whole rather than an intensely concerned portion of it. Commitments to foreign countries and benefits from their commitments to this country moderate, but do not entirely dispel, the force of this argument. Foreign trade is between us and them. The Departments of Commerce, Labor, Interior, and Treasury are concerned with us. The Department of States unpatriotically worries about them.

Coordinating National Action

The problem becomes exacerbated when we go beyond merely refraining from taking action which would benefit one country at the expense of others, to those where it is necessary for two or more countries to coordinate positive steps. In the foregoing pages we have mentioned a number of such occasions:

If it be decided by the developed countries that the less developed countries might appropriately have income redistributed toward them, better than the optimum tariff is a lesser tariff by the less developed countries plus a subsidy to correct the resource misallocation on the part of the developed countries (page 196).

When the incomes of countries are joined in a foreign-trade multiplier with foreign repercussion and spending policies are adopted in both countries for internal and external equilibrium, there are three equations and four unknowns until the countries decide how to divide the burden of the spending policies between the two countries (page 509).

International economic integration calls for more than free trade and an absence of barriers to factor movement. It requires harmonization of tax, wages, foreign exchange, monetary, and fiscal policies (page 181).

The rise of the international corporation, too, may require harmonization of policies in various fields, notably corporate taxation and antitrust, to forestall international corporations from undertaking action affecting one country which is not permitted in another. At the same time the international corporations should not be put in the impossible position of being ordered by two or more governments to take antithetical actions. This is the equivalent of double taxation. Again it calls for harmonization (page 276).

On a flexible-exchange-rate system with government intervention, the governments on both sides of a given exchange rate must collaborate to ensure that they do not each try to push the rate in different directions: the monetary authorities in country A try to depress their rate, offering A currency for B, while those in country B try to depress their rate, offering B currency for A. The result would be mutual acquisitions of the currency of the other, but no change in the exchange rate.

If short-term capital markets are closely linked through such an institution as the Euro-dollar market, monetary authorities tend to lose control of national monetary policy. Pumping money into the money market tends to push it abroad, as the lower interest rate makes funds seek higher rates abroad; taking money out of the system attracts new funds from abroad. To make monetary policy effective, it must be coordinated among the joined money markets, with the monetary authorities operating simultaneously in the same direction. There is something of an asymmetry between New York as the largest financial center and the others: When New York changes its interest rate, it tends to move the whole structure up and down. When other financial centers try to change an interest rate, there is a short period of differential before the mass of foreign funds in, or domestic funds out, restores the old level. This statement exaggerates the position, but the asymmetry is real. There is more need, therefore, for British, French, German, Italian, and so on, representation on the Federal Open Market Committee, perhaps renamed an Atlantic Open-Market Committee, than the other way round. Or perhaps the major central banks of the world, on their way to the ultimate formation of a world central bank, could meanwhile regulate world credit conditions by means of the Euro-currency market.

When a currency is under attack, others must rescue it in the short run, and the rescued currency's country must ensure the rescuers against loss from their aid. In 1931, the Bank of Belgium and the Netherlands Bank both lost substantial sums when sterling was devalued while they maintained large balances in pounds. This proved a costly affair in increasing suspicion and reducing cooperation for the international monetary system. The world's currencies are in the same boat. They can afford one boat rocker, if the others stabilize by leaning against the pushes, but three or four rockers would make the life of the stabilizers difficult. As soon as possible after a Basle-like operation which is sucessful, the purchases of the currency under attack should be paid off through the International Monetary Fund. Should a support operation fail, which is unlikely, the currency on behalf of which the effort had been made must, in the interest of the system, make good any losses of the supporters. If it does not, the system breaks down.

Constitution Writing versus Evolution

The system of international economic collaboration built up in this way is mostly an unwritten one. After the war, the United States took the lead in signing up countries to a host of institutions with elaborate articles of agreement: the United Nations, the IMF, the IBRD, the Havana Charter of the International Trade Organization, Food and Agriculture Organization, and so forth. The IMF had little to do for 10 years. The Havana Charter of the ITO was stillborn, never signed by its sponsor, the United States. The IBRD found it could not tackle reconstruction and was obliged to develop unforeseen techniques in lending for development. The most interesting postwar economic institution in international economics is the Euro-dollar market, which evolved from market forces, more or less by accident and without an origin in economic analysis or international agreement.

The propensity of lawyers is to dot each "i" and cross each "t," providing for every contingency before it occurs. In the international monetary system, this is a bootless and even dangerous inclination. The task of negotiating a precise agreement as to what will happen under a series of imagined catastrophes, who will do what, and how the accounts will be settled, is a disturbing experience. U.S. political processes, moreover, make enacting such an agreement into legislation a long-drawn-out affair, with much unsettling discussion of hypothetical disasters. In the end, it is likely that the economists and lawyers would have failed to foresee exactly the character of the conditions with which the crisis had to cope. Accordingly it is preferable to have what the sociologists call a "diffuse" understanding of the sort that obtains among persons or peoples joined in a community, that in the event of trouble people will help as they can, and that no one will be penalized unfairly for so doing. Lend-Lease was the first of these diffuse international economic understandings. It was a success as the loan contracts of World War I were not. Formal attempts at negotiating major changes in the international economic system seem to emphasize the differences between national points of view. Piecemeal changes in response to felt needs, or evolutionary responses to problems, may fail to provide the assurance needed in advance of difficulty but produce collaboration at a wider and more effective level than would any agreement that could be negotiated in advance.

International Economic Integration

In the last chapter but one, it was suggested that the optimum currency area may well be the world, outside the Soviet bloc. This refers, to be sure, to the developed rather than the less developed countries, in so many of which devaluation and inflation follow one another in dreary succession. The Kennedy Round has reduced tariffs to levels of approximately 10 percent. Capital markets are joined, as is the labor market for highly skilled scientific personnel. International corporations begin slowly to operate by producing in the cheapest market for sale in the dearest, as opposed to the nationalistic system of producing in each market in which they sell. If governmental policies were coordinated and harmonized more fully, the position, with fixed exchange rates, would begin to approach that within a large federal state such as the United States.

Admittedly, the action of the federal government in taxing according to ability to pay and spending without regard to regional lines (for the most part) makes a significant difference. There are, thus far, few international redistributive activities—the United Nations budget, the budgets of specialized agencies, peace-keeping operations in the Congo and, prior to June 1967, in the Gaza strip, and, most important, foreign aid. Even these, however, fall short of the standard applicable inside countrie: The French and Soviet governments chose not to pay a share of the peace-keeping expenses of the Congo or the Gaza strip, and economic aid was partly divided into spheres of influence and partly competitive. The concern of some regions of the United States that they are paying more in taxes than they are receiving in benefits reflects the residual sovereignty of countries that refuse to contribute to world undertakings and is subversive of the national unity.

Apart from the budgetary point, however, with its implication for automatic regional redistribution of income, which probably helps balance the interregional accounts of the less developed and hence poorer regions of the country, the analogy between the spatial economy of the United States and the international system as it appears to be evolving is a striking one. There are no tariffs. Domestic resistance to incursions of national firms—such as the anti-chain-store legislation—is gone. The local firm knows it must compete with firms from outside the region by product differentiation or superior service. National corporations contemplating expansion are bound to no traditional locality. The less developed areas seek to attract them not with tariffs but with tax subsidies. There is a brain drain from the center of the country to the two coasts. Financial centers are organized in a hierarchy with San Francisco, Philadelphia, Boston, Chicago, and New York at the apex. New York performs financial intermediation services for the country as a whole. There is little or no regulation of this function, save for the Securities and Exchange Commission's interest in preventing fraud, state regulation of insurance, and a rather archaic regulation of banking. The local central-bank authorities in the 12 districts perform mainly housekeeping functions. Their contribution to policy is presented in Washington, D.C., with the major responsibility for policy being assumed by New York and Washington.

It is unnecessary to spell out the international parallel to this picture of a national economic system: the weakening influence of tariffs; the rise of the international firm; the efforts of the developed (not the less developed) countries to attract such firms; the movement of skilled personnel; the hierarchical organization of financial centers; the importance of New York (read the Euro-dollar market) in international financial intermediation; and the preponderance of the Federal Reserve System in determining international monetary policy.

National versus International Policy

The policy dilemma remains. In the comfortable classical world, each country, as each person, advances the general interest when it advances its own interest. He governs best who governs least. Free trade, balanced budgets, and the gold standard, or more classical still, the freely flexible exchange rate, put government out of business. Or with world government, a single coherent set of policies would be imposed on the separate countries, now components of a larger entity. With no world government, however, and little prospect of one, countries may achieve the same result by harmonizing policies and coordinating actions. But they have the sovereign right to withhold compliance, or even to take advantage of the opportunities for short-run income maximization and risk minimization which independence gives in a world committed to operate the system.

But suppose the question is not one of taking advantage of the international system but of minding one's own national business. Assume that Europe insists on high interest rates because of its analytical conclusions or prejudices about the relative merits for domestic stabilization of fiscal and monetary policy. Suppose further that this means high interest rates in the United States, to prevent capital outflows, and reduced capital formation and growth. Short-run stability of high-level employment can be achieved with the aid of fiscal policy, but this tends to promote consumption at the expense of capital formation (lower taxes and higher interest rates). If one cares about the rate of growth and the monetary fiscal mix, the insistence of Europe on high interest rates is difficult to support. American domestic economists call for flexible exchange rates, or restrictions on capital outflows to isolate the U.S. money market from the world market and to recapture independence of monetary policy. The international trade economist who puts a high value on the maintenance of international markets for goods and factors urges the coordination of international policies, but he knows well the beliefs or prejudices of the European authorities and is not sanguine that they will alter their position in the interest of an opposing theory in the United States.

Or take administrative convenience. One reason that American economists interested in domestic stability want monetary policy freed of integration into international capital markets is because they are aware that the Federal Reserve System has discretionary power to alter monetary policy, while changes in fiscal policy must be submitted for legislative approval, a time-consuming and even a chancy process. In countries with cabinet responsibility, as the United Kingdom, fiscal policy can be altered as speedily as monetary, and such countries are not always sympathetic with economic policies adopted for the sake of a particular (and inefficient?) political system. Harmonization and coordination of policies are difficult with different traditions, institutions, and pressures.

It is normal for the domestic and the international economist to differ on these issues, normal and, on the whole, salutary. Benevolent despotism is the best form of government, provided that the despot remains not only benevolent, which thus far has been impossible, but also omniscient. In problems with many variables, however (today called system problems), it is difficult and often impossible for the benevolent despot to have in mind all the possible main and side effects coming from a particular policy. It is important to have specialists concerned with various parts of the problem who can look at it from the vantage point of a particular perspective or interest. The clash between the perspectives or interests will illuminate the policy choices to be made and make for more intelligent decisions. But the international trade economist sometimes feels like the Department of State, that the broader interests of the system tend to be subordinated to the interests of the parts, with these being resolved for reasons of convenience and tradition in ways that do not always fit the general weal. Like the Department of State, the international trade economist is probably indulging in the pathetic fallacy when he thinks this way. There is a chemical trace of truth in the contention.

A classical world of competitive markets, including the market for foreign exchange, and no government, or a world government somehow constructed along the lines of a benevolent, omniscient despot, would make an international economic system a reality. One wonders whether governments with power to act, and the need to act in the national interest, in ways dictated by national traditions and within the logic of national institutions, can in fact be sufficiently integrated and coordinated as to constitute an international economic system. Most of the work is still left to be done by the price system. Part of the governments' task is not to interfere, rather than to seek to interfere optimally. Even when it comes time to interfere, more often than not, the interests of the unit and those of the system coincide.

In the limited number of cases when they do not, it is not the task of the international trade economist to uphold the interests of the system against those of the unit. The job is to specify the range of alternatives and their consequences for both.

Summary

The classical economic system with limited government presupposes no conflicts between the interests of the parts and the whole, nor any need to make decisions on the part of a government. On the whole, it is an illusion. With national governments playing roles, the question arises whether they maximize the short-run interest of the country, at the expense of other countries, or adopt longer range policies to uphold the international system, perhaps leaving room for less altruistic governments to take advantage of their restraint. Governments may bind each other to altruistic conduct by agreement. But there will be times when separate parallel action is insufficient, and action must be coordinated. Not all the possibilities can be foreseen and provided for in agreements. Nor can countries be expected to behave in identical fashion, given their different traditions, institutions, and possibly purposes.

The international economic system with governmental intervention is a close analogue to the operations of a national governmental system, save for the redistribution of income, with its effects on payments disequilibriums which go through central budget, and the fact that the decisions are made in many lesser bodies rather than in a single central one. Making separate national decisions in the international economic system calls for harmonized policies and coordinated actions—difficult to achieve.

The role of the economist is not to make choices, especially when the interests of the country and the international economic system clash, but to indicate the alternatives and their implications for the national and system interests.

APPENDIXES

FACTOR SUPPLY,

TECHNOLOGY, AND

PRODUCTION POSSIBILITIES

Derivation of the Transformation Curve from the Production Function and Factor Supplies

A **production function** is a statement of the relationships between physical quantities of inputs of factors and the physical output of a given commodity. Geometrically it can be shown by plotting the various combinations of two factors needed to produce given amounts of the commodity in question. In Figure A.1a, T–T is an **isoquant** representing a given quantity of a single commodity, cloth. T'–T' is a higher isoquant, i.e., a greater amount of cloth such as 200 yards, in comparison with the 100 yards represented by T–T. At a given point such as W, production is in equilibrium if the ratio of marginal physical products of labor and land is equal to the ratio of the prices of the two factors. A line tangent to an isoquant represents the relative price of land and labor. Given the production point, W, one can deduce the relative price of the factors, equal to the slope S–S, or given the quantity to be produced, T–T, and the price of the factors, S–S, one can find the least cost combination, W. OR is an expansion path for the relative price S–S (to which S'–S' is parallel). By adding inputs of land and capital, with the relative prices equal to the slope of S–S, one proceeds to higher isoquants by the path OR. If there are constant returns to scale, the expansion path at constant factor price will be a straight line. This simplest form of production function is called **linear homogeneous.** The isoquant T–T in Figure A.1a shows that labor can fairly easily be substituted physically for land in the production of cloth, and vice versa.

The foregoing is by way of review. In Figure A.1b we show two production functions, for wheat and cloth, in which factor proportions are rigidly fixed but different in each commodity. The expansion paths, OX for cloth and OY for wheat, are straight lines for any positive set of factor prices. Any different set of factor proportions, such as OR instead of OW

461

FIGURE A.1*a*. Production
Function for Cloth

FIGURE A.1*b*. Production
Functions with Fixed Factor
Proportions

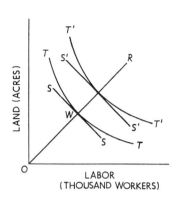

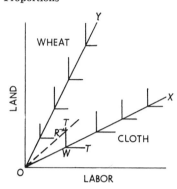

on the isoquant *T–T*, will reduce the marginal physical product of one
factor (in this case land) to zero. Its price will also fall to zero.

In Figure A.1*b* cloth is unambiguously labor intensive and wheat unambiguously land intensive. At any positive relative price of land and
labor, cloth will use more labor relative to land than wheat.

In Figure A.2 we construct a so-called **Edgeworth-Bowley box diagram**,
in which the dimensions of the box represent the amounts of land and
labor in a country, which we shall call Britain. These factor supplies are
assumed to be homogeneous in character and fixed in amount. The production function for cloth is drawn with its origin in the lower left-hand
corner of the box at *O*, and with its isoquants, *T–T*, *T'–T'*, and so on, mov-

FIGURE A.2. Edgeworth-Bowley Box Diagram with Fixed Factor
Proportions

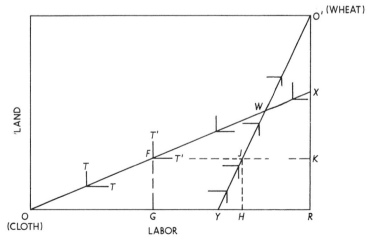

ing out and up to the right. Its expansion path is OX. If all the labor in Britain (OR) were used to make cloth, only RX of land would be required, and O'X of land would be left unemployed. At X, the marginal physical product of land would be zero.

The production function for wheat is drawn reversed and upside down, with its origin at O' and extending downward and to the left. Its expansion path is OY. At Y, all the land would be employed, and YR of labor, but OY of labor would be unemployed. OX and O'Y intersect at W, which is the only production point in the box diagram where there can be full employment and positive prices for both factors. At any other point on either expansion path, say F on OX, land and labor will be able to produce at J on the expansion path for wheat; OG of labor will be engaged in cloth, and HR in wheat. RK of land will be employed in cloth, and O'K' in wheat. But GH of labor will be unemployed.

The curve OWO' as in Figure A.2 is in effect a transformation curve, showing the various combinations of wheat and cloth which can be produced in Britain, given the factor endowments of the country. The only point providing full employment of the two factors and positive factor prices is W. OWO' does not look like a transformation curve, because it is given in terms of physical units of land and labor, rather than physical units of production. If we remap the OWO' curve in Figure A.2 from factor space into commodity space in terms of units of wheat and cloth and turn it right side up, it appears to be a normal production possibilities curve, though kinked at W, as in Figure A.3.

If cloth and wheat were produced with fixed factor coefficients, and these were identical, the two expansion paths would coincide, as in A.4a, and the transformation curve becomes a straight line as in A.4b. But this

FIGURE A.3. Transformation Curve Derived from Edge-worth-Bowley Box Diagram with Fixed Factor Proportions

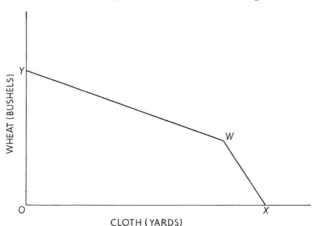

FIGURE A.4a. Constant Op-portunity Costs: Identical Fixed Factor Proportions

FIGURE A.4b. Transformation Curve Derived from Figure A.4a

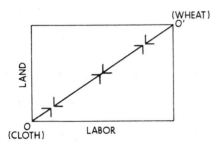

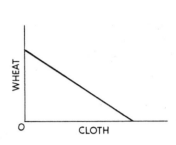

means that land and labor are always used in the same combination so that they might well be regarded as a single factor. This is equivalent to the labor theory of value and its resultant straight-line transformation curve. A similar straight-line transformation curve would be produced by constant costs and identical production functions in the two commodities. It is vital to distinguish between **constant costs** and **constant opportunity costs.** The straight-line transformation curve represents constant opportunity costs. If the production functions for the two commodities differ, the transformation curve will exhibit curvature even though there be constant returns to scale in each commodity taken separately.

When the law of variable proportions holds and there is the possibility of substitution between factors in the production of a commodity, there is no unique expansion path. Instead, a separate expansion path can be drawn for any given set of factor prices, or we can draw in the isoquants for both commodities and trace out a locus of points of tangency between them. This locus represents the efficiency path, or the maximum combinations of production of the two goods which can be produced with the existing factor supply. It is shown in Figure A.5a. Suppose that production

FIGURE A.5a. Maximum Efficiency Locus under Variable Factor Proportions

FIGURE A.5b. Transformation Curve Derived from Figure A.5a

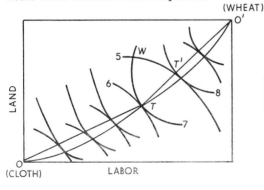

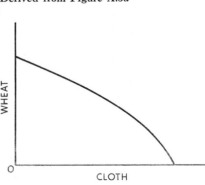

were to take place at W, away from the efficiency locus. W is on cloth isoquant 7, and on wheat isoquant 5. But there is a point T, also on cloth isoquant 7, which is on a higher isoquant (6) of wheat. It would therefore be possible to produce more wheat without giving up any cloth. Or there is a point T' on wheat isoquant 5 which is on cloth isoquant 8. It would equally be possible to produce more cloth and the same amount of wheat. Any point off the locus of trangencies of isoquants of the two production functions is therefore inefficient, insofar as it would be possible to get more output of one commodity without losing any of the other, by moving to the locus.

The efficiency locus is the exact analogue of the "contract curve" in exchange theory. Here the dimensions of the box are given by fixed supplies of commodities, a point off the contract curve represents initial endowments of two individuals, with utility maps measured from origins in the two corners, and the two individuals can improve their utility by moving from the initial endowment point to the contract curve.

When the Edgeworth-Bowley box is used for production, it shows not only the efficient combinations of outputs but also factor combinations and factor prices. Unlike the transformation curve (A.5b), however, it cannot show the relative price of wheat and cloth. If we assume that production is at T, however, the factor proportions in cloth are represented by the slope of OT, and the factor proportions in wheat by $O'T$. It will be obvious that the indicated allocation employs all the land and all the labor. The relative price of land and labor with these outputs is represented by the slope of the tangency to the maximum efficiency locus at T.

Opportunity Costs versus Real Costs

The original theorists who developed the law of comparative costs using the labor theory of value thought of labor as disutility and of the cost of goods as a real cost. With the substitution of the law of variable proportions for the labor theory of value, there was seen to be a difficulty. Land and capital may not involve real costs. One can think not of real costs, but only of the opportunity cost, that is, the cost of giving up something else.

Real-cost theorists, however, have not been willing to abandon their position. In particular, Jacob Viner continued to the end of his life to adhere to a real-cost position, claiming that in many respects one can regard labor as the main cost, or capital as past labor, and clung to something very close to the labor theory of value. Less time is spent in defense, however, than in attack The opportunity cost doctrine was strongly criticized for its assumption that men are indifferent among occupations and willing to work no matter what the price of labor. This assumption of inelastic supplies of factors is evidently unrealistic. If the transformation schedule is built up out of production functions which are statements of physical possibilities, there was no necessary reason, in Viner's view, why a country should be on the frontier of its transformation curve rather than somewhere inside it. The implicit assumption of the transformation curve that the supply of factors is completely inelastic vitiates its validity. The opportunity cost doctrine has no room for the possibility that trade enables a country to work less for the same real income rather than work the same amount and earn a higher return in commodities.

But difficulties are not absent from the real-cost side. It is impermissible to gloss over the question of the absence of real costs in land and the sunk character of real costs in capital. More, the doctrine fails to take account of the possibility that different people have different responses to different kinds of work, so that a given volume of output will represent a different real cost, depending upon who is engaged in it.

Jaroslav Vanek has demonstrated that it is possible to distinguish between two kinds of production possibilities curves, one showing the technical transformation schedules between two goods, which does not allow for reactions of the factors to changes in factor prices, and an economic one, which takes such reactions into account. The economically possible curve lies within the technically feasible curve, except at one or more points where they coincide, since the technical possibilities frontier is an envelope curve of various feasible curves.

SUGGESTED READING

The literature on comparative advantage and factor supply is enormous, and the student is referred to R. E. Caves, *Trade and Economic Structure* (Cambridge, Mass.: Harvard University Press, 1960), chaps. 3, 4 and 5, for a review and bibliography. Two of the outstanding articles: R. Robinson, "Factor Proportions and Comparative Advantage," *QJE*, May 1956, and T. M. Rybczynski, "Factor Endowment and Relative Commodity Prices," *Econ*, November 1955, are gathered in the 1967 American Economics Association, *Readings in International Economics*, part I.

On the controversy between real and opportunity costs, see J. Viner, *Studies in the Theory of International Trade* (New York: Harper & Bros., 1937), pp. 489–93; G. Haberler, *The Theory of International Trade* (London: Macmillan & Co., Ltd., 1937), pp. 126, 175, and J. Vanek, "An Afterthought on the 'Real Cost–Opportunity Cost Dispute' and Some Aspects of General Equilibrium under Conditions of Variable Factor Supplies," *Review of Economic Studies*, June 1959. See also Haberler, "Real Costs and Opportunity Costs," in *International Social Science Bulletin*, Spring 1951.

FACTOR-PRICE

EQUALIZATION

Factor-Price Equalization

There are at least three ways to demonstrate the factor-price equalization theorem. The first, taking off from the Edgeworth-Bowley box, which was explained in Appendix A, is illustrated in Figure B.1. There we construct Edgeworth-Bowley boxes for each of two countries, the United States and Britain, with widely different factor proportions but identical production functions, which differ as between the two commodities, wheat and cloth. The two boxes have a common origin in cloth at O. The different factor proportions result in two separate origins for wheat, Y in the United States and Y' for Britain. Before trade, the two countries are assumed to be producing and consuming at S and T, respectively, determined separately with the help of demand conditions. The land/labor ratio is higher in wheat and cloth, respectively, in the United States than in Britain. (The diagonals are not drawn in, to simplify the diagram, but OS is steeper than OT in cloth, and SY than TY' in wheat.) With more land employed in both commodities in the United States than in Britain, land will be relatively less expensive, compared to labor. Conversely, with a higher labor/land ratio in both commodities, Britain will have a lower return to labor than will the United States.

When trade becomes possible, it is assumed that prices are fully equalized in the two countries because of the absence of transport costs and other barriers to trade. With identical production functions showing constant returns, and something of each good produced in each country, at equal prices, the returns to factors must be identical if the factor proportions in the production of each commodity are identical between countries—if, that is, trade results in production at such points as R and U. At R and U, the equality of factor proportions is demonstrated by the facts that R lies on the straight line OU (there are identical factor proportions in the production of cloth in both countries) and YR and $Y'U$ are parallel.

There are a variety of reasons why two such points as R and U may

FIGURE B.1. Factor-Price Equalization after Trade

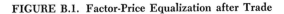

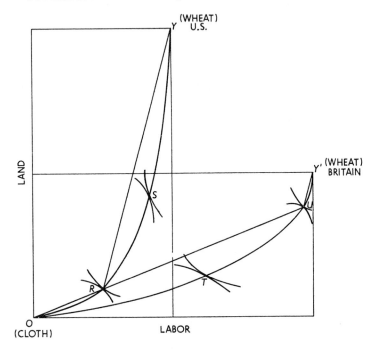

not exist. After trade, one or both countries may be completely specialized, Britain producing cloth at *Y'* or the United States, wheat at *O*. Demand conditions may be so sharply different in the two countries that trade results in shifting production in the United States from *S* toward *Y* rather than toward *O*, so that it would export the labor-intensive good despite its abundance of land. Or land and labor may so substitute for one another in the production of either cloth or wheat that wheat is labor intensive in Britain and land intensive in the United States. This possibility can be illustrated on this diagram but is more conveniently set out in the other two methods.

The second method of illustrating factor-price equalization is one worked out by A. P. Lerner. It is shown with the aid of single isoquants representing the production functions of the two commodities, as in Figure B.2. The trick is to pick isoquants for the two commodities which represent their relative prices, or the quantities in which they are exchanged, after trade is established. Thus the isoquants may represent, say, 3 yards of cloth and 2 bushels of wheat, or 30 yards of cloth and 20 bushels, or 300 and 200. Since the production functions are linear homogeneous, the shape of successive isoquants representing larger quantities is always the same (and the expansion path represented by larger and larger outputs at given factor prices is a straight line). Since the units chosen reflect goods prices

FIGURE B.2. Factor-Price Equalization Illustrated with Production Functions

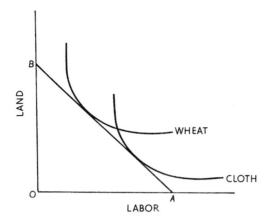

which are the same in the two countries after trade (assuming no transport costs and perfect competition), Figure B.2 applies to the United States and Britain alike. And as the figure is drawn, there can be only one factor-price ratio, the line of tangency to the two isoquants, *A–B*. This then is factor-price equalization.

But notice what happens if the isoquants cross more than once, as in Figure B.3. This situation implies that there is a wide range of factor substitution possible in at least one of the commodities which permits the same goods price to prevail in two countries, but differing factor prices. In Figure B.3, the production function for wheat is the same as in Figure B.2, but there is much more room for factor substitution in cloth. In these circumstances, Britain, with a high labor/land ratio, may produce cloth with the factor proportions represented by the ray from the origin (not drawn) *O–T*, and wheat with the proportions *O–S*, yielding a factor price *A–B*. In this country cloth is relatively labor intensive. But in the United States, land is substituted for labor in producing cloth, and with production at *S'* and *T'*, cloth is land intensive, wheat labor intensive. Factor prices will differ, and one cannot tell from factor endowments which country will export which commodity.

The third method of illustrating factor-price equalization is at the same time the most complex and the most helpful, since it puts factor proportions, goods prices, and factor prices all on the same diagram. Figure B.4 shows the relations between land/labor ratios and wage rates in the upper half of the diagram, and the relationship between wages and goods prices in the lower half. The central horizontal line is the wage/rent ratio, or the wage rate, which rises as it moves to the right. In the upper half of the diagram, land/labor ratios for cloth and wheat are shown rising as wages

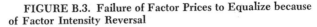

FIGURE B.3. Failure of Factor Prices to Equalize because of Factor Intensity Reversal

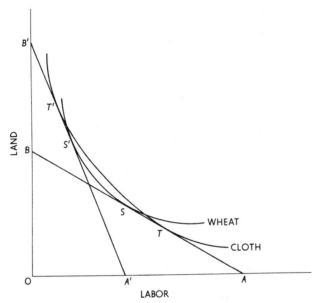

increase: the higher the wage, the more incentive there is for firms to substitute land for labor. Note that cloth is unambiguously more labor intensive, i.e., less land intensive, at every wage rate, since the X–X schedule for cloth lies everywhere below the Y–Y schedule for wheat.

The relation between goods prices and factor prices is shown in the bottom part of the diagram. Here relative goods prices are measured in reverse order, i.e., downwards. The higher the wage, the higher the relative price of cloth, i.e., the higher the P–P line, measured negatively from O. This relationship is obvious enough after the student has become used to handling rising prices upside down: as wages rise, the price of the labor-intensive commodity rises, and cloth is labor intensive at every land/labor ratio portrayed in the diagram.

British and U.S. factor proportions are given by horizontal lines in the upper half of the diagram which show that the United States is relatively land intensive, and Britain, labor intensive. Before trade, production in the separate countries is determined by demand conditions, but as portrayed, the vertical lines for Britain and the United States before trade show that the price of cloth is lower in Britain than in the United States, and the wage rate lower. Conversely, of course, the price of wheat is higher and the rental rate for land higher. When trade is opened up, goods prices have to move together, and under the conditions drawn, the relative wage becomes identical, which means factor-price equalization.

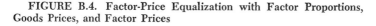

FIGURE B.4. Factor-Price Equalization with Factor Proportions, Goods Prices, and Factor Prices

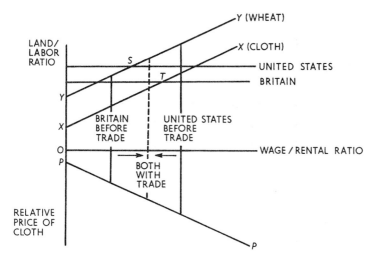

The separate conditions necessary for factor-price equalization can be illustrated by varying this diagram, but we shall content ourselves with word pictures except for factor intensity reversals. Linear homogeneity of production functions is required to have the land/labor ratios for the separate commodities straight lines, as shown. Perfect competition and the absence of transport costs are required to have identical goods prices after trade on the *P–P* line. Lack of complete specialization is a little more difficult to make clear, but if the price line after trade moves to the left of S, where the United States is fully specialized in wheat, or to the right of *T*, where Britain is fully specialized in cloth, goods-price change no longer implies factor-proportion change, and factor proportions are no longer uniquely related to factor prices.

The condition that demands must not be too skewed is to make sure that after trade is opened up the price of cloth in Britain rises, rather than have the country so addicted to cloth that it tries to buy more of it from the United States. Trade should make the price of the goods that are produced intensively by the abundant factor rise not fall.

The condition about factor reversals is illustrated in Figure B.5. In Britain wheat is land intensive relative to cloth, but in the United States, with a much higher land/labor ratio, land is so plentiful that it is copiously substituted for labor in making cloth. This is not very realistic, perhaps, but it might be more confusing to shift the commodities. Notice that as the wage rate rises, the price of cloth rises relative to wheat until the land/labor curves cross. When cloth is more land intensive than wheat, the relative price of cloth declines as wages rise. In these circumstances, it is

FIGURE B.5. Failure of Factor Prices to Equalize because of Factor Intensity Reversal

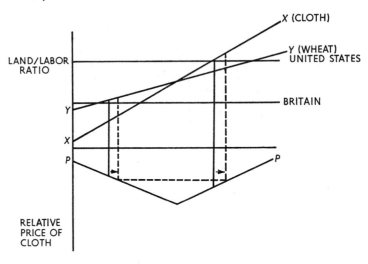

possible to get goods-price equalization without factor-price equalization. After trade, each country exports the labor-intensive good, and trade raises wages in both countries.

Empirical Testing of the Factor-Price Equalization Theorem

There is no doubt that in the world factor prices have not been equalized by trade, which must equalize goods prices because of the assumptions of perfect competition and no transport costs. This means that some of the assumptions of the theorem have not been met. The question, still unanswered, is which. It is obvious that transport costs prevent full equalization of goods prices for many bulky commodities, that tariffs prevent it for others, that perfect competition exists in neither goods nor factor markets, that there is complete specialization (or would be without tariffs) in many manufactured goods and primary products alike. The conditions of the theorem come closest to being met in, say, the Common Market in Europe, where the various economies are roughly similar, adjacent to one another, and incompletely specialized in manufactures. Here the tendency to factor-price equalization through trade is strong. Elsewhere, however, there is much greater doubt of the relevance of the theorem.

The Leontief paradox (mentioned in the text) was developed from input-output analysis of the U.S. economy and showed that contrary to general expectation, U.S. imports were less labor intensive than U.S. exports. A wide variety of explanations for the paradox has been advanced. Many commentators thought that the statistical basis for the demonstration was inadequate. Leontief held that U.S. labor was three times as productive as other labor (and not because of more capital), which made this country really labor intensive. Jaroslav Vanek blames a third factor, natural resources. William Travis asserts that the Leontief paradox is a reflection of tariff interferences in trade, which means that production and trade do not accurately reflect factor proportions. B. S. Minhas and M. Diab, and to some extent the writer, are of the opinion that factor reversals occur in the real world, but some recent research of the National Bureau of Economic Research throws doubt on this explanation for manufactures, even though such reversals occur in agriculture. The question, then, is still open.

SUGGESTED READING

Again the literature is enormous. The classic articles, by Paul Samuelson, "International Trade and the Equalization of Factor Prices," were published in the *EJ* for June 1948, and June 1949. The second of these is reproduced in American Economic Association, *Readings in International Economics*. The original Leontief article, "Domestic Production and Foreign Trade: The American Position Re-examined," is available either in *Economia Internazionale*, February 1954 or in the American Economic Association, *Readings in International Economics*, in the part on empirical testing. If a student goes no further, these are the articles to read. This appendix is based on A. P. Lerner, "Factor Prices and International Trade," *Econ*, February 1952, and H. G. Johnson, "Factor Endowments, International Trade and Factor Prices," in *Manchester School*, September 1957, reprinted in American Economic Association, *Readings in International Economics*, part I. See also the articles by Lancaster, Jones, and Minhas in Bhagwati, *International Trade, Selected Readings*.

For the rest, on factor-price equalization, see R. E. Caves, *Trade and Economic Structure* (Cambridge, Mass.: Harvard University Press, 1960), chap. 3; Meade, *Trade and Welfare*, pp. 331–92; and, for a useful summary of the literature, B. Balassa, "The Factor-Price Equalization Controversy," *Weltwirtschaftliches Archiv*, 1, 1961. On the Leontief paradox, see especially B. S. Minhas, *An International Comparison of Factor Costs and Factor Use* (Amsterdam: North-Holland Publishing Co., 1963); W. P. Travis, *The Theory of Trade and Protection* (Cambridge, Mass.: Harvard University Press, 1964); and J. Vanek, *The Natural Resource Content of United States Foreign Trade, 1870–1955* (Cambridge, Mass.: The M.I.T. Press, 1963).

THE RELATION OF THE OFFER CURVE TO THE PRODUCTION POSSIBILITIES CURVE AND THE CONSUMPTION INDIFFERENCE MAP

John Stuart Mill thought of the offer curve as developed from fixed supplies of commodities to be exchanged. This is the concept to which Frank Graham objected, as he drew attention to the possibility of producing goods, at constant costs, as he thought, for export. But there is no need to limit the offer curve to the case of fixed goods supply. James E. Meade has set out a neat geometric device that builds the offer curve out of the production possibilities curve and the consumption indifference map. The beauty of the technique rests partly in its bridging this gap, but also in that it enables one to demonstrate, neatly and simply, the impact of trade on production, consumption, the gains from trade, and so on. While many students may remain terrified at the prospect of learning still another geometric technique, the braver are encouraged to plunge ahead and acquire a highly useful analytical tool.

The first step is to draw the production block and consumption indifference curve for country A without trade, in the usual way, except for the fact that they are in the northwest rather than the usual northeast quadrant of the system of coordinates. This is done is Figure C.1. Following Meade's notation, the horizontal axis measures A's exportables, which are B's importables; the vertical axis, B's exportables.

Now, holding it level and upright, slide the A production block up and down the no-trade consumption indifference curve, keeping it tangent to the same consumption indifference curve, I. The origin of the block, O, will trace out a trade indifference curve, i. At every point on this curve, A will be indifferent whether it trades or not. It can remain at O and produce and consume at F. Or it can move along the curve to the point where the

FIGURE C.1. The Derivation of the Trade Indifference Map from the Consumption Indifference Map

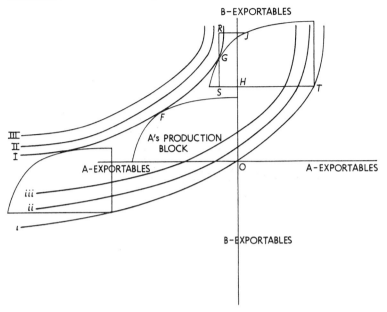

origin of its production possibilities block is at *T*. It will then produce at *G*, and trade *HT* of A-exportables for *HO* of B-exportables. The reason that it is indifferent between *O* and *T* is that it can produce at either *F* or *G* along its production possibilities schedule (transformation along the schedule is assumed to be costless); and *G* is on the same consumption indifference curve as *F*. At *G*, of course, it consumes *GS* + *HO* of B-exportables, and only *SH* of A-exportables.

Note that the trade indifference curve has a different shape than the consumption indifference curve. This is because production has shifted as well as the proportions of goods consumed. If *J* in the upper right-hand position of the A-block corresponds to *F* in the no-trade position, it is clear that in shifting from *O* to *T*, production of A-exportables has increased by *RJ*, and production of B-exportables decreased by *RG*. A trade indifference curve is flatter, to take account of these production changes. When production is fixed and no movement of resources is possible, the trade indifference curve will parallel the consumption one.

There is a trade indifference curve corresponding to every consumption indifference curve, and hence a trade indifference map. A country is better off, the higher the trade indifference curve it is able to reach. Along any single curve, it is indifferent between one position and another. But in Figure C.1 country A is better off the higher the trade indifference curve it can reach (moving from southeast to northwest).

FIGURE C.2. The Derivation of the Offer Curve for Country A from Its Trade Indifference Map

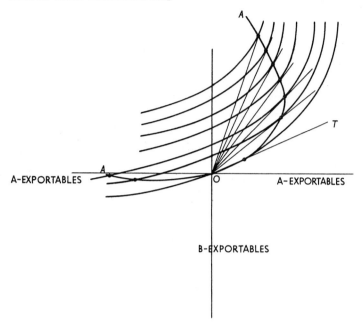

A's offer curve will now be constructed. It represents the locus of a series of tangencies of various price lines to the trade indifference map of successively higher indifference curves. This is shown in Figure C.2. The initial slope of the offer curve through the origin represents the price which would prevail without trade. As higher and higher prices for A-exportables are offered in terms of B-exportables, A will be enabled to move to higher and higher trade indifference curves and will be disposed to offer, as the figure is drawn, first more and more A-goods for larger quantities of B-exportables, and then less. Note that if the price for B-goods gets higher than *OT*, A will export B-exportables in exchange for A-goods. The offer curve moves into the southwest quadrant, but only for very high prices for B-exportables for which the name is belied because they are imported by B.

Country B's offer curve can similarly be traced out from a series of trade indifference curves imposed on the same set of coordinates but developed from sliding B's production possibilities block along its consumption indifference curves in the southeast quadrant. Figure C.3 shows the A and B offer curves intersecting at the balanced trade position where the terms of trade line, *OT*, is tangent to trade indifference curves of A and B and go to the origin. There are other tangencies of trade indifference curves, and a contract curve, *K–K*, may be drawn along them. This contract curve,

FIGURE C.3. The Contract Curve and Trade Equilibrium

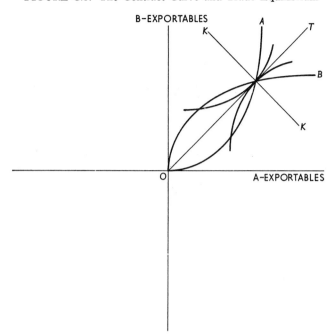

like that of the Edgeworth-Bowley box in Figure A.5a when it is used in exchange and not as an efficiency locus in production, represents different distributions of welfare between A and B. A is better off the further the point of trade is toward the northwest; and B the nearer it is to the south-east. Only at the intersection of OA and OB, however, do the terms of trade balance A's exports and B's imports under free trade.

These three figures neatly show the relationship of the offer curve to consumption indifference curves and to production. The technique can be used in its simple manifestation, however, to show the gains from trade. This is done by leaving the A and B production possibilities blocks at the trading position, as in Figure C.4. Trade and consumption indifference curves and the offer curves are omitted to eliminate clutter.

In Figure C.4, production is measured from the intersection of the origins, T, of the production blocks. In A, production consists of QG of B-exportables and GM of A-exportables. B produces NH of B-exportables and FH of A-exportables. These outputs can readily be added to give production of GJ of A-exportables in the two countries and JH of B-exportables.

Consumption is measured from the original coordinates, intersecting at O. A consumes only GR of A-exportables, but GL of B-exportables; in its turn, B consumes only SH of its G-good, and KH of the A-exportable.

FIGURE C.4. Production and Consumption under Trading

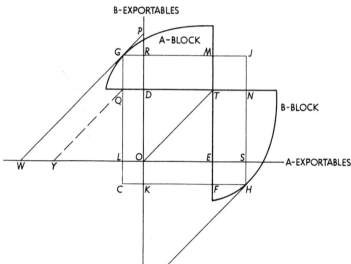

This is made possibly by trade, in which A exchanges DT of the A-good against TE of the B-good, at the terms of trade, OT.

This is a free-trade position, without transport costs. Thus the terms of trade are equal to the internal prices (WG and ZH are parallel to OT and to each other). National income in A is WO expressed in A-exportables, or PO expressed in B's good, whether we take income produced, or income consumed. These are the same because trade is balanced. Income produced directly in A-goods is YO, which is the same as GM or QT (YQ is drawn parallel to OT). That part of income produced which originally consisted of B-goods, GQ, is the equivalent, at the price WG, of WY.

For income consumed, GR of A-exportables is equal to LO, and GL of B-exportables, at the price WG, is the equivalent in A-exportables of WL. $WL + LO = WO$. Similar exercises can be carried through for national income in A measured in B-goods and for income produced and consumed in B in either good.

The gains from trade are more elusive and present an index-number problem. We can measure A's gain in terms of either prices before trade, or prices after trade. In Figure C.5, a and b are the before-trade terms of trade drawn to the A production block after and before trade, respectively. On the other hand, c and d represent the post-trade prices drawn to the same block positions; a, b, c, and d intersect the horizontal axis at A, B, C, and D. The gains from trade in A, expressed in A-exportables, may then

FIGURE C.5. The Gains from Trade Measured in Terms of A-Exportables

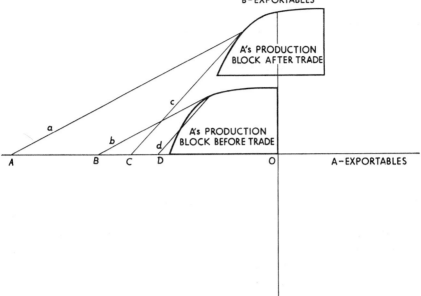

be regarded as *AB*, using the terms of trade before trade, or *CD*, representing it in after-trade prices. But one should not make the mistake of regarding the gains from trade as measured from the national income in the no-trade position at no-trade prices (*BO*) to national income with trade at the with-trade price (*CO*). In that event, the gain from trade would be negative, or a loss (*BC*).

It is true that the gains from trade will be larger, the larger the change in prices before trade and after. The larger the price change, the higher the consumption indifference curve and the higher the trade indifference curve the country can reach. But measurement of the distance between indifference curves requires a scale, and this can be one commodity or the other, but only at a consistent set of prices.

SUGGESTED READING

This appendix is based on Meade, *A Geometry of International Trade*, chaps. 1–4.

THE OPTIMUM TARIFF

A tariff improves the terms of trade if the offer curve facing the imposing country is less than infinitely elastic. But a country must be careful not to raise the tariff too high, or the loss in the quantity of trade will outweigh the improvement in the terms of trade. What is the tariff which will maximize a country's gain, improving the terms of trade more than the volume is reduced?

In Figure D.1, A's and B's offer curves are drawn in the usual way, and at the original free-trade intersection, A has reached its trade indifference curve, as described in Appendix C, which we can designate No. 5. The question is, can it do better? And the answer is that it can. It needs to distort its offer curve by a tariff so as to reach the point where B's offer curve is tangent to its highest trade indifference curve, here numbered 10. Note that a tariff which displaces A's offer curve to the left anywhere short of *F* will leave it better off, but the optimum tariff, as drawn, takes it to its highest possible trade indifference curve, touching B's offer curve. Only points on B's offer curve are feasible, of course, since it takes two to trade.

It should be pointed out that the trade-distorted offer curve in this diagram, which follows the Meade analysis, is different from that in the text of Chapter 7. In the text, the tariff was measured by the distance between the two offer curves, and the proceeds of the tariff were removed from trading by governments and swept under the rug. With the tariff collected as *P'–V* of cloth in Figure 7.4, the new terms of trade are *O–P'*. This is the Lerner diagram. In the Meade analysis, however, the government takes the revenue and gives it back to consumers as subsidies; they spend it on the two goods in their normal fashion. As a consequence of the subsidy, they are in a position to spend more than they earn. The new terms of trade are drawn not to the origin, which is the case only when there is free trade, but to the horizontal axis elsewhere. The terms-of-trade line is drawn tangent to the tariff-imposing country's trade indifference curve. Where it intersects the horizontal axis is a measure of the tariff (*SO* in Figure D.1.) and of the gain through the imposition of the tariff.

FIGURE D.1. The Tariff-Distorted Offer Curve and the Optimum
Tariff

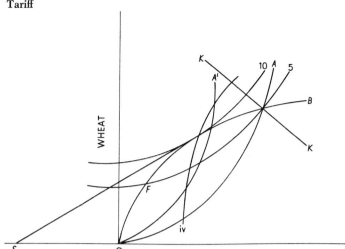

The rate of the optimum tariff can be calculated in terms of the elasticity of the foreign offer curve. In Figure D.2, T is the point where A's tariff-
distorted offer curve cuts B's offer curve. At T, B is willing to trade TQ of
wheat for OQ of cloth. But the price line OT (not drawn) is not tangent
to A's trade indifference curve, and A will not be in equilibrium trading
OQ of cloth. A will trade at T only at a price tangent to its trade indifference
curve at T (also tangent to the offer curve, since this is the optimum tariff).
Draw such a line of tangency and extend it through the vertical axis at R
to the horizontal axis at S. This is the equilibrium price in A. A will trade
along the slope ST and B along OT if exports of cloth are subject to an
export tax of SO/OQ in A, or imports of wheat, UR, are subject to a tax of
RO/UR.

What is the import elasticity of the B offer curve at T? To measure this
elasticity, which represents the change in imports relative to the change
in price of imports, we use the tangent drawn to the relevant axis—in this
case B's—and at the same time drop a perpendicular to it. The elasticity
of the offer curve at the given point is represented by the distance from
the point of intersection of the perpendicular on the vertical axis to the
origin (UO), divided by the distance from the intercept of the tangent
to the origin (RO). If R lies halfway between U and O, the elasticity of
the B offer curve at T is 2. If the offer curve is a straight line from O to L,
the elasticity at L is infinity, since the vertical distance to L divided by O
(where the tangent to the trade indifference line intersects the vertical
axis) is infinity. The import elasticity of the offer curve at M, where the

FIGURE D.2. Calculating the Optimum Tariff

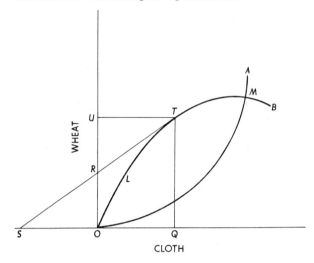

tangent and the perpendicular line are assumed identical, is 1. If the B offer curve slopes downward after M, its elasticity is less than 1, since the tangent intersects the vertical axis further from the origin than the straight line to the axis.

We are now in a position to derive the formula for the optimum tariff. If T is a point on B's offer curve which touches the highest possible trade indifference curve of A, the optimum tariff at point T is SO/OQ. $OQ = UT$. By similar triangles,

$$\frac{SO}{UT} = \frac{RO}{UR} = \frac{1}{\dfrac{UR}{RO}} = \frac{1}{\dfrac{UO - RO}{RO}} = \frac{1}{\dfrac{UO}{RO} - 1}.$$

Since UO/RO is the elasticity of the offer curve at point T, the optimum tariff, SO/OQ, can be expressed as

$$\frac{SO}{OQ} = \frac{1}{\dfrac{UO}{RO} - 1} = \frac{1}{e - 1}.$$

If at point L the elasticity of the offer curve is infinity, the optimum tariff is evidently zero: $1/(\infty - 1) = 0$. Where the offer curve is a straight line, no tariff can improve the terms of trade. At M, where the elasticity of the foreign offer curve is 1, the optimum tariff is infinity $(1/[1-1] = \infty)$, which is to say that the optimum tariff has to be at a point where the elasticity of the opposing offer curve is greater than 1 but less than infinite. At any lower elasticity it is evident that a higher indifference curve can be reached by a tariff.

SUGGESTED READING

Meade, *A Geometry of International Trade,* pp. 76, 87–90; D. B. Marsh, *World Trade and Investment* (New York: Harcourt, Brace & Co., Inc., 1951), chap. 21, and esp. pp. 316–21. See also a series of articles in *Review of Economic Studies* by J. de Graff (1949–50); H. G. Johnson (1950–51 and 1953–54); J. J. Polak (1950–51); and T. Scitovsky, "A Reconsideration of the Theory of Tariffs" in American Economic Association, *Readings in the Theory of International Trade.*

THE MONOPOLY EFFECT

OF A QUOTA

A significant difference between a tariff and a quota is that the conversion of a tariff into a quota which admits exactly the same volume of imports may convert a potential into an actual monopoly and reduce welfare. Figures E.1 and E.2 provide a demonstration.

In Figure E.1, *AR* is the average revenue or demand curve for a commodity in the domestic market. In the absence of international trade, *MR* is the marginal revenue curve facing the domestic industry, and *MC* is the relevant marginal cost curve of the domestic import-competing industry. The world price, assumed to be unchanged by anything which might transpire in the importing country, is *OP*. A tariff, *P–P'*, raises the price at which imports can be sold to *OP'*.

With international trade, and the tariff *P–P'*, *O–P'* is not only the domestic price at which foreigners will supply goods. It also becomes the marginal revenue curve facing the domestic industry (*MR'*). The domestic industry can sell more at the existing price, or infinitesimally below it, so long as it displaces imports. The domestic industry will produce where marginal cost equals marginal revenue, i.e., the amount *OT*. The remaining demand at this price will be supplied by imports, *TW*.

Let us now suppose that the tariff is converted to a quota, and that the licenses are auctioned off. The revenue, terms of trade, and the initial balance-of-payments effects are the same as under the tariff. But the protective, consumption, redistribution, and ultimate balance-of-payments effects are altered because the potential domestic monopoly has been converted to an actual one.

In Figure E.2, the *AR* curve is displaced to the left by the amount of the quota, *TW*, and a new marginal revenue curve, *MR'*, is drawn to the displaced curve, *AR'*. Where the *MC* curve crosses the *MR'* curve will determine domestic production. The price will rise from *OP'* to *OP''*. Imports are the same as before, *TW*, but since no further imports are allowed, the domestic monopoly can raise prices. Welfare is reduced by the shaded

FIGURE E.1. Potential Monopoly in Partial Equilibrium with Tariff

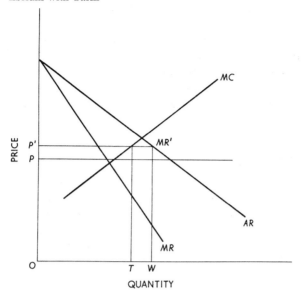

FIGURE E.2. Potential Monopoly Converted to Actual Monopoly under Quota

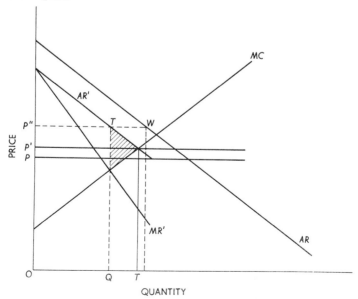

area, representing the reduction in production and consumption, adjusted for the decrease in marginal cost. The student is left to work out the redistribution of welfare.

Conversely, to be sure, the conversion of quota restrictions into tariffs which admit an equal volume of imports will eliminate domestic monopolies by threatening them with potential competition from increased imports. This—that is, the removal of quota restrictions and their conversion to tariffs—is a strong argument for customs unions, and for trade liberalization.

SUGGESTED READING

See H. Heuser, *The Control of International Trade* (London: George Routledge & Sons, Ltd., 1939), chap. 11, especially diagrams 8 and 9.

J. Bhagwati generalizes the possibilities of monopoly among domestic producers, quota holders, and foreign exporters in "On the Equivalence of Tariffs and Quotas," in R. E. Baldwin et al., *Trade, Growth and the Balance of Payments,* Essays in Honor of Gottfried Haberler (Chicago: Rand McNally & Co., 1965).

THE FORWARD

EXCHANGE MARKET

The Forward Exchange Market

The forward market for exchange is not normally a separate market, and it is inaccurate to speak of it as such. It is more properly regarded as a segment of the foreign exchange market as a whole. The link between the forward and the spot rates of exchange is the rate of interest in the two markets involved, and what is known as **interest arbitrage.** In the absence of anticipated movements of the foreign exchange rate, the future rate will be the same as the spot rate if rates of interest are the same in the two money markets concerned. If the three months' interest rate is 6 percent per annum in London and 4 percent in New York, however, three months' sterling should sell at a discount equivalent to 2 percent per annum. This rate, by the way, is $2.388, given a spot rate of $2.40 and a discount of $0.012 (2 percent $\times$ $2.40 $\div$ 4 = $0.012). But a usual way to express the discount or premium is in terms of percent per year.

If forward sterling sold at any higher figure, it would be profitable for banks in New York to put more spot funds in London and sell these forward, because they could earn more than 4 percent without exchange risk. If the discount on the pound were greater or the premium on the dollar more, it would pay London banks to put more money in New York, where it could earn 4 percent per annum plus a premium on forward dollars of more than 2 percent. This would be better than the 6 percent obtainable at home. Interest arbitrage, i.e., the lending of funds at interest in a foreign money market covered by forward sales of the foreign exchange, is the link between the spot and the forward market. In actual practice the discount or premium in the forward market will depart from the **interest differential,** despite arbitrage, by as much as 0.5 percent per annum, which represents the minimum that the banks require as a return to undertake arbitrage. When the differential exceeds 0.5 percent per annum, it is a sign that interest arbitrage is restricted in some fashion.

Interest rates may differ between national markets for a number of reasons. The monetary and banking authorities may be trying to expand or contract lending by the banks, and the rate, therefore, will be low or high, respectively. The rate may be dominated by considerations affecting the government bond market. Or, as we shall see presently, the rate may be changed upward or downward in order to attract or repel foreign funds.

When interest arbitrage is prohibited by the exchange authorities in charge of a currency, in order to limit the outflow of capital, the forward market and the spot market become separate. Discounts or premiums on a currency can now rise to as high as 30, 40, or 50 percent per annum. Rates of this magnitude will mean that the forward market is thin; those people anxious to sell the currency forward must offer a large discount to entice buyers. Any forward sale consummated must find a forward purchaser, since swaps of spot for forward exchange are not permitted. When the forward market is cut adrift from the spot market in this way, it fails to perform its hedging function and provides only a limited outlet for a balanced number of speculative buyers and sellers.

When it is functioning as an integral portion of the foreign exchange market as a whole, through swaps which carry out interest arbitrage, the forward market performs a credit as well as a hedging function. Suppose that a prospective importer in the United States anticipates a need for sterling. Assume that the forward dollar is at a discount and sterling at a premium, because the interest rate is higher in New York than in London. If the importer buys forward sterling, he drives the premium on forward sterling still higher. This encourages a New York bank, let us say, to buy spot sterling and sell it forward at a premium (to the importer). The spot funds transferred to London and held by a New York bank against its forward contract with the U.S. importer may be regarded as those which the importer will ultimately use to make his purchase. Exactly the same result would have been achieved if he had borrowed the amount from a bank in New York, bought spot sterling, and invested it at 4 percent per annum in London until he ultimately needed it in three months. The net cost of covering the exchange risk in this case is the cost of funds in New York less the possible return in London. This is the same as the premium on sterling in the forward market. For the New York banks and for the importer it makes little difference which way the transaction is carried through, except that the importer is less well equipped than the New York banks to handle the London transaction. On this account, the forward market provides him with an alternative way to eliminate the exchange risk to that achievable through borrowing, and the hedging facility has an element of credit connected to it. By the same token, the forward market is either a device which translates the net position taken by nonbank speculators into a short-term capital movement in the spot market, or, if it is cut off from the spot market by fiat and forced to clear itself, a limited device for hedging.

Covered Working Balances

The question may be asked how the New York banks can have a covered position (i.e., assets in foreign currency equal to liabilities) and still have supplies of foreign currency on hand to sell to customers who need it. A covered position means no excess of claims or liabilities; and yet there must be a working balance of sterling to cover the requirements of customers who want to buy telegraphic transfers. The banks cannot expect to be offered each day in telegraphic transfers the foreign currency they sell each day in the same way. Like any business, they must have some inventory.

The answer lies in the forward market and in the fact that the foreign exchange market embraces London as well as New York. All the banks in New York have a minimum need for working balances of, say, £50,000,000. It would be possible to hedge these in the forward market in New York if the banks' customers were willing to buy forward £50,000,000 more than they sold forward. But there is no reason to expect these customers to go long in the forward market by this amount. They, too, may be expected, as a rule, to have a balanced position, with spot and forward claims balanced by net spot and forward liabilities. Under these circumstances, they will not be able to buy £50,000,000 forward from the banks, except in the unlikely situation in which they have in prospect an import surplus of £50,000,000 for which importers require more sterling than exporters are able to provide.

The solution for the banks is found by selling £50,000,000 forward in London. In order to buy this much forward sterling (sell this many dollars forward), the London banks must buy the equivalent number of dollars ($120,000,000 at $2.40) in the spot market. In this fashion, the London and New York foreign exchange markets can be provided with working balances in each other's currencies without undertaking an exchange position, each market contracting to sell the spot exchange forward in the other. New York will then hold £50,000,000 spot and sell the same amount forward in London. London will hold $120,000,000 in New York, which it has sold forward to New York banks. Neither country has an open exchange position. Each has an inventory of exchange for sale to customers desiring it.[1]

If New York banks on balance want to open an exchange position, let

---

[1] It should perhaps be pointed out that the forward contract does not count as a current asset or liability in calculating capital movements. New York owns £50,000,000 and owes $120,000,000 spot. It is therefore on balance neither a borrower nor a lender. Conversely, London has a balance of assets and liabilities. So far as the capital movement is concerned, the currencies in which claims and debts are denominated make no difference. The forward contract is neither an asset nor a liability except in a contingent sense, in which it is both, so that it does not count in reckoning the balance of indebtedness.

us say £2,000,000 short, they can now sell this amount spot or forward. The spot sale will simply eliminate £2,000,000 of their £50,000,000 of working balances (a capital inflow into the United States, it may be observed). If they choose to make a forward sale, however, this must be done in London unless the nonbanking public in the United States fortuitously undertakes an equal exchange position of opposite sign, i.e., is willing to go £2,000,000 long. The forward sale of sterling in London by New York banks will require London banks to sell dollars and buy sterling forward. In order to keep their position covered, the latter will be obliged to buy more dollars spot. In this way the sale of forward sterling by New York banks would result in an increase in London deposits in New York (a capital inflow into the United States) in the amount of $4,800,000.

A debated point is whether the addition of facilities for forward trading to an exchange market alters the character of the exchange market. The general view is that it does. The theoretical possibility exists, however, that it does not. Whether it does or not in the real world, of course, is an empirical question. The answer depends on the relative volume of speculative and arbitrage funds.

Figure F.1 shows a market for three-month forward foreign exchange, with price on the vertical axis and quantity on the horizontal. In the northeast quadrant, supply and demand are positive, in the northwest quadrant, negative. The negatively sloped demand curve from speculators intersects the vertical axis at P_f, the zero quantity at a price which speculators, on balance, think will be the spot exchange rate in three months. At lower rates, they will speculate in favor of the currency; at higher rates their demand will be negative as, on balance, they sell it.

FIGURE F.1. The Speculative Demand and Arbitrage Supply of Three-Month Forward Exchange, Related to the Speculators' View of the Future and the Rate Dictated by the Interest Differential

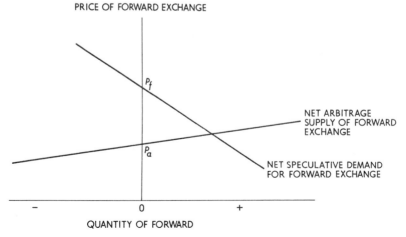

PRICE OF FORWARD EXCHANGE

P_f

NET ARBITRAGE SUPPLY OF FORWARD EXCHANGE

P_a

NET SPECULATIVE DEMAND FOR FORWARD EXCHANGE

−   0   +

QUANTITY OF FORWARD

P_a is the forward rate derived from the spot rate plus the interest differential. At this rate the net supply of forward exchange is zero, because the activity is not profitable. At higher rates of exchange arbitrageurs buy spot and sell forward. At lower rates the supply of forward exchange is negative, as they sell spot and buy forward.

As the figure is drawn, demand and supply for forward foreign exchange intersect in the right-hand quadrant, which means that the speculators have bought forward exchange supplied by arbitrageurs. It is assumed that numbers of speculators are limited and the supply of arbitrage funds is abundant. As a result the price is close to the interest differential, perhaps at the 0.5 percent boundary. If speculators were to change their view of the foreign forward currency and shift the point P_f to the other side of (below) P_a, the intersection would occur in the left-hand quadrant. In this circumstance, speculators would sell foreign forward exchange and arbitrageurs would buy it.

The view that a forward market makes no difference assumes that the interest arbitrage supply schedule is relatively flat, i.e. that there is a large amount of funds willing to invest in interest arbitrage. This means that the forward rate cannot depart widely from the interest differential, P_a, and that any shift in speculative activity in the forward market will be transmitted immediately to the spot market by means of arbitrage. If speculators revise their view of the future rate, for example, so that the demand schedule shifts upward and to the right as they buy more forward exchange, arbitrageurs will supply more at the same price, selling forward and buying spot. The purchase of forward has resulted merely in a purchase of spot—a capital movement—with no great change in the forward rate.

At the other extreme, if there is no arbitrage, the forward rate will be P_f, the rate at which short forward sellers are matched by long forward buyers. A change in the market's view of the three-month prospects will alter the rate. P_a will have no pull.

Between these extremes, of course, there is an infinitude of possibilities, with some slope normal in each schedule and the actual rate likely to end up somewhere between the rate dictated by the spot rate and the interest differential, and that representing the consensus of speculators. That this is an unsensational conclusion probably does not detract from its validity.

SUGGESTED READING

The major work on the subject of forward exchange is P. Einzig's *A Dynamic Theory of Forward Exchange* (London: Macmillan & Co., Ltd., 1961). Mr. Einzig is highly critical of the view expressed here that the addition of a forward market does not greatly alter the way the foreign exchange market performs. See also H. G. Grubel, *Forward Exchange, Speculation and the International Flow of Capital* (Stanford, Calif.: Stanford University Press, 1966), who holds that three-way arbitrage makes a significant difference; J. L. Stein, "The Nature and Efficiency of the Foreign Exchange Market," *EIF*, No. 40, June 1962; P. B. Kenen, "Trade Speculation and the Forward Exchange Rate," in R. E. Baldwin et al., *Trade, Growth, and the Balance of Payments* (Chicago: Rand McNally & Co., 1965); and F. R. Glahe, *An Empirical Study of the Foreign Exchange Market: Test of a Theory*, Princeton Studies in International Finance (Princeton, N.J.: Princeton University Press, 1967). The analysis in Figure F.1 was suggested in a seminar at the Massachusetts Institute of Technology by J. Kesselman. See also his paper on "The Role of Speculation in Forward Rate Determination: The Canadian Flexible Dollar," *Canadian Journal of Economics*, May 1971.

THE MARSHALL-LERNER CONDITION*

In this appendix we examine the model underlying the discussion of the Marshall-Lerner condition in Chapter 19 in a formal and rather exhaustive fashion. Let us assume two countries, A and B. We shall establish the conditions under which devaluation of A's currency improves its balance of trade, expressed in either foreign exchange or domestic currency. The following notation will be employed throughout.

X_A = A's physical quantity of exports.
M_A = A's physical quantity of imports.
X_B = B's physical quantity of exports.
M_B = B's physical quantity of imports.
p_x = Price of A's exports expressed in terms of A's currency.
p_m = Price of A's imports expressed in terms of A's currency.
r = Exchange rate expressed as units of A's currency paid per unit of B's currency.
e_x^A = A's elasticity of supply for exports.
e_m^A = A's elasticity of demand for imports.
e_x^B = B's elasticity of supply for exports.
e_m^B = B's elasticity of demand for imports.
V_m = Value of A's imports expressed in terms of A's currency.
V_x = Value of A's exports expressed in terms of A's currency.
B_d = A's balance of trade expressed in terms of A's currency.
B_f = A's balance of trade expressed in terms of foreign exchange (i.e., B's currency).
T = A's terms of trade, i.e., $\dfrac{p_x}{p_m}$.

Asterisks on p_x and p_m will imply that they are expressed in terms of B's currency.

Before embarking upon the formal analysis the reader is reminded of

---

* By Miltiades Chacholiades.

the following definitions, identities, functional relationships, and assumptions.

Definitions

$$e_x{}^A \equiv \frac{dX_A}{dp_x} \cdot \frac{p_x}{X_A} \equiv X'_A \frac{p_x}{X_A}$$

$$e_m{}^A \equiv \frac{dM_A}{dp_m} \cdot \frac{p_m}{M_A} \equiv M'_A \frac{p_m}{M_A}$$

$$e_x{}^B \equiv \frac{dX_B}{d(p_{m/r})} \cdot \frac{p_m/r}{X_B} \equiv X'_B \frac{p_m}{rX_B}$$

$$e_m{}^B \equiv \frac{dM_B}{d(p_{x/r})} \cdot \frac{p_x/r}{M_B} \equiv M'_B \frac{p_x}{rM_B}$$

$$V_m \equiv p_m M_A \equiv p_m X_B$$

$$V_x \equiv p_x X_A \equiv p_x M_B$$

Identities[1]

$$M_A = X_B \qquad\qquad p_x{}^* = \frac{p_x}{r}$$

$$X_A = M_B \qquad\qquad p_m{}^* = \frac{p_m}{r}$$

Functional Relationships

$$X_A = X_A(p_x)$$
$$M_A = M_A(p_m)$$
$$X_B = X_B(p_m/r)$$
$$M_B = M_B(p_x/r)$$

The independent variables in parentheses that appear in the above relationships will be omitted in what follows in order to simplify the notation. The reader is advised, however, to keep them in mind.

Assumptions

$$\frac{dX_A}{dp_x} \equiv X'_A \geq 0, \qquad \frac{dM_A}{dp_m} \equiv M'_A \leq 0,$$

$$\frac{dX_B}{d(p_m/r)} \equiv X'_B \geq 0, \qquad \frac{dM_B}{d(p_x/r)} \equiv M'_B \leq 0.$$

---

[1] The reader is reminded that these identities hold for the *ex post* (or realized) quantities traded. They should not be confused with the willingness to export or import. However, when the export and import markets are in equilibrium, the two coincide.

Effects of Devaluation on A's Balance of Trade Expressed in Terms of B's Currency

A simplifying assumption usually made to render the arithmetic more easily manageable is that the supply elasticities in both countries are infinite. Thus the domestic prices of each country's exports expressed in terms of its own currency (i.e., p_x and $p_m{}^* = p_m/r$) are constants. This assumption, of course, does some violation to the facts. For this reason it is considered desirable to indicate briefly in the final section of this appendix how the general case can be handled.

A's export revenue expressed in terms of B's currency is equal to $(p_x/r)X_A$. However, since $e_x{}^A$ is assumed infinite, this product does not have much meaning except in relation to B's demand for imports. In other words, under the assumption of infinite supply elasticities, the foreign demand is the limiting factor of the export revenue. Thus, A's export revenue should be written as: $(p_x/r)M_B$. In the same way, A's expenditure on imports expressed in terms of B's currency is equal to: $(p_m/r)M_A \equiv p_m{}^*M_A$. Finally, A's balance of trade expressed in terms of B's currency is defined as follows:

$$B_f = \left(\frac{p_x}{r}\right) M_B - p_m{}^* M_A. \tag{1}$$

Our problem is to find out what happens to B_f when r increases (i.e., when A's currency is devalued). In other words, we are interested in the value of the derivative dB_f/dr. More specifically, we are interested to know whether A's balance of trade improves (i.e., $dB_f/dr > 0$), deteriorates (i.e., $dB_f/dr < 0$), or, remains the same (i.e., $dB_f/dr = 0$). Of course, the precise numerical value of dB_f/dr is of great importance too. Thus, assuming the $dB_f/dr > 0$, the higher the derivative dB_f/dr, the smaller the degree of devaluation necessary to eliminate a certain deficit. In this appendix, however, we are interested only in knowing the conditions under which devaluation is successful, irrespective of the degree of success.[2]

Differentiating[3] B_f with respect to r, we get

$$\frac{dB_f}{dr} = -\frac{p_x}{r^2}M_B - \frac{p_x}{r}M_B'\frac{p_x}{r^2} - p_m{}^*M_A'p_m{}^*$$

$$= \frac{V_x}{r^2}\left(-1 - \frac{M_B'}{M_B}\cdot\frac{p_x}{r} - \frac{V_m}{V_x}\frac{M_A'}{M_A}p_m\right).$$

Using now the definitions of elasticities given previously, we get

---

[2] The student whose calculus is rusty will find in a very brief mathematical note at the end of this appendix all the rules used below. Besides these few rules, only high school algebra is necessary.

[3] We shall adopt the convention of using primes to indicate derivatives, i.e.,

$$\frac{dM_A}{dp_m} = M_A', \quad \frac{dM_B}{dp_x{}^*} = M_B'.$$

$$\frac{dB_f}{dr} = \frac{V_x}{r^2}\left(-1 - e_m{}^B - \frac{V_m}{V_x} e_m{}^A\right).$$ (2)

Devaluation (i.e., an increase in r) improves the balance of trade (i.e., it increases B_f in algebraic terms) when $dB_f/dr > 0$. This occurs when the expression in parenthesis on the right-hand side of equation (2) is greater than zero. In other words, devaluation improves the balance of trade when:

$$-1 - e_m{}^B - \frac{V_m}{V_x} e_m{}^A > 0$$

or

$$-e_m{}^B - \frac{V_m}{V_x} e_m{}^A > 1.$$ (3)

If B's demand for imports is elastic (i.e., $e_m{}^B < -1$), then A's balance of trade always improves with devaluation, as can be verified by inequality (3). If B's demand for imports is inelastic, the outcome can be anything. It will all depend upon the condition of the balance of trade before devaluation (or, more precisely, on the ratio V_m/V_x) and A's elasticity of demand for imports. The larger the ratio V_m/V_x and the higher A's demand elasticity (in absolute terms), the bigger the chance for balance-of-trade improvement.

A country will never consider devaluation unless it suffers from a balance-of-trade deficit. Thus, according to the previous paragraph, the least favorable situation for successful devaluation, as far as the balance of trade is concerned, is when we start with a balanced trade, i.e., $V_m = V_x$. In this case, inequality (3) becomes:

$$-e_m{}^A - e_m{}^B > 1.$$ (4)

Inequality (4) is what is known in the literature as the Marshall-Lerner condition. In words, devaluation always improves the balance of trade expressed in terms of foreign exchange when the sum of the two demand elasticities (taken in absolute terms) is greater than unity. If we start with a balance-of-trade deficit, the Marshall-Lerner condition becomes sufficient. That is because

$$-e_m{}^B - \frac{V_m}{V_x} e_m{}^A \geq -e_m{}^A - e_m{}^B$$

where the equality sign holds when $e_m{}^A = 0$. Thus, when $-e_m{}^A - e_m{}^B > 1$, we must also have $-e_m{}^B - (V_m/V_x)e_m{}^A > 1$. The reverse is not true, however. Hence, the balance of trade might improve even when the Marshall-Lerner condition is not satisfied.

Effects of Devaluation on A's Balance of Trade Expressed in Terms of A's Currency

By definition, $B_d = rB_f$, hence,

$$\frac{dB_d}{dr} = B_f + r\frac{dB_f}{dr}.$$ (5)

If the balance of trade is in equilibrium to begin with, equation (5) takes the form:

$$\frac{dB_d}{dr} = r\,\frac{dB_f}{dr}.$$

Therefore, when $B_d = B_f = 0$, dB_d/dr is positive if and only if dB_f/dr is positive. Thus the previously derived conclusions for improving B_f also guarantee improvement in B_d. However, when the balance of trade is out of equilibrium before devaluation, there emerges a divergence between these conditions. In particular, if we start with a deficit, an improvement in B_d necessarily implies a correcsponding improvement in B_f. But the reverse is not generally true. The real possibility of having an improvement in B_f and a deterioration in B_d exists and cannot be eliminated by any deductive reasoning.

Substituting the values of B_f and dB_f/dr, as given by equations (1) and (2) respectively, into equation (5) and rearranging, we get:

$$\frac{dB_d}{r} = \frac{V_x}{r} - \frac{V_m}{r} + \frac{V_x}{r}\left(-1 - e_m{}^B - \frac{V_m}{V_x}e_m{}^A\right)$$

$$= \frac{V_m}{r}\left(-1 - e_m{}^A - \frac{V_x}{V_m}e_m{}^B\right).$$

Thus, B_d improves with devaluation only when:

$$-(V_x/V_m)e_m{}^B - e_m{}^A > 1. \tag{6}$$

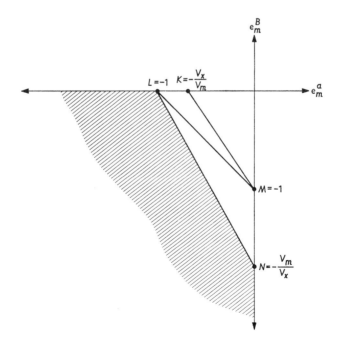

If A's demand for imports is elastic, B_d always improves with devaluation. It should be pointed out, however, that the Marshall-Lerner condition is not sufficient for improving B_d. On the other hand, condition (6) does imply the Marshall-Lerner condition. This is illustrated in the following diagram. Any point in the shaded area satisfies inequalities (3) and (6), as well as the Marshall-Lerner condition. Hence, any combination of demand elasticities lying in this region is sufficient for improving both B_f and B_d. However, any point in the triangle LMN satisfies inequality (3) and the Marshall-Lerner condition (and thus B_f improves), but it does not satisfy condition (6) (and thus B_d deteriorates). Finally, any point in the triangle KLM satisfies only inequality (3). Thus, B_f improves—though the Marshall-Lerner condition is not satisfied—and B_d deteriorates. The areas of these triangles obviously depend on the ratio V_m/V_x. As V_m/V_x increases, points K and N move away from points L and M respectively, and the two triangles become bigger and bigger. On the other hand, as V_m/V_x decreases, both triangles shrink. When $V_m/V_x = 1$, points K and N coincide with points L and M, respectively, and both triangles vanish, together with the paradoxes they give rise to. Finally it should be pointed out that when B's demand elasticity is zero, the Marshall-Lerner condition is sufficient for improving B_d. This is a general proposition which holds irrespective of the values of the supply elasticities.

Effects of Devaluation with Supply Elasticities Less than Infinite[4]

In this general case, the derivative of B_f with respect to r is equal to:

$$\frac{dB_f}{dr} = \frac{V_x}{r^2}\left[\frac{V_m}{V_x}\frac{e_m{}^A(1+e_x{}^B)}{(e_m{}^A - e_x{}^B)} - \frac{e_x{}^A(1+e_m{}^B)}{(e_x{}^A - e_m{}^B)}\right] \tag{7}$$

or

$$\frac{dB_f}{dr} = \frac{e_x{}^A e_x{}^B V_x}{r^2(e_x{}^B - e_m{}^A)(e_x{}^A - e_m{}^B)}\left[\frac{e_m{}^A e_m{}^B}{e_x{}^A e_x{}^B}\left(\frac{V_m}{V_x} + \frac{V_m}{V_x}e_x{}^B + e_x{}^A\right)\right.$$
$$\left. + \frac{e_m{}^A}{e_x{}^B}\left(1 - \frac{V_m}{V_x}\right) + e_m{}^A\frac{V_x - V_m}{V_x} - (1 + e_m{}^A + e_m{}^B)\right]. \tag{8}$$

Further, substituting the values of B_f and dB_f/dr, as given by equations (1) and (7) respectively, into equation (5), we also get:

$$\frac{dB_d}{dr} = \frac{V_x}{r}\left[\frac{V_m}{V_x}\frac{e_x{}^B(1+e_m{}^A)}{e_m{}^A - e_x{}^B} - \frac{e_m{}^B(1+e_x{}^A)}{e_x{}^A - e_m{}^B}\right]. \tag{9}$$

B_f does not change with devaluation (i.e., $dB_f/dr = 0$) in the following two cases: (a) when A's elasticities are zero (i.e., $e_x{}^A = e_m{}^A = 0$) and (b)

[4] See J. Robinson in American Economic Association, *Readings in the Theory of International Trade*, p. 90, n. 8, and J. Vanek, *International Trade Theory and Economic Policy* (Homewood, Ill.: Richard D. Irwin, Inc., 1962), chap. 5.

when the balance of trade is in equilibrium before devaluation and B's elasticities are zero (i.e., $B_f = e_x{}^B = e_m{}^B = 0$). On the other hand, B_d does not change with devaluation in the following two cases: (c) when B's supply elasticities are zero (i.e., $e_x{}^B = e_m{}^B = 0$), and (d) when the balance of trade is in equilibrium before devaluation and A's elasticities are zero (i.e., $B_d = e_x{}^A = e_m{}^A = 0$). These statements can be verified through direct substitution in equations (7) and (9).

When both supply elasticities are zero (i.e., $e_x{}^A = e_x{}^B = 0$), equations (7) and (9) become:

$$\frac{dB_f}{dr} = \frac{V_m}{r^2} > 0$$

and

$$\frac{dB_d}{dr} = \frac{V_x}{r} > 0,$$

respectively. In other words, when both supply elasticities are zero, both B_d and B_f improve with devaluation—excluding, of course, the singular cases (a) through (d) referred to in the previous paragraph.[5]

The right-hand side of equation (8) is the production of a ratio which is generally positive and a long bracketed expression. For $dB_f/dr > 0$, the bracketed expression must be positive. Now, this expression consists of four terms. The first three are always nonnegative, provided the balance of trade is not in surplus to begin with. Hence, if the fourth term is strictly positive, we know that $dB_f/dr > 0$, and therefore the balance of trade improves with devaluation—except in the two cases (a) and (b) referred to above. But the condition that this fourth term be positive is simply the Marshall-Lerner condition. In other words, excluding the two singular cases referred to above, the Marshall-Lerner condition is generally sufficient but not necessary for successful devaluation. It should be observed that when the first three terms of the bracketed expression of equation (8) drop to zero, the Marshall-Lerner condition becomes both necessary and sufficient. This happens in the following three cases: (i) when A's demand elasticity is equal to zero (i.e., $e_m{}^A = 0$), (ii) when the balance of trade is in equilibrium to begin with and B's demand elasticity is equal to zero (i.e., $B_f = e_m{}^B = 0$), and (iii) when the balance of trade is in equilibrium to begin with and both supply elasticities are infinite.

If A's demand for imports is elastic, B_f improves with devaluation except when $B_f = e_x{}^B = e_m{}^B = 0$. Also, if B's demand for imports is elastic, B_f improves with devaluation except when $e_x{}^A = e_m{}^A = 0$. Further, when A's demand for imports is elastic, B_d improves except in the singular case $e_x{}^B = e_m{}^B = 0$. Also, if $e_x{}^B = 0$, B_d always improves except in the two singular cases (c) and (d). It should be pointed out, finally, that the condition $e_m{}^B < -1$ is neither sufficient nor necessary for improving B_d.

---

[5] The cases (i) $e^A = e^B_m = 0$ and (ii) $e^A_m = e^B_x = 0$ should be excluded because the balance of trade cannot be meaningfully defined.

Mathematical Note

Assume that u and v are continuous, differentiable functions of x. The following are the only rules of differentiation used in this appendix.

a) *Differentiation of a Sum.* The derivative of the sum $(u + v)$ with respect to x is given by the formula:

$$\frac{d}{dx}(u + v) = u' + v'.$$

b) *Differentiation of a Product.* The derivative of the product uv with respect to x is given by the formula:

$$\frac{d}{dx}(uv) = vu' + uv'.$$

c) *Differentiation of a Quotient.* The derivative of the quotient u/v with respect to x is given by the formula:

$$\frac{d}{dx}\left(\frac{u}{v}\right) = \frac{vu' - uv'}{v^2}.$$

d) *Differentiation of a Function of a Function.* The derivative of the compound function $f(u)$ with respect to x is given by the formula:

$$\frac{df(u)}{dx} = f'(u)u'.$$

FOREIGN-TRADE MULTIPLIERS*

The Keynesian macroeconomic model underlying the discussion of Chapter 20 is examined more rigorously in this appendix. Although the discussion will not depart from the Keynesian assumptions of the text in any major view, it is formulated in such a general way as to leave the door open for the analysis of more complicated cases. It should be pointed out, however, that in the final section of this appendix some policy problems are considered briefly. These problems do not require any additional mathematical tools other than those required for the rest of this appendix. Nevertheless, they lead to more complicated algebraic expressions. If the student is not particularly interested in these problems, he is advised to skip that section.

The following notation will be used throughout this appendix.

Y_A = National income in country A.
C_A = Total consumption in country A.
I_A = Total investment in country A.
G_A = Total government expenditure in country A.
X_A = Total exports of country A.
M_A = Total importsof country A.
S_A = Total savings in Country A.
Z_A = Total absorption in country A.
C_{Ad} = The part of A's total consumption produced by domestic resources.
I_{Ad} = The part of A's total investment produced by domestic resources.
G_{Ad} = The part of A's total government expenditure on domestic resources.
X_{Ad} = The part of A's total exports produced by domestic resources.
Z_{Ad} = The part of A's total absorption of domestic resources.
C_{Af} = The part of A's consumption produced by foreign resources.
I_{Af} = The part of A's total investment produced by foreign resources.
G_{Af} = The part of A's total goverment expenditure on foreign resources.

---

* By Miltiades Chacholiades.

X_{Af} = The part of A's total exports produced by foreign resources.
Z_{Af} = The part of A's total absorption of foreign resources.
α = Shift parameter.
p_A = Policy parameter in country A.
λ, μ = Arbitrary constants.
T = A's balance of trade.

A similar notation with subscript B applies to country B.

Functional Relationships and Identities

$C_A, C_{Ad}, C_{Af}, I_A, I_{Ad}, I_{Af}, G_A, G_{Ad}, G_{Af}$, and S_A are assumed to be continuous differentiable functions of Y_A; and similarly for country B.[1] M_A is assumed to be a continuous differentiable function of Y_A, α, and P_A, whereas M_B is assumed to be a continuous differentiable function of Y_B, α, and p_B.

We shall adopt the convention of writing "primes" for first partial derivatives of the above variables with respect to Y. In other words,

$$C_A' = \frac{\partial C_A}{\partial Y_A}, \quad I_A' = \frac{\partial I_A}{\partial Y_A},$$

and so forth.

Before embarking upon our main problem, the following identities are worth noting:

$$C_A = C_{Ad} + C_{Af} \tag{1}$$
$$I_A = I_{Ad} + I_{Af} \tag{2}$$
$$G_A = G_{Ad} + G_{Af} \tag{3}$$
$$X_A = X_{Ad} + X_{Af} \tag{4}$$
$$M_A = C_{Af} + I_{Af} + G_{Af} + X_{Af} \tag{5}$$
$$Z_A = C_A + I_A + G_A \tag{6}$$
$$Z_{Ad} = C_{Ad} + I_{Ad} + G_{Ad} \tag{7}$$
$$Z_{Af} = C_{Af} + I_{Af} + G_{Af} = M_A - X_{Af} \tag{8}$$
$$Z_A = Z_{Ad} + Z_{Af} \tag{9}$$
$$M_A = X_B \tag{10}$$
$$M_B = X_A \tag{11}$$
$$T = X_A - M_A = M_B - M_A \tag{12}$$
$$C_A' = C_{Ad}' + C_{Af}' \tag{13}$$
$$I_A' = I_{Ad}' + I_{Af}' \tag{14}$$
$$G_A' = G_{Ad}' + G_{Af}' \tag{15}$$
$$Z_A' = Z_{Ad}' + Z_{Af}' \tag{16}$$

---

[1] It should be pointed out that C is rather a function of disposable income, $Y_d = Y - t$, where t stands for taxes. However, since t is a function of Y, we can consider C as a function of Y directly. This facilitates the algebra. The student should bear in mind, however, that S stands for the sum: private saving (i.e., $Y_d - C$) plus taxes.

$$Y_A = C_A + I_A + G_A + X_A - M_A \tag{17}$$
$$Y_A = C_{Ad} + I_{Ad} + G_{Ad} + X_{Ad} \tag{18}$$
$$Y_A = Z_A + T = Z_{Ad} + X_{Ad} \tag{19}$$
$$S_A = Y_A - C_A \tag{20}$$
$$S_A + M_A = I_A + G_A + X_A \tag{21}$$
$$S_A + C_{Af} = I_{Ad} + G_{Ad} + X_{Ad} \tag{22}$$
$$C_A' + S_A' = 1 \tag{23}$$
$$C_{Ad}' + C_{Af}' + S_A' = 1 \tag{24}$$

If $I_{Af}' = G_{Af}' = 0$, then $M_A' = C_{Af}'$, and identity (24) takes the form:

$$C_{Ad}' + M_A' + S_A' = 1. \tag{25}$$

The same identities hold for country B as well.

In view of the fact that the above identities are elementary in nature, no explanation will be offered.

The Basic Model

The most general form of the basic income identities of the two countries A and B for our purposes is identity (17). Some writers prefer identity (18) over identity (17). This does not give rise to inconsistent results, provided the assumptions of the two groups of writers are identical. Despite the obvious simplicity of identity (18), identity (17) is much richer and permits the formulation of several problems—in particular policy problems—with less effort and complexity. In this appendix we shall work with (17). We thus start with the following system:

$$Y_A = Z_A + M_B - M_A + \mu\alpha \tag{26}$$

$$Y_B = Z_B + M_A - M_B + \lambda\alpha. \tag{27}$$

In the initial equilibrium the parameter α is assumed to be equal to zero. Our problem is what happens to national income when a change occurs, i.e., when α shifts for one reason or another, and how to derive the foreign-trade multiplier $dY/d\alpha$, which will differ for different types of shift in α. We must also explain the constants λ and μ.

The best way to clarify the meaning and function of these parameters is to consider various concrete cases. In so doing, we shall be able to clarify several other points as well.

1. An autonomous increase (decrease) in Z_{Ad} (i.e., an autonomous change in the absorption of domestically produced goods) can be treated as an autonomous increase (decrease) in the parameter α, with the constants μ and λ taking the values 1 and 0, respectively. Further,

$$\frac{\partial M_A}{\partial \alpha} = \frac{\partial M_B}{\partial \alpha} = 0.$$

2. An autonomous increase (decrease) in Z_{Af} (i.e., an autonomous change in A's absorption of B's goods—which has to be distinguished from a shift in the composition of A's expenditure in favor of its imports referred to below—can be treated as an autonomous increase (decrease) in the parameter α, with the constants μ and λ taking the values 1 and 0, respectively. Also $\partial M_A/\partial\alpha = 1$. However, as far as $\partial M_B/\partial\alpha$ is concerned, we have to distinguish between the following two cases: (a) when the autonomous increase in B's exports does not give rise to a simultaneous increase in B's imports, i.e., when only X_{Bd} changes, and (b) when the autonomous increase in B's exports does give rise to a simultaneous increase in B's imports, i.e., when both X_{Bf} and X_{Bd} change. In the first case, we have $\partial M_B/\partial\alpha = 0$. In the second, $\partial M_B/\partial\alpha > 0$.

3. An autonomous increase (decrease) in Z_A may be due to an increase (decrease) in Z_{Ad}, or Z_{Af}, or both. The first two alternatives have been treated in cases 1 and 2, respectively. In the present case, the third alternative (i.e., a change in both Z_{Ad} and Z_{Af}) will be considered. This again can be treated as an autonomous change in α, with the constants μ and λ taking the values 1 and 0, respectively. Further, $\partial M_B/\partial\alpha = 0$, and $0 < \partial M_A/\partial\alpha < 1$.

At this stage it is necessary to point out that the partial derivative $\partial M_A/\partial\alpha$ is not in general equal to A's marginal propensity to import, i.e., M'_A. In the first place, since we are talking about an *autonomous* change, the partial derivative (i.e., the number of cents out of every dollar of the autonomous change in A's expenditure spent on B's products) may take any value whatsoever between 0 and 1. But besides this important reason, there is another more fundamental reason why $\partial M_A/\partial\alpha \neq M'_A$. The marginal propensity to import (M'_A) shows how much out of each extra dollar increase in A's *national income* is spent on imports. On the other hand, the partial derivative $\partial M_A/\partial\alpha$ shows how much out of each extra dollar increase in A's *expenditure* is spent on imports. But when A's national income increases by ΔY_A, A's expenditure does not increase by ΔY_A; it rather increases by $\Delta Y_A(1 - S'_A)$. Further, an increase in expenditure by $\Delta Y_A(1 - S'_A)$ gives rise to an increase in imports equal to:

$$\Delta M_A = \Delta Y_A(1 - S'_A)\frac{\partial M_A}{\partial\alpha}.$$

Hence,

$$\frac{\Delta M_A}{\Delta Y_A} = (1 - S'_A)\frac{\partial M_A}{\partial\alpha}. \tag{28}$$

Thus, if the autonomous change in A's expenditure is divided between expenditure on domestic and on foreign goods according to the existing marginal propensities, the partial derivative $\partial M_A/\partial\alpha$ is not equal to M'_A.

4. An autonomous shift in the *composition* of A's expenditure can be treated as an autonomous change in the parameter α, with the constants

λ and μ being zero. For a shift from domestic goods to foreign, the partial derivative $\partial M_A/\partial \alpha$ takes the value of 1. On the other hand, for a shift from foreign to domestic goods, the partial derivative $\partial M_A/\partial \alpha$ takes the value of -1. The value of $\partial M_B/\partial \alpha$ is determined as in case (2) above.

5. An autonomous increase in X_{Ad} may be due to either an autonomous increase in B's expenditure on A's products or a shift in the composition of B's expenditure in favor of A's products. If the increase in X_{Ad} is due to a net increase in B's expenditure on A's products, then we have the following:

$$\mu = 0, \lambda = 1, \frac{\partial M_A}{\partial \alpha} = 0, \frac{\partial M_B}{\partial \alpha} = 1 .$$

If, on the other hand, the increase in X_{Ad} is due to a shift in B's expenditure in favor of A's products, we have:

$$\mu = 0, \lambda = 0, \frac{\partial M_B}{\partial \alpha} = 1, \frac{\partial M_A}{\partial \alpha} = 0 .$$

For a decrease in X_{Ad}, we must have $\partial M_B/\partial \alpha = -1$ in the above two cases. All other parameters retain the same values.

6. An autonomous increase Z_{Ad} matched exactly by an autonomous decrease in Z_{Bd} can be treated as a change in α, with the constants λ and μ taking the values -1 and 1, respectively. Further,

$$\frac{\partial M_A}{\partial \alpha} = \frac{\partial M_B}{\partial \alpha} = 0 .$$

Other examples of this nature are left to the reader.

The Foreign-Trade Multiplier without Foreign Repercussion

Since the foreign repercussion is absent in this section, we dispense with the subscripts A and B. Thus, the basic income identity takes the form:

$$Y = Z + X - M + \lambda \alpha \qquad (29)$$

where the parameter α has zero value in the initial equilibrium. Differentiating equation (29) totally with respect to α, we get:

$$\frac{dY}{d\alpha} = \frac{\lambda - \dfrac{\partial M}{\partial \alpha}}{1 - Z' + M'} . \qquad (30)$$

We are now ready to study the following specific cases:

a) An autonomous increase in Z_d or X_d, which implies $\lambda = 1, \dfrac{\partial M}{\partial \alpha} = 0$.

b) An autonomous increase in Z or X, which implies $\lambda = 1, \dfrac{\partial M}{\partial \alpha} > 0$, or more specifically, $\dfrac{\partial M}{\partial \alpha} = \dfrac{M'}{1 - S'} .$

c) An autonomous shift in the composition of expenditure in favor of domestic goods, which implies $\lambda = 0$. $\dfrac{\partial M}{\partial \alpha} = < - 1$.

The results are tabulated in table H.1.

TABLE H.1

Case (a)	Case (b)	Case (c)
$\lambda = 1, \dfrac{\partial M}{\partial \alpha} = 0$	$\lambda = 1, \dfrac{\partial M}{\partial \alpha} = \dfrac{M'}{1 - S'}$	$\lambda = 0, \dfrac{\partial M}{\partial \alpha} = -1$
$\dfrac{dY}{d\alpha} = \dfrac{1}{1 - Z' + M'}$	$\dfrac{dY}{d\alpha} = \dfrac{1 - S' - M'}{(1 - Z' + M')(1 - S')}$	$\dfrac{dY}{d\alpha} = \dfrac{1}{1 - Z' + M'}$

Foreign-Trade Multipliers with Foreign Repercussion

Differentiating equations (26), (27), and (12) totally with respect to α, we get:

$$\frac{dY_A}{d\alpha} = Z'_A \frac{dY_A}{d\alpha} + \left(\frac{\partial M_B}{\partial \alpha} + \frac{\partial M_B}{\partial Y_B} \frac{dY_B}{d\alpha} \right) - \left(\frac{\partial M_A}{\partial \alpha} + \frac{\partial M_A}{\partial Y_A} \frac{dY_A}{d\alpha} \right) + \mu \quad (31)$$

$$\frac{dY_B}{d\alpha} = Z'_B \frac{dY_B}{d\alpha} + \left(\frac{\partial M_A}{\partial \alpha} + \frac{\partial M_A}{\partial Y_A} \frac{dY_A}{d\alpha} \right) - \left(\frac{\partial M_B}{\partial \alpha} + \frac{\partial M_B}{\partial Y_B} \frac{dY_B}{d\alpha} \right) + \lambda \quad (32)$$

$$\frac{dT}{\partial \alpha} = \left(\frac{\partial M_B}{\partial \alpha} + \frac{\partial M_B}{\partial Y_B} \frac{dY_B}{d\alpha} \right) - \left(\frac{\partial M_A}{\partial \alpha} + \frac{\partial M_A}{\partial Y_A} \frac{dY_A}{d\alpha} \right) . \quad (33)$$

Solving equations (31) and (32) simultaneously, we get:

$$\frac{dY_A}{d\alpha} = \frac{1}{\Delta} \left[(1 - Z'_B) \left(\frac{\partial M_B}{\partial \alpha} - \frac{\partial M_A}{\partial \alpha} + \mu \right) + (\mu + \lambda) M'_B \right] \quad (34)$$

$$\frac{dY_B}{d\alpha} = \frac{1}{\Delta} \left[(1 - Z'_A) \left(\frac{\partial M_A}{\partial \alpha} - \frac{\partial M_B}{\partial \alpha} + \lambda \right) + (\mu + \lambda) M'_A \right] \quad (35)$$

where

$$\Delta = (1 - Z'_A + M'_A)(1 - Z'_B + M'_B) - M'_A M'_B . \quad (36)$$

Substituting these results into (33), we also get

$$\frac{dT}{d\alpha} = \left(\frac{\partial M_B}{\partial \alpha} - \frac{\partial M_A}{\partial \alpha} \right) + \frac{1}{\Delta} \left[M'_B (1 - Z'_A) \left(\frac{\partial M_A}{\partial \alpha} - \frac{\partial M_B}{\partial \alpha} + \lambda \right) \right.$$
$$\left. - M'_A (1 - Z'_B) \left(\frac{\partial M_B}{\partial \alpha} - \frac{\partial M_A}{\partial \alpha} + \mu \right) \right] . \quad (37)$$

Equations (34) and (35) are the most general forms of the foreign-trade multipliers. We do not plan to apply these multiplier formulas to all cases considered previously. This is left as an exercise for the student. We shall, however, consider one case referred to in the text. Thus, for an autonomous increase in expenditure on A's goods which may come about either through an increase in Z_{Ad} (in which case we have $\lambda = 0$,

$\dfrac{\partial M_B}{\partial \alpha} = 0, \dfrac{\partial M_A}{\partial \alpha} = 0, \mu = 1$), or, an increase in X_{Ad} due to a net increase in

B's expenditure on A's products (in which case we must have $\mu = 0, \lambda = 1$,

$\dfrac{\partial M_A}{\partial \alpha} = 0, \dfrac{\partial M_B}{\partial \alpha} = 1$), the multiplier formulas (34) and (35) take, respec-

tively, the following specific forms:

$$\frac{dY_A}{d\alpha} = \frac{1 - Z'_B + M'_B}{(1 - Z'_A + M'_A)(1 - Z'_B + M'_B) - M'_A M'_B} \tag{38}$$

$$\frac{dY_B}{d\alpha} = \frac{M'_A}{(1 - Z'_A + M'_A)(1 - Z'_B + M'_B) - M'_A M'_B} \tag{39}$$

Further, if $I'_A = G'_A = I'_B = G'_B = 0$, then $Z'_A = C'_A$ and $Z'_B = C'_B$, and equations (38) and (39) become:

$$\frac{dY_A}{d\alpha} = \frac{1 + \dfrac{M'_B}{S'_B}}{S'_A + M'_A + M'_B \dfrac{S'_A}{S'_B}} \tag{40}$$

$$\frac{dY_B}{d\alpha} = \frac{M'_A}{S'_A S'_B + S'_A M'_B + S'_B M'_A} \cdot \tag{41}$$

Policy Considerations

The previous analysis is now extended to cover the case where one or the other or both countries adopt certain policy measures to nullify the effects of an *autonomous* change on a target variable, such as the national income (internal balance) or the balance of trade (external balance). For this purpose, equations (26) and (27) are modified as follows:

$$Y_A = Z_A + M_B - M_A + \mu\alpha + p_A \tag{42}$$

$$Y_B = Z_B + M_A - M_B + \lambda\alpha + p_B \tag{43}$$

In the initial equilibrium position, all parameters (i.e., p_A, p_B and α) are equal to zero. When an autonomous change takes place, it can be treated again as a change in the parameter α, with the constants λ and μ taking the appropriate values as before. But now we have to consider the policy parameters as well. Whenever one country does not pursue any policy whatsoever, its policy parameter does not change when α changes, i.e., $dp/d\alpha = 0$. Thus, when both countries do not pursue any policy, all previous conclusions can also be derived from this general formulation when we put $dp_A/d\alpha = dp_B/d\alpha = 0$. However, when a country does pursue a policy for either internal or external balance, we must have $dp/d\alpha \neq 0$, in general. Further, $dp/d\alpha$ is not a datum, but it has to be determined in such a way as to satisfy the policy objective pursued. The technique of determining the right value for $dp/d\alpha$ will become clear in what follows.

Let us first consider this problem in the simple case where foreign repercussion is absent. We again dispense temporarily with the subscripts A and B. Thus, the basic income identity takes the form:

$$Y = Z + X - M + \lambda\alpha + p, \tag{44}$$

where the parameters α and p have zero values in the initial equilibrium position. Differentiating equation (44) totally with respect to α and rearranging, we get

$$\frac{dY}{d\alpha} = \frac{\lambda - \dfrac{\partial M}{\partial \alpha} - \dfrac{\partial M}{\partial p}\dfrac{dp}{d\alpha} + \dfrac{dp}{d\alpha}}{1 - Z' + M'}. \tag{45}$$

If a policy for internal balance is pursued, we must also have: $dY/d\alpha = 0$. Substituting this into (45), we end up with:

$$\frac{dp}{d\alpha} = \frac{\dfrac{\partial M}{\partial \alpha} - \lambda}{1 - \dfrac{\partial M}{\partial p}}. \tag{46}$$

Equation (46) gives us the required rate of change of the policy parameter per unit change of α, which guarantees internal balance.

If a policy for external balance is pursued, we must have:

$$\frac{dT}{d\alpha} = -\left(\frac{\partial M}{\partial \alpha} + M'\frac{dY}{d\alpha} + \frac{\partial M}{\partial p}\frac{dp}{d\alpha}\right) = 0. \tag{47}$$

Equations (45) and (47) can now be solved simultaneously for $dY/d\alpha$ and $dp/d\alpha$.

In order to allow for foreign repercussion, we differentiate equations (42), (43), and (12) totally with respect to α.

$$\frac{dY_A}{d\alpha} = Z'_A\frac{dY_A}{d\alpha} + \left(\frac{\partial M_B}{\partial \alpha} + \frac{\partial M_B}{\partial p_B}\frac{dp_B}{d\alpha} + \frac{\partial M_B}{\partial Y_B}\frac{dY_B}{d\alpha}\right)$$
$$- \left(\frac{\partial M_A}{\partial \alpha} + \frac{\partial M_A}{\partial p_A}\frac{dp_A}{d\alpha} + \frac{\partial M_A}{\partial Y_A}\frac{dY_A}{d\alpha}\right) + \mu + \frac{dp_A}{d\alpha} \tag{48}$$

$$\frac{dY_B}{d\alpha} = Z'_B\frac{dY_B}{d\alpha} + \left(\frac{\partial M_A}{\partial \alpha} + \frac{\partial M_A}{\partial p_A}\frac{dp_A}{d\alpha} + M'_A\frac{dY_A}{d\alpha}\right)$$
$$- \left(\frac{\partial M_B}{\partial \alpha} + \frac{\partial M_B}{\partial p_B}\frac{dp_B}{d\alpha} + M'_B\frac{dY_B}{d\alpha}\right) + \lambda + \frac{dp_B}{d\alpha} \tag{49}$$

$$\frac{dT}{d\alpha} = \left(\frac{\partial M_B}{\partial \alpha} + \frac{\partial M_B}{\partial p_B} \frac{dp_B}{d\alpha} + M'_B \frac{dY_B}{d\alpha} \right) -$$

$$- \left(\frac{\partial M_A}{\partial \alpha} + \frac{\partial M_A}{\partial p_A} \frac{dp_A}{d\alpha} + \frac{\partial M_A}{\partial Y_A} \frac{dY_A}{d\alpha} \right) \quad (50)$$

The above three equations contain five unknowns, i.e., $dY_A/d\alpha$, $dY_B/d\alpha$, $dp_A/d\alpha$, $dp_B/d\alpha$ and $dT/d\alpha$. Thus, in order to be able to solve this system uniquely, two additional equations must be specified. This is done as soon as we know what policy is pursued by each country. All possible policy combinations are tabulated in Table H.2.

TABLE H.2

A's Policy B's Policy	No policy	Internal balance	External balance
No Policy	$\frac{dp_B}{d\alpha} = \frac{dp_A}{d\alpha} = 0$	$\frac{dp_B}{d\alpha} = 0, \frac{dY_A}{d\alpha} = 0$	$\frac{dp_B}{d\alpha} = 0, \frac{dT}{d\alpha} = 0$
Internal Balance	$\frac{dY_B}{d\alpha} = 0, \frac{dp_A}{d\alpha} = 0$	$\frac{dY_B}{d\alpha} = 0, \frac{dY_A}{d\alpha} = 0$	$\frac{dY_B}{d\alpha} = 0, \frac{dT}{d\alpha} = 0$
External Balance	$\frac{dT}{d\alpha} = 0, \frac{dp_A}{d\alpha} = 0$	$\frac{dT}{d\alpha} = 0, \frac{dY_A}{d\alpha} = 0$	$\frac{dT}{d\alpha} = 0$

Thus, except for the case where both countries are pursuing a policy for external balance, we have two additional equations which, together with equations (48–50), form a system of five equations in five unknowns and which, in general, can be solved uniquely for the five unknowns. The student should not be frightened by the fact that we are talking about a system of five equations, because this is a very simplified system and can be easily solved.

If both countries were pursuing a policy for external balance, we would face a problem of indeterminacy simply because there is only one balance of trade and two policy parameters for achieving balance-of-trade equilibrium. If we know the relative burden of each country in achieving external balance (thus supplying the missing equation), the indeterminacy is removed.

Indexes

INDEX OF NAMES AND AUTHORS

513

INDEX OF SUBJECTS